Would your life be easier if you had an electronic version of your textbook?

MyHistoryLab contains the complete text with icons that link to selected sources. You can print sections of the text to read anytime, anywhere.

Are you overwhelmed by the time it takes to find primary source documents, images, maps, and other sources for your research papers?

MyHistoryLab contains hundreds of primary sources, images, and maps— all in one place —to help make writing your research paper easier and more effective, and to help you better understand the course material.

Martin Luther

Martin Luther's spiritual philosophy advocated that men and women would be saved by faith in God rather than by receiving sacraments from priests and performing charitable acts. One could attain this faith only by contemplating the scriptures. This focus upon individuals reading and studying the Bible further challenged the Catholic Church as the authority on the Bible and its meanings. Luther also claimed that those of faith were equal before God, negating the spiritual divisions between clergy and laity and men and women. These challenges to the Roman Catholic Church and the subsequent spread of Lutheranism ushered in years of religious and political turmoil in Europe.

Photo credit: Erich Lessing/Art Resource, NY

Self-Study Quiz: True-False Questions
Which statements below are true and which are false?

To receive instant feedback for this self-study quiz, click the Check Answers button. Self-study quizzes are not recorded in your course gradebook, and you may take them as many times as you like. These questions are specific to your textbook and have been provided to reinforce chapter materials.
This activity contains 10 questions.

1. [Hint] Most governments realized the crucial role that industrial labor would play in WWI.

○ True
○ False

2. [Hint] The British Restoration of Pre-War Practices Act gave skilled female factory workers two weeks pay and a train ticket home at the end of the war.

○ True
○ False

3. [Hint] *Soviet* is a Russian term for "peasant."

○ True
○ False

Are you sometimes overwhelmed when you study for exams?

MyHistoryLab gives you a quizzing and testing program that shows what you've mastered, as well as where you need more work. Look for these icons on MyHistoryLab:

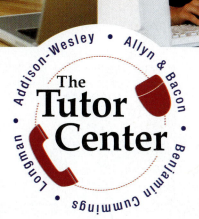

The Tutor Center

Addison-Wesley • Allyn & Bacon • Benjamin Cummings • Longman

Do you sometimes need extra help when your professor isn't in?

Get expert, one-on-one tutoring help with The Tutor Center, available Sunday through Thursday from 5 pm to midnight, Eastern Standard Time – when you're most likely to be completing assignments or preparing for exams, and when your instructor is often unavailable. Tutors can help you use MyHistoryLab to its fullest, or offer advice on writing your research paper.

Did your professor assign other books to read?

MyHistoryLab allows you to read, download, or print over twenty of the most commonly assigned works for this course – all at no additional cost!

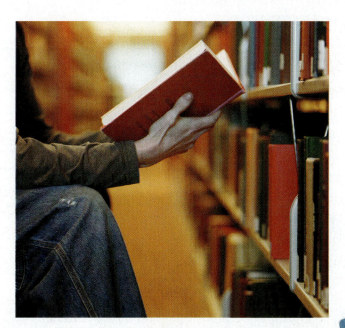

Now, flip through *Civilization Past & Present*. You will find the icons shown on the opposite page. Each icon will direct you to a place in MyHistoryLab to help you better understand the material. For example, when reading about classical China or 19th century European politics, you may find an icon that links you to an original source document by Confucius or Karl Marx.

DOCUMENT

This icon will lead you to primary source documents, so you can see the original documents that pertain to the people and events you're studying.

CASE STUDY

Analyze and interpret two or more primary sources on a similar theme or topic. Includes critical thinking questions.

IMAGE

You'll find photos, cartoons, and artwork that relate to the topic you're reading.

MAP

Interactive maps will help you visualize the geography you are exploring in this course. You will also find printable map activities from one of Longman's workbooks.

History Bookshelf Listing

1. *Aesop's Fables*; date unknown
2. *The Iliad,* Homer; 800 BCE
3. *The Upanishads*; 800 BCE
4. *The Analects*, Confucius; circa 500 BCE
5. *The Tao of Teh King*, Lao-Tze;
6. *Histories*, Herodotus; 440 BCE
7. *The Oedipus Trilogy*, Sophocles; circa 400 BCE
8. *The Republic*, Plato; 360 BCE
9. *The Art of War*, Sun Tzu; 100 BCE
10. *The Arabian Nights*; 10 AD
11. Plutarch's *Lives*; 100 AD
12. *The Bhagavad-Gita*; 200 AD
13. *The Holy Koran*; circa 630 AD
14. *Beowulf*; 1100 AD
15. *The Prince*, Machiavelli; 1505 AD
16. *95 Theses*, Martin Luther; 1517 AD
17. *Gulliver's Travels*, Jonathan Swift; 1726 AD
18. *The Communist Manifesto*, Karl Marx; 1848 AD
19. *Origin of Species*, Charles Darwin; 1859 AD
20. *20,000 Leagues Under the Sea*, Jules Verne; 1869 AD
21. *To the Gold Coast for Gold*, Sir Richard Burton; 1883 AD
22. *The Jungle Book*, Rudyard Kipling; 1894 AD
23. *Heart of Darkness*, Joseph Conrad; 1899 AD

Civilization
Past & Present

Civilization
Past & Present
Eleventh Edition

Volume A: From Antiquity to 1500

Palmira Brummett
UNIVERSITY OF TENNESSEE

Robert R. Edgar
HOWARD UNIVERSITY

Neil J. Hackett
ST. LOUIS UNIVERSITY

George F. Jewsbury
CENTRE D'ÉTUDES DU MONDE RUSSE
ÉCOLE DES HAUTES ÉTUDES EN SCIENCES SOCIALES

Barbara Molony
SANTA CLARA UNIVERSITY

THIS BOOK HAS BENEFITED FROM THE CONTRIBUTIONS
OVER MANY EDITIONS OF THE FOLLOWING AUTHORS:

T. Walter Wallbank (Late)

Alastair M. Taylor

Nels M. Bailkey

Clyde J. Lewis

PEARSON
Longman

New York Boston San Francisco
London Toronto Sydney Tokyo Singapore Madrid
Mexico City Munich Paris Cape Town Hong Kong Montréal

Executive Editor: Michael Boezi
Senior Acquisitions Editor: Janet Lanphier
Senior Development Editor: Dawn Groundwater
Development Editor: Adam Beroud
Executive Marketing Manager: Sue Westmoreland
Media and Supplements Editor: Kristi Olson
Senior Media Editor: Patrick McCarthy
Production Manager: Eric Jorgensen
Project Coordination, Text Design, and Electronic Page Makeup: Electronic Publishing Services
    Inc., NYC
Photo Research: Photosearch, Inc.
Cover Designer/Manager: Nancy Danahy
Cover Image: Panel: Portrait of a Boy. Egyptian. Roman period, ca. 50–100 A.D. The Metropoli-
    tan Museum of Art, Gift of Edward S. Harkness, 1918. (18.9.2) Photograph © 1998 The Met-
    ropolitan Museum of Art.
Manufacturing Buyer: Roy Pickering
Printer and Binder: Courier Corporation
Cover Printer: Coral Graphic Services

Library of Congress Cataloging-in-Publication Data

Civilization past & present / Palmira Brummett ... [et al.].— 11th ed.
    p. cm.
 Includes bibliographical references and index.
 ISBN 0-321-23613-0 — ISBN 0-321-23627-0 — ISBN 0-321-23628-9
 1. Civilization. I. Brummett, Palmira Johnson

CB69.C57 2005
909—dc22   2004029985

Visit us at http://www.ablongman.com.

ISBN 0-321-23613-0 (complete volume)
ISBN 0-321-23627-0 (Volume I)
ISBN 0-321-23628-9 (Volume II)
ISBN 0-321-31775-0 (Volume A)
ISBN 0-321-31776-9 (Volume B)
ISBN 0-321-31777-7 (Volume C)

1 2 3 4 5 6 7 8 9 10—CRK—07 06 05 04

Brief Contents

Detailed Contents

*Each chapter ends with a Conclusion, Suggestions for Web Browsing, Literature and Film, and Suggestions for Reading.

Documents

Maps

Global Issues

Discovery Through Maps

Chapter Opening Image Descriptions

CHAPTER 1

Gold and lapis lazuli Goat and Tree in the form of an offering stand to the Sumerian fertility god Tammuz, from the royal burials at Ur, c. 2600–2500 B.C.E.

CHAPTER 2

The details of the lives of individual human beings in ancient times sometimes become lost in the broader discussions of economic, military, and political events. This image of a Chinese couple playing a board game shows that ordinary life with its amusements remained, and that an artisan thought it moving enough to portray it.

CHAPTER 3

The Lion capital of Sarnath, from an Ashoka column placed at the site of the Buddha's first sermon. This Lion capital is used today as a national emblem of the Republic of India.

CHAPTER 4

A view of the Acropolis of Athens, dominated by the Parthenon, the temple dedicated to the goddess Athena.

CHAPTER 5

The Forum of Rome, with the ruins of the Temple of Vesta and the Column of Phocas.

CHAPTER 6

The gold and silver domes of the Cathedral of Hagia Sophia, Novgorod, built in the mid eleventh century. Though Novgorod lies some 1000 miles to the north of Constantinople, Byzantine cultural influence penetrated deeply into the region that would one day form the heartland of Russia.

CHAPTER 7

Qur'an page with gold lettering by the fifteenth-century calligrapher Sheykh Hamdullah. For Muslims the Qur'an is eternal; craftsmen created beautiful, elaborate Qur'ans for various Muslim rulers.

CHAPTER 8

Brass statue of a queen mother, from the Court of Benin, sixteenth century.

CHAPTER 9

The Gothic-style Benedictine abbey of Mont St. Michel, constructed between the eleventh and sixteenth centuries and built on a rocky inlet amid the sandbanks and tides between Brittany and Normandy, France.

CHAPTER 10

Refined gentlemen of the Tang and Song dynasties, seen in this detail from a scroll by tenth-century artist Gu Hongzhong, displayed their taste and culture in banquets in their own homes. Entertainment by female musicians and courtesans enhanced the opulent foods and rich decorations.

CHAPTER 11

Detail from painted Mayan vase depicting a ceremonially dressed ball player. The ball game served important social, political, and religious functions in Mayan civilization. On a very basic level, it provided the Mayan polity with entertainment. The construction of stone-paved courts, the training of players, and the holding of games also reinforced the prestige of the community. Finally, the game and its players could serve as religious offerings, with losing players sometimes being sacrificed to the gods.

To the Instructor

The eleventh edition of *Civilization Past & Present* continues to present a survey of world history, treating the development and growth of civilization as a global phenomenon in which all the world's culture systems have interacted. This new edition, like its predecessors, includes all the elements of history—social, economic, political, military, religious, aesthetic, legal, and technological—to illustrate that global interaction. One of the most significant changes in the eleventh edition is the addition of our new Asian scholar and co-author, Barbara Molony. Barbara is a professor of history at Santa Clara University and is director of Santa Clara's Program for the Study of Women and Gender. Well-versed in modern Asia, she significantly revised the book's Asian chapters.

With the accelerating tempo of developments in business, communication, and technology, every day each part of the world is brought into closer contact with other parts: economic and political events that happen in even the most remote corners of the world affect each of us individually. An appreciation for and an understanding of all the civilizations of the world must be an essential aim of education. Thus, the eleventh edition of *Civilization Past & Present* emphasizes world trends and carefully avoids placing these trends within a Western conceptual basis.

CHANGES TO ORGANIZATION AND CONTENT

The eleventh edition maintains the many strengths that have made *Civilization Past & Present* a highly respected textbook. As the authors revised the text, they relied on the latest historical scholarship and profited from suggestions from adopters of the text and reviewers. Maintained throughout this compelling survey are a fluid writing style and consistent level of presentation seldom found in multi-authored texts.

While the text retains the basic organization of its predecessors, all chapters have been reviewed and revised in light of the globalization of today's changing world. The authors have carefully evaluated, revised, combined, and rewritten chapters to provide balanced coverage of all parts of the world throughout history.

One of the major changes in the eleventh edition is a new chapter, "Latin America: Independence and Dependence, 1825–1945" (Chapter 25). This new chapter provides detailed coverage of Latin America, including the political, social, and economic challenges following independence and into the twentieth century and relations between the Latin American nations and the United States.

Other chapter changes are as follows:

- **Chapter 1:** "Stone Age Societies and the Earliest Civilizations of the Near East" provides coverage of human prehistory, Egyptian civilization, and the development of smaller Near Eastern states.
- **Chapter 2:** "Ancient China—Origins to Empire: From Prehistory to 220 C.E." and **Chapter 3:** "Ancient India: From Origins to 300 C.E." both include expanded coverage of gender and social history.
- **Chapter 6:** "Byzantium and the Orthodox World: Byzantium, Eastern Europe, and Russia, 325–1500" has been revised to stress the independent development of East Rome and includes enhanced information on the development of the Balkan States.
- **Chapter 9:** "The European Middle Ages: 476–1348 C.E." combines the tenth edition's Chapter 9 and Chapter 10, examining the political, religious, and social history of the entire European Middle Ages in one chapter rather than two.
- **Chapter 10:** "Culture, Power, and Trade in the Era of Asian Hegemony, 220–1350" and **Chapter 13:** "East Asian Cultural and Political Systems, 1300–1650" have been thoroughly revised and expanded, with particular attention to gender and social history.
- **Chapter 14:** "European Cultural and Religious Transformations: The Renaissance and the Reformation 1300–1600" combines the tenth edition's Chapter 15 and Chapter 16, exploring the political, religious, and social connections between the European Renaissance and Reformation in one chapter rather than two.
- **Chapter 15:** "The Development of the European State System: 1300–1650" is a new chapter that examines the growth of the European nation-states from the late Middle Ages through the religious wars of the seventeenth century.
- **Chapter 17:** "Politics in the First Age of Capitalism: 1648–1774: Absolutism and Limited Central Power" places more emphasis on the social crises of the first phase of capitalism.

- Reorganized **Chapter 18:** "New Ideas and Their Political Consequences: The Scientific Revolution, the Enlightenment and the French Revolutions" combines the tenth edition's Chapter 19 and with content from Chapter 22, as the authors believethat intellectual transformations represented by the Enlightenment are directly connected to the political upheavals of French Revolutions and so should be discussed as such in one chapter.
- A recast **Chapter 19:** "Africa, 1650–1850" provides detailed coverage of Africa, including the Atlantic Slave Trade, Islamic Africa, the settlement of South Africa by Africans and Europeans, and state formation in the east and northeast of the continent.
- A recast **Chapter 20:** "Asian and Middle Eastern Empires and Nations, 1650–1815" examines political, social, and cultural developments across Asia, including the Ottoman Empire, Persia, India, China, Korea, Japan, Southeast Asia, and the Pacific.
- **Chapter 21:** "The Americas, 1650–1825: From European Dominance to Independence" offers expanded treatment of the Haitian Revolution.
- Reorganized **Chapter 22:** "Industrialization: Social, Political, and Cultural Transformations," focuses exclusively on the social, ideological, religious, and cultural effects of the Industrial Revolutions in Great Britain, Continental Europe, and the United States.•
- **Chapter 23:** "Africa and the Middle East During the Age of European Imperialism" provides expanded coverage of Islam and Christianity in Africa during the colonial era.
- **Chapter 24:** "Asia, 1815–1914: India, Southeast Asia, China, and Japan" provides expanded coverage of Asian civilizations, with particular emphasis on gender and social history.
- **Chapter 26:** "Politics and Diplomacy in the West: 1815–1914" combines the tenth edition's Chapter 23 and Chapter 27, examining the political changes in Europe between the Congress of Vienna and World War I in one chapter rather than two.
- Expanded **Chapter 28:** "The USSR, Italy, Germany, and Japan: The Failure of Democracy in the Interwar Period" adds coverage of Japan.
- A recast **Chapter 29:** "Forging New Nations in Asia, 1910 to 1950" examines political and social transformations in China, Korea, Southeast Asia, and India.
- A recast **Chapter 30:** "Emerging National Movements in the Middle East and Africa, 1920s to 1950s" explores the rising tide of nationalism in Africa and the Middle East following World War I through the start of the Cold War.
- Expanded **Chapter 31:** "World War II: Origins and Consequences, 1919–1946" adds coverage of the postwar settlements that followed the defeat of the Axis powers in 1945.
- Reorganized **Chapter 32:** "The Bipolar World: Cold War and Decolonization 1945–1991" prefaces its examination of the Cold War by examining the competing economic systems of the United States and the USSR. It also provides a more detailed treatment of decolonization and its relationship to the Cold War.
- Reorganized **Chapter 33:** "The United States and Europe Since 1945: Politics in an Age of Conflict and Change" now stresses the relationship between technology and social change in the United States and Europe and also provides expanded coverage of the Soviet Union and the Russian Republic.
- Reorganized **Chapter 35:** "Asia Since 1945: Political, Economic, and Social Revolutions" integrates coverage of China, Hong Kong, Taiwan, and Singapore.

The eleventh edition of *Civilization Past & Present* is a thorough revision in both its narrative and its pedagogical features. It is intended to provide the reader with an understanding of the legacies of past eras and to illuminate the way in which the study of world history gives insight into the genesis, nature, and direction of global civilization. Given the growing interdependence of the world's nations, the need for this perspective has never been greater.

NEW SPLIT

The split for the two-volume edition has changed for the eleventh edition: Volume I, To 1650, contains Chapters 1–16; Volume II, From 1300, contains Chapters 12–35. The start of Volume II at 1300 accommodates those courses that cover materials beginning earlier than 1650. The eleventh edition also includes a three-volume split edition for schools operating on the quarter system: Volume A, To 1500, contains Chapters 1–11; Volume B, From 500–1815, contains Chapters 9–20; and Volume C, From 1775, contains Chapters 18–35.

FEATURES AND PEDAGOGY

The text has been developed with the dual purpose of helping students acquire a solid knowledge of past events and, equally important, of helping them think more constructively about the significance of those events for the complex times in which we now live. A number of pedagogical features—some well tested in earlier editions and lightly revised here, and a few new ones—will assist students in achieving these goals.

GLOBAL ISSUES

MIGRATION

Why do people move from one place to another?

The history of migration is in a sense the history of humankind. All migrations involve the movement of peoples, cultures, languages, and ideas. As a result, they have shaped history around the world and played a major role in the growth of civilization. The reasons why people migrate vary. Changing environmental conditions, population pressures, economic shifts, political and religious controversies, and war and violence have all compelled people to move from one place to another. Whatever the triggering circumstance may be, the decision to migrate is ultimately driven by the human necessity or desire to find a better or more secure place to live.

Migrations have been an integral part of human experience since our early ancestors took their first tentative steps on the African savanna and began exploring and adapting to new environments. *Homo erectus* migrated from the African continent to Eurasia. Members of *Homo sapiens* followed their predecessor out of Africa and traveled further still, showing considerable ingenuity in overcoming obstacles such as the open sea to reach Australia and the cold of the northern latitudes to traverse the Bering Strait and enter the Americas.

These earliest human movements were small in scale. Extended families or clans would move into a new area and live off the land. Even with small populations, humans often placed considerable environmental strain on the land after only a short time. From 3000 B.C.E. to 500 C.E., Bantu communities migrating into central, eastern, and southern Africa could cultivate an area for only a few years before the soils were exhausted and they had to move to new land.

While environmental degradation caused by human activity has often forced people to migrate, so too have acts of nature such as droughts, floods, cold spells, and crop failures. Severe drought from around 1300 to 1100 B.C.E. likely initiated political disruptions in the eastern Mediterranean and the migrations of the Sea Peoples, Philistines, Sicilians, Sardinians, and Etruscans that followed.[1] More recently, potato blight destroyed the potato crop in Ireland between 1846 and 1850, creating widespread famine and economic hardship. Ireland's population dropped from 8 to 5 million as almost a million people died and the

---

New! *Global Issues* **Essays** These new essays explore seven topics of unique transcultural and transhistorical significance: Migration, Religion and Government, Location and Identity, Technological Exchange, Slavery, Gender, and War and International Law. Each essay employs examples that span both history and the world's many civilizations. As pedagogical tools, the essays are intended to do more than just inform students about global topics; they also reveal challenges that have confronted and still confront civilizations the world over. The essays carefully avoid discussing their topics from a Western conceptual basis and instead strive to examine them using a global framework. Each essay uses art to illustrate its ideas and ends with critical thinking questions. Evenly distributed throughout the book, the essays appear on two-page spreads between chapters.

---

global economy due to transatlantic discoveries and the rise of oceanic merchant empires like those of the Dutch and the English.

The Age of the Köprülü Vizirs

Mehmed IV became sultan in 1648, facing rampant inflation, a Venetian blockade of the Dardanelles, rebellion in the provinces, and a violent struggle among palace factions, including his mother, Turhan (TOOR-hahn) Sultan, and her rival, the old Valide Sultan Kösem (KOO-sem). These senior women wielded considerable influence and controlled considerable wealth in the palace system. In 1651 Turhan ended Kösem's long-term dominance of the harem by having her strangled, but Mehmed remained enmeshed in factional politics. This internal strife was compounded by a vehement struggle between groups of conservative mullahs representing the ***ulama*** (oo-LAH-mah) and **sufis,** both of which were contending for spiritual authority and influence in the capital. By 1656 Istan-

---

ulama—Islamic religious authorities; men versed in Islamic sciences and law.

sufis—Islamic mystics who sought contact with Allah through prayer and ritual dance; considered a heretical movement by conservative Muslims.

New! Pronunciation Guide This new feature will help students correctly pronounce key foreign words. Pronunciations appear in parentheses immediately after the first use of a key foreign term in the text.

New! On-page Glossary This new feature provides students with concise definitions of key historical terms. Glossary definitions appear in the footer of the page in which they are discussed.

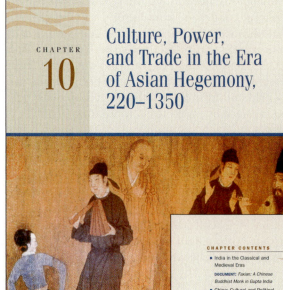

Chapter Opening Pages Chapter opening pages again feature an illustration relevant to a major chapter topic, a chapter outline, and a newly designed, easy-to-read chronology of key events—political, social, religious, and cultural—that are discussed in the chapter. Students can easily refer back to the timeline as they read the chapter.

A short text introduction previews the civilizations and themes to be discussed in the chapter. The chronology then sets the major topics within a framework easy for the student to comprehend at a glance. Chapter opening images reflect a wide range of genres, including sculpture, painting, mosaics, tapestries, and illuminated manuscripts. The images have been carefully selected to invoke a particular culture and engage the student visually.

Chronology Tables Throughout each chapter, brief chronology tables once again highlight the major events occurring within a text section. Whether focusing on general trends, as does Religious Reforms and Reactions (Chapter 14), or on a single country, as does China in the Imperialist Era (Chapter 24), the chronology tables give the student an immediate summary view of a topic, at its point of discussion.

Discovery Through Maps This special feature focusing on primary maps in many chapters offers a unique historical view—be it local, city, country, world, or imagined—of the way a particular culture looked at the world at a particular time. Students tend to take the orientation of a map for granted; however, "An Islamic Map of the World" (Chapter 7) makes clear that not all peoples make the same assumptions. The world map of the famous Arab cartographer al-Idrisi is oriented, as was common at the time, with south at the top. Chapter 19's "The Myth of the Empty Land" shows how European settlers of South Africa laid claim to the South African interior by asserting that they were moving into an unpopulated area.

The discussions accompanying these maps have been expanded to emphasize their connection with the text itself; the addition of review questions helps students better understand the concepts presented by the maps.

Discovery Through Maps

Map of China's Ancient Heartland, circa 1500 C.E.

It is one of the marks of human nature that the center of the world is found in one's self-consciousness, and then in concentric circles in the family, community, and nation. This trait extends across civilizations and continents and can be seen not only in this Chinese map depicting the area known as the *Zhongyuan* (ZHONG-yoo-AHN) or heartland of ancient China, but also in maps created around the same time by Europeans as they made their voyages of discovery. The Chinese map is particularly informative because it reminds its viewers that even within China itself, the heartland was the repository of culture and power.

The map has political implications, in that it shows its viewers that the original heartland of China was the same place as the home of the Ming. This portrayal is difficult, however, for those trained to see geography in terms of a Mercator projection (see, e.g., p. 467). The Mercator projection, like the Ming map, also reflects a worldview that places the map's creators in the center–in the Mercator case, the center is in Europe. Is there any particular reason, for example, why the Greenwich Meridian (from which all longitudes on the surface of the earth are presently measured) should be the central part of the world's geography?

Excerpts from Primary Source Documents Seventeen of the more than 100 primary source documents are new. In "Muslim and Christian: Two Contemporary Perspectives" (Chapter 9), first the Christian knight, then the Muslim physician, write of the bloody fall of Jerusalem with the certainty of religious justification for his cause, and of cultural superiority. Simón Bolívar, in his powerful Proclamation to the People of Venezuela (Chapter 21), addresses his fellow-countrymen to reestablish a republican form of government in the state.

Almost every chapter now includes a document concerning the status of women in general during a particular era or details the accomplishments of a specific woman. In Chapter 35, Benazir Bhutto, Pakistan's first female prime minister, relates the dilemma of being a "foreign" student at Harvard during an era of political turmoil for both Pakistan and the United States.

Headnotes to all have been expanded to better link the documents to the text itself. Several discussion questions now follow each excerpt.

Document   **Letter from Abigail Adams**

Abigail Adams, with her husband John, served as the embodiment of the American republican virtues of plain speaking, lack of ostentation, and sometimes brutal honesty. Her letter to her husband speaks to the openness and strength of their relationship. Her spelling represents the usage of the time.

31 Mar. 1776

I wish you would ever write me a Letter half as long as I write you; and tell me if you may where your Fleet are gone? What sort of Defence Virginia can make against our common Enemy? Whether it is so situated as to make an able Defence? Are not the Gentery Lords and the common people vassals, are they not like the uncivilized Natives Brittain represents us to be? I hope their Riffel Men who have shewen themselves very savage and even Blood thirsty; are not a specimen of the Generality of the people.

I am willing to allow the Colony great merrit for having produced a Washington but they have been shamefully duped by a Dunmore.

I have sometimes been ready to think that the passion for Liberty cannot be Eaquelly Strong in the Breasts of those who have been accustomed to deprive their fellow Creatures of theirs. Of this I am certain that it is not founded upon that generous and christian principal of doing to others as we would that others should do unto us. . . .

I long to hear that you have declared an independancy—and by the way in the new Code of Laws which I suppose it will be necessary for you to make I desire you would Remember the Ladies, and be more generous and favourable to them than your ancestors. Do not put such unlimited power into the hands of the Husbands. Remember all Men would be tyrants if they could. If perticular care and attention is not paid to the Laidies we are determined to foment a Rebelion, and will not hold ourselves bound by any Laws in which we have no voice, or Representation.

That your Sex are Naturally Tyrannical is a Truth so thoroughly established as to admit of no dispute, but such of you as wish to be happy willingly give up the harsh title of Master for the more tender and endearing one of Friend. Why then, not put it out of the power of the vicious and the Lawless to use us with cruelty and indignity with impunity. Men of Sense in all Ages abhor those customs which treat us only as the vassals of your Sex. Regard us then as Beings placed by providence under your protection and in immitation of the Supreem Being make use of that power only for our happiness.

Questions to Consider

1. Why does Abigail Adams fear that the coming political changes will not benefit women?

2. What is Adams's rationale for her critique of the way men sometimes go about doing business?

3. Would Abigail Adams think her descendants living today have fulfilled her hopes for a "proper" place for women in society?

From Abigail Smith Adams, *The Book of Abigail and John: Selected Letters of the Adams Family, 1762–1784,* eds. L. H. Butterfield, et al. (Cambridge, Mass.: Harvard University Press, 1975).

254   CIVILIZATION PAST AND PRESENT

tapping Muslim trading networks. The kingdom of Aksum became a major Red Sea power, serving as a bridge between the Mediterranean and the Indian Ocean. The Swahili city-states on the East African coast and the states of the Zimbabwe Plateau carried on extensive relations with Indian Ocean trading networks. West African savanna kingdoms created the most extensive trading network through their position overseeing trade between North Africa, the savanna, and forest regions to the south. However, within these long-distance trading networks, African states were primarily producers of raw materials.

Although most Africans remained faithful to their traditional religious beliefs and practices, many con-

verted to Christianity and Islam in specific areas. Egypt became an early center of Christianity, while Ethiopia's rulers firmly established Christianity as their kingdom's state religion. Islam became the dominant religion of North Africa, where some rulers and traders in the West African savanna, northeastern Africa, and along the Swahili coast adopted Islam. However, until the eighteenth century, Islam remained primarily a religion of court and commerce in sub-Saharan Africa. It won few followers in small-scale societies that did not have ruling elites. This pattern is similar to other places such as Indonesia where Muslim traders established themselves but did not initially win many converts.

Suggestions for Web Browsing

You can obtain more information about topics included in this chapter at the websites listed below. See also the companion website that accompanies this text, http://www.ablongman.com/ brummett, which contains an online study guide and additional resources.

Internet African History Sourcebook
http://www.fordham.edu/halsall/africa/africasbook.html
Extensive online source for links about the history of ancient Africa, including the kingdoms of Ghana, Mali, and Songhai.

Art of Benin
http://www.si.edu/ofg/Units/sorsnmafa.htm
Site of the Smithsonian Institution's National Museum of African Art displays art objects from the kingdom of Benin before Western dominance.

Great Zimbabwe
http://www.mc.maricopa.edu/~reffland/anthropology/
anthro2003/legacy/africa/zimbabwe/
A 23-slide series, with commentary, that will take you through the ruins of Great Zimbabwe in southern Africa.

The Story of Africa
http://www.bbc.co.uk/worldservice/africa/features/storyofafrica/
index.shtml
The radio service of the BBC presents a history of Africa from the origins of humankind to modern nation-states.

African Voices
http://www.mnh.si.edu/africanvoices/

Ethiopian royal literature, see G. W. B. Huntingford, ed., *Royal Chronicles of Abyssinia: The Glorious Victories of Amda Seyon King of Ethiopia* (Clarendon Press, 1965).

Caravans of Gold (Home Vision, 1984) treats the gold trade between the Sudanic kingdoms of West Africa and the Muslim and European worlds. It is one film in an eight-part series, *Africa: The Story of a Continent*, presented by Basil Davidson, a British writer on African issues. *Lost Cities of the South* (PBS, 1999) presents a discussion of African civilizations of southern Africa, such as Mapungubwe and Great Zimbabwe. It is part of a six-part series, *Wonders of the African World*, narrated by Harvard professor Henry Louis Gates, Jr.

Suggestions for Reading

The best detailed coverage of African history can be found in two multivolume series, each containing chapters by leading scholars: *The Cambridge History of Africa*, 8 Vols. (Cambridge University Press, 1982–1984) and *The UNESCO General History of Africa*. Among other general surveys of African history are Robert July, *A History of the African People*, 4th ed. (Waveland Press, 1992); Erik Gilbert and Jonathan Reynolds, *Africa in World History from Prehistory to the Present* (Pearson Education, 2004); and Christopher Ehret, *The Civilizations of Africa: A History to 1800* (University Press of Virginia, 2002).

The best general reference work on early African history is Joseph Vogel, ed., *Encyclopedia of Precolonial Africa: Archaeology, History, Languages, Cultures, and Environments* (AltaMira Press, 1997). Another general work that examines Africa's history with a disciplinary focus is James Newman, *The Peopling of Africa: A Geographic Interpretation* (Yale University Press, 1995). A general synthesis on women in African history is Iris Berger and E. Frances White, *Women in Sub-Saharan Africa: Restoring* …

Suggestions for Reading To give the student an additional view of the various cultures and time-frames, a *Literature and Film* section at the end of each chapter offers a listing of novels, poetry, films, and videos. Readings have been updated and carefully trimmed of dated entries. Students can consult these general interpretations, monographs, and collections of traditional source materials to expand their understanding of a particular topic or to prepare reports and papers. *Suggestions for Web Browsing* have also been updated throughout.

CHAPTER 6 • *Byzantium and the Orthodox World*   171

silkworms were smuggled out of China about 550 C.E., silk production flourished and became a profitable state monopoly. The state paid close attention to business: controlling the economy through a system of guilds to which all tradesmen and members of professions belonged; setting wages, profits, work hours, and prices; and even organizing bankers and doctors into compulsory corporations.

Justinian and Theodora

The dream of reclaiming the Mediterranean basin and reestablishing the Roman Empire to its former glory, however, did not die until the end of the reign of Justinian (r. 527–565). Aided by his forceful wife, Theodora, and a corps of competent assistants, he made long-lasting contributions to Byzantine and Western civilization, but gained only short-term successes in his foreign policy.

In the 520s and 530s, after earthquakes devastated much of his realm, Justinian carried out a massive

Emperor Justinian. Justinian bequeathed a splendid architectural and legal legacy to Europe. However, his attempt to reclaim the former glory of the Roman Empire gained only temporary success and bankrupted his treasury.

project of urban renewal throughout the empire. He strengthened the walls defending Constantinople and built the monumental Hagia Sophia, which still stands. Forty windows circle the base of this great church's dome, producing a quality of light that creates the illusion that the ceiling is floating.

Justinian also reformed the government and ordered a review of all Roman law. This project led to the publication of the **Code of Justinian**, a digest of Roman and church law, texts, and other instructional materials that became the foundation of modern Western law. Following Constantine's example, Justinian saw himself as the thirteenth apostle and par- …

Photographs The text's more than 500 photos, most in full color, have been carefully revised to present a diverse range of images from all of the world's civilizations. Special care has again been taken to include images of the lifestyles and contributions of women for all eras and areas.

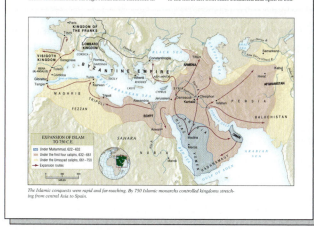

more ... than oth... ...the into ... ... Caliphs
the *ulama* over matters o... ...(as happened with brahmans and kings in India and priests and kings
in Europe). But all Muslim kings, like all Christian kings
in this era, claimed to be defenders of their faith.

THE EXPANSION OF COMMUNITY AND STATE

■ *What factors contributed to the rapid expansion of Islam?*

The Islamic state expanded very rapidly after the death of Muhammad through remarkable successes in

Under the first four caliphs (632–661), the Islamic state rapidly expanded the territory under its control. The wars of expansion were aided by the devotion of the faithful to the concept of *jihad*, a term that is sometimes glossed as "holy war" and sometimes interpreted to mean simply "struggle." Muslims were obliged to extend the faith to unbelievers and to defend Islam from attack. *Jihad* was responsible in part for Islam's early conquests beyond the Arabian peninsula.

But various factors account for the triumph of the early Muslim armies. A long series of wars waged between the Byzantine and Persian (Sassanid) Empires to the north left both sides exhausted and open to con-

The Islamic conquests were rapid and far-reaching. By 750 Islamic monarchs controlled kingdoms stretching from central Asia to Spain.

Maps The use of full color allows students more readily to see distinctions on the more than 100 maps in the text. Some maps make clear the nature of a single distinctive event; others illustrate larger trends. For example, Trade and Cultural Interchange, c. 50 B.C.E. (Chapter 2), makes clear that an interconnected world economy existed long before the advent of modern communication and technology. The specific focus of The Persian Gulf Region, c. 1900 (Chapter 23), foretells some of today's complexities in this area of the world. A caption accompanying each map highlights the significance of the map and its relevance to a specific text topic. Many of the maps have been revised, updated, and/or increased in size. Most of the maps also include insets that show where their territory fits within a larger hemisphere or the globe.

FOR QUALIFIED COLLEGE ADOPTERS

Supplements for Instructors

MyHistoryLab With the best of Longman's multimedia solutions for history in one easy-to-use place, MyHistoryLab offers students and instructors a state-of-the-art interactive instructional solution for the World History survey course. Delivered in Course Compass™, Blackboard™, or WebCT™, MyHistoryLab is designed to be used as a supplement to a traditional lecture course, or to administer a completely online course. MyHistoryLab provides helpful tips, review materials, and activities to make the study of history an enjoyable learning experience. Icons in the book lead students to specific assets.

MyHistoryLab includes the following features, all organized according to the text's table of contents:

- **E-Sources:** Each chapter of the book has its own collection of images, individual documents, and case studies.
- **History Bookshelf:** Read, download, or print more than 20 of the most commonly assigned works like Plato's *The Republic*, Machiavelli's *The Prince*, or Confucius' *The Analects*.
- **History Toolkit:** Guided tutorials help students learn to analyze several types of sources.
- **Map Activities:** Each chapter contains a map activity in which students assess a map from the time period covered and take a brief geography quiz for the chapter.
- **Pre-Test and Post-Test Self-Study Quizzes with Targeted Feedback:** Two quizzes per chapter allow students to review their knowledge of the material and concepts. Chapter feedback provides links that take students directly to the relevant section of the textbook online.
- **Chapter Review Materials:** The Study Guide, PowerPoint™ presentations, flashcards, and other features will help students master the contents of the textbook and prepare for exams.
- **The Textbook Online:** Students can read the book online, or print out sections of the book to read anywhere.
- **Chapter Exam:** Each chapter has a chapter exam whose results report to the CourseCompass™, Blackboard™, or WebCT™ online gradebook.
- **Test Bank:** Create your own exams using the Test Bank from your text, and place them right in MyHistoryLab for your students to take as practice quizzes or as graded exams.
- **The Tutor Center:** On-call qualified help is available to answer student questions about MyHistoryLab when an instructor may not be available. The Tutor Center is open Sunday through Thursday from 5 PM to midnight, EST.
- **Unlimited use of Pearson's Research Navigator™:** The EBSCO ContentSelect, Academic Journal & Abstract Database, *The New York Times* Search by Subject Archive, "Best of the Web" Link Library, and *Financial Times* Article Archive and Company Financials offer thousands of credible and reliable articles and websites to get the research process started.
- **A wealth of instructor support material:** Text-specific materials, such as instructor's manuals, test banks, and PowerPoint™ presentations simplify and enrich the teaching experience.

www.LongmanWorldHistory.com This website offers all the best of MyHistoryLab without course management features or the online e-book. As with MyHistoryLab, icons in the book lead students to specific assets on the website.

Instructor's Manual by Rick Whisonant of Winthrop University. This collection of resources includes chapter outlines, definitions, discussion suggestions, critical thinking exercises, term paper and essay topics, and audiovisual suggestions.

Companion Website (www.ablongman.com/brummett). This online course companion provides a wealth of resources for both students and instructors using *Civilization Past & Present,* Eleventh Edition. Students will find chapter summaries, test questions, and links for further research.

SafariX. SafariX Textbooks Online is an exciting new choice for students looking to save money. As an alternative to purchasing the print textbook, students can subscribe to the same content online and save up to 50% off the suggested list price of the print text. With a SafariX WebBook, students can search the text, make notes online, print out reading assignments that incorporate lecture notes, and bookmark important passages for later review. For more information, or to subscribe to the SafariX Web Book, visit www.safarix.com.

Test Bank and Test Generator by Susan Hellert of the University of Wisconsin at Platteville. This easy-to-customize test bank presents a wealth of multiple-choice, true-false, short-answer, and essay questions. Free to qualified college adopters.

Civilization Past & Present PowerPoint™ Presentations. Updated by Pamela Marquez of Metropolitan State College of Denver, these easy-to-customize Power-Point™ slides outline key points of each chapter of the text and are available for download from the Companion Website (www.ablongman.com/brummett). Free to qualified college adopters.

The History Digital Media Archive CD-ROM. This CD-ROM contains hundreds of images, maps, interactive maps, and audio/video clips ready for classroom presentation, or downloading into PowerPoint™ or any other presentation software. Free to qualified college adopters.

Overhead Transparency Acetates to Accompany Civilization Past & Present. These text-specific acetates are available to all adopters. Every map is represented. Free to qualified college adopters.

Guide to Teaching World History by Palmira Brummett of the University of Tennessee at Knoxville. This guide offers explanations of major issues and themes in world history, sample syllabi and instructions on how to create a manageable syllabus, ideas for cross-cultural and cross-temporal connections, a pronunciation guide, and tips on getting through all the material. Free to qualified college adopters.

Discovering World History Through Maps and Views Overhead Transparency Acetates by Gerald Danzer of the University of Illinois at Chicago. This unique resource contains more than 100 full-color acetates of beautiful reference maps, source maps, urban plans, views, photos, art, and building diagrams. Free to qualified college adopters.

Longman World History Atlas Overhead Transparency Acetates. These acetates are available to instructors who select the *Longman World History Atlas* for their students. Free to qualified college adopters.

Historical Newsreel Video. This 90-minute video contains newsreel excerpts examining U.S. involvement in world affairs over the past 60 years. Free to qualified college adopters.

Longman-Penguin Putnam Inc. Value Bundles. Students and professors alike will love the value and quality of the Penguin books offered at a deep discount when bundled with *Civilization Past & Present,* Eleventh Edition, for qualified college adopters.

Supplements for Students

Companion Website (www.ablongman.com/brummett). This online course companion provides a wealth of resources for both students and instructors using *Civilization Past & Present,* Eleventh Edition. Students will find chapter summaries, test questions, and links for further research.

Student Study Guide in two volumes: Volume 1 (Chapters 1–17) and Volume 2 (Chapters 13–35) revised by Norman Love of El Paso Community College. Each chapter includes chapter overviews, lists of themes and concepts, map exercises, multiple-choice practice tests, and critical thinking and essay questions.

Study Card for World History. Colorful, affordable, and packed with useful information, the *Study Card for World History* makes studying easier, more efficient, and more enjoyable. Course information is distilled down to the basics, helping students quickly master the fundamentals, review a subject for understanding, or prepare for an exam. Because they are laminated for durability, Study Cards can be kept for years to come and be pulled out whenever they are needed for a quick review.

Mapping World History. This workbook was created for use in conjunction with *Discovering World History Through Maps and Views.* Designed to teach students to interpret and analyze cartographic materials as historical documents.

World History Map Workbooks, Second Edition, Volumes I and II. These workbooks, created by Glee Wilson, Kent State University, are designed to explain the correlations between historical events and geography through assignments that involve reading and interpreting maps.

Longman World History Atlas. A comprehensive collection of historical maps that reflects truly global coverage of world history. Each of the atlas's 56 maps are designed to be readable, informative, and accurate as well as beautiful.

Longman Library of World Biography Series. Each interpretive biography in the new Library of World

Biography series focuses on a figure whose actions and ideas significantly influenced the course of world history. Pocket-sized and brief, each book relates the life of its subject to the broader themes and developments of the times. Series titles include:

- *Alexander the Great: Legacy of a Conqueror* by Winthrop Lindsay Adams, University of Utah
- *Benito Mussolini: The First Fascist* by Anthony L. Cardoza, Loyola University of Chicago
- *Fukuzawa Yukichi: From Samurai to Capitalist* by Helen M. Hopper, University of Pittsburg
- *Ignatius of Loyola: Founder of the Jesuits* by John Patrick Donnelly, Marquette University
- *Jacques Coeur: Entrepreneur and King's Bursar* by Kathryn L. Reyerson, University of Minnesota
- *Kato Shidzue: A Japanese Feminist* by Helen M. Hopper, University of Pittsburg
- *Simón Bolívar: Liberation and Disappointment* by

David Bushnell, University of Florida
- *Vasco da Gama: Renaissance Crusader* by Glenn J. Ames, University of Toledo

Longman World History Series. These books focus on the historical significance of a particular movement, experience, or interaction. Concise and inexpensive, they bring the global connections and consequences of these events to the fore, showing students how events that happened long ago or far away can still affect them. Titles include:

- *Colonial Encounters in the Age of High Imperialism* by Scott B. Cook, Rhode Island School of Design.
- *Environmentalism: A Global History* by Ramachandra Guha
- *Expansion and Global Interaction: 1200–1700* by David Ringrose, University of California at San Diego

ACKNOWLEDGMENTS

A special note of appreciation goes to the following reviewers for providing thorough and expert advice for the *Global Issues* essays. Their suggestions have been of tremendous help in the writing of this new feature:

Milan Andrejevich
Indiana University Northwest

Charles E. Bashaw
College of Charleston

Kevin W. Caldwell
Blue Ridge Community College

Peter Fraunholtz
Northeastern University

James C. Godwin II
University of Delaware

Elizabeth P. Hancock
Gainesville College

Frank Karpiel
College of Charleston

Thomas O. Kay
Wheaton College

Laurence W. Marvin
Berry College

Donald T. McGuire
SUNY Buffalo

Fannie T. Rushing
Benedictine University

Mark B. Tauger
West Virginia University

Rick Whisonant
Winthrop University

We are most grateful to the following reviewers who gave generously of their time and knowledge to provide thoughtful evaluations and many helpful suggestions for the revision of this edition.

Henry Abramson
Florida Atlantic University

Lee Annis
Montgomery College—Rockville

Daniel Ayana
Youngstown State University

James W. Brodman
University of Central Arkansas

Thomas Cary
City University

Edward R. Crowther
Adams State College

Cole P. Dawson
Warner Pacific College

Dr. Michael de Nie
State University of West Georgia

Shannon L. Duffy
Loyola University New Orleans

Charles T. Evans
Northern Virginia Community College

Ronald Fritze
University of Central Arkansas

Richard M. Golden
University of North Texas

Elizabeth P. Hancock
Gainesville College

Eric J. Hanne
Florida Atlantic University

Caroline Hoefferle
Wingate University

Roger L. Jungmeyer
Lincoln University of Missouri

Jeffrey W. Myers
Avila University

William R. Rogers
Isothermal Community College

Daniel E. Schafer
Belmont University

Roger Schlesinger
Washington State University

William Seavey
East Carolina University

Deborah A. Symonds
Drake University

Mark B. Tauger
West Virginia University

Ted Weeks
Southern Illinois University

Rick Whisonant
Winthrop University

We also thank the many conscientious reviewers who reviewed previous editions of this book.

Henry Abramson
Florida Atlantic University

Wayne Ackerson
Salisbury State University

Jay Pascal Anglin
University of Southern Mississippi

Lee Annis
Montgomery County Community College—Maryland

Joseph Appiah
J. Sargeant Reynolds Community College

Michael Auslin
Yale University

Mark C. Bartusis
Northern State University

Charlotte Beahan
Murray State University

Martin Berger
Youngstown State University

Joel Berlatsky
Wilkes College

Jackie R. Booker
Kent State University

Mauricio Borrero
St. John's University

Darwin F. Bostwick
Old Dominion University

Robert F. Brinson Jr.
Santa Fe Community College

Robert H. Buchanan
Adams State College

Nancy Cade
Pikeville College

Michael L. Carrafiello
East Carolina University

James O. Catron Jr.
North Florida Junior College

Mark Chavalas
University of Wisconsin

William H. Cobb
East Carolina University

J. L. Collins
Allan Hancock College

J. R. Crawford
Montreat-Anderson College

Edward R. Crowther
Adams State College

Lawrence J. Daly
Bowling Green State University

Demoral Davis
Jackson State University

Anne Dorazio
Westchester Community College

Dawn Duensing
Maui Community College

Ellen Emerick
Georgetown College

William Edward Ezzell
Georgia Perimeter College

John D. Fair
Auburn University at Montgomery

Nancy Fitch
California State University

Robert B. Florian
Salem-Teikyo University

Nels W. Forde
University of Nebraska

Joseph T. Fuhrmann
Murray State University

Lydia Garner
Southwest Texas State University

Robert J. Gentry
University of Southwestern Louisiana

Paul George
Miami Community College, Dade

David Gleason
Armstrong Atlantic State University

Richard Golden
University of North Texas

Oliver Griffin
Weber State University

Michael Hall
Armstrong Atlantic State University

Paul Halsall
University of North Florida

Jeffrey S. Hamilton
Old Dominion University

Donald E. Harpster
College of St. Joseph

Gordon K. Harrington
Weber State University

J. Drew Harrington
Western Kentucky University

Janine Hartman
University of Cincinnati

Geoff Haywood
Beaver College

Thomas Hegarty
University of Tampa

Madonna Hettinger
McHenry County College

David Hill
McHenry County College

Conrad C. Holcomb, Jr
Surry Community College

Thomas Howell
Louisiana College

Clark Hultquist
University of Montevallo

Scott Jessee
Appalachian State University

Roger L. Jungmeyer
Lincoln University of Missouri

Daniel R. Kazmer
Georgetown University

Bernard Kiernan
Concord College

David Koeller
North Park University

Michael L. Krenn
University of Miami

Teresa Lafer
Pennsylvania State University

Harral E. Landry
Texas Women's University

George Longenecker
Norwich University

Norman Love
El Paso Community College

Marsha K. Marks
Alabama A&M University

Caroline T. Marshall
James Madison University

Eleanor McCluskey
Broward Community College

Robert McCormick
Newman University

Christopher McKay
University of Alberta

David A. Meier
Dickinson State University

Arlin Migliazzo
Whitworth College

William C. Moose
Mitchell Community College

Zachary Morgan
William Patterson University

Wayne Morris
Lees-McRae College

John G. Muncie
East Stroudsburg University

Justin Murphy
Howard Payne University

David Owusu-Ansah
James Madison University

George Pesely
Austin-Peay State

Al Pilant
Cumberland College

Jana Pisani
Texas A&M International University

Sr. Jeannette Plante, CSC
Notre Dame College

Norman Pollock
Old Dominion University

J. Graham Provan
Millikin University

George B. Pruden Jr.
Armstrong State College

John D. Ramsbottom
Northeast Missouri State University

Ruth Richard
College of Lake County

Charles Risher
Montreat College

Hugh I. Rodgers
Columbus College

Ruth Rogaski
Princeton University

William Rogers
Isothermal Community College

Patrick J. Rollins
Old Dominion University

Chad Ronnander
University of Minnesota

R. A. Rotz
Indiana University

Robert Rowland
Loyola University

Barry T. Ryan
Westmont College

Bill Schell
Murray State University

Louis E. Schmier
Valdosta State College

William M. Simpson
Louisiana College

Paul J. Smith
Haverford College

Barbara G. Sniffen
University of Wisconsin—Oshkosh

Lawrence Squeri
East Stroudsburg University

Lawrence Stanley
McHenry County College

Terrence S. Sullivan
University of Nebraska at Omaha

John Swanson
Utica College of Syracuse

Edward Tabri
Columbus State Community College

Gordon L. Teffeteller
Valdosta State College

Malcolm R. Thorp
Brigham Young University

Helen M. Tierney
University of Wisconsin—Platteville

Leslie Tischauser
Prairie State College

Arthur L. Tolson
Southern University

Joseph A. Tomberlin
Valdosta State University

Marcia Vaughan
Murray State University

Thomas Dwight Veve
Dalton College

Chris Warren
Copiah-Lincoln Community College

Mary Watrous
Washington State University

David L. White
Appalachian State University

Thomas Whigham
University of Georgia

John R. Willertz
Saginaw Valley State University

To the Student

e set two goals for ourselves when we wrote *Civilization Past & Present*. The first is to provide you with an understanding of the contributions of past eras in all parts of the globe to the shaping of world history. The second is to illuminate the way in which the study of world history gives us insights into the genesis, nature, and direction of our own civilization.

These are challenging tasks. However, given the globalization of all aspects of our lives, they are essential. When economies in East Asia or Latin America are in a state of crisis, the impact is felt on Wall Street. The culture of the New World—especially music and movies—has spread around the globe. When tragedies occur in the Middle East, we are all affected. Long gone are the days when an occurrence that took place far away could be isolated.

Now you are taking a course in world history to understand the development of the cultures of the world—cultures that are coming together to form a multifaceted world civilization. By understanding how and why other civilizations have chosen differing routes to their future, you can gain an understanding of why your part of civilization has succeeded or failed in attaining its potential. With an understanding of world history, you will be able to respond more knowledgeably to the changes through which you will live and to make informed choices as a world citizen.

History is the study of change over time. A historian is a person who focuses on one aspect of changes in the past, poses questions about why a particular event has taken place, proposes answers—hypotheses—and tests those hypotheses against the evidence—all of the evidence. We do not expect you to be historians at this point in your careers—to form your own hypotheses and write monographs. We have written this book, however, to enable you to study change over the entire course of human history.

We have included a number of tools to help you on your voyage through this text. The new **Global Issues essays** explore seven topics of unique transcultural and trans-historical significance: Migration, Religion and Government, Location and Identity, Technological Exchange, Slavery, Gender, and War and International Law. The essays carefully examine these topics using a global framework, employing examples that span both history and the world's many civilizations. The essays are intended to do more than just inform you about global topics; however, they also

reveal challenges that have and still confront civilizations the world over.

As you begin each chapter, take five or ten minutes to look at the **chapter opening pages.** These two pages at the beginning of each chapter reveal what is to come: a photo conceptualizes a main theme of the chapter, and a chapter outline and a timeline allow you to fix beginning and end points in this part of your trip. The chapter introduction sets the stage for the content that follows and indicates the chapter's overall themes—sometimes political or economic, sometimes religious, social, or artistic. Take time to read the introduction and then thumb to the end of the chapter to read the conclusion. Next, go through the chapter reading only the main and secondary headlines. Finally, return to the beginning of the chapter and start to read—knowing in advance where you have come from and which way you are going.

Within each chapter we offer you other tools to gain an understanding of the past. Events take place in a location, and each location has particular features that affect what will happen. Thus the text includes more than 100 full-color **maps,** each with its own explanatory caption. Shaded **insets** on most of the maps help you to locate its territory on its larger hemisphere or the globe. Some maps are designed to make clear the nature of a single distinctive event; others illustrate larger trends.

Each chapter also offers new features to help you better engage with the content. The new **pronunciation guide** will help you correctly pronounce key foreign terms—after each such word within the text a pronunciation appears in parentheses. The new on-page **glossary** provides concise definitions of key historical terms and appears in the footer of the pages in which terms are discussed.

Different civilizations have different visions of themselves and their place in the world. The **Discovery Through Maps** boxes in many of the chapters will give you a notion of the way that various cultures in the world have seen themselves and their relation to the rest of the globe. For example, al-Idrisi's "An Islamic Map of the World" is oriented, as was common in Arab maps of his time, with south at the top; it is centered on the world of his own experience, the sacred city of Mecca in Arabia and the civilized realm of the Mediterranean. A late-nineteenth-century map of southern Africa perpetuated "The Myth of the Empty Land," by which white settlers would claim that they were moving into an unpopulated land and that they had just as much right to it as Africans did.

We also include one or more excerpts from **primary source documents** in each chapter. These excerpts from original sources offer you a window into the way that the people of the time expressed themselves. The documents cover a variety of viewpoints: political, economic, legal, religious, social, artistic, and popular. For example, in "That Was No Brother," two documents—one by an African chief and the other by the English explorer Henry Morton Stanley—give two very different perceptions of the same battle.

The text's 500 **photos,** most in full color, give balanced pictorial coverage of all parts of the world and enhance the reading of each chapter by giving additional context and bringing to life the matters under discussion. For this edition, we have paid special attention in these photos to the lifestyles and contributions of women.

After you have finished each chapter you will find three features to help you prepare a paper or project or simply to learn more. The **Literature and Film** listings offer a listing of novels, poetry, films, and videos. The annotated bibliographies of **Suggestions for Reading** indicate useful general studies, monographs, and source materials. Also included is a list of **Suggestions for Web Browsing** to allow you to hook up to databases, sounds, images, or discussion groups dealing with the topics under consideration.

Robert R. Edgar
Neil J. Hackett
George F. Jewsbury
Barbara Molony

20°E 40°E 60°E 80°E 100°E 120°E 140°E 160°E

ARCTIC OCEAN

BARENTS SEA

S I B E R I A

Lena R.

Ob R.

URAL MTS.

Volga R.

Baikal

BALTIC SEA

NORTH EUROPEAN PLAIN

EUROPE

ASIA

ALPS

CAUCASUS MTS.

Black Sea

Caspian Sea

GOBI
(DESERT)

SEA OF JAPAN

Tigris R.

PLATEAU OF
TIBET

Huang Ho (Yellow R.)

MEDITERRANEAN SEA

Euphrates R.

HIMALAYAS

EAST
CHINA
SEA

Indus R.

Chang Jiang (Yangtze R.)

SAHARA
(D E S E R T)

Nile R.

RED SEA

ARABIAN
DESERT

Ganges R.

THAR
DESERT

PERSIAN
GULF

PACIFIC
OCEAN

AFRICA

ARABIAN
SEA

BAY OF
BENGAL

SOUTH
CHINA
SEA

PHILIPPINE
ISLANDS

Congo (Zaire) R.

L.
Victoria

I N D I A N
O C E A N

MADAGASCAR

AUSTRALIA

KALAHARI
DESERT

GREAT VICTORIA
DESERT

Darling R.

ANTARCTICA

Land Elevation

Feet	Meters
10,000	3,000
5,000	1,500
2,000	600
500	150
0	0
Below sea level	Below sea level

Ice-covered

International
boundaries

0   1,500   3,000 Miles
0   1,500   3,000 Kilometers

**Physical Map
of the World**

Stone Age Societies and the Earliest Civilizations of the Near East

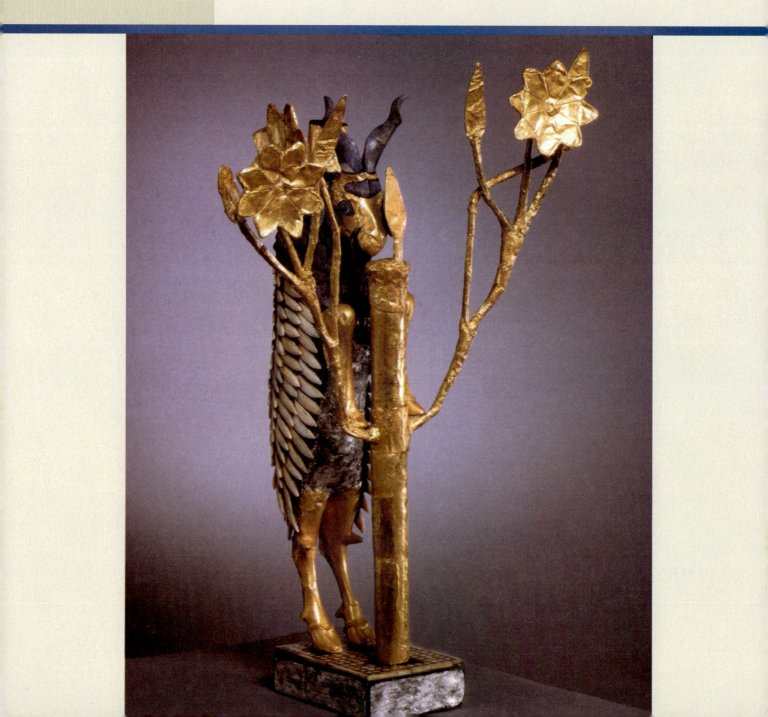

This chapter begins with an overview of the evolution of humankind on the African continent and examines the longest period of human life on the planet when our earliest ancestors invented basic tools and social structures on which all succeeding cultures would build. The skills necessary for survival were mastered over many hundred millennia as humans spread around the world, culminating in the breakthrough to farming with the domestication of plants and animals, and a settled life in villages.

Over the passage of many thousands of years, human societies located throughout Africa, Asia, and Europe continued to develop distinct cultural and technological patterns of life, but change in the patterns of everyday life was something most of the earth's early cultures avoided as frightening and disruptive. Profound change, even if extremely slow in comparison to social change in our modern world, seems to have taken place first in southwestern Asia and northeastern Africa (the Near East), where social developments were accelerated especially by the development of farming and the domestication of animals. There, along the banks of great rivers, villages evolved into towns and cities, and after the fourth millennium B.C.E. the complexity and sophistication of those cultures has led experts to label them as the world's earliest civilizations. The study of these earliest civilizations should furnish us with insights into the nature of some of humankind's most ancient institutions and oldest cultural legacies.

50,000

c. 50,000 B.C.E. *Homo sapiens*

10,000

c. 10,000 End of last ice age

c. 10,000–6000 The Aquatic Age in the Sahara

8000

c. 8000 Neolithic Revolution

6000

c. 6000 Agricultural Revolution: Occupation of Çatul Hüyük

4000

c. 3200 Emergence of civilization in Mesopotamia and Egypt

c. 2800–2300 Old Sumerian Period

c. 2700–2200 Old Kingdom of Egypt (Pyramid Age)

c. 2300–2150 Akkadian Empire

c. 2050–1800 Middle Kingdom of Egypt

2000

c. 2000–1600 Old Babylonian Empire

c. 1570–1090 New Kingdom of Egypt

c. 1450–1200 Hittite Empire

c. 745–612 Assyrian Empire

c. 586–538 Babylonian Captivity of the Jews

c. 550–332 Persian Empire

3

THE ORIGINS OF HUMANKIND

■ *What role did the African environment play in the evolution of* Homo sapiens?

Who are we? Where do we come from? Human beings have probably asked these questions ever since they have had the ability to communicate through language. For thousands of years, humans turned to religion to answer such questions. Indeed, it has only been within the last 150 years that science has put forth the theory that the human species evolved out of lower life forms. The controversy surrounding the theory of evolution continues up to today, although with decreasing intensity as more and more fossil evidence comes to light supporting the theory. Of course, the fossil record will never be complete, and paleontologists (scientists who study fossil remains in order to understand the life of past geological periods) have only skeletal remains to analyze. Nevertheless, the case for evolution appears overwhelming.

According to the theory of evolution, humans belong to the Primate order, which also includes lemurs, tarsiers, monkeys, and apes. A crucial development occurred when the ape family split into branches: tree-dwelling apes and ground-dwelling apes known as *hominids* ("prehumans" or "protohumans"). Over time and in response to environmental pressures, the hominids learned to walk upright, their

legs grew longer than their arms, and their hands—no longer required for locomotion—became more dexterous. Most important, the prehuman head gradually shifted toward a more upright position, rendering superfluous much of the muscle at the back of the neck. This favored expansion of the brain, which ultimately led to modern *Homo sapiens* ("thinking man"), the only survivor of the many-branched hominid tree.

Paleontologists have discovered all of the fossil remains of the earliest ancestors of *Homo sapiens* in Africa. These include *Australopithecus africanus* (ah-STRAH-loh-pi-THEE-kuhs ah-fri-KAH-nus; "southern African ape"). First discovered in South Africa in 1924, it had an erect posture but apelike brain. In 1964 the first representative of the genus *Homo* was found at Olduvai Gorge in Tanzania at a site some 1.75 million years old. In 1973 the partial skeleton of a female named "Lucy" (for the Beatles' hit song "Lucy in the Sky with Diamonds") was found in Ethiopia and dated to about 3.8 to 3 million years ago. One of the most recent discoveries came in 1998, when South African paleontologists discovered a hominid 4 feet tall and some 3.5 million years old, whose virtually complete remains provide uniquely detailed information on the transition from ape to human.

Homo habilis ("skillful man") was the first toolmaker. Dating from about two and a half to two million years ago, *H. habilis* was less than 5 feet tall, walked

An Introduction to the Elements of the Earth

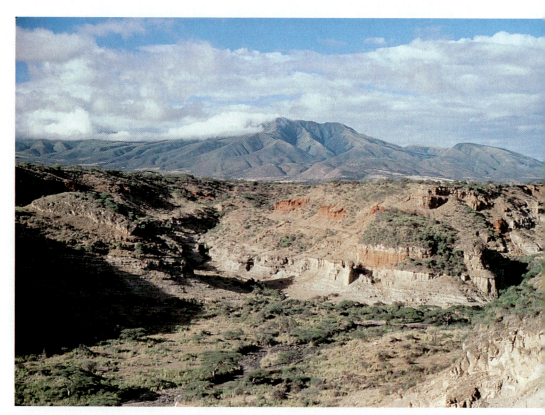

Aerial view of Olduvai Gorge in Tanzania, the site of findings by Mary Leakey and Louis S. B. Leakey, including the first representative fossils of the genus Homo.

erect, and had a well-developed opposable thumb that allowed the species to fashion tools. These fossil remains were found in association with crude tools—rocks cracked and flaked into specialized tools to cut meat and softer plants and to ward off predators. These tools expanded the nutritional options of *H. habilis.*

Later and more advanced species included *Homo ergaster,* which emerged perhaps as long as 2.3 million years ago in Africa. This species was labeled *Homo erectus* in Asia and is more widely known by that name. *H. erectus* had an upright posture, a physique very similar to modern humans, and a brain size of about 1000 cubic centimeters. *Erectus* learned to control and use fire—a major step in extending human habitation into colder latitudes—and perfected the first major standardized all-purpose tool, the Acheulean hand ax. Dubbed the Paleolithic "Swiss army knife" because it could be used for cutting, scraping, chopping, and digging, this ax remained a favorite tool long after the extinction of the species. *Erectus* was the first species to live its life primarily on the ground rather than in the trees and to demonstrate the ability to adapt to varied environments.

Around 1.6 million B.C.E. this species took the bold step of migrating out of Africa, into the Near East and Asia and eventually to the colder climate of Europe. Several theories have been advanced to explain why this movement took place out of Africa. One is that an extended dry period in the region of the present-day Sahara desert may have forced *H. erectus* to move over a wider area to collect foodstuffs. Another argument is that *H. erectus* could have moved into other regions as the species developed an ability to adapt to different environments.

From about 200,000 to 40,000 years ago, during the last ice age, a subspecies of *H. erectus,* the Neanderthals, were the principal inhabitants of Europe and spread to adjacent parts of Asia and Africa. Named for the Neander valley in western Germany where their remains were unearthed in 1856 (*thal* is the German word for "valley"), Neanderthals were slightly taller than 5 feet and had sloping foreheads, with prominent brow ridges, and thickset bodies. They were especially suited to coping with the colder climes of Europe. The inventors of many specialized tools, they were able hunters and adapted to extreme cold by using fire, wearing clothes, and living in caves. One school of thought contended that Neanderthals were the ancestors of modern Europeans until recent DNA testing of a Neanderthal skeleton showed very little overlap with the DNA of *H. sapiens.* Consequently, though sharing a common ancestor, the Neanderthals were probably not a subspecies of *sapiens.*

The culminating phase of the development of the genus *Homo* occurred around 150,000 to 100,000 years ago with the gradual emergence of *H. sapiens.* Up until a few years ago, scientists were engaged in a vigorous debate between the proponents of the "Out of Africa" school—who contend that *H. sapiens* originated exclusively in Africa and spread from there to other continents—and the multiregionalists—who argue that *H. sapiens* evolved independently in Africa, Asia, and Europe. Recent testing of mitochondrial DNA, however, strongly supports the argument for an African origin for *H. sapiens.* Mitochondrial DNA is passed on only through a mother to her offspring. By comparing DNA samples from individuals around the world and calculating the rate of mutations, geneticists have traced our human ancestors back to a hypothetical "Eve" whom they believe lived in eastern Africa some 200,000 years ago.

There is also a lively debate about the interaction between *H. sapiens* and the species of *H. erectus.* In Europe, the Cro-Magnons—*H. sapiens* named after a locality in southern France where their bones were unearthed in 1868—and Neanderthals coexisted for 50,000 years. Around 40,000 years ago, however, the Neanderthals died out, leaving the Cro-Magnons as the only hominids in Europe. Perhaps Cro-Magnons' superior brainpower and communications skills ultimately gave them a decisive advantage over Neanderthals in controlling and using food resources. We don't know for certain, but paleontologists have established that Cro-Magnon skeletons are virtually indistinguishable from those of humans today. Skillfully made flint and bone tools and polychrome paintings found on cave walls indicate that the Cro-Magnon possessed an advanced culture. By 20,000 B.C.E. Cro-Magnon and other representatives of *H. sapiens* inhabited Europe, Asia, Africa, and Australia and had moved into Americas by migrating across the Bering Strait on foot or by traveling in small boats along the coast. Today there is but one existing species of the genus *Homo.*

DOCUMENT

The Long Journey

PRELITERATE CULTURES

▪ *What distinguishes Paleolithic from Neolithic culture?*

In many respects we humans are eclipsed in physical endowments by numerous other creatures—in an all-species Olympic Games, we might not qualify for a medal. We cannot compete with the strength of the elephant or the speed of the antelope on land or any number of marine creatures. Our ability to defy gravity is dwarfed by insects that can jump higher and farther in terms of their size, to say nothing of birds, whose specialized structures enable them to fly and soar. Yet, a number of attributes functioning in concert allowed our species to forge ahead of all others.

They include erect posture, an opposable thumb ideal for fashioning tools, stereoscopic and color vision capable of close visual attention, and a brain whose size and multiple capabilities have enabled it to be termed the "organ of civilization."

Like other creatures, humans possess a practical intelligence for making meaningful responses to the environment. In addition, we are capable of thinking and communicating symbolically through language. The principle of symbolism gives everything a name and makes its functioning universally applicable, rather than restricting it to particular cases. By means of this capability to engage in symbolic thought and communication, humankind has created patterns of behavior and learning that can be termed *culture*. Unlike other creatures, we live also in a symbolic universe that draws on language, myth, art and religion to express aspects of human experience.

Paleolithic Culture

Making and using tools provide the first evidence of humankind's ability to employ reason to solve problems. Stone implements were the most distinctive feature of early human culture; thus, this stage is known as the **Paleolithic** or Old Stone Age. Our earliest ancestors made use of *eoliths* ("dawn stones"), bits of

---

Paleolithic—An era associated with the early Stone Age and the use of simple stone implements and weapons.

stone picked up to perform an immediate job. This simple utilization of what lay at hand was the first major step in toolmaking. The second consisted of *fashioning*, the haphazard preparation of a tool as need arose. The third step was *standardization*, making implements according to certain set traditions. It is with this third stage that we see the importance of symbolic thought in creating patterns of learning and behavior, transmitted in turn from one generation to the next.

In later Paleolithic cultures, toolmaking became progressively sophisticated and efficient. It was marked by a wide range of specialized tools and weapons, including implements whose primary purpose was to make other tools. The fashioning of small, specialized flints, known as *microliths*, represents a compact use of materials—indeed, the ancestor of present-day technological miniaturization. In late Paleolithic cultures, too, our ancestors applied mechanical principles to the movement of weapons. Throwers to launch spears worked on the lever principle to increase the propelling power of a hunter's arm. The bow was also invented to concentrate muscular energy to propel an arrow; it was soon also used to provide a means of twirling a stick, and this led to the invention of the rotary drill. Strictly speaking, *Paleolithic* is a cultural and not a chronological term. In fact, much of our knowledge of Paleolithic culture comes from groups surviving into modern times— for example, indigenous peoples in the rain forests

DOCUMENT

The Tool Maker

As human beings faced an ever-expanding set of challenges to their existence, they invented even more sophisticated tools, as evidenced by these examples of Paleolithic toolmaking.

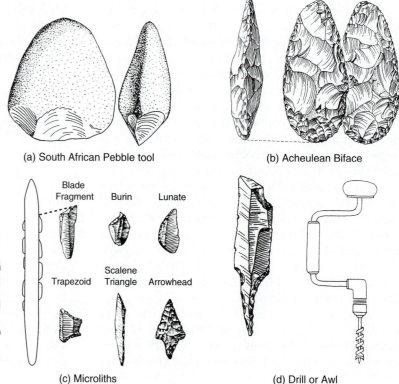

(a) South African Pebble tool

(b) Acheulean Biface

Blade Fragment   Burin   Lunate

Trapezoid   Scalene Triangle   Arrowhead

(c) Microliths

(d) Drill or Awl

Prehistoric art in Los Toldos, Argentina, includes representations of deer and hands. Archaeologists have dated the art to around 15,000 B.C.E.

of Brazil. From an economic standpoint, the Paleolithic is also a food-gathering stage, when humans hunted, fished, and collected wild foodstuffs. Labor was divided according to sex. Men hunted, fished, and protected the group. Women picked wild plants, fruits, and nuts and prepared the food for eating; they also processed animal hides and wood into household objects and cared for the children. Men and women shared such tasks as building dwellings, making ornaments and tools, and training children for adult life.

A special achievement of late Paleolithic cultures around the world was their art. For instance, ani- mated, realistic paintings of bison, reindeer, primitive horses, and other animals, colored in shades of black, red, yellow, and brown, have been found in more than a hundred Cro-Magnon caves in Spain and France dating from about 28,000 to 10,000 B.C.E. Cave art rivals that of civilized artists not only stylistically but also as an expression of significant human experiences. Universal in appeal, the pictures reflect the Paleolithic dependence on an abundance of game animals and success in hunting them. In addition, the artists may have believed they could wield a magical power over the spirits of animals to ensure their availability. Paleolithic artists also chiseled pictures on rock and bone and modeled figures out of clay.

The Neolithic Revolution and Advent of Agriculture

A development of enormous consequence for human societies—the shift to food-producing—took place in the ancient Near East. There, on the flanks of the

mountains bordering the **Fertile Crescent,** an area of rich soil stretching northeast from the Nile River to the Tigris in what is now northern Iraq and then southeast to the Persian Gulf, was adequate rainfall to nourish wild forms of wheat and barley and provide grass for wild sheep, goats, and pigs. By 7000 B.C.E., people in that region had domesticated these grains and animals and lived in villages near their fields and herds. This momentous change ushered in the **Neolithic** or New Stone Age. The best-pre- served village so far uncovered is Çatal Hüyük (chah-tahl HOO-yook; "forked mound") in southern Turkey. This 32-acre site, occupied from around 6500 to 5400 B.C.E., contains some of the most advanced features of Neolithic culture: pottery, woven textiles, mud-brick houses, shrines honoring a mother goddess, and plastered walls decorated with murals and carved reliefs. The most recent archaeological excavations at the site have raised questions about whether settled village life happened at the same time as the domestication of agriculture and whether the community had a political and religious elite.

Neolithic artisans ground and polished stones to produce axes, adzes, and chisels with sharp cutting edges. They devised methods for drilling holes in stone, used boulders for grinding grain, and made stone bowls for storage. Skilled in their earlier role as wild food gatherers, women were responsible now for cultivating the prepared fields. They also made clay pots—decorated with geometric designs—and spun and wove textiles from cultivated flax and animal wool. The Neolithic revolution, with its "migration of skills," spread to the Balkan Peninsula by 5000 B.C.E., Egypt and Central Europe by 4000 B.C.E., and Britain and northwest India by 3000 B.C.E. The Neolithic cultures of sub-Saharan Africa, East Asia, Mesoamerica, and the Andes all developed independently from the Neolithic culture of the Fertile Crescent.

PRELITERATE SOCIETY AND RELIGION

▪ *What were the characteristics of religious beliefs among the earliest human societies?*

How can we know about those features of early cultures that are not apparent from the remains of tools and other objects? In addition to our being able to observe cultures similar to Paleolithic and Neolithic

Fertile Crescent—A geographic region that stretches in a semicircular arc from the eastern Mediterranean to the Persian Gulf.

Neolithic—A time period associated with the later Stone Age and the use of polished stone implements and weapons.

The Oldest Known Map: Çatal Hüyük

This wall painting is perhaps the oldest known map. It is also, for modern viewers, one of the most easily understood ancient maps. It is a city plan painted on two walls of a room in a Neolithic community in south-central Anatolia, near what is still the major land route in Turkey between Europe and the Near East. Radiocarbon dating has placed the image around 6200 B.C.E. It is a very large figure, nearly 9 feet wide.

By the 1960s archaeologists had uncovered 139 rooms in the complex and decided that at least 40 were used for special rites, probably of a religious nature. One of these special rooms, whose walls had often been replastered, contained this large image featuring rows of boxlike shapes. Archaeologists were amazed at the similarity between their own carefully drawn site maps and the painting on the wall. It soon became apparent that the Neolithic image was a map of the community or perhaps of the town that immediately preceded the one the dig was uncovering.

A great deal of information can be gleaned from this map:

- The town site was on a slope, with rows of houses or buildings set on graded terraces.

- The rectangular buildings and the streets set at right angles provide a gridiron look that has characterized much town planning throughout history.

- The elongated, or linear, pattern of the settlement may reflect an orientation to a major road.

- The large figure that looks like a mountain with two peaks beyond the town is, no doubt, Hasan Da-g, a volcano that was active until about 2000 B.C.E. The volcano was the source of the obsidian that was the basis of the settlement's wealth. The glassy, volcanic rock was used for making cutting tools, knives, scrapers, weapons, jewelry, ornaments, and a variety of other artifacts.

The complete map contains about 80 rooms or buildings, somewhat fewer structures than were found in the actual town that was excavated. Since the wall was replastered several times, perhaps the map was "updated." Or it may have served a ceremonial purpose for which the absolute accuracy of a civic map was unnecessary.

This map, certainly the oldest example of landscape art in addition to its function as a map, has perplexed the experts since its excavation in the 1960s. The painting certainly depicts an urban landscape, 2000 years earlier than archaeologists expected such a settlement in the area. Further excavation revealed that the town was very large by contemporary standards—perhaps home to a population exceeding 6000. A settlement of that size could not have grown enough food to support itself while accomplishing all the other tasks that Çatal Hüyük's residents did. Trade and an extensive commercial network had to be present, but there is no archaeological evidence from the site of specialized tools. Yet there is very clear proof that Çatal Hüyük possessed good pottery, well-fashioned textiles, and outstanding artwork. Some experts have speculated that the city may have served primarily as a religious center for an extensive area. In one section of the excavated town, an area of about one acre, archaeologists believe that as many as one of every three buildings may have served as a religious shrine or cult center of some sort.

Questions to Consider

1. What do you think may have been the purpose of the artist or artists who painted this map? Do you think it was intended to impart information?

2. Could the map have been constructed for a religious or ceremonial reason?

3. Why do you think that the volcano plays such a dominant part of this landscape? Could its depiction have a ceremonial or religious significance?

that still exist, the myths of Stone Age peoples throw light on their beliefs and customs. Like ourselves, our Stone Age ancestors sought to account for the origin of the universe and the meaning of existence. In often ascribing the behavior of natural phenomena to supernatural causes, Stone Age mythmakers were nonetheless seeking to make sense of what was familiar in their own lives—such as thunder and lightning and the cycle of the seasons.

Social Organization

Among all peoples, the basic social unit appeared to be the *elementary family*—parents and their offspring. In early human societies, the *extended family* was an individual family, together with a circle of related persons who usually traced their descent through their mothers and were bound together by mutual loyalty. The extended family strengthened the elementary unit in obtaining food and protecting its members against other groups. Land was communally owned but allocated to separate families. A *clan* was a group of extended families that believed that they had a common ancestor. Many peoples identified their clans by a **totem**—an animal or other natural object that was revered. Examples of totemism exist today in military insignia and the emblems of fraternal and sports organizations.

A fourth grouping, the *tribe*, comprised a number of clans. Such a community was characterized by a common speech or distinctive dialect, common cultural heritage, specific inhabited territory, and tribal chief. No community could exist or hold together unless rules governing relations among its members were recognized as binding upon all. Such rules crystallized into precedent or customary law, often attributed to a divine origin.

Correct behavior in preliterate societies consisted of not violating custom. Justice in a group acted to maintain equilibrium. Because theft disturbed economic equilibrium, justice was achieved by a settlement between the injured person and the thief. If the latter restored what had been stolen or its equivalent, the victim was satisfied, and the thief was not punished. Murder and wounding were also private matters, to be avenged by the next of kin on the principle of "an eye for an eye." Certain acts, however, such as treason, witchcraft, and incest were considered dangerous to the whole group and required punishment by the entire community—if need be, by death.

As a general rule, government in these early societies was of a democratic character. Older males—the council of elders—played a dominant role in decision-making because of their greater experience and knowledge of the group's customs and folklore. Serious decisions, such as going to war or electing a chief, required the consent of a general assembly of all adult males. The elected chief was pledged to rule in accordance with custom and in consultation with the council of elders.

Undoubtedly, the strongest single force in the life of preliterate peoples, past and present, has been religion. Religious sensibilities apparently originated in feelings of awe, as our ancestors became conscious of the universe about them. Awe and wonder led to the belief, usually called **animism,** that life exists in everything in nature—winds, stones, animals, and humans. A natural extension was belief in the existence of spirits separable from material bodies. Neanderthal people placed food and implements alongside their carefully buried dead, indicating that they believed in an afterlife and treated their forebears with affection and respect.

DOCUMENT

Early Art: Religion or Worship?

Late Paleolithic people revered the spirits of the animals they hunted as well as the spirit of fertility upon which human and animal life depended. Associated in particular with Neolithic cultures was the worship of a fertility deity, the Earth Mother (or Mother Goddess), known to us from many carved female figures with exaggerated sexual features. Fertility figurines have been excavated from Neolithic sites all over the world. At Çatal Hüyük, 33 representations of the Mother Goddess have been found, but only eight of a god who was either the goddess's son or consort. The relative scarcity of representations of male gods, together with evidence that the cult of the goddess was administered by priestesses rather than priests, supports the view that women occupied a central position in Neolithic society.

Closely associated with ancient religion was the practice of magic. In addition to revering spirits, people wanted to compel them to provide favors. For this purpose they employed magic and turned to shamans to ward off droughts, famines, floods, and plagues through what they believed to be magic powers of communication with the spirits.

Traditionally, magic has been regarded as diametrically opposed to science. Yet, as scholars are increasingly recognizing, both our ancestors and contemporary scientists believe that nature is orderly and that what is immediately perceived by the senses can be systematically classified—such as by the present-day subsistence-level Hanunóo of the Philippines. They have recorded 461 animal types and classified insect forms into 108 named categories,

---

totem—A symbol or emblem, usually an animal or natural object, that is associated with a family or clan.

animism—Generally, the belief that everything in the world is endowed with its own spirit.

including 13 for ants and termites.[1] Preliterate peoples must therefore be credited with a desire to acquire knowledge, both for practical purposes and for its own sake.

Further indications of this avid search for knowledge have been provided by studies of large stone monuments constructed by Neolithic peoples in at least two continents. With a computer, one astronomer found an "astonishing" number of correlations at Stonehenge in England between the alignments of stones, stone holes, and mounds and the solar and lunar positions as of 1500 B.C.E. when Stonehenge was built. These made possible a more accurate calendar and the prediction of the rising and setting of the sun and moon. But the construction of Neolithic astronomical structures had occurred long before Stonehenge. Ancient sandstone monuments in the Nile delta of Egypt indicate that their builders possessed a surprisingly complex knowledge of geometry and astronomy. Between 5000 and 7000 years old, this earliest known astronomical complex shows slabs in various configurations, including a circle that allowed the inhabitants to anticipate sunrise during the summer solstice.[2]

Before we conclude our overview of preliterate cultures, a brief summary is in order. During the first period of humankind's cultural evolution, the Paleolithic or Old Stone Age, our ancestor's toolmaking capability advanced from reliance on very simple implements—such as the standardized, all-purpose hand ax—to ever more sophisticated tools and techniques of operation. This technological evolution enabled *Homo sapiens* to move into and adapt to different environments around the world. By the time of the last glacial phase, our forebears had spread over most of the world.

Paleolithic cultures had food-gathering economies. Then, perhaps about 10,000 years ago, the Neolithic, or New Stone Age, emerged with the appearance of food-producing communities first in the Fertile Crescent of southwestern Asia and then elsewhere. Neolithic cultures are characterized by the cultivation of grains, the domestication of animals, pottery making, and the fashioning of polished stone tools. These advances occurred in different places on earth and at different times.

MESOPOTAMIA: THE FIRST CIVILIZATION

■ *What factors contributed to the development of civilization in Mesopotamia?*

Historians do not agree on how best to define the term *civilization*. But most would accept the view that a civilization is a culture that has attained a degree of complexity, characterized by urban life and the interdependence of those urban residents. In other words, a civilization is a culture capable of sustaining a great number of specialists to furnish the economic, social, political, and religious needs of a large social unit. Other components of a civilization are a system of writing (originating from the need to keep records); monumental, permanent architecture in place of simple buildings; and art that is not merely decorative, like that on Neolithic pottery, but representative of people and their activities. All these characteristics of civilization first appeared together in the southern part of Mesopotamia, which came to be called Sumer.

MAP

The Beginnings of Civilization in the Ancient Near East: City States and International Empires

Around 6000 B.C.E., after the agricultural revolution had begun to spread from its origins on the northern edge of the Fertile Crescent, Neolithic farmers began making their homes in the valleys of the Tigris and Euphrates Rivers themselves. Although the broad plain created by these rivers received insufficient regular rainfall to support agriculture, the eastern section was able to benefit from both rivers as sources of irrigation. Known to the Greeks as Mesopotamia (Greek for "between the rivers"), the lower sections of this plain, beginning near the point where the two rivers nearly converge, was called Babylonia. Babylonia included two geographical areas—Akkad in the north and Sumer, the delta of this river system, in the south.

Sumer had tremendous agricultural potential as long as natural environmental problems could be addressed. The rivers sometimes flooded in uncontrollable torrents. Spring and summer storms were often severe. The valley was virtually exposed on all sides to potential invaders, with no formidable natural boundaries to reduce the possibility of invasion. From the very beginning of habitation, cooperation was necessary for life to succeed. Swamps had to be drained, canals had to be dug to bring water to remote fields, and safeguards had to be constructed against flooding. These and many other related problems were solved by cooperative effort; yet the Mesopotamians continued to live in awe of their gods, whose whims might at any time bring destruction down on them.

In spite of the unpredictable nature of their gods, the Sumerians struggled to bring stability to their society. Sumerian metal workers discovered that copper, when combined with tin, produced an alloy, bronze, which was harder than copper and provided a sharper edge. The beginning of civilization in Sumer is associated with the beginning of this Bronze Age, and the new technology soon spread to Egypt, and later to Europe and Asia. Between 3500 and 3100 B.C.E. the foundations were established for a complex economy and a social order more sophisticated than any previously developed. This far more complex culture, based on large urban centers populated by interdependent and specialized workers, is what experts define as civilization.

Since the Mesopotamian plain had no stone, no metals, and no timber except its soft palm trees, these materials had to be imported, most often from the north. Water transport down the Tigris and Euphrates aided in this process. The oldest sailing boat known is represented by a model found in a Sumerian grave dating to around 3500 B.C.E. Soon after this date, wheeled vehicles appear in the form of war chariots drawn by donkeys. Another important invention was the potter's wheel, first used in Sumer soon after 3500 B.C.E.

The Emergence of Civilization in Sumer, c. 3200–2800 B.C.E.

By 3200 B.C.E. the urban centers in the region known as Sumer had developed the majority of the characteristics required to be called a civilization. Because these included the first evidence of writing, this first phase of Sumerian civilization, to about 2800 B.C.E., is called the **Protoliterate** (meaning "before literate") period.

The Sumerian language is not related to **Semitic** or **Indo-European,** the major language families that appear later in the Near East. The original home of the Semitic-speaking peoples was most likely the Arabian peninsula, and the Indo-Europeans seem to have migrated from regions around the Black and Caspian Seas. A third, much smaller language family, sometimes called Hamitic, included the Egyptians and other peoples of northeastern Africa. But the origin of the Sumerians remains a subject of speculation: Some suggest that migration from the Indus River valley might account for their arrival.

A number of the inventions and innovations of protoliterate Sumer eventually made their way to both

the Nile and the Indus valleys, most likely through trade and commercial contacts. Among these inventions were wheeled vehicles and the potter's wheel. The discovery in Egypt of cylinder seals similar in shape to those used in Sumer attests to contact between the two cultures toward the end of the fourth millennium B.C.E. Certain early Egyptian art themes and architectural forms are also thought to be of Sumerian origin. And it is probable that the example of Sumerian writing stimulated the Egyptians to develop a script of their own.

The symbols on the oldest Sumerian clay tablets, the world's first writing, were pictures of concrete things such as a person's face, a sheep, a star, or a measure of grain. Some of these pictographs also represented ideas; for example, the picture of a foot was used to represent the idea of walking, and a picture of a mouth joined to that for water meant "to drink." This early pictographic writing developed into phonetic (or syllabic) writing when the scribes realized that a sign could represent a sound as

This small but beautifully crafted black diorite statue represents Gudea, the powerful king of the Sumerian city of Lagash in the late third millenium B.C.E. Contemporary poetry and inscriptions indicate that Gudea possessed great wealth and honored his gods by constructing numerous temples and shrines.

well as an object or idea. Thus, the personal name Kuraka could be written by combining the pictographs for mountain (*kur*), water (*a*), and mouth (*ka*). By 2800 B.C.E. the use of syllabic writing had reduced the number of Sumerian signs from nearly 2000 to 600.

When writing, Mesopotamian scribes used a reed stylus to make wedge-shaped impressions in soft clay tablets. This *cuneiform* system of writing (from the Latin *cuneus,* "wedge") was adopted by many other peoples of the Near East, including the Babylonians, the Assyrians, the Hittites, and the Persians.

---

protoliterate—Meaning "before literacy"; the period in a society's development that precedes the development and use of a written language.

Semitic—A group of related languages that include Akkadian, Arabic, Aramaean, Canaanite, and Hebrew. The presumptive source language of these languages is thought to have originated in the Arabian Peninsula, from whence, beginning about 2500 B.C.E., Semitic-speaking tribes migrated to the Mediterranean coast, Mesopotamia, and the Nile delta. The term *Semitic* also refers to the cultures of those who speak Semitic languages.

Indo-European—A family of languages that descended from a single unrecorded language spoken in the Caucasus region more than 5000 years ago. Carried by migrating tribes to Europe and Asia, dialects of the source language eventually evolved into such varied languages as English, German, French, Spanish, Latin, Greek, Persian, and Hindi.

The Old Sumerian Period, c. 2800–2300 B.C.E

By 2800 B.C.E. the Sumerian cities had fully emerged into complex civilizations. This first historical age, called the Old Sumerian period, was characterized by constant warfare as each city attempted to protect or enlarge its land and guarantee its access to water and irrigation. Each city-state was a theocracy, a state in which the chief local god was believed to be the actual ruler. The god's earthly representative was the *ensi*, the high priest and city governor, who acted as the god's caretaker in both religious and civil functions. Though given the power to act for the god by virtue of being the human agent of the divine ruler, the *ensi* was not himself considered a divine being.

The *ensis* were powerful and sometimes autocratic rulers. Most famous is the semilegendary Gilgamesh, ruler of Uruk about 2700 B.C.E., who is known only from several epic tales. Although Gilgamesh is portrayed as an extremely powerful ruler, the epic poem also shows that Sumerian rulers could be questioned, even opposed, by some of the nobles who served as advisers in the city's council.

Early Sumerian society was highly stratified, with priests and officials of the city god and subordinate deities assuming great authority. Each temple administered extensive land holdings; that land served as the god's "estate on earth." In addition to the temple lands, a considerable part of a city's territory originally consisted of land collectively owned by clans, kinship groups comprising a number of extended families. By 2600 B.C.E. these clan lands were becoming the private property of great landowners called *lugals* (literally, "great men"). Deeds of sale record the transfer of clan lands to private owners in return for substantial payments in copper to a few clan leaders and insignificant grants of food to the remaining clan members. These private estates were worked by "clients" whose lives were regulated by the temple authorities.

In time, priests, administrators, and *ensis* began confiscating temple land and other property and asserting their authority over the common people. Their ambitions frequently led to the rise of autocratic leaders who came to power on a wave of popular discontent. Since these despots were usually *lugals*, the term *lugal* became a political title and is now generally translated as "king."

The Sumerians, like their Mesopotamian successors, made extensive use of the institution of slavery, and slaves are recorded to have worked in many capacities—as farm and urban laborers, as servants in homes and temples, and in civic positions, such as in public administration. In some cities, slaves accounted for 40 to 50 percent of the population. Slaves in Mesopotamia were not without rights, and in many cases they were treated with care. Slavery was not based on racial characteristics or cultural differences; people of the same culture became enslaved through conquest or to pay off debt. Perhaps because of the possibility that any city-state might be overtaken and its residents enslaved at the pleasure of the gods, the treatment of slaves in Mesopotamia seems generally to have been more humane than at other times and places in human history.

Sumerian women were able to attain high social prominence, usually depending on the rank of their own or their husbands' families. Men were given the greater authority than their wives in economic and legal matters, and only the husband could initiate divorce proceedings against his wife. Children were under the complete control of their parents until 20 or 21 years of age.

The Akkadian Period, c. 2300–2150 B.C.E.

To the immediate north of Sumer was the region of Akkad, inhabited by Semites who had adopted much of Sumerian culture. Appearing late in the fourth millennium B.C.E, the Akkadians were among the earliest of the Semitic peoples who migrated into Mesopotamia from the Arabian peninsula. Sargon I (2370–2315 B.C.E.), the first Akkadian ruler, conquered Sumer and went on to establish an empire that extended from the Persian Gulf almost to the Mediterranean Sea—the first true empire in history.

Very proud of his lower-class origins, Sargon boasted that his humble, unwed mother had been forced to abandon him, placing him in a reed basket and floating the basket down the river. Rescued and brought up by a gardener, Sargon rose to power through the army. As *lugal*, Sargon claimed to look after the welfare of the lower classes and to aid the rising class of private merchants. At the merchants' request, he once sent his army to far-off Asia Minor to protect a colony of them from interference by a local ruler. Sargon reputedly was a tireless worker on behalf of his people's prosperity and expanded his influence in neighboring lands through almost unending campaigns of conquest.

Early Sumer and Akkad

c. 3200–2800 B.C.E.	Protoliterate period in Sumer
c. 2800–2300 B.C.E.	Old Sumerian period
c. 2370–2315 B.C.E.	Reign of Sargon of Akkad
c. 2300–2150 B.C.E.	Akkadian dominance
c. 2150–2000 B.C.E.	Neo-Sumerian period
c. 2000–1600 B.C.E.	Old Babylonian period
c. 1792–1750 B.C.E.	Reign of Hammurabi
c. 1595 B.C.E.	Sack of Babylon by Hittites

Sargon's successors, however, were unable either to repel the attacks of hostile mountain peoples or to overcome the desire for independence of the priest-dominated Sumerian cities. As a result, the dynasty founded by Sargon collapsed about 2150 B.C.E.

The Neo-Sumerian Period, c. 2150–2000 B.C.E

Order and prosperity were restored by the *lugals* of the powerful Sumerian city of Ur. By creating a highly centralized administration in Sumer and Akkad, these rulers solved the problem of internal rebellion that had been of great concern for Sargon and his successors. The formerly temple-dominated cities became provinces administered by closely regulated governors. Religion became an arm of the state: the high priests were state appointees, and careful oversight and regulation by temple officials gave protection to a newly developing free enterprise economy that Sargon had encouraged. At the head of this bureaucratic state stood the *lugal* of Ur, now considered a living god and celebrated as a heaven-sent authority who brought order and security to the people, who were considered to be his servants.

The earliest of humankind's great civilizations developed in the area that came to be called the Fertile Crescent—where rainfall was adequate to nourish wild forms of grain and grazing animals could find sufficient food.

The *lugals* of Ur, who called themselves the "vigilant shepherds" of their people, presided over a highly centralized and efficient administration. Thousands of records have been preserved from this period, detailing the meticulous regulation of commerce, agriculture, and social standards by the powerful overlords of the city. In addition, Sumerian literature and culture flourished under their direction. But the greatness of Ur lasted for little more than one hundred years.

Disaster struck Ur about 2000 B.C.E., when Elamites from what is now Iran destroyed the city. The Sumerians were never again a dominant force politically, but their cultural influence continued to be powerful throughout all subsequent civilizations in the Tigris-Euphrates valley. The Sumerians themselves disappeared as a people, but the Sumerian language continued to be written and to serve as the language of scholarship and religious ritual.

For more than two centuries following the destruction of Ur, disunity and warfare again plagued Mesopotamia, along with economic stress, a lack of security, and acute hardship for the lower classes. Many merchants, however, used the absence of state controls to become aggressive capitalists who amassed fortunes that they invested in banking operations and land. The stronger local rulers of the period attempted to assert their authority by seizing access to water resources and working toward the establishment of dynastic control.

THE BABYLONIAN EMPIRE, C. 2000–1600 B.C.E.

■ *What distinguished the Babylonians from their Sumerian predecessors?*

Semitic Amorites (from the Akkadian word *Amurru*, "West"), produced one dynasty that based its power on its control of the city of Babylon. This new Babylonian family of rulers defeated its neighboring rivals and began to build their city into a capital that would dominate most of Mesopotamia for the next 300 years. The most outstanding of the kings of this Old Babylonian Empire was Hammurabi (c. 1792–1750 B.C.E.), an extremely successful warrior who succeeded in expanding and securing Babylon's military power north into Assyria, south into Sumer, and east into Elam.

Although he was a tireless warrior, Hammurabi is best known for the code of nearly 300 laws that were given by the king "in order to prevent the powerful from oppressing the weak, in order to give justice to the orphans and widows, in order to give my land fair decisions and to give rights to the oppressed. . . ."[3] The Code of Hammurabi is

Hammurabi's Law Code

a compilation of laws covering a wide variety of topics, such as property disputes, adultery, slavery, prostitution, inheritance, and public order. The collection was not exhaustive, but most likely served as guideposts for judges, as well as educated subjects, in their attempts to administer or anticipate the law. Such compilations of law date back to Sumerian codes 1400 years before Hammurabi's time, and much of the king's code echoes ancient Sumerian precedent. Hammurabi's Code made wide use of corporal punishment for offenses: based on the "eye for an eye, tooth for a tooth" principle of dispensing justice; in many cases Babylonian law was more harsh in its administration of mutilation or death as fitting punishment for crime than that by Sumerian judges, who often levied fines instead of corporal punishment. Babylonian law also made clear the privileged status of the upper classes, who suffered less severe penalties for their offenses as the common citizen, and far less severe punishments than those administered to slaves.

Hammurabi Receives His Law Code from the Gods

Despite the severity of much of Hammurabi's Code, and the disparities in treatment it imposed on the lower classes and slaves, Hammurabi's Code shows an attempt to reduce abusive interest rates and prices, limit slavery for debt to three years, and provide more care to widows and orphans. Minimum wages were established. Other laws protected wives and children; but a wife who had neglected care for her household or husband could be divorced without alimony, or the husband could take another wife and force the first to remain as a servant. Unless a son committed some grave offense, his father could not disinherit him. If the state failed to maintain law and order, the victim of that failure received compensation from the state: the value of the property stolen, or one mina of silver to the relatives of a murder victim.

In the conclusion to the Code, Hammurabi eloquently summed up his efforts to provide social justice for his people:

Let any oppressed man, who has a cause, come before my image as king of righteousness! Let him read the inscription on my monument! Let him give heed to my weighty words! And may my monument enlighten him as to his cause and may he understand his case! May he set his heart at ease! (and he will exclaim): Hammurabi indeed is a ruler who is like a real father to his people. . . .[4]

Mathematics and Science

Building on the work of the Sumerians, the Babylonians made advances in arithmetic, geometry, and algebra. For ease in working with both whole numbers and fractions, they compiled tables for multiplication and division and for square and cube roots.

They knew how to solve linear and quadratic equations, and their knowledge of geometry included the theorem later formulated by the Greek philosopher Pythagoras: The square of the hypotenuse of a right-angled triangle is equal to the sum of the squares of the other two sides. They used the Sumerian system of counting based on the unit 60 (sexagesimal) rather than that based on the number 10 (decimal). The remnants of this sexagesimal system is found today in computing divisions of time—60-minute hours—and the 360-degree circle. They also adopted the Sumerian principle of place-value notation that gave numbers a value according to their position in a series. To represent zero, they employed the character for "not," which is the same as our "naught," still used colloquially for "nothing."

The Babylonians achieved little that today can be called pure science. They were most concerned with observing the natural world so that the future could be predicted. They did observe nature and collect data, the first requirement of the scientific method; but to explain natural phenomena, they were satisfied with the formulation of myths that defined things in terms of the unpredictable whims of the gods. They thought the sun, moon, and five visible planets to be gods who were able to influence human lives; accordingly, their movements were watched, recorded, and interpreted—more the study of astrology than the science of astronomy. But through their study of the world around them in an effort to predict the future, the Mesopotamians were attempting to impose an order on what they found to be a chaotic universe. Through proper reading of the signs given by the gods, some stability in the world might be achieved.

Literature and Religion

The Babylonians borrowed from the Sumerians a body of literature ranging from heroic epics that compare in scope and themes with the *Iliad* and the *Odyssey* to wisdom writings that have their counterparts in the Hebrew Old Testament. The Sumerian *Epic of Gilgamesh* records the great adventures of the heroic ruler of Uruk who supposedly lived about 2700 B.C.E. The epic poem reflects the values of a heroic age, in which great heroes seek to earn undying fame and glory. The supreme value is the eternal reputation achieved through the performance of heroic deeds. After Gilgamesh slays the fierce Bull of Heaven, he stops to proclaim his victory:

> *What man is most impressive now:*
> *Who is finest, firmest, and most fair?*
> *Isn't Gilgamesh that man above men . . . ?*
> *Who is most glorious among men?*[5]

What Gilgamesh fears most is death, which, in the Mesopotamian viewpoint replaces a glorious life on earth with a dismal existence in the House of Dust, "where dust is their fare and clay their food." The epic's central theme is Gilgamesh's search for everlasting life. He seeks out and questions Utnapishtim (oot-nah-PISH-tim), who was granted eternal life because he saved all living creatures from a great flood. (Utnapishtim's story has many similarities with the Hebrew account of Noah and the Flood). But Gilgamesh's search in not successful, and he finally concludes that he must die like all other mortals:

> *There is darkness which lets no person*
> *again see the light of day;*
> *There is a road leading away from*
> *bright and lively life. There dwell those who eat*
> *dry dust*
> *and have no cooling water to quench their*
> *awful thirst.*
> *As I stood there I saw all those who've died*
> *and even kings among those darkened souls*
> *have none of their remote and former glory.*[6]

The ancient Mesopotamians never moved far beyond this early view that immortality was reserved for the gods, and that life after death, if it existed at all, was a gloomy and terrible existence where spirits haunted the world in a continual search for food and water. Unlike the Egyptians, they did not develop an expectation of an attractive life after death as a reward for good behavior on earth. They did come to believe in divine rewards for moral conduct, but these were rewards to be enjoyed in this life—increased worldly goods, numerous offspring, long life.

The ethical content of Babylonian religion was never well developed. Numerous priesthoods—more than 30 different types of priests and priestesses are known—became preoccupied with an elaborate set of rituals, particularly those designed to ward off evil demons and predict the future through observing omens and portents. Good deeds, the priests insisted, could not protect a person from demons that have the power to make their part-human and part-animal bodies invisible. Only the proper spells, incantations, and offerings could ward off evil.

While one large class of priests provided amulets inscribed with incantations and magic formulas to expel demons, another group dealt with predicting the future. Almost anything could be viewed as an omen, but most popular were dreams, the movements of birds and animals, the internal organs of sacrificed animals, the shape taken by oil poured on the surface of water, the casting of dice, and astronomical phenomena. Such practices, called superstitions in the modern world, were in reality attempts

Worshipper statues from the square temple, Eshnunna (now Tel Asmar, Iraq).

by the Mesopotamians to obtain some semblance of control and predictability over a world ruled by chaotic and random forces.

Collapse and Disorder, c. 1600–1200 B.C.E.

The pattern of disunity and warfare, all too familiar in Mesopotamia, reasserted itself following Hammurabi's death. In 1595 B.C.E. the Hittites, an Indo-European people who had established control in Asia Minor, mounted a daring raid down the Euphrates, sacking Babylon and destroying the weakened dynasty of Hammurabi. The swift success of the Hittite raid was made possible by a new means of waging war: the use of lightweight chariots drawn by horses instead of donkeys or oxen. The next five centuries in Mesopotamia were years of disorder about which little is known; political unity dissolved, yet the cultural foundations of Mesopotamian society, and the inheritance that culture owed to the Sumerians, continued to influence the shaping of later Mesopotamian societies.

The beginnings of civilization in Egypt, and the continuous development of that great early civilization, was a development for the most part contemporary with the origins and development of civilization in Mesopotamia. Yet the circumstances under which Egyptian culture took shape, and the very nature of

the Egyptian civilization, stands in contrast to the Mesopotamian achievement.

EGYPT: GIFT OF THE NILE

■ *What effect did the waters of the Nile have on ancient Egyptian political and religious institutions?*

Egypt, one of Africa's earliest civilizations, is literally "the gift of the [Nile] river," as the ancient Greek historian Herodotus observed. The Nile River stretches for 4100 miles, but it is its last valley, extending 750 miles from the First **Cataract** to the Nile delta, that was the heartland of Egyptian civilization. Egyptians called the Nile valley *Kemet* ("the black land") because its soils were renewed annually by the rich black silt deposited by the floodwaters of the Blue Nile and the Apara, rivers descending from the Ethiopian highlands. Unlike the unpredictable floods of Mesopotamia, the Nile's floods rose and fell with unusual precision, reaching Aswan (ahs-WAHN) by late June and peaking in September before beginning to subside. The perennial key to successful farming was con-

---

cataract—Large waterfall or a series of rapids on a river such as the Nile.

trolling the Nile by diverting its floodwaters along the 10- to 20-mile-wide floodplain for irrigation. Egyptian farmers achieved this by building an elaborate network of dikes and canals.

Predynastic Egypt

The first Nile settlers were likely people who moved to the river valley as climatic changes transformed the savanna grasslands west of the Nile into desert. By 4800 B.C.E. the earliest farming communities began to appear in the western Nile delta and spread to the rest of Egypt over the next eight centuries. Recognizing the advantages of creating larger social groupings and the need to cushion themselves from the impact of droughts, floods, and plagues, farming communities started banding together to form regional chiefdoms in Lower Egypt, the area comprising the broad Nile delta north of Memphis, and Upper Egypt, which extended southward along the narrow Nile valley as far as the First Cataract at Aswan. A kingdom emerged in Upper Egypt, while Lower Egypt was divided into a number of districts (later called *nomes*) that had formerly been ruled by independent chieftains.

The Predynastic period ended soon after 3100 B.C.E. when King Menes (also known as *Narmer*) united Upper Egypt and started gradually incorporating Lower Egypt into a new kingdom with its capital at Memphis. This period has become known as the First **Dynasty,** and it marks the beginning of one of the longest-lasting civilizations in history, lasting for 3000 years.

---

dynasty—A series of rulers who belong to the same family or line.

Ancient Egypt	
c. 3100 B.C.E.	Menes unites Upper Egypt
c. 2700 B.C.E.	Construction of Step Pyramid
c. 1720 B.C.E.	Hyksos conquer Egypt
c. 1600 B.C.E.	Oldest medical text
c. 1479–1458 B.C.E.	Regency of Queen Hatshepsut
c. 1458–1436 B.C.E.	Reign of Thutmose III
c. 1363–1347 B.C.E.	Reign of Amenhotep IV (Akhenaton)
c. 1290–1224 B.C.E.	Reign of Ramses II
c. 700s B.C.E.	Conquest of Egypt by Kush

The Old Kingdom, c. 2700–2200 B.C.E.

The kings of the Third through Sixth Dynasties—the period called the Old Kingdom or Pyramid Age—firmly established order and stability, as well as the basic elements of Egyptian civilization. The nobility lost its independence, and all power was centered in the king, or *pharaoh* (*per-ao*, "great house," originally signified the royal palace but during the New Kingdom began to refer to the king). The king had a character both divine and human. Considered a god, he also represented humans before the gods. He had the responsibility to maintain ***maat,*** that is, truth, justice, and order.

The king, along with his relatives, owned extensive tracts of land (from which he made frequent grants to temples, royal funerary cults, and private persons) and received the surplus from the crops produced on the huge royal estates. This surplus supported a large corps of specialists—administrators, priests, scribes, artists, artisans, and merchants—who labored in the pharaoh's service. The pharaoh's power and legitimacy were based on his ability to offer protection and sustain prosperity through abundant harvests. In return, his subjects gave their absolute devotion to the god-king, and Egyptians generally felt a sense of security that was rare in Mesopotamia.

The belief that the pharaoh was divine led to the construction of colossal tombs—pyramids—to preserve the pharaoh's embalmed body for eternity. The ritual of mummification was believed to restore vigor and activity to the dead pharaoh; it was his passport to eternity. The pyramid tombs, especially those of the Fourth Dynasty at Giza near Memphis, which are the most celebrated of all

The Pyramids at Giza

ancient monuments, reflect the great power and wealth of the Old Kingdom pharaohs. Although pyramid building was year-round, most construction took place during the months when the Nile overflowed its banks, and the pharaoh could expect farmers to provide their labor on construction crews. The Egyptian masses performed it primarily as an act of fidelity to their god-king, on whom the security and prosperity of Egypt depended.

Security and prosperity came to an end late in the Sixth Dynasty. The burden of building and maintaining pyramid tombs for each new king exhausted the state. The Nile floods failed, and famines ensued. As the state and its god-king lost credibility, provincial rulers assumed the prerogatives of the pharaohs, including the claim to immortality, and districts became independent. Inscriptions, known as coffin texts, also began to appear in nonroyal coffins. Among other things, the

Two Accounts of an Egyptian Famine

---

maat—A goddess who represented the balance and harmony of the universe as well as a set of ethical concepts that encompassed "truth," "order," and "cosmic balance." One's life and personal behavior should contribute to universal order. Hence, a pharaoh maintained *maat* by ruling justly and serving the gods.

Pharoah Ra-Hotep and his wife Nofret. Ra-Hotep was a pharaoh of the Seventeenth Dynasty who ruled around 1650 B.C.E. as Egypt was under Hyksos rule. These statues raise questions of whether it is fruitful to apply modern racial classifications to ancient Egyptians.

inscriptions expressed the hope that the deceased would be reunited with their families in the afterlife. For about a century and a half, known as the First Intermediate Period (c. 2200–2050 B.C.E.), the pharaoh's central authority weakened as civil war raged among contenders for the throne and local rulers reasserted themselves. Outsiders raided and infiltrated the land. The lot of the common people became unbearable as they faced famine, robbery, and oppression. "All happiness has vanished," related a Middle Kingdom commentary on this troubled era. "I show you the land in turmoil. . . . Each man's heart is for himself. . . . A man sits with his back turned, while one slays another."[7]

The Middle Kingdom, c. 2050–1800 B.C.E

Stability was restored by the pharaohs of the Eleventh and Twelfth Dynasties, who reunited the kingdom.

Stressing their role as watchful shepherds of the people, the Middle Kingdom pharaohs promoted the welfare of the downtrodden. One of them claimed, "I gave to the beggar and brought up the orphan. I gave success to the poor as to the wealthy."[8] The pharaohs of the Twelfth Dynasty revived the building of pyramids as well as the construction of public works. The largest of these, a drainage and irrigation project in the marshy Fayum (fai-YOOM) district south of Memphis, resulted in the reclamation of thousands of acres of arable land.

During the Thirteenth Dynasty, the Hyksos (HIK-sohs; "rulers of foreign lands"), a Semitic people from western Asia, assumed power over much of Egypt. The Hyksos are often portrayed as invaders who conquered Egypt around 1720 B.C.E., but now it is understood that the Hyksos migrated into Lower Egypt during the Middle Kingdom and established trading networks. During the Second Intermediate Period (c. 1800–1570 B.C.E.), they took advantage of weaknesses in the Egyptian state and gradually took control over all of Lower Egypt and many parts of Upper Egypt. The Hyksos did not sweep aside Egyptian institutions and culture. They adapted to existing Egyptian government structures, copied architectural styles and the **hieroglyphic** ("sacred carvings") system of writing, and incorporated Egyptian cults into their religious pantheon. The Hyksos army also introduced new weaponry to the Egyptians: the horse-drawn chariot and bronze weapons such as the curved sword and body armor and helmets.

The New Kingdom or Empire, c. 1570–1090 B.C.E.

Hyksos rule over Egypt lasted several centuries before a resurgent Egyptian dynasty based at Thebes challenged it. Adopting the new weapons introduced by their rulers, the Egyptians expelled the Hyksos and pursued them northwards into Phoenicia. The pharaohs of the Eighteenth Dynasty, who reunited Egypt and founded the New Kingdom, made Phoenicia the nucleus of an Egyptian empire in western Asia and conquered Nubia to the south.

The outstanding representative of this aggressive state was Thutmose III. When the union of Thutmose II and his half-sister, Hatshepsut (hat-SHEP-soot), failed to produce a male heir, Thutmose II fathered Thutmose III with a concubine. When Thutmose II died in 1479 B.C.E., Thutmose was still a child, and Hatshepsut was to act as co-regent until he came of age. Mindful of the Egyptian ideal that a son inherited the throne from the pharaoh, she legitimized her suc-

hieroglyphics—The mode of writing of ancient Egyptians that featured signs or figures to represent words.

cession by claiming that she was the designated successor of Thutmose I. She also stated that she had a divine origin as a daughter of Amon and had an oracle proclaim that Amon had chosen her to become king. She adopted all the customary royal titles; and in many of her statues and helmets, she was even depicted sporting the royal beard.

Because Hatshepsut had her own ambitions, Thutmose III had to wait for more than two decades before he assumed the throne on his own. Toward the end of his reign, he ordered Hatshepsut's name and inscriptions erased, her reliefs effaced, and her statues broken and thrown into a quarry. Historians still speculate whether he was expressing his anger at Hatshepsut or promoting his own accomplishments. Thutmose III is most noted for leading his army on 17 campaigns as far as Syria, where he set up his boundary markers on the banks of the Euphrates, called by the Egyptians "the river that runs backwards." Under his sway, Thutmose III allowed the existing rulers of conquered states to remain on their thrones, but their sons were taken as hostages to Egypt, where they were brought up, thoroughly Egyptianized, and eventually sent home to succeed their fathers as loyal vassals of Egyptian rule. Thutmose III erected *obelisks*—tall, pointed shafts of stone—to commemorate his reign and to record his wish that "his name might endure throughout the future forever and ever." The Egyptian Empire reached its peak under Amenhotep III (c. 1402–1363 B.C.E.). The restored capital at Thebes, with its temples built for the sun-god Amon east of the Nile at Luxor and Karnak, became the most magnificent city in the world. Tribute flowed in from conquered lands, and relations were expanded with Asia and the Mediterranean. To improve ties, the kings of Mitanni and Babylonia offered daughters in marriage to Amenhotep III in return for gold.

During the reign of the succeeding pharaoh, Amenhotep IV (c. 1363–1347 B.C.E.), however, the empire went into a sharp decline as the result of an internal struggle between the pharaoh and the powerful and wealthy priests of Amon, "king of the gods." The pharaoh undertook to revolutionize Egypt's religion by proclaiming the worship of the sun's disk, Aton, in place of Amon and all the other deities. Often called the first monotheist (although, as Aton's son, the pharaoh was also a god and he, not Aton, was worshipped by the Egyptians), Amenhotep changed his name to Akhenaton (akh-NAHT-in; "he who is effective for the Aton"), left Amon's city to found a new capital (Akhetaton,"horizon of Aton"), and concentrated on religious reform. By demoting Amon to a lesser status and taxing his temples, Akhenaton provoked strong opposition from Amon's priesthood. Most of Egypt's tributary princes in Asia defected when their appeals for aid against invaders went unheeded.

Akhenaton's monotheism did not survive his reign. When Akhenaton died, his 9-year-old brother, Tutankhamen (tu-tan-KAHM-in; "King Tut," c. 1347–1338 B.C.E.)—now best remembered for his small but richly furnished tomb, discovered in 1922—returned to the worship of Amon and to Memphis. Amon's priests gained revenge against Akhenaton as Tutankhamen and his successors destroyed Akhenaton's statues and tried to erase all memory of him. When Tutankhamen died in his late teens with no heir, one of his advisers, Horemheb, a general from the Nile delta region, founded the Nineteenth Dynasty (c. 1305–1200 B.C.E.).

Taking the name Ramses I, he sought to reestablish Egyptian control over Palestine and Syria. The result was a long struggle with the Hittites, who in the meantime had pushed south from Asia Minor into Syria. This struggle reached a climax in the reign of Ramses II (c. 1290–1224 B.C.E.) Ramses II regained Palestine, but when he failed to dislodge the Hittites from Syria, he agreed to a treaty. Its strikingly modern character is revealed in clauses providing for nonaggression, mutual assistance, and extradition of fugitives.

The long reign of Ramses II was one of Egypt's last periods of national grandeur. The number and size of Ramses' monuments rival those of the Pyramid Age. Outstanding among them are the great Hypostyle Hall, built for Amon at Karnak, and the temple at Abu Simbel in Nubia, with its four colossal statues of Ramses, which was raised in the 1960s to save it from inundation by the waters of the High Dam at Aswan. After Ramses II, royal authority gradually decayed as the power of the priests of Amon rose.

Third Intermediate Period, 1090–332 B.C.E.

The Third Intermediate Period was another period of transition in which the Amon priesthood at Thebes became so strong that the high priest was able to found his own dynasty and to rule over Upper Egypt. At the same time, merchant princes set up a dynasty of their own in the Nile delta. Libyans from the west moved into central Egypt, where in 940 B.C.E. they established a dynasty whose founder, Shoshenq, was a contemporary of King Solomon of Israel. Two centuries later, Egypt was conquered by the rulers of the kingdom of Kush, who established the Twenty-Fifth Dynasty. Kush's rule came to an end around 670 B.C.E. when the Assyrians of Mesopotamia made Egypt a province of their empire.

Egypt enjoyed a brief reprise of revived glory during the Twenty-Sixth Dynasty (c. 663–525 B.C.E.), which expelled the Assyrians with the aid of Greek mercenaries. The revival of ancient artistic and literary forms proved to be one of the most creative periods in Egyptian history. After attempts to expand into Syria were blocked by Nebuchadnezzar's (neh-boo-kad-NE-zahr) Babylonians, Egypt's rulers concentrated on expanding their commercial linkages throughout the region. To achieve this end, Pharaoh Necho II (c. 610–595 B.C.E.) created the first Egyptian navy. He encouraged the Greeks to establish trading colonies in the Nile delta; he put 12,000 laborers to work, digging a canal between the Nile mouth and the Red Sea (it was completed later by the Persians); and he commissioned a Phoenician expedition to search for new African trade routes.

Egypt came under Persian rule in 525 B.C.E. but was able to regain its independence in 404 B.C.E. After three brief dynasties, Egypt again fell under the Persians before coming within the domain of Alexander the Great (see Chapter 4).

Nubia and the Kingdom of Kush

Egypt's most enduring relationship was with its neighbor to the south, Nubia (NOO-bee-ah; derived from *nub*, the Egyptian word for gold), an area that stretches almost 900 miles from the town of Aswan to Khartoum, the point where the Blue and White Niles converge. The Nile gave Nubian civilization a distinctive character but in ways different from those in Egypt. As the Nile flows northward, its course is interrupted six times by cataracts that served as barriers to river traffic and Nubia's commercial contacts with Egypt. Like Egypt, many parts of Nubia east and west of the Nile are barren, so Nubian agricultural production depended on the Nile's two-mile wide floodplain.

Emerging around 4000 B.C.E., the earliest Nubian culture was made up of hunters, fishermen, farmers, and semi-nomadic pastoralists. This culture was distinguished for its highly skilled sculptures, ceramics, and clay figurines. Nubia also developed a healthy trade with Egypt. After a centralized state emerged in Egypt, Egyptian dynasties regarded Nubia as a source of slaves and raw mate-

rials such as gold, timber, and ivory and made several attempts to colonize Nubia. This state of hostility did not prevent Nubians from marrying into Egyptian royal families and the Egyptian state and army from recruiting Nubian administrators and archers.

Centered in a fertile area of the Nile around the Third Cataract, the Kingdom of Kush emerged around 1600 B.C.E. Its capital was at Kerma, an urban center renowned for its sophisticated temples and palaces. Kush prospered most when Egypt's fortunes declined. Although the basis of Kush's society was agriculture and animal husbandry, Kush engaged in extensive trade with Egypt to the north and African societies to the south and east.

After expelling the Hyksos, Egyptian forces reasserted their dominion over northern Nubia as far south as the Fourth Cataract, including Kerma. For the next four centuries, Egyptian administrators exploited Nubian gold to finance military campaigns in Asia and created an Egyptianized Nubian elite who spoke the Egyptian language and adopted Egyptian deities such as Amon and ritual and burial practices, including erecting pyramids.

Kush did not regain its autonomy until the eighth century B.C.E, when a new line of rulers established themselves at Napata (nah-PAH-tah) between the Third and Fourth Cataracts. The high point of Kush's power came a short time later. Taking advantage of strife in Egypt, the armies of Kush's King Piye swept through Egypt, conquering territory as far north as the Nile Delta. Although Piye proclaimed himself pharaoh

Sections of a wall painting from the tomb chapel of the treasurer Sebekhotep at Thebes show Nubians presenting gold nuggets and rings to King Thutmose IV. It dates from around 1400 B.C.E.

over Egypt and Nubia, he allowed local rulers in Egypt a measure of independence, and he cultivated the priests of the temple of Amon. His brother and successor, Shabaqo, was not so benign. He brought Egypt under the direct control of Kush and moved his capital to Thebes. He and the three pharaohs who succeeded him established the Twenty-Fifth Dynasty, which ruled Kush and Egypt for the next half century until they were forced to retreat following an Assyrian invasion. Kush's capital then moved to Meroe (MEHR-oh-wee), situated at the confluence of the Nile and APara Rivers. This site enjoyed annual rainfalls and supported a larger population. Meroe became a noted center for ironworking and weaving and exporting cotton cloth.

Kush remained in existence until 400 C.E., when it was absorbed into the Ethiopian kingdom of Aksum (ak-soom). Around the second century B.C.E. Kush's rulers started recording their royal annals in a script based on hieroglyphics and a cursive script also derived from hieroglyphics. This language, known as Meroitic, has not been translated to this day.

Egyptian Society and Economy

Egyptian society was highly stratified. Most Egyptians were poor peasants subject to forced labor for the rulers and who paid taxes to those who owned the land—the pharaoh, temples, or wealthy landowners—based on the yields of harvests.

However, class distinctions were not rigid. People could rise to a higher rank in the service of the pharaoh by joining the tiny literate elite. Pupils—usually boys—attended a scribal school for many years in which they learned to read and write hieratic script, a cursive form of hieroglyphics. Students practiced with reed pens on limestone chips or clay tablets. Scribes were in demand by the state for many tasks—writing letters, recording harvests, tracking taxes collected and owed, and keeping accounts for the Egyptian army. The most scholarly scribes assumed positions as priests, doctors, and engineers. Scribes enjoyed secure positions and were free from labor service.

Compared with the Greeks and Romans, Egyptian women enjoyed more rights, although their status at all levels of society was generally lower than that of men. Few women could qualify as scribes and thus were largely excluded from administrative positions. However, women could serve as temple priestesses, musicians, gardeners, farmers, and bakers. Some royal women, because of their positions as wives or mothers of pharaohs, had great influence in royal courts. Business and legal documents show that women shared many of the economic and legal rights of men. Women generally had rights to own, buy, sell, and inherit property without reliance on male legal

Many tomb paintings depict everyday life in Egypt. Here, two servants pick figs at the tomb of Khnumhotpes at Bani Hasan.

guardians; to negotiate legal settlements; to engage in business deals; to make wills; and to initiate litigation and testify in court. In a divorce, a woman kept any property she brought into a marriage as well as one-third of a couple's community property. When Egypt came under Greek rule, most Egyptian women preferred the option of maintaining their legal rights under Egyptian rather than Greek law.

The economy of Egypt was dominated by the divine pharaoh and his state, which owned most of the land and monopolized its commerce and industry. Because of the Nile and the proximity to the Mediterranean and Red seas, most of Egypt's trade was conducted by ships. Boats regularly plied up and down the Nile, which, unlike the Tigris and the Euphrates, is easily navigable in both directions up to the First

Document   "The Great Hymn to the Aton" and Psalm 104

A notable example of New Kingdom Egyptian literature is the pharaoh Akhenaton's "Hymn to the Sun," which was found carved on the tombs of his followers. Akhenaton's Hymn reflected his dramatic break with Egyptian religious beliefs that stressed prayers to gods for health and well-being and prepared the way for "blessed" afterlife. Akhenaton conceived one omnipotent and beneficent Creator and that he was the guarantor of the afterlife. Some scholars argue that his religious reforms may have had a formative effect on the development of monotheism on the Hebrews, many of whom were perhaps enslaved in Egypt at the time of Akhenaton's reforms. The style and subject of Psalm 104 bear a striking resemblance to the king's hymn to the sun:

The Great Hymn to the Aton

Splendid you rise in heaven's lightland,
O living Aton, creator of life!
When you have dawned in eastern lightland,
You fill every land with your beauty.
You are beauteous, great, radiant,
High over every land;
Your rays embrace the lands. . . .
How many are your deeds,
Though hidden from sight;
O Sole God beside whom there is none!
You made the earth as you wished, you alone.
All peoples, herds, and flocks;
All upon earth that walk on legs,
All on high that fly on wings, . . .
You set every man in his place,
You supply their needs;
Everyone has his food,
His lifetime is counted. . .

From Miriam Lichtheim, *Ancient Egyptian Literature: A Book of Readings (Volume II: The New Kingdom)* (Berkeley: University of California Press, 1976, pp. 96–98.

Psalm 104

Bless Yahweh, my soul,
Yahweh my God, how great you are!
Clothed in majesty and glory,
wrapped in a robe of light!
You stretch the heavens out like a tent,
you build your palace on the waters above;
using the clouds as your chariot,
you advance on the wings of the wind;

you use the winds as messengers
and fiery flames as servants.
You fixed the earth on its foundations,
unshakable for ever and ever;
you wrapped it with the deep as with a robe,
the waters overtopping the mountains. . . .
The sun rises, they retire,
going back to lie down in their lairs,
and man goes to work, and to labour until dusk.
Yahweh, what variety you have created
arranging everything so wisely!
Earth is completely full of the things you have
*   made. . . .*
Glory for ever to Yahweh!
May Yahweh find joy in what he creates,
at whose glance the earth trembles,
at whose touch the mountains smoke!

From "Psalm 104," *The Jerusalem Bible*, ed. Alexander Jones (Daarton, Longman & Todd, Ltd., and Doubleday: 1966), pp. 886–888, as quoted in Perry M. Rogers, *Aspects of Western Civilization*, Vol. I (Prentice Hall: 2000), pp. 33–35.

Questions to Consider

1. How do you account for the striking similarities between Akhenaton's Hymn and Psalm 104? Do you think the Hymn might have inspired the writer of Psalm 104?

2. What are the similarities between the Aton and Yahweh? Are there any differences in the manner in which they are described?

3. Why did Akhenaton's monotheism not last beyond his reign, while the Hebrew's monotheism was sustained?

Cataract at Aswan. The current carries ships downstream, and the prevailing north wind enables them to sail upstream easily. Trade reached its height during the empire (c. 1570–1090 B.C.E.), when commerce traveled along four main routes: the Nile River to and from the south; the Red Sea, which was connected by caravan to the Nile bend near Thebes; a caravan route to Mesopotamia and southern Syria; and the Mediterranean Sea, connecting northern Syria, Cyprus, Crete, and Greece with the Nile delta. Egypt's primary imports were timber, copper, tin, and olive oil, paid for with gold from its rich mines, linens, wheat, and **papyrus** rolls made from reeds—the preferred writing materials of the ancient world (the word *paper* is derived from the Greek *papyros*).

Egyptian Religion

Religion played a central role in the everyday life of Egyptians, who attributed everything from the annual cycles of the flooding of the Nile to personal illnesses to acts of gods. The Egyptian pantheon included hundreds of gods and goddesses. Male gods usually represented rulers, creators, and insurers of fertility, while goddesses assumed roles as nurturers, magicians, and sexual temptresses. People made sacrifices and prayed to household gods to protect the well-being and health of their families. They also worshipped deities on a local and regional basis. When the Old Kingdom came into being, ruling families elevated certain local gods and religious centers such as Heliopolis (hel-YOH-POH-lis) and Thebes (in the Middle Kingdom) gained national prominence. The most important gods—such as Osiris, Horus, Re', Amun, and Hathor—had their own temples and priesthoods that conducted rituals, sacrifices, and festivals honoring the god they served. The temples owned vast properties, and the income they generated paid for the salaries and upkeep of priests.

---

papyrus—An early form of writing material made from the stem of the papyrus plant.

Egypt's most popular religious cult was devoted to Osiris, the fertility god of the Nile, whose death and resurrection symbolized the planting of grain and its sprouting. The Egyptian myth of fertility and life after death, according to the priests at Heliopolis, was that Osiris had been murdered by Seth, his brother, who cut the victim's body into many pieces and scattered them around Egypt. When Isis, his bereaved widow, collected all the pieces and wrapped them in linen, Osiris was resurrected so that he could father Horus, the Nile floods resumed, and vegetation revived. The Osiris cult taught that Seth was the god of violence and disorder, that Osiris was the ruler of the dead in the netherworld, and that every mummified Egyptian could become another Osiris, capable of resurrection from the dead and a blessed eternal life.

However, only a soul free of sin would be permitted to live forever. In a ceremony called "counting up character," Osiris presided over a court of 42 gods that weighed the heart of the deceased against the Feather of Truth. If the virtues of the heart were outweighed by the Feather of Truth, a horrible creature devoured it. Charms and magical prayers and spells were sold to the living as insurance policies guaranteeing them a happy outcome in the judgment before Osiris. They constitute much of what is known as the *Book of the Dead,* which was placed in tombs and coffins.

Mathematics and Science

The Egyptians were much less skilled in mathematics than the Mesopotamians. Their arithmetic was limited to addition and subtraction, which also served them when they needed to multiply and divide. They could cope with only simple algebra, but they did have considerable knowledge of practical geometry; the obliteration of field boundaries by the annual flooding of the Nile made the measurement of land a necessity. Knowledge of geometry was also essential in computing the dimensions of ramps for raising stones during the construction of pyramids. In these and other engineering projects, the Egyptians were superior to their

In this scene from the Book of the Dead, *a princess stands in the Hall of Judgment in the Underworld before a set of scales on which the jackal-headed god Anubis weighs her heart against the Feather of Truth. The baboonlike god Thoth records the result. On the left, Isis presents the princess, who has also aided her cause, with an offering to Osiris, a haunch of beef.*

Mesopotamian contemporaries. Like the Mesopotamians, the Egyptians acquired a "necessary" technology without developing a truly scientific method. Yet what has been called the oldest known scientific treatise (c. 1600 B.C.E.) was composed during the New Kingdom. Its author, possibly a military surgeon or a doctor who treated pyramid-building laborers, described cases of head and spinal injuries, dislocations, and broken bones and recommended treatments or, in the case of more serious complications, nothing at all. Other medical writings considered a range of ailments, from pregnancy complications to hippopotamus bites. To Egyptian practitioners, the causes of medical conditions had to be dealt with holistically on a spiritual as well as a physical level. Thus they prescribed a combination of medicines, rituals, magical spells, and amulets.

The Old Kingdom also produced the world's first known solar calendar, the direct ancestor of our own. In order to plan their farming operations in accordance with the annual flooding of the Nile, the Egyptians kept records and divided the calendar into three seasons—flooding, planting and growing crops, and harvesting. Each season contained four months with 30 days in each month. They observed that the Nile flood coincided with the annual appearance of the Dog Star (Sirius) on the eastern horizon at dawn, and they soon associated the two phenomena.

Monumentalism in Architecture

Because of their impressive, enduring tombs and temples, the Egyptians have been called the greatest builders in history. The earliest tomb was the mud-brick Arab *mastaba* (MAS-tuh-buh), so called because of its resemblance to a low bench. By the beginning of the Third Dynasty, stone began to replace brick, and an architectural genius named Imhotep, now honored as the "father of architecture in stone," constructed the first pyramid by piling six huge stone *mastabas* one on top of the other. Adjoining this Step Pyramid was a temple complex whose stone columns were not freestanding but attached to a wall, as though the architect were tentatively feeling his way in the use of the new medium.

The Step Pyramid of Zoser, which was built by piling six huge stone mastabas, *one of top of the other.*

The most celebrated of the true pyramids were built for the Fourth Dynasty pharaohs Khufu, Khafre, and Menkaure. Khufu's pyramid, the largest of the three, covers 13 acres and originally rose 481 feet. It is composed of 2.3 million limestone bricks, some weighing 15 tons, and all pushed and pulled into place by human muscle. This stupendous monument was built without mortar, yet some of the stones were so perfectly fitted that a knife cannot be inserted in the joints. The Old Kingdom's 80 pyramids are a striking expression of Egyptian civilization. Their dignity and massiveness reflect the religious basis of Egyptian society—the dogma that the king was a god who owned the nation and that serving him was the most important task of the people.

Just as the glory and serenity of the Old Kingdom can be seen in its pyramids, constructed as an act of loyalty by its subjects, so the power and wealth of the empire survive in the Amon temples at Thebes, made possible by the booty and tribute of conquest. On the east side of the Nile were built the magnificent temples of Karnak and Luxor. The Hypostyle Hall of the temple of Karnak, built by Ramses II, is larger than the cathedral of Notre Dame in Paris. Its forest of 134 columns is arranged in 16 rows, with the roof over a central aisle raised to allow the entry of light. This technique was later used in Roman basilicas and in Christian churches.

Sculpture and Painting

Egyptian art was essentially religious. Tomb paintings and relief sculpture depict the everyday activities that the deceased wished to continue enjoying in the afterlife, and statues glorify the god-kings in all their serenity and eternity. Since religious art is inherently conservative, Egyptian art seldom departed from the classical tradition established during the vigorous and self-assured Old Kingdom. Sculptors idealized and standardized their subjects, and the human figure is shown either looking directly ahead or in profile, with a rigidity very much in keeping with the austere architectural settings of the statues.

Yet, on two occasions an unprecedented realism appeared in Egyptian sculpture. The faces of some of the Middle Kingdom rulers appear drawn and weary, seemingly reflecting the burden of reconstructing Egypt after the collapse of the Old Kingdom. An even greater realism is seen in the portraits of Akhenaton and his queen, Nefertiti, which continued into the following reign of Tutankhamen. The portraits realistically depict the pharaoh's physical appearance such as his ungainly paunch and his happy but far from god-like family life in informal settings—the pharaoh playing with one of his young daughters on his knee or munching on a bone. The "heretic" pharaoh, who

insisted on what he called "truth" in religion, seems also to have insisted on truth in art.

Painting shows the same precision and mastery of technique that are evident in sculpture. No attempt was made to show objects in perspective, and the scenes seem flat. The effect of distance was conveyed by making objects in a series or by putting one object above another. Another convention employed was to depict everything from its most characteristic angle. Often the head, arms, and legs were shown in side view while the eyes, shoulders, and chest were shown in front view.

Writing and Literary Texts

In Egypt, as in Sumer, writing began with pictures. But unlike the Mesopotamian signs, the Egyptian hieroglyphics remained primarily pictorial. At first, the hieroglyphics represented a mix of pictorial signs and one- and two-consonant signs that later came to stand for ideas and syllables. Early in the Old Kingdom the Egyptians took the further step of using alphabetical characters for 24 consonant sounds. Although they also continued to use the old pictographic and syllabic signs, the use of sound symbols had far-reaching consequences. It influenced their Semitic neighbors in Syria to produce an alphabet that, in its Phoenician form, became the forerunner of our own.

The earliest Egyptian literary works generally recorded the accomplishments of rulers or expressed religious beliefs through prayers, hymns, and funerary inscriptions. Among the latter are the *Pyramid Texts,* a collection of magic spells and ritual texts inscribed on the walls of the burial chambers of Old Kingdom pharaohs. Their recurrent theme is an affirmation that the dead pharaoh is really a god and that no obstacle can prevent him from joining his fellow gods in the heavens.

Old Kingdom literature went on to achieve a classical maturity of style and content—it stresses a "truth" that is "everlasting." Hence *The Instructions of Ptah-hotep,* addressed to the author's sons, insists that "it is the strength of truth that it endures long, and a man can say, 'I learned it from my father.'" Ptah-hotep's maxims stress the values and virtues that are important in fostering positive human relationships. To him, honesty is a good policy because it will gain one wealth and position, while affairs with other men's wives is a bad policy because it will impede one's path to success in life.[9]

DOCUMENT

Elders' Advice to Their Successors

The troubled times that followed the collapse of the Old Kingdom produced the highly personal writings of the First Intermediate Period and the Middle Kingdom. They contain protests against the ills of the day and demands for social justice. In the New Kingdom, writers composed love poems as a means of forgetting misery. The universal appeal of this literature is illustrated by the following lines.

> *I think I'll go home and lie very still,*
> *feigning terminal illness,*
> *Then the neighbors will all troop over to stare,*
> *my love, perhaps among them*
> *How she'll smile while the specialists snarl in*
>   *their teeth!—*
> *She perfectly well knows what ails me.*[10]

MESOPOTAMIAN SUCCESSORS TO BABYLON, c. 1600–550 B.C.E.

■ *What is the legacy left by the states that succeeded the Babylonian Empire?*

The Babylonian Empire came to an end in the sixteenth century B.C.E., most probably through the raids of chariot driving invaders known as the Kassites. Primarily warriors and raiders, they ruled as a minority of conquerors over the native population. Their concern was not with the establishment of lasting political control, but rather with the accumulation of wealth for the dominant warrior class.

The Hittites

Gradually, a people known as the Hittites began to migrate into the region now known as Turkey, settle themselves as a ruling class over the native population, and establish a kingdom that by 1400 B.C.E. became the strongest power in the region and the greatest rival of the Egyptian empire. Very little was known about the Hittites until archaeologists began to unearth the remains of their civilization in Turkey at the beginning of the twentieth century. By 1920 C.E. Hittite writing had been deciphered, and it proved to be the earliest example of an Indo-European language, closely related to Greek, Latin, and Sanskrit. The Hittites began migrating into Asia Minor from the northeast as early as 2000 B.C.E. Their superior military, in particular their mastery of horse-drawn chariot warfare and mass attacks by archers using long-range bows, enabled them to conquer the native people of central Asia Minor and establish a centralized kingdom with its capital city at Hattushash (HAHT-teu-shahsh), which is near the present Turkish capital city, Ankara.

The kings of the early Hittite kingdom were aggressive monarchs who were frequently at odds with their nobles and struggled to establish an orderly succession to the throne. The early effectiveness of the Hittite monarchy was severely limited by this pattern of constant internal strife.

After 1450 B.C.E. a series of energetic Hittite kings succeeded in limiting the independence of their nobles and creating a more centralized empire that included Syria and northern Palestine, which had been left virtually undefended by the Egyptian pharaoh Akhenaton. The pharaoh Ramses II moved north from Palestine in an unsuccessful attempt to reconquer the region in the battle of Kadesh (1285 B.C.E.). Ambushed and forced back to Palestine after a bloody standoff, the pharaoh agreed to a treaty of "good peace and good brotherhood" with the Hittites in 1269 B.C.E.

The Hittite Civilization

The Hittite state under the empire differed in its organization and reflected the traditions of its Indo-European origins rather than the governmental patterns set by the older monarchies of Mesopotamia and Egypt. The king was thought to be the greatest of the nobles, but not a living god or even a god's representative on earth. Hittite nobles held large estates granted by the

The Hittites dedicated animal-shaped drinking vessels to their gods for their own private use. This vessel in the shape of a stag, made of silver with gold inlays, is 7 inches high and dates between the fifteenth to the thirteenth centuries B.C.E.

king and in return provided warriors and served on a council to advise the king and limit his arbitrary power.

The Hittites adopted the Mesopotamian cuneiform script in order to write their Indo-European language. In addition to preserving their own customs, the Hittites readily incorporated features of earlier Mesopotamian civilization that they found appealing. Sumerian and Mesopotamian literature were preserved, and Mesopotamian gods and goddesses were honored with temples and placed on equal footing with their own traditional deities. While their law codes showed great similarity to the Code of Hammurabi, they differed in prescribing more humane punishments. Instead of retaliation ("an eye for an eye"), the Hittite code made greater use of restitution and compensation.

DOCUMENT

Near Eastern
Law Codes

The Hittites left their mark on later peoples of the region primarily as intermediaries. Their skills in metalworking, especially in iron, were passed eventually to their neighbors. Not especially creative in the formulation of law or literature and art, they borrowed extensively from other cultures and in turn passed their knowledge on to others, in particular to the neighboring Phrygians, Lydians, and Greeks.

The Sea Peoples

The Hittites may have been eager for the peace they concluded with Egypt in after the battle at Kadesh because of threats posed by new movements of raiding and displaced peoples—Indo-Europeans and others. A series of disruptions all over the eastern Mediterranean resulted in the overthrow of previously stable regimes now sacked and destroyed. Many survivors of these upheavals, which possibly included the fall of Troy (c. 1150 B.C.E.), fled by sea to seek new lands to plunder or settle. Collectively known as the Sea Peoples, these uprooted people included Philistines (FI-le-steens), Sicilians, Sardinians, and Etruscans. Many gave their names to the areas where they eventually settled. The collapse of the Hittite Empire, shortly after 1200 B.C.E., was partially a result of these migrations and attacks.

Scholars still hotly debate the causes behind the collapses of so many regimes for around 200 years after 1200 B.C.E. Some experts now believe that changes in warfare— especially the reliance on mobile infantry using short swords and javelins in place of the extensive use of chariots—account for the destruction of stable governments and the resulting displacement of peoples.

Population movements, the fall of established states, and even the introduction of new and more effective techniques of producing iron weapons may be some of the reasons for the disruption of the eastern Mediterranean around 1200 B.C.E.

The Beginnings of the Iron Age, c. 1100 B.C.E.

Shortly after the disruptions culminating with the invasion of the Sea Peoples, scholars mark the beginning of the Iron Age in the eastern Mediterranean. In fact, iron had been present in small amounts in Mesopotamia as early as one thousand years before, but the metal was seen as too precious to be employed extensively and not initially more effective than bronze. Iron weapons were used by the Hittites as early as 1400 B.C.E., and the technology used to produce iron was a fiercely guarded secret. Many scholars now suggest that, around 1100 B.C.E., partially because of the collapse of the Hittite Empire, the employment of carbonization in the production of iron tools and weapons, and a shortage in the supply of tin to aid in the manufacture of bronze, the use of iron spread from north to south in the eastern Mediterranean.

After 1200 B.C.E, with the Hittite Empire destroyed, the disorder brought by the incursions of the Sea Peoples, and Egypt in decline, the Semitic peoples of Syria and Palestine were able to assert their territorial claims in the power vacuum created by the weakness of once dominant states. For nearly 500 years, until they were conquered by the Assyrians, these peoples played a significant role in the history of the eastern Mediterranean and southwestern Asia.

The Phoenicians

Phoenicians (foh-NEE-shee-ans) is a name the Greeks gave to those Semitic peoples, called Canaanites (KAY-nah-naits), who lived along the Mediterranean coast of Syria, an area that is today Lebanon. Hemmed in by the Lebanon Mountains to the east, the Phoenicians turned to the sea for their livelihood and empire and by the eleventh century B.C.E. had become the Mediterranean's greatest traders, shipbuilders, navigators, and colonizers. To obtain silver and copper from Spain and tin from Britain, they established Gades (Cadiz) on the Atlantic coast of Spain. Carthage, one of a number of Phoenician trading posts on the shores of the Mediterranean, was a remarkably successful commercial colony and became Rome's chief rival in the third century B.C.E. (see Chapter 5).

Although the Phoenicians were essentially traders, their home cities—notably Tyre, Sidon, and Byblos—also produced manufactured goods. Their most famous export was woolen cloth dyed with the purple dye obtained from shellfish found along their coast. They were also skilled makers of furniture (made from the famous cedars of Lebanon), metalware, glassware, and jewelry. The Greeks called Egyptian papyrus rolls *biblia* ("books") because Byblos was the shipping point for this widely used writing material; later the Hebrew and Christian Scriptures were called "the Book" (Bible).

Culturally, the Phoenicians were not particularly original. They left behind no literature and little innovative art. Yet they made one of the greatest contributions to human progress, the perfection of the alphabet, which had a direct influence on the development later western European scripts. Between 1800 and 1600 B.C.E. Phoenician and neighboring Semitic peoples, influenced by Egypt's semi-alphabetical writing, started to evolve a simplified method of writing. The Phoenician alphabet of 22 consonant symbols (the Greeks later added signs for vowels) is related to the 30-character alphabet of Ugarit, a Canaanite city, which was destroyed about 1200 B.C.E. by the Sea Peoples.

The half-dozen Phoenician cities never united to form a strong state, and in the second half of the eighth century B.C.E. all but Tyre were conquered by the Assyrians. Tyre fell to the Chaldean (kahl-DEE-an) Empire in 571 B.C.E., and the one-time fiercely independent status of the Phoenicians ended with their subjugation first to the Chaldeans, and later to subsequent empires—those of the Persians, Greeks, and Romans.

The Hebrew Kingdoms

In war, diplomacy, technology, and art, the Hebrew contributions to history are of small significance; in religion and ethics, however, their contribution to world civilization was momentous. Out of the Hebrew cultural experience grew three of the world's major religions: Judaism, Christianity, and Islam.

Much of that Hebrew experience is recorded in the Old Testament, the collection of literature that the Hebrews believe was written through divine inspiration. The Old Testament's present content was approved about 90 C.E. by a council of rabbis (spiritual leaders). The Hebrew Bible is an outstanding work of literature and also a valuable source for the study of early Hebrew history and the evolution of Hebrew thought, culture, and religion. The biblical account of the history of the Hebrews (later called Israelites, and then Jews) begins with the account of a **patriarchal** clan leader named Abraham, called "the Hebrew" (a nomad or wanderer). Abraham is said to have led his people out of Ur in Sumer, where they had settled for a time in their wanderings. Most biblical scholars suggest that the date of such a migration should be around 1900 B.C.E. Abraham is then credited with leading his followers to northwestern Mesopotamia. He and his followers remained nomadic—the Bible records that Abraham moved his people to Egypt and back again to

---

patriarchal—"Father rule"; of or relating to a social system in which familial and political authority is wielded exclusively by men.

the north, and Abraham's grandson Jacob (later called Israel, and from whom the Israelites derive their name) eventually led a migration into the land of Canaan, later called Palestine.

Historians and archaeologists have raised many questions about the accuracy of biblical accounts for the early Hebrew community. No archaeological proof exists for a migration of peoples into northern Palestine around 1900 B.C.E. although no evidence exists to negate the possibility. Recently archaeologists have suggested that the culture of the age of the founders of the Hebrew community—that culture described in the early books of the Bible—best describes Hebrew culture around 1100 B.C.E., and not that probably in existence 800 years earlier.[11]

The Old Testament suggests that about 1550 B.C.E., driven by famine, some Hebrews followed Abraham's great-grandson Joseph into Egypt. Joseph's possible rise to power in Egypt and hospitable reception of his people there may be attributed to the presence of the largely Semitic Hyksos, who had conquered Egypt about 1720 B.C.E. Following the expulsion of the Hyksos by the pharaohs of the Eighteenth Dynasty, the biblical account states that the Hebrews were enslaved by the Egyptians. Shortly after 1300 B.C.E. a Hebrew leader named Moses led them out of bondage and into the wilderness of Sinai, where they entered into a pact or covenant with their God, Yahweh. The Sinai Covenant bound the people as a whole—the nation of Israel, as they now called themselves—to worship Yahweh before all other gods and to obey his Law (Torah). In return, Yahweh made the Israelites his chosen people, whom he would protect and to whom he granted Canaan, the Promised Land "flowing with milk and honey." The history of Israel from this time on is held by Jewish people to be the account of the fulfillment of this covenant.

There are no indications in Egyptian sources of a large number of Hebrews enslaved in Egypt after the Hyksos were expelled; at the same time, there are no reasons to believe that such treatment of Semitic peoples who remained in Egypt after the Hyksos did not occur. Hebrew tradition identifies Moses as the leader and eventual liberator of the Hebrews in Egypt and their leader during the Exodus (the "Road Out" in Greek), but Egyptian records give no mention of him, the demands he made of Pharaoh, or the plagues the Hebrew god supposedly visited on Egypt.

The Old Testament account of the Exodus from Egypt ends when the Israelites are led through the Sinai and arrive after 40 years of wandering in sight of Palestine. Here, they had to contend with the Canaanites, whose Semitic ancestors had migrated from Arabia early in the third millennium B.C.E. Joined by other Hebrew tribes already in Palestine, the Israelites formed a **confederacy** of 12 tribes, led by leaders called judges, and in time succeeded in subjugating the Canaanites. The biblical account of the conquest of Palestine records a bloody history of conquest and destruction of those Canaanite cities that resisted Hebrew domination—a feat mainly accomplished through the brilliant military leadership of a hero named Joshua. Recent archaeology reveals a different view: that the Hebrew occupation of Palestine was a long and slow process and that the massive destruction of Canaanite cities by Israelites as recorded in the Old Testament is not affirmed by archaeological remains. Rather, the Hebrews seemed to have absorbed, to have been absorbed, and at times to have lived in peace along with already established Canaanite communities in the region.

Leadership of the Israelites in this effort to claim their promised land seems to have been exercised by both men and women called judges—individuals among the twelve tribes of Israel who had shown uncommon degrees of courage (Judith), strength (Sampson), or divine inspiration (Samuel). The active

In the eighth century B.C.E., *the Hebrew kingdoms of Israel and Judah often found themselves in opposition to each other, as well as being surrounded by potentially more powerful enemies.*

confederacy—A system of government in which power is shared between existing political units with no single unit having authority over the others.

and decisive role the Old Testament attributes to Israelite women reflects the great influence they must have exercised in early Israel. Genesis describes the two sexes as being equal and necessary for human livelihood: "So God created mankind in his image, . . . male and female he created them. And God blessed them and said to them, 'Be fruitful and multiply and fill the earth and subdue it [together]'" (1:27–28). And in the Song of Songs the maiden and the youth share equally in the desire and expression of love; there is no sense of subordination of one to the other. But the continuing dangers that faced the nation led to the creation of a strong centralized monarchy, and with it came male domination and female subordination.

As the Israelites were contesting the Canaanites for dominance of the region, an even more formidable opponent appeared. The Philistines, Sea Peoples that had tried unsuccessfully to invade Egypt, and from whom the name Palestine comes, settled along the coast of Israel about 1175 B.C.E. Aided by the use of iron weapons, which were new to the region and the Hebrews, the Philistines captured the Ark of the Covenant, the sacred chest described as having mysterious powers, in which Moses had placed stone tablets inscribed with the Ten Commandments entrusted to him by Yahweh. By the middle of the eleventh century B.C.E. the Philistines appear to have been on course to dominate the entire land.

Lacking a central authority, the loose 12-tribe confederacy of Israel could not hope to ward off the Philistine danger, and a king, Saul, was chosen to unify resistance to the Philistines.

According to the Bible, Saul's reign (c. 1020–1000 B.C.E.) was not successful. Continuously undercut by

The Hebrews

c. 1800 B.C.E.	Migration of Hebrews to Palestine
c. 1550 B.C.E.	Migration to Egypt
c. 1300–1200 B.C.E.	Exodus from Egypt
c. 1020–1000 B.C.E.	Reign of Saul
c. 1000–961 B.C.E.	Reign of David
961–922 B.C.E.	Reign of Solomon
722 B.C.E.	Northern kingdom destroyed by Assyria
586 B.C.E.	Southern kingdom destroyed by Chaldeans
586–538 B.C.E.	Babylonian Captivity

tribal rivalries and overshadowed by the fame of the boy hero David, who came to prominence by slaying the Philistine giant Goliath in single combat, Saul made no attempt to transform Israel into a centralized monarchy. Saul's successor, the popular David (c. 1000–961 B.C.E.), is credited with restricting the Philistines to a narrow coastal strip to the south of Israel, and also with the consolidation of an impressively large and unified state. David also won Jerusalem from the Canaanites and made it the private domain of his royal court, separate from the existing 12 tribes. His popularity was enhanced when he placed the recovered Ark of the Covenant in his royal chapel, to which he attached a priesthood.

David was succeeded by his son Solomon (961–922 B.C.E.), under whom the Bible says Israel reached its highest degree of power and splendor as a monarchy. But the price of Solomon's vast bureaucracy, building projects (especially the palace complex and the Temple at Jerusalem), standing army (1400 chariots and 12,000 horses), and harem (700 wives and 300 concubines) was great. High taxes, forced labor, and tribal rivalries led to dissension.

Recently, archaeologists have called the Old Testament accounts of the glorious reigns of David and Solomon into question. Some scholars even suggest that a united monarchy never existed, and that even if it did, the extent of its influence is vastly overstated by the Bible. Experts also suggest that the biblical accounts of David's glory and Solomon's wealth are the work of later rulers, dating in particular to the seventh century in the Kingdom of Judah, whose rulers were searching for a glorious past upon which to base their claims of legitimacy.[12] Most archaeologists now concur that the biblical description of David's power and might is exaggerated. Jerusalem appears to have been a hill town of probably no more than 5000 inhabitants in the tenth century B.C.E., and traces of Solomon's great temple have so far evaded the archaeologists. The existence of a dynasty of kings descended from David (the so-called House of David) has been claimed to be proven by the recent discovery of several inscriptions dating to the eighth century, but other scholars question their authenticity.

The Old Testament records that when Solomon died in 922 B.C.E., the kingdom split in two—Israel in the north and Judah in the south. These two weak kingdoms were in no position to defend themselves when new, powerful empires rose again in Mesopotamia. In 722 B.C.E. the Assyrians captured Samaria, the capital of the northern kingdom, taking 27,290 Israelites into captivity (the famous "ten lost tribes" of Israel; two remained in the southern kingdom) and settling other subjects of their empire. The resulting population, called Samaritans, was ethnically, culturally, and religiously mixed, as well as deprived of any political role.

The southern kingdom of Judah held out until 586 B.C.E., when Nebuchadnezzar, the Chaldean ruler of Babylon, destroyed Jerusalem and carried away a large number of its residents to his capital city. This deportation began the so-called Babylonian Captivity of the Jews (Judeans), which lasted until 538 B.C.E. While held in Babylon, the Jews were considered to be free people, allowed to engage in commerce and industry, and to practice their own religion. Some Jews abandoned their religious traditions, but most seem to have held strongly to them. It was in Babylon that the first synagogues (Greek for "gathering together") came into existence, as the Jewish communities assembled for worship and study.

DOCUMENT

Suffering Explained

In 538 B.C.E. Cyrus the Great, the king of Persia, conquered Babylon, and allowed the captives to return to Jerusalem. In 515 B.C.E. the returning exiles completed the reconstruction of the Temple destroyed by Nebuchadnezzar. But large numbers of believers never returned to Judah, which was now referred to as Judea by the Persian governors who administered it. These Jews, scattered all over the region, formed communities of worship in their cities of residence, and membership in these communities of believers became an essential component in the lives of the participants. By 500 B.C.E. the majority of Jewish believers lived outside Palestine. This "scattering" (*diaspora* in Greek) was to be a significant characteristic of Jewish existence from this time forward in their history.

The mostly peaceful Persian rule in Judea was followed by the conquest of Palestine by Alexander the Great in 332 B.C.E. After Alexander's death Judea was part of the empire ruled by the Ptolemaic dynasty of Egypt, and in 63 B.C.E. it became a Roman protectorate. Roman administration proved especially rigid and unpopular with the Jews. In 70 C.E. a revolt of the Jews against their Roman rulers was crushed, the city of Jerusalem and the temple destroyed, and the history of the Jews as a political entity ended until the twentieth century. The resulting *diaspora* from their troubled homeland sent the Jews to all the major cities of the Mediterranean, where many became influenced by the culture of the Greco-Roman world, even while others strictly adhered to their traditional beliefs and customs emphasized through instruction in the synagogues.

Hebrew Religion

The Bible states that from the time of Abraham, the Hebrews worshiped one stern, warlike tribal god whose name was not revealed to the Hebrews until the time of Moses. Yet there are traces in the Old Testament of an earlier stage of religious development that shows evidence of animism and a reverence for spirits associated with the winds, stones, and sacred springs. Gradually, beliefs became more sophisticated and developed into a worship of **anthropomorphic** gods. The god of Abraham was a god closely associated with Abraham's clan or tribe. Hebrew religion entered a more sophisticated stage of development around the thirteenth century B.C.E., when Moses is credited with directing the Hebrews toward the worship of a national god, the god of Abraham now revealed to be named Yahweh. The religion of Moses may be called monolatry—the belief that there is one god for that god's select people, but that there may exist other gods for other peoples.

Moses is credited in the Bible with being the recipient of God's law in the form of the Ten Commandments, and the leader who, with Yahweh's assistance, led the Hebrews from Egypt to the Promised Land. After their entrance into Palestine, many Hebrews adopted the **polytheism** of the Canaanites as well as the luxurious Canaanite manner of living. As a result, prophets arose who "spoke for" Yahweh (*prophetes* is Greek for "one who speaks for God"), insisting on strict adherence to the laws delivered by Moses. Between 750 and 550 B.C.E. a series of these prophets wrote down their messages and insisted that disaster would result if Yahweh's chosen people strayed from proper worship. They also developed the idea of a coming Messiah (the "anointed one" of God), a descendant of King David, who would begin a reign of peace and justice.

The destruction of Jerusalem in 586 B.C.E. and the exile in Babylon was another formative event in the evolution of Jewish thought. In accord with the prophetic warnings, Yahweh had punished his chosen people, yet the prophets also foretold that they would be allowed to return to Jerusalem and be reconfirmed as the chosen of God. Many scholars believe that the time spent in Babylon was crucial to the final achievement of true monotheism by Jewish thinkers: the destruction of Yahweh's holy city was not a sign of His weakness, but rather a sign of His power and universality, and His people's journey would serve as proof to all mankind of His glory. The Jews who returned from the Babylonian Captivity were provided a renewed faith in their destiny and a new understanding of their significance in human history.

The Aramaeans

Closely related to the Hebrews were the Aramaeans (ah-rah-MAY-ens), who occupied Syria east of the Lebanon Mountains. The most important of their little kingdoms was centered at Damascus, one of the oldest

---

anthropomorphic—Literally, "human shaped"; endowed with human characteristics.

polytheism—Belief in many gods. Though Judaism, Christianity, and Islam are monotheistic, most other religions throughout history have been polytheistic. The numerous gods may be dominated by a supreme god or a group of gods.

continuously inhabited cities in the world. The Aramaeans dominated the camel caravan trade connecting Mesopotamia, Phoenicia, and Egypt and continued to do so even after Damascus fell to the Assyrians in 732 B.C.E. The Aramaic language, which used an alphabet similar to the Phoenician, became the international language of the Mesopotamian region and the northeastern Mediterranean coast by the fifth century B.C.E. In Judea it was more commonly spoken than Hebrew among the lower classes, and was the language spoken by Jesus and his disciples.

The Assyrian Empire, c. 550–331 B.C.E.

By 700 B.C.E. the era of small states had ended with the emergence of a powerful Assyrian Empire. Two of the greatest achievements of the Assyrians were the forcible unification of weak, unstable regions of Mesopotamia and the establishment of an efficient and centralized imperial organization.

For two centuries before 700 B.C.E. the Assyrians had been attempting to transform the growing economic prosperity of northern and central Mesopotamia into a political unity. The Assyrian attempt to dominate the region began in the ninth century B.C.E; after a short period of weakness, the Assyrian monarchy regained its effectiveness in the eighth century, when the state also took over Babylon. By 671 B.C.E. the Assyrians had annexed Egypt and were the masters of the entire Fertile Crescent.

A Semitic people long residing in the hilly region of the upper Tigris, the Assyrians had experienced a thousand years of constant warfare. But their matchless army was only one of several factors that explain the success of Assyrian imperialism: a policy of calculated terrorism, an efficient system of political administration, and the support of the commercial classes that wanted political stability and unrestricted trade over large areas.

The Assyrian army, with its chariots, mounted cavalry, and sophisticated siege engines, was the most powerful ever seen in the ancient world before 700 B.C.E. Neither troops nor walls could long resist the Assyrians, whose military might seemed unstoppable. Conquered peoples were held firmly in control by systematic policies designed to terrorize. Mass deportations, like that of the Israelites, were employed as an effective means of destroying national feeling.

The well-coordinated Assyrian system of political administration was another factor in the success of the empire. Conquered lands became provinces ruled by governors who exercised extensive military, judicial, and financial powers. Their chief tasks were to ensure the regular collection of tribute (payments demanded by the conquerors) and the raising of troops for the per-

Assyria

c. 1350 B.C.E.	Assyrian rise to power
704–681 B.C.E.	Military power at height
669–626 B.C.E.	Reign of Ashurbanipal
612 B.C.E.	Fall of Nineveh

manent and professional army that eventually replaced the native militia of sturdy Assyrian peasants. An efficient system of communications carried the "king's word" to the governors as well as the latter's reports to the royal court—including one prophetic dispatch reading: "The king knows that all lands hate us." Nevertheless, the Assyrians should be credited with laying the foundations for some elements of the later more humane administrative systems of their successors, the Persians and Alexander the Great of Macedonia.

Assyrian Culture

The Assyrians borrowed from the cultures of other peoples and unified the elements into a new product. This is evident in Assyrian architecture and sculpture, the work of subject artisans and artists. Both arts glorified the power of the Assyrian king. The palace, serving as both residence and administrative center, replaced the temple as the characteristic architectural form. A feature of Assyrian palace architecture was the structural use of the arch and the column, both

This ancient Assyrian relief, The Dying Lion, is an example of a common theme in royal Assyrian sculpture. The prowess of the Assyrian king as hunter and leader was often emphasized through such artistic themes.

borrowed from Babylonia. Palaces were decorated with splendid relief sculptures that glorified the king as warrior and hunter. Assyrian sculptors were especially skilled in portraying realistically the ferocity and agony of charging and dying lions.

Assyrian kings were interested in preserving written as well as pictorial records of their reigns. King Ashurbanipal (ah-shoor-BAH-ni-pahl; 669–626 B.C.E.), for example, left a record of his great efforts in collecting the literary heritage of Sumer and Babylon. The 22,000 clay tablets found in the ruins of his palace at Nineveh (NI-neh-vah), in today's northern Iraq, provided modern scholars with their first direct knowledge of the bulk of this literature, which included the Sumerian *Epic of Gilgamesh.*

Downfall of the Assyrian Empire

Revolt against Assyrian terror and tribute was inevitable when Assyria's strength weakened and united opposition to Assyrian terror arose. By the middle of the seventh century B.C.E. the Assyrians had been destroyed by wars, and the Assyrian kings had to use unreliable mercenary troops and conscripted subjects. Egypt regained its independence from the Assyrians under the Twenty-Sixth Dynasty, and the Medes to the north refused to pay further tribute. The Chaldeans, tribal groups of Semites who had migrated into Babylonia, revolted in 626 B.C.E. In 612 B.C.E. they joined the Medes in destroying Nineveh, the Assyrian capital. With the fall of the capital city, Assyrian dominance was ended, much to the general satisfaction of the subjects of the Assyrian overlords.

The Lydians and the Medes

The fall of Assyria left four states to struggle over the remains of their empire: the Chaldeans and Egypt fought for control of Syria and Palestine, and Media and Lydia clashed over eastern Asia Minor.

After the collapse of the Hittite Empire about 1200 B.C.E., the Lydians succeeded in establishing a kingdom in western Asia Minor. When Assyria fell, the Lydians expanded eastward until stopped by the Medes at the Halys River, in central Turkey. Lydia profited from being in control of part of the commercial land route between Mesopotamia and the Aegean Sea, and from the possession of valuable gold-bearing streams. About 675 B.C.E. the Lydians invented coinage, which replaced the silver bars in general use up to that time. Lydia's most famous king was Croesus (KREE-sus), a monarch whose wealth was legendary. With the king's defeat by the Persians in 547 B.C.E., Lydia ceased to exist as an independent state.

The Medes were an Indo-European people who by 1000 B.C.E. had established themselves on the Iranian plateau east of Assyria. By the seventh century B.C.E. they had created in Media a strong kingdom with Ecbatana (ek-bah-TAH-nah) as its capital and with the Persians, their kinsmen to the south, as their subjects. Following the collapse of Assyria, the Medes expanded into Armenia and eastern Asia Minor, but their short-lived empire ended in 550 B.C.E. when they, too, were absorbed by the Persians.

The Chaldean (New Babylonian) Empire

While the Median kingdom controlled the northern Iranian plateau, the Chaldeans, with their capital at Babylon, became masters of the fertile crescent. Nebuchadnezzar, who had become king of the Chaldeans in 604 B.C.E., raised Babylonia to another epoch of brilliance after more than a thousand years of eclipse. By defeating the Egyptians in Syria, Nebuchadnezzar ended Egyptian hopes of recreating their empire. As we have seen, he destroyed Jerusalem in 586 B.C.E. and took thousands of captured Jews to Babylonia.

Nebuchadnezzar rebuilt the city of Babylon, making it the largest and most impressive urban center of its day. The tremendous city walls were wide enough at the top to have rows of small houses on either side. In the center of Babylon ran the famous Procession Street, which passed through the Ishtar Gate. This arch, which was adorned with brilliant tile animals, is the best remaining example of Babylonian architecture. The immense palace of Nebuchadnezzar towered terrace upon terrace, each decorated with masses of ferns, flowers, and trees. These roof gardens, the famous Hanging Gardens of Babylon, were so beautiful that they were regarded by the Greeks as one of the seven wonders of the ancient world.

Nebuchadnezzar was the last great Mesopotamian ruler, and Chaldean power quickly crumbled after his death in 562 B.C.E. Chaldean priests, whose interests included political intrigue as well as astrology, continually undermined the monarchy. Finally, in 539 B.C.E. they opened the gates of Babylon to Cyrus the Persian, allowing him to add Babylon to his impressive new empire.

THE PERSIAN EMPIRE, 550–331 B.C.E.

■ *In what ways were the Persians innovators, and how did they also incorporate the legacies of earlier Mesopotamian societies?*

Cyrus the Persian was the greatest conqueror in the history of the ancient Near East. In 550 B.C.E. he ended Persian subjugation to the Medes by captur-

After the seventh century B.C.E. three great empires dominated the Mesopotamian region and sought to extend their control. The Assyrian Empire extended its might into Egypt, the Chaldean into the region of the Fertile Crescent, and the Persian from Egypt in the west to the Indus River in the east.

ing Ecbatana and ending the Median dynasty. Most of the Medes readily accepted their vigorous new ruler, who soon demonstrated that he deserved to be called "the Great." When King Croesus of Lydia moved across the Halys River in 547 B.C.E. to pick up some of the pieces of the collapsed Median Empire, Cyrus defeated him and annexed Lydia, including Greek cities on the coast of Asia Minor that were under Lydia's nominal control. Then he turned his attention eastward, establishing his power as far as the frontier of India. Babylon and its empire were also annexed to the great Persian Empire.

After Cyrus died, his son Cambyses (cam-BAI-seez; 530–522 B.C.E.) conquered Egypt. The next ruler, Darius I (522–486 B.C.E.), added the Punjab region in India and Thrace in Europe. He also began a conflict with the Greeks that continued intermittently for more than 150 years until the Persians were conquered by Alexander the Great in 331 B.C.E.

DOCUMENT

Darius the Great

Persian Government

Although built on the Assyrian model, the Persian administrative system was far more efficient and humane. The empire was divided into 20 *satrapies,* or provinces, each ruled by a governor called a *satrap.* To check the satraps, a secretary and a military official representing the "Great King, King of Kings" were installed in every province. Also, special inspectors, "the Eyes and Ears of the King," traveled throughout the realm. Imperial post roads connected the important cities. Along the Royal Road between Sardis and Susa there was a post station every 14 miles, where the king's couriers could obtain fresh horses, enabling them to cover the 1600-mile route in a week.

The Persian Empire was the first to attempt to govern many different racial groups on the principle

Persia	
c. 600 B.C.E.	Union under Achaemenid kings
559–530 B.C.E.	Reign of Cyrus the Great
550 B.C.E.	Conquest of Median Empire
539 B.C.E.	Conquest of Babylon
530–522 B.C.E.	Reign of Cambyses
522–486 B.C.E.	Reign of Darius I

of equal responsibilities and rights for all peoples. So long as subjects paid their taxes and kept the peace, the king did not interfere with local religion, customs, or trade. Indeed, Darius was called "the shopkeeper" because he stimulated trade by introducing a uniform system of gold and silver coinage on the Lydian model.

Persian Religion and Art

The humaneness of the Persian rulers may have stemmed from the ethical religion founded by the prophet Zoroaster, who lived in the early sixth century B.C.E. Zoroaster attempted to replace what he called "the lie"—ritualistic, idol-worshipping cults and their Magi priests—with a religion centered on the sole god Ahura-Mazda ("Wise Lord"). This "father of Justice" demanded "good thoughts of the mind, good deeds of the hand, and good words of the tongue" from those who would attain paradise (a Persian word). This new higher religion made little progress until first Darius and then the Magi adopted it. The Magi revived many old gods as lesser deities, added much ritual, and replaced monotheism with dualism by transforming what Zoroaster had called the principle or spirit of evil into the powerful god Ahriman (the model for the Jewish Satan), the rival of Ahura-Mazda, "between which each man must choose for himself."

The complicated evolution of Zoroastrianism is revealed in its holy book, the Avesta ("The Law"), assembled in its present form between the fourth and sixth centuries C.E. Zoroastrian **eschatology**—the "doctrine

---

eschatology—Theological doctrine of the "last things," or the end of the world.

Document | ## The Majesty of Darius the Great: A Persian Royal Inscription

The Persian kings ruled their vast empire with absolute authority. But these kings were not regarded as divine beings ruling without responsibility. The power of the king had to be exercised in a reasonable and ethical manner, and in accord with the precepts of the great god of the Persians, Ahura-Mazda. The following inscription, attributed to King Darius the Great, was intended to show the Persian people that the king was an able and powerful monarch, but in addition a just and merciful administrator of his responsibilities:

A great god is Ahuramazda who created this excellent work which one sees; who created happiness for man; who bestowed wisdom and energy upon Darius the king. Says Darius the king: by the favour of Ahuramazda I am of such a kind that I am a friend to what is right, I am no friend to what is wrong. It is not my wish that to the weak is done wrong because of the mighty, it is not my wish that the weak is hurt because of the mighty, that the mighty is hurt because of the weak. What is right, that is my wish. I am no friend of the man who is a follower of the lie. I am not hot-tempered. When I feel anger rising, I keep that under control by my thinking power. I control firmly my impulses. The man who co-operates, him do I reward according to his co-operation. He who does harm, him I punish according to the damage. It is not my wish that a man does harm, it is certainly not my wish that a man if he causes damage be not punished. What a man says against a man, that does not convince me, until I have heard testimony(?) from both parties. What a man does or performs according to his powers, satisfies me, therewith I am satisfied and it gives me great pleasure and I am very satisfied and I give much to faithful men.

I am trained with both hands and feet. As a horseman I am a good horseman. As a bowman I am a good bowman, both afoot and on horseback. As a spearman I am a good spearman, both afoot and on horseback. And the skills which Ahuramazda has bestowed upon me and I have had the strength to use them, by the favour of Ahuramazda, what has been done by me, I have done with these skills which Ahuramazda has bestowed upon me.

Questions to Consider

1. What might have been the purpose of this inscription? What might have been its effect on the king's subjects who read it?

2. How does the inscription give the impression that the king's authority is unquestioned?

3. Why do you think that references to the king's skill as a hunter and a bowman are included? Are his exploits overstated or modestly listed? What purpose did these references to physical skills have?

From B. Gharib, "A Newly Found Inscription of Xerxes," *Franica Antiqua*, 1968, as quoted in Amélie Kuhrt, *The Ancient Near East: c. 3000–330 B.C.E.*, Vol. 2 (London: Routledge, 1995), p. 681.

of final things" such as the resurrection of the dead and a last judgment—also influenced later Judaism. Following the Muslim conquest of Persia in the seventh century C.E., Zoroastrianism virtually disappeared in its homeland. It exists today among the Parsees in India and in scattered communities worldwide.

In art the Persians borrowed largely from their predecessors in the fertile crescent, particularly the Assyrians. Their most important contribution was in palace architecture, the best remains of which are now found at Persepolis. Built on a high terrace in southern Iran, the royal residence was reached by a grand stairway faced with beautiful reliefs. Instead of the warfare and violence that characterized Assyrian sculpture, these reliefs depict hundreds of soldiers, courtiers, and representatives of 23 nations of the empire bringing gifts to the king for the festival of the new year.

CONCLUSION

During the Paleolithic and Neolithic periods, several technological and agricultural advances gave humans the opportunity to spread and adapt to different parts of the world. Increasingly sophisticated tools and techniques of operation allowed humans to hunt and gain control over diverse environments, while the transition from good gathering to food production made it possible for the development of the first significant civilizations along the banks of rivers.

In the second half of the fourth millennium B.C.E, the first major civilizations, Mesopotamia and Egypt, originated in river valleys: one by the Tigris and Euphrates and one by the Nile. In each instance, the complex society we call a civilization was the result of organized and cooperative efforts that were necessary to make the rivers useful to humans living along them.

Cooperation and centralized leadership resulted in interdependent urban living—the quest for order in a challenging, disorderly world. Through centralized control of religion, these early civilizations sought to understand the gods and establish harmony with them.

Through creativity and inventiveness—bronze tools and weapons, the wheel, writing, and law, either in written form or revealed through the person of pharaoh—social order was established in the first cities.

Mesopotamian civilization originated in the land called Sumer. The achievements of the Sumerians served as a foundation for later Mesopotamian civilizations established by Semitic peoples migrating into the river valleys. The most significant of these later Semitic civilizations was the Babylonian Empire ruled by Hammurabi. Babylon was sacked by the Indo-European Hittites of Asia Minor, who went on to duel with Egypt over control of Syria and Palestine.

In Egypt a great civilization arose on the banks of the Nile, a civilization both monumental and timeless. The temples and tombs of the Egyptian monarchs were designed to endure forever and to preserve the satisfying and stable existence of this world into eternity. Egypt centered on the absolute rule of the pharaohs—god-kings who eventually extended their domain from Nubia to the Euphrates River.

By 1200 B.C.E. the great Near Eastern empires—Babylonian, Egyptian, and Hittite—had weakened, allowing the Semitic peoples of Syria and Palestine more opportunity to make their own cultural contributions. Although never a powerful political force in the ancient world, Israel would have a momentous impact on the future through its development of a sophisticated and influential religious tradition. Political diversity had ended by the rise of the Assyrian Empire, which unified the ancient Near East for the first time. After the fall of Assyria, the Chaldean Nebuchadnezzar constructed a new Babylonian Empire, but it was soon engulfed by the expansion of Persia. Stretching from India to Europe, the Persian Empire gave the Near East its greatest extension and power.

The achievements of these early civilizations would become the inheritance of the Greeks and eventually the Romans. Much of the social and cultural legacy of the ancient Near East remains preserved in the fabric of those Mediterranean societies, which rose to political and cultural prominence after the first civilizations declined in vitality.

Suggestions for Web Browsing

You can obtain more information about topics included in this chapter at the websites listed below. See also the companion website that accompanies this text, **http://www.ablongman.com/brummett,** which contains an online study guide and additional resources.

Fossil Hominids: Mary Leakey
http://www.talkorigins.org/faqs/homs/mleakey.html

Discussion, with images, of the life and findings of one of the twentieth century's most famous archaeologists. Links to husband Louis Leakey, son Richard Leakey, Olduvai Gorge, and fossil findings.

Human Prehistory: An Exhibition
http://users.hol.gr/~dilos/prehis.htm

Walk through six rooms of text and vivid images that discuss the works of Lyell, Huxley, and Darwin; the first humans; the first human creations; the first villages, including Çatal Hüyük, and artworks of Neolithic Greece.

Chauvet Cave
http://www.culture.gouv.fr/culture/arcnat/chauvet/en/

A French government site on a major discovery of prehistoric cave art. Contains information about the findings and many views of cave paintings at this location and others in France.

Neanderthal Museum
http://www.neanderthal.de/

Site of a German museum whose goals are to maintain and popularize the cultural heritage of the Neanderthals.

Oriental Institute Virtual Museum
http://www-oi.uchicago.edu/OI/MUS/QTVR96/QTVR96.html

An integral part of the University of Chicago's Oriental Institute, the Oriental Institute Museum offers a virtual showcase of the history, art, and archaeology of the ancient Near East.

Hammurabi
http://home.echo-on.net/~smithda/hammurabi.html

A short biography of Hammurabi, in addition to a discussion of the legal concepts he espoused in his code and a virtual recreation of the Hanging Gardens of Babylon.

Egyptian Museum
http://www.egyptianmuseum.gov.eg/

Website of the Egyptian Museum in Cairo, highlighting images of accessories and jewelry, sculptures, furniture, mummies, and written documents of ancient Egypt from the museum's enormous collection.

Museums of the Vatican: Gregorian Egyptian Museum
http://www.christusrex.org/www1/vaticano/EG-Egiziano.html

The Vatican Museum's Egyptian Museum provides images and descriptions of many of the significant objects in one of the world's best ancient Egyptian museums.

Nubia: The Land Upriver
http://ancientneareast.tripod.com/Nubia.html

The geography and early history of the Nubian peoples, from prehistoric times to the kingdom of Kush.

The Hittite Home Page
http://www.asor.org/HITTITE/HittiteHP.html

A website devoted to all things Hittite, including a useful list of links to various universities conducting excavations of Hittite sites.

Material Culture of the Ancient Canaanites, Israelites, and Related Peoples: An Information Database from Excavations
http://www.bu.edu/anep/

This site contains hundreds of images of artifacts such as weapons, tools, and jewelry, with brief histories of the cultures described.

World Cultures: Mesopotamia and Persia
http://www.wsu.edu:8080/~dee/MESO/PERSIANS.HTM

This site gives valuable information on the influence of geography on early Persian civilization, reviews Persian military history, and discusses the importance of Persian religion.

Literature and Film

Selections of Egyptian literature are presented in John Foster, *Echoes of Egyptian Voices: An Anthology of Ancient Egyptian Poetry* (University of Oklahoma Press, 1992), and R. B. Parkinson, trans. and ed., *Voices from Ancient Egypt: An Anthology of Middle Kingdom Writings* (University of Oklahoma Press, 1991).

Stephanie Dalley, ed., *Myths from Mesopotamia: Creation, the Flood, Gilgamesh, and Others* (Oxford University Press, 1998), is an excellent compilation from a variety of Mesopotamian cultures. Danny Jackson et al., eds., *The Epic of Gilgamesh* (Bolchazy Carducci, 1997), is a unique modern translation of the epic poem.

Two excellent videos are *Ancient Mesopotamia* (Schlessinger Media, 1998), and the six-video set presented by Bill Moyers on *Genesis* (PBS, 1998), in which an impressive array of experts discuss the implications and meaning of the biblical account.

Three other videos stand out: *Egypt—Beyond the Pyramids* (History Channel, 2001). This film investigates recent archaeological discoveries in Egypt, including tombs of pharaohs, temples, and cemeteries. *In Search of Human Origins* (NOVA PBS, 1994) is a three-part documentary that explores the search for human origins by scientists. *In search of History: Akhenaten: Egypt's Heretic King* (Arts and Entertainment, 1998) is a documentary portrait of Akhenaton's life and his impact on Egyptian religion and art and an exploration of his capital city, Akhetaton.

Suggestions for Reading

For comprehensive accounts of the human fossil record, the evolution of the human brain and cognitive powers, and the significance of lithic art, see Ian Tattersall, *Becoming Human: Evolution and Human Uniqueness* (Harcourt Brace, 1998), and Donald C. Johanson and Blake Edgar, *From Lucy to Language* (Simon & Schuster, 1996).

On human evolution and the spread of humankind from Africa to the rest of the world, see Noel T. Boaz, *Eco Homo: How the Human Being Emerged from the Cataclysmic History of the Earth* (HarperCollins, 1997); Ian Tattersall, *The Last Neanderthal: The Rise, Success, and Mysterious Extinction of Our Closest Relatives* (Westview Press, 1999); and Christopher Stringer and Robin McKie, *African Exodus: The Origins of Modern Humanity* (Henry Holt, 1997). Jared Diamond's *Guns, Germs and Steel: The Fates of Human Societies* (W. W. Norton, 1997) examines the impact of environment on the development of human societies in different parts of the world.

A work that deals with the origins of toolmaking in a broad cultural matrix is Kathy Schick and Nicholas Toth, *Making Silent Stones Speak: Human Evolution and the Dawn of Technology* (Simon & Schuster, 1993). On early communities, see Tim Megarry, *Society in Prehistory: The Origins of Human Culture* (New York University Press, 1996).

Fundamental forms of expression in primeval art, symbolization, the role of animals, depiction of the human figure (including fertility figurines), and the conception of space in prehistory are dealt with in Sigfried Giedion's *The Eternal Present: The Beginnings of Art* (Pantheon, 1962).

The debate between the "Out of Africa" and multiregional schools is treated in Milford Wolpoff and Rachel Caspari, *Race and Human Evolution: A Fatal Attraction* (Simon & Schuster, 1997) and Christopher Stringer and Rachel McKie, *African Exodus: The Origins of Modern Humans* (Henry Holt, 1997).

Amélie Kuhrt, *The Ancient Near East*, 2 vols. (Routledge, 1995), is an outstanding and useful overview of Mesopotamia to 330 B.C.E. William W. Hallo and William Kelly Simpson, *The Ancient Near East: A History* (Harcourt Brace, 1998), remains a good standard text. Jean Bottero et al., *Everyday Life in Ancient Mesopotamia* (Johns Hopkins University Press, 2001) gives an excellent account of the culture. Surveys of Egyptian history include Nicolas Grimal, *A History of Ancient Egypt*, trans. Ian Shaw (Blackwell, 1992), and the 14-volume *Cambridge Ancient History* (Cambridge University Press, 1970–1997). The history of Nubia and the kingdom of Kush is examined in Derek Welsby, *The Kingdom of Kush* (Wiener, 1998) and Stanley Burstein, ed., *Ancient African Civilizations: Kush and Axum* (Wiener, 1998). For the history and significance of the Hittites, see Trevor Bryce, *The Kingdom of the Hittites* (Oxford University Press, 1998). For two contrasting but well-researched interpretations of ancient Israel, see David J. Goldberg and John D. Rayner, *The Jewish People: Their History and Their Religion* (Viking, 1987), and I. Finkelstein and N. A. Silberman, *The Bible Unearthed* (The Free Press, 2001). Don Nardo, *The Persian Empire* (Lucent Books, 1998) and J. M. Cook, *The Persian Empire* (Barnes & Noble, 1998), are two of the best studies on ancient Persian history and culture.

CHAPTER 2

Ancient China—Origins to Empire

Prehistory to 220 C.E.

The Neolithic Chinese people were a series of distinct, regional groups or cultures that have been traced back almost 10,000 years. By 200 C.E., the Chinese people belonged to an empire supported by trade routes in Asia and Africa, by a written history, and by rule by kings: they had a sense of commonality as Chinese. They also shared legendary heroes and heroines. Within both the empire and contending philosophies, there were strong attempts to maintain social differences—to keep an order that distinguished between Chinese and non-Chinese, rich and poor, and the feminine and the masculine both inside and outside the household. Such attempts at establishing and maintaining these distinctions did not always work.

Even with the maintenance of social differences during this formative period, in the face of often cataclysmic disasters, the Chinese maintained a zest for life. They reacted to human suffering by pursuing religious answers and by instituting ambitious innovations in all aspects of society from philosophy to economics. Throughout, the state retained its theoretical focus toward the amelioration of social evils and the relief of distress.

THE ORIGINS OF CHINA, 6500–221 B.C.E.

■ *What developments in culture, politics, and philosophy molded prehistoric China into a civilization?*

The Neolithic Age: c. 6500–c. 1600 B.C.E.

As in other parts of the world, there were tool-using humanoids *(homo erectus)* some 600,000 to 800,000 years ago on the Chinese subcontinent. Modern humans *(homo sapiens)* appeared in China around 100,000 years ago, and were hunters and gatherers during the Paleolithic period (c. 100,000–10,000 B.C.E.). They lived in a vast watershed, extending over 1000 miles from north to south and east to west and drained by two river systems that rise on the high Tibetan plateau and flow eastward to the Pacific. Three mountain ranges crisscross the river systems, diminishing in altitude as they slope eastward. The Huanghe (HWAHNG-HUH) or Yellow River crosses the highlands of the west, the deserts of the north, the hills filled with yellow silt called "loess," and the entire alluvial plain. The silt gradually builds up along the river bottom, requiring extensive dykes and river control to permit the development of agriculture. The Yangzi (YAHNG-zih) River forms the second river system. Emerging from the Tibetan highlands, it moves through gorges with cliffs 1000 or more feet high. Extensive drainage of the Yangzi valley over several centuries allowed rice agriculture to emerge in China's heartland.

Within the Chinese subcontinent, geographers have identified at least eight different ecosystems, ranging from the semitropical southeast, receiving as much as 5 feet of rain each year, to the desert-like northwest, which gets less than 4 inches of rain annu-

Ancient China's establishment and expansion were determined by key geographical factors. In addition to such divisions as those separating northern and southern cultures, determined by the Huanghe and Yangzi Rivers, there was geographic expansion incorporating independent peoples and states into one bureaucratic entity. By the end of the Han Empire, China had come close to achieving its natural geographic frontiers from the South China Sea to the Eurasian Steppes to the north, and the Himalayan mountains to the west. China was thus open to invasion from the north, west, and south, but conflict with "barbarians" was a stimulus to enormous cultural change.

ally. Geography, along with shifts in climate, determined the emergence of two main regional cultures by the Neolithic era.

Archaeological discoveries confirm the presence of Neolithic settlements in China before 5000 B.C.E. In each region, climate and rainfall affected the kinds of crops that were domesticated. Rice and water plants such as lotus and water chestnuts were grown in the warm, moist Yangzi valley and south of the Yangzi. Millet and wheat grew well in the drier climate of the north. In both north and south China, dogs, cattle, and pigs were raised, while buffalo were more common in the north and sheep in the south. Domestication of plants and animals in the Neolithic period may have been influenced by similar developments in West Asia, showing a sophisticated ability to adopt and develop techniques used elsewhere in Eurasia. Neolithic culture can also be divided into eastern and western geographic regions. The Yangshao (yahng-SHOW) culture of the western region (5000–3000 B.C.E.) produced geometrically painted pottery. The eastern region's culture produced beautifully crafted jade figurines and jewelry. By the late Neolithic period (3000–2000 B.C.E.), the techniques and skills were blended, as geometric designs moved westward and styles of pottery were shared. Interpreting cracks on heated bones inscribed with questions, called oracle bones, was also practiced in both areas. There is evidence that metallurgy began to be used to make weapons in this period.

Settlements surrounded by packed-earth walls appeared throughout North China. Located along the rivers, they sheltered their residents from aggressive actions of other communities. China's communities were very diverse in the Neolithic era. Some people lived in towns; some were nomadic. While the towns made institutional and technological advances, especially in the area of defense, the nomadic bands created their own effective weapons. The tension between the settled communities and the more nomadic bands had a decisive effect on the development of Chinese politics and culture.

Historians do not agree if a well-organized dynasty existed in China before the Shang dynasty in the

Preimperial History

before 1600 B.C.E.	"Xia"
c. 1600–1027 B.C.E.	Shang
1027–770 B.C.E.	Western Zhou
770–256 B.C.E.	Eastern Zhou
722–481 B.C.E.	Spring and Autumn period
403–221 B.C.E.	Warring States period

Bronze Age. But the founding myths of China constructed a country defined by government and technology bequeathed by sage rulers. According to these myths, the earliest sages were Fu Xi (FOO SHEE), the Ox-tamer, credited with inventing the family and domesticating animals; Shen Nong, the Divine Farmer, who invented farming; and Huang Di (hoo-AHNG DEE), the Yellow King, who invented writing, silk, and pottery and was deemed the first of the **Five Sover-**

The sophistication of c. 4000 B.C.E. artisans can be seen in this Neolithic vessel. At the same time practical and pleasing to the eye, this bowl testifies to the aesthetic standards of everyday Chinese civilization.

eigns. The last two of these five were Yao, who invented rituals, and Shun, a paragon of filial piety, who appointed wise officials. Shun's successor, Yu, is credited with developing flood control. Early historians considered Yu and his son the founders of a dynasty called Xia (shee-AH). Though such a centralized dynasty may not have existed (and is the object of debate among historians in China), the kinds of values attributed to its kings and sagely men before them created lasting Chinese institutions.

Five Sovereigns—Mythical ancient kings who are believed to have ruled before hereditary dynastic succession was established.

The Bronze Age: The Shang Dynasty (c. 1600–c. 1027 B.C.E.)

The diverse cultures of northern China gave rise to a complex Bronze Age civilization sometime in the centuries after 2000 B.C.E. Several cultures remained in North China for a few centuries while one, the Shang, came to predominate by 1600 B.C.E. The Shang supposedly arose to conquer a particularly oppressive Xia overlord; the idea that sagely rule could give way, in later generations, to rule by corrupt descendents, had begun to take root. Over the 600 years of Shang rule, China developed even more complex systems of government, cities, writing, class and occupational stratification, religious ritual as the basis of the state, and sophisticated metallurgy.

Shang territorial control was not extensive, being located primarily around the Huanghe. But the spread of Shang culture stretched all the way to the Yangzi valley. In the area of Shang control, archaeological evidence of Shang capitals such as Zhengzhou (juhng-JOH) and, later, Anyang, indicates that the kings could exercise enormous power. They could demand the work of a large number of laborers and craftsmen to build their palaces and tombs. Zhengzhou, for instance, was surrounded by walls 2385 feet long, 60 feet wide, and 30 feet high. As their political and military fortunes varied, the rulers moved their capitals frequently during the six centuries of the Shang dynasty. The final Shang capital was at Anyang where the marshaling of resources and skills for the production of bronze artifacts also points to a concentration of power.

The Shang dynasty differed from its predecessors in more than simply the development of a sophisticated bronze metallurgy. Shang artisans, who lived in production centers surrounding the capital's power core with its palaces and temples, used bronze to make elaborate ceremonial and drinking vessels, weapons, pottery, and stone carvings. Not only were the bronze and other productions practical, but they were also works of art with both incised and high-relief designs. A common design was the animal mask, or *taotie* (TOW-tee-eh).

The Shang people used a system of writing that probably originated before their rule, as graphs are

DOCUMENT

Oracle Bones and Chinese Characters

found on Neolithic pottery, though no documents predating Shang rule have yet been found. Shang writing can still be deciphered, because it was an early form of the same characters used in modern Chinese today. Shang writing was based on several thousand characters, some of which are **pictographs** and some of which represent sounds or meanings. Some Chinese characters consisted of two parts: one part indicating the topic of the word and the second expressing the

sound. An example of the combination of two elements is the word for "family" or "home," which consists of the character for pig placed under a roof.

The Chinese writing system in later centuries served as the foundation for other written languages in East Asia, including Korean and Japanese. Because the writing system was not phonetic, it could be used to represent other languages as well as variations of Chinese in different locations and across the centuries. It could be imposed on conquered peoples who already spoke Chinese or a related language. Shang culture could even be extended beyond the boundaries of the king's control—including to those who spoke different languages—through transmission of ideas written in Chinese characters. Over the next three millennia, a certain degree of ideological conformity could be maintained even as diverse cultures and technological advances produced fundamental differences within China. Writing also served to advance government functions and increasingly sophisticated intellectual activities.

IMAGE

An Inscribed Oracle Bone

Most Shang writing is found on thousands of oracle bones, fragments of animal bones and tortoise shells. The religious diviners of the Shang kings dried the shells and bones and dug hollows in them to make the bones crack more easily. After the king relayed his question, the priests put a hot poker to the bones and interpreted the resulting cracks. Engravers then recorded these interpretations onto the bones. The written questions were directed at the ancestral spirits, who were believed to be closely tied to their living descendants as members of the family group. The living would ask the dead such questions as "Will the king's child be a son?" and "If we raise an army of 3000 men to drive X away from Y, will we succeed?" The practice of oracle bone divination was a form of religious ritual, accompanied by music, dancing, and animal or human sacrifices.

As the state and its activities grew more complex, the kings had to oversee not only fighting but also taxing and governing, processes facilitated by writing and record keeping. The leaders needed to record their decisions and to transmit them to their often distant subjects. These tasks were done by scribes, who became increasingly useful to the kings. Later, the scribes would grow in power to become trusted officials who would defend the monarch's power when the kings were off fighting wars or interacting with communities outside the region around the capital.

Religion played the key connective role in the maintenance of social order. The king was at the top of the Shang power structure because his ancestors were deemed best able to communicate with the supreme deity, Di, and the Shang king himself was best able to communicate with his own ancestors. The king and people worshiped other deities, including the gods controlling the Huanghe River and the mountains as well as the long-dead ancestors and recently deceased members

---

pictographs—Characters that depict an object or idea; thus, the character for "tree" originated in a drawing of a tree.

of the royal family. Ancestor worship, a key element of Shang royal power, continued in later times as veneration of ancestors and, in a particular case, as filial piety, or veneration of one's parents, the closest ancestors.

No distinction was made between the king's religious and secular powers, and his government was replicated in the structure of the patriarchal family—the state was a household that had to be managed. The Shang kings were to communicate with Di via dialogue with deceased royal kin. Such communication was accompanied by offerings to the king's ancestors in a ceremony. Offerings took various forms, including sacrifice of humans or offerings of rich foods to ancestors. Below the king on the social ladder were members of his family line or lineage who comprised the Shang aristocracy, court officials, lords who owned land, and finally what the oracle bones termed "the multitude"—common people who, unlike the kings and nobles, had no recorded ancestors and did not belong to a clan. Common people included artisans who worked in jade, bronze, wood, or leather; spun and wove silk; and devised a rich material culture, as well as peasants who lived in villages in houses partially below ground level. At the very bottom of the social order were the prisoners of war who were enslaved and forced to work on massive building projects. After their work was completed, many prisoners' heads and limbs were cut off before burial. Members of the nobility often accompanied the king to his death, and oracle bone inscriptions reveal that over 7000 captive slaves, many from the neighboring Qiang (chee-AHNG) people, were sacrificed in order to win the aid or avoid the displeasure of the spirits. As part

of the ritual of human and animal sacrifice, a beerlike liquor was poured on the ground.

Unlike the common people, the kings and nobles had recorded ancestors and belonged to a clan. They were the descendants in the male line from a common ancestor whom they worshipped. The lesser levels of society each had their local gods, to whom requests to guarantee good harvests and long life were addressed. The peasants belonged to no clans, and there is no evidence that they worshipped their ancestors. Instead, their gods were the fundamental forces of nature, such as rivers, mountains, earth, wind, rain, and the stars and planets.

During the Shang period, a special group of Chinese became skilled in the use of magic, with which they attempted to manipulate the two forces of the world. They called these two opposed but complementary forces *yang* and *yin*. Yang was associated with the sun and all things male, strong, warm, and active; yin was associated with the moon and all things female, dark, cold, weak, and passive. Many centuries later, in the fourth century B.C.E., scholars speculated about these forces. In later ages Chinese thinkers would also employ these concepts to compel greater obedience and passivity from women.

The power of the kings and nobles rested on their ownership of the land, their monopoly of bronze metallurgy, their chariots, the king's religious functions and his frequent visits to subordinate domains, and a bureaucracy that was considered divine. We can see proof of the power of the Shang kings and their nobles in their imposing buildings, military superiority, and tombs. They often entered into battle across North

Chariots, whose appearance around 1200 B.C.E. attests to contact with cultures to the west of China, were a symbol of kingly power in the Shang and Zhou and were therefore sometimes buried with rulers, as in this pit in Hebei.

China and, for centuries, gained victory by using chariots, a potent technological advantage around the year 1200 B.C.E. that suggests contact with other chariot-using societies in western Asia. After death, the Shang kings' power continued when they were buried in sumptuous tombs along with those chariots and still-living servants and war captives.

Peasants might be legally free, but they had little mobility. They rarely owned land and worked plots periodically assigned to them by royal and noble landowners. They collectively cultivated the fields retained by their lords. Farming methods were primitive, not having advanced beyond the Neolithic level. Bronze was used for weapons and artwork, but not for farm tools or implements, and the peasants continued to reap wheat and millet with stone sickles and till their allotted fields with wooden plows. The inequity between the power of the king and the powerlessness of his impoverished subjects was evident by the eleventh century B.C.E. It was replaced by a new power that claimed political legitimacy due to its greater virtue.

The Zhou Dynasty (1027?–221 B.C.E.)

Around 1050 B.C.E. the Zhou frontier state, which had adopted the material advances of the Shang while preserving the cultural traditions of pre-Shang Neolithic societies, overthrew the Shang dynasty. An early Zhou history, *The Book of Documents*, later included among the classics, explained that the Shang had become corrupt and dissolute and their conquest by the virtuous Zhou was to be expected. The Zhou leader announced that Heaven *(Tian)* had given him a mandate to replace the Shang. Because the concept that Heaven indicated its will through uprisings and natural disasters was new in China, the Zhou seizure of power as *Tian*'s will was probably, in part, a rationalization for the Zhou overthrow of Shang rule. The idea of a mandate of Heaven introduced a new and very long-lasting aspect of Chinese thought: The cosmos is ruled by an impersonal and all-powerful Heaven that sits in judgment over the human ruler who links Heaven's commands and human fate. Without approval or mandate from Heaven, in other words, kingly rule was not possible. The king came to be called the "Son of Heaven."

The Zhou were a powerful western frontier tribe that took advantage of the opportunities of the wealth and increasing weakness of Shang rule. Given the Zhou's military strength, the other Chinese tribes wisely switched their loyalty to them. The Zhou went on to establish a dynasty that lasted, in one form or another, for almost 900 years (c. 1027–221 B.C.E.).

Three Zhou rulers are credited in early texts with establishing the stable Zhou state. The founder, King Wen, formed alliances with neighboring states while the Shang ruled with cruelty; Wen's son, King Wu, moved the capital eastward to Luoyang (lo-YANG) and began to fight the Shang; and the Duke of Zhou, Wu's brother, intelligently and benevolently ruled as regent for Wu's young son. After building a beautiful capital at Luoyang and conquering other states in the Yangzi valley, the Duke of Zhou stepped down to let his nephew rule.

Spread out over most of North China and the Yangzi valley, the very size of the Zhou domain made it impossible to be ruled directly from the center. States on the periphery were either ruled by Zhou relatives sent out as their representatives or allowed to stay under the jurisdiction of local chiefs. These chiefs were given hereditary titles and sent tribute to the Zhou. They also had armies that fought alongside the Zhou king's army. The king and these subordinate lords (later called vassals) were linked by kinship. Some were partrilineally related; others were related through marriage. The num-

Bronze vessels, such as this one from the early tenth century B.C.E., were designed to contain water, wine, meat, or grain used during the sacrificial rites in which the Shang and Zhou prayed to the spirits of their ancestors. Animals were a major motif of ritual bronzes.

bers of these subordinate rulers fluctuated greatly over the long centuries of Zhou rule. Around 800 B.C.E., there were approximately 200 domains, of which 25 or so were large enough to be important. With their hereditary officials and various types of aristocrats, Zhou society was hierarchically arranged from the Son of Heaven on top, down through domain lords, great officials, lesser officials, and ordinary commoners.

The early Zhou kings were strong leaders who kept the allegiance of their vassals, the lords of the peripheral territories, while fighting off attacks on the frontiers. However, after two centuries, complacency set in, and a succession of weak kings led to a reduction in the central throne's power over its subordinates; taking advantage of advances in military technology, the vassals became more independent. By the eighth century B.C.E. the vassals no longer went to the Zhou capital for investiture by the Son of Heaven. As the Zhou monarchs became weaker, court officials increased their influence. Under the feudal politics of the Zhou, bureaucratic documentation became ever more complex, as the center had to define its relations with the 50 major vassal dependencies and continually changing foreign contacts. The kings' scribes, clerks, and officials wrote the documents that defined hierarchy and order and mastered the political precedents that the military men needed to exercise legitimate authority. As the state became more complex, the qualifications for state servants became more specific. Now the officials of the state, along with the nobles, could gain rank, land, wealth, and an assured future for their family, but such a bureaucracy did not ensure the strength of the reign.

The remnants of Zhou royal power disappeared completely in 771 B.C.E., when an alliance of disloyal vassals and border-area tribesmen destroyed the capital and killed the king. Part of the royal family managed to escape eastward to Luoyang, however, where the dynasty survived for another five centuries (until around 250 B.C.E.), doing little more than performing state religious rituals as the Sons of Heaven. The period before 771 is often called the "Western Zhou" to distinguish it from the era after 771 B.C.E., referred to as the "Eastern Zhou" for the location of the capital. In 335 B.C.E. some of the stronger vassals began calling themselves "kings" *(wang)*, thereby ending the sovereignty of the Zhou monarchs. Some conquered their weaker neighbors. Some pioneered new policies, based on new schools of thought developed in the East. Warfare among emerging states was incessant. During the early Eastern Zhou, also called the Spring and Autumn Period (722–481 B.C.E.), warfare often took a chivalrous form, but it turned more violent during the two and a half centuries known as the period of Warring States (403–221 B.C.E.). By 221 B.C.E. the ruler of the Qin (CHIN), the most successful of the seven largest states still existing in 300 B.C.E., had conquered all of his rivals and established a unified empire over which he was the absolute ruler.

The art of horseback riding, common among the nomads of Central Asia, greatly influenced later Zhou military strategies, supplanting the chariot-based strategy of earlier centuries. Rulers in the north developed cavalry as a defense against nomadic forces and later used their new cavalry against other Chinese states. Infantry forces drafted from the farm population were also effective against chariots. Rulers of the Warring States period began constructing increasingly complex defensive walls. The infantry adapted to new conditions by wearing tunics and trousers adopted from the nomads, an example of the interactions of non-Chinese and Chinese culture. In later centuries, the mutual influence of Chinese and "barbarian" culture would encompass military, political, intellectual and material culture. Large populations were essential to build defensive walls and raise armies. Effective rulers devised new economic and sociopolitical ways to enrich their growing populations and their resources.

Zhou Economy and Society

The contestants for power—the Jin (divided during the Warring States era into Han and Wei) in the north, the Qi (CHEE) in the east, the Chu in the Yangzi region, and the Qin in the west—recognized the connection between wealth and power. Prosperous rulers could field large armies of soldiers and laborers. New lands were claimed for agriculture from marginal fields and marshes, and the states encouraged trade in textiles, metals, woods, jade, bamboo, seafood, pearls, and animal products. During the seventh century B.C.E., the Chinese mastered the use of iron and mass-produced cast iron objects from molds, which were in wide use by the end of the third century B.C.E. The ox-drawn iron-tipped plow, together with the use of manure and the growth of large-scale irrigation and water-control projects, led to a more dependable and productive food supply and greater population growth. Zhou-era rulers also understood the necessity to build canals to improve their realm's economy and communication. The canals made it possible to move food and useful items dependably over long distances. Commerce and wealth thus grew rapidly. At the beginning of the Zhou dynasty, brightly colored shells, bolts of silk, and ingots of precious metals were used as forms of exchange; by the end of the dynasty, small round copper coins with square holes had taken their place.

Under the Zhou dynasty, merchant and artisan classes played an economically prominent, if not socially recognized, role as wealth spread beyond the nobles and court servants. Indicative of the rise in the general economic level, chopsticks and finely lacquered objects, today universally considered as symbols of Chinese and East Asian culture, were in general use by the end of the period. The continued importance of the intertwining of political power and cultural beliefs, as in the Shang era, is evident from inscriptions on bronzes. From them we know that Zhou kings, like the Shang kings, worshipped their ancestors. The Zhou kings had elaborate rituals in family temples, where they made offerings to their ancestors. The nobility, for their benefit, recorded honors they had received from the Zhou kings onto commissioned pieces of bronze. These messages were inscribed inside food containers or hidden on the backs of bells because they were meant only for the eyes of the ancestors.

Other vessels, no longer shaped in the *taotie* or animal mask form of the Shang dynasty, appear to have been used in rituals viewed by an audience. Many were inscribed with texts, suggesting their owners may have been thinking about their descendants.

The early Zhou years gave birth to the first collection of poetry, *The Book of Songs,* later canonized as one of China's great classics. The poems, composed between 1000 B.C.E. and 600 B.C.E., included love poems, poems about government officials, and poems that depict everyday lives of commoners. One poem laments the role played in the Zhou court by the powerful wives of rulers, which was a reflection of their role in the frequent disputes over succession to the throne:

> *Clever men build cities,*
> *Clever women topple them . . .*
> *Disorder does not come down from heaven;*
> *It is produced by women.*[1]

Not all royal women, however, were so poorly regarded by their contemporaries. The excavation of the tomb of Lady Hao, wife of King Wu (c. 1200 B.C.E.) contains oracle bones showing she led military expeditions, managed an estate, and carried out rituals.

It was during the time of political and social disruption of the Eastern Zhou that teachers and philosophers, longing for an idealized "good old days" of social stability of the Western Zhou, played an important role in defining and teaching values that, in continually evolving forms, would dominate Chinese society into the twentieth century. This new form of leadership found a willing audience among the people who had the most to gain from order and hierarchy, the clerks and officials who increased their influence, wealth, and legal privileges during the Zhou dynasty.

Nostalgia for the imagined past led to the conceptualizing of an entire hierarchical social order developed around an idealized monarch, with each inferior in the descending scale owing respect and obedience to his superior.

The peasant masses stood at the bottom of the hierarchy. They were controlled by government officials, landed gentry, and rural moneylenders, although, ostensibly, they were free to buy and sell land or change occupation. Most, like peasants elsewhere, were tied to their villages, where they worked as tenants or serfs and struggled to eke out an existence. Some were forced into debt slavery. To increase production and control of farmers, some rulers used their own officials rather than local intermediaries to govern the farm population. Officials gained opportunities for advancement through good performance in these jobs, and farmers were increasingly rewarded by freedom from serfdom by their own good performance. By the end of the Warring States era, rulers with more effective centralized bureaucratic control and increasingly free peasants found themselves emerging on top.

The Philosophical Schools

The rich streams of thought that appeared during the latter part of the Zhou period emerged from the very disquiet and instability of the times. During the next three centuries, some great teachers and philosophers thought deeply about the nature of humanity and the problems of society. They created a range of philosophies on how people should live. These ideas went from the extremes of living for society to living for one's own soul, and they continued to change through the centuries and shape Chinese society even today.

Confucianism: The Foundation

The first, most famous, and certainly most influential Chinese philosopher and teacher was Kong Fuzi (KONG FOO-dzih; "Master Kong, the Sage," c. 551–c. 479 B.C.E.), known in the West as Confucius after Jesuit missionaries to China in the seventeenth century Latinized his name. He was one in a line of teachers who tried to explain the universe and the place of the Chinese people within it as well as the appropriate behavior among human beings in society. Eventually viewed as the central figure in orthodox Chinese philosophy, many of his students believed the master composed or edited what were often called the Confucian classics—*The Book of Songs, The Book of Poetry, The Book of Documents, The Analects,* and other texts. The only work that can be accurately attributed to Confucius is *The Analects* ("Selected Sayings"), a collection of his responses to questions posed by his disciples that was passed on after his death.

Confucius belonged to the lower aristocracy of a minor state, Lu, which had been under the Duke of Zhou, idealized by Confucius and later made into a model by the master's students. Confucius was more or less a contemporary of the Buddha in India,

Document The Wisdom of Confucius

The wisdom of Confucius is celebrated across the world. Unlike some wise ancient texts that seem limited to the time in which they were written, the thoughts of the great Chinese philosopher have a relevance that transcends the moment they were expressed. In these extracts, Confucius reflects on the notions of family, power, and education.

1:1 The Master said, "To learn, and at due times to practice what one has learned, is that not also a pleasure? To have friends come from afar, is that not also a joy? To go unrecognized, yet without being embittered, is that not also to be a noble person?"

1:2 Master You [You Ruo] said, "Among those who are filial toward their parents and fraternal toward their brothers, those who are inclined to offend against their superiors are few indeed. Among those who are disinclined to offend against their superiors, there have never been any who are yet inclined to create disorder. The noble person concerns himself with the root; when the root is established, the Way is born. Being filial and fraternal—is this not the root of humaneness?"

1:3 The Master said, "Those who are clever in their words and pretentious in their appearance, yet are humane, are few indeed."

1:4 Zengzi said, "Each day I examine myself on three things: In planning on behalf of others, have I failed to be loyal? When dealing with friends, have I failed to be trustworthy? On receiving what has been transmitted, have I failed to practice it?"

1:5 The Master said, "In ruling a state of a thousand chariots, one is reverent in the handling of affairs and shows himself to be trustworthy. One is economical in expenditures, loves the people, and uses them only at the proper season."

1:7 Zixia said, "One who esteems the worthy and has little regard for sexual attraction, who in serving his parents is able to summon up his entire strength, who in serving his ruler is able to avoid himself with utmost devotion, who in interacting with friends shows himself trustworthy in his words—though it may be said of him that he has not studied. I would definitely call him learned."

1:8 The Master said, "If the noble person is not serious, he will not inspire awe, nor will his learning be sound. One should abide in loyalty and trustworthiness and should have no friends who are not his equal. If one has faults, one should not be afraid to change." . . .

1:16 The Master said. "One should not grieve that one is unrecognized by others; rather, one should grieve that one fails to recognize others." . . .

2:1 The Master said. "One who governs through virtue may be compared to the polestar, which occupies its place while the host of other stars pay homage to it." . . .

2:11 The Master said, "One who reanimates the old so as to understand the new may become a teacher."

2:12 The Master said, "The noble person is not a tool."

2:14 The Master said, "The noble person is inclusive, not exclusive: the small person is exclusive, not inclusive."

2:15 The Master said, "To learn without thinking, is unavailing; to think without learning is dangerous."

Questions to Consider

1. What do you think Confucius considers to be the traits of a "serious" person?
2. Does your professor fit the qualification expressed in 2:11? If so, why? If not, why not?
3. According to Confucius, what should be the ruler's attitude toward his people?

From the *Analects,* in William Theodore de Bary et al., eds., *Sources of Chinese Tradition*, 2nd ed., Vol. 1 (New York: Columbia University Press, 1999).

Zoroaster in Persia, and the early philosophers of Greece. To achieve his goal of improving society, Confucius did not look to the gods and spirits for assistance; he accepted the existence of Heaven *(Tian)* and spirits, but he insisted in the *Analects* that it was more important "to know the essential duties of man living in a society of men."

"We don't know yet how to serve men," he said, "How can we know about serving the spirits?" And, "We don't yet know about life, so how can we know about death?" Confucius hoped to become an adviser to a ruler, but he turned to teaching after traveling from court to court in an unsuccessful search for a ruler who would make use of his ideas.

He tried to inspire his students to be moral and prepared them to serve in government even if he himself was unable to do so. He honored the roles of learned men who served their rulers in ritual practice, record keeping, divination, and reception of guests and envoys from other rulers. He stressed that following honorable conventions and accepting hierarchy produced social harmony. Confucius advocated a fairly conservative order, though his words were reinterpreted constantly over the centuries to offer a variety of approaches to organizing the state and society.

Confucius was deeply disappointed with the condition of his own society, which he viewed as characterized by selfishness, lack of benevolence, and greed. Nobility, he contended, was not transmitted by birth but by acquiring wisdom and virtue. The ideal man was a *junzi* (JOON-zih), often translated as "gentleman," though without the hereditary connotations with which the word is associated in English. A *junzi* should be virtuous, righteous, humane, wise, and brave. Interactions among people should be governed by *li*, a term which covers the modern English-language connotations of propriety, manners, and ceremonial and sacred ritual. *Li* performed with a sincere heart rendered an individual human. Though *li* was manifested in each of the Five Relationships—the relationships between parent and child, ruler and subject, husband and wife, elder brother and younger brother, and friend and friend—it was most important in the family. Confucius emphasized filial piety, the respect of a child for his or her parents, above all. If the interests of one's ruler and one's parents conflicted, one's support of the parent came first. A son should never turn his father in for theft, for example.

DOCUMENT

Government and the Superior "Man"

At the same time, Confucius believed that the improvement of society was the responsibility of the ruler and that the quality of government depended on the ruler's moral character: "The way (Dao) of learning to be great consists in shining with the illustrious power of moral personality, in making a new people, in abiding in the highest goodness," he wrote.[2] Confucius's definition of the Dao as "moral personality" and the "highest goodness" was in decided contrast to the old premoral Dao, in which gods and spirits, propitiated by offerings and ritual, regulated human life for good or ill. Above all, Confucius's "new way" meant a concern for the rights of others, an adherence to a type of Golden Rule. When a disciple asked, "Is there any

Throughout the ages, Confucius became idealized as the authority to whom one could look for instruction on proper government and behavior.

saying that one can act on all day, every day?" Confucius replied, "Perhaps the saying about consideration: 'Never do to others what you would not like them to do to you.'"

Confucius's view of society was hierarchical. Even though four of the Five Relationships connected a superior and an inferior (only the relationship of friend to friend was equal), all relationships were to be grounded in *ren* (often translated as benevolence, humanity, or human-relatedness), a virtue applied to all without any hierarchical dimensions.

Although Confucius called himself "a transmitter and not a creator," his redefinition of Dao and his teachings produced an ethical program for this world, by this world.[3] His desire to reemphasize the propriety and humanity of *li*, which he felt were being ignored in his day, and his redirecting of the concept of the *junzi,* or gentleman, to one whose character rather than birth defined his nobility, underscore his new ethical emphasis. As he noted, "The noble man understands what is right; the inferior man understands what is profitable."[4]

Mozi (MOH-dzih; c. 490–391 B.C.E.), born around the time of Confucius's death, took issue with Confucius's placing of priority on one's family. Mozi stressed universal love instead, though he also believed in a hierarchy headed up by those who were capable and educated. Mozi disdained wars of aggression for territorial gain and excessive mourning rituals. Though Mozi, like numerous other philosophers of the Spring and Autumn era, had a lively following in his day, his school of thought did not survive the end of the Warring States period. In the end, historians stress the contributions of Confucianists, Daoists, and Legalists because of their continuing influence on Chinese thought, but scholars like Mozi were part of a very active intellectual climate.

Mencius: The Mandate of Heaven

Mencius, or Mengzi (MUNG-dzih; c. 372–c. 289 B.C.E.) was one of two scholars whose work was largely responsible for the emergence of Confucianism as the most widely accepted philosophy in China. Born a century after the death of Confucius, Mencius was raised by a mother who, according to legend, sacrificed her own happiness to support her son's education in scholarship and righteous behavior. Mencius's mother, revered as a paragon of virtue, is supposed to have expressed the long-lasting prescription for women's position in the family: as a child, a girl is subordinate to her father; as a young adult, a woman is subordinate to her husband; and as a widow, to her son.

Mencius is best known for adding important new dimensions to Confucian thought in terms of conceptions of human nature and of the right to govern. Whereas Confucius had only implied that human nature is good, Mencius emphatically insisted that all people are innately good and tend to seek the good, just as water tends to run downhill. But goodness must be cultivated by virtuous and wise rulers. He compared human nature to a mountain, once beautiful and lush, made barren by humans and animals denuding it of vegetation. Just as the mountain's nature was not to be barren, so, too, human nature was not to be corrupt. But both needed the right conditions to flourish.

Mencius believed good kings had ruled benevolently in the past and urged rulers of his day to practice benevolence as well, by reducing taxes and making punishments less severe. In that way, he stressed, kings would gain their people's support and be invincible. Mencius went further, proposing a system of land distribution believed to have been used by ancient sage rulers. This system, called the "well-field" system, called for eight families to farm fields shaped like the Chinese character for *well* (like a modern day tic-tac-toe board), with one field in the middle farmed by all eight families for taxes. This way, Mencius argued, everyone's needs would be satisfied fairly. When the people were happy, they would support their ruler.

If the ruler was not wise and benevolent, government would be corrupt, the people hungry, and natural disasters destructive of the people's livelihood. This, Mencius averred, was Heaven's sign that the ruler was not really a true ruler. By the Confucian principle of "rectification of names," a person who was not a ruler should be removed. Such a ruler had lost the mandate of Heaven. If the Son of Heaven ruled by virtue of the permission (or mandate) of Heaven, Heaven also had the right to withdraw the mandate. Mencius's great contribution to Confucian thought was his suggestion that people's rebellion was a sign of the loss of the mandate. In fact, the phrase "removing the mandate" became the basis for the modern Chinese and Japanese terms for "revolution."

As we have seen, this concept had been used by the Zhou to justify their revolt against the Shang whom they considered corrupt. On that occasion the concept had a religious meaning. The people were to obey the Zhou ruler as the Son of Heaven, just as they worshipped Heaven through rites and rituals. Mencius, however, secularized the mandate of Heaven when he declared, "Heaven hears as the people hear; Heaven sees as the people see."[5] By redefining the concept of a heavenly mandate in this way, Mencius made the welfare of the people the ultimate standard for judging the virtue of government. Mencius advocated responsible monarchy, supporting this concept because he believed there was a need for a new, unifying leadership that could end the warring between regional states during the late Zhou period, not, however, because he believed that people had a right to express their political views. Nonetheless, the idea of the mandate of Heaven came to be associated with the idea of the people's right to rebel and to overthrow the unjust leadership of a leader who had "lost the mandate of Heaven."

Xunzi: Human Nature as Antisocial

Xunzi (SHOON-dzih; c. 310–c. 220 B.C.E.), like Mencius, interpreted and extended Confucius's ideas. Contrary to Mencius, however, Xunzi argued that human nature tended to be antisocial and needed guidance to turn toward virtue. Wise leadership, proper rituals, and even strict laws (which Mencius rejected) would make humans capable of living good lives, filled with filial piety and morality. Once a person recognizes what is good, Xunzi argued, he or she will practice goodness. Xunzi differed from some other Confucianists by arguing that an impartial Heaven did not respond to prayers or ritual: It will rain whether or not one prays for rain. But he did not reject ritual and prayer; rather he stated that ritual, like music, was an excellent way for people to express their emotions, to provide social harmony, and to order social hierarchy.

Legalism

Legalism: The Way of the State

Xunzi is appropriately considered a Confucian thinker. Two of his students, however, took some of his ideas and applied them to a different philosophical tradition that came to be called Legalism due to its emphasis on laws. Decades before Xunzi interpreted Confucianism, Lord Shang (d. 338 B.C.E.), a minister in the state of Qin, described his work as Legalist. He got rid of Qin's aristocracy; determined his subordinates' military rank by the number of heads they cut off in battle; organized territory into counties; attracted farmers to those counties by offering them houses, land, and freedom from serfdom; made people responsible for crimes committed by members of their mutual responsibility groups; and codified laws, applying them harshly without consideration for rank.

Xunzi's student Han Feizi (HAN FAY-dzih; d. 233 B.C.E.) followed in Lord Shang's tradition. He advocated harsh application of laws, unmodified by family concerns. It was shocking to Confucianists that he suggested that rulers should not be expected to be moral leaders who treated their subjects with kindness. Indeed, he said, since even parents treated their newborn sons and daughters differently, thereby showing little parental love for their own daughters, how could a ruler be expected to rule subjects, with whom they had no familial bond, with morality and virtue? Equal application of the law was the only answer. Han Feizi's contemporary, Li Si (d. 208 B.C.E.), also a former student of Xunzi, put Legalist political theory into practice in Qin as its leading minister.

The Legalists argued for an elaborate system of laws defining fixed penalties for each offense, with no consideration for rank, class, or circumstances, with the important exception of the ruler, who was above the law. Judges were not to use their own consciences in estimating the gravity of a crime and arbitrarily deciding on the punishment. Their task was solely to define the crime correctly; the punishment was provided automatically by the code of law. This clashed with Confucian prioritization, in the name of human kindness, of the family, and with the notion that *ren* (benevolence) itself was a motivation for the people to support their ruler.

Daoism

Daoism: The Way and Virtue

A third, lasting school of thought emerged in the late Zhou era. **Daoism** contrasted greatly with Confucian ideals and practices, as it focused on natural harmony rather than social harmony. In its very earliest forms, Daoism had some political aspects, but in the third century B.C.E. its leading philosopher, Zuangzi (JWAHNG-dzih) (c. 369–c. 286 B.C.E.), embraced relativism and spiritual freedom and was adamantly apolitical. Daoists, unlike Confucianists, did not welcome rulers' intervention to improve people's livelihoods. For Confucianists, the Dao ("the way") was the ethical path for rulers' humanity in a human-centered world; for Daoists, the Dao was the way of nature with which humans should seek harmony rather than dominance.

Two Daoist texts survive. The earliest, the *Daodejing* (DOW-deh-JING) or *Laozi* (LOW-dzih), is often attributed to Lao Dai, a sixth-century contemporary of Confucius. Most likely the book was compiled three centuries later. This poetic text is cryptic and paradoxical and open to many interpretations, because, as it suggests, the Dao itself cannot be defined. There are a few ideas that are strongly encouraged, however: that nonaction and nonbeing triumph over action and being and that silence is superior to words. Rulers should not take actions, but rather allow nature to take its course. As the *Laozi* explained, "Do not honor the worthy, and the people will not compete. Do not value rare treasures, and the people will not steal. . . . A sage governs this way: He empties people's minds and fills their bellies. . . . Engage in no action and order will prevail."[6]

The other Daoist text, the *Zhuangzi*, goes much farther in rejecting politics and engagement with society. While the *Laozi* had some political uses—for instance, some rulers believed that by doing nothing their state or society could be strengthened—the *Zhuangzi* strongly rejected politics. Zhuangzi himself, believed to be the book's author, turned down government jobs and titles, preferring, he said, to drag his tail in the mud like a turtle rather than having his bones venerated after his death. Here Zhuangzi rejects both political power, which he likens to the impotence of dead bones, and social respect, suggested by his rejection of the veneration ("ancestor worship") of his bones.

Daoism was a revolt not only against society but also against the intellect's limitations. Intuition, not reason, was the source of true knowledge; and books, Daoists said, are "the dregs and refuse of the ancients." Zhuangzi even questioned the reality of the world of

Daoism—A philosophical school, later a religion, focusing on natural harmony and nonaction.

Document # Legalism: The Theories of Han Feizi (d. 233 B.C.E.)

Throughout history, philosophers and leaders have generally differed in their notions of human nature. Some, like Confucius, counseled a due respect for the people, while others like Mencius saw the need for the people's consent in the affairs of state. The thinker Han Feizi disagreed with both Confucius and Mencius, viewing human nature as essentially evil and the average human being as incompetent.

When the sage rules the state, he does not count on people doing good of themselves, but employs such measures as will keep them from doing any evil. If he counts on people doing good of themselves, there will not be enough such people to be numbered by the tens in the whole country. But if he employs such measures as will keep them from doing evil, then the entire state can be brought up to a uniform standard. Inasmuch as the administrator has to consider the many but disregard the few, he does not busy himself with morals but with laws.

. . . Therefore, the intelligent ruler upholds solid facts and discards useless frills. He does not speak about deeds of humanity and righteousness, and he does not listen to the words of learned men.

Those who are ignorant about government insistently say: "Win the hearts of the people." If order could be procured by winning the hearts of the people, then even the wise ministers Yi Yin and Guan Zhong would be of no use. For all that the ruler would need to do would be just to listen to the people. Actually, the intelligence of the people is not to be relied upon any more than the mind of a baby. If the baby does not have his head shaved, his sores will recur; if he does not have his boil cut open, his illness will go from bad to worse. However, in order to shave his head or open the boil someone has to hold the baby while the affectionate mother is performing the work, and yet he keeps crying and yelling incessantly. The baby does not understand that suffering a small pain is the way to obtain a great benefit.

. . . The sage considers the conditions of the times . . . and governs the people accordingly. Thus though penalties are light, it is not due to charity; though punishment is heavy, it is not due to cruelty. Whatever is done is done in accordance with the circumstances of the age. Therefore circumstances go according to their time, and the course of action is planned in accordance with the circumstances.

. . . Now take a young fellow who is a bad character. His parents may get angry at him, but he never makes any change. The villagers may reprove him, but he is not moved. His teachers and elders may admonish him, but he never reforms. The love of his parents, the efforts of the villagers, and the wisdom of his teachers and elders—all the three excellent disciplines are applied to him, and yet not even a hair on his shins is altered. It is only after the district magistrate sends out his soldiers and in the name of the law searches for wicked individuals that the young man becomes afraid and changes his ways and alters his deeds. So while the love of parents is not sufficient to discipline the children, the severe penalties of the district magistrate are. This is because men become naturally spoiled by love, but are submissive to authority. . . .

That being so, rewards should be rich and certain so that the people will be attracted by them; punishments should be severe and definite so that the people will fear them; and laws should be uniform and steadfast so that the people will be familiar with them. Consequently, the sovereign should show no wavering in bestowing rewards and grant no pardon in administering punishments, and he should add honor to rewards and disgrace to punishments—when this is done, then both the worthy and the unworthy will want to exert themselves.

Questions to Consider

1. What is the function of the law, according to Legalist thinker Han Feizi?
2. What does the author believe to be the intellectual capacity of "the people?"
3. According to Han Feizi, how should a leader behave in regard to those who do good and those who do not?

From *Sources of Chinese Tradition*, 2nd ed., Vol. 1, eds. William Theodore de Bary, et al. Copyright © 1999 Columbia University Press. Reprinted with the permission of the publisher.

the senses. He said that he once dreamed that he was a butterfly, "flying about enjoying itself." When he awakened, he was confused: "I do not know whether I was Zhuangzi dreaming that I was a butterfly, or whether now I am a butterfly dreaming that I am Zhuangzi."

Anecdotes and allegories abound in both texts, as in all mystical teachings that deal with subjects that are difficult to put into words. As the *Daodejing* put it, "The one who knows does not speak, and the one who speaks does not know." In later centuries, Daoism, which was primarily philosophical in its formative years, adopted a religious aspect. At the end of the Han dynasty, also discussed in this chapter, Daoism took on a religious coloration, and Daoists then used their beliefs in political movements and in the quest for immortality through alchemy and sexual practices. Although Confucianism and Daoism frequently sniped at each other, they never became mutually exclusive outlooks on life. Daoist intuition complemented Confucian rationalism in the search for the true way, and during the centuries to come, Chinese often attempted to follow Confucianist precepts in their social relations, while at the same time maintaining Daoist beliefs.

The diverse philosophers of the Warring States centuries reflected not only a variety of responses to the brutality of war but also the different cultural or regional environments in which they emerged. Those that left a record in the form of silk scrolls were not only attached to their time and place but also were able, through the constancy of the Chinese written language, to transcend their time. In time, these written works became part of the "Classics" considered to be the heart of Chinese philosophy.

THE QIN AND HAN EMPIRES, 221 B.C.E.–220 C.E.

■ *How did Chinese leaders use Confucian and Daoist ideas to justify conflicting state policies in the name of promoting the people's welfare and the growth of the state?*

The Qin Dynasty: Unification

Two dynasties, the Qin and the Han, unified China and created a centralized empire. The Qin dynasty collapsed soon after the death of its founder, but the Han lasted for about four centuries. Together, these dynasties transformed China, but the changes were the culmination of earlier philosophical, political, and economic developments that had emerged during the turmoil of the Warring States period.

Throughout the Warring States period, there had been a widely shared hope that a king would unite China and inaugurate a great new age of peace and stability. Whereas the Confucianists believed that such a king would accomplish the task by means of his outstanding moral virtue, the Legalists substituted kingly power and rule of law as the essential elements of effective government. The rise to preeminence of the Qin state began in 361 B.C.E. when its ruler selected Lord Shang, a man imbued with Legalist principles, to be chief minister. Recognizing that the growth of Qin power depended on a more efficient and centralized bureaucratic structure, Lord Shang undermined the old hereditary nobility and created a new aristocracy based on military merit. He also undermined their privileged place in society by introducing a universal draft beginning at approximately age 15. This produced an effect of leveling social difference, as chariot and cavalry warfare, in which the nobility had played the leading role, was replaced in importance by masses of peasant infantry equipped with iron weapons. Economically, Lord Shang further weakened the old landowning nobility by granting peasants ownership of the plots they tilled. Thereafter, the peasants paid taxes directly to the local state, thus increasing its wealth and power. These reforms were essential to Qin's rise to power during the Warring States period.

Nearly a century later, King Zheng ascended the throne as a boy of nine in 247. Nine years earlier, the last Zhou king had been deposed. Aided by two ministers, former merchant Lu Buwei (LOO boo-WAY; d. 235 B.C.E.) and Li Si, King Zheng conquered the neighboring states of Han, Zhao, Wei, Chu, and Qi, thereby unifying China in 221 B.C.E. The king then declared himself *Shi Huangdi* (SHIH HWAHNG-dee) or the "First August Supreme Ruler" of the Qin, or First Emperor, as his new title is more commonly translated. Huangdi ("emperor") endured as the royal title until 1911. Shi Huangdi also enlarged China—a name derived from the word Qin—by conquests in the south as far as the coast of South China. Military expeditions

The Early Empires

221–206 B.C.E.	Qin
206 B.C.E.–9 C.E.	Former (Western) Han
9–23 C.E.	Reign of Wang Mang
23–220 C.E.	Later (Eastern) Han

entered Vietnam and Inner Mongolia as well. The emperor stated that his dynasty would endure 10,000 generations. Although it lasted just 15 years, the idea of a united China ruled by an emperor would persist into the twentieth century.

China's Struggle for Cultural and Political Unity, 400 B.C.E. to 400

The First Emperor further weakened the power of the nobility by moving hundreds of thousands of leading families to the capital at Xianyang (shee-AHN-yahng), near Xi'an, where they could be closely watched. To block rebellion, he ordered the entire civilian population to surrender their weapons to the state. A single legal code replaced all local laws. Modeled on the social structure of Lord Shang, the population was organized into groups of ten families, and each person was held responsible for the actions of all the members of the group. This structure ensured that all crimes would be reported; it also increased loyalty to the state at the expense of loyalty to the family.

As part of the unifying process, the entire realm was divided into 36 commanderies which were subdivided into counties directly ruled by the emperor's centrally controlled civil and military appointees sent to replace the local families who had been moved to Xianyang. To destroy the source of the aristocracy's power and to permit the emperor's agents to tax every farmer's harvest, private ownership of land by peasants, promoted a century earlier in the state of Qin by Lord Shang, was decreed for all of China. Thus the Qin Empire reflected emerging social forces at work in China: the peasants freed from serfdom, a new military and administrative upper class, and merchants eager to increase their wealth within a larger political arena. In place of the hereditary power of the nobility, the entire population was divided into 20 ranks, each entitled to different rights, including access to a certain type of clothing and a specified amount of land, slaves, and housing. The new bureaucracy was a meritocracy in both the civil and military realms. As late as the early Zhou period, cowrie shells and cloth had been used as currency, but money had begun to circulate broadly around 500 B.C.E., and by the outset of

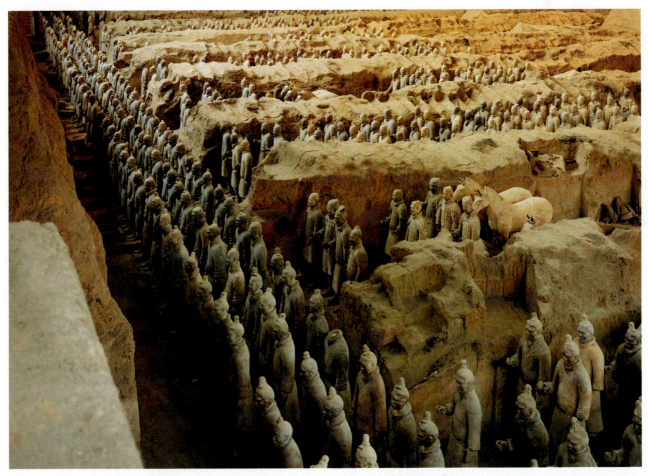

The tombs of the First Emperor, 210 B.C.E., have yielded most of the surviving art of that period in China. The more than 6000 figures, including these terra-cotta warriors, were not discovered until 1974 in one of the greatest archaeological finds in history.

Qin rule, the centuries of unrest had stimulated an economic boom manifested not only in support for military endeavors, but in trade routes and networks, regional specialization, and the growth of cities.

Economic growth under the First Qin Emperor's short reign was also stimulated by public works, the standardization of the written language and of currency, and the erecting of walls to keep non-Chinese nomads out. All construction was by forced labor, and under the First Emperor, 4000 miles of roads and thousands of miles of canals and waterways, one of which connected the Yangzi to the Xi River and Guangzhou (gwahng-JOH), were completed. (This surpassed the system of the Roman Empire, which was estimated to be somewhat shorter—3740 miles.) The standardization of writing entailed the introduction of new, simpler written language, and no variation was allowed. These Chinese characters, central to unification, would be used until 1949, when an even more streamlined method of writing was created.

The new, unified currency could be threaded together in strings. Moreover, weights and measures and even the length of axles (so that cart wheels would fit the grooves cut in the highways) were made uniform. Although the First Emperor, like some Warring States rulers before him, built walls to impede the incursion of nomadic tribes from central Asia, it is no longer believed that he built the 1400-mile Great Wall of China. In its present form the Great Wall was mainly the work of the sixteenth-century Ming dynasty.[7]

IMAGE

The Great Wall of China

The First Emperor tried to enforce intellectual conformity and to cast the Qin Legalist system as the only natural political order. He suppressed all other schools of thought, especially the Confucianists, who idealized the Zhou political order. To break the hold of the past, the emperor put into effect a Legalist proposal requiring that all privately owned books reflecting past traditions be burned and that opponents of government in the name of antiquity be beheaded. Books burned included the Confucian classics and any statements of political philosophy that countered the Qin concern for control. Legend has it that the Qin emperor had 460 Confucian scholars buried alive, but the anti-Qin hostility of later generations of Confucian scholars makes it impossible to prove whether this really happened.

DOCUMENT

Li Si and Legalist Policies of Qin Shi Huang

The First Emperor created a new cultural elite of state-appointed teachers who would give an approved reading of the traditions and lessons of history. This set in motion the precedent that "imperial governments would henceforth insist that approved texts and suitable interpretations would be used for this purpose and that teaching would be conducted along recognized lines." As recent scholarship has argued, however, much of Chinese thought was based on oral traditions handed down, and therefore the burning of books and state control of intellectual life did not eradicate late Zhou learning.[8]

The First Emperor's control of the lives of his subjects did not erase his fear of death. Three assassination attempts gave him reason to be concerned. He dispatched a group of young men and women on a fruitless quest for the mythical islands of immortality. In addition, his fear of death, along with the Qin need to demonstrate its power, led to the emperor's employment of over half a million laborers to construct a huge burial mound near the Qin capital. The location of the mound was to be kept a secret from the people, however. All artisans and laborers involved in the construction of the tomb were locked inside the tomb while alive. Nearby, over 6000 terra-cotta soldiers were presented in military formation, in three large pits. These sculptures represented figures of the Emperor's imperial guard, and no two faces of these life-size figures are alike—each head is a personal portrait.

When the First Emperor took ill and died in 210 B.C.E. while on one of his frequent tours of inspection to control his realm, he was succeeded by an inept son who was unable to control the rivalry among his father's chief aides. Qin policies had alienated not only the intellectuals and the old nobility but also the peasants, who were subjected to ruinous taxation and forced labor. Rebel armies thus rose in every province of the empire; some led by peasants, others by aristocrats. Anarchy followed, and by 206 B.C.E. the Qin dynasty had disappeared. But the idea of a unified Chinese empire, though it often failed to be created, would last until 1912, when China became a republic.

At issue in the fighting that continued for another 4 years after the end of the Qin dynasty was not only the question of succession to the throne but also the form of government. The peasant and aristocratic leaders, first allied against the Qin, became engaged in a ruthless civil war. The aristocrats, led by the brilliant general Xiang Yu (shee-AHNG YOO; 233 B.C.E.–202 B.C.E.), sought to restore the power they had possessed before the Legalist consolidation of imperial rule. Their opponents, whose main leader was Liu Bang (LEE-oo BAHNG), a peasant who became a minor government functionary, desired a centralized state. In this contest between the old order and the new, the new was the victor—China would stay united under the Han emperors and by a bureaucratic culture, based on merit, and dedicated to rule from the center.

The Han Dynasty

The Empire Consolidated

In 206 B.C.E. Liu Bang, known to history as the Emperor Gaozu (GOW-dzoo; r. 202–195 B.C.E.), defeated his aristocratic rival and established the Han

Classical China

dynasty, building a capital at Chang'an (modern Xi'an). It lasted for more than 400 years and is traditionally divided into two parts: the Former Han (206 B.C.E.–8 C.E.) and the Later Han (23–220 C.E.). The impact of these four centuries is illustrated by the fact that ethnic Chinese still call themselves "people of Han."

The empire and power sought by Gaozu and his successors were those of the Qin, but they succeeded where the Qin had failed because they attempted to balance *wu* ("military power") with *wen* ("ethical civilian rule"). To indicate his opposition to the centralized rule of the tyrannical Qin, Gaozu had initially distributed domains to supporters who would govern them as somewhat autonomous vassal states. He soon realized, however, that effective rule required centralization. He then appointed officials to carry out legal and administrative functions in the provinces. To placate the peasants, Gaozu lowered taxes and reduced forced labor. The Han tied the empire together physically as well. By100 B.C.E., the Han had established a road system that made it possible for a traveler to go from the far north to the far south in 56 days on foot or in 32 days on horseback. But the most effective tool to gain acceptance was to enlist the support of the Confucian intellectuals. The emperors recognized that an educated bureaucracy was necessary for governing their vast empire. They lifted the Qin ban on the Confucian classics and other Zhou literature. The way was open for a revival of intellectual life that had been suppressed under the Qin, and the result was yet another reformulation of Confucian thought.

In accordance with Legalist principles, now tempered by Confucian insistence on the ethical basis of government, the Han emperors established administrative organs, staffed by a salaried bureaucracy with as many as 20 levels, to rule their empire. Government officials hailed mainly from rich families who were able to educate their sons, but the door to a government career was, in principle, open to all capable men. Emperor Wudi (r. 141–87 B.C.E., "Martial Emperor"), the Han dynasty's most vigorous emperor, established a university to train future officials. The first student body numbered 50. By 8 B.C.E., there were 3000 students; the number increased to 30,000 in the Later Han. The curriculum focused on Confucianism, endearing the emperor to many scholars and legitimizing the dynasty in their skeptical eyes. The formal examination system to select officials (developed in later centuries) did not yet exist; all officials were selected after they gave evidence of their scholarly abilities. Though these officials owed their positions to political appointments, they were men of conviction. Many suffered when their convictions differed with the opinions of their rulers.

The Han dynasty devised effective ways to maintain control of power, but they were unable to address one major challenge to their control. The families of emperors' wives emerged as powerful political actors. Gaozu's widow ruled and promoted her family's interests for 15 years after Gaozu's death. At the end of the Former Han, Wang Mang, a relative of an emperor's widow, came to power briefly, attempting to establish his own dynasty, the Xin (SHIN; 9 C.E.–23 C.E.).

Wudi

After 60 years of consolidation, the Han dynasty achieved its greatest size and zenith of achievements during the long reign of Wudi. At the same time, however, Wudi raised the peasants' taxes. In addition, he increased the amount of labor and military service the peasants were forced to contribute to the state. Those taxes were lowered after his death.

Even before Wudi's reign, Han officials were concerned about the burden of taxes on the ordinary peasants. Estate holders could generally evade taxation, so peasants began to turn their land over to estate holders to whom they paid rents that were lower than

Officials conspicuously indicated their rank by the retinues of attendants that accompanied them on their travels to their posts. Officials' tombs often contained paintings, statues, or friezes depicting these retinues. This scene, carved on a tomb brick during the Later Han, shows carriages, horses, and runners.

official taxes. The government responded by lowering taxes on peasants and finding new revenue sources. To pay for his military expansion, Wudi increased taxes on businesses, confiscated some nobles' lands, and most controversially, started government monopolies in salt and iron production in 119 B.C.E. Salt and iron were both necessities, and the government monopolies raised a lot of money. Confucianists were horrified, however, that the Son of Heaven should be involved in something they disdained—the quest for profits. A great debate about the economic role of the state—should the state promote profit making for the people's benefit or should it stay away from enterprise for the benefit of government morality?—engaged scholars in 81 B.C.E. This classic debate is still the basis of discussions on the role and scope of government, in China and throughout the world. Should the government play an economic role, or are laissez-faire policies more effective?

Wudi may also have initiated policies concerning grain, but the timing of those policies is unclear. Certainly by 51 B.C.E. (after Wudi's death), the Ever-Normal Granary Policy had the government buy grain when it was plentiful, allowing farmers to earn a good profit, and storing it until shortfalls hit, as they always did, saving the people from famine. The price and the quantity of rice available were, thus, stabilized.

Wudi justified his expansionist policies in terms of self-defense against nomadic tribes, including the Xiongnu (SHONG-noo), known later to Europeans as the Huns. The nomads' threats had caused the Emperor Gaozu to construct a wall and to send the nomads gifts and imperial princesses as brides. In 133 B.C.E., Wudi reversed the conciliatory policy and sent huge armies to the far west, establishing military colonies there and forcing local chieftains to send their sons to China for education, in effect making them hostages. Wudi annexed a large corridor extending through the Tarim River basin of central Asia to the Pamir Mountains, close to Bactria.

Wudi sent an envoy westward to seek allies against the Xiongnu. Captured and held prisoner for ten years, this envoy eventually reached Bactria and Ferghana. His reports of the interest shown in Chinese silks by the peoples of the area is an excellent example of increasing Chinese cultural, economic, and political interaction with non-Chinese. Commercial exchanges between China and other civilizations farther west were already underway. By 101 B.C.E., Wudi conquered Ferghana, thus controlling trade routes across Central Asia. This was the beginning of centuries of what came to be called "Silk Roads," major trade routes that carried a variety of products in addition to the popular silks.

Wudi also outflanked the Xiongnu in the east by the conquest of southern Manchuria and northern Korea. In addition, he completed the conquest of South China, begun by the Qin, and added northern Vietnam to the Chinese Empire. Chinese settlers moved into all the conquered lands. In fact, just as the armies of the Roman Republic were laying the foundation of the Pax Romana in the West, the Martial Emperor was consolidating power in the East.

Han Decline

Wudi's conquests led to overextension of the empire. As costs increased and many peasants fled to the protection of the great estates, taxes on the remaining peasants increased. Advances in agricultural technology, especially new plows and irrigation systems, permitted increased output. The donkey, brought from the west by the Xiongnu, was a helpful pack animal. These improvements led to population growth—the Han Empire had more people than Rome in 2 B.C.E.—but life for farmers was precarious. The custom of multiple inheritance led to tiny farms. The central government had to rely more and more on local military commanders and great landowners for control of the population, giving them great power and prestige at its own expense. More and more peasants fell behind in their rents and were forced to sell themselves or their children into debt slavery. This decline after an initial period of increasing prosperity and power made it appear that the Han were in danger of losing the mandate of Heaven.

Wudi was followed by less powerful rulers. Two child emperors, with Wang Mang as their regent, weakened Han control. At the same time, the rise of a messianic religious movement inspired by the cult of a goddess called the Queen Mother of the West suggested that the end of the dynasty was near. Wang Mang took over the throne in 9 C.E., seeming to fulfill the cult's prophecy. Wang Mang united Confucian ethics with Legalist practice. His goal was the rejuvenation of society by employing the power of the state. Because the number of large tax-free estates had greatly increased while the number of tax-paying peasant holdings had declined in the decades before Wang Mang's rise to power, he resurrected the well-field system, cut court expenses, issued new coins, abolished slavery, and reinvigorated the Ever-Normal Granary Policy. He tried to bring back Zhou-style offices. (In 1938 a chance reading of Wang Mang's proposal inspired the "ever-normal granary" program of the American New Deal!)[9]

Wang Mang's reform program failed. The conservative bureaucracy was unequal to the difficult administrative task. The powerful landowners rebelled against the ruler who proposed to confiscate their land. To make matters worse, in 11 C.E., the Huanghe changed course dramatically, flooding enormous tracts of land. The peasants joined the wealthy in opposition to Wang Mang. Although Wang Mang rescinded his reforms, he was killed by the rebels in 23 C.E. The conflicts over landownership and tenancy, along with the concentration of power of great families, became—and remained—a major problem in Chinese history.

The Later Han dynasty never reached the heights of its predecessors. Warlords who were members of the rich landowner class seized more and more power, and widespread peasant rebellions sapped the state's resources.

Religious uprising abounded, including one led by Daoist Mother Lu. Rivalries between Confucian scholars and court **eunuchs** had always been a problem, but in the second century of the Later Han, these erupted in murderous attacks on one another. Eunuchs were in control of the throne by the 170s. The previous decades saw plagues of locusts and horrific floods. By the 180s, rebellions were occurring everywhere. The uprising of the Yellow Turbans (so named because of the yellow scarves they wore) in 184 C.E. was particularly destructive to the Later Han. This was a messianic movement joined by thousands of poverty-stricken people, who believed in what they called *Taipingdao* (tai-PING-DOW) or "The Way of Great Peace." Emerging from economic need, this movement combined folk religious Daoism with the political goal of ending the dynasty. The Yellow Turbans did not achieve their goal, but they left behind a legacy in terms of setting a precedent for other grassroots revolts.

The general who subdued the Yellow Turbans went on to slaughter over 2000 eunuchs, along with beardless men mistaken for eunuchs. Luoyang was sacked in 189.

Surviving in name only during its last 30 years, the Han dynasty ended in 220 C.E., when the throne was usurped by the son of a famous warlord. Three and a half centuries of disunity and turbulence followed—the longest period of strife in China's long history. But China eventually succeeded in reuniting. In 589 the Sui dynasty united China again. By the end of the sixth century, as a result of centuries of political and cultural transformation, China had been created.

Han Scholarship, Art, and Technology

Scholarship flourished under the Han. A major concern of scholars was the collecting and interpreting of the classics of Chinese thought produced in the Zhou period. Many of the texts destroyed under the Qin were reproduced by scholars who had memorized

---

eunuchs—Castrated men used to guard the Emperor's wives and concubines because they posed no sexual threat.

them earlier. When some documents assumed to be original classics were unearthed in the first century B.C.E., disputes over authenticity arose. The recovered volumes were venerated as a repository of past wisdom, while the texts written down from memory accorded more closely with scholarly currents of the Han dynasty. This encouraged studies of the past, including historical studies and the production of the world's first dictionary. This dictionary, containing 9000 characters with their meanings and pronunciations, was written by Xu Shen (SHOO SHEN; c. 54–120 C.E.). Han scholars venerated Confucius, who moved in the popular imagination from being a teacher, a man like any other, to becoming the ideal thinker and a being regarded as in some ways divine. Confucianism became the official philosophy of the state. Antiquarian interest spurred the research of Sima Qian (SIH-mah CHEN; c.145–90 B.C.E.) and Ban Gu (BAHN GOO; d. 92 C.E.). Sima Qian's work, a comprehensive history of China, the *Historical Records (Shiji)*, is a huge and highly detailed work of 130 chapters beginning with the Xia dynasty, including narratives of political events, chronological tables, and biographies. Sima Qian carefully quoted from documents, weighing evidence and bringing sophisticated historical methods to his study. He was so dedicated to his work that he chose castration over death for the crime of defending a general who had surrendered to an enemy in order to complete the *Historical Records*. Ban Gu's *History of the Former Han* was the first dynastic history written during and later approved by the following dynasty. Ban Gu, like Sima Qian, strove for historical accuracy and objectivity. Thereafter, it became customary for each dynasty to write the official history of its immediate predecessor.

DOCUMENT

Sima Qian on Qin Shi Huang

Other scholars made an important mark as well. Dong Zhongshu (DONG JONG-shoo; c. 179–104 B.C.E.), Wudi's adviser, stressed the ruler's central role in leading the people to understand the goodness in their nature. He also stressed that earthquakes, eclipses, and weather disasters were signs of a ruler's immorality and pending loss of the mandate of Heaven. The Chinese believed that the successes and failures of the past provided guidance for one's own time and for the future. As stated in the *Historical Records*, "Events of the past, if not forgotten, are teachings about the future." The state-sponsored Chinese historians wrote to affirm the intimate and unchanging and essential link—the emperor—between the heavenly order and politics, caught up in supposedly predictable cycles.[10]

Han scholars also made use of archaeological investigation as an aid to the writing of history. One scholar anticipated modern archaeologists by more than a thousand years in classifying human history by "ages": "stone" (Old Stone Age), "jade" (New Stone Age), "bronze," and "the present age" when "weapons are made of iron."[11]

Han art was clearly creative. The largely decorative art of the past, which served a religious purpose, was replaced by a realistic pictorial art (foreshadowed earlier by the individually sculpted soldiers buried near the First Emperor's tomb) portraying ordinary life. The result was the first great Chinese flowering of sculpture. Some of the finest examples of this realistic secular art are the models of the tall and spirited horses that Wudi imported from Bactria. The Han greatly admired these proud "celestial" and "blood-sweating" horses from the west, and their artists brilliantly captured the beasts' high spirit. Human figures, models, and tiles depicting everyday life are among

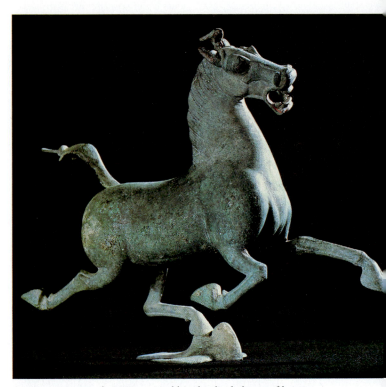

A masterpiece nearly 2000 years old is this lively horse of bronze, galloping and neighing with its head and tail high. To show its speed, the unknown artist, with bold imagination, placed its left hind hoof on a flying swallow, and the other three hooves in the air. The craftsmanship is extremely fine and conforms to the principles of mechanics.

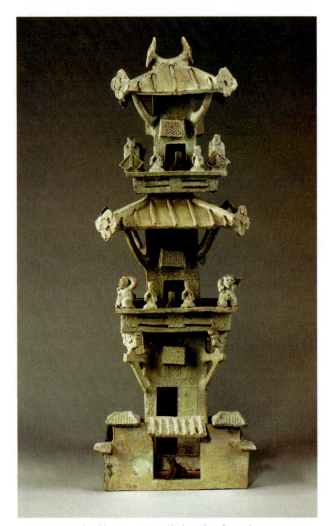

Because Han buildings were made largely of wood, none remain. Ceramic models show us how houses and towers were constructed. This Han-era model of a tower, which might have been part of a single- or multistory housing compound surrounding a courtyard, indicates the use of tile, plaster, wood, and other materials.

the fine art forms. The flair for ornamentation in the visual arts and architecture are replicated in the vibrant poetry.

During the Han period, China surpassed the level of technological development in the rest of the world. Notable inventions included a simple seismograph capable of indicating earthquakes several hundred miles away; the use of water power to grind grain and to operate a piston bellows for iron smelting; the horse collar, which greatly increased the pulling power of horses; paper made from cloth rags, which replaced cumbersome bamboo strips and expensive silk cloth as a writing surface; a sophisticated, labor-saving plow; and the humble but extremely useful wheelbarrow. By the end of the first century B.C.E., the Han Chinese had recognized sunspots and accurately determined the length of the calendar year, an example of the high level gained in their mathematical and observational astronomy.[12]

The Confucian Woman of the Han

Confucius had placed wives in a position subordinate to their husbands, and yin-yang theory had held that men and women were fundamentally different, but few scholars discussed women before the Han dynasty. Poetry and art had depicted women, but two writers in the Han wrote works that had the most long-lasting effects on the status of women. The first work, *Biographies of Heroic Women* by Liu Xiang (lee-OO SHANG; 79–8 B.C.E.), is a major collection of biographies of 125 exemplary women, notable for their filial piety, wise counsel to their husbands, and valor in the defense of their chastity. Such biographies were common didactic vehicles for men, and Liu Xiang's work parallels those with examples of women.

The other work was by Ban Zhao (BAN JOW; 45–116 C.E.), sister of Ban Gu, and a teacher to the girls and women in the palace. Her *Lessons for Women* were strict rules for the separation of men's and women's spheres. She elaborated on what propriety meant for women, listing four "womanly qualifications": womanly virtue, womanly words, womanly bearing, and womanly work that included sewing, weaving, and the ordering of wine and food for guests. Women were to guard their chastity and exhibit modesty and self-control, to choose their words with care, to wear clean clothing and ornaments, and to keep their bodies clean. She stated that wives should be obedient to their husbands, parents-in-law, and brothers- and sisters-in-law.

Because she knew that courtesy and righteousness could only be attained if women were educated, she stressed education. She asked: "Only to teach men and not to teach women, is that not ignoring the essential relation between them?"[13] *Lessons for Women* was passed down from Chinese men and women to girls into the twentieth century, and Ban Zhao's approach to womanhood influenced ideas in Japan and Korea as well as China.

Religious Daoism and Buddhism

The philosophical Daoism of the late Zhou era was joined by a new form of religious Daoism in the Han. While it was not until the last century of the Later Han that religious Daoism developed a written body of sacred texts and clergy able to interpret them—concepts that would have seemed alien to Zhuangzi and Laozi—other uses of Daoism emerged as early as the founding of the Qin. Both the first emperor of the Qin and Wudi of Han consulted Daoist specialists on extending their lives through elixirs, diet, and talismans in addition to sexual practices and breathing exercises. These techniques were performed by men in power and were not yet a form of popular religious expression.

By the second century of the Later Han, these Daoist-inspired practices for extending longevity were joined by an interest in alchemy to produce elixirs and combined with folk beliefs in local gods and shamanistic rituals to create a more organized religion. From these roots, religious Daoism produced several leaders able to transform peasant discontent into massive religious movements, such as the Red Eyebrows and the Yellow Turbans. Religious Daoism continued to evolve in the next several centuries.

The breakdown of the political and social order during the Later Han also produced an upsurge in philosophical Daoism. Because they had no faith in the political order or in social action that could eradicate the widespread discontent and were discouraged with Confucianism and its concern for society, educated Chinese began to turn inward. The Mahayana school of Buddhism, first mentioned in China around 66 C.E. and brought in by missionaries and traders through central Asia, provided another answer to the need for religious assurance. (For the history and beliefs of Buddhism in its country of origin, India, see the next chapter.) At first, Buddhism in China was practiced by foreigners and was not a single system of beliefs but a wide array of sects and approaches. Mahayana Buddhism came to China along with meditation, monasticism, and magic. About 148 C.E. a Buddhist missionary established a center for the translation of Buddhist writings into Chinese at the Later Han capital. Relatively few Chinese, however, were attracted to the religion during the Han dynasty. Buddhism's great attraction to converts and its influence on Chinese culture came after the fall of the Han dynasty when renewed political turmoil made its emphasis on otherworldly salvation appealing to the great majority of Chinese and its stress on compassion, transcending gender and ethnicity, particularly attractive to women. Indeed, some scholars refer to the next half millennium as China's Buddhist age, when the religion permeated culture, arts, and governance. Ten thousand temples transformed the Chinese countryside within 300 years of the fall of the Han. Religious Daoism became increasingly sophisticated and experienced great growth, too, but new Chinese developments in Buddhism particularly endeared the latter to the masses.

China and Foreign Trade

Chinese leaders had ambivalent feelings about trade with foreigners. On the one hand, they did not want to provide "the barbarians" with the means to become richer or the technology to become stronger. But to ensure stability on the northern frontier and with their

Document   From *The Book of Songs:* "A Simple Rustic You Seemed"

Every Confucian gentleman was expected to memorize *The Book of Songs*, one of the five Chinese Confucian classics, along with *The Book of History, The Book of Rites,* and *The Book of Change.* The poems of *The Book of Songs* were composed between 1000 and 600 B.C.E. This particular poem is attributed to the Daoist "old master" Laozi.

A Simple Rustic You Seemed

A simple rustic you seemed,
Carrying cloth to barter for silk.
But you did not come to buy silk;
You came with a design on me.
I saw you off, wading the river Ch'i
As far as Tun-ch'iu.
"It is not that I'd put off the date,
But no good go-between you have,
Please, do not be angry;
Autumn is the time we meet again."
I climbed that ruined wall
To look towards Fu-kuan.
I did not see Fu-kuan;
My tears flowed in streams.
After I had seen Fu-kuan,
How I laughed and talked!
You'd consulted the shell and the stalks,
And there was nothing inauspicious.
You came with your carriage
And carried me away and my goods.
Before shedding from the mulberry tree,
How glossy green the leaves are!
Alas, you turtledove,
Eat not the mulberries!
Alas, you women,
Do not dally with men!
When a man dallies,
He will still be pardoned;
But when a woman dallies,
No pardon will she have.
The mulberry leaves have fallen,
All yellow and sere.
Since I came to you,
Three years I have lasted poverty.
The waters of the Ch'i are full;
They wet the curtains of my carriage.
The woman remains constant,
But the man has altered his ways;
He is lacking in faith

And changeable in his conduct.
Three years I was your wife,
I never tired of household chores.
Early I rose and late I went to bed
Not a morning was I without work.
First you found fault with me,
Then treated me with violence,
My brothers, not knowing this,
Jeered and laughed at me.
Quietly I brood over it
And myself I pity.
Together with you I was to grow old;
Old, it has made me wretched!
The Ch'i, at least, has its banks,
And the swamp, its shores.
At the feast of the "tufted hair,"
We talked and laughed gaily.
You pledged solemnly your truth,
Little reckoning that it would be broken.
No, I never thought that it could be broken,
And that this should be the end.

(*Trans. Wu-chi Liu*)

Questions to Consider

1. This poem gives us an indication of the role of gender in classical China. What sense do you now have regarding how expectations for women differed from expectations for men?
2. *The Book of Songs* contained folk songs, military songs, religious hymns, and love songs. The poem "A Simple Rustic" is one of the love songs. Do you think the ideas and emotions expressed here can be compared to the thoughts and sentiments in contemporary love songs? If so, why and if not, why not?
3. Do you think that this poem can be read as an expression of protest, or do you see it more as an acceptance of the composer's personal history?

From Wu-chi Liu and Irving Yuchang, eds., *Sunflower Splendor. Three Thousand Years of Chinese Poetry* (Garden City: Anchor Books, 1975), pp. 97–101.

Central Asian neighbors, the Chinese engaged in trade, especially in silk. In return they received the horses and woolen goods they needed. The Han government began to actively promote the silk business in the first century B.C.E. Some of the caravans carrying silk reached the Mediterranean basin via middlemen along trade routes stretching from Rome to China. In late nineteenth-century Europe the idea of the existence of one Silk Road was first popularized, but, in fact, there were numerous routes, most of which led to India or Persia. We have evidence of the trade from the Roman writer Pliny who criticized the decadence of those in Rome who were purchasing silk. The Latin word *serica* ("silk") came from *Seres,* the Greek word for China. Just as China was forced to form relationships beyond its borders, others were beginning to formulate images and policies for China.

In 138 B.C.E. the Han emperor Wudi sent an envoy to Bactria to seek allies against the Xiongnu. The information he brought back amounted to the Chinese discovery of western Eurasia. Intrigued above all by his envoy's report of interest in Chinese silks and his description of Central Asia's magnificent horses, Wudi resolved to open trade relations with his western neighbors. His armies pushed across the Pamir Mountains to a location close to Alexandria Eschate (Khojend), founded by Alexander the Great as the northern limit of his empire. Shortly after 100 B.C.E. silk began arriving in the Mediterranean basin, conveyed by the Parthians. Wealthy private merchants carried on this trade, which required large outlays of capital. They organized their cargoes into caravans of shaggy packhorses and two-humped Bactrian camels. When the Chinese armies moved back across the Pamirs, the

Kushans of India became their middlemen, selling the silk to the Parthians and later to European merchants coming by sea to India.

It was not until about 120 C.E. that the Parthians allowed some merchants from the west to cross their land. The information they brought back about the Chinese was used by Ptolemy in constructing his map of the world. During the first and second centuries C.E.—the prosperous years of the Pax Romana—the peoples of the Roman Empire had a voracious appetite for Chinese silk, which the Romans believed was produced from the leaves of trees. In 166 C.E., according to the *History of the Later Han Dynasty,* some merchants from Da Qin ("Great Qin," the Chinese name for Rome), claiming to represent "King Antun" (Emperor Marcus Aurelius Antoninus), arrived in South China by sea across the Bay of Bengal and around the Malay peninsula.

To satisfy the Roman world's insatiable appetite for luxury goods, trade with China grew immensely in the first two centuries of the Common Era. But because such Roman exports to the East as wool, linen, glass, and metalware did not match in value Rome's imports of silk, spices, perfumes, gems, and

An interconnected world economy existed long before the advent of modern communications and technology. During the first century B.C.E., Africa, Asia, and Europe were drawn together in a trade cycle of raw materials and finished goods. Many items were traded across Eurasia, but the predominance of silk in the trade between the Han and Roman empires led to the routes across Central Asia being dubbed the "Silk Road."

other luxuries, the West suffered seriously from an adverse balance of trade. Gold and silver had to be continually exported to Asia. Late in the first century C.E., Pliny estimated that China and Arabia drained away annually at least 100 million sesterces (the daily wage of an unskilled Roman laborer was 4 sesterces).

For the Chinese, trade with what would come to be Europe was the least important aspect of its international commerce during the Han dynasty and continued to be so until the nineteenth century. There were, however, relations between China and the West through central Asia. Indochina, Korea, Japan, India, and the lands to the north would all come together in the next millennium to form the first global trading zone, in conjunction with the Arab markets, and would enrich and stimulate China.[14]

MAP
Early China

in place. These would take highly different forms throughout the centuries. Nonetheless, the idea of a centralized kingdom under the mandate of Heaven was now a powerful force.

Confucian presumptions about social relationships, including the interaction between women and men in the family and between the dead and the living, had taken a strong hold. So had the Daoist philosophical and religious stream of thought that provided a counterpoint to Confucianism because of its emphasis on nonaction over social interaction and on supernatural beliefs. Buddhism was beginning to transform the entire religious landscape. The Chinese state was based primarily on Confucian concerns, however, focusing on the secular amelioration of social evils and the relief of distress.

Finally, a domestic bureaucratic model that relied on both Confucian and Legalist goals and methods was in place by the beginning of the Common Era. China was seen as a united entity inhabited by a people with shared culture and power. The imperial ambitions that had coalesced many kingdoms into one was channeled into a lively trade with the outside world, and the dynamic interaction between China and its neighbors resulted in cultural innovations and enormous social change.

CONCLUSION

China was created because of, not in spite of, constant turmoil over the centuries. By the third century C.E. institutions of kingship, kinship, and empire would be

---

Suggestions for Web Browsing

You can obtain more information about topics included in this chapter at the websites listed below. See also the companion website that accompanies this text, **http://www.ablongman.com/ brummett,** which contains an online study guide and additional resources.

Ancient Dynasties
http://www-chaos.umd.edu/history/ancient1.html

Images and text present a view of early China, from prehistory to the era of the Warring States, 221 B.C.E.

China the Beautiful
http://www.chinapage.com/chinese.html

Extensive site exploring the art, calligraphy, poetry, literature, and music of China throughout its lengthy history.

Ancient China
http://www.wsu.edu:8080/~dee/ANCCHINA/ANCCHINA.HTM

Chinese history from 4000 to 256 B.C.E., with details about philosophy and culture.

Literature and Film

Selected Poems of Chu Yuan, ed. Dayu Sun (Universe Inc., 1999) presents a translation of representative poems by the man considered the first great Chinese poet. In the classic *Pan Chao: Foremost Woman Scholar of China* (published 1932; reprinted with an introduction by Susan Mann, Center for Chinese Stud-

ies, 2001), Nancy Lee Swann paints an insightful picture of the famous Chinese woman intellectual—a sketch of the Eastern Han period when Pan Chao (Ban Zhao) lived and wrote, of her family background, and of the literary milieu of which she was a part. In addition, Swann provides translations of writings definitively identified with Ban that survive from the years when she was active (c. 89–105 C.E.).

The Tomb of the Terra Cotta Warriors offers viewers a detailed look at one of the most surprising and important archaeological discoveries in history (The History Channel, 2001).

Suggestions for Reading

Insightful surveys and analyses of ancient China include John K. Fairbank, *China: A New History* (Belknap, 1998); Jacques Gernet, *A History of Chinese Civilization,* 2nd ed. (Cambridge University Press, 1996); Derk Bodde, Charles le Blanc, and Dorothy Borei, *Essays on Chinese Civilization* (Princeton University Press, 1981); Charles Holcombe, *The Genesis of East Asia* (University of Hawaii Press, 2002); David Keightly, ed., *The Origins of Chinese Civilization* (University of California Press, 1983); Michael Loewe, *The Pride That Was China* (St. Martin's Press, 1990); Kwang-Chih Chang, *The Archaeology of Ancient China,* 4th ed. (Yale University Press, 1987), and *Shang Civilization* (Yale University Press, 1982); Michael Loewe, John K. Fairbank, and Denis C. Twitchett, eds., *The Ch'in and Han Empires, 221 B.C.–A.D. 220* (Cambridge University Press, 1986); and Patricia Buckley Ebrey, *Cambridge Illustrated History of China* (Cambridge University Press, 1996).

The following are excellent treatments of intellectual and religious traditions: Benjamin Schwartz, *The World of Thought in Ancient China* (Harvard University Press, 1985); Frederick W. Mote, *Intellectual Foundations of China*, 2nd ed. (McGraw-Hill, 1989); A. C. Graham, *Disputers of the Tao* (Open Court Publishing, 1989); Isabelle Robinet, *Daoism: Growth of a Religion,* trans. Phyllis Brooks (Stanford University Press, 1997); and Daniel Overmyer, *Religions of China* (Harper and Row, 1986). On the fine arts, see Michael Sullivan, *The Arts of China,* 4th ed. (University of California Press, 2000), and Wen Fong, ed., *The Great Bronze Age of China* (Metropolitan Museum of Art/Knopf, 1980).

CHAPTER 3

Ancient India

From Origins to 300 C.E.

The Indian subcontinent since ancient times has functioned as a matrix for networks of trade and culture. It has been the target of conquerors and empire builders and the origination point of philosophical and artistic trends that have radiated outward along the land-based routes linking Asia with Europe and the seaborne routes connecting South Asia to Africa, the Middle East, Southeast Asia, and East Asia. The civilizations of classical India have had a profound effect that endures to this day on the arts, literature, religion, and philosophical beliefs of the world.

The subcontinent called India was a land of sometimes dense settlement as early as the Stone Age, dating back 500,000 years. An area diverse in climate, geography, language, and ethnicity, it was, like all premodern societies, primarily a village-based agricultural society. In the ancient times discussed here, India produced an extensive civilization in the Indus valley of the northwest that ultimately declined, adopted culture and language from people who immigrated from the Iranian plateau, and later generated a second large-scale state, centered in the northeast but including large blocks of territory elsewhere throughout much of the subcontinent. Other empires rose and fell, especially in the south, throughout antiquity. Synthesizing the social ideas and the philosophical and religious beliefs and practices arising from immigration and temporary contact with those of indigenous people, India developed three major religious traditions during this time, Hinduism, Jainism, and Buddhism, the last of which spread far beyond the bounds of India to become a pan-Asian and today global religion.

2500 B.C.E.

c. 2500 Indus valley civilization develops

c. 1900–1000 Composition of the early *Rig-Veda*

c. 1900–1700 Growth of Aryan culture

1000

c. 600 Composition of the earliest *Upanishads*

500

c. 481 (perhaps as late as 400) Death of Gautama Buddha

c. 468 (perhaps as late as 447) Death of Jain Tirthamkara Mahavira

c. 400 Composition of early *Mahabharata* and *Ramayana*

321 Chandragupta Maurya establishes Mauryan kingdom

269–232 Reign of Ashoka

1

40 C.E.–200 C.E. Kushana Empire rules northern India

First century Development of Mahayana Buddhism

EARLY INDIA

■ *How did indigenous culture and outside influences come together to create ancient Indian civilization?*

In this chapter we trace the important threads of Indian history to the third century C.E. This period was the formative age of Indian civilization, when its basic institutions and cultural patterns were determined.

Early Civilization in India

The term *India* is used here to refer to the entire subcontinent, an area encompassing the modern nations of Pakistan, India, Nepal, Bhutan, Bangladesh, and Sri Lanka. The term *subcontinent* is frequently used to refer to this large area. It could also be used to refer to other discrete parts of Eurasia, such as China or Europe, but such uses are not common. The Indian subcontinent is a large, irregular diamond, the lower sides of which are bounded by the warm waters of the Indian Ocean and the upper sides by the mountain walls of the Himalayas on the north and several smaller ranges on the west. The highest mountains in the world, the Himalayas, and their western counterparts divide India from the rest of Asia, making it a geographically discrete area, though never cut off from the great movements of civilization and culture. Through the Khyber Pass and other mountain passes in the northwest and across the Indian Ocean have come the armed conquerors, restless tribes, merchants, and travelers who did much to shape India's turbulent history.

In addition to the northern mountain belt, which shields India from arctic winds, the subcontinent comprises two other major geographical regions. In the north is the great plain (which came to be known as *Hindustan* after the Muslim invasions), extending from the Indus valley to the Bay of Bengal. It spans the watersheds of two great river systems, the Indus and the Ganges, which have their sources in the Himalayas. South of this great plain and separated from it in the west by the Vindhya mountain range, rises a semiarid plateau, the Deccan ("southland").

India's climate and the rhythms of Indian life are governed by the dry northeast monsoon wind of the winter and the wet southwest monsoon wind of the summer. Most parts of India receive the majority of their rainfall during the summer and autumn months of the southwest monsoon, which blows in from the Arabian Sea. The Western Ghats cause the summer monsoon to drop most of its rain on the thin Malabar Coast, making it one of the wettest areas of the globe, but the western Deccan, directly east of the Ghat range, has a semiarid climate.

India comprises an area comparable to Europe in size and internal diversity. The regions and peoples of India came to be roughly divided into two major language groups, the Indo-European in the north and the Dravidian in the south; each group embraces a number of separate languages. In the centuries between 1900 B.C.E. and 300 C.E., the emerging Hindu cultural synthesis, though modified by diverse philosophies and religions, gave the subcontinent a general cultural

India is a peninsula protected on its northern frontiers by the Himalaya, Kirthar, and Sulaiman mountain ranges.

unity similar to the unity afforded to Europe by the spread of the Christianity in the first millennium C.E.

The Indus Civilization, c. 2500–1500 B.C.E.

Sometime before 2500 B.C.E., a counterpart of the civilizations that had emerged along the Tigris and Euphrates and the Nile appeared along the Indus River in northwestern India. This area, called the Punjab (poon-JAHB) or "land of the five rivers, is made up of an alluvial plain watered by the upper Indus and its tributaries, and the region of the lower Indus (called Sind, from *sindhu*, meaning "river," and the origin of the terms *Hindu* and *India*). This Indus valley civilization flourished until about 1700 B.C.E. Among its major cities, Mohenjo-Daro (moh-HEN-joh dah-ROH), located north of Karachi in present-day Pakistan, is believed to have been one of the largest Bronze Age cities of the world.

Archaeologists believe that the Indus valley civilization began declining sometime around 1900 B.C.E. Around that time, or perhaps a few hundred years earlier, migrants began to move into the subcontinent from the Iranian plateau. Their culture and language gradually came to dominate the north of India, as people adopted important aspects of the migrants' culture and intermixed with them. The migrants' religion, cultivated by their **Brahmans** (BRAH-muhns; seers and priests), became the foundation for much of the later cultural development of the entire subcontinent.

The rise of civilization in the Indus valley around 2500 B.C.E. resembled what had occurred in Mesopotamia nearly a thousand years earlier. In India Neolithic farmers had been living in food-producing villages situated on the hilly flanks of large river valleys since around 4000 B.C.E. These settlements spread out along the river valleys, capitalizing on their abundant water and fertile soil. Here they developed the more complex way of life we call a civilization. Some of these farming villages had grown into large cities with as many as 40,000 inhabitants by 2300 B.C.E. Excavations of two of these cities, Mohenjo-Daro in Sind and Harappa (hah-RAP-pah)

Brahmans—The priestly *varna*; highest in Hindu caste hierarchy.

The ruins at Mohenjo-Daro, a city of an estimated 30,000 to 50,000 people, are still impressive more than four millennia after the city was established. There has been much speculation concerning the function of Mohenjo-Daro's largest buildings. Were they temples, administrative centers, or perhaps granaries? Only the function of the large public bath seems at least relatively clear.

This tiny figure of a girl who may be dancing was unearthed at Mohenjo-Daro and probably dates from around 2000 B.C.E.

in the Punjab, have provided much of our knowledge of the Indus valley civilization, but other sites were widely dispersed across the whole of northwestern India. Reaching its height in the centuries around 2000 B.C.E., the Indus valley civilization produced highly organized towns and uniform weights, measures, and pottery.

Although Mohenjo-Daro and Harappa were 400 miles apart, similarities in the cities' construction and layout suggest that the Indus River made possible the maintenance of a uniform administration and economy over the entire area. The cities appear to have been carefully planned, with residential blocks arranged on a north-south grid and an elaborate drainage system with underground channels. The spacious two-storied houses of the well-to-do contained bathrooms and were constructed with the same type of baked bricks used for roads. Indeed, it was the durable bricks produced by Indus valley builders that led, in part, to the discovery of Harappa after a nineteenth-century work crew found and "recycled" its ancient bricks for a railway project.

The economy of the Indus civilization, like that of Mesopotamia and Egypt, was based on irrigation farming. Wheat and barley were the chief crops, and the state collected these grains as taxes and stored them in huge granaries. For the first known time in history, chickens were domesticated as a food source during the Indus civilization, and cotton was grown and used in making textiles. Cotton textiles would ultimately become a world trade good and an important source of wealth for South Asia. The spinning and weaving of cotton remains today one of the subcontinent's chief industries.

The nature of the society that produced Indus valley civilization is the subject of considerable controversy. Unlike Egyptian hieroglyphics, which were deciphered by modern scholars using the Rosetta Stone, the Indus valley script (400 pictographic signs) has never been deciphered. Thus, the Indus valley writings, used on engraved stamp-seals, have given rise to modern claims and counterclaims about their "true" meaning. Indus stamp seals depict bulls, rhinoceroses, and crocodiles—but they also depict horned humans, unicorns, and large figures that may or may not be gods, generating considerable speculation about the beliefs and social organization of Indus peoples.

Numerous clay mother goddess figurines have been unearthed, indicating an early version of mother-goddess worship still important in India. Such figures are also found in various forms throughout the Mediterranean world, although their exact meaning in India and elsewhere is the subject of

Excavations at Mohenjo-Daro have unearthed what are often called "mother goddess figurines" such as this terra-cotta female. The figure, with her elaborate headdress, may well be a symbol of fertility but that conclusion is speculative.

considerable debate. Another controversial question is whether the Indus valley peoples were peaceful or warlike. Copper and bronze were used for tools and weapons, but the rarity of weapons has been used by some scholars to suggest that Indus society was peaceful. An interesting archaeological find is a set of three double graves, each with a male and a female. These may be married couples buried in single graves, which may suggest an early form of a wife's duty to her husband, called *sati,* so strongly praised in later centuries.

We cannot yet solve the Indus valley controversies, but what the archaeological evidence does make clear is that the Indus valley civilization was prosperous and well organized. Trade was sufficiently well organized to obtain needed raw materials—copper, tin, silver, gold, and timber—from the mountain regions to the west; and there were active trade contacts with Mesopotamia, some 1500 miles away, as early as 2300 B.C.E. (the time of Sargon of Akkad). In addition, Indus valley seals have been found in Sumerian sites.

Excavations at Mohenjo-Daro show that decline was well underway when a series of great floods caused by earthquakes altered the course of the Indus around 1700 B.C.E and apparently severely affected the settlements along it. Other Indus valley cities, such as Harappa to the north, appear to have suffered a similar fate, although some others continued to carry on long after the decline of these two great cities. The culture of migrants entering the Indus valley through the northwest passes around 1900 B.C.E. was thus able to influence the language, religion, and culture of north India as the great Indus valley civilization was on the decline.

The Introduction of Aryan Ways in the Early Vedic Age, 1900–1000 B.C.E.

The question of the end of the Indus valley civilization and its replacement in north India by different languages and customs is a topic of heated debate among historians. While some assert that a large wave of people called Aryans invaded and conquered north India, bringing their culture with them, other historians stress that Indians already living in the north adopted the culture of a much smaller though influential group of people who immigrated from the Iranian plateau and merged with them. Thus, those who called themselves Aryans included many local people who used the term to distinguish themselves from those who did not share their culture; the distinction, these historians assert, was not between an indigenous ethnic group and immigrants from outside India, but was based more on cultural differences.

People of Aryan culture who lived in northeastern India and eastern Afghanistan inhabited tribal villages and herded cattle, sheep, goats, and horses. Their language, an early form of Sanskrit, belonged to a group of languages called Indo-European, which include Sanskrit, Persian, Celtic, English, Germanic, Italian, and Greek languages. Whether one accepts the view that a wave of semibarbaric Aryan nomads skilled at chariot warfare contributed to the weakening of the Indus valley civilization or accepts the increasingly common view that local people gradually adopted Aryan culture as they mixed with them, Aryan language and culture certainly became indigenized and dominant in northern India in the first five or six centuries after their arrival. Not all indigenous populations of the subcontinent adopted Aryan languages and cultures. Some, located in the Deccan, retained their own, which were part of the Dravidian language group. The Aryans referred to these people as *Dasas,* which had a negative connotation of "dark" enemies.

During the centuries in which Aryan culture was absorbed in north India, Aryans worshipped their gods with sacrificial rituals that were accompanied by specially composed "verses of praise and adoration," *ric* verses, which would be recited together in "hymns." The *ric* verses and the hymns they made up were regarded as the sacred compositions of inspired seers (the Brahmans), who could see the gods and understood their ways and were thus able to compose verses that could influence the gods to favor and bless Aryan men and their families. Over 1000 such hymns were gathered together in the *Rig-Veda* (reeg-VAY-dah), a collection that has been memorized and used in worship continuously for over 3500 years. (*Veda* means "knowledge," a reference to the Brahman's knowing all the hymns by memory.) The earliest part of the *Rig-Veda* was probably composed between 1900 and 1500 B.C.E., and later portions were added until about 1000 B.C.E. Both religious and secular hymns are included in the *Rig-Veda;* in the latter, the structure of society, with its occupational classifications, is revealed. Thanks to the *Rig-Veda* we know more about the Aryans than we know about the Indus civilization, for which we must still rely only on archaeological evidence because their writings have not yet been deciphered.

The early Aryan religion involved making sacrificial offerings of grain, cakes, dairy products, and animals to the gods, who embodied and controlled the forces of what we today call "nature," in return for such material gains as long life, health, many offspring, victory in war, and life in the "bright place in the sky" (heaven). The god worshipped most in the *Rig-Veda* was Indra, storm-god and patron of warriors, who is described as leading the Aryans in destroying the forts of the Dasas. Virile and boisterous, Indra personified the heroic virtues of the Aryan warrior aristocracy as he drove his chariot across the sky, wielded his thunderbolts, ate the meat of dozens of sacrificed bulls and buffaloes, and quaffed entire lakes of the stimulating ritual drink *soma,* which might have been alcoholic, narcotic, or psychedelic.

Next to Indra in popularity was Agni, the benevolent god of fire, who performed many services for the

IMAGE

Statue of Indra, God of War

Document   *Rig-Veda:* Creation and the Kinds of Men

Like other ancient peoples, the societies of India developed a variety of creation myths. Such myths often involve stories of sacrifice and explanations for the hierarchy of beings. The Purusha Sutra of the *Rig-Veda* provides the first suggestion in ancient Vedic texts of the notion of the *varnas,* the idea that humankind is divided into four classes and their differences are based in Creation itself. The four classes are priests (Brahmans), rulers and warriors (Rajanyas or Kshatriyas), herders and merchants (Vaishyas), and the low-class workers or servants (Shudras). In this Vedic story, Purusha (the "primordial cosmic man") serves as the victim in the cosmic sacrifice from which the universe originates.

The sacrificial victim, namely Purusha, born at the very beginning, they [the gods] sprinkled with sacred water upon the sacrificial grass. With him as oblation, the gods performed the sacrifice, and also the *Sadhyas* [a class of semidivine beings] and the *rishis* [ancient seers].

From that wholly offered sacrificial oblation were born the verses and the sacred chants. . . . From it the horses were born and also those animals who have double rows of teeth; cows were born from it, from it were born goats and sheep.

When they divided Purusha, in how many different portions did they arrange him? What became of his mouth, what of his two arms? What were his two thighs and his two feet called?

His mouth became the brahman; his arms were made into the rajanya; his two thighs the vaishyas; from his two feet the shudra was born.

The moon was born from his mind, from the eye the sun was born; from the mouth Indra and Agni [Vedic gods], from the breath the wind was born.

From the navel was the atmosphere created, from the head the heaven issued forth; from the two feet was born the earth and the quarters [the four cardinal directions] from the ear. Thus did they fashion the worlds.

. . . With this sacrificial oblation did the gods offer the sacrifice. These were the first norms [dharma] of sacrifice. These greatnesses reached to the sky wherein live the ancient *Sadhyas* and gods.

Questions to Consider

1. Think about the many different ways that people can be divided. What is the system of division in this myth based on?
2. What does this myth suggest about the roles of the gods and of sacrifice in Indian society?
3. Think about other creation myths you have heard or read. How is this one similar or different?

From Ainslie T. Embree, ed., *Sources of Indian Tradition,* Vol. 1, 2nd ed. (New York: Columbia University Press, 1988), pp. 18–19.

Aryans, not least of which was conveying their ritual offerings up to the other gods. Another major Aryan god was Varuna, the sky-god. Viewed as the king of the gods, he lived in a great palace in the heavens where one of his associates was a sun-god, Mitra, known as Mithras to the Persians and, a thousand years later, widely worshipped in the Roman Empire. Varuna was the guardian of *rita,* the "right order of things." *Rita* was both the cosmic law of nature (the regularity of the seasons, for example) and the customary tribal law of the Aryans. Varuna was, thus, the divine judge.

The *Rig-Veda* is the earliest surviving work of literature in an Indo-European language, and it gives some insight into the institutions and ideas of the Early Vedic Age. Each tribe was headed by a war leader called *raja,* a word related to the Latin word for king, *rex.* Like the early kings of Sumer, Greece, and Rome, the raja was only the first among equals. Two tribal assemblies, one a small council of the great men of the tribe and the other a larger gathering of the heads of families, approved his accession to office and advised him on important matters.

The hymns in the *Rig-Veda* mention three social categories **(varnas),** the Brahmans or priests, the **Kshatriyas** (kuh-SHAH-tree-yas) or nobility, and the **Vaishyas** (VAI-shas) or commoners. A fourth class, the **Shudras,** the non-Aryan population of workers and serfs, was then added at the bottom of the social scale.

varnas—Originally occupational groups; later also four status groups connected to purity and prestige at sacred rituals.

Kshatriyas—The *varna* associated with governing and military power; second in the *varna* hierarchy.

Vaishyas—Commoner *varna;* merchants and landlords; third in the *varna* hierarchy.

Shudras—Menial workers; lowest in *varna* hierarchy.

In one of the later hymns of the *Rig-Veda*, these four social categories are described as emerging from the sacrifice of the Cosmic Man, Purusha, with priestly Brahmans coming from his mouth, ruling Kshatriyas from his arms, Vaishyas from his thighs, and Shudras from his feet.

The Later Vedic Age, c. 1000–600 B.C.E.

Most of our knowledge about the years between 1000 and 600 B.C.E. derives from religious texts the Brahmans composed during this period or from later texts such as the two great epics of **Hinduism,** the *Mahabharata* (mah-hah-BAH-rah-tah) and the *Ramayana* (rah-mah-YAH-nah). All these texts tell us a great deal about religious and philosophical thought during this time, but what we know of this period's political, social, and economic institutions we must glean from religious texts or infer from the convergence of the archaeological record with later texts.

By about 1000 B.C.E. Aryans and their culture had moved into the critical territory that lies between the Indus watershed and the Ganges watershed. During the Later Vedic Age, they continued their movement both to the east, passing into the Doab ("land of two rivers") between the Yamuna and the Ganges and on down the Ganges valley, and to the south, toward the Vindhya Mountains. The area between the two watersheds came to be known as *Kurukshetra* ("the field of King Kuru"), and it became the sacred heartland of the Aryans in the Later Vedic Age. Kurukshetra (koo-roo-KSHET-rah) was the site of the fabled Bharata (BAH-rah-tah) war (the story of which is told in the *Mahabharata*), and many other battles critical to the history of India over the next 3000 years were fought in this vicinity. The sense of space, particularly sacred space, is very important in Indian thought, and the ways such spaces have been articulated remain a critical factor in Indian politics today.

This era seems to have been a golden age for the Brahmans and their Vedic religion. During this period, some of the hymns of the *Rig-Veda* were set to melodies (called *samans*) collected in a separate *Veda* called the *Sama-Veda*. The *Yajur-Veda* was a compilation of prayers and instructions for priests performing sacrifices. Different families of Brahmans would specialize in learning one or the other of these three *Vedas;* and spectacularly large *soma* sacrifices developed that employed Brahmans of each kind. A fourth *Veda,* the *Atharva-Veda,* was formed from a large collection of sacred formulas that, when correctly uttered, were supposed to solve many of life's mundane problems: baldness, impotence, skin rashes, and so on. These hymns and prayers suggest the ways in which the Brahmans, as keepers of the *Vedas,* gained power in Indian society.

As the number of Brahman priests and *Vedas* increased, the focus of Vedic religion shifted from the gods to the power of the sacrifice itself, and especially to the holy energy contained in the sacred words of the different Vedic songs, chants, recitations, and prayers. The Brahmans' perfect singing or chanting of Vedic verses (now called *mantras*) came to be regarded as the embodiment of the sacred energy at the heart of the ritual—the energy, called **brahman** (not to be confused with the priestly Brahmans; the energy force will be italicized in this text), that kept the world going, the energy that had brought the world into being. Even kings, those with the power over violence, had to depend on the spiritual power of the priestly Brahmans.

The Brahmans also composed, now in prose rather than verse, a whole new kind of text, the *Brahmanas* (bra-MAH-nahs), which explained the philosophy of the rituals and the background meaning and use of the Vedic mantras employed in the rituals. During the Early Vedic Age sacrifice had been a means of influencing the gods in favor of the offerer; now in the later Vedic Age the Brahmans regarded sacrifices to the gods as working automatically to produce the good results people wanted, provided that the ritual was performed exactly right. The sacrifices were supposed to bring long life, many sons, victory over one's enemies, general prosperity, and heaven; they made the world a good place for all beings. Since only the priests possessed the knowledge to perform the complex and lengthy rites of sacrifice (a few of which could last for months), and since the slightest variation in ritual was thought to bring harm to the people and the land, the Brahmans gained great prestige and power.

By the beginning of the Later Vedic Age the Aryans had learned iron metallurgy, possibly from people of the Iranian plateau. As in other parts of the world, iron-based tools increased the potential for agricultural exploitation and made warriors with access to iron weapons more deadly and effective. These developments set the stage for the emergence in the eastern Ganges valley of cities, territory-based kingdoms, standing armies, and stronger institutions of kingship.

Although some Indian kingdoms in this period were oligarchic republics, most were ruled by rajas, maharajas (mah-hah-RAH-jas, "great kings"), or samrajas ("universal kings," as some called themselves).

Hinduism—The largest religion in India, this heterodox faith stresses adherence to sacred texts such as the *Vedas* and *Upanishads* and the proper ritual worship of gods, Vishnu, Shiva, and Devi and their various manifestations being the most prominent. Hinduism emphasizes proper behavior for one's station in life and the eventual release (*moksha*) from the cycle of rebirth.

brahman—As first described in the *Upanishads,* the divine force or energy that created and sustains the universe.

Despite the preservation of advisory councils of nobles and priests, the kings' powers were greater than those of the Aryan tribal leaders of the earlier period. They now lived in palaces and collected taxes—in the form of goods from the villages—in order to sustain their courts and armies. The cities that arose were often administrative centers connected to a palace, and some were also commercial centers. Of course, cities did not just appear. They had to be built; and large building projects meant the mobilization of labor: some people doing the work while others gave the orders.

Village, Caste, and Family

In the Later Vedic Age, the three pillars of traditional Indian society—the autonomous village, caste, and the joint or extended family—were established. India has always been primarily agricultural, and its countryside is still a patchwork of villages. The ancient village was made up of joint families governed by a headman and a council of elders. Villages enjoyed considerable autonomy; the raja's government hardly interfered at all as long as it received its quota of taxes.

DOCUMENT

Hindu Creation Myth and the Caste System

As noted earlier, Hindu society came to be divided into four occupational categories, or *varnas*—Brahmans (priests), Kshatriyas (nobles), Vaishyas (commoners), and Shudras (workers or servants). The Portuguese in the sixteenth century labeled this the *caste system*, and the name stuck in Western descriptions of Indian society. Medieval Brahmans wrote that within the framework of these four *varnas* society was divided into thousands of subgroups, or **jatis** (literally, "species"), each with a special social, occupational, or religious character. For example, they wrote, occupational groups of merchants or shopkeepers formed many *jatis* within the Vaishya caste.

In ancient times, however, and even today, *varna* and *jati* had different meanings. *Varna* categories described one's actual occupation and could change when one changed jobs. In antiquity, *varnas* were important during rituals involving the whole community because they determined one's task or physical placement for those rituals or sacrifices. *Jati*, on the other hand, were originally kinship groups and, thus, were not changeable as were *varnas*. In time, certain occupations became associated with certain *jati*, and the *jati* came to be ranked by the level of respect each occupation had. Later, the *jati* were associated with particular *varnas*. But there was never a consensus as

to which *varna* a *jati* belonged; disagreement continues today. Those whose occupations were the most menial and degrading—scavengers (who remove human waste) and tanners (because they handle the carcasses of dead animals)—also formed numerous *jatis* but were perceived as outside and beneath the people of the four *varnas*. These outcasts were called *Untouchables* because their touch was considered defiling to members of the *varnas*.

The third pillar of Indian society was the three-generation household, a patriarchal system. In these households, seniority brought status to both men and women. Sons were subordinate to their fathers, and young wives were subordinate to their mothers-in-law. When a woman married, she went from the house of her father to the house of her husband's father. As in many traditional societies, children were considered the property of the father, not the mother. When the patriarch died, his authority was transferred to his eldest son, but his property was divided equally among all his sons. Women were subordinate to men and required a male protector: father, husband, brother, or son. They could not inherit property, nor could they participate in sacrifices to the gods; their presence at the sacrifice was considered a source of pollution. A common Vedic prayer asked for "manly, heroic" sons. Daughters, who needed a dowry to get married, were seen as having little value to their families. Senior women, however, had status as elders and bearers of sons. Ideally, they were revered and served by their daughters-in-law.

DOCUMENT

Women in Classical India

The emphasis placed on communal interests rather than on the individual is a common denominator of the three pillars of Indian society. Thus, Indian society has always been concerned with stability, respect for elders, and family and group solidarity.

DRAMATIC DEVELOPMENTS IN RELIGION AND CULTURE, 600–320 B.C.E.

■ *What characteristics of Indian religion and culture of this era made them so appealing far beyond India's borders?*

Out of all these new political and economic developments came dramatic cultural changes that after 600 B.C.E. elevated an entirely different kind of religion to highest status and eventually gave rise to whole new religions that challenged Brahman hegemony and created important new institutions. The first of these

---

jatis—Literally "species"; originally a term meaning kinship groups, later associated with occupation. Usually what Indians mean by the Western concept of caste.

developments, beginning around 600 B.C.E, was the composition of texts called the **Upanishads** (oo-PAHN-ee-shads). The second was the rise of the new non-Vedic, even anti-Vedic, monastic religions of Jainism and Buddhism sometime in the fifth century B.C.E.

In the 600s B.C.E. a radical minority of Brahmans began to embrace ascetic and mystical religious ideas and practices (early forms of yoga, meaning "spiritual discipline" and usually involving some kind of meditation) that ultimately rejected the goals and means of Vedic ritual religion and the settled village and family life that Vedic religion presumed. Some of these radical mystics recorded the *Upanishads,* which taught "secret, mystical understandings" of the human body, the breath, the mind, and the soul. The most important of these understandings was the assertion that the light of consciousness within a person was nothing less than the undiluted energy of *brahman,* the eternal, sacred creative energy that is the source and the end of all that exists (equivalent to God in monotheistic religions).

Most of the *Upanishads* taught that all things that exist—from the most sublime ideas a person could think to the crudest forms of matter—came from *brahman* energy and eventually returned to *brahman,* the only permanent reality. Beyond these ideas, the *Upanishads* taught a way for ethically pure, worthy persons (usually only Aryans, but not necessarily just Brahmans) to immerse themselves into *brahman,* which the *Upanishads* described as unsurpassably blissful. These ideas gained great power after their presentation in the *Upanishads*. A relatively tiny minority of people followed this yoga (most Aryan people continued to make use of Brahman priests and Vedic rituals). But the basic ideas, values, and meditative techniques over time greatly influenced South Asian society and came to be regarded as the supreme form of Brahman religion.

The Vedic Brahmans had thought that people live only once and that the fate of their soul is determined in that one life. (The same general idea is found in all three of the Western Abrahamic religions: Judaism, Christianity, and Islam.) Vedic Aryans hoped to live up in the heavens with the sky-gods after their death. The *Upanishads,* however, introduced the idea of the transmigration of the soul, which was entirely new in Brahman thought. (Some scholars have speculated that this idea was part of pre-Aryan culture, but there is no solid evidence of this.) Then, in texts called the *Brahmanas,* the idea was put forward that a person's deeds stayed with him or her in the form of an unseen power that would act after that person's death and condition the

Upanishads—Sacred Brahmanic scriptures collected in sixth century B.C.E. that stress *brahman* force and idea of cyclical rebirth until release through *moksha.*

Developments in Culture and Religion in India

c. 600 B.C.E.	Earliest *Upanishads*
c. 481 (perhaps as late as 400) B.C.E.	Death of Gautama Buddha
c. 468 (perhaps as late as 447) B.C.E.	Death of Mahavira
c. 300 B.C.E.	Jainism gains support in North and South India

fate of the departed soul. A deed or action was called *karman* in Sanskrit, and the unseen power of past deeds was called *karman* as well (karma in contemporary English).

The latest *Brahmana* texts sometimes express a fear that people "die again"—the accumulation of their good works, their good karma, supports them in heaven when they die, but the karma gets used up keeping the soul in heaven, and the soul then "dies" again, in heaven. This fear leads directly to the idea that when the soul dies in heaven, it descends to earth, reincarnated in another body. This new person lives and dies, and the soul goes to heaven once again, if the earthly actions of this latest lifetime have been good (that is, if they conformed with the law, or dharma [DAR-mah] as revealed in the *Vedas*). Bad deeds, bad karma, lead the soul to hell.

Eventually, the idea emerged that rebirth in subhuman forms of life was a natural consequence of violating dharma. After living a life as some kind of animal, a soul automatically moves up the ladder of life forms toward an eventual human incarnation because animals cannot violate dharma. The rebirth of the soul in a new body is called *samsara* (sam-SAH-rah), and the *Upanishads* regarded continual, unending samsara as dreary and unpleasant. The *Upanishads* taught that good deeds, including Vedic rituals, could do nothing more for a person than provide a temporary spell in heaven between incarnations. Bad deeds, of course, had far more unpleasant consequences; but worse than either hell or heaven was the prospect of living, acting, and dying over and over, forever without end. In the face of this bleak prospect, the *Upanishads* said the only truly good thing a person can do is try to escape perpetual samsara through release from desire and eventually from rebirth. That release was called *moksha* (MOHK-sha). Achieving *moksha* involves permanently escaping from karma, from

DOCUMENT

Transmigration of Souls in the *Upanishads*

samsara, and from all the pain and suffering encountered in countless lives. According to the *Upanishads,* by permanently immersing oneself in *brahman* through meditation, a person can dissolve the soul back into the holy oneness that is its ultimate source and end. The soul has "returned home"—its journey through samsara is over.

The *Upanishads* depict the first Indian gurus wandering in the forests as ascetics; there they meditated and taught their disciples. One of them summed up their quest as follows:

> *From the unreal lead me to the real!*
> *From darkness lead me to light!*
> *From death lead me to immortality!*

Of course, most Indian people did not become gurus or devote their lives to meditation and asceticism; most Indians lived the life of the agriculturalist. But the powerful ideas of rebirth and *moksha* presented in the *Upanishads* and the *Brahmanas* had an enormous impact on subsequent Indian thought and social organization.

The Jains, Defenders of All Beings

Beyond the changes just noted in Vedic religious thought, two non-Vedic religions also emerged in South Asia during this time: Jainism and Buddhism. Jainism contributed to all of India (and today to the rest of the world) the unique ethical claim that the most important duty of a person is **ahimsa** (ah-

---

ahimsa—The practice of nonviolence toward all living things; a belief central to Jainism initially but also adopted by Buddhism and Hinduism.

Document   The Jains on the Souls in All Things

The Jains, like the Buddhists, believe in conquering desire as a way of achieving Enlightenment and escaping from the cycle of rebirth. But the Jains emphasize the existence of souls in all living things. They believe all beings experience pleasure, pain, terror, and unhappiness. Hence Jain texts reveal a heightened sensitivity to the pain man can inflict by harming all things, animate and inanimate. This verse passage is taken from a Jain text depicting the speech of a prince who is trying to persuade his parents to allow him to take up a life of religion. He tries to express to them the terrible agonies suffered by beings at various levels of creation.

From clubs and knives, stakes and maces,
  breaking my limbs,
An infinite number of times I have suffered
  without hope.
By keen edged razors, by knives and shears,
Many times I have been drawn and quartered,
  torn apart and skinned.
Helpless in snares and traps, a deer,
I have been caught and bound and fastened, and
  often I have been killed.
A helpless fish, I have been caught with hooks and
  nets;
An infinite number of times I have been killed and
  scraped, split and gutted.
A bird, I have been caught by hawks or trapped in
  nets,
Or held fast by birdlime, and I have been killed an
  infinite number of times.
A tree, with axes and adzes by the carpenters
An infinite number of times I have been felled,
  stripped of my bark, cut up, and sawn into
  planks.
As iron, with hammer and tongs by blacksmiths

An infinite number of times I have been struck
  and beaten, split and filed. . . .
Ever afraid, trembling in pain and suffering,
I have felt the utmost sorrow and agony. . . .
In every kind of existence I have suffered
Pains that have scarcely known reprieve for a
  moment.

Questions to Consider

1. What problems might the Jain teachers have encountered in trying to persuade others to accept their beliefs?

2. If someone truly believed that such suffering was endured by all beings, how might it affect that person and change his or her behavior?

3. Like the Buddha, the "speaker" in this text is a prince going against the wishes of his family. What does this speech suggest about generations, change, and a family's ambitions for its sons?

From Ainslie T. Embree, ed., *Sources of Indian Tradition,* Vol. 1, 2nd ed. (New York: Columbia University Press, 1988), pp. 62–63.

HEEM-sah), which is to practice nonviolence and to cause no harm or pain to any being. Buddhism also adopted the idea of ahimsa, and, over time, many, but not all, Brahmans and their followers eventually did likewise.

Jainism places a special emphasis on the idea that all beings (including plants, insects, and minerals) have "souls" *(jiva)* and experience pain. Thus, causing pain to any other sentient beings is the biggest source of the worst possible karma. Jain texts, for example, explain in graphic detail the suffering caused to the tiny beings living in wood when it is cast upon the fire. While it is inevitable that a believer will cause pain (by drinking water and the beings that are in it, for example), a person should avoid such destructive acts as much as possible. Some Jains, who practice their faith most rigorously, gently sweep the path before them with a broom as they walk to avoid stepping on living things; they may tie cloths over their mouths to avoid inhaling any small creatures in the air.

The most significant figure in Jain belief is Mahavira (mah-hah-VEE-rah; c. 559–c. 468 B.C.E.), the faith's founder. Mahavira means "great hero." He is called the *Jina* (JEE-nah, "victor," "conqueror"), and his followers are called *Jainas* (those who "follow the Jina"), hence the Western name *Jainism* for the religion as a whole. According to Jain tradition, Mahavira was a Kshatriya prince who at the age of 30 renounced the world—his home and family and all property and status that went with them.

For over a dozen years Mahavira followed the teachings of an earlier religious teacher, Parshvanatha (parsh-vah-NAH-tah). During those years Mahavira wandered naked from place to place, lived on handouts, engaged in meditation, debated with other men who were also on holy quests, observed celibacy, and engaged in various painful ascetic practices in order to purify his soul of past karma. Nudity was a form of asceticism because it exposed the genitals and invited the painful ridicule of ordinary people. The practice of nudity was the subject of debate among later Jain ascetics and gradually died out.

Mahavira gained a great reputation as a wise and holy man, attracting many followers. Thirteen years after he resolved to starve himself to death to achieve release from the bondage of his past karma, he died after seating himself in the posture of meditation with the intention of never moving again. This deliberate form of death by inaction is seen not as an act of suicide but as the most heroic and ascetic form of non-action humanly possible. For those whose souls were still fouled with karma, this mode of death was regarded as highly purifying, and many Jain saints have died this way throughout history.

The Jains accept the reality of samsara and karma and regard *moksha* (release from rebirth) to be the only sensible goal to pursue in life; but their way of pursuing *moksha* was very different from that of the Brahmans of the *Upanishads*. The path to *moksha* that Mahavira preached centers on the practice of asceticism, although one does not have to practice the most rigorous forms to be considered a pious Jain. To gain *moksha* a Jain must sooner or later, in this life or a future life, renounce the world and become a wandering monk or nun. But a person may be a pious lay Jaina, supporting the monks and nuns with handouts of food, clothing, and shelter and living a life that conforms to the Jain ethic (which emphasizes nonviolence but also forbids liquor, sex outside of marriage, lying, and stealing) until he or she is convinced that the time for renunciation has come.

Jains believe Mahavira died in 527 B.C.E., but modern, non-Jain historians believe he died 60 to 80 years later. Jains believe Mahavira was the twenty-fourth and last great *tirthamkara* (teer-tahm-KAH-rah; a "ford-maker," who aids his followers in crossing the swirling flood of samsara, the cycle of rebirth) in a long series of wise and powerful men in this current age. For Jains time revolves in endless cycles like a great cosmic wheel. In every age, *tirthamkara*s like Mahavira are born to teach the doctrines of Jainism to humanity. Every era consists of millions of years. The Jains also believe that when a soul gains *moksha* and escapes the cycle of rebirth forever, it ascends to the topmost point of the universe, where it exists in complete purity forever. This differs dramatically from the idea of the *Upanishads* that every individual's soul is completely submerged into *brahman*, the single "soul" of the whole universe.

DOCUMENT

Jainism: From *The Book of Sermons, The Book of Good Conduct*

Socially, Jainism was distinctive. It rejected the sacredness of the *Vedas* and thereby rejected the social stratification that assigned preeminence to the Brahmans. Interestingly, Jainism was also the first Indian religion formally to allow women to become renouncers and pursue *moksha* as nuns. The Buddha only reluctantly and belatedly allowed Buddhist laywomen to become nuns; and although some Hindu women did renounce the world from time to time, the Hindu dharma (sacred law) never formally sanctioned their doing so.

In the centuries after Mahavira the number of Jains has always been significant but never tremendously large. In spite of always being a minority religion in India, the Jains have consistently exerted greater influence than their numbers would lead anyone to expect. By 300 B.C.E. Jainism had gained significant political recognition in various kingdoms of north and south India. Also, because the ethics of their religion basically forbade farming for pious lay followers of the Jina (because tilling the soil kills so many small creatures), lay Jains were usually merchants living in cities. They often became wealthy and poured much of their wealth into the support of their religion. As a result, the Jain religion has contributed a great number of learned Jain scholars and libraries to India's cultural history.

The Middle Way of Gautama Buddha

About the same time that Mahavira lived, another ascetic and monastic religion arose in northern India. This religion, Buddhism, became popular and important in India and remained influential there for many centuries. It also spread outside India to all of Asia and today continues its expansion around the globe. Buddhism had some basic similarities to Jainism, but its root ideas were profoundly different. Both religions derive from the life and teachings of a great man; both stress the humanity of their teacher and do not rely on gods or divine rites to pursue the highest goal of life; both developed monastic institutions in which celibate men and women lived in spiritual communities, supported by a devoted laity. There is an archaic quality to many Jain doctrines, probably due to the fact that the Jain religion was never taken up by people outside of India. Buddhist doctrines, by contrast, seem very modern in certain ways, which may in part account for Buddhism's appeal to non-Indian peoples, including Europeans and Americans in the twenty-first century.

Whereas Jainism stresses purification of the soul and ascetic pain and its leader is described in military terms as a "great hero" and "victor," Buddhism's founder was a man whose leadership was the result of his "waking up," having his understanding boosted to a higher level of insight. The word *buddha* means basically "someone who has awakened from sleep." Buddhists see the Buddha's Great Awakening *(Bodhi)* as the greatest discovery of the truth of life that has ever been made. As Jains follow Mahavira's soldierly example, Buddhists seek to use the Buddha's example and his teachings so that they too may wake up and realize the benefits of Awakening (often also called Enlightenment).

The man who became the Buddha was born Siddhartha Gautama (sid-HAR-ta gow-TAH-ma), a prince of the Shakyas (SHA-kee-ahs), whose small oligarchic state was located at the foot of the Himalayas. As with many of the world's great figures, the traditional accounts of the Buddha's life contain many legends and miracles. Accordingly, Gautama was conceived when his mother dreamed one night that a white elephant entered her right side. Later the baby was born from her right side, and right after birth the baby stood up and announced that this would be his last life. Seers predicted that Gautama would become either a great king or a great sage who would see four special sights of human suffering—a sick man, an old man, a dead man, and an ascetic holy man seeking to escape suffering—after which he would renounce the world and discover a way to relieve the world's suffering.

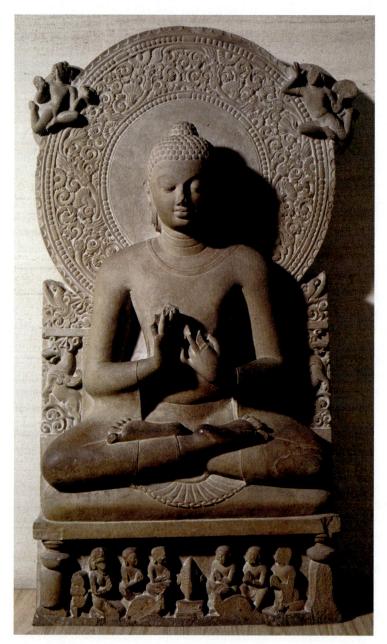

This seated Buddha from Sarnath shows the elongated earlobes, heavy-lidded eyes, knot of hair, hand gestures, and expression of deep repose that are symbolic of the Buddha.

The traditions tell us that Gautama's father, King Shuddodana (SHOOD-doh-DAH-nah), raised him in luxury and went to great lengths to prevent the prince from ever seeing the sick, the old, or the dead.

In the prince's twenty-ninth year, however, all his father's protections proved vain in the face of fate: On three separate occasions the prince happened to see a sick man, an old man, and a dead man. These sights shocked him, and he was troubled to learn, from his chariot driver, that all people suffer sickness, old age, and death. He then happened to see a wandering ascetic who was in quest of *moksha*, and this encounter made him think very deeply about how to free himself from life's suffering. To his father's great disappointment, Gautama decided to follow that ascetic's example. He renounced his wealth and position, forsaking his wife and child.

Gautama studied meditation for a year with two different teachers, abandoning both after a while because their doctrines did not satisfy him. Then, like Mahavira, he took up the most painful and demanding forms of asceticism and practiced them with great determination and devotion. Gautama almost died from this fasting and self-torture, and after five years he concluded that these ascetic practices weakened the mind and would not lead to the end of suffering.

Gautama left his ascetic companions, who ridiculed him for his "weakness," walked down to a river and had his first bath in five years, then sat down under an expansive banyan tree (the Indian fig tree) to rest in the cool shade. (Asceticism was regarded as a kind of purifying heat by ancient Indians.) Gautama was then given a refreshing meal by a rich woman who offered a special meal once a year to the spirit of that tree. Clean, refreshed, and reinvigorated by food, Gautama was vibrantly awake as night fell. He sat up meditating all through the night; as the night progressed, his mind examined the world and its workings, and he came to understand more and more the fundamental causes for all that happens. Shortly before the dawn, he attained the key insights for understanding and then eliminating suffering, but not, according to legendary tradition, before the demon Mara (Death) and his daughters Greed, Lust, and Anger did all in their powers to prevent his grasping the truth.

Gautama summarized the truth to which he "woke up" during this Great Awakening as the Four Noble Truths, which succinctly express the entire system of Buddhist thought. The religious way of life to which the Four Noble Truths lead is often called the Middle Way. It is the way of life that is in between the normal human life of sensation, desire, and action, on the one hand, and the life of harsh asceticism, on the other. The Middle Way involves the moderate asceticism of renunciation, celibacy, and the Buddhist monastic way of life as opposed to the much more rigorous asceticism of Indian groups such as the Jains. The whole philosophy, which the Buddha taught to others, and the religious way of life to which those ideas lead is referred to in Buddhism as the *Dharma*. (The root sense of *dharma* for Hindus is "religious law" or "religious good deeds leading to a good afterlife"; Dharma, for Buddhists, has a broader meaning.)

Buddha's Four Noble Truths are these:

1. Suffering dominates our experience.
2. The cause of suffering is desire or craving.
3. It is possible to extinguish suffering by extinguishing its cause, thereby attaining nirvana. (*Nirvana* originally referred to a fire's going out; the Buddha's idea was to let the fire of desire go out by depriving it of its normal fuel. It resembled *moksha*.)
4. The Noble Eightfold Path leads to the extinction of desire—that is, it leads to nirvana.

The Noble Eightfold Path consists of pursuing the following eight ideals:

1. *Right views*—the intellectual conviction that the Four Noble Truths are "the Truth."
2. *Right resolve*—the decision to act according to the Four Noble Truths.
3. *Right speech*—having words be governed by the Five Moral Precepts of right conduct: do not harm any living being (ahimsa); do not take what is not given to you; do not speak falsely; do not drink intoxicating drinks; do not be sexually unchaste.
4. *Right conduct*—having deeds, like words, be governed by the Five Moral Precepts.
5. *Right livelihood*—conducting oneself ethically even in earning a living; hence such occupations as farming (which could lead to the killing of small creatures), soldiering, prostitution, and tavern keeping are disallowed.
6. *Right effort*—following the path with all one's heart and energy by renouncing the world and becoming a monk or nun.
7. *Right mindfulness*—a form of meditation that eventually produces "wisdom"; wisdom undermines desire because the wise person no longer sees his or her own self as particularly important in the world.
8. *Right concentration*—a form of meditation that uses trances to make the nonrational and unconscious layers of the person completely calm and tranquil.

DOCUMENT

Buddha's Sermon at Benares and The Edicts of Ashoka

Buddhism claims that desire is extinguished and nirvana attained when steps 7 and 8 of the path have been perfected—that is, when the person on the path has the wisdom to see that he or she is just one more sentient being among many and is no more valuable or important than any other (this removes the natural instinct to fight for success and even survival) and when "concentration meditation" has stilled all the powerful impulses and drives that condition every sentient being's mind. A person who has reached this nirvana of desire simply looks at his or her own condition at any given moment as "what is" and does not wish it to be otherwise, is not driven to improve it, does not envy anyone else, and does not suffer. Physical pain may be present, but the person who has reached nirvana is dissociated from it and simply sees it as one more fact of the situation of the moment. Nirvana is a happy, friendly state (in which the Buddha lived for 45 years after his Awakening), but it is not an "altered state" of consciousness and certainly not a paradise or any kind of heavenly world. Later developments in Chinese and Japanese Buddhism did create ideas about rebirth in paradise and suffering in hell, but the Buddha himself did not suggest these.

In Buddhist thought the essential element of action is the desire to get something for oneself. So, the Buddhists believe that a person who has extinguished desire no longer really performs actions, even if his or her body may be going through the motions. In other words, such a person accumulates no karma and has escaped the round of samsara. For Buddhists this nirvana amounts to gaining *moksha.*

Many peoples over time have struggled with the question of what, if anything, comes after death. The Buddha's followers were no exception. But when they asked him what happens after the devotee escapes the cycle of rebirth, the Buddha told them that the question could not be answered and was pointless anyway. Such a question, he said, "tends not to edify"; that is, it does not contribute to the one important goal. The only important thing a person can do in life is deal with suffering.

Dressed in a simple yellow robe, with begging bowl in hand, Gautama wandered through the plain of the Ganges, speaking with everyone (regardless of social class) and attracting disciples to a growing community (called the *Sangha;* SAN-gah) of monks walking the Path. He taught many sermons (the Sutras; SOO-trahs) and laid down the Rules specifying many details of the monks' daily life (the Vinaya [vee-NAH-yah] analogous to the much later Rule of St. Benedict in Medieval Europe). Resisting at first, the Buddha eventually acquiesced to demands that women be allowed to renounce the world and pursue the path and its advanced meditations on a full-time basis as nuns. Buddhist history states that while the Buddha lived, it was relatively easy to accomplish the nirvana of desire and suffering and that a great number of disciples actually did so.

At last, 80 years old and enfeebled, the Buddha was invited by a poor blacksmith to a meal. According to legend, the food included tainted mushrooms, but Gautama ate the meal rather than offend his host. Later in the day the Buddha had severe pains, and he knew death was near. Calling his disciples together, he gave them this parting message: "Be ye lamps unto yourselves. Be a refuge to yourselves. Hold fast to the truth as to a lamp. Look not for refuge to anyone beside yourselves." The Buddha had instructed that his body be burned. According to legend, his followers quarreled over possession of his ashes, which were divided into eight parts and ensconced in shrines called *stupas* (STOO-pas). Buddhist tradition credits the third century B.C.E. king Ashoka with construction of tens of thousands of stupas all over his realm, into which the ashes from the eight original stupas were subdivided. Whether or not Ashoka actually carried out this holy task, there are now stupas all over South Asia.

The Buddha stressed the fact that each person could overcome suffering only through her or his own efforts, another aspect of Buddhism that would be modified a millennium after his death by Buddhists in East Asia. Nonetheless, his followers developed a profound affection for him and were very attached to him. After his death (even to some extent during his life) many of his followers believed that mere contact with him would somehow benefit them. What the Buddha taught is a philosophy, but the movement developed by his followers, which we call Buddhism, is a religion. That religion has had a profound effect on the society, politics, and economy of South Asia and other areas, like China, Japan, and Vietnam, where Buddhism spread.

The Buddha, the Dharma he taught, and the Sangha, the community of Buddha's followers, are regarded by Buddhists as the Three Precious Jewels. Historically, as in the Jain religion, the majority of the Buddhist community are laypeople who live in the world until they sense the time is right to take the sixth step of the path, right effort, and become a monk or a nun. (In some Buddhist countries, lay Buddhists often make short retreats to a monastery for instruction from the monks and practice in meditation.) In addition to restricting their speech, conduct, and livelihood by the Five Moral Precepts, they cultivate the virtues of generosity, friendliness, and compassion. Buddhists believe that only people with great amounts of good karma ever hear the Buddhist teachings; and only those with even more good karma possess the courage and determination actually to become a monk or a nun. In the end one does not want any karma at all, good or bad, but whatever good karma a lay Buddhist accumulates will help carry that person further along the Path in this or a future life.

Buddhist Religious Site

Buddhists who became monks or nuns donned the yellow (or orange) robe worn by all renouncers in India except the Jains (who wore white if they wore anything). Unlike their Hindu and Jain counterparts—who usually lived alone or in small assemblies without any Rule—Buddhist renouncers created the world's first monastic communities, in which people pursuing spiritual goals lived together under strict rules.

Often the Buddhists lived in caves that rich lay Buddhists had cut into the sides of mountains or rock cliffs. Their only possessions were their sandals, robe, and begging bowl. They ate only one meal a day and ate only what they had received from begging. Periodically all the monks in a given area recited together all the rules of monastic life, and anyone who had violated any rule was required to make a public confession. Four sins warranted permanent expulsion from the community: fornication, stealing, murder, and making false claims of one's spiritual attainments. Large parts of the day were given over to meditation, and monks who had accomplished nirvana were known as *arhats* (AHR-hahts; "worthy ones").

The Buddha was a critic of all religious and philosophical thinkers who came before him. He censured the *Vedas* and the rites of the Brahmans, considered the *Upanishads* wrong about *brahman*, and thought Mahavira's religion of ascetic purification futile. The Buddha took an agnostic stance on what really might lie beyond this world; he claimed that we, as finite, conditioned beings, had no way of knowing anything about infinite, unconditioned beings. He thought that anyone, regardless of social status, could gain nirvana, but he did not himself try to change Indian society. Though Shudras and women were admitted to Buddhist monasteries, those monasteries still tended to mirror the social structures and habits of the larger Indian society.

As with Mahavira, there is great uncertainty about exactly when the man who became the Buddha died. Buddhists have traditionally taught that he died in 526 B.C.E. Modern, non-Buddhist historians believed for many decades that 481 B.C.E. was a more accurate date. Current historical scholarship is energetically reconsidering this date and pushing it down toward 400 B.C.E. or possibly even later. Whatever the exact dates of Gautama Buddha and his contemporary Mahavira, both lived and taught in eastern India as powerful new kingdoms were in the process of turning into the Mauryan (MOW-ree-ahn) Empire (inaugurated about 320 B.C.E.). Buddhism in particular

would have a significant impact on the organization of that empire.

THE MAURYAN EMPIRE AND OTHER KINGDOMS, 320 B.C.E.–300 C.E.

■ *Why was Ashoka ancient India's most revered king?*

By the sixth century B.C.E., 16 major kingdoms and tribal oligarchies stretched across northern India, from modern Pakistan to Bengal. The richest and most powerful kingdom was Magadha (mah-GAH-dah), located in the eastern region that included the Ganges River. The Magadha kingdom's support of Buddhism was key to the new religion's survival and growth. The kingdom's important role in trade is seen in the presence of its coins in the far northwest of India as well. Nevertheless, it took an outside stimulus for the Magadha kingdom to attempt to build an empire. Two centuries later, a conquering general, Alexander the Great, appeared in the region. Son of a Macedonian warlord, this famous general conquered the Persian Empire (see Chapter 4), and in 326 B.C.E. brought his phalanxes into the Indus valley, defeating local Punjabi rulers. Despite his apparent ambitions to conquer India, the Punjab proved to be the easternmost territory of Alexander's empire. His weary troops refused to advance farther eastward. So, Alexander constructed a fleet and sailed to the mouth of the Indus; he then returned overland to Babylon while his fleet skirted the coast of the Arabian Sea, sailing west to the Persian Gulf.

Classical India

After Alexander's death in 323 B.C.E., the empire he had built so rapidly quickly disintegrated, and within two years his kingdom in the Punjab had completely disappeared. He had, however, helped open routes between India and countries to the West and,

The Mauryan Empire	
326 B.C.E.	Alexander the Great invades India
321 B.C.E.	Chandragupta seizes Magadha
305 B.C.E.	Chandragupta defeats Seleucus
269–232 B.C.E.	Reign of Ashoka
c. 185 B.C.E.	Brahman-led revolt against last Mauryan emperor

by destroying the petty states in the Punjab, facilitated the conquests of India's own first emperor.

The Founding of the Mauryan Empire (326–184 B.C.E.)

A new era began in India in 321 B.C.E., when Chandragupta (chahn-drah-GOOP-tah) Maurya seized Pataliputra (pah-tah-li-PU-trah), capital of the state of Magadha in the Ganges valley. Chandragupta conquered northern India from this sophisticated city and founded the Mauryan dynasty, which endured until about 184 B.C.E. At its height, the empire spanned most of the subcontinent except the extreme south, although many of its territories were separated by lands ruled by other kings.

India's first empire reflected the imperial vision of its founder. Chandragupta created an administrative system of remarkable efficiency. He was also a brilliant general who extended his control westward beyond the Indus River. In 305 B.C.E. he concluded a treaty with Seleucus, the general who had inherited the major part of Alexander the Great's empire in western Asia, that ceded all territories east of Kabul to the Mauryans in return for an exchange of ambassadors and a gift of 500 war elephants to Seleucus.

DOCUMENT

Lessons in Statecraft

Life in the Mauryan Empire

Seleucus's ambassador to the court of Chandragupta, Megasthenes, wrote a detailed account of his experiences in India in his diary, fragments of which have survived. They give a fascinating picture of life in the empire. Chandragupta's capital, Pataliputra (known today as *Patna*), covered 18 square miles and was probably the largest city in the world at the time. Outside its massive wooden walls was a deep trench used for defense and the disposal of sewage.

The remarkably advanced Mauryan Empire was divided and subdivided into provinces, districts, and villages whose headmen were appointed by the state. The old customary law, preserved and administered by the Brahman priesthood, was superseded by an extensive legal code that provided for royal interference in all matters. A series of courts, ranging from the village court presided over by the headman to the emperor's imperial court, administered the law. So busy was Chandragupta with the details of his highly organized administration that, according to Megasthenes, he had to hear court cases during his daily massage.

CASE STUDY

Hinduism and the Mauryan Empire

Two other factors struck Megasthenes as important in the administration of the empire. One was the professional army, which he reports was an enormous

force of 700,000 men, 9000 elephants, and 10,000 chariots. The other was the secret police, whose numbers were so large that the Greek ambassador concluded that spies constituted a separate class in Indian society. Chandragupta, fearing conspiracies, was said to have lived in strict seclusion, attended only by women who cooked his food and in the evening bore him to his apartment, where they lulled him to sleep with music.

Of course, the historian cannot take literally the details or the numbers in Megasthenes's account. They were impressionistic and designed to create certain effects on his audience at home. Ambassadors had limited knowledge of and exposure to the daily lives of kings, and the stories of rulers and their female companions are often myths based on hearsay and conjecture. Furthermore, the counts of armies, especially of one's enemies, tended to be inflated. Nonetheless, it is clear that Megasthenes was impressed by the urban development, political organization, and military force of Chandragupta's empire.

An important indigenous source of information on Chandragupta's reign is a remarkable book, called the *Arthashastra* (ar-tah-SHAS-trah), or *Treatise on Material Gain*, written by Kautilya (kow-TIL-ya) as a guide for the king and his ministers. Said to be Chandragupta's chief adviser, Kautilya exalted royal power as the means of establishing and maintaining political and economic stability. The great evil, according to the *Arthashastra*, is anarchy, such as had existed among the small warring states in northern India. To achieve the aims of statecraft, a single authority (the king), who must employ force when necessary, was needed. Kautilya advised the king to make war on weaker kings and make peace with those who had equal or greater power. Attacking a stronger king, he said, is like "engaging . . . in a fight on foot with an elephant," while attacking an equal was like striking two unbaked jars together—both would be smashed. The king must also be wary of sons, "who are inclined to devour their begetters." Kautilya advised the king that princes should be carefully trained; but he also suggested making sacrifices in advance while the queen was pregnant and arranging for specialists to supervise her nourishment and childbirth.[1]

The *Arthashastra* is an early example of a whole genre of literature, sometimes called "mirrors for princes," that provided advice to monarchs on the best and most effective ways to rule. Later examples are found in the Middle East and Europe—for example, the medieval Persian work of Qai Qa'us and that of the Renaissance author Machiavelli. Machiavelli, like Kautilya, would advocate deception or unscrupulous means to attain desired ends. The *Arthashastra* remains in print today and has been translated into many languages. Modern leaders have been known to consult its pages.

The Mauryan state controlled and encouraged economic life. Kautilya's treatise, which is thought to reflect much actual practice, advises the ruler to "facilitate mining operations," "encourage manufacturers," "exploit forest wealth," "provide amenities" for cattle breeding and commerce, and "construct highways both on land and on water." Price controls are advocated because "all goods should be sold to the people at favorable prices," and foreign trade should be subsidized: "Shippers and traders dealing in foreign goods should be given tax exemptions to aid them in making profits."[2] Foreign trade did flourish, and the bazaars of Pataliputra displayed goods from southern India, China, Mesopotamia, and Asia Minor. Agriculture, however, remained the chief source of wealth. In theory, all land belonged to the state, which collected one-fourth of the produce as taxes. Irrigation and crop rotation were practiced, and Megasthenes states that there were no famines. The ability of the ruler to insure a regular supply of food for his kingdom was, of course, a primary measure of success.

Ashoka, India's Greatest King

Following Chandragupta's death, his son and grandson expanded the Mauryan Empire southward into the Deccan peninsula. His grandson, Ashoka (ah-SHOH-kah; r. 269–232 B.C.E.), the most renowned of all ancient Indian rulers, however, gained a reputation for being more committed to peace than to war. After eight years of expansion by military means, Ashoka attacked the kingdom of Kalinga with great brutality. The cruelty of that campaign horrified him, and he resolved never again to permit such acts of butchery. Ashoka adopted the Buddhist law of nonviolence (ahimsa) in his realm in the tenth year of his reign. The story of Ashoka's horror at the carnage of war is similar in some ways to the account of Yudhishthira (yoo-deesh-TEE-rah) in the *Mahabharata*, which also relates a king's remorse in the aftermath of battle. Scholars have pointed out that Ashoka did not renounce violence until he had completed his conquest. But for our purposes, the story of Ashoka illustrates the inherent contradictions between the idea of nonviolence and the idea that a king was by nature a warrior whose duty it was to preside over violence and death.

Throughout his empire, Ashoka had his edicts carved on rocks and stone pillars. They remain today as the oldest written documents in India yet deciphered (the Indus valley texts have not yet been deciphered) and are especially valuable for appreciating Ashoka's own construction of the spirit and purpose of his rule. For example, they contain his conception of the duty of a ruler:

He shall . . . personally attend the business . . . of earth, of sacred places, of minors, the aged, the afflicted, and the helpless, and of women. . . . In the happiness of his subjects lies his happiness.[3]

Although Ashoka made Buddhism Maurya's state religion, he did not persecute the Brahmans and Hindus but proclaimed religious toleration as an official policy:

The king . . . honors every form of religious faith . . . whereof this is the root, to reverence one's own faith and never to revile that of others. Whoever acts differently injures his own religion while he wrongs another's.[4]

Ashoka was a successful propagator of Buddhism. He supported the building of temples and stupas all over his empire, and the remains of many are still standing. He sent Buddhist missionaries to various lands—the Himalayan regions, Tamil Land (India's far south), Sri Lanka (Ceylon), Burma, and even as far away as Syria and Egypt, transforming Buddhism from a small Indian sect to a missionary faith. Modern Indians revere his memory, and the famous lion on the capital of one of his pillars has been adopted as the national seal of the present Indian republic.

Ashoka (c. 268–233) left a written record of his reign inscribed on rocks and stone pillars all over the Mauryan Empire.

Fall of the Mauryan Empire

As so often happens, almost immediately after Ashoka's death in 233 B.C.E., the Mauryan Empire began to disintegrate. The last emperor was assassinated about 185 B.C.E. in a palace uprising led by a Brahman general. Once again, the subcontinent was politically fragmented. Northern India was overrun by a series of invaders, and the south, never controlled by the north, maintained its separate status.

The sudden collapse of the powerful Mauryan state and the grave consequences that ensued have provoked much scholarly speculation. Some historians have believed that the fall of the Mauryans can be traced to a hostile Brahman reaction against Ashoka's patronage of Buddhism. Others believe that Ashoka's inclination toward nonviolence curbed the military ardor of his people and left them vulnerable to invaders. More plausible explanations for the fall of the Mauryan state take into account the transportation and communications problems facing an empire that spanned much of the Indian subcontinent, with unsubdued areas separating territory under Mauryan control; the difficulty of financing a vast army and bureaucracy; and the intrigues of discontented regional groups within the empire.

In fact, one might argue that political division is a more natural state for large multiethnic, multilingual landmasses with diverse terrain; empires that endure and unite vast expanses of territory are the exception. No one person could directly rule all of the subcontinent; like the later Roman and Ottoman empires elsewhere, the Mauryan kingdom survived through a combination of talented leadership, economic success, flexible rule, and delegated authority.

Bactrian Greeks and Kushanas

The Mauryan Empire was the first of two attempts to unify much of north and even central India in ancient times. The second—the work of the Gupta dynasty (c. 320–550 C.E.)—was more limited in its geographical reach, but was a glorious empire nonetheless (see Chapter 10). In the five centuries between these two eras of imperial splendor, a succession of foreign invaders entered South Asia from the northwest and added new cultural elements to the Indian scene.

The first of the new invaders of India were Greeks from Bactria. They were descendants of the soldiers settled there by Alexander the Great to serve his empire in the East. After Alexander, Bactria continued as a province of the Seleucid Empire, a bastion against the attacks of nomadic tribesmen from the north and a center for trade with India to the southeast. The decline of the Seleucid Empire allowed the Bactrian Greeks to establish an independent kingdom about 245 B.C.E.

In 183 B.C.E., two years after the death of the last Mauryan emperor of India, the fourth Bactrian king, Demetrius, crossed the Hindu Kush mountains as Alexander had done 150 years earlier and occupied the northern Punjab. From his base at Taxila, Demetrius and his successors ruled Bactria and the entire Pun-

Coins provide interesting evidence of cross-cultural artistic influences and of the self-definitions of rulers and peoples. This Bactrian coin from 170–159 B.C.E. shows the influence of Greek portraiture on South Asian money.

jab (modern Afghanistan and northern Pakistan), while Taxila functioned as an important nexus of both the east-west and north-south trade.

The Greeks in India established the farthest outpost of Hellenism in the Hellenistic Age (see Chapter 4). Their cities were not Greek enclaves in a hostile land, like Alexandria in Egypt and Antioch in Syria. The South Asian peoples were enrolled as citizens, a bilingual coinage was issued bearing Greek inscriptions on one side and Indian on the other, and at least one king, Menander, became a Buddhist. The Indo-Greek Buddhist art in the Gandhara (gahn-DAH-ra) was the greatest legacy of the era of Greek control. Some other Greeks in Bactria adopted aspects of Indian culture, including Hindu worship.

But soon after 150 B.C.E. Bactria was overrun by nomadic tribesmen. Thereafter, Greek rule in the northern subcontinent steadily declined until the last remnants disappeared late in the first century B.C.E. Hordes of nomadic peoples, migrating out of Central Asia, replaced the Greeks in Bactria and northwestern India. First to arrive were the Indo-European Scythians, who had been pushed out of Central Asia by other Indo-European nomads known in Chinese sources as the Yuezhi (yoo-EH-zhih). In their turn, the Yuezhi occupied Bactria, and about 40 C.E. they crossed the

Hindu Kush and conquered the Punjab. The Yuezhi divided into four tribes, and one, Kushana (koo-SHAH-na), took over in north India, expanding eastward to the middle Ganges valley and southward perhaps as far as the borders of the Deccan.

In contrast to the more centralized Mauryan Empire, the Kushana state was more like a loose federation—its kings were overlords rather than direct rulers—yet it gave northern India two centuries of peace and prosperity. The Kushana kingdom acted as a hub for trade routes linking India, China, and the West. Its greatest ruler, Kanishka (kah-NEESH-ka; fl. c. 120 C.E.), produced a multicultural coinage that employed Chinese, Greek, Persian, Hindu, and Buddhist devices. Kanishka gained fame as a patron of the arts and of a new form of Buddhism called **Mahayana** (MAH-hah-YAH-nah).

South India

To a large extent, India can be divided culturally into north and south. Although the south was often penetrated by northern conquerors, in general its civilizations developed in a fashion distinct from those of the north. The vast tableland of South India—the Deccan—and its fertile coastal plains remained outside the main forces of political change in the north, except, in some cases, for the 150 years of Mauryan imperial rule. The peoples of this area differed in appearance, culture, and very importantly, language—their languages were part of the Dravidian language family rather than Aryan—from the Aryan-speaking peoples of the north. Gradually, however, as Brahman priests and Buddhist monks infiltrated the south, Hinduism and Buddhism were grafted onto the existing Dravidian culture.

Politically, the south remained divided into numerous warring states. Prominent among them were three well-developed Tamil (an old Dravidian language) kingdoms in the southern third of the Deccan peninsula. These three kingdoms—Chera, Pandya, and Chola—alternated between allying to fend off northern attacks and rivalrous warfare among themselves. In the early fourth century C.E., a new dynasty, the Pallavas, took over in Chola. Under the patronage of the kings of these three states, the Tamil language developed a classically exquisite literature in the first few centuries of the Common Era. This tradition, known as the *Sangam* ("Academy") tradition, was based in the old city of Madurai in Tamil Nadu ("Tamil Land"), and it produced several anthologies of poetry, several unique epics, and a superb handbook of lan-

guage and poetics. Love was an important theme in the Tamil poetry:

> *As a little white snake*
> *with lovely stripes on its young body*
> *troubles the jungle elephant*
> *this slip of a girl*
> *her teeth like sprouts of new rice*
> *her wrists stacked with bangles*
> *troubles me.*[5]

Tamil society differed in several key respects from northern society. The divisions among groups of Tamils were based on their geographic origin as hill people, forest people, coastal people, and so on. Social structure was possibly matriarchal rather than patriarchal, and matrilineal inheritance was practiced until recently. Both men and women took part in the production of art, music, and dance.

By the first century B.C.E., Tamil Nadu had become an intermediary in the maritime trade extending eastward to the East Indies and westward to the Hellenistic kingdoms. Indeed, a major factor that distinguishes south India from north India is the former's orientation toward the sea. On the east and west coasts of southern India, ports developed that became important entrepots for the East-West trade and important points of cultural contact with foreign states and peoples. There, large jugs called *amphorae* have been found, evidence either of South Asian taste for Roman wine or of the Roman traders' need to bring their favored drink with them on voyages to India. The ships that brought these amphorae, as well as copper, lead, tin, and large numbers of gold coins, sailed back bearing South and Southeast Asian pepper, cotton goods, silks, cinnamon, cloves, and jewels.

EMERGENT HINDUISM AND BUDDHISM, 200 B.C.E.–300 C.E.

■ *How did Hinduism develop as a religion based on worship of deities and Buddhism branch into two major divisions?*

Hinduism and Buddhism were not static or fixed in time; they were evolving during the classical era. In the years 200 B.C.E. to 300 C.E. the religion called Hinduism was formulating a synthesis and meeting the challenge of Buddhism. Buddhism, in turn, split into two distinct strands of interpretation. These developments were set in the context of the Indian social order that was wedded to village life, caste hierarchies, and a household based on the extended family.

Mahayana—"Greater Vehicle" branch of Buddhism; focuses on bodhisattvas who lead others to nirvana.

The Hindu Synthesis

Hinduism is not one single doctrine. It is an array of highly diverse beliefs that include the various texts of the Vedic Age, pre-Aryan Indian practices, and an evolving set of deities and rituals. Essential to Hinduism are the beliefs in the cycle of birth, death, and rebirth (samsara) and a society structured by social status and proper behavior. Beings may be born as humans in various *jatis* or as lesser creatures, depending on their actions in the previous life. A believer who accumulates good actions ascends in the hierarchy of beings in subsequent births and may ultimately escape rebirth and be absorbed into *brahman* energy.

Three Traditions of Worship and Theology: Vishnu, Shiva, and Devi

Early Aryan religion had focused on sacrifices and rituals, but later Brahmanic religion stressed personal devotion to a deity. This marked the emergence of Hinduism as a religion with increasing popular appeal. The first steps toward this were taken by Brahmans who incorporated Upanishadic thought into their teaching. In doing so, they gave the caste system additional religious support by linking it to karma and the process of reincarnation. The priests made individual salvation, now a conspicuous part of Indian religion, dependent on the uncomplaining acceptance of one's position at birth and the performance of one's dharma, which varied by caste. The belief that a person was born into a caste and died in that caste was given religious support. Marriage out-

side one's caste was forbidden. Of course, in practice, as in all religious systems, social reality did not always match religious ideals. In fact, some people did marry across caste lines, and some groups did apparently change caste over time. But Brahman and social sanctions against violating caste boundaries made such changes difficult.

The Upanishadic doctrine of salvation by absorption of the individual soul into *brahman* was too intellectual and remote for the average person to grasp fully. Thus, devotion to personal savior gods also emerged as an important element in Hinduism. This devotion centered on anthropomorphic deities with rich personalities and long histories.

The major Vedic gods gradually faded into the background, and three virtually monotheistic gods emerged as paramount in Hinduism: Vishnu (VISH-noo); Shiva (SHEE-va); and Devi (DAY-vee), the Goddess (sometimes called Kali (KAH-lee)). Each one of these gods became immensely popular in Hindu worship. Vishnu, Shiva, and Devi evolved from Vedic and indigenous Indian origins, and each came to be regarded by one or several different traditions as the uniquely supreme and holy God, creator of the universe. The theologies of Vishnu and Shiva were already well developed by about 200 B.C.E.; that of the Goddess was not fully developed until some time later. The theologies of these gods, as in other religious traditions, did not remain static and fixed over the ensuing centuries. In the old Vedic pantheon of the Aryans, Vishnu was a relatively minor god associated with the sun. He then developed into a pacific father-god, comforter, and savior who works continuously for the welfare of humanity. "No devotee of mine is lost," is Vishnu's

Vishnu and his consort, Lakshmi, recline upon the serpent Shesha floating on the waters of creation. Emerging out of Vishnu's navel is a lotus that serves as a throne for the god Brahma, who creates the world. This is a representation of just one of the varied Hindu creation myths. It suggests lushness, fertility, and water as the source of life. Some variants of this particular creation story note that Vishnu also created two demons who were arrogant and boastful. These demons tormented Brahma while he was trying to meditate and attacked Vishnu, thinking they were stronger than he.

promise. His followers believe that he has appeared in nine major "descents" in human form to save the world from disaster. (A predicted tenth descent has yet to happen.) Two of Vishnu's incarnations are described in the great Indian epics, as Krishna in the *Mahabharata* and as Rama (RAH-ma), the hero of the *Ramayana*. Rama saves the human race from the oppressions of a great demon, rules for many years in the city of Ayodhya, and then returns to the "City of the Gods," resuming the form of Vishnu.

Shiva, the other great popular god of classical and modern Hinduism, evolved from a minor Aryan Vedic god who was the guardian of healing herbs but whose arrows also brought disease. It is possible that another prototype of Shiva was a pre-Aryan fertility god who was worshipped in the cities of the Indus civilization. Shiva is often associated with phallic symbols. His spouse, Parvati, is the earliest expression in the Brahman texts of a powerful female goddess who was eventually recognized as a separate deity in her own right (under other names) and elevated to the status of a unique supreme and holy divinity.

Shiva's followers believe he is superior to the other gods. He personifies the cosmic force of change that destroys in order to build anew; he is often depicted with a necklace of skulls. Some representations show Shiva as the Lord of Dancers; the rhythm of his dance is that of a world continuously forming, dissolving, and reforming. He also exemplifies another major characteristic of Hinduism, the reconciliation of extremes: violence and passivity, eroticism and asceticism. Shiva is portrayed as remaining unmoved in meditation for years on end. When he emerges from his meditations, however, he is often lustful and violent.

As already noted, Shiva's wife, Parvati (followed by Vishnu's wife, Lakshmi (LAHKSH-mee)), marked the first appearance in Hinduism of a powerful female divinity. Archaeological and other evidence suggests that goddesses were worshipped in India from the time of the Indus valley civilization. But only toward the Gupta period (fourth and fifth centuries C.E.) did fully developed theologies of a supreme Goddess, Devi (the word *devi* simply means "goddess"), begin to appear. As with the development of Shiva and Vishnu, the development of Devi involved the fusion of numerous local deities into a single complex figure. The Goddess presents two faces to the world: She is a tender mother to her devotees and a ferocious warrior to those who threaten her devotees. Called "Mother" or "Bestower of Food" (Annapurna) in her benevolent moods, she can also be "the Black One" (Kali), wearing a necklace of the skulls of her victims, or Durga, a many-armed warrior riding on the back of a lion to do battle with demons. As the creative power of the universe (similar to the Vedic idea of *brahman*), she is

Lakshmi, Vishnu's consort and goddess of prosperity, beauty, and precious things, emerged from the foam of the ocean. This statuette was found half a world away from India in the ruins of ancient Pompeii in Italy, thus demonstrating the extent of trade both in Indian cultural objects and Indian ideas in the first century C.E.

referred to as Shakti ("Power," "Creative Energy"), and theologies focused on Devi as the Supreme Being of the universe are referred to as Shaktism.

As mentioned earlier, there is no centralized authority in Hinduism. The resulting "flexibility" makes Hinduism seem extremely complicated to outsiders who are used to more structured religious traditions. One aspect of this flexibility is that many versions of the theology and mythology of these deities are mixed together. For example, worshippers of Shiva often recognize Vishnu as an important and exalted creature fashioned by Shiva but who in no way rivals Shiva's divine supremacy. Worshippers of Vishnu often fit Shiva into their theology in similar ways. They also eventually included the Buddha as one of Vishnu's incarnations, and in modern times some Hindus have incorporated the Christians' Jesus into their devotions. Today many Hindus worship Jesus as a divine incarnation, but they do so as Hindus in Hindu ways; they are not Christian converts.

Most Hindus today are devotees of either Vishnu, Shiva, or Devi and their respective incarnations. But animals (especially the cow), vegetation, water, and even stones are also worshipped by some as symbols of the divine. Over time, literally thousands of deities, demigods, and lesser spirits came to form the Hindu pantheon, the world's largest.

Because the authority to teach normative ideas in Hinduism was vested in the Brahmans as a class, Hinduism is probably the world's most flexible religion. Brahmans were present in villages and towns throughout the subcontinent, and many local ideas and practices were "normalized" as "compatible with the *Vedas*." Hinduism possesses no canon, such as the Bible or the Qur'an; no single personal founder, such as Christ or Muhammad; and no precise body of authoritative doctrine. Hindu beliefs vary dramatically among the faithful.

The Epics

The *Mahabharata* is the great Hindu epic. Composed in verse, it contains over 75,000 stanzas, the longest work of literature in the world. It tells the tale of an all-encompassing war between rival sets of cousins, the Pandavas (pahn-DAH-vas) and the Kauravas (kow-RAH-vas). These cousins are fighting for the throne of the Bharata kingdom, in the upper Ganges plain in the region of modern Delhi. But in the epic, this great battle, lasting 18 days, is not simply a struggle for an earthly kingdom; it is ultimately a cosmic struggle between virtue and evil, a battle to set the world right.

As in the Greek *Iliad*'s account of the Trojan War, the *Mahabharata* presents a dramatic tale of heroism, vengeance, and sacrifice in which the gods directly intervene in the affairs of men. In the great Indian epic, however, it is duty that must govern the actions of kings; only through war will the proper order of the universe be restored. When the war is over and the victorious Pandavas view the horrendous slaughter of their sons, cousins, teachers, and friends, Yudhishthira, the intended king, is so shocked and horrified by the carnage that he refuses to accept the throne and wishes to retreat into the forest. Eventually, however, he is persuaded to become king. It is not his own desires or wishes that Yudhishthira must follow, but his duty.

The *Mahabharata* was shaped and embellished over time. It was incorporated into royal sacrificial ritual, and a long succession of priestly editors added many long passages on religious duties, morals, and statecraft. One of the most famous additions, incorporated into the *Mahabharata* around 200 B.C.E., was the *Bhagavad-Gita* (BAH-gah-vad GEE-tah, "The Lord's Song"), a philosophical dialogue that stressed the performance of duty (dharma) and the overcom-

The serene and reclining god Vishnu is shown here in a sculpture from a sixth-century C.E. Hindu temple. Beneath Vishnu are the five Pandavas, heroes of the Mahabharata, *and their shared wife, Draupadi. Draupadi, along with Sita, stands as a model of Hindu womanhood: virtuous, honorable, and strong.*

ing of passion and fear. It is still the most treasured piece in Hindu literature.

The dialogue in the *Bhagavad-Gita* takes place between Arjuna (AR-joo-na), the greatest warrior of the Pandava brothers, and Krishna, an incarnation of the god Vishnu, who takes human form and acts as Arjuna's charioteer. Arjuna is shaken by the prospect of killing his kinsmen. But Krishna, who gradually reveals himself as no ordinary charioteer, instructs Arjuna that he must give up worldly desire and personal attachment and devote himself to discipline and duty. In so doing, he will be able to attain freedom, overcome despair, and act according to his dharma, fulfilling his role in the cosmic struggle. Krishna tells Arjuna:

> *Knowledge is obscured*
> *by the wise man's eternal enemy*
> *which takes form as desire,*
> *an insatiable fire, Arjuna.*
> *The senses, mind, and understanding*
> *are said to harbor desire;*

with these desire obscures knowledge
and confounds the embodied self.
Therefore, first restrain
your senses, Arjuna,
then kill this evil
that ruins knowledge and judgment.[6]

The universal appeal of Arjuna's internal struggle and Krishna's advice has made the *Bhagavad-Gita* a world classic; it has been translated into many languages. Once Arjuna realizes that he is receiving advice from a god, he wants to know more. He wants to see the god as he really is, so he asks Krishna to reveal himself in all his majesty. Krishna obliges the unwitting Arjuna by giving him a "divine eye" with which he can see the whole universe inscribed in the god's body. But this fearful vision of world-devouring time is too much for the awestruck Arjuna. So Krishna takes mercy on him and reverts to his human form.

The other great Hindu epic, the *Ramayana*, which appears to predate the *Mahabharata*, has been likened to the Greek *Odyssey*. It recounts the tale of the exiled prince Rama and his faithful wife Sita (SEE-ta). During their banishment to the forest, Sita is kidnapped by the demon Ravana. Rama searches valiantly for his wife, whom he eventually finds, and vanquishes the

---

Document The *Ramayana:* The Trial of Sita

In the great Hindu epic, the *Ramayana,* King Rama rescues his wife Sita from her captor, the demon Ravana, after a lengthy struggle. Rama is overjoyed to see Sita but tormented by the shame of knowing she was touched by another male. The doubt thus cast upon her virtue forces him to repudiate her. Devastated at this rejection by her lord, Sita nevertheless proudly answers in her own defense. In a dramatic speech, she demands that a pyre be built on which she can immolate herself. The ideas of devotion, sexual purity, and masculine and feminine honor expressed here are not limited to the society of classical India. They are common in many traditional societies and continue to influence gender relations in the present day.

Rama speaks to his beloved Sita: Oh illustrious Princess, I have re-won thee and mine enemy has been defeated on the battlefield; I have accomplished all that fortitude could do; my wrath is appeased; and the insult and the one who offered it have both been obliterated by me. . . . As ordained by destiny the stain of thy separation and thine abduction by that fickle-minded titan has been expunged by me, a mortal. . . . [However] a suspicion has arisen with regard to thy conduct, and thy presence is as painful to me as a lamp to one whose eye is diseased! Henceforth go where it pleaseth thee, I give thee leave, O Daughter of Janaka. O Lovely One, the ten regions are at thy disposal; I can have nothing more to do with thee! What man of honor would give rein to his passion so far as to permit himself to take back a woman who has dwelt in the house of another? Thou hast been taken into Ravana's lap and he has cast lustful glances on thee; how can I reclaim thee, I who boast of belonging to an illustrious House [family]? . . .

Sita replies with passion: Why dost thou address such words to me, O Hero, as a common man addresses an ordinary woman? I swear to thee, O Long-Armed Warrior, that my conduct is worthy of thy respect! It is the behavior of other women that has filled thee with distrust! Relinquish thy doubts since I am known to thee! If my limbs came in contact with another's it was against my will, O Lord, and not through any inclination on my part; it was brought about by fate. That which is under my control, my heart, has ever remained faithful to thee. . . . If despite the proofs of love that I gave thee whilst I lived with thee, I am still a stranger to thee, O Proud Prince, my loss is irrevocable. . . . Raise a pyre for me, O Saumitri, this is the only remedy for my misery! These unjust reproaches have destroyed me, I cannot go on living! Publicly renounced by mine husband, who is insensible to my virtue, there is only one redress for me, to undergo the ordeal by fire!

Questions to Consider

1. Why might such an abduction be considered equivalent to a rape, even though Ravana never had sexual relations with Sita?
2. Ordeal by fire is an idea and practice found historically in a variety of regions. What does Sita's willingness to undergo such an ordeal suggest about ancient Indian society's beliefs? Why fire?
3. Why are both male and female honor so dependent upon a woman's sexual purity?
4. Why must Rama, as a king, be particularly conscious of his reputation and that of his wife?

From *The Ramayana of Valmiki,* Vol. 3, trans. Hari Prasad Shastri (London: Shanti Sadan, 1970), pp. 336–337.

enemy. Rama then gains his rightful throne. In the course of time, priestly editors transformed this simple adventure story into a book of devotion. Rama, like Krishna in the *Bhagavad-Gita*, was an incarnation of the great god Vishnu. He was viewed as the ideal ruler: a truly virtuous, mighty man who exemplifies "proper conduct and is benevolent to all creatures. Who is learned, capable, and a pleasure to behold."[7] Sita emerged as the perfect woman, devoted and faithful to her husband, yet strangely powerful. Her words were memorized by almost every Hindu bride:

> *Car and steed and gilded palace,*
> *vain are these to woman's life;*
> *Dearer is her husband's shadow*
> *to the loved and loving wife.*

Sita's abduction by the demon Ravana launches another cosmic battle between the forces of good and evil. Rama, though victorious, is dishonored because Ravana had touched his wife and taken her to his palace. He feels compelled to repudiate Sita; her abduction is viewed as a rape even though she rejected Ravana's advances. One of the most moving scenes of the *Ramayana* is that in which the loyal Sita proposes to immolate herself rather than live separated from her lord. The gods save her from the flames, thus allowing Rama honorably to take her back. But years later, wagging tongues revive the question of her "tainted" virtue, and the heroine is once again prompted to prove her purity. The figure of Sita endures as an emblem of ideal Hindu womanhood. In the Indian nationalist struggles of the twentieth century, Sita served as a symbol of femininity and of the nation itself.

Counting Time

There are many ways to understand a civilization: through its art, its buildings, its political systems, its religions, its gender relations. One interesting way to envision a people is to examine its imaginings of time. Past societies have counted time in diverse ways, and those ways then shape the people's myths. Christians and Muslims, for example, trace their histories from a creation that includes the first man, Adam. Then each faith begins counting time from the life of its particular savior or prophet, Jesus and Muhammad, respectively. Of the three great religious traditions that emerged earlier in India, Jainism and Buddhism also focus on the lives of particular holy men who taught the way of Enlightenment. But the belief in reincarnation, shared by Hindus, Buddhists, and Jains, makes Indian notions of time radically different from those of traditions in which humans have only one lifetime. In the Indian traditions, humans

can and will have thousands of lifetimes. The question "What comes after death?" is intimately linked to the imagining of time.

Hindu civilization is unique among ancient world civilizations in its crafting of a particularly grand and elaborate scheme for counting time. There are many Indian creation myths, and these stories merged and shifted over time. One common Indian notion of the creation and destruction of the universe is that time is counted in eras called *mahayugas* (mah-hah-YOO-gahs). Just as individuals die and then are reborn, at the end of each era the world dissolves and then reemerges to begin a new era. Each era consists of one complete cycle of four ages: the Golden Age (1,440,000 human years), in which all beings are good and all life is comfortable; the Age of Trey (1,080,000 human years), in which some evil appears along with some suffering and difficulty in life; the Age of Deuce (720,000 human years), in which there is more evil, pain, and suffering; and the Age of Dissolution (360,000 human years), in which evil, pain, and distress predominate in human life. Before and after each age are "twilight periods" of varying length that altogether add another 720,000 years to the length of a whole cycle.

This vast expanse of human time, however, is nothing compared to the life of the god Brahma. One thousand *mahayugas* make up only one day in his existence, which lasts for 100 years of 360 days each; and as each Brahma dies, a new one is born from an egg that grows within *brahman*. In this Hindu cosmology, there have already been billions of Brahmas. According to certain ancient Hindu texts, the world is currently in an Age of Dissolution; in other words, we are approaching the end of a *mahayuga* and the halfway point in the current day of the current Brahma.

Buddhism After the Buddha

Buddhism was increasingly supported by rulers and wealthy merchants in the third century B.C.E. Its compelling message of escape from suffering and its rejection of the caste system later enhanced its popularity among other segments of society. It maintained an important position for several hundred years after that and, although other religions surpassed it in popular appeal, it survived in India until it was exterminated in the thirteenth century C.E. in the aftermath of the Muslim invasions.

The Brahmans did not sit quietly by while Buddhism challenged their power. They launched a countermovement in the second century B.C.E., reasserting their authority in the face of Buddhist successes and winning back political and economic support. This Brahman effort played a major role in giving rise to a movement of Buddhist rejuvenation, called Mahayana that began to flower about 100 B.C.E. Its followers called this movement the "Great Vehicle." Mahayana Buddhism stressed that pious Buddhists should not just seek their own personal nirvana or release from rebirth. Rather, they should imitate the Buddha directly by trying to relieve others' suffering with the message of the Dharma.

Earlier forms of Buddhism focused on the salvation of the pious individual. Mahayana Buddhism stressed the centrality of bodhisattvas (boh-dee-SAT-vas), those who postpone their own entry into the final nirvana in order to act as a compassionate and loving guide to others still suffering in the world. The Mahayana movement criticized the older forms of Buddhism calling them *Hinayana* (HEE-nah-YAH-nah) or "Lesser Vehicle" because, it said, their focus on salvation was selfish. One school of older Buddhism, Theravada (TAY-rah-VAH-dah), the so-called Doctrine of the Elders, did continue to thrive in India, but Mahayana Buddhism became more popular.

Buddhism, of course was not just a set of religious and philosophical ideas; it was a way of life. Thousands of men and women became monks and nuns, while many other lay Buddhists contributed to their support. Over time, Buddhists built monasteries, some of which became important centers of learning and way stations for traders and travelers. Monks transcribed Buddhist texts, which made their way to China and beyond, and Indian artisans carved thousands of statues of the Buddha to meet burgeoning demand. Gifts of the seven treasures (the luxury trade items gold, silver, lapis lazuli, crystal, pearl, rubies, and coral) were presented to monasteries by donors hoping to secure religious merit, good health, or nirvana for their loved ones. Some devotees venerated the Buddha along with Hindu deities, demonstrating that the lines dividing one religion from another were never as rigid in actual social practice as they often seemed. Even Roman merchants offered gifts to Buddhist monasteries; and some scholars have suggested that certain monasteries functioned as centers of trade and finance.

Buddhism (both the older Theravada and the newer Mahayana) spread outside of India and thrived in all parts of Asia. According to Sri Lankan chronicles, Buddhism was brought to Sri Lanka by missionaries sent there by the Mauryan emperor Ashoka around 250 B.C.E. After 100 B.C.E. Buddhists spread the Dharma beyond the boundaries of the subcontinent into China and central, western, and southeastern Asia. In most of those areas it took permanent root, establishing Buddhist societies, states, and monasteries that function to this day. Today the older form of Buddhism survives only in Sri Lanka and Southeast Asia, and the Mahayana is absent there; Mahayana survives in Tibet, Korea, Japan, and China. The translation of the very numerous books of the Buddhist scriptures from Sanskrit into Chinese took place during the second, third, and fourth centuries C.E., an intellectual achievement as fascinating as it is staggering. A small revival of Buddhism occurred in Maharashtra, India, in the 1950s when the Untouchable leader Dr. B. R. Ambedkar led a mass conversion of 50,000 Untouchables to Buddhism so that they might escape the oppression of Hindu "untouchability."

THE MEETING OF EAST AND WEST: NETWORKS OF EXCHANGE

■ *What role did India play in Eurasian trade?*

In the centuries immediately preceding and following the birth of Christ, the great civilizations of the world—Indian, Chinese, and Roman—were connected by a complex network of commercial, intellectual, and diplomatic exchanges. North India and south India played different roles in these networks of exchange, one oriented primarily towards the land and the other towards the sea. Travelers and monks from China visited the holy sites in India, the monsoons carried merchants to and fro across the Indian Ocean, and the goods and ideas of the East continued to enhance and alter the societies of the Mediterranean world.

Buddhist Sculpture and Architecture

Indian thought and art would have a profound effect on the eastern and western ends of Eurasia. Conversely, the most lasting Western influence on India in the Classical Age was the influence of Greek art on Buddhist sculpture. Before the Kushana period, Indian artists were influenced by the Buddha's prohibitions against idolatry, and they refrained from portraying the Buddha in human form. His presence was indicated by symbols only, such as his footprints, his umbrella, or the tree under which he attained Enlightenment. Beginning in the first century C.E., however, the Buddha himself was portrayed in numerous statues and reliefs. Most of these early Buddha figures come from Gandhara, the center of the Kushana Empire and the earlier Greco-Bactrian kingdom.

The primary inspiration for this Gandharan Buddhist art came from Mahayana Buddhism, which viewed the Buddha as a savior. This devotional form of Buddhism used images for worship, and statues of the Buddha as well as of many bodhisattva saints were produced in large numbers. Indeed the demand for images of the Buddha and bodhisattvas was so great that it affected the economy and artistic production of South Asia. Wealthy patrons like the Kushana king Kanishka hoped to gain spiritual favor or answers to their prayers by patronizing Buddhist monks and nuns. They paid artisans to create statues, build monasteries, and carve cells in rock cliffs to accommodate the flourishing communities of monks. The overland routes which carried traders, monks, and the message of Buddhism into China are marked by these monasteries, statues of the Buddha, and rock-carved caves. A second inspiration for Gandha-

The Great Stupa at Sanchi, built in the first century B.C.E., contains this detailed and elegant scene from the life of the Buddha. Numerous stupas were built by King Ashoka, starting in the third century, to hold the funeral relics of the Buddha.

ran art came from Greece. Apparently, Hellenistic sculptors and craftsmen migrated to Gandhara via the Central Asian trade routes. The result was an execution of Indian themes through the use of Greek artistic techniques. Thus Mahayana Buddhism and Greco-Buddhist images of the Buddha, both of which developed in the Kushana Empire, spread together throughout eastern Asia.

The magnificent buildings of the Mauryan emperors have disappeared, although archaeologists have found the ruins of a huge pillared hall at the site of the Mauryan capital which probably dates from the time of Chandragupta. Buddhist stupas, the dome-shaped monuments that were used as funeral mounds to enshrine the relics of the Buddha and Buddhist saints or to mark a holy spot, remain in great numbers. Originally made only of earth, more elaborate mounds were later fashioned out of earth faced with brick and surrounded by railings and four richly carved gateways of stone. On top of the dome was a boxlike structure surmounted by a carved umbrella, the Indian emblem that symbolizes the Buddha's princely birth. As centuries passed, the low dome was heightened in some areas into a tall, tapered structure more like a tower. Later, when Buddhism spread to other countries, the stupa type of architecture went along. Its gateway was widely copied, and the stupa itself was the prototype of the multistoried Buddhist pagodas that are common in East Asia today.

Beyond the Indian Frontiers

The Mauryan Empire had already declined by the time the Han dynasty arose in China and the Roman Empire emerged in the Mediterranean. Both empires were connected to India through trade, and the Tamil states, with their excellent ports, were well positioned to promote international commerce. While Rome experienced the prosperous years of the Pax Romana during the first and second centuries C.E., Indian merchants supplied goods to the Roman entrepots in the Middle East. South Asian ports acted as staging points for sales of Chinese silk and Indian cottons demanded in the West. Indian traders exchanged textiles for African gold and ivory and traded rice, oils, precious woods, jewels, and spices in the ports of the Arabian Sea.

Even earlier, in the years after Alexander the Great's death, India had maintained trade contacts with the Seleucid and Ptolemaic kingdoms of the Hellenistic Age over two routes, one by land and the other by sea. The most frequented route was the caravan road that extended from West Asia and Syria, crossed Mesopotamia, and then skirted the Iranian plateau to either Bactria or Kandahar before crossing the Hindu

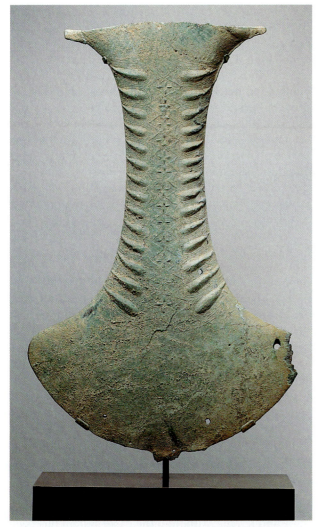

South and Southeast Asia were famous for metalworking. Bronze objects used for practical and ritual purposes (like this ceremonial blade) were highly prized and widely traded throughout the Indian Ocean region.

Vessel in the Form of an Ax. Bronze. The Metropolitan Museum of Art, Purchase, George McFadden Gift and Edit Perry Chapman Fund, 1993. (1993.525) Photograph by Bruce White © 1993 The Metropolitan Museum of Art.

Kush to reach Taxila in South Asia. The sea route that linked the eastern and western ends of Eurasia extended from China and Southeast Asia across the Bay of Bengal to India and Sri Lanka and thence across the Indian Ocean to the Red Sea ports or to the head of the Persian Gulf. From those two waterways, goods then proceeded overland and via the Mediterranean to the Middle East and into Africa and Europe.

The courts of kings and seats of power were great consumers of the goods of the East-West trade. The Mauryan and Kushana kings developed the trade passing through northern India in order to provide the foreign commodities that embellished their palace life. The Roman appetite for luxury goods from India and Southeast Asia—ivory, pearls, spices, dyes, and cotton—greatly stimulated trade in the southern kingdoms of India. Rulers vied to control and tax this lucrative commerce.

But no monarch, however great, could maintain control over the whole vast expanse of territory crossed by these trade routes. There were always middlemen. The Parthians, whose kingdom extended from the Euphrates to the borders of Bactria, levied heavy tolls on the caravan trade. The Kushanas acted as middlemen for the Chinese silk trade, selling the silk to the Parthians and later to Mediterranean merchants coming by sea to India. The Sabaean Arabs of southwestern Arabia seized the Red Sea route at Aden and were in control of much of the Mediterranean world's overseas trade with India. From Aden, the Sabaeans sent Indian goods north by caravan to Petra, which grew rich as a distribution point to Egypt via Gaza and to the north via Damascus.

So great was the demand and so lucrative the trade in Indian goods that the Roman emperor Augustus Caesar tried to break the hold of the Parthian and Arab middlemen on the Eastern trade, establishing direct commercial connections by sea with India. By 1 B.C.E. he had gained control of the Red Sea, forcing the Sabaeans out of Aden and converting the city into a Roman naval base. Ships were soon sailing from Aden directly to India across the Arabian Sea, blown by the monsoon winds.

From May to October the monsoon blows from the southwest across the Arabian Sea; between November and March the counter-monsoon blows from the northeast. Thus direct round-trip voyages, eliminating middlemen and the tedious journey along the coasts, could be made in eight months. Strabo, a Greek geographer during the time of Augustus, stated that 120 ships sailed to India every year from Egyptian ports on the Red Sea. This was an era in which early circuits of world trade developed.

When Augustus became head of the Roman world, the Tamil and Kushana rulers sent him congratulatory embassies. At least nine other embassies from India visited the Roman emperors, and Roman-Indian trade flourished. Indian birds (particularly talking parrots, costing more than human slaves) became the pets of wealthy Roman ladies, and Indian animals (lions, tigers, and buffaloes) were used in the wild beast shows of Roman emperors.

During the first century C.E., when Roman-financed ships reached the rich markets of southern India and Sri Lanka, Christianity may have accompanied them. Indian Christians today claim that their small group of about two million was founded by St. Thomas, one of Jesus' original 12 disciples, who may have sailed to India about 50 C.E. Thus, the trade routes carried more than goods. They bore travelers, envoys, pilgrims, and missionaries. Though the story of St. Thomas in India may be legendary, Buddhist philosophy was certainly spreading east and south into China and Southeast Asia.

The Balance of Trade

The balance of trade between the east and west of Eurasia from ancient times until the modern era tended to favor the countries of the East. Although Western trade with the East grew immensely in the first two centuries C.E., Roman exports such as wool, linen, glass, and metalware to the East did not match in value Rome's imports of silk, spices, perfumes, gems, and other luxuries. To make up the difference, gold and silver had continually to be exported to Asia. The discovery of large hoards of Roman coins in India seems to support claims that the Romans had to pay cash for some significant portion of their Indian goods.

Beginning in the third century, contacts between the eastern and western countries gradually declined. India entered a period of change and transition after the Mauryan Empire fell and the Kushana Empire in northeast India collapsed. In China, the Han dynasty in China broke apart. At the Western end of the trade routes, the Roman Empire's power was also circumscribed, and the hegemony of the Romans challenged. These political upheavals disrupted long-range cultural and commercial interchange but certainly did not eliminate it. The desire for diverse goods, commercial profits, and information insured the continuity of trade.

CONCLUSION

During India's formative age, three major religions were evolving on the subcontinent. Hinduism became the dominant social and religious force in India, with its notions of dharma (duty) allocated by caste. Jainism fostered the notion of ahimsa (nonviolence), which would play a powerful role in the twentieth-century Indian independence movement. Buddhism challenged the Brahman order and spread beyond the frontiers of India, ultimately to become a world religion. The great bulk of Indian thought sought not to challenge the existing social order but to explain and justify it; dharma dominated. Individual rights and desires in this world were ideally overshadowed by the requirements of eternal salvation, and freedom meant escape from the cycle of birth, death, and rebirth.

As in China, both local indigenous cultures and new languages, ideas, religions, and cultures came together to form the Indian society of antiquity. Forces of cultural and political integration at various times produced empires that spread across north India and penetrated the south. Unlike China, the written historical record can only be deciphered to the fourth century B.C.E., leaving historians more dependent on archaeological remains and engendering more heated debates about India's cultural origins.

India is today the heir of one of the longest-living civilizations in the world. By the beginning of the third century C.E., this civilization had produced a set of religious, philosophical, and literary traditions that endures to the present day. Television broadcasts of the *Ramayana* and the *Mahabharata* have been enormously successful in India in recent years. Rama and Sita remain as significant models for the virtuous male and female. Although the caste system has been challenged by the nation-state politics of modern India, it remains an essential element of Hindu identity: shaping social convention, determining political allegiance, and providing a framework for the practice of religion.

Suggestions for Web Browsing

You can obtain more information about topics included in this chapter at the websites listed below. See also the companion website that accompanies this text, **http://www.ablongman.com/ brummett,** which contains an online study guide and additional resources.

Itihaas: Chronology—Ancient India
http://sify.com/itihaas/fullstory.php?id=13225643

Lengthy chronology of ancient India, 2700 B.C.E. to 1000 C.E.; most entries include subsites with text and images.

India
http://www.art-and-archaeology.com/timelines/india/india.html

Site discussing the history, sites and monuments, and classical texts of India, 600 B.C.E. to 1256 C.E.

Jainism
http://www.cs.colostate.edu/~malaiya/jainhlinks.html

Extensive site discusses the principles, traditions, and practices of Jainism and includes numerous related links.

The Buddhist Age, 500 B.C.E. to 319 C.E.
http://www.stockton.edu/~gilmorew/consorti/1cindia. htm#religdone

Text and images detail Buddha's life, the Four Truths, and the evolution of Buddhism. Related links offer analyses of Buddhist texts and a lengthy list of primary texts.

Ancient Indian History
http://www.fordham.edu/halsall/India/indiasbook.html

Comprehensive collection of documents, secondary sources on India.

The *Ramayana*: An Enduring Tradition
http://www.maxwell.syr.edu/maxpages/special/ramayana/

The Ramayana is one of the most important literary and oral texts of South Asia. This extensive site from Syracuse University offers both a short and complete story of Rama, history, images, and maps.

Literature and Film

On Indian literature, see *The Rig-Veda,* trans. Wendy Doniger (Penguin, 1986); *Upanisads,* trans. Patrick Olivelle (Oxford University Press, 1996); and *The Laws of Manu,* trans. George Bühler (Cosmo Books, 2004). For the *Mahabharata,* see J. A. van Buitenen, ed. and trans., *The Mahabharata,* 3 Vols. (University of Chicago Press, 1973–1978), and the theatrical adaptation by Jean-Claude Carrière, *The Mahabharata* (Harper & Row, 1985). The scholarly edition of the *Ramayana* is Robert P. Goldman, et al., trans., *The Ramayana of Valmiki: An Epic of Ancient India,* 7 vols. (Princeton University Press, 1984–1998). See also Nigel Frith, *The Legend of Krishna* (Schocken, 1976). Ancient Indian literature also treats intimate matters; see, e.g., Wendy Doniger and Sudhir Kakar, trans., *Kamasutra* (Oxford University Press, 2002)

Tamil literature can be sampled in A. K. Ramanujan, trans., *The Interior Landscape: Love Poems from a Classical Tamil Anthology* (Oxford University Press, 1994); and R. Parthasarathy, trans., *The Cilappatikaram of Ilanko Atikal: An Epic of South India* (Columbia University Press, 1993).

Mahabharata, directed by Peter Brooks, is based on the version by Jean-Claude Carrière. The six-hour film (1989) is highly stylized, and its interpretation of the Indian epic has been controversial. The opera *Satyagraha* by composer Philip Glass and librettist Constance De Jong premiered in 1980; a film version was made in 1983. It focuses on Gandhi but is based on the *Bhagavad-Gita. Satyagraha* was Gandhi's idea of vehemently holding to the truth against all odds and temptations.

Suggestions for Reading

Excellent surveys of ancient India may be found in Romila Thapar, ed., *Recent Perspectives of Early Indian History* (Popular Prakashan, 1995), and Stanley A. Wolpert, *A New History of India,* 7th ed. (Oxford University Press, 2004).

On pre-Aryan society see, Gregory L. Possehl, *The Indus Civilization: A Contemporary Perspective* (Altamira Press, 2003). The question of who the Aryans were is discussed in Frank Raymond Allchin, ed., *The Archaeology of Early Historic South Asia* (Cambridge University Press, 1995); Edwin Bryant, *The Quest for the Origins of Vedic Culture* (Oxford University Press, 2001); and George Erdosy, ed., *The Indo-Aryans of Ancient South Asia* (Walter de Gruyter Press, 1995). On Bactria see Frank Lee Holt, *Thundering Zeus*: *The Making of Hellenistic Bactria* (University California, 1999). The Mauryan civilization is analyzed by Romila Thapar, *Ashoka and the Decline of the Mauryas,* 2nd ed. (Oxford University Press, 1997).

On seafaring and India's trade, see Kenneth MacPherson, *The Indian Ocean* (Oxford University Press, 1998), and Xinru Liu, *Ancient India and Ancient China: Trade and Religious Exchanges 1–600* (Oxford University Press, 1988).

There are a number of studies of Indian religions. On Buddhism, Edward Conze, *A Short History of Buddhism* (Allen & Unwin, 1980), is a good introduction. See also Edward J. Thomas, *The Life of Buddha as Legend and History* (Routledge, 1975); Richard H. Robinson, Willard L. Johnson, and Sandra A. Wawrytko, *The Buddhist Religion: A Historical Introduction,* 4th ed. (Wadsworth, 1996); T. W. Rhys Davids, trans., *Buddhist Suttas* (Book Tree, 2000); and John S. Strong, *The Experience of Buddhism* (Wadsworth, 1995). On Hinduism, see Gavin Flood, *An Introduction to Hinduism* (Cambridge University Press, 1996); Pratima Bowes, *The Hindu Religious Tradition* (Routledge, 1978); and Sarvepalli Radhakrishnan, *The Hindu View of Life* (Allen & Unwin, 1980). For primary documents, see Ainslie Embree, ed., *Sources of Indian Tradition,* Vol. 1, 2nd ed., (Columbia University Press, 1988).

On Indian art, see Benjamin Rowland, *The Art and Architecture of India: Buddhist, Hindu, Jain,* 3rd ed. (Penguin, 1970); John Marshall, *The Buddhist Art of Gandhara* (Cambridge University Press, 1960); Heinrich Zimmer, *The Art of Indian Asia* (Princeton University Press, 1960); and Michael W. Meister, *Encyclopedia of Indian Temple Architecture,* 2 Vols. (Princeton University Press, 1983–1992).

MIGRATION

Why do people move from one place to another?

Spanish Civil Guard watching over illegal immigrants from North Africa.

The history of migration is in a sense the history of humankind. All migrations involve the movement of peoples, cultures, languages, and ideas. As a result, they have shaped history around the world and played a major role in the growth of civilization. The reasons why people migrate vary. Changing environmental conditions, population pressures, economic shifts, political and religious controversies, and war and violence have all compelled people to move from one place to another.

Migrations have been an integral part of human experience since our early ancestors took their first tentative steps on the African savanna and began exploring and adapting to new environments. *Homo erectus* migrated from the African continent to Eurasia. Members of *Homo sapiens* followed their predecessor out of Africa and traveled further still, showing considerable ingenuity in overcoming obstacles such as the open sea to reach Australia and the cold of the northern latitudes to traverse the Bering Strait and enter the Americas.

These earliest human movements were small in scale. Extended families or clans would move into a new area and live off the land. Even with small populations, humans often placed considerable environmental strain on the land after only a short time. From 3000 B.C.E. to 500 C.E., Bantu communities migrating into central, eastern, and southern Africa could cultivate an area for only a few years before the soils were exhausted and they had to move to new land.

While environmental degradation caused by human activity has often forced people to migrate, so too have acts of nature such as droughts, floods, cold spells, and crop failures. Severe drought from around 1300 to 1100 B.C.E. likely initiated political disruptions in the eastern Mediterranean and the migrations of the Sea Peoples, Philistines, Sicilians, Sardinians, and Etruscans that followed.[1] More recently, potato blight destroyed the potato crops in Ireland between 1846 and 1850, creating widespread famine and economic hardship. Ireland's population dropped from 8.5 to 5 million as about a million people died of starvation and disease and hundreds of thousands migrated to Britain and the United States. In the United States, as the Great Depression took hold in the 1930s and a 7-year drought hit the Great Plains states, tenant farmers went deeply into debt and banks called in their loans. In the hope of generating more income, farmers cultivated their fields more intensively, leading to soil erosion. Hundreds of thousands of migrants fled the "Dust Bowl" and headed west along Route 66 seeking a "promised land" in California.

From the sixteenth century onward, an important component of European conquests around the globe was the migration of its citizens to new colonies. European languages and cultures left deep imprints on the colonized societies. English settlers were especially adept at creating "Little Englands" in places such as Australia, New Zealand, Canada, and the American colonies. A common feature of these settler colonies and the states that grew out of them was the expulsion of indigenous peoples from their lands. As American settlers pushed westwards, they moved Amerindian peoples to reservations. In 1838 the U.S. government went a step further by expelling Cherokees from Georgia and sending them on the Trail of Tears to Oklahoma, a territory initially set aside for Indians. This forced migration claimed some 4000 lives.

The largest forced migration in history was the trans-Atlantic slave trade, which, over the span of 300 years, wrenched an estimated 12 million people from West and Central Africa to work as slaves on sugar plantations in Latin America, the Caribbean, and the United States. Many more millions of African slaves were taken from West Africa across the Sahara and from East Africa across the Indian Ocean to states in North Africa and the Middle East.

War and conflict have also triggered huge shifts in populations. In the fourth century C.E. the nomadic Huns of Central Asia drove westwards across the steppes into the lands occupied by Germanic tribes. The violent movement of the Huns, in turn, caused German tribes to flee further westward and eventually confront and overrun the declining western Roman Empire. The subsequent resettling of the former Roman domains by the Germanic tribes eventually led to the creation of nations such as France and England.

In the last century, wars and political conflicts have continued to be a major cause of migration. Before and during World War II, Jews in Germany and eastern Europe fled to escape persecution by the Nazis; many of those who did not manage to escape were killed. After the war millions of ethnic Germans were forcibly relocated from eastern Europe to Germany. When Communist regimes took over in Russia, China, Vietnam, and Cambodia, huge numbers of political refugees sought asylum in other countries. In the 1970s and 1980s, as civil wars erupted between guerilla groups and repressive regimes throughout Central America, hundreds of thousands of refugees fled the fighting, many of them to the United States. This trend shows no signs of abating. In 2003 the UN High Commissioner of Refugees put the total number of refugees around the world at 20.5 million.

Religion has also brought about migrations as religious minorities have sought places to practice their faiths without persecution. After the Muslim conquest of Persia in the seventh century C.E., a group of Zoroastrians migrated to India in the tenth century to escape a forced conversion to the Islamic faith. In 1685 Louis XIV of France revoked the Edict of Nantes of 1598 that guaranteed Protestant Huguenots the right to freedom of worship and made them liable to torture or jail for their beliefs. As a result, about 300,000 Huguenots left France. In 1947, the partition of British India into the new nations of India and Pakistan led to the migration of at least 10 million people who feared religious oppression. Muslims in Hindu India fled for Pakistan while Hindus and Sikhs in Muslim Pakistan fled for India. The resulting religious violence left hundreds of thousands dead.

Economic changes and population growth have also generated migrations of people from rural ar-

eas to urban centers. As European nations industrialized in the nineteenth century, rural people seeking work in factories swelled the populations of many cities and leading to problems in housing, sanitation, law enforcement, and transportation. Dramatic population growth and unemployment late in that century also led 40 million Europeans to migrate from the continent to the Americas and Australia. The ethnic makeup and national identity of countries such as Argentina were transformed as a result.

Not all economic migrations, however, have been to cities. A century ago the economic policies of European colonizers in Africa heavily favored exports from coastal areas, which forced seasonal migrants from the interior to seek work on plantations nearer the coast. With the discovery of mineral resources in southern Africa in the late nineteenth century, hundreds of thousands of male migrant workers flocked to the mines for short periods of time leaving their families behind. In both cases, the movements of these migrants between home and places of employment have continued to the present day.

In recent years, migrant workers in foreign countries have been called by many names, for example, "guest workers," "illegal aliens," and "temporary sojourners." Local people have often resented the presence of economic migrants because they are seen as threats to their jobs or way of life. Many governments have been challenged to define the status of foreign migrants and to devise policies for controlling how they enter and where and how long they stay. During the apartheid era (1948–1994) in South Africa, the white-ruled government tried to control the movements of black adults by issuing them passbooks that contained permits allowing them to work and live in areas reserved for whites.

Migration has been an integral feature of history as individuals and groups of people have moved from one place to another for a host of reasons. Some people have moved voluntarily, but over the last five centuries, many migrants have been forced to leave their homes because of war and conquest, oppressive regimes, religious intolerance, and exploitative economic systems. The result is that migration has left few countries in the modern world untouched. The United States often prides itself on being a "nation of immigrants," but as one considers the global reach of migrations, have we reached a point where it is more accurate to refer to a "world of immigrants"?

Questions

1 Why have so many people emigrated to the United States in the last 25 years?

2. How has migration been a part of your own family's history?

3. What were the causes of the world's largest migrations?

Greece

Minoan, Mycenaean, Hellenic, and Hellenistic Civilizations, 2000–30 B.C.E.

CHAPTER CONTENTS

S carred by time, war, weather, and modern pollution, the ruins of the Athenian Acropolis stand today under a smoggy sky and overlook the trees and buildings of a vibrant city that has been modernized and beautified for the 2004 Olympic games. Because of the recent Olympics in Athens, ancient Greek civilization has received renewed attention worldwide. The renovation of the highways and subway system and new construction in preparation for the games have resulted in archaeological discoveries that add greatly to our knowledge of life in this ancient city. Celebration of contemporary Olympics in their birthplace has brought global recognition to the ancient Greeks and the significance of their cultural achievement.

In the fifth century B.C.E. the temples and statues of the Acropolis were new and gleaming, fresh from the hands of confident architects and sculptors. Today those temples, civic centers, and works of art remain ruins, yet ancient Athens and the civilization that was centered there have retained a lasting significance. The accomplishments of the ancient Greeks proved to be enduring. Their magnificent intellectual and artistic legacy helped shape much of the cultural heritage of western Europe and effect political and cultural development in Asia and Africa.

In the past historians and other scholars who specialize in western European civilization have generally tended to overemphasize the originality of Greek civilization and the positive contributions the Greeks made to their cultural heirs. Now we are able to reconstruct a more balanced picture of the ancient Greeks: one that more accurately assesses their cultural inheritance along with their original contributions. We are now much more aware of the formative influences of earlier neighboring civilizations in Africa and Asia that played an important role in influencing the shape of Greek history and culture. Our image of the ancient Greeks has become more balanced, and the recent focus of world attention on modern Athens has resulted in a renewed appreciation of the ancient Greek achievement.

2000 B.C.E.

c. 2000–1200 Minoan and Mycenaean civilizations

1628? Eruption of Thera

1500 B.C.E.

1450–1150 Mycenaeans in Crete

1150–750 Greek Middle Age

1000 B.C.E.

c. 800 Homer

c. 750 Greek city-states emerge

508–502 Cleisthenes establishes democracy in Athens

500 B.C.E.

490–478 Persian Wars

470–399 Socrates

431–404 Peloponnesian War

427–347 Plato

384–322 Aristotle

359–336 Reign of Philip II of Macedonia

336–323 Reign of Alexander the Great

200 B.C.E.

200–300 Rome annexes Hellenistic states

MINOAN AND MYCENAEAN CIVILIZATIONS, C. 2000–1200 B.C.E.

■ *In what ways did these two early Aegean societies interact with each other?*

More than one thousand years before the emergence of the Greek civilization we call classical, two advanced cultures, one on the mainland of Greece and another centered on the island of Crete, had taken shape. Minoan (mi-NO-an) civilization with Crete as its center and the surrounding Aegean (ay-GEE-an) islands its commercial partners, was highly developed by 2000 B.C.E.; Mycenaean (mai-se-NEE-an) civilization on the mainland seems to have reached its greatest power between 1450 and 1200 B.C.E. Both civilizations appear to have collapsed shortly after 1200 B.C.E. And both of them contained elements that were to influence the development of the later so-called classical civilization of Greece.

The Minoans

The earliest of these Aegean cultures to reach a high degree of sophistication is now referred to as Minoan

civilization, named after the legendary king of Crete, Minos (MEE-nos). From its center on Crete, Minoan civilization spread to the surrounding Aegean Islands, the coast of Asia Minor, and to mainland Greece itself. A narrow, 160-mile-long island, Crete served as a stepping-stone for extensive trading contacts with Europe, Asia, and Africa. Established by immigrants from Asia Minor, and made prosperous and powerful by economic and cultural contacts with Mesopotamia, Egypt, and more southern Africa, Minoan civilization achieved a high level of sophistication by 2000 B.C.E.

Minoan prosperity was based on a large-scale trading network that ranged throughout the Mediterranean: from Sicily, Greece, Asia Minor, and Syria to Africa, Sicily, and probably even Britain. The Minoans employed well-constructed ships capable of long voyages over the open sea. Chief exports were olive oil, wine, metalware, and magnificent pottery. This trading network was overseen as the monopoly of an efficient bureaucratic government under a powerful ruler whose administrative records came to be written on clay tablets, first in a form of picture writing (**hieroglyphics**)

---

hieroglyphics—Written characters that are pictorial in nature such as the ancient Egyptian written script. The word is Greek in origin (hieros="holy"; glyphos="writing").

Both the Minoan and Mycenaean civilizations established wide-ranging networks throughout the Mediterranean. Evidence of trading contacts from as far away as Kush (south of Egypt) and Afghanistan has been found in Aegean Bronze Age archaeological sites.

Preclassical Greece

c. 2000–1200 B.C.E.	Minoan and Mycenaean civilizations
1628? B.C.E.	Eruption of Thera
1450–1200 B.C.E.	Mycenaeans in Crete
1150–750 B.C.E.	Greek Dark Ages

and later in a script known as Linear A, whose 87 signs represented syllables. Since neither of these early scripts has been deciphered, our knowledge of the earliest stages of Minoan civilization is incomplete and imprecise; most of what we know is derived from the material remains—walls, temples, houses, and pottery and tablet fragments—uncovered by archaeologists.

The spectacular discoveries of English archaeologist Sir Arthur Evans a century ago first brought to light this impressive civilization, whose existence had previously only been mentioned in the epics of Homer and in Greek legends such as that of the Minotaur, half bull and half man, who devoured young Greek men and women sent to it as tribute from subject Greek cities. Between 1900 and 1905 Evans excavated the ruins of a great palace at Knossos, the largest and most prosperous city in Crete after 1700 B.C.E. Rising at least three stories high and sprawling over nearly 6 acres, this "Palace of Minos," built of brick and limestone and employing unusual downward-tapering columns of wood, was a maze of royal apartments, storerooms, corridors, open courtyards, and broad stairways. Equipped with running water, the palace had a sanitation system that surpassed anything else constructed in Europe until Roman times. Walls were painted with elaborate frescoes in which the Minoans appear as a happy, peaceful people with an enthusiasm for dancing, festivals, and athletic contests. Women are shown enjoying a freedom and prominence rarely matched either in the ancient Near East or even in later classical Greece. They are not secluded in the home but are portrayed sitting with men and taking an equal part in public festivities—even as athletes and participants in religious rituals. Their dresses are very elaborate, with bright patterns and colors, pleats, and puffed sleeves.

Their dresses are open in front to the waist, and their hair is carefully curled and arranged—a certain indication that Minoan women of high standing had sufficient time and wealth to devote to elaborate fashion.

One of the most notable features of Minoan culture was its art, varied in its themes, full of color, motion, and even humor. Art seems to have been an essential part of everyday life and not, as in the ancient Near East, intended to impart a religious or political message. What little is known of Minoan religion also contrasts sharply with earlier religious patterns in the Near East: There is no evidence of great temples, powerful priesthoods, or large cult statues of the gods. The principal deity was probably a Mother Goddess; her importance seems to reflect the prominence women held in Minoan society. A number of recovered statuettes show her dressed like the fashionable Minoan women who are portrayed in the murals that decorated the palace at Knossos. The Minoan Mother Goddess was perhaps an early inspiration for such later Greek goddesses as Athena, Demeter, and Aphrodite.

The Mycenaeans

Around or shortly after 2000 B.C.E., the first Indo-European Greek tribes, usually called Achaeans (ah-KEE-ahns), invaded Greece from the north, either conquered or absorbed the earlier settlers, and ruled from palaces on fortified hills at Mycenae, Pylos, Athens, and other sites in the south of Greece. By 1600 B.C.E. these Greeks—or Mycenaeans, as they are called today, after the richest of their fortresses at Mycenae—had absorbed much of the culture of the Minoans through trading contacts. But unlike

Vivid frescoes decorated the walls of many of the rooms in the Palace of Knossos. This famous Dolphin Frieze in the so-called Queen's Chamber illustrates the importance of the sea and of animals in Minoan life and art.

rooms and apartments, fresco-lined walls, floors of painted stucco, and large storerooms. Impressive also were the royal tombs constructed by Mycenaean kings after 1500 B.C.E. These beehivelike tombs, constructed of cut stones over several tons in weight and averaging over 40 feet in height, show proof of the power and control these Mycenaean kings exercised.

The desire to expand wealth and power led the Mycenaeans to establish colonies in the eastern Mediterranean (Hittite sources refer to Achaeans in Asia Minor) and even to the conquest of Knossos about 1450 B.C.E. This Mycenaean takeover was made possible by the destruction of the mazelike palace at Knossos by fire, perhaps in the aftermath of an earthquake that weakened the palace's defenses. Minoan dominance in the Aegean and prosperity on Crete had already been reduced by the destruction caused by the spectacular eruption of the volcanic island of Thera (modern Santorini), 80 miles north of Crete, and a resultant massive tidal wave that may have struck the northern shore of the island at a height of nearly half a mile. Archaeologists and **volcanologists** now place this great eruption in 1628 B.C.E., but the resulting damage to buildings, crops, and the merchant fleet of the Minoans probably contributed to making the civilization vulnerable to Mycenaean raids. The palace at Knossos was rebuilt by the Mycenaeans only to be destroyed about 1380 B.C.E. by earthquake and fire, after which the center of civilization in the Aegean shifted to the Greek mainland.

Many of the details regarding Minoan-Mycenaean relations were unknown until after 1952, when a young English architect, Michael Ventris, startled the scholarly world by deciphering a late type of Minoan script known as Linear B, many examples of which had been found by Evans at Knossos and by later archaeologists at mainland Greek sites such as Pylos, Mycenae, and Tiryns. Before Ventris's translation, most scholars thought that Linear B had to be a written version of the Minoan language. But Ventris proved that Linear B was actually an early form of Greek written in syllabic characters. Since Linear B was Greek, the rulers of Knossos after 1450 B.C.E. must have been Mycenaean Greeks who had come to power in Crete through invasion or piracy and adopted the Minoan script to write their own language.

The Linear B texts, which are administrative documents and inventories, add greatly to our

In contrast to some of the rigid and grandiose Mesopotamian and Egyptian statues, those of the Minoans were small and animated. This little priestess holds snakes, possibly reflecting Minoan religious rituals.

the Minoans, the Mycenaeans seemed to have been a more warlike people and sailed the seas as raiders as well as traders. Mycenaean women adopted Minoan fashions and added to Minoan styles their own cultural preferences in cosmetics, dress, and jewelry.

The Mycenaeans accumulated their wealth through agricultural production, the manufacture of superior pottery and metal tools and weapons, international trade, and probably piracy. Some of the great wealth accumulated by the kings of Mycenae—the greatest single hoard of gold, silver, and ivory objects found anywhere before the discovery of Tutankhamen's tomb—was excavated in 1876 by the amateur German archaeologist Heinrich Schliemann (1822–1890), a few years after his sensational discoveries at Troy. The royal palace on the acropolis, or citadel, of Mycenae had spacious audience

---

volcanologists—Those who study the formation, distribution, and classification of volcanoes and their eruptions.

knowledge of Mycenaean life. The Mycenaean centers were fortified palaces and administrative offices and not, as in Crete, true cities. The bulk of the population lived in scattered villages where they worked either communal land or land held by nobles or kings. The nobles were under the close control of the kings, whose administrative records were kept daily by a large number of scribes. Prominent in these records are details of the distribution of grain and wine as wages and the collection of taxes. The most important item of income was olive oil, the major article in the wide-ranging network of Mycenaean trade, which was operated as a royal monopoly. Perhaps it was their role as merchant adventurers that led the Mycenaean kings about 1250 B.C.E. to launch an expedition against Troy to eliminate a powerful commercial rival.

Troy—Site of Homer's *Iliad*?

DOCUMENT

Homer, *The Iliad*

The city most authorities believe to have been Troy, as described to us first by the poet Homer, occupied a strategic position on the Hellespont (the strait from the Aegean to the Black Sea, now known as the Dardanelles). In such an important location, this city could command both sea traffic through the straits and land routes between Asia and Europe. For many years scholars thought that Troy existed only in the epic poems of Homer; however, Heinrich Schliemann believed otherwise. As a young man he had read Homer's *Iliad,* and he became firmly convinced that the city had truly existed. At the age of 48, having made fortunes in the California gold rush and in worldwide trade, Schliemann retired from business to prove that his dreams of ancient Troy's existence were real.

In 1870 Schliemann began excavations at the legendary site of Troy, where he unearthed nine buried cities, built one on top of the other. He discovered a treasure of golden earrings, hairpins, necklaces, and bracelets in the second city (Troy II), which led him to believe that this was the city described by Homer. Excavations in the 1930s, however, showed that Troy II had been destroyed about 2200 B.C.E., far too early to have been the scene of the Trojan War. Scholars now believe that Troy VI or VII (c. 1200–1125 B.C.E) was probably the city made famous by Homer.

Homer's account tells us that the Trojan War began because of the abduction of Helen, queen of Sparta, by the Trojan prince Paris. Under the leadership of Agamemnon, king of Mycenae, the wrathful Achaeans besieged Troy for ten long years. Homer's *Iliad* actually describes only a period of a few weeks during the tenth year of the supposed siege. There is no archaeological proof of Homer's account. But we do know that Troy VII was destroyed by fire, and there are indications that the city was besieged. Were the attackers from Greece, or perhaps did the city fall victim to the piracy and disorder associated with the coming of the Sea Peoples or the collapse of the Hittite empire around 1200 B.C.E.? Folktales of the demise of the great city passed from Mycenaean times through oral tradition and elaboration down to the eighth century, when the account attributed to the poet Homer took written form. But the facts behind the destruction of the great city on the Hellespont remain clouded in mystery.

In 1876, when Heinrich Schliemann found this gold death mask at Mycenae, he excitedly telegraphed a friend: "I have looked upon the face of Agamemnon." The mask, however, dates from about 1500 B.C.E., nearly three centuries before the Trojan War, during which Agamemnon is said to have reigned.

The Fall of Mycenaean Civilization

Greek traditions recorded that around 1200 B.C.E. a new wave of Greek invaders, materially aided by weapons made of iron instead of bronze, invaded Greece from the north and conquered the Mycenaean strongholds. These newcomers may have followed in the path of the devastation caused by raiding Sea Peoples (see Chapter 1); some archaeologists suggest that invasions of new peoples caused less damage to Mycenaean sites than did the revolts of the lower classes against their powerful and autocratic overlords. First of the Mycenaean strongholds to fall was Pylos, whose Linear B archives contain numerous references to quickly undertaken preparations to meet military emergencies. We find orders directing women and children to places of safety and instructions given to makers of weapons, the navy, and food suppliers. The preparations were not in time. Pylos was sacked and burned, and all of the other major Mycenaean citadels were likewise destroyed.

THE RISE OF HELLENIC CIVILIZATION, c. 1150–500 B.C.E.

■ *How did a distinct Hellenic civilization evolve out of the Greek Dark Ages?*

The four centuries from around 1150 to 750 B.C.E., called the Greek Dark Ages, were marked by drastic depopulation and the disappearance of the major characteristics of Mycenaean civilization—centralized and bureaucratic administration, wide-ranging commerce, sophisticated art forms, monumental architecture, and writing. Although the fall of Mycenaean civilization was a catastrophic event, the end of Mycenaean dominance eventually gave rise to the emergence of a new and different civilization, called the Hellenic. Hellenic civilization receives its name from the Greek hero Hellen, a mortal who is credited with bringing humans to first inhabit Greece (Greeks ancient and modern call their country Hellas).

The Influence of Geography

MAP

The Early Aegean

Geographical factors played an important part in shaping the events of Greek history. The numerous mountain ranges that crisscross the peninsula, which is about the size of the state of Maine, severely restricted internal communication and led to the development of fiercely independent city-states and the reluctance of the Greeks to unite into a single nation. The mountains cover two-thirds of the peninsula, and along the west coast, they come close to the sea, leaving few harbors or arable plains. Elsewhere the deeply indented coast provides many natural harbors. A narrow isthmus at the Gulf of Corinth made southern Greece almost an island—in fact, it was called the Peloponnesus (pe-loh-poh-NEE-sus) for "Pelop's island." The jagged coastline and the many islands offshore stimulated seagoing trade, and the rocky soil (less than a fifth of Greece is agriculturally productive) and few natural resources encouraged the Greeks to establish colonies abroad.

The Homeric Age

Most of our information about the Greek Dark Ages comes from the epic poems put in written form around 750 B.C.E. and attributed to a supposedly blind Greek poet named Homer. Controversy surrounds the question of Homer's existence and whether he alone or several poets composed the *Iliad* and the *Odyssey*. The Homeric epics retain something of the material side of the Mycenaean period, handed down to Homer's time by a continuous oral tradition. But in terms of the details of political, economic, and social life, religious beliefs and practices, and the ideals that gave meaning to life, the poet could only describe what was familiar to him in his own age, probably soon after 800 B.C.E.

The values held by Homer to give meaning to life in the Homeric Age were predominantly heroic values—the strength, skill, and valor of the dominating warrior. Such was the earliest meaning of *arête* (AH-re-te), "excellence" or "virtue," a term whose meaning changed as values changed during the course of Greek culture. To obtain *arête*—defined by one Homeric hero as "to fight ever in the forefront and outdo my companions"—and the undying fame that was its reward, men would endure hardship, struggle, and even death. Honor was the just reward for one who demonstrated *arête*, and the greatest of human injustices was the denial of honor due to a great hero. Homer makes such a denial the theme of the *Iliad*, "The ruinous wrath of Achilles that brought countless ills upon the Achaeans," when Achilles, insulted by Agamemnon, withdraws from battle.

The Homeric king was essentially a war leader, hardly more than the "first among equals" among his companions—his fellow nobles who sat in his council to advise him and to check any attempt he might make to exercise arbitrary power. There was also a popular

The Development of Hellenic Civilization	
c. 1150–c. 750 B.C.E.	Greek "Dark Ages"
c. 800–750 B.C.E.	Establishment of the Greek *polis* (city-state)
c. 750–550 B.C.E.	Great age of Greek colonization
c. 650 B.C.E.	Age of Greek tyrants; *helot* revolt in Sparta
c. 600 B.C.E.	Coinage introduced in Greece
594 B.C.E.	Solon named sole *archon* in Athens
c. 560 B.C.E.	Pisistratus is tyrant in Athens
508–502 B.C.E.	Cleisthenes establishes democracy in Athens

Document   Homer—*The Iliad*: Andromache and Hector

Homer's *Iliad* is mostly a story of war and carnage. Yet this great work also contains vivid and moving accounts of life and even love during the respites between battles. Homer's work served as inspiration to the Greeks of the classical period; much of the actions of heroic men and women were held up as examples of ideal conduct in times of crisis. Such inspiration can be taken from the description of an interaction between the Trojan hero Hector and his loyal wife Andromache (an-DRO-ma-kee) before Hector went out to meet certain death at the hands of the Greek Achilles:

A flash of his helmet
And off he strode and quickly reached his sturdy,
well-built house. But white-armed Andromache—
Hector could not find her in the halls.
She and the boy and a servant finely gowned
were standing on the tower, sobbing, grieving.
. . . Hector spun and rushed from his house,
back by the same way down the wide, well-paved
    streets
throughout the city until he reached the Scaean
    Gates,
the last point he would pass to gain the field of
    battle.
There his warm, generous wife came running up to
meet him,
. . . She joined him now, and following in her steps
a servant holding the boy against her breast
in the first flush of life, only a baby
Hector's son, the darling of his eyes
and radiant as a star . . .
The great man of war breaking into a broad smile,
his gaze fixed on his son, in silence. Andromache,
pressing close beside him and weeping freely now,
clung to his hand, and urged him, called him:
    "Reckless one,
my Hector—your own fiery courage will destroy
    you!
Have you no pity for him, our helpless son? Or me,
and the destiny that weighs me down, your widow

now so soon. Yes, soon they will kill you off,
all the Achaean forces massed for assault, and
    then,
bereft of you, better for me to sink beneath the
    earth.
What other warmth, what comfort's left for me,
once you have met your doom? Nothing but
    torment!
I have lost my father. Mother's gone as well.
. . . You, Hector—you are my father now, my noble
    mother,

a brother too, and you are my husband, young
    and
warm
and strong."

Questions to Consider

1. Do you think Hector and Andromache are displaying ideal conduct in this exchange?

2. Is Andromache in any way receptive to concerns *other* than her own security? What seem to be Andromache's primary goals in her conversation with Hector?

3. Is Andromache helpless to do something other than her husband's bidding? Why?

From Homer, *Iliad*, 6, 439–509, trans. Robert Fagles (New York: Penguin, 1990).

assembly of arms-bearing men, whose consent was asked whenever a crisis occurred, such as war or the recognition of a new king.

Noble women were freed from agricultural labor, but still had major responsibility for maintaining the order of the household and its accounts, supervising the upbringing of the children, and overseeing the activities of any servants attached to the estate. In most circumstances noble women had to manage the estates of their husbands when war or other duties demanded their attention. They are described by Homer as active participants in the life of their communities and even in the banquet hall conversations alongside the men. But the opportunity for leisure like that possessed by their Minoan and Mycenaean predecessors was a luxury most of these noble women probably could not enjoy.

Society was clearly aristocratic; nobles were recognized as such because of their ownership of larger estates, and their resulting influential position within

Greek civilization flourished in the mountainous lands of the eastern Mediterranean. Mainland Greece lacked arable land and navigable rivers, but its extensive coastline and fine harbors drew the Greeks to the sea for sustenance and commerce. All of the eastern Mediterranean became involved in the war between Athens and Sparta. The Spartans, surrounded by Athens's growing power, concluded that they had to go to war to prevent eventual Athenian dominance.

the tribes. Only the nobles, the *aristoi* ("best"), possessed *arête*—and the common man was reprimanded and beaten when he dared to question his superiors. Yet the commoners had certain political rights as members of the tribes; they were able to sit in the popular assembly, own land, and enjoy the protection of law as interpreted by the king.

The economy was a simple, self-sufficient agricultural system in which private ownership of land replaced the collective group ownership of Mycenaean times. Slavery was not a widely employed institution in the Greek Dark Age. Most of the estates were small, and most agricultural and domestic labor was provided by free, landless peasants. Slaves were not numerous; if slaves were to be found they were mostly employed as domestic servants on the estates of the wealthiest of the nobles.

From Oligarchy to Tyranny

The *polis* (pl. *poleis*), the term which later comes to mean the city-state—the political unit comprising the city and its people— did not carry the same meaning for the Greeks of Dark Ages. The word originally described only the physical city itself. The center of every polis was the high, fortified site, the *acropolis*, where people could take refuge from attack. In time this defensive center took on added significance as the focus of political and religious life. When commerce revived in the eighth and seventh centuries B.C.E., a trading center (*agora*) developed below the acropolis. The two areas and the surrounding territory, usually smaller than a modern county, in combination with its citizens, came to give new meaning to the word *polis*: the city and the people who share a common citizenship.

The political development of the polis was so rich and varied that it is difficult to find of a form of government not experienced—and given a lasting name—by the Greeks: monarchy, oligarchy, tyranny, and democracy. For most of the Greek Dark Ages, monarchy had been the typical form of government. But by the middle of the eighth century B.C.E., the nobles, who wished to share in the authority exercised by monarchs, had taken over the government of most city-states, ushering in an age of aristocracy ("government by the best") or **oligarchy** ("government by the few"). Exercising their superior power, the nobles in many locations abolished the popular assembly, acquired a monopoly of the best land, reduced many commoners to virtual serfdom, and forced others to seek a living on rocky, barren soil. Often the poor found relief only by emigrating overseas. In many city-states the wealthy promoted colonization as a safety valve to ward off a threatened political and economic explosion from the lower classes.

But the colonization movement was much more than just an effort to relieve the distress of the landless poor. From 750 to 550 B.C.E. the Greeks planted colonies throughout most of the Mediterranean world. Colonies were founded along the northern coast of the Aegean and around the Black Sea. So many Greeks migrated to southern Italy and eastern Sicily that the region became known as *Magna Graecia*, Great Greece. Col-

VIDEO
Ephesus

onies were also founded as far west as present-day France—at Massilia (modern Marseilles), for example—and Spain and on parts of the African coast. Unique was Naucratis (NAH-krah-tis) in Egypt, not a true colony but a trading post whose residents gained extraterritorial rights (their own magistrates and law courts) from the Egyptians.

Colonization not only lessened some of Greece's social problems but also stimulated rapid and significant economic development. By 600 B.C.E. economic progress and the use of coined money, probably inspired by the Lydians, had fostered the beginnings of a middle class. The Greek poleis gradually became "industrialized" as a result of concentrating on the production of specialized goods—vases, metal products, textiles, olive oil, and wine—for export in exchange for food and raw materials. But before this economic revolution was completed, the continuing land hunger of the poor contributed to a political revolution.

After 650 B.C.E. rulers known as *tyrants* seized power in many Greek states and, supported by both poorer citizens and the rising middle classes, took control of government from the nobility. Tyrants were supported also by the newly developed heavily armed infantry force: the hoplite phalanx—a formation of foot soldiers carrying overlapping shields and long spears, which replaced the aristocratic cavalry as the most important element in Greek warfare. Most tyrants were commanders of the hoplite phalanx. The hoplites, common citizens wealthy enough to furnish their own equipment, supported their commander's efforts to seize power in turn for the promise of more partici-

---

A sixth-century B.C.E. amphora from the polis of Corinth. Corinthian pottery was the most popular of all such merchandise produced in Greece for two hundred years, and many examples of it are found throughout the Mediterranean region, even as far into Asia as modern Iran.

---

pation in the affairs of the polis once the tyranny was established.

The tyrants (the word meant simply "absolute ruler" and did not at first have today's connotation of brutality) sometimes distributed land to the landless poor and, by promoting further colonization, trade, and industry, increased economic prosperity and generally made their poleis better places to live for all residents. At first exceptionally popular leaders, tyrants attempted to keep a dynastic control of their poleis by passing on their power to their sons. Within a few generations, these dynastic tyrannies tended to grow more autocratic and unpopular with the citizens, and almost all were eventually overthrown. Most Greek poleis then reverted to an aristocratic form of government with control in the hands of the nobility. The two notable exceptions to this pattern are two of the most unique of poleis: Athens and Sparta.

Athens to 500 B.C.E.

Athens and Sparta, the two city-states destined to dominate the political history of Greece during the classical period (the fifth century B.C.E. and most of the fourth), had radically different courses of development during the period prior to 500 B.C.E. The

---

oligarchy—Government by the few, from the Greek word oligos ("few"); political domination by a limited number of families or individuals.

political, economic, and social evolution of Athens was typical of most Greek states, but Sparta's development produced a unique way of life that inspired the admiration of other Greeks, and often their astonishment as well.

In Athens during the seventh century B.C.E., the council of nobles became most influential. The popular assembly rarely met, and the king's authority was replaced by nine magistrates, called *archons* ("rulers"), chosen annually by the aristocratic council to exercise the king's civil, military, and religious powers. While the nobles prospered on their large estates, the small farmers and sharecroppers suffered. Bad years and poor land forced them to borrow seed from the wealthy nobles, and when they were unable to repay their debts, they were sold into slavery. Small farmers called out for the cancellation of debts and the end to debt slavery, and those without any land demanded a redistribution of the land claimed by the aristocrats.

The majority of Athenian nobles finally realized that their failure to address the demand for reform might result in the rise of a tyrant, and they agreed to a policy of compromise advocated by the aristocrat Solon. In 594 B.C.E. Solon was made sole archon, with broad authority to revise the constitution of Athens in order to avoid class conflict. Solon, widely respected in Athens for his wisdom and fair dealing, instituted middle-of-the-road reforms intended to save Athens from social revolution and economic disaster.

For the lower classes, Solon agreed to canceling all debts and forbidding future debt slavery, but he rejected as too radical the demand for the redistribution of the land. His long-range solution to the economic problem was to seek full employment by stimulating trade and industry. To achieve this goal, Solon required fathers to teach their sons a trade, granted citizenship to foreign artisans and merchants who settled in Athens, and encouraged the intensive production of wine and olive oil for export.

All citizens in Athens, women included, were encouraged to work—most Athenian women citizens who did so worked at home-based small industries. Solon regulated prostitution in Athens, although such an occupation was considered unacceptable for any but foreign noncitizens.

Moderation also characterized Solon's political reforms—the common people were granted important political rights but not complete equality. Although laws continued to originate in a newly instituted Council of Four Hundred controlled by the nobles, they now had to be ratified by the popular assembly, to which Solon gave more power. And since wealth, not birth, became the qualification for membership in the new council and for the archonships, wealthy commoners could acquire full political equality. Furthermore, the assembly could now act as a court to hear appeals from the decisions of the archons and to try the archons for misdeeds in office.

Solon's reforms were very popular with the middle classes but did not completely satisfy the rich or the poor. The poor had received neither land nor full political equality, while the nobles thought Solon too radical of a reformer who had betrayed his own class. But both classes were given more political power and a sense of participation and involvement in the life of the polis. Solon's reforms moved Athens closer to the implementation of a more fully democratic constitution.

Solon advised the Athenians to accept his reforms, and then left the city and its politics for ten years, in the hope that his new constitutional reforms would take root without his interference. But rivalries between the nobles, the middle class, and the poor resulted in years of civil conflict. In 560 B.C.E., after several attempts to dominate Athens, Pisistratus (pai-SIS-tra-tus), a military hero and champion of the commoners, seized power as tyrant. He addressed the economic problems by banishing many nobles, whose lands he distributed among the poor, and by promoting commerce and industry. Together with extensive public works projects and state sponsorship of the arts—starting Athens on the road to cultural leadership in Greece—these reforms gave rise to a popular saying that "life under Pisistratus was paradise on earth." Like Solon, Pisistratus moved Athens closer to the acceptance of a more fully developed democracy by giving both the middle class and especially the commoners a real possibility to participate in governing the polis.

Pisistratus was succeeded by his son, Hippias (HIP-i-as), who proved unable to retain his father's popularity and soon became tyrannical in the modern sense of the word. The nobles, aided by a Spartan army, took the opportunity to restore aristocracy, but the majority of Athenian citizens by this time supported establishing a more democratic form of government that empowered the middle and lower classes to a greater degree than the nobles supported. The leader of the democrats, a noble named Cleisthenes (KLAIS-the-neez), established order in Athens with the cooperation of even the nobles when they were faced with the possibility of further Spartan interference.

From 508 to 502 B.C.E. Cleisthenes was given power to enact constitutional reforms that greatly reduced the remaining power of the nobility. He disbanded the old noble-dominated tribes and created ten new ones, each embracing citizens of all classes from widely scattered districts. The popular assembly acquired the right to initiate legislation and became the sovereign power in the state; there could be no appeal from its decisions. A new democratic Council of the Five Hundred, selected by lot from the ten tribes, advised the assembly and supervised the administrative actions of the archons.

Cleisthenes also has been credited with instituting the institution of *ostracism,* an annual referendum in which a quorum of citizens could vote to exile for ten years any individual thought to be a threat to the new Athenian democracy. (A quorum consisted of 6000 of the 50,000 male citizens over the age of 18. The average attendance at an Athenian assembly, whose ordinary meetings were held every ten days, was about 5000.) By 500 B.C.E. the Athenian polis had established a form of government more thoroughly democratic than in any other city in the ancient world.

The establishment of democratic government at Athens owed a great debt to the reforms of Solon and to the policies of Pisistratus, as both Athenian leaders encouraged greater participation in governance by the commoners. But the idealism of Cleisthenes was mainly responsible for establishing the democracy. Cleisthenes diminished the power and influence of the nobles in Athenian politics by reducing their ability to influence voting through their control of the tribal structure and their neighborhoods. He abolished the four Athenian tribes into which all Athenian citizens were born, and instituted in their place ten new tribes, based on neighborhood units called *demes,* which were distributed among the new tribes in such a way that no tribe could dominate a region. All citizens were enrolled on lists kept by the demes, and even if a citizen moved away from the deme in which in which he was originally enrolled, he had to return to that deme to vote and to register for military service. Cleisthenes also awarded citizenship to many resident aliens, most of whom were productive members of the middle classes. A council of 500 was established to replace the old council of 400; now 50 citizens from each of the new 10 tribes constituted this new body that was charged primarily to prepare legislation for the assembly's consideration. But final authority was given to the assembly of all citizens over the age of 18, in which any member might propose legislation, initiate debate, or argue for or against a proposal.

Comparing Athens and Sparta

By the beginning of the fifth century B.C.E., Athens was fully involved in the implementation of its new democratic institution but unsure of its security against the threat of Spartan intervention and the possibility of Persian expansion into the Aegean. Its large population and great potential for economic advantage through international trade gave the city-state great potential for growth and prosperity. But the greatest test the polis would face came from the Persian suppression of the revolt of the Greek poleis on the coast of Asia Minor and the subsequent Persian invasion of Greece.

Sparta to 500 B.C.E.

The early history of Sparta seems very similar to that of many Greek poleis. Sparta took steps to move from a powerful monarchy to oligarchy when the nobles installed five annually elected aristocratic magistrates, called *ephors* ("overseers"), to supervise the kings' activities. Instead of sending out colonists to satisfy the Spartans' desire for more land, the Spartans turned instead to the conquest of the neighboring region of Messenia, whose residents were forced to become state slaves *(helots).* Around 650 B.C.E., however, the Messenians revolted, and it took Sparta nearly 20 years to crush the rebellion. During this emergency that threatened the very existence of the polis, the aristocrats were forced to seek the aid of the Spartan commoners. In return, the nobles agreed to the commoners' demand for land division and more political participation. Private ownership of land was abolished, and the land allotments were divided equally among the 9000 Spartan male citizens. These land allotments were to remain with the original claimants and often came to be held by women when no male heirs to the property remained alive to claim inheritance.

DOCUMENT

Plutarch on Life in Sparta

In addition, the nobles established an assembly of all Spartan citizens with the right to elect the ephors and to approve or veto the proposals of the 30-member Council of Elders. While the Athenian state required only two years of military training for young men, the Spartan system—traditionally attributed to a legendary lawgiver named Lycurgus (lai-KUR-guz)—was designed to make every Spartan man a professional soldier and to keep him in a constant state of readiness for war, especially the ever-present danger of a helot revolt. To this end, Spartan society enforced an absolute subordination of the individual to the preservation of the state.

Spartan officials examined all newborn children, and any found sickly or deformed were abandoned. At the age of 7 a boy was taken from his family and placed in the charge of state educators, who taught him to bear hardship, endure discipline, and devote his life to the state. At 20 the young Spartan enrolled in the army and continued to live in barracks, where he contributed food from his allotment of land granted by the state and worked by helots. He was allowed to marry, but he continued to live in barracks, sneaking back to visit his wife only at night. After 30 he could live at home, but continued to take his meals with his company of male comrades. Finally, at 60, he was released from the army and could live at home with his family. This lifelong pattern of discipline produced some of the most formidable soldiers in human history and inspired Spartan citizens with the sense of purpose, obedience, and respect for Spartan law.

Spartan girls also received state training in order to become healthy mothers of warrior sons. Their primary service to the state was thought to be giving birth to male babies, and to that end they were instructed to strengthen their bodies for childbirth. Clad in short tunics, which other Greeks thought immodest, they engaged in running, wrestling, and throwing the discus and javelin. Their characters were to be as strong and resolute as their husbands'. As their men marched off to war, Spartan women gave them a **laconic** farewell (Laconia was another name for the Spartan homeland): "Come back *with* your shield—or *on* it."

Although many Greeks admired the Spartan way of life, few would ever desire to be a part of the Spartan regimen. The typical Spartan was an unsophisticated, uncultured fighting machine. Spartan discipline was almost universally admired, although no other Greek would wish to trade places with a Spartan who avoided the corruptions of fine food and good wine.

Although Sparta developed the finest infantry force in Greece, the state purposely remained backward culturally and economically. Trade and travel were prohibited because the city fathers feared that foreign ideas might threaten Spartan discipline. Sparta is a classic example of how intellectual stagnation accompanies rigid social conformity and military regimentation. But, through conscious design to preserve the state and the privileged status of the citizen elite, the Spartans purposely froze the natural evolution of their political and cultural institutions.

To provide additional assurance that its helots remained uncontaminated by democratic ideas, Sparta allied itself with oligarchic parties in other Peloponnesian (pe-le-pon-NEE-si-an) states and aided them in suppressing their democratic opponents. The resulting Spartan League of oligarchic states, in operation by the end of the sixth century B.C.E., was shortly to be opposed by an Athenian-led alliance of more democratic states.

---

laconic—Using few words, but expressing much. From Laconia, the region in which Sparta was located. Esessentially, to be laconic is to speak in a terse manner, as a Spartan did.

Persian Wars

before c. 540 B.C.E.	Persian control of Greek cities in Asia Minor
499–495 B.C.E.	Rebellion of Ionian cities in Asia Minor
490 B.C.E.	Battle of Marathon
480–479 B.C.E.	Xerxes' invasion of Greece
480 B.C.E.	Battles of Thermopylae and Salamis
479 B.C.E.	Battle of Plataea

THE GOLDEN AGE OF GREECE, 500–336 B.C.E.

■ *What about this period justifies the idea of a Greek "Golden Age"?*

The leaders of a Greek economic and cultural revival after 750 B.C.E. were the Ionian Greeks, who had settled on the Aegean coast of central Asia Minor and the nearby offshore islands and the mainland region of Attica—the Athenians were also Ionian Greeks. Influenced by contacts with Phoenician traders (from whom they borrowed the alphabet in the eighth century B.C.E.) and neighboring Lydia and Egypt, the Ionians became innovators in art, science, philosophy, and literature. Ionian creativity was also evident in their commercial ventures, which spread throughout the Aegean region. It was especially because of their economic prosperity that they became the first of the Greeks to face conflict with the great powers of the Near East.

The Persian Wars

When the Persian empire and its young king Cyrus conquered Lydia in 547 B.C.E., they also took over the Ionian poleis, which had been fairly content under moderate Lydian rule. In open opposition to their Persian-appointed overlords, the Ionian cities revolted in 499 B.C.E., established democratic regimes, and appealed to the Athenians, their kinsmen, for assistance. Athens sent 20 ships—token help, and far too few to prevail over the Persians. By 494 B.C.E. the Persian king Darius I had crushed the revolt, burning the Greek polis of Miletus in revenge.

King Darius knew that Ionia was insecure as long as Athens remained free to incite the Ionian Greeks to revolt again. In 490 B.C.E. a Persian force of about 20,000 infantry and cavalry sailed across the Aegean, conquering the Greek island states along their path, and eventually encamped on the plain of Marathon, 24 miles northwest of Athens. Darius's attempt to eliminate the interference of Athens was ended when the Athenian army, half the size of the Persian force, won an overwhelming victory, slaying as many as 6400 of the invaders while losing only 192 themselves.

The battle of Marathon was one of the most decisive in ancient history. It destroyed the Greek suspicion of Persian invincibility and demonstrated, according to a contemporary Greek historian, that "free men fight better than slaves." Ten years later the Greeks were forced to prepare for a new Persian invasion under Xerxes, Darius's successor, whose objective this time was the subjection of all of Greece. Athens now had 200 warships, the largest fleet in Greece, and Sparta had agreed to head a defensive alliance of 31 states.

The Persian army was too huge to be transported by ship. Crossing the swift-flowing, mile-wide Hellespont near Troy on two pontoon bridges—a notable feat of engineering—the army marched along the Aegean coast accompanied by a great fleet carrying provisions. The Spartans wanted to abandon all of Greece except the Peloponnesus to the invaders but finally agreed to a holding action at the narrow pass of Thermopylae (ther-MO-poh-lee) in central Greece. Here 300 Spartans and a few thousand other Greeks held back the Persians for three days until the Persians discovered a mountain path to the rear of the Greek position. The Spartans fought magnificently until all were killed, along with at least 700 other Greeks. The Spartan dead were immortalized on a monument erected later at the pass, with the inscription "Go Stranger, and tell the Spartans that we lie here, obedient to their word."

The Persians then sacked Athens, whose inhabitants had been evacuated to the Peloponnesus and the islands near the bay of Salamis. Themistocles (the-MI-stoh-kleez), the leader of the democrats at Athens, had long been a strong advocate for the construction of a strong naval force, and now the Athenians were prepared to put their confidence in their ships to defeat the Persian navy in the Bay of Salamis. The battle that took place in the spring, after the Persians had spent the winter in Athens preparing for the event, was an overwhelming Greek victory. Taking full advantage of the Persians' ignorance of the tides and the inability of their ships to outmaneuver the heavier Athenian vessels designed for ramming and close combat, the Persian navy suffered near complete defeat. With 200 of his 350 ships destroyed and his lines of communication cut, Xerxes saw no alternative but to retreat to Asia, although he left a strong force in Greece. The following summer (479 B.C.E.) the Greek army, with the Spartan army in the forefront, defeated the Persian force in central Greece at Plataea. The Persian threat to the Greek mainland was ended, and the Greeks immediately began plans for campaigns to drive the Persians from the Aegean island and the Ionian coast of Asia Minor.

Athens After the Persian Wars

The prominent role the Athenians played in the Greek victory over the mighty Persian Empire exhilarated the polis and gave Athens the confidence and energy to try to assert their leadership of the Greek world during most of the remainder of the fifth century B.C.E. During this period, often described as the Golden Age of Greece, the Athenians also achieved the fullest development of their democracy, and at the same time established a formidable empire on both land and sea.

For more than 30 years (461–429 B.C.E.) during this period, the great statesman Pericles (PE-ri-kleez) guided Athenian policy. In Pericles' time actual executive power no longer resided in the archons, who were chosen by lot, but in a board of ten generals elected annually. The generals urged the popular assembly to adopt specific measures, and the success or failure of their policies determined whether they would be reelected at the end of their annual term. Pericles failed in reelection only once, and so great was his influence on the Athenians that, in the words of his contemporary, the historian Thucydides (thu-SI-di-deez), the Athenian democracy was in reality completely dominated by Pericles and his policies.

To enable even the poorest citizen to participate in government, Pericles extended payment to jurors (a panel of 6000 citizens chosen annually by lot) and to members of the assembly. Although his conservative opponents called this political bribery, Pericles insisted that it was essential to the success of democracy that all the citizens be able to participate, and so those who could not afford to miss a day's wage would be compensated at state expense.

Athenian Society

Despite the many democratic aspects of Athenian society, not all residents of Athens were given the opportunity to be fully participating citizens. Women, slaves, and resident foreigners (with the exception of those to whom Cleisthenes had granted it) were denied citizenship and had no voice in the government. Legally, Athenian women were first the property of their fathers and then of their husbands. They could not possess property in their own name, make legal contracts, testify in the courts, or initiate divorce proceedings. The exclusion of Athenian women from public life seems significant, given the extent to which the participation in the democracy was extended to males of every social class.

An Athenian wife's function was to bear children and manage the home, where she was restricted to the women's quarters when her husband entertained his friends. Men did not marry until they were about 30, and they usually married girls half their age or less. Marriages were normally arranged through agreements between families, and prospective brides and bridegrooms seldom met before their marriage was agreed upon. Families were small, with usually no more than two children, and infanticide, usually by exposure, of unwanted infants was practiced as a means of population control. The average life expectancy in Athens was little more than 30 years, but if one were able to survive childhood, a longer life could be anticipated.

Sexual activity for men outside marriage was not a matter for negative public comment in Athens, and prostitution was common. An acceptable social institution intended to serve the needs and desires of upper-class Athenian men was spending one's leisure time with female "companions" (*hetaerae;* he-TAI-rai). These prostitutes were normally resident foreigners and therefore not subject to the social restrictions imposed on Athenian women. A few of the *hetaerae,* such as Aspasia (as-PAY-zhah), the mistress and later wife of Pericles, were cultivated women who entertained at gatherings frequented by prominent Athenian political and cultural leaders.

Although there are representations of outspoken and assertive women left for us by Athenian dramatists, actual examples of Athenian women who were publicly prominent are almost nonexistent, and the women themselves accepted their status. Athenian women enjoyed less freedom of movement and participation in the public life of the polis than most other Greek states, even Sparta. Veiled from public view, forbidden to converse with men other than their husbands, restricted to their own quarters in the home when their husbands entertained their guests—the private life of an Athenian wife was known only to her household. Yet married life seems to have been stable and peaceful. Athenian gravestones in particular attest to the love spouses felt for one another. The tie to their children was strong, and

the community set high store on the honor owed by sons and daughters to their parents.

Homosexuality was an acceptable form of social conduct for Athenian men during certain periods of their lives. A sexual relationship between a mature man and a young boy just before or after the youth attained puberty was common practice. The relationship was viewed not only as sexual, but educational—a rite of initiation into adult society—and such relationships were most common among Athenian soldiers. However, male homosexuality that continued into the years when Athenians were expected to marry and produce children, as well as homosexual prostitution at any time, was not condoned. Such relationships were regarded as unnatural, and the Athenian government issued strong legal prohibitions against them.

In fifth-century Athens scholars estimate that one out of every four persons was a slave. Some were war captives and others were children of slaves, but most came from outside Greece through slave dealers. No large collections of slaves were used on agricultural estates. Small landowners might own one or more slaves, who worked in the fields alongside their masters. Those who owned many slaves—one rich Athenian owned a thousand—hired them out to private individuals or to the state, where they worked alongside Athenian citizens and received comparable wages.

Other slaves were taught a trade and set up in business. They were allowed to keep one-sixth of their wages, and many of them were able to purchase their freedom. Although a very few voices argued that slavery was contrary to nature and that all people were equal, the Greek world as a whole agreed with Aristotle that some people—non-Greeks in particular—were incapable of full human reason, and so they were by nature of inferior status and likely in need of the guidance of a master.

Athenian Imperialism

The Greek victory over Persia had been made possible by a temporary cooperation of the leading Greek city-states, but that unity quickly dissolved after the war when Sparta, envious of Athenian naval superiority and fearful of helot rebellion at home, recalled its troops and resumed its policy of isolation. Because the Persians still ruled the Ionian cities and another invasion of Greece seemed possible, Athens in 478 B.C.E. invited the city-states of the Aegean to join them in forming a defensive alliance called the Delian League. The small island of Delos, sacred to the Ionian Greeks, was chosen to be the league's headquarters and the

Document　Aristophanes on the Shortcomings of Athenian Democracy

In *The Frogs*, the comic dramatist Aristophanes (445–385 B.C.E.) exhorts the Athenians to elect better-quality leaders.

[The leader of the chorus comes forward and addresses the audience.]

We chorus folk two privileges prize:
To amuse you, citizens, and to advise.
So, mid the fun that marks this sacred day,
We'll put on serious looks, and say our say. . . .
But if we choose to strut and put on airs
While Athens founders in a sea of cares,
In days to come, when history is penned,
They'll say we must have gone clean round the
*　bend. . . .*
I'll tell you what I think about the way
This city treats her soundest men today:
By a coincidence more sad than funny,
It's very like the way we treat our money.
The noble silver drachma, that of old
We were so proud of, and the recent gold,
Coins that rang true, clean-stamped and worth
*　their weight*
Throughout the world, have ceased to circulate.
Instead, the purses of Athenian shoppers
Are full of shoddy silver-plated coppers.
Just so, when men are needed by the nation,
The best have been withdrawn from circulation.
Men of good birth and breeding, men of parts,
Well schooled in wrestling and in gentler arts,

These we abuse, and trust instead to knaves,
Newcomers, aliens, copper-pated slaves,
All rascals—honestly, what men to choose!
There was a time when you'd have scorned to use
Men so debased, so far beyond the pale,
Even as scapegoats to be dragged from jail
And flogged to death outside the city gate.
My foolish friends, change now, it's not too late!
Try the good ones again: if they succeed,
You will have proved that you have sense indeed.

Questions to Consider

1. What do you think the reaction of the Athenian theatergoers might have been to this sort of criticism?
2. What elements of Aristophanes' criticism of Athens' situation seem timeless? In what ways could a modern day satirist get by with making the same remarks?
3. Aristophanes complains that the Athens of his time is not as good as the "good old days." Are you able to understand why Aristophanes might make that remark from the section given above, and the fact that he lived and wrote during the Peloponnesian War?

From Aristophanes, *The Frogs and Other Plays*, trans. David Barrett (Baltimore: Penguin, 1964), pp. 181–183.

location of the league treasury. To maintain a 200-ship navy that would drive the Persians out and then police the seas, each state was assessed an annual payment of either ships or money, in proportion to its wealth, to the league treasury. From the beginning, Athens dominated the league. Since almost all of the 173 member states paid their assessments in money, which Athens was eager to collect, the Athenians furnished the necessary ships by building them to Athenian specifications in Athenian harbors, with cash collected from their allies.

By 468 B.C.E., after the Ionian cities had been set free and the Persian fleet had been destroyed, various league members thought it unnecessary to continue league membership. In putting down all attempts to withdraw from the league, the Athenians were motivated to some extent by the fear that a Persian danger still existed but mainly by the desire to maintain and protect the large free trade area necessary for Greek—and especially Athenian—commerce and industry. The treasury of the league was moved from Delos and incorporated into that of Athens—further indication to the league's members that Athens was in total control. The Athenians created an empire because they dared not disband the Delian League and because the league was very beneficial to a vibrant Athenian economy. By aiding in the suppression of local aristocratic factions within its subject states and at times imposing democratic governments on the allied states, Athens both eased the task of controlling its empire and emerged as the leader of a union of "democratic" states subject to Athenian control.

To many Greeks—above all to the Spartans and their allies—Athens had become an autocratic and arrogant state interested only in extending its own authority. Athens' leaders, however, justified Athenian **imperialism** on the grounds that it brought freedom, security, and prosperity to the states that recognized Athenian leadership.

The Peloponnesian War

In 431 B.C.E. the Peloponnesian War broke out between the Spartan League and the Athenian Empire. Although commercial rivalry between Athens and Sparta's major ally, Corinth, was an important factor, the conflict is a classic example of how fear of an enemy's growing power can generate a war unwanted by either side. Several incidents served to ignite the underlying tension, and Sparta finally felt it unavoidable to declare war on the Athenians, whom they considered to be the aggressors.

Sparta's hope for victory lay in its army's ability to lay siege to Athens and destroy the crops in the Athenian countryside. Pericles, for his part, relied on Athens's unrivaled navy to import sufficient food and to harass its enemies' coasts.

But Pericles' careful plans to defeat the Spartans were upset by an unexpected turn of events. In the second year of the war a plague, probably an outbreak of **typhus,** killed a third of the Athenian population, including Pericles himself. His death was a great blow to Athens, for leadership of the government passed to leaders of lesser vision and talent.

Eight more years of indecisive warfare ended in 421 B.C.E. with agreement on a compromise peace treaty. During the succeeding period Athenian imperialism was revealed in its worst form through the actions of Pericles' less able successors. In 416 B.C.E. an expedition embarked for Melos (MEE-los), a neutral Aegean island, to force it to join the Athenian Empire. When the Melians refused to join the Empire and argued that they preferred merely to be left alone, the Athenians executed all the men of military age and sold the women and children into slavery.

The war resumed in 415 B.C.E. with an Athenian expedition against Syracuse, the major Greek state in Sicily. The campaign was hastily put together and badly planned, with complete disaster as a result.

Acting on the invitation of states that feared Syracusan expansion, the Athenians hoped to add Sicily to their empire and so become powerful enough to control nearly the entire Mediterranean. But bad luck and incompetent leadership resulted in the destruction of two Athenian fleets and a large Athenian army by the Syracusans, who were also supported by Sparta. The war dragged on until 404 B.C.E., when Athens surrendered after its last fleet was destroyed by a Spartan fleet, which was built with money received from Persia in exchange for possession of the Greek cities in Ionia. At home, Athens had been weakened by the plots and schemes of oligarchic politicians to whom Sparta now turned over the government. The once powerful city-state was stripped of its empire, its fleet, the defense walls that led to the port, and its army and navy.

Aftermath of the War

Anarchy and depression were the political and economic legacies of the Peloponnesian War. Having ended the threat of Athenian domination of Greece, the Spartans substituted their own form of rule that made Athenian imperialism seem mild in comparison. Everywhere, democracies were replaced by oligarchies supported by Spartan troops. The bloody regimes of these unimaginative oligarchs soon led to successful democratic revolutions at Athens and elsewhere. As one of their generals admitted, the Spartans did not know how to govern free people. Incessant warfare between city-states involved in a bewildering series of shifting alliances became typical of Greece in the fourth century B.C.E. Some alliances were even financed by Persia, which wanted to keep the Greek states disunited and weak.

Political instability in turn contributed to the economic and social problems that plagued Greece during this period. Commerce and industry lagged, and the unemployed who did not go abroad as soldiers of fortune supported authoritarian leaders and their radical schemes for redistribution of wealth. The wealthy, for their part, became increasingly reactionary and uncompromising. Many intellectuals and philosophers—including Plato and Aristotle—lost faith in democracy and joined with the wealthy in looking for an inspirational leader who would bring order and security to Greece. They found him, finally, in the person of the king of Macedonia.

imperialism—The policy of a government to build and widen its authority by controlling other states or regions through military, political, and economic domination.

typhus—A disease characterized by exhaustion, fever, and the eruption of reddish spots on the body. Probably spread by a microorganism carried by lice and fleas.

The Macedonian Unification of Greece

To the north of Greece was Macedonia (ma-si-DOH-ni-ah), a region inhabited by people of the same

Forensic facial reconstruction of Philip II, father of Alexander the Great, based on remains of his skull found in his tomb in Macedonia. The king had suffered an arrow wound to the eye during battle.

After unifying all of his home country—including a number of Greek colonies that had been established along the Macedonian coast during the earlier centuries of Macedonia's weakness—Philip turned to the Greek city-states, whose wars afforded him the opportunity first to participate through intervention and then to dominate by military superiority. Demosthenes (de-MOS-the-neez), a prominent Athenian orator and an advocate of democracy, warned constantly of the threat he believed Philip to be to Greek freedom, and urged the Athenians and other Greeks to stop the king's expansion before it was too late. Ultimately, Athens and Thebes did attempt to stop Philip's advance, but their combined forces were shattered at Chaeronea (KAY-ro-NEE-yah) in 338 B.C.E. Philip then forced the Greeks to form a league in which each state, while retaining self-government, swore to make peace and to furnish Philip with men and supplies for a campaign against Persia. Two years later, before setting out for Asia Minor, Philip was assassinated by a Macedonian noble, leaving the war against Persia as a legacy for his gifted son Alexander.

With the Macedonian victory in 338 B.C.E. and the formation of the league of Greek states firmly under the control of King Philip, the warfare between Greek states that had been almost constant for more than one hundred years came to an end. But one of the costs of this peace was the independence and self-government so prized by Greek poleis. With the Macedonian victory came changes not only in the political fabric of traditional Greek life, but cultural adaptations so significant that many scholars detect in them the beginnings of a new political and cultural order in the Mediterranean world.

descent as the Greeks in the south who spoke a Greek dialect. But the Greeks considered the Macedonians backward and almost barbaric. No city-states had ever developed in Macedonia, and the land continued to be ruled by kings who were often assassinated by their own nobles if they attempted to assert too much power. But in the fourth century Macedonia emerged as a centralized, powerful state under a young and brilliant King Philip II (359–336 B.C.E.), who created the most formidable Greek army yet known by joining the well-trained Macedonian cavalry of nobles with the hoplite infantry used by the Greeks. When he was a youth, Philip had been held as a hostage at Thebes, where he acquired an appreciation of Greek culture, an understanding of Greek political weaknesses, and a desire to win for Macedonia a place of honor and power in the Greek world.

THE GREEK CULTURAL ACHIEVEMENT

■ *How did the cultural achievements of the Greeks have an impact on Western civilization and other succeeding world cultures?*

The Greeks were the first to formulate many of the Western world's fundamental concepts in politics, philosophy, science, and art. How was it that a relatively small number of people could leave such a great legacy to later civilizations? The definitive answer may always escape students, but a good part of the explanation might be found in environmental and social factors.

Unlike the older Near Eastern monarchies, the polis was not governed by a "divine" ruler, nor were the thoughts and activities of its citizens restricted by

Classical Greek Literature and Culture

c. 800 B.C.E.	Homer, *The Iliad*
c. 700–480 B.C.E.	Archaic period of Greek art
c. 700 B.C.E.	Hesiod, *Works and Days*
c. 600 B.C.E.	Thales of Miletus, "father of philosophy"
525–456 B.C.E.	Aeschylus, *Oresteia*
c. 496–406 B.C.E.	Sophocles, *Oedipus*
c. 484–c. 425 B.C.E.	Herodotus, "father of history"
c. 480–406 B.C.E.	Euripides, Athenian tragedian
c. 470–399 B.C.E.	Socrates' quest for truth
460–400 B.C.E.	Thucydides, scientific historian
c. 445–385 B.C.E.	Aristophanes, *The Frogs*
427–347 B.C.E.	Plato, *Republic*
c. 420 B.C.E.	Hippocrates' medical school
384–322 B.C.E.	Aristotle's Lyceum

powerful priesthoods. Many Greeks, and most notably the Athenians, were fond of good, wide-ranging conversation and loved debate and argument. The Greeks were religious people, but in most regards they were not overpowered by their gods and regulated by their priests. Their most creative thinkers believed that most significant questions about the world and their place within it could be answered through human resourcefulness and speculation.

The Greek Character

The Greeks felt a need to discover order and meaning both in nature and in human life. This outlook produced exceptional results in science, philosophy, and the arts. As early as the poet Hesiod (c. 700 B.C.E.), the Greeks stressed the virtue of *sophrosyne* (soh-froh-SEE-nay), moderation and self-control, as the key to happiness and fulfillment in life. Working against this virtue was *hubris*, meaning pride, arrogance, and unbridled ambition. The result of human excess and the basic cause of personal misfortune and social injustice, hubris always inspired *nemesis*, or retribution. According to the Greeks, an unavoidable law would cause the downfall or disgrace of anyone guilty of hubris. The

Athenian dramatists emphasized this theme in their tragedies, and Herodotus attributed the Persian defeat by the Greeks to Xerxes' overpowering pride.

The Greeks had all the usual human frailties and failings—at times they were irrational, vindictive, and cruel. But at their best they were guided by the ideals that are described in their intellectual and artistic legacy. The philosopher Protagoras (proh-TA-goh-rahs) is credited with the statement, "Man is the measure of all things"—a statement that typifies the fundamental humanistic character of Greek thought and art.

Greek Religion

Early Greek religion, like almost all religious expressions of early civilizations, abounded in gods and goddesses who personified the forces of nature. Zeus, sky-god and wielder of thunderbolts, ruled the world from Mount Olympus with the aid of lesser deities, many of whom were his children. His power was limited only by the mysterious decrees of Fate. These gods and goddesses as described by Homer act like humans—capable of evil deeds, favoritism, and jealousy, differing from ordinary people only in their immortality. Zeus was often the unknowing victim of the plots of his wife, Hera, and other deities, and he asserted his authority through threats of violence. Hades, the place of the dead, was a subterranean land of dust and darkness, and Achilles, as Homer tells us in the *Odyssey,* would prefer to be a slave on earth than a king in Hades.

By the time of Hesiod, a more sophisticated religious interpretation had changed the vengeful and unpredictable gods of Homer into more rational dispensers of justice who rewarded the good and punished the wicked. Zeus's stature was increased when he was newly identified as the source of Fate, which was no longer considered a separate mysterious power. And from the famous **oracle** at Delphi the voice of Zeus's son Apollo urged all Greeks to follow the ideal of moderation: "Nothing in excess" and "Know yourself."

A century after Hesiod, the Orphic and Eleusinian (el-eu-SI-ni-uhn) mystery cults emerged as a type of Greek higher religion. Their initiates *(mystae)* were promised salvation in an afterlife of bliss in Elysium,

---

oracle—In ancient Greece, a divine message made by a god through a priest or priestess, or even through the rustling of wind through trees. Oracles were usually delivered in answer to an inquiry from an individual or polis, and the response was typically given in a form that was open to several interpretations. At Delphi, the oracle sometimes refers to the priestess who delivered the god's message.

formerly the home after death of a few heroes only. The basis of the Orphic cult was an old myth about Dionysus, a son of Zeus, who was killed and eaten by the evil Titans before Zeus arrived on the scene and burned them to ashes with his lightning bolts. Orpheus, a legendary figure, taught that Zeus then created man from the Titans' ashes. Human nature, therefore, is composed of two distinct and opposing elements: the evil Titanic element (the body) and the divine Dionysian element (the soul). Death, which frees the divine soul from the evil body, is therefore to be welcomed.

Early Greek Philosophy

What the Greeks were the first to call *philosophy* ("love of wisdom") arose from their curiosity about nature. The early Greek philosophers were called *physikoi* ("physicists") because their main interest was the investigation of the physical world. ("It is according to their wonder," wrote Aristotle, "that men begin to philosophize, pursuing science in order to know.") Later, and primarily due to the influence of Socrates, the chief concern of philosophy was not natural science but *ethics*—how people ought to act in light of moral principles.

The Mesopotamians, as noted in Chapter 1, were skilled observers of astronomical phenomena, which, like the early Greeks, they attributed to the action of the gods. But early Greek philosophers, beginning with Thales of Miletus around 600 B.C.E., changed the course of human knowledge by insisting that the phenomena of the universe could be explained by natural rather than supernatural causes. This rejection of mythological explanations led the Greeks to emphasize the use of human reason to explain the world around them.

Called the "father of philosophy," Thales speculated about the nature of the basic substance of which everything in the universe is composed. He concluded that it was water, which exists in different states and is indispensable to the maintenance and growth of organisms. Thales's successors in Ionia proposed elements other than water as this primal substance in the universe. One called it the "boundless," apparently a general concept for matter; another proposed "air," out of which all things come by a process of "rarefying and condensing"; a third asserted that fire was the "most mobile, most transformable, most active, most life-giving" element. This search for a material substance as the first principle or cause of all things culminated two centuries after Thales in the atomic theory of Democritus (de-MO-kri-tus). To Democritus (c. 460–370 B.C.E.), reality was the mechanical motion of indivisible particles, which differed in shape, size, position, and arrangement but not in quality. Moving about continuously, these particles combined to create objects.

While these and other early Greek philosophers were proposing some form of matter as the basic element in nature, Pythagoras of Samos (c. 582–500 B.C.E.) countered with the profoundly significant idea that the "nature of things" was something nonmaterial: numbers. By experimenting with a vibrating chord, Pythagoras discovered that musical harmony is based on arithmetical proportions, and he intuitively concluded that the universe was constructed of numbers and their relationships. His mystical, nonmaterial interpretation of nature, together with his belief that the human body was distinct from the soul, greatly influenced the thinking of Plato.

An important result of early Greek philosophical speculation was the further questioning of conventional beliefs and traditions. In religion, for example, Anaximander argued that thunder and lightning were caused by blasts of wind and not by Zeus's thunderbolts. Xenophanes (ze-NO-fah-neez) went on to ridicule the traditional view of the gods: "If oxen and lions had hands, . . . they would make portraits and statues of their gods in their own image."

The eroding of traditional beliefs was intensified during the last half of the fifth century B.C.E. by the activity of professional teachers, called Sophists ("intellectuals"). They taught a variety of subjects—the nucleus of our present arts and sciences—that they claimed would lead to material success. The most popular subjects they taught were methods of persuasion and successful argumentation; some even claimed to be able to teach virtue and wisdom to students who paid for their knowledge. The Sophists tried to put all conventional beliefs to the test of rational criticism and subjected human beliefs, customs, and even laws to rational analysis. Some even concluded that truth itself was relative, having no firm existence other than in the decisions and institutions of society. Such speculation questioned the existence of fixed universal standards to guide human actions.

The Contribution of Socrates

A contemporary of the early Sophists but opposed to many of their conclusions was the Athenian Socrates (SO-kra-teez). Like the Sophists, Socrates (c. 470–399 B.C.E.) turned from concern with the gods to human affairs. But unlike them, Socrates believed that by asking meaningful questions and subjecting the answers to logical analysis, agreement could be reached about ethical standards and rules of conduct in human affairs. And so he would question his fellow citizens who possessed a certain skill or particular talent in hopes of learning more about the principles that determine human behavior. He found that his fellow citizens possessed no such knowledge. Instead, he found that he was accused of undermining the institutions and values of the city-state through his constant questioning of socially accepted customs and institutions. His dislike of democracy, which he believed to be a government in which important decisions were usually made by badly informed or even totally ignorant participants, earned him the hostility of most of his fellow citizens. In spite of the growing suspicion that he was a subversive, he continued to emphasize his own individualism and his belief that the pursuit of philosophy was the best way to improve the soul and to assert that he was an ignorant man in search of knowledge, rather than a teacher of others.

In time Socrates' quest for truth led to conflict with the state. In 399 B.C.E. the Athenians, unnerved by their defeat in the Peloponnesian War and concerned about subversion from within, put Socrates on trial for introducing new gods into Athens and corrupting the youth. He was found guilty and was condemned to death. Although he was given a chance to escape that fate, he refused to do so, choosing instead to observe the polis's laws, but still retaining the right to question and analyze them.

Plato and His Theory of Ideas

After Socrates' death, philosophical leadership passed to his most famous student, Plato (427–347 B.C.E.). Like Socrates, Plato believed that truth exists, but only in the realm of thought, the spiritual world of ideas or forms. Such universal truths as beauty, good, and justice exist apart from the material world, and the beauty, good, and justice encountered in the world of the senses are only imperfect reflections of eternal and changeless ideas. The task for humans is to come to know the true reality—the eternal ideas—behind these imperfect reflections. Only the soul and the "soul's pilot," reason, can accomplish this goal, for the human soul is spiritual and immortal, and in its original state it existed beyond the "heavens" where ultimate truth also is found.

Disillusioned with the democracy that had led Athens to ruin in the Peloponnesian War and that had condemned Socrates to death, Plato put forward his concept of an ideal state in the *Republic*, the first systematic work on political science. The state's basic function, founded on the idea of justice, was the satisfaction of the common good. Plato described a kind of ideal polis in which the state regulated every aspect of life, including thought. Accordingly, poets and forms of

music considered unworthy were prohibited. Private property was abolished on the grounds that it bred selfishness. Plato believed there was no essential difference between men and women; therefore, women received the same education and held the same occupations as men, including military training. Individuals belonged to one of three classes and found happiness only through their contribution to the community: workers by producing the necessities of life, warriors by guarding the state, and philosophers by ruling in the best interests of all the people.

Plato founded the Academy in Athens, the famous school that existed from about 388 B.C.E. until 529 C.E., when it was closed by the Christian emperor Justinian. Here Plato taught and encouraged his students, whom he expected to become the intellectual elite who would go on to reform society.

Aristotle, the Encyclopedic Philosopher

Plato's greatest pupil was Aristotle (384–322 B.C.E.), who set up his own school, the Lyceum (lai-SEE-um), at Athens. Reacting against the otherworldly directions of Plato's thought, Aristotle insisted that ideas have no separate existence apart from the material world—knowledge of universal ideas is the result of the painstaking collection and organization of particular facts. Aristotle's Lyceum, accordingly, became a center for the analysis of data from many branches of learning.

DOCUMENT

Aristotle on Slavery

Aristotle's works remain among the most influential contributions to Western thought. Much of his speculation deals with what he called the "philosophy of human affairs," whose object is the acquisition and maintenance of human happiness. Two kinds of virtue *(arête)*, intellectual and moral, which produce two types of happiness, are described in the *Ethics*. Intellectual virtue is the product of reason, and only such people as philosophers and scientists ever attain it. Much more important for the good of society is moral virtue—virtues of character, such as justice, bravery, and temperance—which is the product less of reason than of habit and thus can be acquired by all. In this connection Aristotle introduced his "doctrine of the mean" as a guide for good conduct. He considered all moral virtues to be means between extremes; courage, for example, is the mean between cowardice and rashness. In the *Politics* Aristotle viewed the state as necessary "for the sake of the good life," because its laws and educational system provide the most effective training needed for the attainment of moral virtue and, as a result of that moral virtue—happiness. To Aristotle, the viewpoint that the state stands in opposition to the individual would not be valid.

There have probably been few geniuses whose interests were as widespread as Aristotle's. He investigated such diverse fields as biology (his minute observations include the life cycle of the gnat), mathematics, astronomy, physics, literary criticism (the concept of *catharsis*—art as a release of emotion), rhetoric, logic (deductive and inductive), politics (he analyzed 158 Greek and foreign constitutions), ethics, and metaphysics. His knowledge was so encyclopedic that there is hardly a college course today that does not take note of what Aristotle had to say on the subject. Although his works on natural science are now mostly historical curiosities, they held a place of undisputed authority until the scientific revolution of the sixteenth and seventeenth centuries. But in no important sense are his humanistic studies, such as the *Ethics* and the *Politics*, out of date.

Medicine

Superstitions about the human body held back the development of medical science until 420 B.C.E., when Hippocrates (hip-PO-kra-teez), the "father of medicine," founded a school in which he emphasized the value of observation and the careful interpretation of symptoms. Such modern medical terms as *crisis*, *acute*, and *chronic* were first used by Hippocrates. He was firmly convinced that disease resulted from natural, not supernatural, causes. The Hippocratic school also gave medicine a sense of service to humanity that it has never lost. All members took the famous Hippocratic Oath, still in use today.

Despite using the empirical approach, the Hippocratic school adopted the theory that the body contained four liquids or *humors*—blood, phlegm, black bile, and yellow bile—whose proper balance was the basis of health. This popular doctrine was to impede medical progress in Europe until the seventeenth century.

The Writing of History

If history is defined as an honest attempt to find out what happened and then to explain why it happened, Herodotus (he-RO-doh-tuhs) of Halicarnassus (c. 484–c. 425 B.C.E.) deserves to be called the founder of that discipline. In his well-researched and highly entertaining history of the Persian Wars, he identified the clash of two distinct civilizations, the Greek and the Near Eastern. His portrayal of both the

DOCUMENT
Herodotus, *Histories*

Greeks and the Persians was in most cases impartial, but his fondness for a good story often led him to include tall tales in his work. As he stated more than once, "My duty is to report what has been said, but I do not have to believe it."

The first truly scientific historian was Thucydides (460–400 B.C.E.), who wrote a notably objective account of the Peloponnesian War. Although Thucydides was a contemporary of the events and a loyal Athenian, a reader can scarcely detect whether he favored Athens or Sparta. Thucydides believed that his history would become a useful tool for those who desire a clear picture of what has happened and, human nature being as it is, what is likely to be repeated in the future. His belief was based on his remarkable ability to analyze and explain human behavior and the nature of politics.

DOCUMENT
Thucydides on Athens

Greek Poetry and Drama

Greek literary periods can be classified according to the dominant poetic forms that reflect particular stages of the culture's development. First came the time of great epic poems, followed by periods in which lyric poetry and then drama flourished.

Sometime during the eighth century B.C.E. in Ionia, the *Iliad* and the *Odyssey*, the two great epics attributed to Homer, were set down in their present form. The *Iliad*, describing the clash of arms between the Greeks and Trojans, glorifies heroic bravery and physical strength against a background of divine intervention in human affairs. The *Odyssey*, relating the adventure-filled wanderings of Odysseus on his return to Greece after Troy's fall, places less stress on divine intervention and more on the cool resourcefulness of the hero in escaping from danger and in regaining his kingdom. These stirring epics have provided inspiration and source material for many generations of poets.

As Greek society continued to develop and seek new varieties of artistic expression, a new type of poetry, written to be sung to the accompaniment of a small stringed instrument called a lyre, became popular among the Ionian Greeks. Unlike Homer, authors of this lyric poetry sang not of legendary events but of present delights and sorrows.

DOCUMENT
Greek Poetry

Drama (also in verse) developed from the religious rites of Dionysus (son of Zeus from an affair with the daughter of the king of Tyre) in which a large chorus and its leader sang and danced. The legendary Thespis, supposedly a contemporary of Solon, added an actor called the "answerer" (*hypocrites*, the origin of our word *hypocrite*) to converse with the chorus and its leader. This innovation made dramatic dialogue possible. By

---

catharsis—A word which means "cleansing" in Greek, but in its application to ancient Greek tragedy, its meaning is more specifically "a purging of pity and fear"—the desired effect of the performance on the audience.

The World According to Herodotus, c. 450 B.C.E.

This map depicts the known world at the time of the Greek historian Herodotus, who lived and worked around 450–425 B.C.E. The map is a modern rendition of what we know Herodotus thought to be the world, as described in his writings, the *Histories*. The *Histories* was written to describe the events and circumstances that led the Greeks and the Persians to engage in war—a war that Herodotus believed changed the direction of human history. To understand why these two great powers came into conflict, the historian believed he would have to examine the origins, geographical setting, culture, and traditions of the whole empire of the Persians, as well as the background of the Greek city-states. The *Histories* became not just a listing of chronological events but an exploration of geography, sociology, and anthropology as well.

We are certain that Herodotus himself traveled extensively throughout his world in order to learn firsthand of the people he described. Most of his geographical knowledge came from his own observations or from interviews with the people he met. He seems to have believed that the earth was a flat disk, although he must have been familiar with contemporary theories that the world might be a sphere. He differed from most of his contemporaries in not picturing Europe, Africa (which he called Libya), and Asia as approximately the same size. He described Europe as being as long as both Asia and Africa put together. Yet Herodotus did not travel to the farthest reaches of the continent but relied on accounts of others; he knew nothing of the existence of Britain or Scandinavia, for example, and he did not know if Europe was surrounded by water to the west or north. His knowledge of Asia was limited to the lands of the Persian Empire. He knew that the Caspian Sea was an inland sea and not, as most of his contemporaries believed, a sea that emptied into the band of ocean that encircled the earth. He also knew that Africa was surrounded by water—a fact that the geographer Ptolemy missed 500 years later.

Questions to Consider

1. How might you account for some of the major errors in Herodotus's geographical knowledge?
2. Are there any features of the map which you find to be remarkably accurate for Herodotus's time?
3. Do you see any significance in the proportions of the map, and what region is placed in the center?

the fifth century B.C.E. in Athens, two distinct forms, tragedy and comedy, had evolved. Borrowing from the old familiar legends of gods and heroes for their plots, the tragedians reinterpreted them from the point of view of the values and problems of their own times.

In reworking the old legends of the heroic age, Aeschylus (ES-kuh-luhs; 525–456 B.C.E.) attempted to present the new values being considered regarding Greek religion, first expressed in Hesiod's work, by showing how following the old unsophisticated beliefs leads to suffering. In his trilogy, the *Oresteia*, for example, he concerned himself with hubris as applied to the murder of the hero Agamemnon by his queen following his return from the Trojan War. Aeschylus then proceeded to work out its effects—one murder after another murder until people, through suffering, learn to substitute the moral law of Zeus for the primitive law of the blood feud.

A generation later, Sophocles (c. 496–406 B.C.E.) continued to explore the themes of divine justice, morality, and ethics, while concentrating, in addition, on character development and psychological themes. Euripides (eu-RI-pi-deez; c. 480–406 B.C.E.), the last of the great Athenian tragedians, reflects the rationalism and critical spirit of the late fifth century B.C.E. His plays concentrate more on the personalities of his characters and their interesting behavior, rather than on the overriding power of fate or the gods.

Greek comedies were full of satire and scathing criticism of contemporary prominent citizens. There were no libel laws in Athens, and Aristophanes (a-ri-STO-fah-neez; c. 445–385 B.C.E.), the famous comic-dramatist and a conservative in outlook, brilliantly satirized Athenian democracy as a mob led by demagogues, the Sophists (among whom he included Socrates) as subversive, and Euripides as an opponent of civic spirit and traditional values.

Greek Architecture

During the formative, archaic period of Greek art (c. 700–480 B.C.E.), architecture flourished in Ionia, Greece, and the Greek colonies in Sicily and southern

In the Parthenon, great care was taken to design a perfect building, both structurally and visually. The topics of the Doric columns lean toward the center, and the columns are more widely spaced in the middle of each row than at the ends. All these refinements create an illusion of perfect regularity that would be lacking if the parts were actually regular. Sculpture adorned the triangular gables and part of the frieze just below the gables; another sculptured frieze ran around the walls inside the colonnade. The whole building was once painted in bright colors.

Italy. Reflecting the prosperity produced by colonization, large stone temples were constructed. Their form may have developed from wooden structures that had been influenced by the remains of Mycenaean palaces, and perhaps by Egyptian temples or the religious architecture of the Near East.

The classical phase of Greek architecture reached its zenith in Athens during the second half of the fifth century B.C.E. The Parthenon, the Erechtheum (e-rek-THEE-um), and the other temples on the Acropolis in Athens exhibit the highly developed features that make Greek structures so pleasing to the eye. All relationships, such as column spacing and height and the slight curvature of floor and roof lines, were calculated and executed with remarkable precision to achieve the illusion of a perfect balance, both structurally and visually. The three orders, or styles, usually identified by the characteristics of the columns, were the **Doric,** which was used in the Parthenon; the **Ionic,** seen in the Erechtheum; and the later and more ornate **Corinthian.**

Erectheion, Athens

Greek temples afford an interesting comparison with those of Egypt. Egyptian temples were enclosed by walls and only priests and royalty could enter the inner rooms, but the Greek temple was open, with a colonnade porch and an inside room containing a statue of the god or goddess. Animal sacrifice and ritual took place outside the temple, where the sacrificial altar was placed.

Other types of buildings, notably the theaters, stadia, and gymnasia, also express the Greek spirit and way of life. In the open-air theaters, the circular shape of the spectators' sections and the plan of the orchestra section set a style that has survived to the present day.

Greek Sculpture and Pottery

Greek sculpture is usually described as having passed through three stages of development: the archaic, the classical, and the Hellenistic periods. Greek sculpture of the archaic period, although crude in its representation of human anatomy, displays the freshness and liveliness of youth. Influenced clearly by Egyptian models, the statues of nude youths and draped maidens usually stand stiffly with clenched fists and with one foot thrust awkwardly forward. The fixed smile and formalized treatment of hair and drapery also reveal the sculptors' struggle to master the technique of their art.

The mastery of technique by 480 B.C.E. began the classical period of fifth-century Greek sculpture, whose principles of harmony and proportion shaped the development of art in the West for centuries after the Greeks. Sculpture from this period displays both the end of technical immaturity and the beginning of idealization of the human form, which reached its culmination in the dignity and poise of Phidias's (FI-dee-uhs) figures in the continuous **frieze** and **pediments** of the Parthenon. Carved with restraint and proportion, the frieze represents the citizens of Athens participating in a procession in honor of their patron goddess, Athena, which took place every four years.

The more relaxed nature of fourth-century B.C.E. Greek sculpture, while still considered classical, lacks some of the grandeur and dignity of fifth-century art. Charm, grace, and individuality characterize the work of Praxiteles (prax-IT-el-eez), the most famous sculptor of the century. These qualities can be seen in his flowing statues of the god Hermes holding the young Dionysus and of Aphrodite stepping into her bath.

The making of pottery, the oldest Greek art, started at the beginning of the Greek Middle Age (c. 1150 B.C.E.) with crude imitations of late Mycenaean forms. Soon the old Mycenaean patterns were replaced by abstract geometrical designs. With the coming of the archaic period came paintings of scenes from mythology and daily life. We are able to form an impression of what Greek painting, now lost, must have been like from surviving Greek pottery and mosaics. The buildings and sculpture we observe today as stark white marble creations were in all likelihood lavishly and brightly painted in the colors the Greeks obviously loved.

THE HELLENISTIC AGE, 336–30 B.C.E.

■ *How did the Hellenistic Age differ from the Greek civilization that preceded it?*

The Hellenistic Age is the three-century period beginning with the career of Alexander the Great to the rise

---

Doric—Specific form of the capital (or crown) of a Greek column. A capital in the Doric order is squat and simple without elaborate decoration and originated in wooden temples.

Ionic—Specific form of the capital (or crown) of a Greek column. A capital of the Ionic order is usually decorated with scrolls (or volutes).

Corinthian—Specific form of the capital (or crown) of a Greek column. Corinthian capitals are the most highly decorated of the three orders of Greek columns, with carved acanthus leaves and scrolls.

---

frieze—In Greek architecture, a long, narrow, horizontal panel often decorated with relief sculpture and placed around the walls of a room or a temple.

pediment—The most dominant feature of the front of a Greek temple. A triangular construction that sits on top of the temple's facade.

Alexander the Great

When Philip of Macedonia was assassinated in 336 B.C.E., his authority was claimed by his 20-year-old son, Alexander. Alexander proved himself a remarkably gifted individual from the very beginning of his reign by gaining the support of the Macedonian nobles, even though some of them suspected the young man of being involved in Philip's murder. Alexander persuaded his father's old generals and comrades to swear their loyalty to him and proceeded to demand the loyalty of the Greek League, which had been founded by his father. When the Greek city of Thebes responded to a rumor that Alexander had been killed in battle by rebelling against the Macedonians, the young king marched his army quickly to the south and ruthlessly crushed the city, selling its remaining inhabitants into slavery. The Greeks were horrified at such brutal action, but a lesson was learned, and few states dared consider rebellion in the years ahead.

Alexander is one of history's most remarkable individuals. Of average height and looks for a Macedonian, he nevertheless impressed his contemporaries as a gifted athlete, a charismatic personality, and a natural leader. Both his father, Philip, and his mother, Olympias, a princess from Illyria, were strong influ-

Macedonia and Alexander

359–336 B.C.E.	Reign of Philip II
338 B.C.E.	Philip conquers Greek city-states
336–323 B.C.E.	Reign of Alexander the Great
334 B.C.E.	Alexander invades Persian Empire
331 B.C.E.	Battle at Gaugamela
327 B.C.E.	Alexander enters India
323 B.C.E.	Alexander dies

Alexander the Great and the Hellenistic Age

of Augustus Caesar, the first of the Roman emperors, who completed Rome's domination of the Mediterranean world by adding Greek-ruled Egypt to Rome's empire in 30 B.C.E. The Hellenistic Age, begun by the creation of Alexander the Great's vast conquests, was a period of economic expansion, cosmopolitanism, striking intellectual and artistic achievements, and the wide distribution of Greek culture.

This small but expertly crafted ivory is thought to be a representation of King Philip, his second wife Olympias, and their young son Alexander (the Great). The three figures are probably represented as participants in a religious ritual dedicated to the god Dionysus. The object was found among the royal graves of the Macedonian monarchs in Vergina.

ences on him. Philip earned his son's respect as a king and a general, and Olympias was a forceful woman who wished great things for her son and who constantly assured the boy that his true father was not Philip, but the god Zeus.

DOCUMENT
Plutarch on Alexander the Great

Having been tutored by Aristotle, Alexander was taught the superiority of Greek culture and wished to be the fulfillment of the Greek ideal. Reveling in the heroic deeds of the *Iliad*, which he always kept at his bedside, Alexander saw himself as a new Achilles waging war against barbarians when he planned to complete his father's desire to avenge the Persian attacks on Greece by conquering the Persian Empire. In 334 B.C.E. he set out with an army of 35,000 soldiers recruited from Macedonia and the Greek League. In quick succession he subdued Asia Minor, Syria, and Palestine, defeating the Persians in two great battles. He marched into Egypt, where the Egyptians welcomed him as a deliverer from their Persian masters and recognized him as pharaoh, the living god-king of Egypt.

Greatly impressed with Egypt and its traditions, Alexander wished to spend more time there. But Darius III, the Persian king, was gathering one more massive army to oppose the invader, and Alexander marched into Mesopotamia to meet the Persians for a final battle. In 331 B.C.E., at Gaugamela, near the ancient city of Nineveh, the Macedonians defeated the Persian forces. Darius III was executed by his own relatives as he fled, and Alexander became Great King of the Persian Empire. Alexander led his victorious troops to the ancient Persian capital city of Persepolis (per-SE-poh-lis), but his campaigns did not end there. He wished to command the loyalty of all Persian lands and to extend the great empire to even farther reaches. He led his troops north through Media and Bactria, then south and east into present-day Afghanistan, finally venturing as far east as the rich river valleys of India. There his weary and frightened soldiers, many of whom had been away from home for more than ten years, forced him to turn back.

DOCUMENT
Descriptions of Alexandria, Egypt

In 323 B.C.E. Alexander fell ill with a mysterious fever. Perhaps he had contracted malaria in India; perhaps he fell victim to his accumulated battle wounds;

At the time of his death, Alexander had laid claim to a vast empire. One biographer claims that Alexander was planning more conquests when he recovered from his illness—perhaps north into what is now Russia or along the northern coast of Africa and eventually to Rome.

Document   Arrian: Alexander the Leader

Arrian wrote his account of Alexander's campaigns in the second century C.E., almost 500 years after Alexander's death. Yet we can have great trust in most of his account, since Arrian evidently had access to accounts and diaries contemporary with Alexander. The following is a description of Alexander's inspirational leadership during an extremely difficult crossing of the southern Iranian desert in hopes of returning to Babylon:

The army was crossing a desert of sand; the sun was already blazing down upon them, but they were struggling on under the necessity of reaching water, which was still far away. Alexander, like everyone else, was tormented by thirst, but he was nonetheless marching on foot at the head of his men. It was all he could do to keep going, but he did so, and the result (as always) was that the men were better able to endure their misery when they saw that it was equally shared. As they toiled on, a party of light infantry which had gone off looking for water found some—just a wretched little trickle collected in a shallow gully. They scooped up with difficulty what they could and hurried back, with their priceless treasure, to Alexander; then, just before they reached him, they tipped the water into a helmet and gave it to him. Alexander, with a word of thanks for the gift, took the helmet and gave it full view of his troops, poured the water on the ground. So extraordinary was the effect of this action that the water wasted by Alexander was as good as a drink for every man in the army. I cannot praise this act too highly; it was a proof, if anything was, not only of his power of endurance, but also of his genius for leadership.

Questions to Consider

1. Do you think that this account could be factual, or is it most likely propaganda? Why?
2. How could such an act of wastefulness be an inspiration to an army?
3. Do you think that the myth of Alexander was, and is, perhaps more important than the historical reality of the man? Give several reasons for your answer.

From Arrian, *Anabasis*, 6.26 in A. de Selincourt, *The Campaigns of Alexander* (New York: Penguin Books, 1958).

---

perhaps his years of heavy drinking had taken their toll; perhaps, as rumor had it, he had been slowly poisoned by his enemies in the Macedonian camp. Whatever the case, after a short illness, and without designating an heir to his empire, Alexander died in Babylon at the age of 32.

Alexander the Great is a puzzling figure to modern historians. Some view him as a ruthless conqueror who never lost a battle and a despot who ordered even his fellow Macedonians to prostrate themselves in his presence. Others picture him as a farsighted visionary hoping to unite East and West in one world and seeking the eventual "brotherhood of man" by establishing equality for all individuals through the unity of a common Greek culture.

IMAGE

Mosaic of Alexander the Great

Some of Alexander's military and administrative policies sought to unify the lands he conquered and to promote what he himself called "concord and partnership in the empire" between easterners and westerners. He blended Persians with Greeks and Macedonians in his army and administration; he founded numerous cities—70, according to tradition—in the East and settled many of his followers in them; and he married two oriental princesses and encouraged his officers and men to take foreign wives. Finally, for perhaps egotistical and certainly for political reasons, he ordered the Greek city-states to accord him "divine honors."

Alexander was a remarkable blend of the romantic idealist and the practical realist, contrasting traits that he may have inherited from his parents. His mother, Olympias, who practiced the rites of the cult of Dionysus and claimed to be a descendant of the Greek hero Achilles, instilled in her son the consciousness of a divine mission that drove him onward, even to seeking the end of the earth beyond India. Much like his father, he demonstrated remarkable abilities as military commander, expert diplomat, and able political administrator. Alexander was a self-confident idealist who was excited by challenges, but meeting those challenges forced him to take actions that were practical and pragmatic. For example, he could not merely conquer the Great King of Persia; he had to act as his successor as well. Alexander ruled for only 13 years, but in many ways a large part of the world was never again the same.

The Division of Alexander's Empire

With the Greeks now masters of the ancient Near East, a new and distinctly **cosmopolitan** period in their history and culture began—the Hellenistic ("Greek-like") Age. For several decades following Alexander's sudden death, his generals competed against each other for the spoils of empire. Three major Hellenistic kingdoms emerged and maintained an uneasy balance of power until the Roman conquests of the second and first centuries B.C.E.: Egypt, ruled by Alexander's friend and general Ptolemy (TO-le-mee) and his successors; Asia, comprising most of the remaining provinces of the Persian Empire and held together with great difficulty by the dynasty founded by Seleucus (se-LEU-kus); and Macedonia and Greece, ruled by the descendants of Antigonus (an-TI-go-nuhs) the One-Eyed.

While the Antigonids in Macedonia followed the model of Alexander's father, Philip, in ruling as national kings selected by the army, the Ptolemies ruled Egypt as divine pharaohs, and some of the Seleucids attempted to have themselves recognized as "saviors" and "benefactors" of their subjects. Ptolemaic and Seleucid administrations were centralized in bureaucracies staffed mainly by Greeks, an arrangement that created a vast gulf between rulers and ruled.

Plagued by native revolts, dynastic troubles, and civil war, the Hellenistic kingdoms eventually began to crumble. Macedonia lost effective control of Greece by 250 B.C.E. when Athens asserted its independence and most of the other Greek states resisted Macedonian domination by forming two federal leagues, the Achaean and the Aetolian (a-TOH-li-an). Toward the end of the third century B.C.E. the Romans became involved in the rivalries

of the city-state and Macedonian monarchy and eventually added all Greece and Macedonia into their growing empire.

The eastern reaches of Alexander's empire—Parthia, Bactria, and India—gradually broke out of Seleucid control. Pergamum, in northwestern Asia Minor, renounced its allegiance to the Seleucids and became an independent kingdom famous for its artists and scholars. By 200 B.C.E. the Romans had entered the scene, and by 30 B.C.E. Rome had annexed all but the last remaining Hellenistic state, Egypt; in that very year Cleopatra, the last reigning member of the dynasty founded by Ptolemy, was captured by the Romans and committed suicide.

HELLENISTIC SOCIETY AND CULTURE

■ *What were the results of the expansion of Hellenistic civilization?*

The Hellenistic Age was a time of economic expansion and social change. In the wake of Alexander's conquests, thousands of Greeks moved eastward to begin a new era of Greek colonization, ending the long economic depression that followed the breakup of the Athenian Empire. An economic union of East and West permitted the free flow of trade, and prosperity was stimulated further when Alexander put into circulation huge amounts of Persian gold and silver and introduced a uniform coinage. The result was a much larger and more affluent middle class than had existed previously. The condition of the poor, however, was made worse by rising prices.

By the third century B.C.E. the center of trade had shifted from Greece to the Near East. Largest of the Hellenistic cities, and much larger than any cities in Greece itself, were Antioch, in northern Syria, and Alexandria, in Egypt. The riches of India, Persia, Arabia, and the Fertile Crescent were brought by sea and land to these Mediterranean ports.

Alexandria outdistanced all other Hellenistic cities as a commercial center. Its merchants supplied the ancient world with wheat, linen, papyrus, glass, and jewelry. Boasting a population of nearly a million, the city had a double harbor in which a great lighthouse, judged one of the wonders of the ancient world, rose to a height estimated at 370 feet. Its busy streets were filled with a mixture of peoples—Greeks, Macedonians, Jews, and Egyptians. As in all other Hellenistic cities in the Near East, the privileged

VIDEO
Greek Heritage in Turkey

cosmopolitan—A person or thing that belongs to all the world; free from local or national prejudices or limitations. From Greek *cosmopolites* ("citizen of the world").

Greeks and Macedonians were at the top of the social scale and the mass of native population at the bottom; the large Jewish population lived apart and was allowed a significant degree of self-government. Labor was so cheap that slavery hardly existed in Hellenistic Egypt. As a consequence, worker-organized strikes were frequent.

Hellenistic Philosophy

Developments in philosophical thought reflected the changed conditions of the Hellenistic Age. With a growing sense that individual significance was decreased in the large Hellenistic states, in which the vitality of the polis seemed to give way to a more isolated existence, philosophers concerned themselves less with the reform of society and more with the attainment of happiness for the individual. "There is no point in saving the Greeks" is the way one Hellenistic philosopher summed up the new outlook, quite in contrast to that of Socrates, Plato, and Aristotle. This emphasis on peace of mind for the individual living in an insecure world led to the rise of four principal schools of Hellenistic philosophy, all of which had their beginnings in Athens.

The Skeptics and Cynics reflected most clearly the doubts and misgivings of the times. The Skeptics hoped to achieve freedom from anxiety by denying the possibility of finding truth. The wise, they argued, will suspend judgment and not preach to others because they had learned that sensory experience, the only source of knowledge, is deceptive. They believed that real knowledge was impossible to achieve, and that it was not crucial to achieve it anyway. The Skeptics busied themselves with pointing out the errors they identified in the other opposing schools of philosophy. The Cynics believed that withdrawing from the world was the best way to deal with the miseries life held for humans. They advocated rejection of virtually all social conventions, traditions, and religious values. Cynic philosophers, most notably Diogenes of Sinope (c. 400–325 B.C.E.), wandered from city to city, dressed in rags, begging, and performing lewd acts in public to call attention to his rejection of conformity.

More socially acceptable and popular were the schools of Epicureanism and Stoicism. The Athenian Epicurus (342–270 B.C.E.) taught that happiness could be achieved simply by freeing the body from pain and the mind from fear—particularly the fear of death. To reach this dual goal, people must avoid bodily excesses, including sensual pleasures, and accept the scientific teaching of Democritus that both body and soul are composed of atoms that fall apart at death. Beyond death there is no existence and nothing to fear. Epicurus maintained that the finest pleasures are intellectual and that the gods do not concern themselves with humans, but instead spend their time pursuing true pleasure, like good Epicureans.

The Stoics, followers of Zeno (c. 336–c. 264 B.C.E.), a Semite who settled in Athens, argued in contrast to Epicureanism that the universe is controlled by some power—variously called destiny, reason, natural law, providence, or God—that determines everything that happens. Fortified by this knowledge, wise Stoics conform their will to be in harmony with natural order and "stoically" accept whatever part fortune gives to them in the drama of life. The Epicurean retreated from worldly responsibilities, but the Stoic urged participation. Stoicism's stern sense of duty and belief in the equality of all people under a single ruling force made it particularly attractive to the Roman successors to power in the Hellenistic world conquerors of the ancient world.

Science and Mathematics

The Greek concern for rational, impartial inquiry reached a high level of development in the Hellenistic period, particularly in Alexandria, where the dynasty of the Ptolemies subsidized a great research institute, the Museum, and a library of more than half a million books. Emphasizing specialization and experimentation and enriched by the inheritance of Near Eastern astronomy and mathematics, Greek science in the third century B.C.E. achieved results unmatched until the seventeenth century.

The expansion of geographical knowledge resulting from Alexander's conquests inspired scientists to make more accurate maps and to estimate the size of the earth, which had been identified as a globe through observation of its shadow in a lunar eclipse. Eratosthenes (e-rah-TOS-the-neez), the outstanding geographer of the century, drew parallels of latitude and longitude on his map of the inhabited world and calculated the circumference of the globe (within 1 percent, an error of 195 miles) by measuring the difference in the angles of the noonday sun's shadows at Aswan and Alexandria. In astronomy, Aristarchus (a-ri-STAR-kus) put forward the radical theory that the earth rotates on its axis and moves in an orbit around the sun. Most of his contemporaries, however, held to a belief in the prevailing geocentric theory, which stated that the earth was stationary and the sun revolved around it. Not only was this view supported by the powerful authority of Aristotle, but it also seemed to explain all the known facts of celestial motion. This was particularly true after Hipparchus (hi-PAR-kus) in the next century added the new idea of *epicycles*—each planet revolves in its own small orbit while moving around the earth. Aristarchus's **heliocentric theory** was forgotten until the sixteenth century C.E., when it was revived by Copernicus.

Mathematics also made great advances in the third century B.C.E. Euclid (EU-klid) systematized the theorems of plane and solid geometry, and Archimedes (ar-ke-MEE-deez) of Syracuse, who had studied at Alexandria, calculated the value of *pi*, invented a terminology for expressing numbers up to any magnitude, and established the rudiments of calculus. Archimedes also discovered specific gravity by noticing that he displaced water when submerged in his bath. And, despite his dislike for making practical use of his knowledge, he invented the compound pulley and the windlass—a lifting device consisting of a horizontal cylinder turned by a crank on which a rope or cable is wound.

The Hellenistic Greeks also contributed to the advances in medicine made earlier by Hippocrates and his school. By dissecting bodies of dead criminals, they were able to trace the outlines of the nervous system, to understand the principle of the circulation of the blood, and to ascertain that the brain, not the heart, is the true center of consciousness.

Hellenistic Art and Literature

The large number of new cities that sprang up in Hellenistic times served as a tremendous impetus to new developments and experiments in architecture. These new municipalities benefited from town planning; the streets were laid out on a rectangular grid. The great public buildings were elaborate and highly ornamented; this was an age that preferred the ornate Corinthian column to the simpler Doric and Ionic styles of decoration.

Hellenistic sculptors continued and intensified the realistic, dramatic, and emotional approach that began to appear in late classical sculpture. Supported by rulers and other rich patrons in such affluent cities as Alexandria, Antioch, Rhodes, and Pergamum, they displayed their technical virtuosity by representing violent scenes, writhing forms, and dramatic poses, all

This representation of the goddess of erotic love, Aphrodite (Venus in Latin), being defended by her young son Eros (Cupid) from the advances of the god Pan, was crafted around 100 B.C.E. and is now in the Acropolis Museum in Athens. It is an excellent example of the realism, emotion, and even humor conveyed by much of Hellenistic sculpture.

with a realism that could make stone simulate flesh. Like most postclassical art, little evidence remained of the balance and restraint of classical Greek sculpture. Much of Hellenistic sculpture, with its twisted poses, contorted faces, and swollen muscles, stands in obvious contrast to the works of classical Greece seeking balance, harmony, and restraint.

Literature produced in the Hellenistic Age was generally more narrow and scholarly in its appeal than the earlier literary forms of the classical period. Scholarship flourished, and we are in debt for the

---

heliocentric theory—An astronomical theory, now proven as fact, that the sun resides at the center of the planetary system. *Heliocentric* in Greek literally means "sun centered."

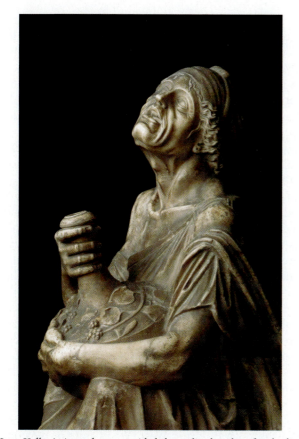

Late Hellenistic sculptors avoided the stylized and perfect bodies preferred by the artists of the classical period and chose instead to portray the realistic and commonplace in their work. This famous sculpture of a drunken old woman shows not only the great skill of the artist, but also the radical shift in artistic themes now more popular and acceptable in the Hellenistic Age.

preservation of much of Greek classical literature to the subsidized scholars who worked at the Library of Alexandria. They composed epics in imitation of Homer (one new feature was romantic love, not found in Homer), long poems on fundamental subjects like the weather, and short, witty epigrams—all in a highly polished style. These sophisticated scholars also invented a new type of romantic, escapist literature: pastoral poetry extolling the unspoiled life and loves of shepherds and their rustic love interests. Some of the best of the new poetry was written at Alexandria in the third century B.C.E. by Theocritus (thee-OH-kra-tus), who also composed very realistic verses.

The Hellenistic Contribution

The greatest contribution of the Hellenistic Age was the diffusion of Greek culture throughout the

ancient East and the newly rising Roman West. In the East, the cities that Alexander and his successors built were the agents for spreading Hellenistic culture from the Aegean Sea to India. Literate Asians learned Greek to facilitate trade and to read Greek literature. In Judea, upper class Jews built Greek theaters and **gymnasia** and adopted Greek speech, dress, and names.

For a time the Seleucid Empire provided the peace and economic stability necessary to ensure the partial Hellenization of a vast area. But with an insufficient number of Greeks to colonize so large an area as the Near East, the Greek cities remained only islands in an Asian ocean. As time passed, this ocean encroached more and more on the Hellenized outposts.

The gradual weakening of the loosely knit Seleucid Empire eventually resulted in the creation of independent kingdoms on the edge of the Greek world. In the middle of the third century, a nomad chieftain founded the kingdom of Parthia, situated between the Seleucid and Bactrian kingdoms. Claiming to be the heirs of the more ancient Persians, the Parthians expanded until 130 B.C.E., when they were able to take Babylonia away from Seleucid control. Although Parthia was essentially a native Iranian state, its inhabitants absorbed some Hellenistic culture. Cut off from Seleucid rule by the Parthian kingdom, Bactria also became independent. Its Greek rulers, descendants of Alexander's veterans, controlled the caravan route to India and issued some of the most beautiful of Greek coins. In 183 B.C.E. the Bactrians crossed into India and conquered the province of Gandhara. One result of the conquest was a strong Greek influence on Indian art (see Chapter 3).

In the history of western European civilization, there are few developments of greater significance than Rome's absorption of Hellenistic Greek culture and its transference of that Greek cultural heritage to later European tradition. The culture of the cosmopolitan Hellenistic Age, drawn mainly from its Greek origins, served as the vehicle through which Greece left its imprint on the Roman world. The process by which the Roman West absorbed the cultural legacy of the Greeks will be described in the next chapter.

---

gymnasia—The plural of gymnasium—an area or a room in which Greeks, usually younger men, came to exercise and converse. From Greek *gymnos* ("naked") and *gymnazein* ("to train").

CONCLUSION

The civilization developed by the ancient Greeks is certainly one of the most outstanding in the history of humanity at any time and at any place on our planet. Those cultures we usually call Western correctly look upon the ancient Greeks as one of the most significant influences in the formation of their cultures. For centuries, these Western cultures considered the Greeks to have been the sole originators of Western civilization, but more recent generations have properly recognized that the Greeks, although highly creative and original, still were influenced by the earlier civilizations of Asia and Egypt. Trade and commerce with these peoples brought knowledge of their skills and past achievements, from metalworking, war, and art to religion. The Greeks did not invent Western civilization in a vacuum.

But the ancient Greeks do deserve great admiration. They developed a culture that was quite different than any previous social achievement. Theirs was a culture that was human-centered; although observant of religion, the Greeks did not believe they were owned by the gods. The Greeks rivaled their own gods in their attempts to gain true knowledge of the secrets of philosophy and science, to produce perfection in art, architecture, and even government. Human self-confidence had never been as high, and the resulting achievements of Greek culture still remain as timeless contributions to human cultures worldwide.

Often it seems the most significant factor explaining the success of a culture contains the seeds of its greatest liability. One might propose that the independence of both individuals and city-states led to outstanding achievements. But that individuality also seems to have made it impossible for the Greeks to unify for any significant length of time or to avoid bitter rivalries and destructive war. In time, the Macedonian king Philip, and later his son Alexander, forced the Greeks to cooperate with the formation of a unified Greece, but much of the originality and creativity of that earlier vibrant Greek culture was lost in the process.

The final chapter of ancient Greek history is called the Hellenistic Age, in which Alexander and then his successors hoped to rule their new subjects in Greek fashion, imposing a superior Greek culture over their new subjects. The attempt was eventually unsuccessful. Alexander's conquest of the Persian empire has been hailed throughout the history of the West as a remarkable achievement, and largely as a noble effort to bring a superior civilization to a broader world. Even today the memory of that Western conquest of the East is remembered in Asia as one of the first of many attempts of the West to impose its brand of civilization on unwelcoming victims. Cultural exchange as well as suspicions over cultural motivations is as old as the ancient civilizations of both East and West. Yet in spite of the complexities brought about when the modern world attempts to find explanations of its difficulties in ancient rivalries, the lasting achievements of the Greeks deserve the admiration of us all. Their creativity, vitality, and humanness have left to the whole world a timeless cultural legacy.

Suggestions for Web Browsing

You can obtain more information about topics included in this chapter at the websites listed below. See also the companion website that accompanies this text, **http://www.ablongman.com/ brummett,** which contains an online study guide and additional resources.

Minoan Palaces
http://dilos.com/region/crete/minoan_pictures.html

Images and text from major Minoan archaeological sites, including Knossos.

Ancient Greek World
http://www.museum.upenn.edu/Greek_World/Index.html

A presentation by the University of Pennsylvania Museum of Archaeology and Anthropology. Text and museum artifacts tell the vivid story of life in ancient Greece: land and time; daily life, economy, religion, and death.

Perseus Project
http://www.perseus.tufts.edu/

An impressive compilation of information on Greek art, architecture, and literature. One of the most useful but also scholarly sites dealing with ancient Greece.

Vatican Museum: Greek Collection
http://www.christusrex.org/www1/vaticano/GP-Profano.html

The excellent works in the Vatican's Greek collection are displayed and discussed in this outstanding site.

Daily Life in Ancient Greece
http://members.aol.com/Donnclass/Greeklife.html

A wonderfully entertaining site on ancient Greek life—gives a feel for what life would be like in a variety of Greek city-states.

Women's Life in Greece and Rome

http://www.stoa.org/diotima/anthology/wlgr/

Details about the private life and legal status of women, in addition to biographies of prominent women of ancient Greece and Rome.

Diotima: Women and Gender in the Ancient World

http://www.stoa.org/diotima/

An excellent site for information on women in ancient Greece—their political influence, occupations, dress, diet. A great range of information.

Alexander the Great

http://united-states.asinah.net/american-encyclopedia/wikipedia/a/al/alexander_the_great.html

Web page detailing the life of the king of Macedonia and conqueror of the Persian Empire.

Ancient Olympics

http://www.perseus.tufts.edu/Olympics/

Compare ancient and modern Olympic sports and read about the Olympic athletes who were famous in antiquity.

Greek Warfare

http://www.dean.usma.edu/history/web03/atlases/ancient%20warfare/ancient%20warfare%20index.htm

Informative site for ancient Greek battles, logistics, and tactics. Excellent maps and diagrams of military campaigns.

Literature and Film

Mary Renault, *The King Must Die* (Bantam, 1974), is an absorbing novel set in Mycenaean times. Several new and excellent works of historical fiction are Steven Pressfield, *Gates of Fire* (Bantam, 1999) and *The Tides of War* (Doubleday, 2000), dealing with the battle of Thermopylae and the general Alcibiades, respectively. Also outstanding are Tom Holt's *The Walled Orchard* (Warner, 1997) and *Olympiad* (Abacus, 2001). Anna Apostolou, *A Murder in Macedon* (St. Martin's, 1998), is a well-done novel dealing with the assassination of Philip, Alexander's father.

Some excellent video presentations dealing with ancient Greece are *The Mystery of the Minoans* (1999), *Atlantis—In Search of a Lost Continent* (1996; 2 tapes, Questar Edition), and *The Greeks: Crucible of Civilization* (2000; 2 tapes, PBS Home Video). Greek art and architecture are beautifully reviewed in *Art in Ancient Greece* (1994; 2 tapes, Kultur Video). *In the Footsteps of Alexander the Great* (1996; 2 tapes, PBS Home Video) is a modern trek over Alexander's ancient route through Asia.

Suggestions for Reading

John Boardman, Jasper Griffin, and Oswyn Murray, eds., *The Oxford History of the Classical World* (Oxford University Press, 1986) is one of the most comprehensive studies of ancient Greece and its culture. A shorter yet still excellent history is J. V. A. Fine, *The Ancient Greeks: A Critical History* (Belknap/Harvard University Press, 1983). John Chadwick's *The Mycenaean World* (Cambridge University Press, 1976) and Robert Drews's *The Coming of the Greeks* (Princeton University Press, 1988) are both excellent studies of the early Greek experience. For the classical period, some outstanding studies are Donald Kagan, *The Peloponnesian War* (Viking Press, 2003), and Sarah Pomeroy, *Goddesses, Whores, Wives, and Slaves: Women in Classical Antiquity* (Schocken, 1975). James Davidson's *Courtesans and Fishcakes* (St. Martin's, 1998) is a delightful study of Athenian manners and private life. Mark Munn, *The School of History: Athens in the Age of Socrates* (University of California Press, 2002) is an outstanding cultural history. For the Hellenistic period, see Peter Green's *Hellenistic History and Culture* (University of California Press, 1993) and his excellent biography of Alexander, *Alexander of Macedon: 356–323 B.C.* (Praeger, 1970).

CHAPTER 5

Roman Civilization

The Roman World, c. 900 B.C.E. to 476 C.E.

The remains of the Roman Forum stand today in the center of a vibrant city of more than a million people—in the capital of Italy, a center of world commerce, diplomacy, and culture. That same description holds true for the Forum and the city as it was more than two thousand years ago. Originally used as a cemetery as early as the ninth century B.C.E., the Forum became a marketplace and a center of political activity two hundred years later. As Roman conquests in Italy and throughout the Mediterranean world grew, so did the importance of the Forum as the symbolic center of Rome's dominance.

Over centuries, the Romans decorated the Forum with triumphal arches and columns commemorating military conquests—constant reminders that Rome was the capital of a world state that extended from Britain to Persia, from Africa to Germany. The public buildings and temples in the Forum were Greek in style and inspiration, although more monumental and immense in appearance. And in that very design and presentation, we see two important elements of Roman culture: they readily borrowed ideas from others, especially the Greeks, if they found those ideas preferable to their own, and they very often modified and made improvements on what they borrowed. Roman ability to adapt and modify may be observed even in the empire's structure: Rome brought political stability to the Mediterranean world and in the same process perpetuated the intellectual and cultural contributions of their conquered subjects. As Rome's empire expanded, the cultural legacies of the ancient world were preserved and spread westward throughout most of Europe.

From their beginning as a simple farming community on the banks of the Tiber River to the largest and longest lasting empire of the ancient world, the Romans met one challenge after another by attempting practical solutions and efficient governmental approaches—and almost always prevailed. In the company of its formidable legions went engineers and architects, so that today, throughout the lands that were once under the rule of Rome, the remains of walls, baths, temples, amphitheaters, and aqueducts survive as reminders of the Roman contribution to shaping European civilization.

EARLY ITALY AND THE ORIGINS OF ROME: C. 900–509 B.C.E.

■ *What impact did Italian geography and the various peoples of Italy have on the development of Rome?*

The history of Rome begins with small agricultural settlements in the region that eventually became the city of Rome around 900 B.C.E. The Romans themselves, however, believed that the city actually began in 753 B.C.E.—the traditional date for the founding of the city by Romulus, Rome's legendary first king. It is equally difficult to assign an end date to Rome, because long after the political dominance of Rome came to an end, the social and cultural legacies of the empire continued to influence life in lands impacted by Roman occupation. A great variety of dates might be offered to indicate the end of the empire; one such significant milestone took place in 476 C.E., when the German chieftain Odovacer (c. 435–493 C.E.) assassinated Romulus Augustulus, the

last emperor to ruler the western half of the Roman world. The first period in this remarkable span of more than a thousand years of dominance, however, ended in 509 B.C.E., according to Roman tradition, with the expulsion of the Etruscan monarch Tarquin the Proud, the seventh and last of Rome's kings, and the establishment of an aristocratic republic.

Geography and Early Settlers of Italy

Geography was crucial in shaping the course of events in Italy. The Italian peninsula is 600 miles long and about four times the size of Greece, or two-thirds that of California. A great mountainous backbone, the Apennine range, runs almost the entire length of the peninsula. But the land is not as rugged as Greece, and the mountains did not create a formidable barrier to political unification. Unlike in Greece, a network of roads could be built to link the peninsula. Furthermore, the plain of Latium (LAH-tee-um) and its major city, Rome, occupied a strategic position. The hills near what became Rome were relatively easy to defend, and once

The great variety of peoples and cultures of early Italy are portrayed on this map. Roman institutions and culture were influenced greatly by these early residents.

ITALY BEFORE THE ROMAN EMPIRE

the Romans had begun to establish themselves as successful conquerors, they occupied a central position on the peninsula, which made it difficult for their enemies to unite successfully against them. The important central position of Rome was duplicated on a larger scale by the location of Italy itself. Italy juts into what is almost the center of the great Mediterranean sea. Once Italy was unified, its central position aided Rome in dominating the entire Mediterranean region.

Italy's most imposing valleys and useful harbors are on the western slopes of the Apennines, and the Italian peninsula extends into the western Mediterranean, not eastward. For much of its early history, therefore, cultural development in Italy was not as rapid as it might have been if the two peoples had come into close cultural contact sooner.

Both Greeks and Romans were descendants of a common Indo-European stock, and settlement of the Greek and Italian peninsulas followed broadly parallel stages. Between 2000 and 1000 B.C.E., when Indo-European peoples invaded the Aegean world, a western wing of this nomadic migration filtered into the Italian peninsula, then inhabited by indigenous Neolithic peoples. The first invaders, skilled in the use of copper and bronze, settled in the Po valley. Another wave of Indo-Europeans, equipped with iron weapons and tools, followed; in time the newer and older settlers intermingled and spread throughout the peninsula. One group, the Latins, settled in the plain of Latium, in the lower valley of the Tiber River.

As the Iron Age began in the western Mediterranean, the cultures of Italy became increasingly complex. During the ninth century B.C.E., a people known as the Etruscans established dominance throughout most of central Italy. The exact origin of the Etruscans remains uncertain. Some experts believe them to have been a non-Indo-European people who came to Italy by sea from Asia Minor. Others believe that their origin is explained through a rapid and creative growth of already resident iron-using peoples in northern Italy. Perhaps a combination of the two explanations is most likely—that native creativity fueled by contact with immigrants from the East resulted in a distinctly vibrant and creative culture. Expanding from the west

Etruscan tombs were often elaborately painted with scenes of feasting and entertainment. On these tombs youths celebrate with music and wine.

coast up to the Po valley and south to the Bay of Naples, the Etruscans organized the less-advanced and disparate Italic peoples into a loose confederation of Etruscan-dominated city-states.

In the sixth century B.C.E., Rome became one of the cities controlled by the Etruscans, at a time when that city was not highly developed politically or culturally. The Etruscans brought with them a highly effective political system under the strong direction of kings, an aristocracy of landholding nobles, and a military organization superior to any they encountered among the Italic peoples. Etruscan cultural influence was particularly strong among their Roman subjects. Much of the area around the city was made more useful through Etruscan engineering skill, marsh drainage, and agricultural technology. Their religion, which included many Eastern elements such as the worship of numerous gods and goddesses, powerful priesthoods, rituals, and sacrifices to please the gods and ward off evil, also greatly influenced the development of Roman religious belief. Their funeral customs, which helped to shape Roman practices, show the prominent role of women in Etruscan society. They are usually portrayed in Etruscan tomb paintings as appearing in public, participating in banquets along with their husbands, and in general sharing in the pleasures of life on an equal footing with men.

After 750 B.C.E. Greek colonists migrated to southern Italy and Sicily, where their colonies provided a protective buffer against powerful and prosperous Carthage, a Phoenician colony established in North Africa about 800 B.C.E. The Greeks, along with the Etruscans, had a lasting influence on Roman culture—particularly with regard to religion and their sophisticated accomplishments in art and architecture.

Rome's Origins

Legend held that Rome was founded in 753 B.C.E. by Romulus. He and his twin brother, Remus, were sons of a nearby king's daughter who had been raped by Mars, the god of war. Thrown into the Tiber River by their wicked uncle who had seized the throne, they were rescued and nurtured by a she-wolf. Other legends told the story that Romulus's ancestor was Aeneas (ay-NEE-uhs), a Trojan hero who, after the fall of Troy, founded a settlement in Latium, near what came to be Rome. The Aeneas story, perhaps invented by later mythmakers, pleased the Romans because it linked their history with that of the Greeks, whose culture they thought more sophisticated than their own.

Turning from fable to fact, modern scholars believe that in the eighth century B.C.E. the inhabitants of some small Latin settlements on hills in the Tiber valley united and established a common meeting place, the Forum, around which the city of Rome

grew. Situated at a convenient place for fording the river and protected from invaders by surrounding hills and marshes, Rome was strategically located on excellent passes to both north and south. Because of their interest in gaining access to trade with the Greeks in the south, the expanding Etruscans conquered Rome about 625 B.C.E., and under their direction Rome became an important city.

Rome, Italy, and Empire

The Roman Monarchy, 753–509 B.C.E.

Rome's political growth followed a pattern of development similar to that of the Greek city-states: monarchy similar to that described by Homer, oligarchy, modified democracy, and, finally, the permanent dictatorship of the Roman emperors. In moving from oligarchy to democracy, the Romans succeeded in avoiding the intermediate Greek stage of tyranny.

The executive power, both civil and military, of Rome's seven kings (the last three were Etruscans) was called the *imperium*, (the root word for both *imperialism* and *empire*) which was symbolized by an ax bound in a bundle of rods (*fasces*; FAS-kees). Imperium was officially conferred on the king by a popular assembly made up of male citizens, and the king was expected to turn for advice to a council of nobles called the Senate. Senators held their positions for life, and they and their families belonged to the *patrician* class, the fathers of the state (*pater* means "father"). The other class of Romans, the *plebeians*, or commoners, included small farmers, artisans, and many clients, or dependents, of patrician landowners. In 509 B.C.E. the patricians, with some plebeian assistance, overthrew the Etruscan monarchy and established an aristocratic form of government, known as the Republic.

THE REPUBLIC AND THE ROMAN CONQUEST OF ITALY: 509–133 B.C.E.

■ *How did the Romans conquer all of Italy and much of the Mediterranean by 130 B.C.E.?*

The history of the Roman Republic can be divided into two distinct periods. During the first, from 509 to 133 B.C.E., two themes are dominant: a change from aristocracy to a more democratic constitution, the result of the gradual extension of political and social equality to the plebeian lower class; and the expansion of Roman military and political control, first in Italy, and then throughout the Mediterranean region.

The Early Wars of Rome

509 B.C.E.	Etruscans expelled from Rome
390 B.C.E.	Gauls attack and plunder Rome
338 B.C.E.	Rome emerges victor in wars with members of the Latin League
264–241 B.C.E.	Rome wins Sicily in First Punic War
218–201 B.C.E.	Rome defeats Hannibal in Second Punic War
149–146 B.C.E.	Carthage destroyed in Third Punic War

Establishment of the Republic

In 509 B.C.E. the patricians forced out the last Etruscan king, Tarquin the Proud (Tarquinius Superbus), claiming he had acted despotically. According to the Roman historian Livy, Tarquin was the first of the Roman kings to ignore the advice of the Senate and govern in a selfish and irresponsible manner. The patricians replaced the monarchy with an aristocracy they called a *republic* (*res publica*, "commonwealth"). The imperium of the one king was shared by two new magistrates, called *consuls*. Elected annually from the patrician class, the consuls exercised power in the interest of that class. In the event of war or serious domestic emergency, an "extraordinary" magistrate called a *dictator* could be substituted for the two consuls, but the man was given absolute power for six months only. The popular assembly was retained because the patricians could control it through their plebeian clients who, in return for a livelihood, voted as their patrons directed them.

Struggle of the Orders

For more than two centuries following the establishment of the Republic, the plebeians struggled for political and social equality. Outright civil war was avoided by the willingness of the patricians to accept the demands of the plebeians, even though patrician acceptance was often reluctant and usually slow. Much of the plebeians' success in this struggle was due to their having been granted the right to organize themselves as a corporate body capable of collective action. This permission to organize, granted by the Senate early in the fifth century B.C.E., after the plebeians threatened to leave Rome and found a city elsewhere, established a sort of state within a state known as the *Concilium Plebis* (kun-SIL-I-um PLAY-bis) or "gathering of the plebeians." This assembly was presided over by plebeian leaders called *tribunes* and could pass *plebiscites* ("plebeian decrees") that were binding only on the plebeian community. The tribunes were given sacred status, *sacrosanctitas* (sak-roh-SANG-ti-tahs), by the plebeian assembly in an effort to furnish them protection from any bodily harm that might come their way from patrician opponents. Tribunes also assumed the right to stop unjust or oppressive acts of the patrician consuls and Senate by uttering the word *veto* ("I forbid.").

Another major concession to plebeian interests was in the field of law. Because the consuls often interpreted Rome's unwritten customary law to suit patrician interests, the plebeians demanded that it be written down and made available for all to see. As a result, about 450 B.C.E., the law was inscribed on a dozen tablets of bronze and set up publicly in the Forum. This Code of the Twelve Tables was the first landmark development in the long history of Roman law.

In time the plebeians acquired other fundamental rights and safeguards: the rights to appeal a death sentence imposed by a consul and to be retried before the popular assembly were secured; marriage between patricians and plebeians, prohibited by the Code of the Twelve Tables, was legalized; and the enslavement of citizens for debt was abolished.

That their service in the Roman army was indispensable to the patricians greatly increased the plebeians' bargaining position in the state. Since Rome was almost constantly at war during these years, the patrician leaders of the state were more ready to accommodate plebeian demands than to face the possibility of a withdrawal of military participation by the commoners. In addition, trade and commerce in early Rome came to be dominated by the plebeian class, since the patricians avoided commercial activities in favor of concentrating their wealth on the acquisition of land and country estates.

Little by little the plebeians acquired more power in the government. In 367 B.C.E. one consulship was reserved for the plebeians, and before the end of the century, plebeians were eligible to hold other important magistracies that the patricians had created in the meantime. Among these new offices, whose powers had originally been held by the consuls, were the *praetor* (PREE-tor; in charge of the administration of justice), *quaestor* (KWEE-ster; treasurer), and *censor* (supervisor of public morals and the granting of state contracts).

The long struggle for equal status ended in 287 B.C.E. when the *Concilium Plebis* was recognized as a constitutional body, which then became known as the Tribal Assembly, and its plebiscites became laws binding on all citizens, patrician as well as plebeian.

The Roman Republic was technically a democracy, although in actual practice a senatorial aristocracy of noble patricians and rich plebeians continued to control the state. Having gained political and social equality, the plebeians were usually willing to allow the more experienced Senate to run the government from this time until 133 B.C.E., a period of almost constant warfare.

After 287 B.C.E. conflict in Roman society gradually assumed a new form. Before this time, the issue of greatest domestic importance had primarily been social and political inequality

This statue of a patrician with busts of his ancestors dates from either the first century B.C.E. or the first century C.E. The patricians were the aristocracy of Rome, and during the later Republic they came increasingly into conflict with senators and generals who took the part of the plebeians.

between the classes of patricians and plebeians. After equal political status was achieved, many rich plebeians were elected to the highest offices and became members of an expanded senatorial aristocracy. The new Roman "establishment" was prepared to guard its privileges even more fiercely than the old patricians had done. This fact became evident in 133 B.C.E. when a popular leader, Tiberius Gracchus (tai-BEE-ri-uhs GRAH-kuhs), arose to challenge the establishment.

The Conquest of Italy

The growth of Rome from a small city-state to the dominant power in the Mediterranean world in less than 400 years (509–133 B.C.E.) was a remarkable achievement. Roman expansion was not deliberately planned; rather, it was the result of dealing with unsettled conditions, first in Italy and then abroad, which were thought to threaten Rome's security. Rome always claimed that its wars were defensive, waged to protect itself from potentially hostile neighbors—Etruscans in the north, land-hungry hill tribes in central Italy, and Greeks in the south. Rome subdued them all after a long, determined effort and found itself master of all Italy south of the Po valley. In the process the Romans developed the administrative skills and traits of character—both fair-mindedness and ruthlessness—that would lead to the acquisition of an empire with possessions on three continents.

Soon after driving out their Etruscan overlords in 509 B.C.E., Rome and the Latin League, composed of other Latin peoples in Latium, entered into a defensive alliance against the Etruscans. This new combination was so successful that by the beginning of the fourth century B.C.E., it had become the chief power in central Italy. But at this time (390 B.C.E.), a major disaster almost ended the history of Rome. A raiding army of Celts, called *Gauls* by the Romans, invaded Italy from central Europe, wiped out the Roman army, and almost destroyed the city by fire. The elderly members of the Senate, according to the traditional account, sat awaiting their fate with quiet dignity before they were massacred. Only a garrison on the Capitoline Hill held out under siege. After seven months and the receipt of a huge ransom in gold, the Gauls withdrew. The stubborn Romans rebuilt their city and protected it with a stone wall, part of which still stands. They also remodeled their army by replacing the solid line of fixed spears of the phalanx formation, borrowed from the Etruscans and Greeks, with much more maneuverable small units of 120 men, called *maniples*, armed with javelins instead of spears. It would be 800 years before another barbarian army would be able to conquer the city of Rome. In the years that followed Rome's recovery from the attack of the Gauls, the Latin League grew more and more alarmed at Rome's increasing strength, and war broke out between the former allies. Upon Rome's victory in 338 B.C.E. the league was dissolved, and the Latin cities were forced to sign individual treaties with Rome.

But soon after the Roman victory over the Latin League, border clashes with aggressive mountain tribes of Samnium led to three fiercely fought Samnite wars and the extension of Rome's frontiers to the Greek colonies in southern Italy by 290 B.C.E. Fearing Roman conquest, the Greeks prepared for war and called in the mercenary army of the Greek king, Pyrrhus (PEER-uhs) of Epirus, who dreamed of becoming a second Alexander the Great. Pyrrhus's war elephants, unknown in Italy, twice defeated the Romans, but at so heavy a cost that such a triumph is still called a "Pyrrhic victory." When a third battle failed to persuade the Romans to make peace, Pyrrhus returned to his homeland. By 270 B.C.E. the Roman army had subdued the Greek city-states in

Italy, and the peninsula south of the Po River was under their control.

Treatment of Conquered Peoples

Instead of killing or enslaving their defeated opponents in Italy, the Romans treated them fairly, a policy which in time created a strong loyalty to Rome throughout the peninsula. Roman citizenship was a prized possession that was not extended to all peoples in Italy until the first century B.C.E. Most defeated states were required to sign a treaty of alliance with Rome, which bound them to accept Rome's foreign policy and to supply troops for the Roman army. No tribute was required, and each allied state retained local self-government. Rome did, however, annex about one-fifth of the land its **legions** conquered in Italy, on which nearly 30 colonies were established by 250 B.C.E.

CASE STUDY

Greek and Roman Slavery

The First Punic War

After 270 B.C.E. Rome's only serious rival for dominance in the western Mediterranean was the city-state of Carthage. This prosperous state located near the modern city of Tunis began as a Phoenician colony on the northern African coast in the ninth century B.C.E. By the sixth century, Carthage had become not only independent but also the dominant commercial power in the western Mediterranean. Much more wealthy and populous than Rome, Carthage's magnificent navy controlled the northern coast of Africa, Sardinia, Corsica, western Sicily, and much of Spain. The city and its empire were governed by a commercial oligarchy of Semitic descendants of Carthage's founders. The native population was forced into service in agriculture or in the army and navy; mercenaries were also hired to secure the interests of the ruling minority.

There had been almost no conflicts of interest between Rome and Carthage before the First Punic War (from *Punicus*, Latin for "Phoenician") broke out in 264 B.C.E. In that year, Rome answered an appeal from a group of Italian mercenaries who were in control of the city of Messana, on the northern tip of Sicily next to Italy. These mercenaries were opposed by a Carthaginian force, and when the Roman Senate agreed to send an army to aid the mercenaries, a war between Carthage and Rome was the obvious result.

The First Punic War was a costly one for both combatants. Roman ground forces were quickly successful

---

legion—A military organizational division, originally the largest permanent unit in the Roman army. The legion was the basis of the military system by which imperial Rome conquered and ruled its empire.

in gaining control of most of Sicily, but the Carthaginian navy was unopposed, since the Romans had no need of a navy in their conquest of Italy. Rome constructed its fleet in hurried fashion and sent it against the Carthaginians with surprising initial success. Roman engineers furnished their new vessels with an invention called the *corvus*, or "crow," a boarding bridge at the bow of a ship that, when lowered, turned a naval engagement into a land battle. After a stunning defeat of the Carthaginian navy, the Romans invaded the African coast, lost decisively, and suffered the losses of large numbers of ships through violent storms in attempting to return home. Eventually, victory for Rome came through another victory over the Carthaginian navy, but the costs of victory were high; Rome and its Italian allies lost more than 500 ships in naval engagements and storms before Carthage asked for peace in 241 B.C.E. Sicily, Sardinia, and Corsica were annexed as the first prizes in Rome's overseas empire, regulated and taxed—in contrast to Rome's allies in Italy—by Roman officials called *governors*.

The Contest with Hannibal

Stunned by its defeat in the First Punic War, Carthage concentrated on enlarging its empire in Spain. Rome's determination to prevent this led to the most famous and most difficult war in Roman history. While both powers sought a position of advantage, a young Carthaginian general, Hannibal, precipitated the Second Punic War by attacking Saguntum, a Spanish town claimed by Rome as an ally. Rome declared war, and Hannibal, seizing the initiative, in 218 B.C.E. led an army of about 40,000 men, 9000 cavalry troops, and a detachment of African elephants across the Alps into Italy. Although the crossing had cost him nearly half of his men and all but one of his elephants, Hannibal defeated the Romans in three major battles within three years, while ranging throughout Italy but not attacking Rome.

Hannibal's forces never matched those of the Romans in numbers, and the Carthaginian general was never given the reinforcements he requested from his home state. Nevertheless, Hannibal's brilliance as a commander was obvious. At the battle of Cannae (KAN-ee), in 216 B.C.E., Hannibal won his greatest victory by surrounding an army of nearly 80,000 Romans with 50,000 Carthaginians. Almost the entire Roman force was killed or captured. Even at this darkest hour of defeat, the Senate displayed the determination that was to become legendary. When the one consul who survived the battle returned to Rome to give his report, he was congratulated by the senators for "not despairing of the Republic."

The Romans ultimately produced a general, Scipio (SI-pee-oh), who was Hannibal's match in military strategy and who was bold enough to invade Africa. Asked to return home after 15 years spent on Italian soil, Hannibal clashed with Scipio's legions at Zama, where the Carthaginians suffered a complete defeat. The power of Carthage was broken forever by a harsh treaty imposed in 201 B.C.E. Carthage was forced to pay a huge **war indemnity,** disarm its forces, and turn Spain over to the Romans. Hannibal fled to the Seleucid Empire, where he attempted to encourage anti-Roman sentiment, and eventually committed suicide in order to avoid Roman capture.

Roman Intervention East and West

The defeat of Carthage freed Rome to turn eastward and deal with King Philip V of Macedonia. Fearful of Rome's growing power, Philip had allied himself with Hannibal during the Second Punic War. In 200 B.C.E., Rome was ready to act, following an appeal from Pergamum and Rhodes for aid in protecting the smaller Hellenistic states from Philip, who was advancing in the Aegean, and from the Seleucid emperor, who was moving into Asia Minor. The heavy Macedonian phalanxes were no match for the mobile Roman legions, and in 197 B.C.E. Philip was soundly defeated in Macedonia. His dreams of empire were ended when Rome destroyed his navy and military bases in Greece. The Romans then proclaimed the independence of Greece and were praised as liberators by the grateful Greeks.

A few years later Rome declared war on the Seleucid emperor, who had moved into Greece, urged on by Hannibal and number of Greek states that resented Rome's interference. The Romans forced the emperor to move out of Greece and Asia Minor, pay a huge indemnity, and give up his warships and war elephants. The Seleucids were checked again in 168 B.C.E. when a Roman ultimatum halted their invasion of Egypt. A Roman envoy met the advancing Seleucid army and, drawing a ring in the sand around the emperor, demanded that he decide on war or on peace with Rome before stepping out of it.

DOCUMENT

Plutarch,
*The Life
of Cato
the Elder*

In the middle of the second century B.C.E. anti-Romanism became widespread in Greece, particularly among the poorer classes, who resented Rome's support of conservative governments and the status quo in general. In 146 B.C.E., after many Greeks had supported an attempted Macedonian revival, Rome destroyed Corinth, a hotbed of anti-Romanism, as an object lesson. The Romans also supported the oligarchic factions in all Greek states and placed Greece under the watchful eye of the governor of Macedonia, a recently established Roman province.

In the West, meanwhile, Rome's more aggressive imperialism led to suspicion of Carthage's reviving prosperity and to a demand by Roman extremists for war—*Carthago delenda est* ("Carthage must be obliterated."). Obviously provoking the Third Punic War, the Romans besieged Carthage, which resisted for three years. Rome destroyed the city in 146 B.C.E. (the same year they destroyed Corinth), killed or enslaved almost all of its surviving inhabitants, leveled the buildings, and poured salt over its borders so that nothing would ever take root on its soil again. The powerful state that had dared to defy Rome was now obliterated, and the province of Africa was created in its place.

In 133 B.C.E. Rome acquired its first province in Asia when the king of Pergamum, dying without an heir, left his kingdom to Rome. The Senate accepted the bequest and created a new province, called Asia. With provinces on three continents—Europe, Africa, and Asia—the once obscure Roman Republic was now supreme in the ancient world.

Society and Religion in Early Rome

The most important unit of early Roman society was the family. The power of the family father (*pater familias*) was absolute, and strict discipline was imposed to instill in children the virtues to which the Romans attached particular importance—loyalty, courage, self-control, and respect for laws and ancestral customs. The Romans of the early Republic were stern, hardworking, and practical. The conservative values of an agrarian society formed the values of both Roman men and women. With much of a Roman man's time taken up with military or political concerns, women had great responsibilities in supervising the upbringing of children and maintaining estates and farms.

In contrast to the frequency of divorce in the late Republic, marriage in the early Republic was viewed as a lifelong union; patrician marriages were usually arranged between families and were undertaken primarily for the creation of children, but on many occasions such marriages resulted in mutual affection between husband and wife. Nonetheless, the authority of the Roman male within his own household was usually unchallenged.

The religion of the early Romans, before their contacts with the Etruscans and Greeks, is very difficult for scholars to describe with confidence. Available evidence for their views on life after death is vague. Religious practices were concerned with appeasing and honoring the spirits (*numina*) of the family and the state by the repetition of complicated rituals and formulas. Mispronunciation of even a sin-

---

war indemnity—A payment to compensate for losses sustained or expenses incurred as a result of war. The Romans regularly imposed such war indemnities on their conquered enemies.

gle syllable was enough to cause the ritual to become ineffective. Under Etruscan influence, major gods and goddesses were personified. The sky-spirit Jupiter became the patron god of Rome; Mars, spirit of vegetation, became god of war and agriculture; and Janus, whose temple doors remained open when the army was away at war, was originally the spirit guarding the city gate.

Although early Roman religion did not have great concern with morals, it had much to do with morale. It strengthened family solidarity and enhanced a patriotic devotion to the state and its gods. But the early Romans' respect for hard work, frugality, and family and state gods was to be challenged by the effects of Rome's expansion in Italy and over much of the Mediterranean area during the early Republic.

The Late Republic	
133–123 B.C.E.	Reform movement of the Gracchi
88–82 B.C.E.	First Civil War (Marius vs. Sulla)
58–49 B.C.E.	Caesar conquers Gaul
49–45 B.C.E.	Second Civil War (Pompey vs. Caesar)
44 B.C.E.	Caesar assassinated
31 B.C.E.	Third Civil War (Octavian vs. Antony)
27 B.C.E.	Octavian (Augustus) becomes ruler of Rome

THE LATE REPUBLIC: 133–30 B.C.E.

■ *What were the main reasons for the failure of the Roman Republic and the consolidation of power by Augustus?*

The century following 133 B.C.E. during which Rome's frontiers reached the Euphrates and the Rhine, witnessed the failure of the Republic to solve problems generated in part by the acquisition of an empire. These years serve as a good example of the failure of a democracy and its replacement by a dictatorship. The experience of the late Republic gives support to Thucydides' judgment that a democracy is incapable of running an empire. Athens kept its democracy but lost its empire; Rome would keep its empire and loss its democracy.

Effects of Roman Expansion

The political history of Rome to 133 B.C.E. possessed two dominant themes: the gradual extension of citizenship rights in Italy and the expansion of Roman dominion over the Mediterranean world. Largely as a result of this expansion, Rome faced critical social and economic problems by the middle of the second century B.C.E.

One of the most pressing problems Rome faced was the decline in the number of small landowners, whose service and devotion had made Rome great. Burdened by frequent military service, their farms and buildings destroyed by Hannibal, and unable to compete with the cheap grain imported from the new Roman province of Sicily, small farmers sold out and moved to the great city. Here they joined the unemployed and discontented *proletariat,* so called because their only contribution was *proles,* "children." The proletariat soon were the majority of the citizens in the city.

At the same time, improved farming methods learned from the Greeks and Carthaginians encouraged rich aristocrats to buy more and more land. Abandoning the cultivation of grain, they introduced large-scale scientific production of olive oil and wine, sheep, and cattle. This change was especially profitable because an abundance of cheaply purchased slaves from conquered territory was available to work on the estates. With the increase in the availability of slave labor came worsening treatment of the labor force, as well as deteriorating conditions for the declining numbers of free laborers on these large estates. These large slave plantations, called *latifundia* (lah-ti-FUN-dee-uh), became common in many parts of Italy.

The land problem was further complicated by the government's practice of leasing part of the territory acquired in the conquest of the Italian peninsula to anyone willing to pay a percentage of the crop or animals raised on it. Only the wealthy could afford to lease large tracts of this public land, and in time, they treated it as if it were their own property. Plebeian protests led to an attempt to limit the holdings of a single individual to 320 acres of public land, but the law enacted for that purpose was never enforced.

Corruption in the government was another sign of the growing problems of the Roman Republic. Provincial officials took advantage of the opportunity to engage in graft for great profit, and aggressive Roman businessmen scrambled selfishly for the profitable state contracts to supply the armies, collect taxes and loan money in the provinces, and lease state-owned mines and forests.

Although in theory the government allowed for an unhindered participation of all male citizens, in practice it remained a senatorial oligarchy. Wars tend to strengthen the executive power in a state, and in Rome the Senate traditionally had such power. Even the tribunes, guardians of the people's rights, became, for the most part, tools of the Senate. By the middle of the second century B.C.E. the government was in the hands of a wealthy, self-serving Senate, which became increasingly incapable of coping with the problems of governing a world-state. Ordinary citizens were mostly impoverished and landless, and Rome swarmed with fortune hunters, imported slaves, unemployed farmers, and discontented war veterans. The poverty of the many, coupled with the great wealth of the few, contrasted dramatically with the old Roman traits of discipline, simplicity, and respect for authority. The next century (133–30 B.C.E.) saw Rome torn apart by internal conflict, which led to the establishment of a permanent dictatorship and the end of the Republic.

Document   Columella: Roman Farm Women

Columella was a Roman citizen from Spain in the first century C.E. He served with the Roman legions and later retired to an agricultural estate, where he wrote his suggestions for how Roman farming could most efficiently be undertaken. The following excerpt from his works on agriculture describes the duties he believes should be given to the forewomen on Roman estates. Such women were usually under the supervision of a foreman; both were often slaves. Columella's listing of the forewoman's tasks gives us an insight into the wide range of duties for which such Roman farm women were held responsible:

The forewoman must not only store and guard the items which have been brought into the house and delivered to her; she should also inspect and examine them from time to time so that the furniture and clothing which have been stored do not disintegrate because of mold, and the fruits and vegetables and other necessities do not go rotten because of her neglect and slothfulness. On rainy days, or when a woman cannot do field work out of doors because of cold or frost, she should return to wool-working. Therefore, wool should be prepared and carded in advance so that she can more easily undertake and complete the required allotment of wool-working. For it will be beneficial if clothing is made at home for her and the stewards and the other valued slaves so the financial accounts of the *paterfamilias* are less strained. She ought to stay in one place as little as possible, for her job is not a sedentary one. At one moment she will have to go to the loom and teach the weavers whatever she knows better than them or, if she knows less, learn from someone who understands more. At another moment, she will have to check on those slaves who are preparing the food for the *familia*. Then she will also have to see that the kitchen, cowsheds, and even the stables are cleaned. And she will also have to open up the sickrooms occasionally, even if they are empty of patients, and keep them free of dirt, so that, when circumstance demands, a well-ordered and healthy environment is provided for the sick. She will, in addition, have to be in attendance when the stewards of the pantry and cellar are weighing something, and also be present when the shepherds are milking in the stables or bringing the lambs or calves to nurse. But she will also certainly need to be present when the sheep are sheared, and to examine the wool carefully and compare the number of fleeces with the number of sheep. Then she must turn her attention to the slaves in the house and insist that they air out the furniture and clean and polish the metal items and free them from rust, and take to the craftsmen for repair other items which require mending.

Questions to Consider

1. How do you think the responsibilities of Roman forewomen compare to modern positions of responsibility on farms?

2. Do you find it surprising that such heavy responsibilities were often given to slave women? What might be the reasons for this?

3. What duties are omitted from the list of responsibilities given by Columella, and do you see any significance in their omission?

From Columella, *On Agriculture*, 12.3.5, 6, 8, and 9, in Jo-Ann Shelton, *As the Romans Did*, 2nd ed. (New York: Oxford University Press, 1998), p. 304.

Reform Movement of the Gracchi

An awareness of Rome's serious social and economic problems led to the reform program of an idealistic and ambitious young aristocrat named Tiberius Gracchus. His reforming spirit was partly the product of newly imported philosophical arguments from Greece and an awareness that the old Roman values and customs were fast slipping away. He sought to stop Roman decline by restoring the backbone of the old Roman society, the small landowner. Supported by a **faction** of senators, Tiberius was elected tribune for the year 133 B.C.E. at the age of 29.

Tiberius proposed to the Tribal Assembly that the act limiting the holding of public land to 320 acres per male citizen, plus 160 acres for each of two grown-up sons, be reenacted. Much of the public land would continue to be held by the present occupants and their heirs as private property, but the rest was to be taken back and granted to the poor in small plots of 9 to 18 acres. The recipients were to pay a small rent and could not sell their holdings. When it became evident that the Tribal Assembly would adopt Tiberius's proposal, opposing senators persuaded one of the other tribunes to veto the measure. On the ground that a tribune who opposed the will of the people had no right to his office, Tiberius took a fateful—and, the Senate claimed, unconstitutional—step by having the assembly depose the tribune in question. The agrarian bill was then passed.

To ensure the implementation of his agrarian reform, Tiberius again violated custom by standing for reelection in the Tribal Assembly after completing his one-year term. Claiming that he sought to make himself king, partisans of the Senate murdered Tiberius and 300 of his followers.

Tiberius's work was taken up by his younger brother, Gaius Gracchus, who was elected tribune for 123 B.C.E. In addition to the allocation of public land to the poor, Gaius proposed establishing Roman colonies in southern Italy and in Africa—his enemies said near the site of Carthage. To protect the poor against speculation in the grain market (especially in times of famine), Gaius committed the government to the purchase, storage, and distribution of wheat to the urban poor at about half the actual market price. Unfortunately, what Gaius intended as a relief measure later became a dole, through which nearly free food was distributed—all too often for the advancement of astute politicians—to the entire proletariat.

Another of Gaius's proposals would have granted citizenship to Rome's Italian allies, who felt they were being mistreated by Roman officials. This proposal

cost Gaius the support of the Roman proletariat, which did not wish to share the privileges of citizenship or share its control of the Tribal Assembly. In 121 B.C.E. Gaius failed to be reelected to a third term as tribune. In a further effort to guard against Gaius's leadership, the Senate again resorted to force. It decreed that the consuls could take any action deemed necessary "to protect the state and suppress the tyrants." Three thousand of Gaius's followers were killed in rioting or were arrested and executed, a fate Gaius avoided by committing suicide.

Through these actions, the Senate had shown that it had no intention of initiating needed domestic reforms or of allowing others to do so, and the deaths of Tiberius and Gaius were ominous signals of the way the Republic would decide its internal disputes in the future. In foreign affairs as well, the Senate demonstrated ineptness. Rome was forced to grant citizenship to its Italian allies after the Senate's failure to deal with their grievances pushed them into open revolt (90–88 B.C.E.). Other shortsighted actions led to the first of the three civil wars that assisted in the destruction of the Republic.

The First Civil War: Marius Against Sulla

Between 111 and 105 B.C.E. Roman armies, dispatched by the Senate and commanded by senators, failed to protect Roman business interests in Numidia, a kingdom in North Africa allied to Rome. Nor were they able to prevent Germanic tribes from overrunning southern Gaul, then a Roman province, and threatening Italy itself. Accusing the Senate of neglect and incompetence in directing Rome's foreign affairs, the Roman commercial class and common people joined together to elect Gaius Marius consul in 107 B.C.E., and the Tribal Assembly commissioned him to raise an army to put down the foreign danger. Marius first pacified North Africa and then crushed the first German threat to Rome. In the process, he created a new-style Roman army that was destined to play a major role in the turbulent history of the late Republic.

Unlike the old Roman army, which was composed of conscripts who owned their own land and thought of themselves as loyal citizens of the Republic, the new army created by Marius was recruited from landless citizens for long terms of service. These professional soldiers identified their own interests with those of their commanders, to whom they swore loyalty and looked to for bonuses of land and money, since the Senate had refused their requests for such support. Thus the character of the army changed from a militia of draftees to a "personal army" in which loyalty to the state was replaced with loyalty to the commander.

---

faction—A like-minded, organized group that operates within another group or government. In Rome, various factions rivaled each other for political power in the state.

Plutarch—The Murder of Tiberius Gracchus

In 133 B.C.E., a tribune named Tiberius Gracchus proposed a solution to a major crisis in the Roman state. Redistribution of land to the landless and unemployed residents of the city would allow these individuals to become productive citizens, strengthen the economy, and enable the Roman system of military service, which was dependent on land-owning citizens, to function more effectively. Even though such reform was thought to be necessary by many in the Roman aristocracy, Tiberius was resented for the power and prestige his land law gave him, and he was assassinated by rival aristocrats. The tradition of nonviolent domestic reform through compromise and debate was ended in Rome; many students of Roman history see in the assassination of Tiberius, and of his younger brother Gaius ten years after, the first indications of the breakdown of the Roman Republic:

... Flavius got to (Tiberius), and informed him that the rich men, in a sitting of the senate, seeing they could not prevail upon the consul to espouse their quarrel, had come to a final determination amongst themselves that he should be assassinated, and to that purpose had a great number of their friends and servants ready armed to accomplish it. Tiberius no sooner communicated this confederacy to those about him, but they immediately tucked up their gowns, broke the halberts which the officers used to keep the crowd off into pieces, and distributed them among themselves, resolving to resist the attack with these. Those who stood at a distance wondered, and asked what was the occasion; Tiberius, knowing they could not hear him at that distance, lifted his hand to his head wishing to intimate the great danger which he apprehended himself to be in. His Adversaries, taking notice of that action, ran off at once to the senate-house, and declared that Tiberius desired the people to bestow a crown upon him, as if this were the meaning of his touching his head. This news created general confusion in the senators, and Nasica at once called upon the consul to punish the tyrant, and defend the government. The consul mildly replied that he would not be the first to do any violence.... But Nasica, rising from his seat, "Since the consul," said he, "regards not the safety of the commonwealth, let every one who will defend the laws, follow me." He then, casting the skirt of his gown over his head, hastened to the capitol; those who bore him company, wrapped their gowns also about their arms, and forced their way after him. And as they were persons of the greatest authority in the city, the common people did not venture to obstruct their passing but were rather so eager to clear the way for them, that they tumbled over one another in haste. The attendants they brought with them had furnished themselves with clubs and staves from their houses, and they themselves picked up the feet and other fragments of stools and chairs, which were broken by the hasty flight of the common people. Thus armed, they made towards Tiberius, knocking down those whom they found in front of him, and those were soon wholly dispersed and many of them slain. Tiberius tried to save himself by flight. As he was running, he was stopped by one who caught hold of him by the gown; but he threw it off, and fled in his under-garment only. And stumbling over those who before had been knocked down, as he was endeavouring to get up again, Publius Satureius, a tribune, one of his colleagues was observed to give him the first fatal stroke, by hitting him upon the head with the foot of a stool. The second blow was claimed, as though it had been a deed to be proud of, by Lucius Rufus. And of the rest there fell above three hundred killed by clubs and staves only, none by an iron weapon.

This, we are told, was the first sedition amongst the Romans, since the abrogation of kingly government, that ended in the effusion of blood.... Tiberius himself might then have been easily induced, by mere persuasion, to give way, and certainly, if attacked at all, must have yielded without any recourse to violence and bloodshed.... But it is evident, that this conspiracy was fomented against him, more out of the hatred and malice which the rich men had to his person, than for the reasons which they commonly pretended against him. In testimony of which we may adduce the cruelty and unnatural insults which they used to his dead body. For they would not suffer his own brother, though he earnestly begged the favour, to bury him in the night, but threw him, together with the other corpses, into the river. Neither did their animosity stop here; for they banished some of his friends without legal process, and slew as many of the others as they could lay their hands on; amongst whom Diphanes, the orator, was slain, and one Caius Villius cruelly murdered by being shut up in a large tun with vipers and serpents.

Questions to Consider

1. Do you think that Tiberius's assassination could represent a crucial step in the decline of the Roman Republic?

2. Does Plutarch's description of the assassination give you the impression that the assassination was a well-thought-out plan, or action taken in haste? Why?

3. If Tiberius Gracchus's assassination was planned by the Senatorial opposition, what did this group have to gain by Tiberius's death? Why did they resort to violence?

From Plutarch, *Life of Tiberius Gracchus*, 16–20, in *Readings in Ancient History*, vol. 2, ed. William Davis (Boston: Allyn and Bacon, 1913) pp. 108–109.

Ambitious generals were in a position to use their military power to seize the government.

Encouraged by growing anti-Roman sentiment in the province of Asia and in Greece caused by corrupt governors, tax collectors, and moneylenders, in 88 B.C.E. the king of Pontus, in Asia Minor, declared war on Rome. The Senate ordered Cornelius Sulla, an able general and a strong supporter of the Senate's authority, to march east and restore order. As a countermove, the Tribal Assembly chose Marius for the eastern command. In effect both the Senate and the Tribal Assembly, whose power the Gracchi had revived, claimed to be the ultimate authority in the state. The result was the first of a series of civil wars between rival generals, each claiming to champion the cause of either the Senate or the Tribal Assembly. The first civil war ended in a complete victory for Sulla, who in 82 B.C.E. was appointed dictator by the Senate, not for a maximum of six months but for an unlimited term as "dictator for the revision of the constitution."

Sulla intended to restore the preeminence of the Senate. He drastically reduced the powers of the tribunes and the Tribal Assembly, giving the Senate virtually complete control of all legislation. Having massacred several thousand of the opposition, Sulla was convinced that his constitutional improvements would be permanent, and in 79 B.C.E., he voluntarily resigned his dictatorship and retired from public life.

The Second Civil War: Pompey Against Caesar

The first of the civil wars and its aftermath increased both discontent and division in the state and fueled the ambitions of younger individuals eager for personal power. The first of these men to come forward was Pompey (106–48 B.C.E.), who had won fame as a military leader. In 70 B.C.E. he was elected consul. Although he was a former supporter of Sulla, he won popularity with the commoners by repealing Sulla's laws limiting the

power of the tribunes and the Tribal Assembly. Pompey then put an end to disorder in the East caused by piracy (the result of the Senate's neglect of the Roman navy), the continuing threats of the king of Pontus, and the political uncertainty caused by the collapse of the Seleucid Empire. New Roman provinces and **client states** set up by Pompey brought order eastward as far as the Euphrates. These included the province of Syria—the last remnant of the once vast Seleucid Empire—and the client state of Judea, supervised by the governor of Syria.

Marcus Crassus (MAR-kuhs KRAS-suhs) was another ambitious member of the Senate who was also reputed to be the richest man in Rome resulting from his shrewd business dealings throughout the empire. Crassus was given special military command in 71 B.C.E. to crush the rebellion of nearly 70,000 slaves in southern and central Italy led by the gladiator Spartacus.

A magnificent and idealized representation of Julius Caesar (100–44 B.C.E.), consummate politician, military strategist, and the first Roman to be awarded the title Dictator for Life. Caesar, in possession of more power than any previous Roman political leader, was assassinated in 44 B.C.E. by opponents who feared that he would destroy the Republic.

Still another ambitious and able leader beginning his public career in the 60s was Gaius Julius Caesar (100–44 B.C.E.) From a noble family, Caesar nonetheless chose to appeal to the commoners for most of his support.

Pompey, Crassus, and Caesar all found that the Senate stood in the way of their desires for more control in the state. To negate senatorial opposition, these three politicians agreed to cooperate with one another in an informal arrangement later called the First Triumvirate. All three politicians would pool their resources to help each individual member reach his personal goals in the state and subvert the opposition of the Senate. In 59 B.C.E. Julius Caesar was elected consul and worked to enact legislation favored by Pompey and Crassus. Following his consulship, Caesar spent nine years conquering Gaul, under the pretext of protecting the Gauls from the Germans across the Rhine. He accumulated a fortune in plunder and trained a loyal army of veterans. During his absence from Rome, he kept his name before the citizens by publishing an attractively written account of his military feats, *Commentaries on the Gallic War.*

---

client state—A kingdom or region that Rome considered to be dependent on Rome's patronage. Such states enjoyed some measure of independence but were expected to seek approval from Rome for any major undertaking. If client states failed to satisfy Roman expectations, Rome usually moved to establish permanent control.

Crassus was killed in battle against the Parthians of Persia in 53 B.C.E. Steadily becoming more fearful of Caesar's growing power, Pompey associated himself with the Senate in order to limit Caesar's authority. When the Senate demanded in 49 B.C.E. that Caesar disband his army, he crossed the Rubicon, the river in northern Italy that formed the boundary of his province, and in effect declared war on Pompey and the Senate. He marched on Rome while Pompey and most of the Senate fled to Greece, where Caesar eventually defeated them at Pharsalus (FAR-sa-luhs) in 48 B.C.E. Pompey was killed in Egypt when he sought refuge there. By 45 B.C.E. Caesar had eliminated all military threats against him, and he returned in triumph to Rome to exercise what he hoped would be unlimited power.

As he assumed the title of "dictator for the administration of public affairs," Caesar initiated far-reaching reforms. He granted citizenship to the Gauls and packed the Senate with many new non-Italian members, making it a more truly representative body as well as a rubber stamp for his policies. In the interest of the poorer citizens, he reduced debts, inaugurated a public works program, established colonies outside Italy, and decreed that one-third of the laborers on the slave-worked estates in Italy be persons of free birth. As a result, he was able to reduce from 320,000 to 150,000 the number of people in the city of Rome receiving free grain. (The population of Rome is estimated to have been 500,000 at this time.) His most enduring act was the reform of the calendar in the light of Egyptian knowledge; with minor changes, this calendar of 365 1/4 days is still in use today.

Caesar realized that the Republic was dead. In his own words, "The Republic is merely a name, without form or substance." He believed that only intelligent autocratic leadership could save Rome from continued civil war and collapse. But Caesar inspired the hatred of many, particularly those who viewed him as a high-handed egomaniac who not only had destroyed the Republic but also even aspired to having himself recognized as a god. On the Ides (fifteenth day) of March, 44 B.C.E., a group of conspirators, led by Brutus and other ex-Pompeians whom Caesar had pardoned, stabbed him to death in the Senate, and Rome was once more drawn into conflict.

The Third Civil War: Antony Versus Octavian

Following Caesar's death, his 18-year-old grandnephew and heir, Octavian (63 B.C.E.–14 C.E.), allied himself with Caesar's chief lieutenant, Mark Antony, against the conspirators and the Senate. The conspirators' armies were defeated at Philippi in Macedonia in 42 B.C.E. Then for more than a decade, Octavian and Antony exercised dictatorial power and divided the Roman world between them. But the ambitions of each man proved too great for the alliance to endure.

Antony, who took charge of the eastern half of the empire, became completely infatuated with Queen Cleopatra, the last of the Egyptian Ptolemies. He even went so far as to transfer Roman territories to her control. Octavian took advantage of Antony's blunders to propagandize Rome and Italy against Antony and his foreign lover-queen. The resulting struggle was portrayed by Octavian as a war between the Roman West and the "oriental" East. When Octavian's fleet met Antony's near Actium in Greece, first Cleopatra and then Antony deserted the battle and fled to Egypt. There Antony committed suicide, as Cleopatra did soon afterward when Alexandria was captured by Octavian in 30 B.C.E.

THE ROMAN EMPIRE AND THE PAX ROMANA: 30 B.C.E.–476 C.E.

■ *What were the most significant achievements of the Roman Empire, and what were its greatest failures?*

At the end of a century of civil violence, Rome was at last united under one leader, Octavian, who was hailed by the grateful Romans as the "father of his country." The Republic gave way to the permanent dictatorship of the empire, and two centuries of imperial greatness, known as the *Pax Romana* ("Roman Peace"), followed. But in the third century, the empire was beset with challenges that proved disastrous: economic stagnation, Germanic invasions, and finally the loss of imperial control of the empire in the west.

Reconstruction Under Augustus

Following his triumphal return to Rome, Octavian in 27 B.C.E. announced that he would "restore the Republic." But he did so only outwardly by blending republican institutions with his own strong personal leadership. He consulted the Senate on important issues, allowed it to retain control over Italy and half of the provinces, and gave it the legislative functions of the nearly unused Tribal Assembly. The Senate in return bestowed on Octavian the title *Augustus* ("The Revered," a title previously used for gods), by which he was known thereafter.

DOCUMENT

Excerpt from Suetonius, *The Life of Augustus*

During the rest of his 45-year rule, Augustus never again held the office of dictator, and he seldom held the consulship. Throughout his career he kept the powers of a tribune, which gave him the right to initi-

The Roman Empire

14–68 C.E.	Period of the Julio-Claudian emperors
64 C.E.	Rome destroyed by fire; Emperor Nero attributes fire to Christians
69–96 C.E.	Period of the Flavian emperors
79 C.E.	Mount Vesuvius erupts, destroying Pompeii
96–180 C.E.	Period of the Antonine emperors
313 C.E.	Emperor Constantine issues Edict of Milan; Christians free to worship
378 C.E.	Battle of Adrianople; Germanic invasions into Roman Empire begin
395 C.E.	Roman Empire divided into eastern and western empires
476 C.E.	Last Roman emperor in the West assassinated

challenged. From his military title, *imperator* ("victorious general"), is derived our modern term *emperor*.

Augustus constructed a constitution in which his power was in reality almost unlimited, yet disguised through his masterful use of the institutions of the old republic. He preferred the modest title of *princeps*, "first citizen" or "leader," that he felt best described his position, and his form of virtual dictatorship is therefore known as the Principate. At the beginning of the empire, then, political power was in appearances divided between the princeps and the senatorial aristocrats. This arrangement was continued by most of Augustus's successors during the next two centuries.

Seeking to heal the scars of more than a century of civil strife, Augustus concentrated on internal reform. He annexed Egypt and extended the Roman frontier to the Danube as a defense against barbarian invasions, but he failed in an attempt to conquer Germany up to the Elbe River. As a result, the Germans were never Romanized, as the Celts of Gaul and Spain were.

Through legislation and propaganda, Augustus attempted to check moral and social decline and revive the old Roman ideals and traditions. He rebuilt deteriorated temples, revived old priesthoods, and restored religious festivals. He attempted to reestablish the integrity of the family by legislating against adultery, the chief grounds for divorce, which had become quite common during the late Republic. A permanent court

ate legislation and to veto the legislative and administrative acts of others. He also kept for himself the governorship of the frontier provinces, where the armies were stationed. Augustus's nearly total control of the army meant that his power could not be successfully

The Roman Empire at the time of Augustus.

was set up to prosecute adulterous wives and their lovers. Among those found guilty and banished from Rome were Augustus's own daughter and granddaughter. Finally, to disarm the gangs that had been terrorizing citizens, he outlawed the carrying of daggers.

Augustus greatly reduced the corruption and exploitation that had flourished in the late Republic by creating a well-paid civil service, open to all classes. He also established a permanent standing army, stationed in the frontier provinces and kept out of politics. More than 40 colonies of retired soldiers were founded throughout the empire. Augustus's reforms also gave rise to a new optimism and patriotism that were reflected in the art and literature of the Augustan Age.

DOCUMENT

Augustus on his accomplishments

The Julio-Claudian and Flavian Emperors

Augustus was followed by four descendants from among his family, the line of the Julio-Claudians, who ruled from 14 to 68 C.E. Augustus's stepson Tiberius, whom the Senate accepted as his successor, and Claudius were fairly efficient and devoted rulers; in Claudius's reign the Roman occupation of Britain began in 43 C.E. The other two rulers of this imperial line disregarded the appearance that they were only the first among all citizens: Caligula (Ka-LIG-eu-lah), Tiberius's nephew and successor, was a megalomaniac who demanded to be worshiped as a god and considered the idea of having his favorite horse elected to high office in Rome; Nero, Claudius's adopted son and successor, was notorious for his immorality, for the

murders of his wife and his mother, and for beginning the persecutions of Christians in Rome. Caligula and Nero have been immortalized through history for their excesses and depravity, yet both functioned effectively as emperors for at least some duration of their reigns. Nero in particular was recognized to be intelligent and accomplished by some of his contemporaries.

The Julio-Claudian line ended in 68 C.E. when Nero, declared a public enemy by the Senate and facing army revolts, committed suicide. In the following year, four emperors were proclaimed by rival armies, with Vespasian (ves-PAY-si-an) the final victor. For nearly 30 years (69–96 C.E.) the Flavian dynasty (Vespasian followed by his two sons, Titus and Domitian) provided the empire with effective but autocratic rule. The fiction of republican institutions gave way to a scarcely veiled monarchy as the Flavians openly treated the office of emperor as theirs by right of conquest and inheritance.

The Antonines: "Five Good Emperors"

An end to autocracy and a return to the Augustan principle of an administration of equals—emperor and Senate—characterized the rule of the Antonine emperors (96–180 C.E.), under whom the empire reached the height of its prosperity and power. Selected on the basis of proven ability, these "good emperors" succeeded in establishing a spirit of confidence and optimism among the governing classes throughout the empire. Two of these emperors are especially worthy of mention.

Hadrian reigned from 117 to 138 C.E. His first important act was to stabilize the boundaries of the

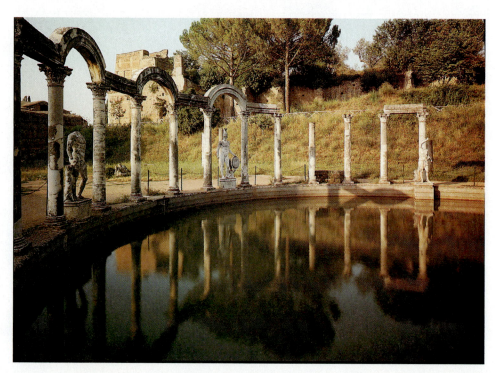

The villa of the emperor Hadrian at Tivoli, a short distance away from Rome's congestion. Hadrian had the villa landscaped and decorated with replicas of famous Greek and oriental monuments.

empire. He gave up as indefensible recently conquered Armenia and Mesopotamia and erected protective walls in Germany and Britain. Hadrian traveled extensively, inspecting almost every province of the empire. New cities were founded, old ones were restored, and many public works were constructed, among them the famous Pantheon, still standing in Rome.

The last of the "five good emperors" was Marcus Aurelius (MAHR-kuhs ah-REE-lee-uhs), who ruled from 161 to 180 C.E. He preferred the study of philosophy and the quiet contemplation of his books to the blood and brutality of the battlefield. Yet he was repeatedly troubled by the invasions of the Parthians from the east and Germans from across the Danube. While engaged in his Germanic campaigns, he wrote his *Meditations,* a collection of personal thoughts notable for its Stoic idealism and love of humanity. Like a good Stoic, Marcus Aurelius died at his post at Vindobona (Vienna); at Rome his equestrian statue still stands on the Capitoline Hill.

The Pax Romana

DOCUMENT

Excerpt from Aelius Aristides, *The Roman Oration*

In its finest period, the empire was a vast area stretching from Britain to the Euphrates and populated by more than 100 million people. It was welded together into an orderly and generally peaceful state, bringing stability and prosperity to the Mediterranean region and beyond. Non-Romans were equally conscious of the rich benefits derived from the Pax Romana, which began with Augustus and reached its fullest development under the Five Good Emperors. They welcomed the peace, prosperity, and administrative efficiency of the empire. Cities increased in number and were largely self-governed by their own upper-class magistrates and senates.

Economic Prosperity

Rome's unification of the ancient Mediterranean world had far-reaching economic consequences. The

The Roman Empire was situated at one end of a vast trading network that spread, by land and sea, across Europe, Asia, and North Africa. At the other end of the network, in China, stood the Han Empire.

TRADE ROUTES OF THE ROMAN EMPIRE
— Principal sea routes
— Principal land routes

Pax Romana was responsible for the elimination of tolls and other artificial barriers, the suppression of piracy and lawlessness, and the establishment of a reliable coinage. Such factors, in addition to the longest period of peace the West has ever enjoyed, explain in large measure the great expansion of commerce that occurred in the first and second centuries C.E. Industry was also stimulated, but its expansion was limited since wealth remained concentrated and no mass market for industrial goods was created. Industry remained organized on a small-shop basis, with producers widely scattered, resulting in self-sufficiency.

The economy of the empire remained basically agricultural, and huge estates, the *latifundia*, prospered. On these tracts, usually belonging to absentee owners, large numbers of *coloni*, free tenants, tilled the soil as sharecroppers. The *coloni* were replacing slave labor, which was becoming increasingly hard to secure with the disappearance of the flow of war captives.

Early Evidence of Economic Stagnation

Late in the first century C.E. the first sign of economic stagnation appeared in Italy. Italian agriculture began to suffer from overproduction as a result of the loss of Italy's markets for wine and olive oil in Roman Gaul, Spain, and North Africa, which were becoming self-sufficient in those products. To aid the Italian wine producers, the Flavian emperor Domitian created an artificial scarcity by forbidding the planting of new vineyards in Italy and by ordering half the existing vineyards in the provinces to be plowed under. A century later the Five Good Emperors sought to solve the continuing problem of overproduction in Italy by subsidizing the buying power of consumers. Loans at 5 percent interest were made to ailing landowners, with the interest to be paid into the treasuries of Italian municipalities and earmarked "for girls and boys of needy parents to be supported at public expense." This system of state subsidies was soon extended to the provinces.

Also contributing to Roman economic stagnation was the continuing drain of money to the East for the purchase of such luxury goods as silks and spices and the failure of city governments within the empire to keep their finances in order, thus making it necessary for the imperial government to intervene. Such early evidence of declining prosperity foreshadowed the economic crisis of the third century C.E., when political anarchy and monetary inflation caused the economy of the empire to collapse.

Roman Society During the Empire

The social structure of Rome and of the entire empire underwent slow but significant change in the early centuries of the Common Era. At the top of the Roman social order were the old senatorial families who lived as absentee owners of huge estates and left commerce and finance to a large and wealthy middle class. In contrast to the tenements of the poor, the homes of the rich were palatial, as revealed by excavations at Pompeii, which was buried and so preserved by the eruption of the volcano Vesuvius in 79 C.E. These elaborate villas contained courts and gardens with fountains, rooms with marble walls, mosaics on the floors, and numerous frescoes and other works of art. An interesting feature of Roman furniture was the abundance of couches

Wall painting of an imaginary garden, recently excavated in the villa of Livia Drusilla, the wife of the emperor Augustus. The scene is painted on the wall of Livia's triclinium, a large living and dining area within the villa, and dates to circa 10 B.C.E. Trees, fruits, birds, and flowers of all varieties are portrayed to create a perfect natural setting.

A fresco portrait of a young woman from Pompeii. She seems to be caught in thought as she prepares to make an entry in her diary.

and the scarcity of chairs. People usually reclined, even at meals.

Roman women in the early empire were still very much the subjects of their fathers or husbands. They could not vote, they had almost no opportunity to represent their own interests in the law courts, nor could they initiate divorce proceedings unless a husband could be convicted of sorcery or murder. Women of very high social status continued to be looked upon as valuable assets in creating marriage alliances between families for eventual political or economic advantage. Wives of many emperors were regarded as representations of the ideal Roman woman, but most such highborn women were given little actual power. With the steady increase in the west of the number of noble women from the eastern empire, where women were permitted more independence of character and action, and through the growing popularity of eastern **mystery religions,** which highlighted the significance of women, the western empire began slowly to grant more rights to its female citizens.

The lower classes in the cities found recreation in social clubs, or guilds, called *collegia* (co-LEE-gee-ah), each comprising the workers of one trade. The activity of the collegia did not center on economic goals, like modern trade unions, but on the worship of a god and on feasts, celebrations, and decent burials for members. The social conditions of slaves varied greatly. Those in domestic service were often treated humanely, with their years of efficient service sometimes rewarded by emancipation or a less demanding retirement from service. Freed slaves were sometimes able to rise to positions of significance in business, letters, and the imperial service. But conditions among slaves on the large estates could be indescribably harsh. Beginning with Augustus, however, legal restrictions protected slaves from mistreatment.

DOCUMENT

Slaves in Roman Law

---

mystery religion—Secret religious cults popular in both Greece and Rome. They reached their peak of popularity in the first three centuries C.E. Their members met secretly to share meals and take part in dances and ceremonies, especially initiation rites. Observance of the proper rites and rituals were thought to provide the initiated with a blessed and blissful existence in the afterlife.

Portrait of a young Egyptian man flanked by folding doors depicting the goddess Isis (left) and the god Serapis, both of whom were associated with death and the afterlife. These paintings on wood panels date to circa 180–200 C.E. and are some of the very few remaining representations of Greco-Roman portraiture used in connection with Egyptian rites for the dead.

Recreation played a key role in Roman social life. Both rich and poor were exceedingly fond of their public baths, which in the capital alone numbered 800 during the early days of the empire. The larger baths contained enclosed gardens, promenades, gymnasia, libraries, and famous works of art as well as a sequence of cleansing rooms through which one moved—the sweat room, the warm room where sweat was scraped off by a slave (soap was unknown), the tepid room for cooling off, and the invigorating cold bath. Another popular room was the lavatory, with its long row of marble toilets equipped with comfortable arm rests.

Footraces, boxing, and wrestling were popular sports, but chariot racing and gladiatorial contests were the chief amusements. By the first century C.E. the Roman calendar had as many as 100 days set aside as holidays, the majority of which were given over to games furnished at public expense. The most spectacular sport was chariot racing. The largest of six racecourses at Rome was the Circus Maximus, a huge marble-faced structure seating about 150,000 spectators. The games, which included as many as 24 races each day, were presided over by the emperor or his representative. The crowds bet furiously on their favorite charioteers, whose fame equaled that of the sports heroes of our own day.

Of equal or greater popularity were the gladiatorial contests, organized by both emperors and private promoters as regular features on the amusement calendar. These spectacles were held in arenas, the largest and most famous of which was the Colosseum, opened in 80 C.E. The contests took various forms. Ferocious animals were pitted against armed combatants

IMAGE

Roman
Colosseum

or occasionally even against unarmed men and women who had been condemned to death. Another type of contest was the fight to the death between gladiators, generally equipped with different types of weapons but matched on equal terms. It was not uncommon for the life of a defeated gladiator who had fought courageously to be spared at the request of the spectators. Although many Romans considered these bloodletting contests barbaric, they continued until the fifth century, when Christian rulers outlawed them.

THE RISE OF CHRISTIANITY

■ *How did Christianity grow from humble beginnings to become the sole religion of the Roman Empire?*

The growth of the Christian religion, from its modest beginnings in an obscure part of the Roman Empire to its eventual dominance as the one and only religion tolerated by that same empire that had once persecuted its followers, is a remarkable story. The rise and ultimate victory of Christianity in the Roman world has even been identified by many observers throughout Europe's history as perhaps the most significant reason for the ultimate decline and fall from dominance of the Roman Empire itself. Whether Christianity was the primary cause of Rome's demise remains a highly debated topic, but there is no controversy about the fact that the religion's growth and development in the ancient world changed not just the course of European but also of world history.

A mosaic from the third century B.C.E. depicting gladiators. Introduced to Rome by the Etruscans, gladiatorial contests grew in popularity and cruelty as Rome grew in power and population.

A partially unrolled section of the texts known as the Dead Sea Scrolls, now preserved and displayed at the Hebrew University in Jerusalem. The Scrolls were preserved by the Essenes, a sect of Jewish militant and religious zealots, whose nearby monastery was destroyed by the Romans in the Jewish revolt of 66–70 B.C.E.

The Jewish Background

Following the conquests of Alexander the Great in the Near East, the Ptolemies and then the Seleucids ruled Palestine. After the Jews returned from exile in Babylonia in 538 B.C.E. (see Chapter 1), they attempted to create a theocratic community based on God's law (the *Torah*) as contained in the *Pentateuch* (PEN-tah-teuk), the first five books of the Old Testament. Later they added to this record the teachings of the prophets and the writings of priests and scholars.

Jewish religious life in Jerusalem centered on the Temple at Jerusalem, and Jewish groups outside Palestine—the Jews of the Diaspora, those who did not return to Palestine after the Babylonian exile—met in local *synagogues* (from the Greek word for "assembly") for public worship and instruction in the Scriptures.

During the Hellenistic Age, Greek philosophy and culture constantly influenced the Jews outside Palestine, most of whom spoke Greek, and contributed to factionalism among the Jews in Palestine. Religious conflict often developed into open warfare.

It was in the midst of a civil war that the Roman legions first made their appearance. In 63 B.C.E. Pompey, who was then completing his pacification of Asia Minor and Syria, made Judea a Roman dependancy, subject to the Roman governor of Syria. Later, Herod the Great, a half-Jewish, half-Arab leader from Edom, was appointed king of Judea by Mark Antony and reigned from 37 to 4 B.C.E. Soon after Herod's death, Judea became a Roman administrative unit ruled by officials called *procurators*. The best-known procurator was Pontius Pilate, who ruled from 26 to 36 C.E. and under whose government Jesus was crucified. The Jews remained unhappy and divided under Roman domination. For centuries the prophets had taught that God would one day create a new Israel under a Messiah—a leader anointed by God. Many Jews lost hope in a political Messiah and an earthly kingdom and instead began to hope for a Messiah who would lead all the righteous to a spiritual kingdom.

The Life and Teaching of Jesus

The Jewish sect that became Christianity bears the unmistakable imprint of the personality of its founder, Jesus of Nazareth. According to the biblical accounts pieced together from the four Gospels, he was born in Bethlehem during Herod's reign; therefore, he must have been born by the time of Herod's death in 4 B.C.E.— probably not in the year that traditionally begins the Christian or Common Era, 1 C.E. After spending the first years of his adult life as a carpenter in the village of Nazareth, Jesus began preaching love for one's fellow human beings and urging people to turn away from sin.

DOCUMENT

Excerpt from the Gospel According to Luke

Reports of Jesus's miracles, such as casting out demons, healing the sick, raising the dead, and walking on water, spread among the Jews as he and his 12 apostles traveled from village to village. When he came to Jerusalem to observe the feast of the Passover, huge crowds greeted him enthusiastically as the promised Messiah. But his opponents, most importantly the influential sect of the **Pharisees,** accused him of distortion

---

Pharisees—Jewish religious party that emerged c. 160 B.C.E. in Palestine. The Pharisees believed that the Jewish oral tradition was as valid as the law presented in the Old Testament. Their belief that reason must be applied in the interpretation of the Old Testament and its application to contemporary problems has now become basic to Jewish theology.

of Jewish religious law, and with treason for claiming to be king of the Jews. He was crucified, a standard Roman penalty for treason, probably in 30 C.E.

The Spread of Christianity

Soon after Jesus's death, word spread that he had been seen alive after his crucifixion and had spoken to his disciples, giving them comfort and reassurance. Initially, there were few converts in Palestine, but the Hellenized Jews living in foreign lands, in contact with new ideas and modes of living, were less firmly committed to traditional Jewish **doctrines.** The new faith first made rapid headway among the Jewish communities in such cities as Damascus, Antioch (where its followers were first called "Christians" by the Greeks), Corinth, and Rome.

The Spread of Christianity to 300 C.E.

The first followers of Jesus had no thought of breaking away from Judaism. But because they adhered to the requirements of the Jewish law, their new message did not easily attract non-Jews. These obstacles were largely removed through more liberal and cosmopolitan teachings of an early Christian convert now known as Saint Paul. Because of his powerful influence, he has been called the second founder of Christianity.

Originally named Saul, Paul was of Jewish ancestry but a Roman citizen by birth. He was raised in the cosmopolitan city of Tarsus, in Asia Minor, and possessed a thorough knowledge of Greek culture. He was also a strict Pharisee who considered Christians to be traitors to the sacred law, and he took an active part in their persecution. One day about 33 C.E., while traveling to Damascus to prosecute the Christian community there, Saul experienced a conversion to the very beliefs he had been vigorously opposing. His conversion caused him to change his name, and also the whole course of his life—from an opponent of the new religion into the greatest of the early Christian missionaries.

Paul taught that Jesus was the Christ (from the Greek *Christos,* "Messiah"), the Son of God, and that he had died to atone for the sins of all people, and to bring salvation to Jews and Gentiles (non-Jews) alike. Adherence to the complexities of the Jewish law was unnecessary.

After covering 8000 miles teaching and preaching, Paul supposedly was put to death in Rome about 65 C.E., the same year as Peter, founder of the church at Rome, during the reign of Nero. By that time Christian communities had been established in all the major cities in the East and at Rome. Paul had performed a very important service to these infant communities of believers by instructing them, either through visits or letters, in the fundamental beliefs of the new religion. He had served as an authority by which standardization of belief could be achieved.

Reasons for the Spread of Christianity

The popular mystery religions that the Romans had embraced from Greece and the Near East during the troubled last century of the Republic gave spiritual satisfaction not provided by Rome's early ritualistic forms of worship. These mystery religions included the worship of the Phrygian Cybele (Si-BEH-lee), the Great Mother *(Magna Mater);* the Egyptian Isis, sister and wife of Osiris; the Greek Dionysus, called Bacchus by the Romans; and the Persian sun-god Mithras, the intermediary between humans and Ahura-Mazda, the great Lord of Light, whose sacred day of worship was called Sunday and from whose cult women were excluded. Common to all the mystery religions were the notions of a divine savior and the promise of everlasting life.

Followers of these mystery cults found Christian beliefs and practices familiar enough to convert easily to the new faith. But Christianity had far more to offer than the mystery religions did. Its founder was not a creature of myth, like the gods and goddesses of the mystery cults, but a real person whose ethical teachings were preserved by his followers and later written down. Shared with the Jews was the concept of a single omnipotent God, the God of the Hebrew Scriptures, now the God of all humanity. Moreover, Christianity was a dynamic, aggressive faith. It upheld the spiritual equality of all people—rich and poor, slave and freeborn, male and female. Women were among Jesus's audiences, and Paul's letters give much evidence of women active in the early church. One of Jesus's closest and favored followers was said to have been Mary Magdalene, a former prostitute. According to the so-called Gnostic Gospels, which the church declared heretical in the early fourth century and ordered destroyed, "Christ loved her more than all the disciples."

Christianity taught that God, the loving Father, had sent his only Son to atone for human sins and offered a vision of immortality and an opportunity to be "born again," cleansed of sin. Its converts were bound together by faith and hope, and they took seriously their obligation of caring for orphans, widows, and other unfortunates. The courage with which some of their number faced death and persecution impressed even their bitterest enemies.

Persecution of the Christians

The Roman government tolerated any religion that did not threaten the safety and stability of the empire. Christianity, however, initially was perceived as a sub-

---

doctrine—A specific position that is taught or advocated. In a religious context, a doctrine is an official position that must be accepted by those who wish to consider themselves believers.

versive danger to society and the state. Christians, as monotheists, refused to offer sacrifice to the state cults on behalf of the emperor—not even a few grains of incense cast upon an altar. Offering sacrifice to the state cults was considered an essential patriotic rite uniting all Roman subjects in common loyalty to the imperial government. For Christians, however, there was only one God: they could sacrifice to no others. In the eyes of many Roman officials, this attitude branded them as traitors.

To the Romans, the Christians were a secret antisocial group forming a state within a state—"walling themselves off from the rest of mankind," as a pagan writer observed. Many were pacifists who refused to serve in the army, denied the legitimacy of other religious sects, and refused to associate with pagans or take part in social functions that they considered sinful or degrading.

During the first two centuries after Jesus's crucifixion, persecution of Christians was sporadic and local, such as that at Rome under Nero. But during the late third and fourth centuries, when the empire was in danger of collapse, three organized efforts were launched to suppress Christianity throughout the empire. By far the longest and most systematic campaign against the Christians, who made up perhaps one-tenth of the population in the early fourth century, was instigated by the emperor Diocletian (dai-o-KLEE-shan) from 303 to 311. He stringently imposed the death penalty on anyone who refused to sacrifice to Roman gods. But the inspired defiance of the Christian **martyrs,** who seemed to welcome death, had a persuasive effect on many observers. "The blood of the martyrs is the seed of the church" became a Christian slogan.

Church Organization

Viewing the present world as something that would end quickly with the imminent second coming of Christ and the last judgment of the living and the dead, the earliest Christians saw no need to build a formal religious bureaucracy. But after it became clear that the second coming would not be immediate, a church organization emerged to manage the day-to-day business of defining, maintaining, and spreading the faith.

At first there was little or no distinction between laity and **clergy.** Traveling teachers visited Christian communities, preaching and giving advice. But the steady growth in the number of Christians made necessary special church officials who could devote all their time to religious work, clarifying the body of Christian doctrine, conducting services, and collecting money for charitable purposes.

The earliest officials were called *presbyters* ("elders"), *deacons* ("servers"), or *bishops* ("overseers"). By the second century, the offices of bishop and presbyter had become distinct. Christian communities in villages near the main church, which was usually located in a city, were administered by priests who were responsible to a bishop. The *diocese,* a territorial administrative division under the jurisdiction of a bishop, usually corresponded to a Roman administrative district of the same name. The bishops were reputed to be the direct successors of the apostles and, like them, the guardians of Christian teaching and traditions.

A number of dioceses made up a *province.* The bishop of the most important city in each province enjoyed more prestige than his fellows and was known as an *archbishop* or *metropolitan.* The provinces were grouped into larger administrative divisions called *patriarchates.* The title of *patriarch* was applied to the bishop of such great cities as Rome, Constantinople, and Alexandria.

The bishop of Rome rose to a position of preeminence in the hierarchy of the church in the western empire. At first only one of several patriarchs, the Roman bishop gradually became recognized as the leader of the church in the West and was given the title of *pope,* from the Greek word for "father." Many factors explain the emergence of the papacy (the office and jurisdiction of the pope) at Rome. As the largest city in the West and the capital of the empire, Rome had an aura of prestige that was transferred to its bishop. After political Rome had fallen, religious Rome remained. When the empire in the West collapsed in the fifth century, the bishop of Rome emerged as a stable and dominant figure looked up to by all. The primacy of Rome was fully evident during the pontificate of Leo I, the Great (440–461), who provided both the leadership that saved Italy from invasion by the Huns (see page 158) and the major theoretical support for papal leadership of the church, the Petrine theory. This doctrine held that because Peter, whom Jesus had made leader of the apostles, was the first bishop of Rome, his authority over all Christians was handed on to his successors at Rome. The church in the East, insisting on the equality of all the apostles, never accepted the Petrine theory.

Foundations of Christian Doctrine and Worship

While the administrative structure of the church adapted to changing conditions in the West, a combination of theologians and church administrators

---

martyrs—Those who voluntarily suffer death rather than deny their religious convictions. The early Christian church saw the suffering of martyrs as a test of their faith. Many saints of the early church underwent martyrdom during the persecutions imposed by Roman authorities.

clergy—The recognized group or body of persons who are officials of a religious organization. In the early Christian church, the clergy were ordained (recognized as officials through ceremonial appointment) and considered apart from the laity, or the believers who were not officials of the church.

defined and systematized Christian beliefs, sometimes by arbitrary means. This process of fixing Christian doctrine, or *dogma,* began with Paul, who stressed Jesus's divinity and explained his death as an atonement for the sins of all humanity.

In time, differences of opinion over doctrinal matters caused many controversies. One of the most important was over a belief called *Arianism.* At issue was the relative position of the three persons of the Trinity: God the Father, God the Son, and God the Holy Spirit. The view that Father and Son were equal was vigorously denied by Arius (256–336), a priest from Alexandria. He believed that Christ logically could not fully be God because he was not of a substance identical with God and, as a created being, was not coeternal with his creator. The controversy became so serious that in 325 the emperor Constantine convened the first ecumenical church council to resolve the problem. This Council of Nicaea (ni-SEE-a) was the first of such councils in early church history. With Constantine presiding, the council found the Arian position to be a **heresy**—an opinion or doctrine contrary to the official teaching of the church—and Christ was declared to be of the same substance as God, uncreated and coeternal with him. This mystical concept of the Trinity, essential to the central Christian doctrine of the *incarnation*—God becoming man in Christ—received official formulation in the Nicene Creed. However, Arius's views found acceptance among the Germans, and his version of the doctrine of the Trinity was adopted throughout Europe and North Africa.

The **liturgy** of the early churches was plain and simple, consisting of prayer, Scripture reading, hymns, and preaching. Early Christians worshipped God and sought salvation through individual efforts. Following the growth of church organization and proclamation of official dogma, however, the church came to be viewed as the indispensable intermediary between God and humans. Without the church, the individual could not hope for salvation.

The development of the church's dogma owed much to the church fathers of the second through fifth centuries. Since most of them were intellectuals who came to Christianity thoroughly equipped with a classical education, they maintained that Greek philoso-

heresy—Any belief rejected as false by religious authorities. In Christianity, the official teachings of the church were believed to be based on divine revelation, and so heretics were viewed as perversely rejecting the guidance of the church. Numerous Christian heresies appeared from the second century onwards.

liturgy—The organization of services for public worship. A standardized and formal presentation of services usually associated with public worship. In the early Christian context, the formal organization of services usually connected with the Eucharist.

phy and Christianity were compatible. Because reason (*logos* in Greek) and truth came from God, philosophy was considered a proper tool with which one could discover God's perfection. Thus Christianity was viewed as a superior philosophy that could supersede all pagan philosophies and religions.

In the West three church fathers made highly significant contributions to the formation of Christian dogma and organization. The scholarship of Jerome (340–420) made possible the church-authorized translation of the Bible into Latin. In a revised form, it is still the official translation of the Roman Catholic Church. Jerome also justified Christian use of the literature and learning of the classical world.

Another of the church fathers, St. Ambrose (340–397), resigned his government post to become bishop of Milan, where he employed his great administrative skills to establish a model bishopric. By criticizing the actions of the strong emperor Theodosius I and forcing him to do public penance, Ambrose was the first to assert the church's superiority over the state in spiritual matters.

St. Augustine (354 – 430) was the most influential of all the church fathers in the west. At the age of 32, as he relates in his *Confessions,* one of the world's great autobiographies, he found in Christianity the answer to his long search for meaning in life. Before, he had shared the doubts of men who search for spiritual satisfaction. He blended classical logic and philosophy with Christian belief to lay the foundation of much of the church's theology.

The Regular Clergy

The secular clergy moved through the world (*saeculum;* SAI-keu-lum), administering the church's services and communicating its teachings to the laity, the common people. But another type of clergy also arose: the regular clergy, so called because they lived by a rule (*regula*) within monasteries. These monks sought seclusion from the distractions of this world in order to prepare themselves for the next. In so doing, they helped preserve and spread the heritage of the classical world along with the faith.

The monastic way of life was older than formalized Christianity, having existed among the Essenes, a militant Jewish communal group. Christian ascetics, who had abandoned worldly life to live as hermits, could be found in Egypt and the East as early as the first century C.E. They pursued spiritual perfection by denying their physical feelings, torturing themselves, and fasting. In Syria, for example, St. Simeon Stylites sat for 33 years atop a 60-foot-high pillar. A disciple then surpassed his record by three months.

In a more moderate expression of **asceticism,** Christian monks in Egypt developed a monastic life in which, seeking a common spiritual goal, they lived together under a common set of regulations. St. Basil (330–379), a Greek bishop in Asia Minor, drew up a rule based on work, charity, and a communal life that still allowed each monk to retain most of his independence. The Rule of St. Basil became the standard system in the eastern church.

In the West the work of St. Benedict (c. 480–543) paralleled St. Basil's efforts in the East. About 529 Benedict led a band of followers to a high hill between Rome and Naples, named Monte Cassino, where they erected a monastery on the site of an ancient pagan temple. For his monks Benedict composed a rule that gave order and discipline to western monasticism. Benedictine monks took three basic vows—of poverty, chastity, and obedience to the *abbot,* the head of the monastery. The daily activities of the Benedictine monks were closely regulated: They participated in eight divine services, labored in fields or workshops for six or seven hours, and spent about two hours studying and preserving the writing of Latin antiquity at a time when illiteracy was widespread throughout western Europe. Benedictine monasticism was to be one of the most dynamic civilizing forces in early medieval Europe.

Women also played an important role in monastic Christianity. In Egypt an early-fifth-century bishop declared that 20,000 women—twice the number of men—were living in desert communities as nuns. In the West several fourth-century biographies of aristocratic women describe how they turned their villas and palaces into monasteries for women of all classes and remained firmly in control of their institutions. These communities became famous for their social and educational services, in addition to providing a different way of life for women who sought alternatives to the usual pattern of marriage, motherhood, and family life.

Official Recognition and Acceptance of Christianity

In 311 the emperor Galerius (ga-LEH-ree-uhs) recognized that persecution of Christians had failed to eliminate the belief and issued an edict of toleration, making Christianity a legal religion in the East. Two years later Constantine granted Christians freedom of worship throughout the empire by issuing, in 313, the Edict of Milan, an order decreeing that Christianity would be tolerated throughout the empire.

Why Constantine did this is open to debate. His Christian biographers assert that the night before a decisive battle at the Milvian Bridge, he looked to the sky and saw a cross with the words *"Hoc vinces"* ("By this, conquer") written on it. The next day, Constantine led his troops to victory, raising the cross as his symbol. The victory also played a role in his embrace of Christianity, which allowed him to build on the support of Christians, who, at 20 percent of the empire, constituted the most organized and unified segment of the population. His actions at the Council of Nicaea (see p. 154) as a self-proclaimed "thirteenth apostle" showed that the Christian Church was to be his state church. Constantine and his mother, Helena, remained deeply committed to Christianity, but he waited until just before his death to be baptized. All of his successors but one were Christian.

This sole exception was Julian the Apostate (361–363), a military hero and scholar who had been raised a Christian but then renounced his faith and sought to revive paganism. But Julian did not persecute the Christians, and his efforts to revive paganism failed.

The emperor Theodosius I (379–395) made Christianity the official religion of the empire. Paganism was now persecuted, Christian authorities sentenced large numbers of pagan philosophers to death, pagan philosophical schools (including Plato's Academy) were closed, and non-Christian works of art and literature were destroyed. Even the Olympic games were suppressed. One famous victim of this persecution *by* Christians was the philosopher Hypatia (hi-PAY-shi-ah), who in 415 was killed by a Christian mob in Alexandria. By the age of 25, she had become famous throughout the eastern half of the empire as a lecturer on Greek philosophy. Her popularity and beauty aroused the resentment of Cyril, the archbishop of Alexandria, who had already led a mob in destroying the homes and businesses of the city's Jews. He incited the mob to abduct Hypatia, who was dragged into a nearby church and hacked to death.

The Roman Crisis of the Third Century

In the third century C.E., internal anarchy and foreign invasion drastically transformed the Roman Empire. Augustus's constitutional monarchy, in which the emperor shared power with the Senate, had changed to a despotic absolute monarchy, in which the emperors made no attempt to hide the fact that they were backed by the military and would tolerate no senatorial influence. By the late third century, the emperor was no

---

asceticism—The denial of physical or psychological desires in order to achieve a spiritual ideal or goal. The quest for spiritual purity, the need for forgiveness, and the wish to earn merit or gain access to supernatural powers all are reasons for ascetic practice. Common forms of ascetic self-denial include celibacy, abstinence, and fasting.

longer addressed as *princeps,* "first among equals," but as *dominus et deus,* "lord and god." The Principate had been replaced by the absolute rule known as the Dominate.

The transformation of the Roman Empire in the third century was foreshadowed by the reign of Commodus (KOM-moh-duhs), who in 180 C.E. began a 12-year rule characterized by incompetence, corruption, cruelty, and neglect of affairs of state. He was strangled in 192, and civil war followed for a year until the establishment of the Severan dynasty (193–235). The Severan dynasty was intimidated by the military, whose commanders the emperors attempted to placate through bribes and exorbitant favors.

After 235, when the last member of the Severan dynasty was murdered by his own troops, 50 years of bloody civil wars, Germanic invasions, and new foreign threats ensued. Of the 26 men who claimed the title of emperor during this time, only one died a natural death. Prolonged economic decline was equally deadly to the well-being of the empire as military anarchy and foreign invasions. The economy became static, inflation set in, and the concentration of land ownership in the hands of the few destroyed the small farming classes. The *latifundia,* with their fortified villas, grew as the number of *coloni*—sharecroppers—grew. As the rural tax base declined, chaotic conditions took their toll on trade, and by the end of the period, the government refused to accept its own money for taxes and required payment in goods and services.

A much needed reconstruction of the empire was accomplished by Diocletian (285–305), a rough-hewn soldier and shrewd administrator. To increase the strength of the government, he completed the trend toward autocracy, leaving the Senate in a greatly diminished role. He attempted to restructure the empire to ensure better government and an efficient succession scheme. Diocletian also tried to stop the economic decay of the empire by issuing new coins based on silver and gold and by imposing a freeze on prices and wages.

Diocletian's succession scheme collapsed when Constantine (306–337) overcame his rivals to take power. Constantine continued

Diocletian's attempts to ensure the production of essential goods and services as well as the collection of taxes. He imposed decrees tying people and their children to the same occupation in the same place. Most important, he moved the capital to the site of the old Greek colony of Byzantium, renaming it Constantinople (see Chapter 6). By doing so, he, in effect, left Rome open to the attacks of the advancing Germanic peoples but ensured the continuation of Roman government in a new, safer location.

The Germanic Tribes

Waves of restless and diverse Germanic tribes were drawn into the power vacuum created during the two centuries of Rome's decline after 180. While the west-

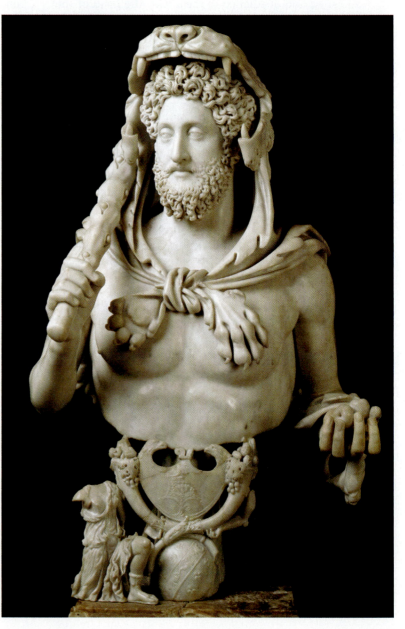

Bust of the emperor Commodus (177–192 C.E.) portrayed as Hercules. The son of the philosopher-emperor Marcus Aurelius, Commodus was physically impressive and often dressed as Hercules and performed as a gladiator. He was one of Rome's most corrupt and despised rulers.

ernmost German tribes (Franks, Angles, and Saxons) had achieved a settled agricultural life in the third and early fourth centuries, the Goths, Vandals, and Lombards remained largely nomadic.

The economic and legal practices of the Germanic tribes set them apart from the Romans. They engaged in so little commerce that cattle, rather than money, sufficed as a measure of value. A basic factor behind Germanic restlessness seems to have been land hunger. Their numbers were increasing, much of their land was forest and swamp, and their agricultural methods were inefficient. In an effort to eliminate blood feuds, the tribal law codes of the Germans encouraged the payment of compensation as an alternative for an aggrieved kin or family seeking vengeance. For the infliction of specific injuries, a stipulated payment, termed a *bot,* was required. The amount of compensation varied according to the severity of the crime and the social position of the victim.

Lack of written laws made it necessary to hold trials to determine guilt or innocence. A person standing trial could produce oath-helpers who would swear to his innocence. If unable to obtain oath-helpers, the accused was subjected to trial by ordeal, of which there were three kinds. In the first, the defendant had to lift a small stone out of a vessel of boiling water; unless his scalded arm healed within a prescribed number of days, he was judged guilty. In the second, he had to walk blindfolded and barefoot across a floor on which lay pieces of red-hot metal; success in avoiding the metal was a sign of innocence. In the third, the bound defendant was thrown into a stream; if he sank he was innocent, but if he floated, he was guilty because water was considered a divine element that would not accept a guilty person.

According to the Roman historian Tacitus, the Germans were notorious as heavy drinkers and gamblers, but Tacitus praised their courage, respect for women, and freedom from many Roman vices. A favorite amusement was listening to the tribal bards recite old tales of heroes and gods. Each warrior leader had a retinue of followers who were linked to him by personal loyalty. The war band—*comitatus* (ko-mi-TAH-tus) in Latin—had an important bearing on the origin of medieval political patterns, which were based on similar personal bonds between vassals and their lords. The heroic values associated with the *comitatus* also continued into the Middle Ages, where they contributed to the basis of the value system of the nobility.

DOCUMENT

Tacitus, *Germania*

During the many centuries that the Romans and Germans faced each other across the Rhine-Danube frontier, there was much contact—peaceful as well as warlike—between the two peoples. Roman trade reached into German territory, and Germans entered the Roman Empire as slaves. During the troubled third century, many Germans were invited to settle on vacated lands within the empire or to serve in the Roman legions. By the fourth century, the bulk of the Roman army and its generals in the west were German.

The Germans beyond the frontiers were kept in check by force of arms, by frontier walls, by diplomacy and gifts, and by playing off one tribe against another. In the last decades of the fourth century, however, these methods proved insufficient to prevent a series of new invasions.

The Germanic Invasions

The impetus behind the increasing German activity on the frontiers in the late fourth century was the approach of the Huns. These nomads—superb horsemen and fighters from central Asia—had plundered and slain their Asian neighbors for centuries. In 372 they crossed the Volga River and soon subjugated the easternmost Germanic tribe, the Ostrogoths. Terrified at the prospect of being conquered, the Visigoths, who found themselves next in the path of the advancing Huns, petitioned the Romans to allow them to settle as allies inside the empire. Permission was granted, and in 376 the entire tribe of Visigoths crossed the Danube into Roman territory. But corrupt Roman officials soon cheated and mistreated them, and the proud Germanic tribe went on a rampage. Valens (VAH-lens), the East Roman emperor, tried to stop them, but he lost both his army and his life in the battle of Adrianople in 378.

Adrianople has been described as one of history's decisive battles since it destroyed the legend of the invincibility of the Roman legions and ushered in a century and a half of chaos. For a few years, the emperor Theodosius I held back the Visigoths, but after his death in 395, they began to migrate and pillage under their leader, Alaric. He invaded Italy, and in 410 his followers sacked Rome. The weak West Roman emperor ceded southern Gaul to the Visigoths, who soon expanded into Spain. Their Spanish kingdom lasted until the Muslim conquest of the eighth century.

To counter Alaric's threat to Italy, the Romans had withdrawn most of their troops from the Rhine frontier in 406 and from Britain the following year. A flood of Germanic tribes soon surged across the unguarded frontiers. The Vandals pushed their way through Gaul to Spain and, after pressure from the Visigoths, moved on to Africa, the granary of the empire. In 455 a Vandal raiding force sailed over from Africa, and Rome was sacked a second time. Meanwhile, the Burgundians settled in the Rhone valley, the Franks gradually spread across Gaul, and the Angles, Saxons, and Jutes invaded Britain. Although each of these tribes set up a German-ruled kingdom within the confines of the empire, only the Franks in Gaul and the Angles and Saxons in Britain managed to establish kingdoms that lasted longer than a few generations.

Meanwhile, the Huns pushed farther into Europe. Led by Attila, the "scourge of God," the mounted nomads crossed the Rhine in 451. The remaining Roman forces in Gaul, joined by the Visigoths, defeated the Huns near Troyes, France. Attila then plundered northern Italy and planned to take Rome, but disease, lack of supplies, and the dramatic appeal of Pope Leo I, whose actions brought great prestige to the papacy, caused him to return to the plains of eastern Europe. The Huns' threat disintegrated after 453, when Attila died on the night of his marriage to a Germanic princess.

The End of the West Roman Empire, 395–476 C.E.

After the death of Theodosius I in 395, the Roman Empire was divided between his two sons. The decline of Roman rule in the West was hastened as a series of weakened emperors abandoned Rome and sought safety behind the marshes at the northern Italian city of Ravenna. The leaders of the imperial army, whose ranks were now mainly German, exercised the real power.

In 475 Orestes, a German army commander, forced the Senate to elect his young son Romulus Augustulus ("Little Augustus") emperor in the West. The following year another German chieftain, Odovacar, murdered Romulus Augustulus and named himself head of the government. The murder of this boy, who ironically bore the names of the legendary founder of Rome and the founder of the empire, marks the traditional "fall" of the Roman Empire in the West, since no emperor was named to carry on the succession. Instead, the emperor in Constantinople commissioned Theodoric (thee-O-doh-rik), king of the Germanic tribe of the Ostrogoths, to lead his people into Italy and establish order. The Ostrogothic Kingdom of Italy, with its capital now at Ravenna, restored order on the peninsula, but the political unity of the western empire fell into steady decline. Because he appreciated the culture he had seen at Constantinople, Theodoric attempted to preserve much of the culture of the Roman West, but the basic fabric of society in western Europe was in gradual transition into a new construct which combined useful institutions of both older Roman and new Germanic elements. A new society was evolving.

THE ROMAN LEGACY

■ *What seem to be the greatest cultural achievements of the ancient Romans, and what effects, if any, do they continue to have on the modern world?*

The Romans left a remarkable legacy to their successors. They excelled in the art of government and created a workable and enduring world-state that brought peace and order to extensive lands on three continents. For a time during the empire, probably one-third of the world's population owed allegiance to the Roman superpower. In addition to their skills in administration, the formulation and application of law, and their gifts as architects and engineers, Roman achievements in the arts, literature, philosophy, and religious thought were also greatly influential on the peoples and cultures that were the heir of their accomplishments.

Evolution of Roman Law

Of the many contributions made by the Romans in government, Roman law is one of the most significant. Roman law evolved slowly over a period of about a thousand years. At first, as in all early societies, the law was unwritten custom, handed down from the remote past, and harsh in its judgments. As noted earlier, in the fifth century B.C.E. this law was put in writing in the Code of the Twelve Tables, as the result of plebeian demand. During the remainder of the Republic, the body of Roman law (*jus civile*, "law of the citizen") was enlarged by legislation passed by the Senate and the assembly and by judicial interpretation of existing law to meet new conditions. By the second century C.E. the emperor had become the sole source of law, a responsibility he entrusted to scholars "skilled in the law" (*jurisprudentes*). These scholars were loyal to the principle of equity ("Follow the beneficial interpretation"; "The letter of the law is the height of injustice") and to Stoic philosophy with its concept of a "law of nature" (*jus naturale*) common to all people and obtainable by human reason. As a result, the absolute power of the Roman father over the family was weakened, women gained control over their property, and the principle that an accused person was innocent until proven guilty was established. Finally, in the sixth century C.E. the enormous bulk of Roman law from all sources was codified and so preserved for the future.

Roman Engineering and Architecture

Always at the hub of the sprawling empire was Rome, with close to a million inhabitants by the early days of the empire. Augustus boasted that he had found a city of brick and had left it one of marble. Nonetheless, Rome presented a great contrast of magnificence and slums, of splendid public buildings and poorly constructed tenements, which often collapsed or caught fire.

The empire's needs required a communication system of paved roads and bridges as well as huge public buildings and aqueducts. As road builders, the Romans surpassed all previous peoples. Constructed of layers of stone and gravel according to sound engineering principles, their roads were planned for the use of armies and messengers and were kept in constant repair. The earliest and best-known main Roman highway was the Appian Way. Running from Rome to the Bay of Naples, it was built about 300 B.C.E. to facilitate Rome's expansion southward. It has been said that the speed of travel possible on Roman highways was not surpassed until the early nineteenth century. In designing their bridges and aqueducts, the Romans placed a series of stone arches next to one another to provide mutual support. At times several tiers of arches were used, one above the other. Fourteen aqueducts, stretching a total of 265 miles, supplied some 50 gallons of water daily for each inhabitant of Rome.

At first the Romans copied Etruscan architectural models, but later they combined basic Greek elements with distinctly Roman innovations. By using concrete—a Roman invention—faced with brick or stone, they developed new methods for enclosing space. The Greeks' static post-and-lintel system was replaced by the more dynamic techniques of vaulting derived from the arch, also borrowed from the Etruscans.

Heavy concrete barrel vaults, cross (or groin) vaults, and domes—all so solid that they exerted no sidewise thrust—made possible the vast interiors that distinguish Roman architecture. The barrel vault was essentially a series of connected arches resembling a tunnel, and the cross vault consisted of two barrel vaults intersecting at right angles. The largest Roman domed structure is the Pantheon, the oldest massive roofed building in the world that is still intact. As its name indicates, it was dedicated to "all the gods" by the emperor Hadrian as a symbol of the union of Greeks and Romans on equal terms. The great dome rests on thick round walls of poured concrete with no window openings to weaken them. The only light enters through a great hole, 30 feet wide, at the top of the dome. The size of the dome remained unsurpassed until the twentieth century.

The Interior of the Pantheon, Rome

The typical Roman **basilica,** which served as a social and commercial center and as a law court, was not domed or vaulted. It was a rectangular structure with a light wooden ceiling held up by rows of columns that divided the interior into a central **nave** and side aisles. The roof over the nave was raised to admit light. The Roman basilica would eventually evolve into the Christian church.

Roman buildings were built to last, and their size, grandeur, and decorative richness aptly symbolized the proud imperial spirit of Rome. Whereas the Greeks designed the temple, theater, and stadium, the Romans contributed the triumphal arch, bath, basilica, amphitheater, and multistoried apartment house. Perhaps the most famous Roman building is the Colosseum, a huge amphitheater about 1/4 mile in circumference and with a seating capacity of about 45,000. On the exterior, its arches are decorated with Doric, Ionic, and Corinthian columns.

Marble representation of a dying Gallic woman and her husband committing suicide rather than be taken prisoner by the Romans. The Romans regarded the Gauls as courageous but unsophisticated in politics and culture.

Sculpture and Painting

After the conquest of Greece, many Romans acquired a passion for Greek art. The homes of the wealthy were filled with statues, either brought to Rome as plunder or copied in Greece and shipped to Rome in great number.

Although strongly influenced by Etruscan and Greek models, the Romans developed a distinctive sculpture of their own, particularly portrait sculpture, which was remarkably realistic. Their skill in

basilica—Originally a secular public building in ancient Rome, typically a large rectangular structure with an open hall and a raised platform at one or both ends. "Basilica" is also a title of honor given to a Roman Catholic or Greek Orthodox church distinguished by its antiquity or its role as an international center of worship.

nave—Main part of a Christian church, extending from the entrance (the narthex) to the transept or chancel (area around the altar). In a basilican church (see basilica), which has side aisles, nave refers only to the central section.

portraiture probably originated in the early practice of making and preserving wax images of the heads of important deceased family members. During the Principate, portraiture and relief sculpture tended to idealize the likenesses of the emperors. The Romans developed a great number of decorative motifs, such as cupids, garlands of flowers, and scrolls of various patterns, which are still used today.

What little Roman painting has been preserved clearly reflects the influence of Hellenistic Greek models. The Romans were particularly skilled in producing floor mosaics—often copies of Hellenistic paintings—and in painting frescoes. The frescoes still to be seen in Pompeii and elsewhere show that the artists drew objects in clear though idealized perspective.

Literary Rome

In literature as in art, the Romans originally turned to the Greeks for their models. Roman epic, dramatic, and lyric poetry forms were usually written in conscious imitation of the Greek masterpieces. Although first conforming to Greek examples and standards, Latin prose and poetry developed an originality and substance that ensure its value as one of the world's great literatures. Its influence was extremely strong on medieval and Renaissance literary efforts, and it continues even now on western literary themes and styles.

The Golden and Silver Ages of Latin Literature, c. 100 B.C.E.–138 C.E.

106–43 B.C.E.	Cicero: Orations and letters
c. 87–54 B.C.E.	Catullus: Poems and epigrams
c. 99–55 B.C.E.	Lucretius: Philosophical poem *On the Nature of Things*
70–19 B.C.E.	Virgil: Epic poem *Aeneid*
65–8 B.C.E.	Horace: Poems
43 B.C.E.–17 C.E.	Ovid: *The Art of Love; Metamorphoses*
59 B.C.E.–17 C.E.	Livy: *History of Rome*
c. 55 B.C.E.–117 C.E.	Tacitus: *Annals, Histories, Agricula*
c. 50 B.C.E.–127 C.E.	Juvenal: *Satires*
c. 46–c. 126 C.E.	Plutarch: *Parallel Lives*

Formal Latin literature did not begin until the mid-third century B.C.E. when a Greek slave named Livius Andronicus translated Homer's *Odyssey* and several Greek plays into Latin. By the end of that century the first of a series of Latin epics dealing with Rome's past was composed. Only a few fragments have survived.

The oldest examples of Latin literature to survive intact are the 21 comedies of Plautus (c. 254–184 B.C.E.), which were adapted from Hellenistic Greek originals but with many Roman allusions, colloquialisms, and customs added. Plautus's comedies are bawdy and vigorously humorous, and their rollicking plots of illicit love and character portraits reveal the level of culture and taste in early Rome. The works of Plautus suggest many of the types that modern comedy has assumed, including farce, burlesque, and comedy of manners.

Literature of the Late Republic and Empire

Latin literature came of age in the first century B.C.E., when an outpouring of intellectual effort coincided with the last years of the Republic. This era is often called the Ciceronian period because of the stature and lasting influence of Marcus Tullius Cicero (106–43 B.C.E.), one of the greatest masters of Latin prose and an outstanding intellectual force in Roman history.

Acclaimed as the greatest orator of his day, Cicero found time during his busy public life to write extensively on philosophy, political theory, and rhetoric. Some 900 of his letters survive. Together with 58 speeches, they give us insight into Cicero's personality as well as life in the late Republic. Cicero also made a rich contribution by passing on to the Romans and to later ages much of Greek thought—especially that of Plato and the Stoics—and at the same time interpreting philosophical concepts from the standpoint of a Roman intellectual and practical man of affairs.

Two notable poets of the Ciceronian period were Catullus (Kah-TUHL-luhs) and Lucretius (loo-KREE-shuhs). Catullus (c. 87–54 B.C.E.) was a socially active young man who wrote highly personal lyric poetry. His best-known poems are addressed to "Lesbia," an unprincipled noblewoman ten years older than he, with whom he carried on a passionate affair. Catullus's contemporary Lucretius (c. 99–55 B.C.E.) found in the philosophy of Epicurus (e-pee-KEU-ruhs) an antidote to his profound disillusionment with his fellow citizens, whom he criticized for their lack of morals and obsession for wealth and sensual pleasures.

Augustus provided the Roman world with a stability and confidence that encouraged a further outpouring of literary creativity. The literature of the Augustan Age was notable particularly for its poetry. Virgil (70–19 B.C.E.) is considered the greatest of all Roman poets. His masterpiece, the great epic poem called the *Aeneid* (ay-NEE-id), glorified the work of Augustus and emphasized Rome's destiny to conquer and rule the world. Using Homer's *Iliad* and *Odyssey* as his models, Virgil recounted the fortunes of Aeneas, the legendary founder of the Latin people, who came from Troy to Italy to fulfill his destiny.

As the most noted poet after Vergil, Horace (65–8 B.C.E.) often praised the work of Augustus and the emperor's great mission. But most of Horace's poetry is concerned with everyday human interests and moods, and succeeding generations up to the present have been attracted by his serene outlook on life.

Quite a different sort of poet was Ovid (43 B.C.E.–17 C.E.). His preference for themes of sensual love in his *Art of Love* and other poems caused Augustus to exile him from Rome. But Ovid was also a first-rate story-teller, and it is largely through his *Metamorphoses*, a witty verse collection of Greek stories about the life of the gods—not neglecting their love lives—that classical mythology was transmitted to the modern world.

DOCUMENT

Juvenal, *Satires*

The literature of the later empire, especially the period between the deaths of Augustus and Hadrian (14–138 C.E.), substituted a more critical and negative spirit for the patriotism and optimism of the Augustan Age. Despite a great emphasis on artificial stylistic devices, the period was memorable for the moral emphasis of much of its literature, seen in the historical works of Tacitus and Plutarch, the philosophical works of Seneca, and especially the poetry of Juvenal (c. 50 B.C.E.–127 C.E.), who has been called one of the greatest satiric poets, who attacked the shortcomings of Roman society and its overwhelming concern for material gain and sensual pleasures.

The Writing of History

Two Roman historians produced notable works of lasting significance during the Augustan age and the early empire. The first, Livy (59 B.C.E.–17 C.E.), was a contemporary of Vergil. His immense *History of Rome*, like the *Aeneid*, is of epic proportions and glorifies Rome's conquests and ancestral greatness. By assembling the legends and traditions of early Roman history and folding them into a continuous narrative, Livy, like Vergil, intended to advance Augustus's program of moral and social regeneration. He praised the virtues of the ancient Romans and sought to draw moral lessons from an idealized past.

Tacitus (55–117 C.E.), like his contemporary Juvenal, was concerned with the declining morality of both the Roman nobility and common citizens. In his *Germania* he contrasted the life of the idealized, simple Germanic tribes with the corrupt and immoral existence of the Roman upper classes. In the *Annals* and *Histories* he used his vivid, succinct prose to depict the shortcomings of the emperors and their courts from the death of Augustus to 96 C.E. Tacitus idealized the earlier Republic, and because he viewed the emperors as tyrants, he could not do justice to the positive contributions of imperial government.

The most famous Greek author in the empire was Plutarch (c. 46–c. 126 C.E.). He lectured on philosophy in Rome before retiring to his small hometown to pursue research on the outstanding figures in Roman and Greek history in order to discover what qualities make people great or unworthy. His *Parallel Lives*, containing 46 biographies of famous Greeks and Romans arranged in pairs for the purpose of comparison, is one of the great readable classics of world literature. Because many of the sources Plutarch used have been lost, his *Lives* is a treasure house of valuable information for the historian.

Religion and Philosophy

The turmoil of the late Republic helped erode the traditions, values, and religion of earlier Rome. For spiritual satisfaction and salvation, many Romans turned increasingly to the mystery cults of Greece (see Chapter 4) or to the Near East. Among the latter were Cybele, the Great Mother, and the Egyptian goddess Isis, who attracted the greatest number of women followers. A faithful mother herself, she extended a mother's arms to the weary of this world.

But the more intellectually sophisticated of Romans turned to Greek philosophy, particularly Epicureanism and Stoicism, for meaning. As young men, both Vergil and Horace embraced Epicureanism, but Lucretius became the most important Roman interpreter of this philosophy. In *On the Nature of Things*, Lucretius followed Epicurus in basing his explanation of the "nature of things" on materialism and atomism. He called on people to free themselves from the fear of death—which was drawing them to the emotional mystery religions of Greece and the East—since souls, like bodies, are composed of atoms that fall apart when death comes. Lucretius urged his readers to seek pleasure in the study of philosophy and not from material gain or such sensual excitements as love.

More in line with Roman taste, especially in the days of the empire, was Stoicism. The emphasis of Roman Stoicism was on living a just life, constancy to duty, courage in adversity, and service to humanity. Stoic influence had a humanizing effect on Roman law by introducing such concepts as the law of nature and the brotherhood of all, including slaves. The law of nature, as defined by Cicero, was an eternal truth that ordered all the rational thought upon which human law must be based.

One of the outstanding Roman Stoics was Seneca (4 B.C.E.–65 C.E.), Nero's tutor and a writer of moral essays and tragedies. He was regarded with high favor by the leaders of the early Christian church, for his Stoicism, like that of the ex-slave Epictetus (eh-pik-TEE-tuhs) (d. 135 C.E.) and the emperor Marcus Aurelius, had the appearance of a religious creed. He stressed an all-wise Providence, or God, and believed that each person possessed a spark of the divine.

Science in the Roman Empire

The Romans were accomplished at putting the findings of Hellenistic science to practical use, and they became extremely skilled in engineering, applied medicine, and public health. The Romans pioneered in public health service and developed the extensive practice of *hydrotherapy*, the use of mineral baths for healing. Beginning in the early empire, doctors were employed in infirmaries where soldiers, officials, and the poor could obtain free medical care. Great aqueducts and admirable drainage systems also indicate Roman concern for public health.

Characteristic of their utilitarian approach to science was their interest in amassing large encyclopedias. The most important of these was the *Natural History*, compiled by Pliny (PLI-nee) the Elder (23–79 C.E), an enthusiastic collector of all kinds of scientific odds and ends. In writing his massive work, Pliny is reputed to have read more than 2000 books. The result is an intriguing mixture of fact and fable thrown together with scarcely any method of classification. Nevertheless, it was the most widely read work on science during the empire and the early medieval period in Europe.

Two of the last great scientific minds of the ancient world were two Greeks, Claudius Ptolemy and Galen, both of whom lived in the second century C.E., an era succeeding the greatness of Hellenic civilization and the growing dominance of Rome. Ptolemy resided at Alexandria, where he became celebrated as a geographer, astronomer, and mathematician. His maps show a comparatively accurate knowledge of a broad section of the known world. But he exaggerated the size of Asia, an error that influenced Columbus to underestimate the width of the Atlantic and to set sail from Spain in search of Asia. His work on astronomy, usually called the *Almagest* ("The Great Work") from the title of the Ara-bic translation, presented the geocentric (earth-centered) view of the universe that prevailed until the sixteenth century. In mathematics, Ptolemy's work in improving and developing trigonometry became the basis for modern knowledge of the subject.

Galen, born in Pergamum, in Asia Minor, was a physician for a school of gladiators. His fame spread, and he was called to Rome, where he became physician to the emperor Marcus Aurelius. Galen was responsible for notable advances in physiology and anatomy; for example, he was the first to explain the mechanism of respiration. Forbidden by the Roman government to dissect human bodies, Galen experimented with animals and demonstrated that an excised heart can continue to beat outside the body and that injuries to one side of the brain produce effects in the opposite side of the body. Galen's medical encyclopedia, in which he summarized the medical knowledge of antiquity, remained the standard authority until the sixteenth century.

CONCLUSION

The story of Rome's rise from a collection of insignificant and unsophisticated villages along the banks of the Tiber to the mighty capital of an empire that included most of western Europe, the Mediterranean region, and the Near East will always remain one of the most fascinating stories in world history. Through the creation of a unified and cosmopolitan empire, the heritage of earlier near Eastern and Greek cultures was preserved, synthesized, and disseminated—and of course the Romans made significant original contributions of their own. They excelled in political theory, governmental administration, and jurisprudence. Roman military might, conquest, and pacification also enabled the growth and development of trade and commerce throughout the Mediterranean and beyond. The security of the empire, and its vast network of roads, fostered a thriving exchange of ideas as well as tangible goods. The growth and triumph of the Christian religion in the West was due in large part to the material benefits provided by the empire's infrastructure, along with the Roman capacity to adapt and refine the innovations of others.

Rome's greatest achievement was perhaps the establishment of peace and prosperity over a vast area for long periods under a stable and acceptable government. The long-enduring empire and its success in uniting a great variety of cultures and peoples under one system of government had a lasting effect on nations and peoples that came after the fall of the empire in western Europe. The cosmopolitan nature of the Roman experience and Rome's long lasting success in bringing unity and peace for centuries, and to a vast amount of territory and diverse peoples, might also serve as an example that such achievements are not impossible accomplishments.

Suggestions for Web Browsing

You can obtain more information about topics included in this chapter at the websites listed below. See also the companion website that accompanies this text, **www.ablongman.com/brummett**, which contains an online study guide and additional resources.

Museums of the Vatican: Gregorian Etruscan Museum
http://www.christusrex.org/www1/vaticano/ET1-Etrusco.html
http://www.christusrex.org/www1/vaticano/ET2-Etrusco.html

Two sites within the extensive pages of the Museums of the Vatican offer numerous images from the Etruscan period.

Timeline
http://www.exovedate.com/ancient_timeline_one.html

The history of ancient Rome, with a chronological index and links to Internet resources. Emphasis is placed on the roles of women in ancient times.

Roman Empire
http://library.advanced.org/10805/rome/html

The history of the empire is illustrated through maps and timelines. Examinations of the sources of our knowledge through Roman writers is emphasized. An extensive history of ancient Rome.

Online Encyclopedia of the Roman Empire
http://www.roman-emperors.org/

A massive site emphasizing the study of Roman history through coins and through maps of the empire.

Pompeii Forum Project
http://pompeii.virginia.edu/forummap.html

Constructed by historians and archaeologists from the University of Virginia, this site examines ancient Pompeii through a variety of photographs.

Vesuvius
http://volcano.und.nodak.edu/vwdocs/volc_images/img_vesuvius.html

A beautiful exploration of Mount Vesuvius in ancient Rome and as it appears today. Speculation on the next eruption as well.

Women's Life in Greece and Rome
http://www.stoa.org/diotima/anthology/wlgr/

Details about the private life and legal status of women, in addition to biographies of prominent women of ancient Rome.

Roman Art and Architecture
http://harpy.uccs.edu/roman/html/romarch.html

A collection of images of Roman architecture.

Literature and Film

Recommended historical novels dealing with Republican and Imperial Rome are a continuing series of mystery novels set in late Republican Rome by Steven Saylor, the most recent of which is *The Judgment of Caesar* (St. Martin's Press, 2004); Thornton Wilder, *The Ides of March* (Avon, 1975); John Williams, *Augustus* (Penguin, 1979); Robert Graves, *I Claudius* (Vintage, 1977); Marguerite Yourcenar, *Memoirs of Hadrian* (Modern Library, 1984); Lindsey Davis, *Time to Depart* (Warner, 1995); and a continuing series of novels dealing with the Roman Republic by Colleen McCullough, beginning with *The First Man in Rome* (Morrow, 1990).

A number of excellent videos available deal with Roman and early Christian themes. Outstanding Hollywood movies, spectacular for their recreations of ancient scenes, are *Ben Hur* (1959), *Spartacus* (1960), and most recently *Gladiator* (2000). More scholarly in content are *Ancient Rome: Story of an Empire* (1998; 4 tapes); *Rome: The Power and the Glory* (2001; Questar); *Catacombs of Rome* (2001; A&E Home Video); and *Rome's Lost Harbor* (2000, A&E Home Video), an excellent account of ancient Ostia. *From Jesus to Christ: The First Christians* (1998; 4 tapes, PBS Home Video) is a very good account of the beginnings of the religion. Finally, *I, Claudius* (1996; 7 tapes, BBC Production) is a classic presentation of the novel by Robert Graves.

Suggestions for Reading

H. H. Scullard, *A History of the Roman World, 753–146 B.C.*, 5th edition (Methuen, 1980); and Michael Grant, *History of Rome* (Scribner, 1979), are highly recommended general historical accounts. Also an excellent general study is Max Cary and Howard H. Scullard, *A History of Rome: Down to the Reign of Constantine*, 3rd ed. (St. Martin's Press, 1976). Ellen Macnamara, *The Etruscans* (Cambridge, 1991), is an informative study of these intriguing people. Three valuable studies of Roman society and morals are Keith Bradley, *Slavery and Society at Rome* (Cambridge University Press, 1994); Florence Dupont, *Daily Life in Ancient Rome* (Oxford University Press, 1992); and Roland Auguet, *Cruelty and Civilization: The Roman Games* (Routledge, 1994). Tom Holland, *Rubicon: The Last Years of the Roman Republic* (Doubleday, 2003) is an outstanding study of the fall of the Republic and Julius Caesar.

For the beginnings of Christianity see J. H. Hexter, *The Judeo-Christian Tradition*, 2nd ed. (Yale University Press, 1995), a brief but valuable survey; Rodney Stark, *The Rise of Christianity* (HarperCollins, 1996); and Richard E. Rubenstein, *When Jesus Became God: The Struggle to Define Christianity during the Last Days of Rome* (Harvest Books, 2000). For the later Roman Empire see Averil Cameron, *The Later Roman Empire: A.D. 284–430* (Harvard University Press, 1993), and Peter Brown, *The Making of Late Antiquity* (Harvard University Press, 1978).

CHAPTER 6

Byzantium and the Orthodox World

Byzantium, Eastern Europe, and Russia, 325–1500

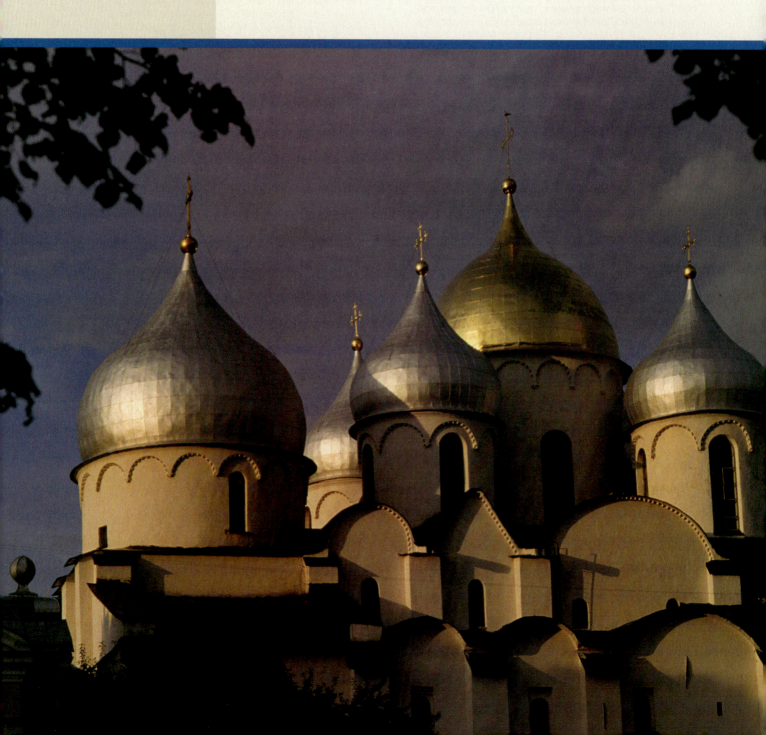

At its height the Roman Empire controlled the Mediterranean world, a zone that extended from the Straits of Gibraltar on the Atlantic Ocean to the Red Sea and the Black Sea. Roman bureaucrats ran a centralized administration that dictated details as small as mosaic patterns on floors in cities as distant as the present-day Constanta, Romania, and Colchester, England. Roman military leaders carried on battles in present-day Persia and along the Danube.

In the power vacuum that followed in the wake of Rome's decline, three civilizations, each sharing common Judeo-Christian roots, emerged to occupy the Mediterranean world. The civilization of western Europe, initially the weakest and most fragmented of the three civilizations, developed under the creative tension between the religious center at Rome and the political structures, such as France, north of the Alps (see Chapter 9). The Islamic world dominated the region in southwest Asia and North Africa (see Chapter 7). The Byzantine Empire, dominating the northwestern part of the Mediterranean world, carried on and modified the Roman traditions, in time transmitting a political and civilizational legacy to the peoples of the Balkans and Russia—the Orthodox world.

In this chapter we will consider the origins and development of the Orthodox world, from the founding of the Eastern Roman capitol at Constantinople—the Second Rome—to the rise of the Russian state at Moscow, the city that claimed the title of the Third Rome after the Ottoman Turks took Constantinople in 1453. When the *tsar* (the Russian word for caesar) Ivan III proclaimed Moscow to be the arena for the playing out of God's divine plan, the end of the world, and the second coming of Christ, he was embracing ideas established first in the Byzantine Empire.

BYZANTIUM: THE LATIN PHASE, 325–610

■ *Why did the East Roman—and not the West—part of the Empire survive the Germanic invasions in the two centuries after 325?*

In his wide-ranging reforms, the Roman emperor Diocletian (die-oh-KLEE-shun; r. 285–305) had wanted to bring order to the governing of the empire. To that end he imposed a new autocratic model for the emperor. He also wanted to make the transfer of power more systematic by dividing up the empire into eastern and western parts, governed by two caesars and two *augusti.* In theory, as each *augustus* would retire, the caesar-in-waiting would advance to take his place. Instead of resolving the problems of civil wars and regime change, Diocletian's solution led to yet another conflict, this one over control of the western half of the empire to be decided in a conflict between Maxentius and Constantine (306–337) at the battle of the Milvian Bridge in 312.

Constantine and Constantinople

Constantine's biographers assert that during the night before the battle, Constantine looked to the sky and saw a cross with the words, *"In hoc signo vinces"* ("By this, conquer") written on it. The next day, after Christ is said to have appeared in his dreams, Constantine led his troops to victory, raising the cross as his symbol. Thereafter he made an alliance with the Christians that turned a minority, though active, sect into a state religion.

DOCUMENT

Eusebius on Constantine The Great

The Roman political tide had turned quickly in the favor of the Christians at the beginning of the fourth century, a time in which they constituted only 20 percent of the empire, though its most organized and motivated population. Diocletian had sanctioned widespread persecution of the Christian faithful but he had succeeded only in creating more martyrs. In 311, the emperor Galerius recognized that persecution had failed to stop the growth of Christianity and issued an edict of toleration, making Christianity a legal religion in the East. Two years later, Constantine and Licinius granted Christians freedom of worship throughout the empire by issuing, in 313, the **Edict of Milan.**

---

augusti—Plural of *augustus*, the title granted the first Roman emperor by the Senate in 27 B.C.E. The title passed to all of his successors. Under Diocletian's plan, the empire would be split into eastern and western parts, governed by two caesars and two *augusti.*

Edict of Milan—Constantine and Licinius in 313 granted Christians the freedom openly to worship their religion throughout the Roman Empire.

In 325, a number of factors convinced Constantine to move his capitol to the site of the old Greek city of Byzantium, including his new affiliation with the Christians (who were then primarily concentrated in the East), the political and defensive disadvantages of Rome, and the wealth of the eastern part of the empire. Constantine named the city after himself and dedicated it as the first Christian city on May 11, 330. He chose a site on the frontier of Europe and Asia dominating the waterway connecting the Mediterranean and Black Seas and protected on three sides by cliffs. The emperor and his successors fortified the fourth side with an impenetrable three-wall network. In the first two centuries, Visigoths, Huns, and Ostrogoths unsuccessfully threatened the city. In the seventh, eighth, and ninth centuries first Persians, then Arab forces, and finally Bulgarians besieged but failed to take Constantinople. The fortress city withstood all assaults until the Fourth Crusade in 1204. The East Roman Empire survived more 1000 years because of the security and wealth provided by Constantinople's setting.

Constantine set out enthusiastically to defend his new faith. At the Council of Nicaea, a gathering of religious leaders held to combat the **Arian heresy,** Constantine declared himself to be the "thirteenth apostle." By combining the function of head of church with that of head of state, Constantine established **caesaropapism,** a system which bestowed on the Byzantine ruler the power to impose his control over all aspects of life in his realm, both spiritual and temporal. Despite his commitment to the church, Constantine waited until just before his death to be baptized. All of his successors but one would be Christian.

Aside from his embrace and use of Christianity, Constantine continued the basic trend of Diocletian's economic and social policies. Upon his death in 337, his three sons took power as coemperors. They, in the tradition of the late Roman Empire, fell into dispute with each other until one, Constantius, emerged victorious. As they built on their father's advances, the successors faced challenges not only from the Germans, but also from the Persians. The East Romans alternately fought with and bribed the Persians, who would remain a continual threat to the East until the rise of Islam.

Arian heresy—The theological doctrine that affirmed that Christ demonstrably, by his suffering on the cross, was not of the same substance as God the father and therefore was less than his father.

caesaropapism—The political system in which the ruler controls all aspects of life in his realm, both secular and spiritual—he is both caesar and pope.

THE SPREAD OF CHRISTIANITY

- Christians: 50% or more of population, 300 C.E.
- Christians: 30%–50% of population, 300 C.E.
- Paul's travels
- ■ Christian communities in the first century C.E.

Christianity spread rapidly as the result of missionary activity along the Roman road system. The first major theological centers were Alexandria, Antioch, Ephesus, and Corinth.

This colossal head of Constantine captures the emperor's vision of himself as a strong man in control.

Julian: The Last Pagan

By aligning himself with Christianity, transferring his capitol to Constantinople, and installing a new form of government, Constantine began the Roman world's transition from a pagan to a Christian world. But, in going from Rome to the East, Constantine moved from the Latin world—centered around law, government, and public works—to the Greek, more specifically the pagan, Hellenistic world, home of the synthesis constructed by Alexander the Great that combined grandeur, polytheistic mystery cults, and Hellenic civilization. As the role of the Christian church grew between Constantine and Theodosius, the pagan world made some counterattacks.

The most prominent attempt to turn back the Christian tide was that made by Julian, called the **Apostate** (r. 361–363). Julian, a nephew of Constantine, saw three of his brothers killed by their uncles during the succession crisis after 337. Because of his age he was spared and sent into exile in the far-off city of Cappadocia. There, he received a classical Greek education, along with a thorough grounding in the study of Christianity. Even though he was baptized, he remained true to pagan Greek literature and not the Christian catechism. In 347, at the age of sixteen, he was allowed to come back to Constantinople,

Apostate—A person who abandons or renounces his religion.

where he continued his studies in Greek philosophy. In 351, he secretly renounced Christianity and continued the pursuit of **Neo-Platonism.** Four years later he went to Athens, where he was initiated into the Eleusinian cults.

In 357 Julian set out to do battle in Gaul, winning several battles along the Rhine and—at the same time—the love and loyalty of his troops, who proclaimed him to be the new Augustus. In 360 he led his forces back to Constantinople, ready to launch a revolt. Constantius, the emperor, died, however, and Julian took power peacefully. Inspired by the example of Marcus Aurelius and Octavian, he set out to be a modest and humane ruler, clearing out corrupt bureaucrats and imposing a just system of taxes. Because he served as emperor only two years, however, his style of government did not make any significant changes in the East Roman system.

Julian saw himself as a divine person, who was descended from the sun god, and carried out his rule as a religious leader. Even though he declared himself to be openly pagan, he advocated a policy of religious tolerance for all, including the anathematized Arians in Alexandria. The longer he ruled, however, the more he became opposed to the Christians, and he began to exclude them from serving in public offices. In the schools he removed Christian teachings and blocked Christians from teaching literature and philosophy. But Julian did not persecute the Christians, and his efforts to revive paganism failed. In 363, he died from wounds suffered in combat with the Persians. The two years of his reign were not enough to turn the Christian tide.

Thereafter the East Roman state resumed its attack on paganism. Theodosius the Great suppressed the Olympic Games in 393. Individual pagans faced attacks by Christian mobs. One well-known victim of this persecution was the philosopher Hypatia of Alexandria, who in 415 was killed by a Christian gang. Justinian made another attack on the 1000-year-old Greek literary and artistic traditions. He gave pagan professors an ultimatum to convert or lose the right to teach. In 528–530, when they refused to convert to Christianity, he closed Plato's Academy along with other schools in Athens. Justinian made the Christian victory complete.

Orthodoxy and Heresies

Continual theological crises occupied most of the 1128 years of the East Roman state. By establishing the precedent of the emperor as the "thirteenth apostle," Constantine gained important support from the

Neo-Platonism—A fusing of Plato's philosophy with Aristotelian, Jewish, and Near-Eastern concepts that led logically to the belief in a universal, perfect One with which the individual soul could commune.

church, and the church itself profited by becoming a state church. In a single-centered-society, heresy was not only a religious issue, but—by definition—a political crime as well. Therefore, the East Roman leaders became embroiled in the theological controversies involved in defining Orthodox Christian theology until the eighth century. Thereafter, Rome and Constantinople competed on questions of doctrine and conversions until the **Great Schism** of 1054, which split European Christianity into Roman and Greek Orthodox communities and remains to the present day.

From its origins, Christianity has been a religion that has produced important controversies. The notions of the composition of the **Trinity,** the nature of Christ, and the **Incarnation** are difficult concepts to define, let alone agree on. Added to these theological controversies was the political competition posed by the establishment of the new Christian city of Constantinople, which had no apostolic traditions such as those found at the older centers at Alexandria, Ephesus, Chalcedon, Antioch, and Rome. The head of the Orthodox church in Constantinople, the **Patriarch,** and the head of the Catholic church in Rome, the Pope, were in general accord for the first four centuries as they constructed the basis of Orthodox Christianity through their readings of the scriptures and the deliberations of the first seven ecumenical councils, which are: "assembl[ies] under the presidency of the Emperor, where every inter-communicating church was represented [and which] was the inspired body whose decisions were binding on Christendom."

In the modern, pragmatic age, the arguments over the Trinity, the nature of Christ, and the Incarnation strike secular people as being particularly abstruse and abstract. But these theological differences had important consequences, not only for the East Roman Empire but also for the development of Christianity. The Arian heresy remained strong in the West—especially in Spain—until the eighth century, and made church unity difficult. When the Muslims began their expansion in 632, people believing in **Monophysite,** Nestorian, and other heretical beliefs—especially the

Great Schism—In 1054, the last in a series of breaks between the churches of Rome and Constantinople occurred. After over 950 years the two churches remain separated.

Trinity—The Christian doctrine asserting that the Father (God), the Son (Jesus Christ), and the Holy Spirit exist as a perfect unity in one godhead.

Incarnation—The putting into human form of a spirit or god. In Christianity, the appearance of the son, Jesus Christ, in human form.

Patriarch—The head of the Orthodox Church in Constantinople, or the head of the churches of Alexandria, Antioch, Moscow, and Jerusalem among others.

Monophysite—A person who believes that God the son has one single, divine nature. This is against the Orthodox view that asserts that Christ was perfect God and perfect man.

Document The Ecumenical Councils and Heresies

First Ecumenical Council: Nicaea I, 325

Attacked the widely followed Arian heresy that asserted Christ was not of the same substance, and therefore less than the father. Instead, affirmed the full divinity of Jesus and of His being of the same substance as God the father.

Produced the creed defining Orthodox Christianity, which, with changes added in the Second Council and in the fifth century is essentially the same as that recited by Christians today. Established the date on which Easter would be celebrated.

Second Ecumenical Council: Constantinople I, 381

Once again, Arianism condemned.

Defined the nature of the Trinity, affirmed the divinity and equality of the Holy Ghost in the Trinity.

Constantinople recognized as second in status among Christian cities, after Rome.

Third Ecumenical Council: Ephesus, 431

Declared Mary to be Mother of God and reaffirmed the single nature of Christ, in opposition to the Nestorian view of the two natures—human and divine—and two persons of Christ, with the implied, reduced role of the Virgin Mary.

Position of Constantinople within the hierarchy of the Church strengthened.

Fourth Ecumenical Council: Chalcedon, 451

Established the Orthodox definition of Christ as having two natures (divine and human) coexisting in one person—perfect God and perfect man, and not one single, divine nature as advanced by the Monophysites living in the east of the empire.

Fifth Ecumenical Council: Constantinople II, 553

Another unsuccessful attempt to reconcile the Nestorian and Monophysite beliefs and bring unity to the empire.

Sixth Ecumenical Council: Constantinople III, 680

In an attempt to heal the divisions within the empire over the Christological controversies, the doctrine of Monotheletism had emerged. In an attempt to bridge the gap between those affirming that Christ had one single, divine nature and the Orthodox position of the two natures of Christ, Monotheletism split the difference and said that Christ had one nature, but that His will was divine-human. This approach was popular in the East, but was found to be heretical at this council.

Seventh Ecumenical Council: Nicaea II, 787

Allowed and encouraged the use of holy images in churches, thus temporarily ending the iconoclastic crisis.

Taken from Steven Runciman, *Byzantine Civilization* (Cleveland and New York: World Publishing Company, 1961), *The Cambridge Medieval History*, Vol. IV, pts. 1 and 2, (Cambridge: Cambridge University Press, 1966).

Copts in Egypt and the Syrians—accepted and even welcomed the invaders, because Islam was more tolerant to them than were the Orthodox Christians. Deeply held differences over the nature of Christ produced substantial political and diplomatic impacts.

The German Challenges

As we saw in Chapter 5, after the end of the first century, the Roman Empire faced the continual pressure of the German migrations. The Rhine-Danube frontier held for the better part of the second century C.E., but the pressure of these migrations, themselves part of a larger, 1000-year-long movement that saw people continually moving to the West from the Chinese frontier to the Atlantic, eventually caused the Rhine-Danube defensive perimeter to fall apart. During the fifth century the western part of the empire became a region dominated by the various German tribes.

The Eastern Roman capitol at Constantinople also found itself on the path of these huge and continuous population movements. Toward the end of the fourth century the Huns, a nomadic tribe of skilled horseman, left Central Asia and began moving to the West. They conquered the Ostrogoths and forced the terrified Visigoths to flee to the West. The Visigoths petitioned the Romans to allow them to settle as allies in the empire. Permission was granted in 376, and the entire tribe crossed the Danube into Roman territory. They were badly treated by corrupt Roman officials, and soon they revolted. The Emperor Valens led his forces from the safe haven of the walls of Constantinople in 378 and tried to stop them at the battle of Adrianople. Aided by the use of the stirrup and long, slashing swords, Visigoth cavalry slaughtered both the emperor and his army. This ended what was left of the Roman army's prestige. The Visigoths soon moved on to the West into Italy, and the eastern capital recovered behind its impenetrable walls. With the exception of Valens's defeat, the Germanic tribes never seriously threatened Constantinople.

Valens' successor, the Spaniard Theodosius (later called "The Great"), pacified the Visigoths and the Ostrogoths who came after them, converting a hostile invasion into a peaceful one. He agreed to make Christianity the official religion of the empire, sought to suppress other beliefs and religions, and advocated

conversion of the Jews. After his death, the western portion of the Empire went into a rapid decline, until its final "fall" in 476.

East Rome, however, became stronger, maintaining its defenses against the waves of migration, codifying its laws, and becoming wealthier. Those fortunate enough to live in Constantinople enjoyed the highest standard of living in medieval Europe. The city became a world trade center by the end of the fifth century and enjoyed the continuous use of a money economy in contrast to the barter system found in western Europe. The Byzantines' wealth and taxes supported a strong military force and financed an effective government. The city built excellent sewage and water systems that permitted an increased life span. Food was abundant, with grain from Egypt and Anatolia and fish from the Aegean. Constantinople could feed as many as 1 million people when it was difficult to find a city in Europe able to sustain more than 50,000. Unlike Rome, Constantinople had several industries producing luxury goods, military supplies, hardware, and textiles. Until Justinian's reign (r. 527–565), all raw silk had been imported from China, but after

BYZANTIUM AND
GERMANIC EUROPE
c. Fifth Century C.E.

☐ Barbarian Europe
☐ Eastern Roman Empire

0   200   400
MILES

By about 481 C.E. the Germanic invasions had nearly eliminated the unity of the West Roman Empire, but the fate of the East was quite different.

silkworms were smuggled out of China about 550 C.E., silk production flourished and became a profitable state monopoly. The state paid close attention to business: controlling the economy through a system of guilds to which all tradesmen and members of professions belonged; setting wages, profits, work hours, and prices; and even organizing bankers and doctors into compulsory corporations.

Justinian and Theodora

The dream of reclaiming the Mediterranean basin and reestablishing the Roman Empire to its former glory, however, did not die until the end of the reign of Justinian (r. 527–565). Aided by his forceful wife, Theodora, and a corps of competent assistants, he made long-lasting contributions to Byzantine and Western civilization, but gained only short-term successes in his foreign policy.

In the 520s and 530s, after earthquakes devastated much of his realm, Justinian carried out a massive

Emperor Justinian bequeathed a splendid architectural and legal legacy to Europe. However, his attempt to reclaim the former glory of the Roman Empire gained only temporary success and bankrupted his treasury.

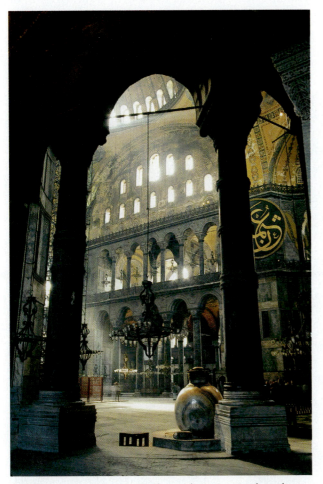

Hagia Sophia remains intact today, and visitors can share the awe of the Russians who visited the structure in the tenth century and said, "We knew not whether we were in heaven or on earth."

project of urban renewal throughout the empire. He strengthened the walls defending Constantinople and built the monumental Hagia Sophia, which still stands. Forty windows circle the base of this great church's dome, producing a quality of light that creates the illusion that the ceiling is floating.

Justinian also reformed the government and ordered a review of all Roman law. This project led to the publication of the **Code of Justinian,** a digest of Roman and church law, texts, and other instructional materials that became the foundation of modern Western law. Following Constantine's example, Justinian saw himself as the thirteenth apostle and participated actively in the religious arguments of his day.

The costs of Justinian's ambitious projects triggered violence among the gangs of Constantinople. Since ancient times, groups throughout the Mediterranean

Code of Justinian—A review of all Roman laws since the beginning of the Roman Republic led to the publication of the Code, a digest of Roman and church law, texts, and other instructional materials. This became the basis of modern Western law.

pushed competitively for their own economic, social, and religious goals. Much like contemporary urban gangs, they lived in separate and well-defined neighborhoods, moved about in groups, and congregated at public events. When the factions had complaints with the emperor's policies, they chanted them in unison when Justinian was present at the circus. The most important of these were the Greens and the Blues, factions that often came to the Hippodrome—a structure that could hold 80,000 people—to support competing chariot racers in the circus.

A general dislike of Justinian's wife, Theodora, the daughter of a circus animal trainer (a background that made her almost untouchable in polite society), provided another point of contention. Her enemies believed that she behaved in an outrageous manner, espoused a heretical variant of Christianity, and had too much influence over her husband. Usually, the gangs neutralized each other's efforts. In 532, however, the Blues and the Greens joined forces to try to force Justinian from the throne. The so-called Nika rebellion, named after the victory cry of the rioters, almost succeeded. We know from Procopius's *Secret Histories* that Justinian was on the verge of fleeing until Theodora stopped him and told the emperor:

> *I do not choose to flee. Those who have worn the crown should never survive its loss. Never shall I see the day when I am not saluted as empress. If you mean to flee, Caesar, well and good. You have the money, the ships are ready, the sea is open. As for me, I shall stay.*[1]

Assisted by his generals, the emperor remained and destroyed the rebellion.

Justinian momentarily achieved his dream of reestablishing the Mediterranean rim of the Roman Empire. To carry out his plan to regain the half of the empire lost to the Germanic invaders, Justinian first had to buy the neutrality of the Persian kings who threatened not only Constantinople but also Syria and Asia Minor. After securing his eastern flank through diplomacy and bribery, he took North Africa in 533 and the islands of the western Mediterranean from the Vandals. His generals also reclaimed the southern part of Spain from the Visigoths, but no serious attempt was ever made to recover Gaul, Britain, or southern Germany.

The grandeur of the Byzantine court can be seen in this mosaic presentation of the Empress Theodora in the St. Vitale Church in Ravenna, Italy.

The old Roman tradition of the Mediterranean as Mare Nostrum *("Our Sea") died hard for Justinian.
Twenty years of fighting allowed one last glimmer of the old days but exhausted his army and his treasury.
A half-century after his reign, the western holdings would be lost, and the East Roman Empire would be
redefined around an Anatolian, not a Mediterranean, base.*

Following Theodoric's death without a male heir
in 526, civil war broke out in Italy, paving the way for
Justinian's 20-year war of reconquest (535–555). Italy
was ravaged from end to end by the fighting, and the
classical civilization that Theodoric had carefully preserved was in large part destroyed in Rome, with
Ravenna suffering extensive damage. To achieve this
victory Justinian drained his treasury. Ironically, in
568, three years after his death, the last wave of Germanic invaders, the Lombards, reputed to have been
the most brutal and fierce of all the Germans, poured
into Italy. The emperor in the East held on to southern Italy, as well as Ravenna and Venice, but left Rome
to the pope, who became the most powerful person in
the city.

By a decade after Justinian's death, most of the
territory he had reconquered had been lost. The
Moors in Africa, Germanic peoples across Europe,
and waves of nomadic tribes from Asia threatened
Byzantium's boundaries. Ancient enemies such as
the Persians, who had been bribed into a peaceful
relationship, returned to threaten Constantinople
when the money ran out, setting in motion a half-
century-long battle. In addition, the full weight of
the Slavic migrations came to be felt. Peaceful
though they may have been, the Slavs severely
strained and sometimes broke the administrative
links of the state in the Balkans. Finally, the empire
was split by debates regarding Christian doctrine.

The stress of trying to maintain order under these
burdens drove two of Justinian's successors insane.

THE AGE OF CONSOLIDATION: 610–1071

■ *What were the institutional changes made by
Heraclius that permitted the Byzantine Empire
to maintain its dominance for the next four
centuries? Why did the system finally fall?*

At the beginning of the seventh century, the East
Roman Empire appeared to be on the brink of extinction. Salvation appeared from the west when Heraclius (r. 610–641), the Byzantine governor of North
Africa, returned to Constantinople in 610 to overthrow
the mad emperor Phocas (r. 602–610). When Heraclius
arrived in the capital, conditions were so bad and the
future appeared so perilous that he considered moving the government from Constantinople to Carthage
in North Africa. Heraclius abandoned the hope of
reunifying the old Roman Empire around its Mediterranean base and, instead, determined that Anatolia
would be the foundation of the empire. During this
time the use of Latin as an official language came to
an end, and Greek—the language of the great majority of the population—took its place. But even with

A Sixth-Century Map: The Madaba Mosaic

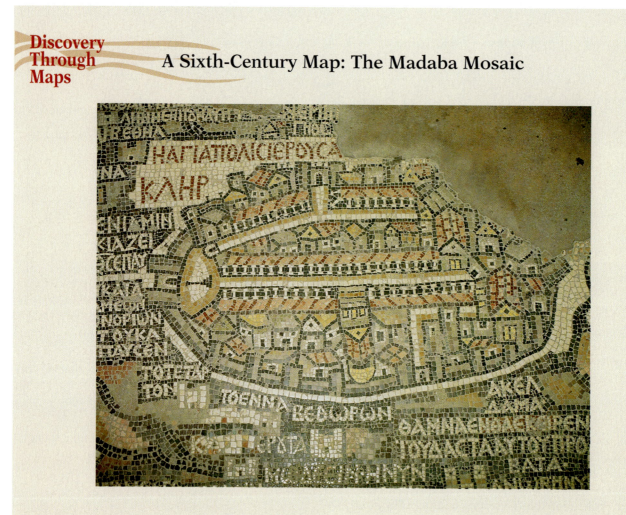

During the first part of Justinian's reign a series of earthquakes shattered buildings around the eastern Mediterranean. The emperor, who had a full treasury, embarked on a massive reconstruction program that adhered to a classical style that was copied all over the empire, even in places that had not suffered from natural disasters. One of the most impressive results of this architectural explosion was Hagia Sophia Church in Constantinople. Another, more subtle but equally revealing, was the Madaba mosaic map, found in present-day Jordan.

Although Justinian was one of the last Latin-speaking emperors of East Rome, the language used in the mosaic map is Greek, a testimony to the existence of the Greek cultural zone established by Alexander the Great in the fourth century B.C.E. that at its height extended from Gibraltar to the Indus River.

Just as Hagia Sophia spoke volumes about the wealth and power of the Christian church, this map, roughly 50 feet by 18 feet, gives remarkable detail about the eastern part of the empire. More than 150 places in present-day Israel, Jordan, Saudi Arabia,

Syria, Lebanon, and part of Egypt—the area of the 12 biblical tribes, or the boundaries of Canaan promised to Abraham—are identified, along with an accurate portrayal of the roads, rivers, deserts, seas, and mountains of the region. Unlike modern maps, which are constructed with a north-south orientation, this map points to the east—toward the altar. The importance of a town can be seen by the way it is described—a small town is depicted as having a small church, whereas the unique qualities of the larger places such as Jerusalem are given more elaborate representations.

There are also other details, such as precise illustrations of places mentioned in the Bible, palm trees to indicate oases, and points at which to cross rivers on foot or by ferry boat. It is obvious that the mosaic map profited from the accounts of travelers. The care with which the unique qualities of various sites are illustrated shows that the map had more than just a decorative function: it was also to be used by Christians making pilgrimages—both those from the West and locally.

A little more than a century later, the region would be swept up in the Islamic advances, and Arabic would begin to replace Greek as the dominant language of the region. Even with that, pilgrims would continue to make their quest through the coming centuries, and the Madaba Mosaic would speak clearly to them.

To gain some notion of a modern perspective, see the map of the Spread of Christianity.

this linguistic change, the rulers referred to themselves as Romans.

Heraclius

The situation did not improve soon for the Byzantines after Heraclius's arrival. The Persians marched seemingly at will through Syria, took Jerusalem, capturing the "true cross"—the cross on which Christians believed Christ was crucified—and advanced into Egypt. The loss of Egypt to the Persians cost Constantinople a large part of its grain supply. Two fierce Asiatic invaders, the Avars and the Bulgars, pushed against Byzantium from the north. Pirates controlled the sea-lanes, and the Slavs, who had begun to move into southeast Europe in the sixth century, cut land communication across the Balkans. Facing ultimate peril, the emperor abandoned the state structure of Diocletian and Constantine.

Byzantium

325	Constantine the Great establishes capitol in Constantinople (city dedicated May 11, 330)
378	Battle of Adrianople; Visigoths defeat Roman armies, Emperor Valens killed
410	Alaric invades Italy
527–565	Reign of Justinian, construction of Hagia Sophia Cathedral
674–678	Arab sieges of Constantinople
842–1071	Golden Age of Byzantine culture and power
1054	Great schism between the Eastern Orthodox and Roman Catholic churches
1204	Fourth Crusade; Byzantium disappears until 1261
1453	Fall of Constantinople, end of East Roman Empire

Heraclius instituted a new system that strengthened his armies, tapped the support of the church and the people, and erected a more efficient, streamlined administration. He determined that the nucleus of the empire would be Anatolia (Asia Minor, the area of present-day Turkey) and that the main source of fighting men for his army would be the free peasants living there rather than mercenaries. Instead of the sprawling realm passed on by Justinian, Heraclius designed a compact state and an administration conceived to deal simultaneously with the needs of government and the challenges of defense.

This system, the **theme system,** had been tested when Heraclius ruled North Africa. Acting on the lessons of the past four centuries, he assumed that defense was a constant need and that free peasant soldiers living in the theme ("district") they were defending would be the most effective and efficient force. He installed the system in Anatolia, and his successors then spread it throughout the empire over the next two centuries. Heraclius's scheme provided sound administration and effective defense at half the former cost. As long as the theme system—with its self-supporting, landowning, free peasantry—endured, Byzantium remained strong. When the theme system and its free peasantry were abandoned in the eleventh century, the empire became weak and vulnerable.

Heraclius, buttressed by the church, fought a holy war to reclaim Jerusalem. During the 620s he applied some of the lessons of Hannibal's mobile warfare to attack Persian strength and took the enemy heartland. In 626 Heraclius stood ready to strike the final blow and refused to be drawn away by the Avar siege of Constantinople. He defeated the Persians at Nineva, marched on to Ctesiphon, and finally—symbolic of his victories—reclaimed the "true cross" and returned it to Jerusalem in 630.

The Byzantines were unable to savor their victory for long, however, because the advance of a new force, the Muslims, posed an even more dangerous threat to

---

theme system—Heraclius divided his realm, first in Asia Minor and then in other regions, into districts called "themes." Understanding that defense would be a continual necessity, he empowered the free peasant soldiers living in the theme to be responsible, under the leadership of a district commander, for the protection of their homelands.

The Byzantine navy coupled its prowess in battle with the secret and powerful weapon known as Greek fire, depicted here in a fourteenth-century manuscript illumination.

Byzantium than the Persians. Byzantium and Persia had previously dominated the Near East, but they were exhausted after 20 years of war. Aided by a superior cavalry, the Muslims took Syria and Palestine at the battle of Yarmuk in 636. Persia fell to them in 637, Egypt in 640. In Syria and Egypt, their advances were assisted by the anti-Constantinople sentiment provoked during the Christological controversies. Under the more tolerant Muslims, those who had a different view of the nature of Christ could freely follow their faith. A millennium of Greco-Roman rule in the eastern Mediterranean ended in a mere five years.

Constantinople's walls and the redefined Byzantine state withstood the challenge, enduring two Arab sieges in 674–678 and 717. Both times the capital faced severe land and naval attack. The Byzantines triumphed by using new techniques such as Greek fire and germ warfare. Greek fire was the medieval equivalent of napalm. It caught fire on contact with water and stuck to the hulls of the Arabs' wooden ships. The germ warfare was accomplished by sending people with small pox and other diseases into enemy camps. At the same time, the Byzantines faced the serious threats of the Bulgarians—continuing their four-century-long pressure on Constantinople—and the Slavs. Heraclius's successors built on his strong foundations by extending the theme system and protecting the free peasants—a source of taxes and soldiers.

The Heraclian dynasty saved the Byzantine state three times: in 610 and during the two Arab sieges. In the end, however, this dynasty proved the point that the political succession in East Rome was never an orderly process. Beginning with the conflicts among the sons of Constantine and continuing at least once in every century thereafter, civil war erupted around the issue of succession, usually with great violence. Notable among these episodes was that of Justinian II, Rhinometus (r. 685–695 and 705–711). His opponents removed him in 695 and, to insure that he wouldn't return, slit his nose and his tongue. He was sent off to exile across the Black Sea, in Crimea. His expulsion led to a 22-year period in which Byzantium had seven different rulers, including the exiled Justinian Rhinometus for a second tour as emperor in 705.

The Iconoclastic Period

As we have seen, from Constantine on, the Byzantine emperors played active roles in calling church councils to debate the questions concerning the nature of Christ and His relationship with the Father and the Holy Spirit. In a structure in which the emperor was both the political and spiritual leader an Orthodox Christian doctrine had to be established as a base to deal with both the secular and spiritual opponents of Constantinople. During times of war, such as the Persian invasions during Heraclius's reign, the combined force of church and state provided great strength. At other times, as in the eighth century, when arguments raged between Rome and Constantinople over the use of icons and the propagation of their particular branches of the faith, the emperor's mixing in matters of faith hurt the East Roman state.

Byzantine Emperors

306–337	Constantine the Great
361–363	Julian the Apostate
364–378	Valens
527–565	Justinian I
610–641	Heraclius I
717–741	Leo III, the Isaurian
797–802	Irene
829–842	Theophilus
867–886	Basil I, the Macedonian
886–912	Leo VI, the Wise
912–959	Constantine VII, Porphyrogenetus
963–1025	Basil II, Bulgaroctonus
1449–1453	Constantine XI

When Constantinople faced a three-sided invasion from the Arabs, Avars, and Bulgarians in 717, another powerful leader, Leo the Isaurian (r. 717–741), came forward to turn back the invaders. Over the next decade Leo rebuilt the areas ruined by war and strengthened the theme system. He reformed the law, limiting capital punishment to crimes involving treason and increasing the use of mutilation for a wide range of common crimes.

Leo took seriously his role as religious leader. He vigorously persecuted heretics and Jews, decreeing that the latter group must be baptized. In 726 he launched a theological crusade against the use of icons, pictures, and statues of religious figures such as Christ and the saints. He was concerned that icons played too prominent a role in Byzantine life and that their common use as godparents, witnesses at weddings, and objects of adoration went against the Old Testament prohibition of the worship of graven images. Accordingly, the emperor ordered the army to destroy icons. The destruction of the icons caused a violent reaction in the western part of the empire, especially in the monasteries. The government responded by mercilessly persecuting the iconophiles ("icon lovers"). The eastern part of the empire, centered in Anatolia, supported the **iconoclasm.** By trying to

---

iconoclasm—The breaking of images. Under the reign of Leo the Isaurian, the empire split over the role of icons (holy images) in the life of believers. Leo wanted to destroy icons, seeing them as a worship of graven images.

remove what he saw to be an abuse, Leo split his empire in two and drove a deeper wedge between the church in Rome and the church in Constantinople.

In Byzantium the religious conflict over destruction of the icons had far-reaching cultural, political, and social implications. Pope Gregory II condemned iconoclasm in 731. Leo's decision to attack icons stressed the fracture lines that had existed between East and West for the past four centuries, typified by the linguistic differences between the Latin West and Greek East. As Leo's successors carried on his religious and political policies, Pope Stephen II turned to the north and struck an alliance with the Frankish king, Pepin, in 754. This was the first step in a process that a half-century later would lead to the birth of the Holy Roman Empire and the formal political split of Europe into East and West.

Empress Irene and Iconophilism

Women played a prominent role in Byzantine political life, whether openly as was the case with Justinian's wife Theodora, or more commonly as powers behind the throne. When succession led to the ascendancy of a minor, a regency council or a single regent would exercise power. Several times in Byzantine history, the Dowager Empress—the mother of the emperor in power—ruled. In 1042 the last of the Macedonian dynasty, sisters Zoe and Theodora, ruled briefly. Later on, Theodora ruled on her own in 1055. Anna Comnena (see Document), wrote of the importance of her mother and grandmother in the affairs of state.

The best-known woman who ruled in her own right was the Empress Irene. Irene was from Athens and an iconophile, a curious choice for the wife of Leo IV. She became regent for—and coemperor with—her 10-year-old son Constantine VI at Leo's death in 780, at the age of 30. She resisted attempts to overthrow her and her son and consolidated their power. In addition, she slowly worked to reverse the iconoclastic policies of her predecessors and called the Seventh Ecumenical Council to bring concord with Rome and reinstall the use of icons.

Irene extended her power during the latter part of the 780s and even after her son reached the age at which he was eligible to rule, she refused to yield any of her power. The iconoclasts rallied around Constantine VI while the iconophiles supported Irene, and finally she was forced out after the army declared its loyalty to her son in 790. Two years later, she was back after Constantine suffered defeat in several battles and proved to be incompetent and even vicious in his actions—when he sensed a potential coup from his uncles, he blinded them and cut their tongues out. His personal behavior, including openly adulterous

Document — Anna Comnena

Anna Comnena, the first woman historian, was a prominent representative of the rich Byzantine intellectual life. She entered this calling after being blocked by the birth of her brother in her drive to become Byzantium's second empress and in other, later political activities. At the age of 55 she was sent off to a forced retirement and began to write a number of books, the best known of which is *The Alexiad*. She lived at the time of the first crusades, seen by the Byzantines as a western European barbarian invasion, and her descriptions of events show a marked disdain for the crusaders so revered in Western accounts. As she described herself, she was "nurtured and born in the purple, not without my full share of letters, for I carried to its highest point the art of writing Greek, nor did I neglect the study of rhetoric: I read with care the system of Aristotle and the dialogues of Plato, and fortified my mind with the quadrivium of sciences." (Quoted in Norman Baynes, *Byzantium*, Oxford: The Clarendon Press, 1961, p. 258).

On Peter the Hermit and the First Crusade

A Celt named Peter, called "Peter the Hermit," left to worship at the Holy Sepulcher. After having suffered much bad treatment at the hands of the Turks and the Saracens who were ravaging all of Asia he returned to his home only with great difficulty. Since he could not bear to have failed in his aim, he decided to begin the same voyage over again. But he understood that he should not retravel the route to the Holy Sepulcher alone for fear that a worse mishap might occur to him; and he thought up a clever scheme, which was to preach throughout all the countries of the Latins as follows: "A divine voice has ordered me to proclaim before all the nobles of France that they should all leave their homes to go worship at the Holy Sepulcher and try with all their ability and with all their passion to free Jerusalem from the domination of the [Saracens]."

Since they did [not] march in ranks or troops, they [later] fell into a Turkish ambush near Drakon and were wretchedly massacred. So many Celts and Normans were victims of the[ir] . . . swords that when the bodies of the slaughtered warriors which were scattered about were [put together they formed] a high mountain of considerable dimensions, so great was the mass of bones.

From Paul Brians, trans., in *Reading About the World*, Vol. I, eds. Paul Brians et al., published by Harcourt Brace Custom Books.

Anna Comnena also wrote compellingly of the brilliance of her grandmother.

It may cause some surprise that my father the Emperor had raised his mother to such a position of honor, and that he had handed complete power over to her. Yielding up the reins of government, one might say, he ran alongside her as she drove the imperial chariot. . . .

My father reserved for himself the waging of wars against the barbarians, while he entrusted to his mother the administration of state affairs, the choosing of civil servants, and the fiscal management of the empire's revenues and expenses. One might perhaps, in reading this, blame my father's decision to entrust the imperial government to the gyneceum (the quarter of the palace reserved for women). But once you understood the ability of this woman, her excellence, her good sense, and her remarkable capacity for hard work, you would turn from criticism to admiration.

For my grandmother really had the gift of conducting the affairs of state. She knew so well how to organize and administer that she was capable of governing not only the Roman Empire but also every other kingdom under the sun. . . . She was very shrewd in seizing on whatever was called for, and clever in carrying it out with certitude. Not only did she have an outstanding intelligence, but her powers of speech matched it. She was a truly persuasive orator, in no way wordy or long-winded. . . .

She was ripe in years when she ascended the imperial throne, at the moment when her mental powers were at their most vigorous. . . .

As for her compassion toward the poor and the lavishness of her hand toward the destitute, how can words describe these things? Her house was a shelter for her needy relatives, and it was no less a haven for strangers. . . . Her expression, which revealed her true character, demanded the worship of the angels but struck terror among demons. . . .

From "The Writings of Medieval Women," Vol. 14, ed. and trans. M. Thiebaux, *Garland Library of Medieval Literature* (New York, 1987).

Questions to Consider

1. Compare and contrast the leadership qualities Anna Comnena portrays in her father and in her grandmother.

2. How would you characterize the Byzantines' attitudes toward the Crusaders? Were these caused more by civilizational or by political considerations?

3. Note Anna's description of herself in the introduction. Can you describe any other women in your study that measure up to her intellectual attainments? As you continue your study of other civilizations at this same time, cite other women you find as equals to Anna and note why.

4. Compare and contrast the frustrations faced by women in the Byzantine setting with those that continue into twenty-first century industrialized societies.

behavior—not a thing usually expected from the thirteenth apostle—led to his being increasingly isolated. Finally, in 797, Irene ordered him taken to the Purple Room, the place in which he was born, and blinded. Irene now ruled the empire in her own name—but as emperor, not empress.

Once in power she cut many taxes to gain the support of her people, gave lucrative gifts to the monasteries, and cut import duties. She gained a moment of popularity, but the state treasuries were drained. She failed to

The Empress Irene (r. 797–802) sought to change the anti-icon policies of her realm and make an alliance with Charlemagne, before being deposed.

win lasting support among the eastern part of the empire for her pro-icon policies; nor could she arrange a marriage alliance with the newly proclaimed western emperor, Charlemagne, before being overthrown—a union that would have brought together the forces of East and West. As Irene spent the treasury into bankruptcy, her enemies increased. Finally, in 802 they deposed her and sent her into exile on the island of Lesbos.

The iconoclastic controversy and Irene's failed policies placed the empire in jeopardy once again. Her successor, Nicepherous (r. 802–811), after struggling to restore the bases of Byzantine power, was captured in battle with the Bulgarians in 811. Khan Krum beheaded him in July and turned his skull into a drinking cup. The iconoclasts had made a comeback, but this phase of image-breaking lacked the vigor of the first, and by 842 the policy was abandoned.

The clash over icons marked the final split between East and West. Eastern emperors were strongly impressed by Islamic culture, especially with its prohibition of images. The Emperor Theophilus (r. 829–842), for example, was a student of Muslim art and culture, and Constantinople's painting, architecture, and universities benefited from the vigor of Islamic culture. This focus on the East may have led to the final split with the West, but, by the middle of the ninth century, it also produced an East Roman state with its theological house finally in order and its borders fairly secure.

Missionary Activities

During the ninth and tenth centuries, Constantinople made its major contributions to eastern Europe and Russia. Missionaries from Constantinople set out to convert the Bulgarians and Slavic peoples in the 860s and, in the process, organized their language, laws, aesthetics, political patterns, and ethics as well as their religion. But these activities did not take place without competition. Conflict increasingly marked the relationship between the Byzantine and Roman churches. A prime example of this conflict was the competition between Patriarch Photius and Pope Nicholas I in the middle of the ninth century.

Photius excelled both as a scholar and as a religious leader. He made impressive contributions to schools in the Byzantine Empire and worked to increase Orthodoxy's influence throughout the realm. Nicholas I was Photius's equal in ambition, ego, and intellect. They collided over the attempt to convert the pagan peoples, such as the Bulgarians, caught between their spheres of influence.

Khan Boris of Bulgaria, who was as cunning and shrewd as Photius and Nicholas, saw the trend toward conversion in Europe that had been developing since the sixth century and realized the increased power he could gain with church approval of his rule. But he also wanted a separate patriarch and church for his own people and dealt with the side that gave him the better bargain. From 864 to 866 Boris changed his mind three times on the question of following Rome or Constantinople. Finally, the Byzantines gave the Bulgarians the equivalent of an autonomous (independent) church, and in return the Bulgarians entered the Byzantine cultural orbit. The resulting schism proclaimed between the churches in 867 set off a sputtering sequence of Christian warfare that continued for centuries.

The work of the Byzantine missionary brothers Cyril and Methodius was more important than Bulgarian ambitions or churchly competition. The men were natives of Thessalonica (thes-sa-LON-ee-ka), a city at the mouth of the Vardar-Morava water highway that gave access to the Slavic lands. Versed in the Slavic language, the two led a mission to Moravia, ruled by King Rastislav. He no doubt wanted to convert to Orthodoxy and enter the orbit of distant Constantinople in order to preserve as much independence for his land as he could in the face of pressure from his powerful German neighbors. Cyril and Methodius carried the faith northward in the **vernacular.** Cyril adapted Greek letters to devise an alphabet for the Slavs, and the brothers translated the liturgy and many religious books into the Slavic language. Although Germanic missionaries eventually converted the Moravians, the work of Cyril and Methodius profoundly affected all of the Slavic peoples.

Byzantium's Golden Age, 842–1071

For two centuries, a period coinciding roughly with the reign of the Macedonian dynasty (867–1056), Byzantium enjoyed political and cultural superiority over its western and eastern foes. Western Europe staggered under the blows dealt by the Saracens, Vikings, and Magyars, and the Arabs lost the momentum that had carried them forward for two centuries. Constantinople enjoyed the relative calm, wealth, and balance bequeathed by the theme system and promoted by a series of powerful rulers. The time was marked by the flowering of artists, scholars, and theologians as much as it was by the presence of great warriors. Byzantium's security and wealth encouraged an active political, cultural, and intellectual life. The widespread literacy and education among men and women of various segments of society would not be matched in Europe until eighteenth-century Paris. Unfortunately this time of well-being would come to an end at the beginning of the twelfth century.

During the Golden Age, the population lived within the theoretical stability of the autocratic framework in which all things—political, religious, military, economic, and social—flowed from the emperor. Underneath that caesaropapistic unity, however, were the political, social, and economic struggles found in all societies. In Anatolia, the theme system based on the free soldier-peasants remained until the end of the eleventh century. The rich soil of the area combined with the dignity of self-defense to produce proud and independent families. Life was difficult, but from time to time there were religious feasts, fairs, and the occasional wandering entertainers. Still, there was always the possibility of an early frost that would wipe out a harvest and bring debt, and there were always the tax collectors. Women guaranteed the functioning of the home while also carrying on the work of the farm when their husbands were fulfilling their military obligations.

In Constantinople, a dependable supply of affordable food was guaranteed by the state and the church, again until the end of the eleventh century. Despite the wars and upheavals, the population levels remained constant in Constantinople through to 1204 and the Fourth Crusade. Among the 800,000 or so inhabitants of the city there were of, course, the homeless, numbering perhaps 30,000, and the criminal element, numbering perhaps the same. The population of the city was divided into three major groups: those who worked for the state, those who were in commerce and manufacturing, and the workers, poor people, and slaves.

The civil servants in the ninth century were the foremost proponents of Greek language and civilization, and—like the Chinese scholar gentry—their learning was as essential to their work as to the advancement of their civilization. Their pride in their position made them intolerant of foreigners, especially people from western Europe. The civil servants also carried a deep contempt for the military, who in their eyes were barbarians. For the clever and ambitious from all levels of society, the means to upward mobility was through education in the Greek classics.

Those in the second category, who made and sold things, remained subject to strict governmental controls over their work. They were frozen into a system of guilds and price controls until the theme system died at the end of the eleventh century. But with all of that, the living conditions were comparatively good—even for those who worked for the owners and merchants. The government remembered its Roman past and worked hard to keep the loyalties of the citizens of the capitol. As long as bread was cheap, the emperors had the support of the citizens of Constantinople. Free bread had ended with the loss of Egypt. The cost of food was kept low afterwards, as the supplies from Anatolia were consistent. Along with bread, a diet of

---

vernacular—Using the language of the people of a local, particular region.

dried peas and beans, green vegetables, and fish was possible even for the poorest inhabitant. If food was plentiful and cheap, clothing and shelter were less available and expensive. The homeless were the first to suffer from the bubonic plague of the eighth century and the Black Plague of the fourteenth—not to mention the always-constant small pox.

At the lower levels of society, few lived beyond the age of 60—but this was a longer life span than that found in western Europe at the same time. The life of the common laborer was difficult, jobs were aggressively sought after, and pay was low. Threatening their status from below were the large numbers of slaves kept in the Byzantine Empire. The status of slave, beyond removing one's legal identity, applied equally to some who lived very well, doing important work for their masters, as well as to those who lived an abusive life, performing the most brutal manual labor.

Except for members of the elite, such as the historian Anna Comnena, the social role of women was

DOCUMENT

Anna
Comnena,
The Alexiad

limited. For the most part, women of the top levels of society remained secluded and rarely went out of their houses without wearing a veil. At home it was rare for a woman to share a meal with a stranger. Within this seclusion, however, there was a lively society, an often-rich family life, and a comparatively high level of literacy and knowledge of the Greek classics. At the lower levels, women rarely were permitted by the guild structure to pursue a craft. Prostitution, which had a restricted legal standing under Constantine the Great, was practiced by a large number of women—in the thousands—in all periods of the Byzantine Empire. For women at all levels, death in childbirth was a common tragedy, and those that lived often saw their babies unable to survive the first winter, as infant mortality rates were extremely high.

Byzantium continued its military as well as its theological dynamism. Arab armies made repeated thrusts, including one at Thessalonica in 904 that led to the loss of 22,000 people. But during the tenth century, a decline in Muslim combativeness, combined with the solidity of Byzantine defenses, brought an end to that chapter of conflict. Basil II (r. 963—1025), surnamed Bulgaroctonus (bul-ga-ROK-to-nus) or "Bulgar slayer," stopped Bulgarian challenges for more than a century at the battle of Balathista in 1014. At the same time, the Macedonian emperors dealt from a position of strength with western European powers, especially where their interests clashed in Italy. Western diplomats visiting the Byzantine court expressed outrage at the benign contempt with which the eastern emperors treated them. But the attitude merely reflected Constantinople's understanding of its role in the world.

The Byzantines continued their sometimes violent political traditions. Emperor Romanus Lecapenus I

(r. 920–944) was overthrown by his sons, and in the eleventh century, succession to the throne degenerated into a power struggle between the civil and military aristocracies. Yet through all the political strife, the secular and theological schools flourished, and the emperors proved to be generous patrons of the arts. Basil I (r. 867–886) and Leo VI (r. 886–912) oversaw the collection and reform of the law codes. Leo, the most prolific lawgiver since Justinian, sponsored the greatest collection of laws of the medieval Byzantine Empire, a work that would affect jurisprudence throughout Europe. Constantine VII Porphyrogenitus (por-phi-ro-GEN-ee-tus; r. 912–959) excelled as a military leader, lover of books, promoter of an encyclopedia, and surveyor of the empire's provinces. At a time when scholarship in western Europe was almost nonexistent, Constantinople society featured a rich cultural life and widespread literacy among men and women of different classes.

The greatest contribution to European civilization from Byzantium's Golden Age was the preservation of ancient learning, especially in the areas of law, Greek science and literature, and Platonic and Aristotelian philosophy. Whereas in the West the church maintained scholarship, the men and women of Byzantium perpetuated the Greek tradition in philosophy, literature, and science. Perhaps because of this rich secular intellectual life, Byzantine monasteries—which produced many saints and mystics–showed little interest in learning or teaching about this world.

WESTERN AND TURKISH INVASIONS: 1071–1453

■ *Why did the Byzantine Empire pass from being the dominant power in the region in 1015 to being so weak by 1095?*

Empires more often succumb to internal ailments than to external takeovers. This was the case with the Byzantine Empire. As long as Constantinople strengthened the foundations laid by Heraclius—the theme system and reliance on the free soldier-peasant—the empire withstood the military attacks of the strongest armies of the time. When the Byzantine leaders abandoned the pillars of their success, the state succumbed to the slightest pressure.

Byzantine Decline and the Seljuk Advance

Inflation and ambition ate away at the Heraclian structure. Too much money chased too few goods during the Golden Age. Land came to be the most profitable investment the rich could make, and the landowning magnates needed labor. Rising prices meant increased taxes. The peasant villages were collectively responsible for paying taxes, and the rising tax burden overwhelmed them. In many parts of the empire, villages sought relief by placing themselves under the control of large landowners, thus taking themselves out of the tax pool and lowering the number of peasant-soldiers. Both the state treasury and the army suffered as a result.

Until Basil II, the Macedonian emperors had tried to protect the peasantry through legislation, but the trend could not be reversed. Even though the free peasantry never entirely disappeared and each free person was still theoretically a citizen of the empire, economic and social pressures effectively destroyed the theme system. An additional factor contributing to the empire's decline was the growth of the church's holdings and the large percentage of the population taking holy orders, thus becoming exempt from taxation.

For 50 years following Basil II's death in 1025, the illusion that eternal peace had been achieved after his defeat of the Bulgarians in 1014 encouraged the oppor-

tunistic civil aristocracy, which controlled the state, to weaken the army and neglect the provinces. The next time danger arose, no strong rulers appeared to save Byzantium, perhaps because no enemies massed dramatically outside the walls of Constantinople.

New foes challenged Byzantium. The Turkish peoples, who had migrated from the region north of China to southwestern Asia around the sixth century, converted gradually to Islam. Warrior bands that formed among them fought first with and then against the Persians, Byzantines, and Arabs. The first of these Turkish bands to invade the Middle East and, eventually Anatolia, were the Seljuks (SEL-yukes). When the Seljuk Turk leader Alp Arslan (the "Victorious Lion") made a tentative probe into the empire's eastern perimeter near Lake Van in 1071, the multilingual mercenary army sent out from Constantinople fell apart even before fighting began at Manzikert. With the disintegration of the army, the only thing that could stop the Seljuk Turks' march for the next decade was the extent of their own ambition and energy.

Byzantium lost the heart of its empire when it lost Anatolia, and with it the reserves of soldiers, leaders, taxes, and food that had enabled it to survive

The Byzantine Empire went from a major to a minor power in the century and a half portrayed on this map. After the Turkish defeat at Manzikert in 1071, the Byzantines maintained effective control of only a small fringe of Anatolia to the east and to the north, giving in to the pressure of the Slavic migrations which had begun around the fifth century C.E. The arrival of the Hungarians in the ninth and tenth centuries drove a wedge that prevented the Slavs from unifying.

for four centuries. From its weakened position, the empire confronted Venice, a powerful commercial, and later political, rival. By the end of the eleventh century the Venetians had achieved undisputed trading supremacy in the Adriatic and turned their attention to the eastern Mediterranean. The Byzantines also faced the challenges of the Normans, led by Robert Guiscard, who took the last Byzantine stronghold in Italy.

The Western Crusades

The fracture in the relationship between Rome and Constantinople that had been opened during the iconoclastic controversy steadily grew into a theological gulf during the conversion competition of the ninth century. Thereafter, Rome and Constantinople developed in different ways. The Pope stood at the head of a growing community of independent states while the Emperor and his Patriarch could look to the west and north and see their allied Orthodox countries. The events leading up to the Great Schism in 1054 centered around the competition between Pope Leo IX and Patriarch Michael Cerularius. Each was ambitious for his own cause; neither cared further to maintain the fiction of Christian unity. The issues had been previously discussed: the western doctrine of the double procession of the Holy Ghost and fasting on Sunday and the eastern practices of a married clergy and the use of leavened bread in the communion service. The face-off between Pope and Patriarch led, in July of 1054, to the Roman excommunication of the eastern church's leaders and Constantinople's excommunication of the Roman church's officials. The schism between the two has never been healed.

In 1081 a politically astute and brilliant family, the Comnenians, claimed the Byzantine throne. In earlier times, with the empire at its strongest, these new rulers might have accomplished great things. But the best they could do in the eleventh and twelfth centuries after the defeat at Lake Van was to play a balance-of-power game between East and West, so well described by Anna Comnena in *The Alexiad*. In 1096 the first crusaders appeared, partly in response to the Council of Clermont, partly in response to the lure of gold and glory (see Chapter 9). Alexius Comnenus (r. 1081–1118) had appealed to Pope Urban II for help against the Seljuks, but he did not bargain on finding a host of crusaders, including the dreaded Normans and fanatic and disorganized peasants, on his doorstep. Alexius quickly got the crusaders—both peasant and noble—across the Straits of Bosporus and Dardanelles, where they won some battles that allowed the Byzantines to reclaim land lost in the previous 15 years.

Dueling Crusaders

The envy, hatred, and frustration that had been building up between the Byzantines and the Crusaders during the twelfth century finally erupted during the Fourth Crusade. The Venetians, who wanted to extend

The Crusades, viewed from the Western perspective as an epoch of bravery, were for the Byzantines and the Arabs a time of barbaric invasions. The crusaders not only failed in the long term to reclaim the Holy Land but also failed to stem the Islamic advance. By the sixteenth century, Turkish forces would be threatening Vienna.

their trade dominance in the eastern Mediterranean and the Black Sea, had control of the ships and money for this crusade. When the crusaders proved unable to pay for Venetian services rendered, they persuaded the crusaders to attack the Christian city of Zadar in Dalmatia—a commercial rival of Venice and Constantinople—before going on to the Holy Land. Constantinople itself was paralyzed by factional strife, and in 1204 for the first time an invading force captured and sacked the city. A French noble described the scene:

> *The fire . . . continued to rage for a whole week and no one could put it out. . . . What damage was done, or what riches and possessions were destroyed in the flames, was beyond the power of man to calculate. . . . The army . . . gained much booty; so much, indeed, that no one could estimate its amount or its value. It included gold and silver, table-services and precious stones, satin and silk, mantles of squirrel fur, ermine and miniver, and every choicest thing to be found on this earth. . . . So much booty had never been gained in any city since the creation of the world.*[2]

The Venetians made sure they got their share of the spoils, such as the bronze horses now found at St. Mark's Cathedral in Venice, and played a key role in placing a new emperor on the throne. The invaders ruled Constantinople until 1261. The Venetians put a stranglehold on commerce in the region and turned their hostility toward the Genoese, who threatened their trade monopoly.

The Ottoman Victory

The empire's last two centuries under the final dynasty, the Paleologus (1261–1453), saw the formerly glorious realm become a pawn in a new game. Greeks regained control of the church and the state, but there was precious little strength to carry on the ancient traditions. Byzantine coinage, which had retained its value from the fourth through the eleventh centuries, fell victim to inflation and weakness. The church, once a major pillar to help the state, became embroiled in continual doctrinal disputes. Slavic peoples such as the Bulgarians and the Serbs under Stephen Nemanja (r. 1168–1196) and Stephen Dushan (r. 1331–1355), who had posed no danger to the empire in its former strength, became threats. After Mongol invasions in the thirteenth century destroyed the exhausted Seljuk Turks, a new more formidable foe, the Ottoman or Osmanli Turks, appeared.

The Ottomans emerged from the groups of elite Turkish warriors, the *ghazis*, which came together on the northwestern frontier of Anatolia. They participated in the complex political and diplomatic relations in the Aegean area in the wake of the Fourth Crusade and were ready to take advantage of the weakened Byzantine Empire. Blessed after 1296 with a strong line of male successors and good fortune, the Ottomans rapidly expanded their power through the Balkans. They crossed the Straits into Europe in 1354 and moved up the Vardar and Morava valleys to take Serres (1383), Sofia (1385), Nis (1386), Thessalonica (1387), and finally Kosovo from the South Slavs in 1389.

The Ottoman Turks' overwhelming infantry and cavalry superiority gave them their military victories. But their administrative effectiveness, which combined strength and flexibility, solidified their rule in areas they conquered. In contrast to the Christians, both Roman and Byzantine, who were intolerant of theological differences, the Turks allowed monotheists or any believers in a "religion of the book" (the Bible, Torah, or Qur'an) to retain their faith and be ruled by a religious superior through the **millet system,** a network of religious ghettos.

In response to the Ottoman advance, the West mounted a poorly conceived and ill-fated crusade against them. The confrontation at Nicopolis on the Danube in 1396 resulted in the capture and slaughter of 10,000 knights and their attendants. Only the overwhelming force of Tamerlane (Timur the Magnificent), a Turco-Mongol ruler who defeated the Ottoman army in 1402, gave Constantinople and Europe some breathing space.

DOCUMENT
Kritovoulos on the Fall of Constantinople

The end for Constantinople came in May 1453. The last emperor, Constantine XI, and his force of 9000, half of whom were Genoese, held off 160,000 Ottomans for seven weeks. Finally, with the help of Hungarian artillerymen, the Turks breached the once impenetrable walls of the depopulated city. After 1123 years, the shining fortress fell.

DOCUMENT
Nestor-Iskander on the Fall of Constantinople

SOUTHEASTERN EUROPE TO 1500

■ *What role did religion play in the formation of the various Balkan nations?*

Following in the wake of the Germanic tribes' westward march, the dominant people of eastern Europe, the Slavs, spread from the Pripet marshes west to the Elbe, east to the Urals, north to Finland, and south to the Peloponnesus. As they settled throughout eastern

---

millet system—The Ottoman Turks ruled in accord with religious law and governed their holdings as a theocratic state. Non-Turks were ruled according to their religious faith, and responsibilities for governance were handed over to the chief figures of each religious area, or millet.

and southern Europe from the sixth through the ninth centuries, they absorbed most of the original inhabitants of the region. This mixing of peoples produced the resulting blends of nations that make up the present-day complexity of eastern Europe and Russia.

Compared to the wealth and sophistication of the Byzantines, the Slavs' economic and cultural lives were primitive, and their political and military structures were weak. Outsiders—Byzantines, Germans, Magyars, Mongols, or Turks—often ruled the various Slavic groups. Yet, before the imposition of Ottoman control, each of the Balkan peoples would have a moment of glory—the two Bulgarian empires, the Serbs under Stephen Nemanja and Stephen Dushan—in which each would create its own image of Byzantium.

Bulgaria

During the great migrations of the peoples, a warlike Finno-Tatar group arrived in the late seventh century—at a time when the Byzantine Empire was fighting for its life against the Arabs—and occupied the lands between the Balkan and the Rhodope Mountain ranges of the Balkans. Like the Huns, they were fighters and not farmers, and so after easily conquering the Slavic peoples of the region, they lived off the fruits of their subjects' labors while consolidating their positions against other invaders.

As was the case with other nomadic warrior bands, the Bulgarians within a couple of generations were absorbed by the more numerous Slavs, and became, for all intents and purposes, like other South Slavs in language and culture. They still retained their military tradition and their leadership by their Khans, however. And during the ninth and tenth centuries they posed a constant challenge to Constantinople. The great Khan Krum defeated the Emperor Nicepherous, and he led his armies far to the south of the Balkans. He even reached the walls of Constantinople, but as other leaders in the previous half-millennium, he did not possess the strength or technology to take the city.

Khan Boris cleverly set Roman and Byzantine missionaries against each other in order to gain the most advantageous terms for his conversion to Christianity. In fact he was given a national church with its own hierarchy of bishops and archbishops. Once he had joined the Byzantine side, Boris encouraged the work of missionaries from Constantinople to convert his people, and in the process accepted a Slavonic alphabet for the translations of scripture and church documents.

The First Bulgarian Empire hits its high point in the reign of Symeon (r. 893–927), a person who had been educated in Constantinople and had developed not only an appreciation for, but also a mastery of, Greek culture. Bulgaria served as the main transmission line for the spreading of Orthodoxy throughout the Balkans and into Russia. Symeon's admiration for Byzantine culture did not stop him from attempting to set up his own, independent empire however. He controlled most of the land south of present day Belgrade, up to the suburbs of Constantinople. His empire was short-lived, however, because he was in the path of yet another set of invaders coming from the east to the west: the Magyars (Hungarians), the Pechenegs, and the rising power of Russia. Finally Basil Bulgaroctonus defeated the major Bulgarian force and blinded all those who survived the battle 1014.

Bulgaria remained subdued for the next two centuries until 1185 when Peter and John Asen rebelled against Byzantine authority and successful established the Second Bulgarian Empire, and Bulgaria was a serious competitor with the weakened Byzantine Empire. Until the 1240s, Bulgaria briefly became the most important state in the Balkans, with its imitation Byzantine court and ritual. In the middle of the

In the Balkans, the new Serbian, Bulgarian, and Hungarian states grew powerful. Even though the Byzantines claimed control over the region and farther to the north and east, the Bohemian and Polish states and Russia came into existence.

thirteenth century, it fell to the Serbian Empire, and then a century later was overrun by the Ottoman Turks. Despite these reversals, the Bulgarians remained important missionaries and teachers in the spread of the Orthodox Church.

Serbia

The Serbs, a Slavic people, converted to Orthodox Christianity at roughly the same time as the Bulgarians. They too were caught in the Rome-Constantinople conversion competition, and their brothers the Croats and the Slovenes became Catholics. Despite their linguistic and ethnic similarities, the fact that the Serbs became Orthodox and the Croats and Slovenes Catholics established the foundation for centuries of tragic conflict right up to the wars in the former Yugoslavia in the 1990s.

At first the Serbs were dominated by the Bulgars, but by the 1180s, Stephen Nemanja, the Grand Zhupan, united the Serbian people. He successfully

fought off both the Bulgarians and the weakened Byzantines to establish a kingdom along the Vardar and Morava river basins. His son, Stephen Nemanja II (r. 1196–1228) took advantage of the chaos created by the Fourth Crusade to consolidate his power. Like Khan Basil centuries earlier, he skillfully gained the status of king and also a Serbian national church by appealing to Rome and Constantinople for legitimacy.

Stephen Dushan (r. 1308–1355—at various times king and tsar) brought Serbia to its historic high point geographically, politically, and culturally. The Serbian ruler gained control over most of the Balkans north of Saloniki and south of the Sava River. Politically, he raised himself to the dignity of a *tsar*, or caesar—even to the point of challenging the weakened Byzantines in 1355, seeking help from both the Pope and the Turks. He died as his troops marched to Constantinople, and after that his empire fell apart. The legacy of his empire was a rich Serbian culture, based on Byzantine models, but also combining indigenous qualities and Italian influences.

As the Turks patiently advanced in the Balkans in the 1380s, the usually feuding Slavs finally united at the battle of Kosovo. After a long day of valiant fighting, which saw both the Turkish Sultan and the Serbian king die, the Ottomans emerged victorious—with control of the Balkans for the next five centuries. For the Balkan Slavs, especially the Serbs, the memory of the battle of Kosovo would be passed from generation to generation to be used by politicians in the 1990s as a tragedy to unite their people.

The collapse of Dushan's empire created such instability in the Balkans that the Ottoman Turks advanced with very little challenge. Under Sultan Murad (r. 1359–1389) they defeated the South Slavs in 1389 at the Battle of Kosovo—a date of mourning that still unites Serbian patriots today.

Romania

The Romanians, who see themselves today as "an island of Latins in a sea of Slavs," entered history as the Dacian people, settled on both sides of the Carpathian Mountain chain. They stood in the way of the Roman advance in the first century C.E. and irritated the caesars by their incursions into Roman-controlled provinces south of the Danube. The Emperor Trajan managed to defeat the Dacians and to turn the province into a productive part of the empire. These people remained under Roman rule from circa 100 to circa 275 B.C.E. and became thoroughly latinized, so much so that the Dacian culture and language died out.

The area served as a crossroads for the waves of migrating peoples coming from East to West—follow-

ing the natural geographic path from the steppe frontier to the Danube valley, and from the end of Roman times to the thirteenth century, the Romanians essentially disappeared from history. After the thirteenth century the regions they inhabited became provinces: Moldavia, Wallachia, Bukovina, Bessarabia, and Transylvania. After the thirteenth century two independent, but weak, states emerged—Moldavia and Wallachia. They were threatened on all sides by the Mongols, the Russians, the Hungarians, the Bulgarians, and the Serbs. By the end of the fifteenth century they rested firmly under Ottoman control.

The Romanians were drawn into the religious orbits of whichever dominant power was the closest to where they lived. Thus, the Transylvanians became Catholic, the Wallachians became Orthodox following Serbian and Bulgarian models, and Moldavians became Orthodox with very strong influences from Russia.

Albania

The Albanians are the only indigenous Bronze Age people in the Balkans who have managed to preserve their own unique language and some of their culture. With a small population and little political and military power, they were from the first caught up in the Greek political strife of the Hellenic age, when they were subjects of the Macedonians under Philip and Alexander. In the second century B.C.E., they fell under Roman domination and their homeland became the province of Illyria (EE-lee-ree-ah). Albanians served in the Roman armies and bureaucracy—even providing several emperors, including Diocletian.

The Albanians were overwhelmed by first the Germanic and the Slavic migrations but did not assimilate with either group. They passed from being dominated by the Byzantines, to being harassed by the Bulgarians and then dominated by the Angevines during the early Crusades. Finally, after the death of Stephen Dushan, Albania entered a period of strife-filled independence, having to fight off the attentions of the Venetians and the Turks, until the arrival of their national hero Skanderbeg (r. 1443–1468). Led by Skanderbeg, Albania became a major player in Balkan affairs for one of the few times in its history. After Skanderbeg's death, however, Albania fell to the Turks. With most of the population eventually adopting Islam, Albania earned a favored position within the Ottoman Empire.

RUSSIA TO 1500

- *Of all the Slavic peoples in the Byzantine zone, why did Russia become the Third Rome and, eventually, a great power?*

Like that of eastern Europe, Russia's history is largely a product of its geography. The vast expanse of land combined with a comparatively small population has made the domination of the peasants by the landed interests, both individuals and state, one of the continuing themes in Russian history. Russia's difficulty in gaining access to the sea has had important economic and cultural consequences, stunting the growth of a merchant class and encouraging the formation of an inward-looking population.

Russia's waterways, however, have played a key role in the development of the country. The rivers, which flow north or south across the land, have served as thoroughfares for trade and cultural exchange as well as routes for invasion. Unconnected to the western European region, the rivers dictated a line of communication that led early Russian traders south to Constantinople rather than to the West. The Volkhov and Dnieper network tied together the Varangians (also known as the Vikings) and the Greeks through Russia, while the Volkhov and Volga system reached toward Central Asia.

Kiev Rus' and Vladimir

In the sixth century C.E. the eastern Slavs began moving out of the area near the Pripet marshes. The various clans went as far north as the White Sea, as far east as the Urals, and to the region south of Kiev. (Kiev Rus' describes the Kievan phase of Russian history, especially the introduction of a stronger Ukrainian historiographical tradition. The apostrophe stands for a diacritical mark in the writing of the word *Rus'* in Russian and Ukrainian.) To the north, around Lake Ilmen, the Slavs established a number of trading towns such as Novgorod, from which they founded other trading bases. By the ninth century they had accumulated sufficient wealth to attract the attention of the Varangians, who came down from the Baltic to dominate the trading routes, especially those going from the Dvina to the Dnieper to Constantinople.

Russian history is said to begin with the entry of the Varangians into eastern Slavic affairs in the 860s. One of the key controversies in Russian history revolves around the question of the Varangians' role. Did they impose themselves on the Slavs and form them into their first political units, or were the Varangians invited in by the already sophisticated, though feuding, Slavic tribes? Varying interpretations of the so-called Norman controversy can best be addressed by noting that the Slavs, like most other Europeans, fell under the wave of the northern invaders but, within two generations, assimilated them and incorporated their capabilities.

The Varangian Oleg (c. 882–913) established his seat of government at Kiev, at the transition point between the forest and steppe zones. During the tenth century Oleg and Sviatoslav (SVYAH-toe-slaf; r. 964–972) created a state that was the equal of contemporary France. Oleg took control of both Kiev and Novgorod and, with the strength gained, launched an attack on Constantinople. Sviatoslav carried Kievan power to the Danube and the lower Volga. He fell victim to the knives of Asiatic invaders, the Patzinaks. However, he left a state strong enough to endure almost a decade of internal power struggles.

The most important ruler in the Kievan phase of Russian history was Vladimir, who overcame his brothers to dominate his country from 980 to 1015. Vladimir learned his political lessons dealing with the Byzantines, and he consolidated his power in Kiev. At first, he based his rule on the pagan religion and erected statues to gods such as Perun (the god of thunder) and Volos (the god of wealth). He made peace with the Volga Bulgars to the east and worked with the Byzantines against the Bulgarians in pursuit of his diplomatic and political goals.

CASE STUDY

Constantine I, Vladimir, and the Selection of Christianity

Vladimir acknowledged the fact that the nations surrounding him were converting to one organized

Document   The Acceptance of Christianity

The Christian conversion of European pagan leaders involved a complex formula of political advantage, internal rivalries, and piety. Beginning with Constantine's conversion, as described by Eusebius, the spiritual element is always emphasized as the primary cause for becoming Christian. Vladimir's conversion to Orthodoxy was a fundamental step in the division of Europe between East and West, perhaps a far more important step than any other taken in Russian history. This excerpt from the *Russian Primary Chronicle* explains in touching, if naive, detail how the decision was made.

6494 (986). Vladimir was visited by Volga Bulgars of Mohammedan [Muslim] faith. . . . Then came the Germans, asserting that they came as emissaries of the Pope. . . . The Jewish Khazars heard of these missions, and came themselves. . . . Then the Greeks sent to Vladimir a scholar. . . .

6495 (987). Vladimir summoned together his vassals and the city elders, and said to them, "Behold, the Volga Bulgars came before me urging me to accept their religion. Then came the Germans and praised their own faith; and after them came the Jews. Finally the Greeks appeared, criticizing all other faiths but commending their own, and they spoke at length, telling the history of the whole world from its beginning. . . ."

. . . The Prince and all the people chose good and wise men to the number of ten, and directed them to go first among the Volga Bulgars and inspect their faith. The emissaries went their way, and when they arrived at their destination they beheld the disgraceful actions of the Volga Bulgars and their worship in the mosque; then they returned to their own country. Vladimir then instructed them to go likewise among the Germans, and examine their faith, and finally to visit the Greeks. They thus went into Germany, and after viewing the German ceremonial, they proceeded to Tsargrad [Constantinople], where they appeared before the Emperor. . . .

Thus they returned to their own country, and the Prince called together his vassals and the elders. Vladimir then announced the return of the envoys who had been sent out, and suggested that their report be heard. He thus commanded them to speak out before his vassals. The envoys reported, "When we journeyed among the Volga Bulgars, we beheld how they worship in their temple, called a mosque, while they stand ungirt. The Volga Bulgar bows, sits down, looks hither and thither like one possessed, and there is no happiness among them, but instead only sorrow and a dreadful stench. Their religion is not good. Then we went among the Germans, and saw them performing many ceremonies in their temples; but we beheld no glory there. Then we went on to Greece, and the Greeks led us to the edifices where they worship their God, and we knew not whether we were in heaven or on earth. For on earth there is no such splendor or such beauty, and we are at a loss how to describe it. We only know that God dwells there among men, and their service is fairer than the ceremonies of other nations. . . ." Then the vassals spoke and said, "If the Greek faith were evil, it would not have been adopted by your grandmother Olga, who was wiser than all other men." Vladimir then inquired where they should all accept baptism, and they replied that the decision rested with him. . . .

By divine agency, Vladimir was suffering at that moment from a disease of the eyes, and could see nothing, being in great distress. The Princess declared to him that if he desired to be relieved of this disease, he should be baptized with all speed, otherwise it could not be cured. . . . The Bishop of Kherson, together with the Princess' priests, after announcing the tidings, baptized Vladimir, and as the Bishop laid his hand upon him, he straightway received his sight. Upon experiencing this miraculous cure, Vladimir glorified God, saying, "I have now perceived the one true God." When his followers beheld this miracle, many of them were also baptized.

Questions to Consider

1. Why do you think that Vladimir felt compelled to convert to one religion or another? Were spiritual or secular concerns more important? What did he gain by conversion?

2. Which of the possible options—Catholicism, Islam, Judaism, Orthodoxy—gave the most important advantages to Vladimir? Consider each choice and make a list of negative and positive points for the Russian ruler.

3. If you have access to a genealogy of your family, try to identify how your ancestors come to find their particular religious—or nonreligious—persuasions.

From *The Russian Primary Chronicle*, trans. Samuel H. Cross. In *Harvard Studies and Notes in Philology and Literature*, Vol. 12 (Cambridge, Mass.: Harvard University Press, 1953), pp. 183–213 passim. Reprinted by permission.

religion or another: the Poles and Hungarians to Roman Catholicism, the Khazars to Judaism, the Volga Bulgars to Islam, and the Bulgarians to Orthodox Christianity. His shrewd grandmother, Olga, had accepted Orthodox Christianity from Constantinople in 956, as had other members of his family. During the 980s Vladimir sent observers to judge the various religious alternatives. According to *The Russian Primary Chronicle*, they visited Hagia Sophia at Constantinople in 988 and were impressed with the power and wealth of the city. The observers recommended that Vladimir choose the Orthodox faith.

DOCUMENT

Vladimir's Acceptance of Christianity

The story, though interesting, ignores the many concrete advantages Vladimir derived from his decision. As part of the negotiation package, Vladimir agreed to help the Byzantine emperor Basil against his enemies. In return, upon converting to Orthodoxy, he would receive the hand of the emperor's sister in marriage. After a successful campaign, Basil delayed in carrying out his part of the bargain. Vladimir moved quickly to make his point and marched into the Crimea and took the Byzantine city of Cherson. The Kiev-Byzantine arrangements were finally carried out in 990. Vladimir, now a member of the Byzantine royal family, brought his country into the Byzantine, Orthodox orbit. Even before "becoming a saint," the Chronicle tells us he destroyed the pagan statues, converted his many concubines to nuns, and forced his people to become Christians.[3] Eventually the Russians gained their own church, received their own metropolitan, and adapted Byzantine ritual, theology, and monastic practices to their own use. They also applied Byzantine governmental theories to their own social hierarchy.

After Vladimir, few great monarchs ruled during the Kievan period of Russian history. Instead, political fragmentation began to intensify. During the reign of Yaroslav the Wise (r. 1019–1054), the Kievan state reached its high point. It was the cultural and economic equal of any government in Europe, with cities larger than those found in the West. Yaroslav undertook major building projects, revised the law code, and promoted the growth of the church. He formed a dynastic alliance with Henry I of France. Unfortunately, Kiev did not long maintain its prestigious position. Yaroslav introduced a principle of succession based on the seniority system, passing the rule of Kiev from brother to brother in a given generation. This practice is in contrast with the Western one of primogeniture, under which rule is handed down to the eldest son of the ruler. Within two generations, the seniority system led to the political breakup of Kiev, although the city maintained its theoretical superiority within Russia.

Kiev also came under attack from both east and west and suffered as well from the economic decline of Constantinople. Under Vladimir Monomakh

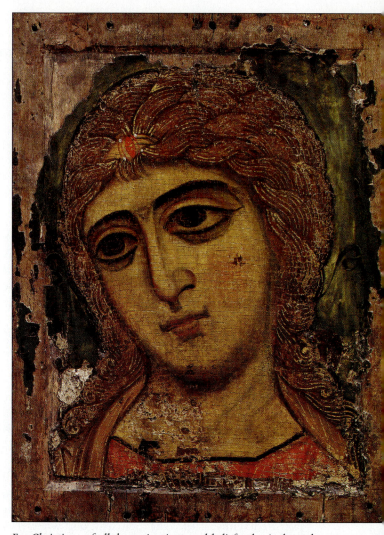

For Christians of all denominations and beliefs, the Archangel Gabriel is one of the most beloved angels. He is the angel of mercy, the messenger of the incarnation and resurrection, and the bringer of consolation. It is no wonder that he figured heavily in the iconography of the Orthodox Church.

(r. 1113–1125), Kiev reemerged briefly as a center of power, but a half-century of decline soon followed. Competing centers arose at Suzdal; Galicia, where the local aristocracy dominated; Vladimir, where the prince emerged all-powerful; and Novgorod, where the assembled citizens—the *veche*—were the major force. Even before the Mongols totally destroyed the city in 1240, Kiev's era of prominence was effectively over.

Novgorod, Moscow, and the Mongols

For more than two centuries, from 1240 to 1480, Mongols dominated Russia, and during that time, much of the land was cut off from contact with the outside world. During this period a new center of power, Moscow, emerged to serve for most of the time as collector of tribute for the Mongol court. New internal markets developed, and the Orthodox Church, unhampered by the Mongols, grew in strength and influence. The Russian city of Novgorod also managed to carry on despite the oriental overlord.

Novgorod had come under the control of the Varangians in the ninth century. However, in 997, the citizens received a charter granting them self-government, and for the next five centuries this *veche* elected its own rulers. The city boasted an aggressive and prosperous merchant class, which exploited the region from the Ural Mountains to the Baltic Sea and held its own against German merchants from the Baltic area. Novgorod was the equal of most of the cities found along the Baltic and North seas. In the middle of the thirteenth century, Alexander Nevsky, the prince of Novgorod, led his fellow citizens in struggles to repel the Teutonic Knights and the Swedes. A few years later, he showed exceptional diplomatic skill in paying homage to the Mongols, even though they had halted 60 miles outside the city and left Novgorod untouched. At a time when the rest of Russia suffered mightily under the first phase of Mongol domination, the *veche*-elected oligarchy continued to rule Novgorod.

The city's wealth and traditions permitted the *veche* to rule. These male citizens elected their princes and forced them to sign a contract setting out what they could and could not do. In the words of a typical document between ruler and city, the citizens could show their prince "the way out" if he failed to live up to the terms of his agreement. The prince could act as a leader of Novgorod only when he remained within the city's limits. The city's method of government permitted the rise of class divisions that led to more than 20 major outbreaks of violence in the thirteenth and fourteenth centuries. Changes in trade routes in the fifteenth century led to a decline in Baltic commerce, and Novgorod became dependent on Moscow for its grain supply. That dependence, in addition to the class conflict, weakened Novgorod, and in 1478 Moscow absorbed the town.

The obscure fortress town of Moscow, first mentioned in records in 1147, became the core of the new Russia. Even before the Mongol invasion, a large num-

The Rise of Moscow

ber of Slavs moved toward the north and east, and this migration continued for centuries as that frontier offered opportunities for the oppressed. Moscow was well-placed along a north-south river route in a protective setting of marshes and forests.

One of Alexander Nevsky's sons, Daniel, founded the Grand Duchy of Moscow, and he and subsequent rulers inherited Nevsky's ability to get along with the Mongols. As the Moscow princes skillfully acknowledged their inferior position to the Mongol khans, who sought tribute and recruits, the Muscovites improved their political position in relation to the other Russians by monopolizing the tax collection function for the

Beginning as a small fortress town, first mentioned in the chronicles in the mid-twelfth century, Moscow grew rapidly by 1500.

Mongols. In addition, at the beginning of the fourteenth century they made sure that the seat of the Russian Orthodox Church would be in Moscow, a reflection of the city's prestige.

In the first century after the Mongol invasion, the Muscovite princes showed a great deal of ambition and ability, albeit in a sometimes unattractive way. For example, during his reign Ivan I Kalita (r. 1328–1341), whose surname means "moneybags," greatly increased the wealth and power of Moscow through aggressive tax collection practices.

IMAGE

St. Basil's Cathedral, Moscow

On the surface, the fourteenth century appeared to be a time of decline, of Mongol domination and gains by the European states at Russian expense along the western boundary. The reality, however, was that Russia was laying foundations for its future with Moscow as the country's religious and political center. In 1380 Dmitri Donskoi (r. 1359–1389) defeated the Mongols at Kulikovo. Although Mongol strength was far from broken, the Russian victory had great symbolic significance.

Ivan III and the Third Rome

Civil war and invasions threatened the Moscow-based country throughout the fifteenth century. Finally, Ivan III (r. 1462–1505) made major strides to build the modern Russian state. He took Novgorod and two years later ceased acknowledging Mongol domination. He then began to advance toward the south and east against the Turks and Mongols, setting in motion a drive of expansion that lasted for centuries.

In developments of considerable symbolic importance, the Russians embraced many elements of the Roman tradition. Ivan III married the niece of the last East Roman emperor, an alliance arranged by the pope. Russians espoused the theory that Moscow was the Third Rome, the logical successor to Constantinople as the center of Christianity. In 1492 (the year 7000 in the Orthodox calendar and the beginning of a new millennium), the Muscovite metropolitan, Zosima, stated that Ivan III was "the new Emperor Constantine of the new Constantinople Moscow." Zosima for the first time called Moscow an imperial city. Philotheus of Pskov (SKOV) expounded the theory of Third Rome in full detail in the 1520s. Ivan began to use the title *tsar* ("caesar") and adopted the Roman two-headed eagle as the symbol of the Russian throne.

DOCUMENT

Filofei and the Christian Role of Moscow

Ivan opened the doors to the West ever so slightly. He established diplomatic relations with a number of European powers. He brought in Italian technicians and architects such as Aristotele Fieravanti and Pietro Antonio Solari to work on the churches, palaces, and walls of the Kremlin: the vastly expanded site of the original fortress that was the center of the town three centuries earlier. The Italian artistic tradition had no lasting cultural impact on Russia, but use of Italian artists nonetheless signified an awareness of the West. In recognition of the need to establish a standing army, Ivan began the difficult process of building up a modern state structure and increased restrictions on the Russian peasants. During the fifteenth century, Ivan was the equal of his western European colleagues Henry VII of England and Louis XI of France. After three centuries of isolation under the Mongols, the Russians were again interacting with Europe.

CONCLUSION

Byzantium made important contributions to European civilization: Greek language and learning were preserved for posterity—especially after the transmission of documents and texts to Italy, an important stage in the opening of the Renaissance; the Roman imperial system was continued and Roman law codified; and missionary activity spread Christianity throughout much of eastern Europe and Russia and fostered the development of a splendid new art dedicated to the glorification of the Christian religion. Situated at the crossroads of the East and the West, Constantinople acted as the disseminator of culture for all peoples who came in contact with the empire. This rich and turbulent city was to the early Middle Ages what Athens and Rome had been to classical times. Most importantly, by merging Roman political institutions with the Christian Church, Constantine created the form of political legitimacy that would last in Europe until the French Revolution in 1789.

From the fourth through the ninth centuries, as the Slavs moved to their new homelands, they came under the influence of dominant outside forces. In Russia and the Balkans, Byzantine patterns and traditions shaped their lives. After its initial Kievan phase, in which Vladimir made the choice to follow East Roman precedents, the Russians remained under Mongol domination even when Russia's political and religious center moved to Moscow. When the Russians regained their independence in the fifteenth century, they redefined their polity in Roman and Christian terms, claiming the legacy of the fallen city of Constantinople.

From Constantine onward, ambitious Christian leaders strengthened their control through the powerful fusion of Roman symbolism and the Christian Church. Not until the development of modern political ideologies after the French Revolution did a more potent combination of theories and symbols help governments motivate and dominate their people. In its turn, the politicians' embrace of Christ's message profoundly altered the form, if not the substance, of Christianity.

Suggestions for Web Browsing

You can obtain more information about topics included in this chapter at the websites listed below. See also the companion website that accompanies this text, **http://www.ablongman.com/ brummett**, which contains an online study guide and additional resources.

Access to the Metropolitan Museum of Arts Byzantine Collection
http://www.metmuseum.org/explore/Byzantium/byzhome.html
A site providing a wide-ranging selection of Byzantine architectural and artistic triumphs.

Byzantium Studies on the Internet
http://www.fordham.edu/halsall/byzantium/

Byzantine Art
http://www.fordham.edu/halsall/byzantium/images.html

> *This site includes many images of icons, monasteries, Ravenna, and Hagia Sophia; it details Byzantine life in Jerusalem and offers links to related websites.*

Byzantine Architecture
http://www.byzantium1200.com

> *See a unique experience at computer reconstructions of major Byzantine structures as they might have been in the year 1200.*

Historical Tour of Jerusalem: Byzantine Period
http://gurukul.ucc.american.edu/TED/hpages/jeruselum/byzantin.htm

> *Short history of Jerusalem, from 324 to 638 C.E., including an image and discussion of the Madaba mosaic showing the Jerusalem Gate.*

Women in Byzantium
http://www.wooster.edu/ART/wb.html

> *Extensive bibliography of primary and secondary sources regarding women in Byzantium.*

Byzantium Through Arab Eyes
http://www.fordham.edu/halsall/source/byz-arabambas.html

> *An original account of a mission to Constantinople by an Arab ambassador in the late tenth century.*

Literature and Film

One of the finest novels written about Byzantium is Gore Vidal's celebration of the last pagan emperor, *Julian* (Vintage, 2003). Superbly written, it is unabashedly pro-Julian and makes the fourth-century Christian hierarchy appear to be narrow and even backward in the face of the emperor's learning and sophistication. Michael Ennis gives a lively view of the tenth century in his *Byzantium* (Atlantic Monthly Press, 1989). The fortress city is seen through Viking eyes. A classic, time-travel science-fiction treatment of the reign of Justinian and his Italian campaign is provided by L. Sprague de Camp in *Lest Darkness Fall* (Prime Press, 1949), available in combined edition with David Drake's *To Bring the Light* (Baen, 1996). The author is very good at picking up the religious competition between the Arian Goth and the Orthodox Byzantines. For the most complete selection of novels, poetry, plays, movies, and music of and about Byzantium go to http://www.fordham.edu/halsall/byzantium/texts/byznov.html.

Suggestions for Reading

Two works by Arnold Hugh Martin Jones, *The Decline of the Ancient World* (Longman, 1977), and *The Later Roman Empire, 284–602: A Social, Economic, and Administrative Survey*, 2 vols. (Johns Hopkins University Press, 1986), are indispensable. Two recent and valuable studies on the impacts of the German infiltration and, later, invasions of the Roman Empire are Herwig Wolfram, *The Roman Empire and its Germanic Peoples* (University of California Press, 1998), and Leslie Webster and Michelle Brown, eds., *The Transformation of the Roman World: AD 400–900* (University of California Press, 1997).

For an exhaustive treatment of all aspects of Byzantine life, see *The Cambridge Medieval History* (Cambridge University Press, 2004, replacing Vol. 4 of the 1966–1967 edition). George Ostrogorsky, *History of the Byzantine State* (Rutgers University Press, 1957), provides a clear institutional overview. Joan M. Hussey's *The Orthodox Church in the Byzantine Empire* (Oxford University Press, 1986) is the best introduction in English to the development of the eastern variant of Christianity. Warren Treadgold provides a view of the sophistication of one period of medieval Byzantium in his *The Byzantine Revival, 780–842* (Stanford University Press, 1991). Francis Dvornik, *The Photian Schism: History and Legend* (Rutgers University Press, 1970), and *The Slavs in European History and Civilization* (Rutgers University Press, 1970), address the matters of conversion.

Charles M. Brand, *Byzantium Confronts the West, 1180–1204* (Harvard University Press, 1968), and Donald E. Queller, ed., *The Latin Conquest of Constantinople* (John Wiley & Sons, 1971), describe the tragedy of the Crusades for Byzantium and complement Steven Runciman's three-volume *History of the Crusades* (Cambridge University Press, 1987). For a view from the other side, see Amin Maalouf, *The Crusade Through Arab Eyes* (Shocken Books, 1989). Donald Nicol, *The Last Centuries of Byzantium*, 2nd ed. (Cambridge University Press, 1993), discusses the empire in its state of weakness. For an excellent discussion of the military reorganization that made the survival of the Byzantine Empire possible, see Warren Treadgold, *Byzantium and Its Army: 284–1081* (Stanford University Press, 1995). Paul Stephenson's study, *Byzantium's Balkan Frontier: A Political Study of the Northern Balkans: 900–1204* (Cambridge University Press, 2000), is a much-needed contribution to the opening chapters of the political history of the peoples of the Balkans.

John Fennell, *The Crisis of Medieval Russia, 1200–1304* (Longman, 1983), and Robert O. Crummey, *The Formation of Muscovy, 1304-1613* (Longman, 1987), are two first-rate surveys of the early phases of Russian history. Oscar Halecki, *Borderlands of Western Civilization* (Random House, 1984), gives the outlines of eastern European history, especially the northern region.

Islam

From Its Origins to 1300

600

622 Hijra, Muhammad's flight from Mecca to Medina

632–661 Rashidun caliphs; Islam spreads in Near East, Persia, and North Africa

661–750 Umayyad dynasty; Islam expands into Central Asia, Indus valley, Maghrib, and Spain

700

750–1258 Abbasid dynasty, high point of classical Islamic civilization

756–1031 Umayyad dynasty reestablished in Spain and North Africa

900

900–1100 Golden Age of Muslim scholarship

909–1171 Fatimid dynasty, first in North Africa, then in Egypt and Syria

1000

1095 First Crusade called

1200

1250 Mamluks seize power in Egypt

1258 Mongols conquer Baghdad

Arabia was the birthplace of the Islamic religion; out of this desert peninsula with its commercial entrepots and oases there emerged a new vision of the world and of people's relation to the divine. That vision was based on a single, powerful god, a final prophet, and a belief in revelation. It provided a system of law, a guide for social organization, and a framework for what would become a highly diverse cultural synthesis. Human time began with the first man and woman, Adam and Eve; each believer lived in expectation of a Judgment Day, while the afterlife promised a gardenlike heaven and a fiery hell. For kingdoms and their rulers, Islam provided a universal law extending to all subjects, Muslim and non-Muslim alike. It legitimized sovereigns and promised justice to subjects. The ideal society envisioned in its sacred text, the Qur'an (or *Koran*), was one in which marriage was a preferred state, women were subordinate to men, the wealthy took care of the poor, and competing allegiances were set aside in favor of a primary allegiance to the community of believers (the *umma*). This worldview both challenged and reflected the social order of Arabia. Of course, societies and states never adhere absolutely to the ideals embedded in their sacred texts, and religious messages are interpreted in diverse ways as they extend over time and across space. Like other religious messages, the message of Islam was codified and contested. But the unity embodied in the idea of the *umma* and in the universal Sharia law has prompted some scholars to call Islamic civilization the "first world civilization." Within one century after Muhammad disseminated its message in the seventh century C.E., the power of Islam would be felt from the Indian Ocean to the Atlantic; it would transfigure age-old religious, intellectual, and political patterns.

ARABIA BEFORE
THE PROPHET

■ *How did the desert environment of Arabia influence Arabic culture?*

The Arabian peninsula is one-third the size of the continental United States. Most of its land is desert; rainfall is scarce, vegetation is scant, and very little of the land is suitable for agriculture. Arabia before the birth of Muhammad was a culturally isolated and economically underdeveloped region. In the relatively more fertile southwestern corner of the peninsula, however, several small Arab kingdoms once flourished in the area now known as Yemen. The most notable of these early kingdoms, Saba' (the biblical Sheba), existed as early as the eighth century B.C.E. and lasted until the third century C.E., when it was taken by the Himyarites (HEEM-yar-aits) from the south.

Aided by the domestication of the camel and the expanding trade in frankincense and spices, these kingdoms became prosperous; they formed part of a commercial network of kingdoms within and beyond the Arabian peninsula. In the north of Arabia, several kingdoms were able to establish contacts with the Byzantine and the Persian (Sassanid) empires as early as the fifth century C.E. Among the most notable of these small kingdoms were Nabataea in northwestern Arabia, which dominated Arabian trade routes until the Romans annexed the kingdom in the second century C.E., and the realm of the Lakhmids in the northeast, whose prominence was greatest around 250 to 600 C.E., until the kingdom was destroyed by the Sassanids. But in the interior of Arabia, a vast desert dotted sparsely with oases, a nomadic life based on herding was the only successful existence.

The Bedouin

The desert nomads, or *Bedouin* (BED-eu-in), lived according to ancient tribal patterns; at the head of the tribe was the male elder, or *shaykh* (SHAYK), elected and advised by the heads of the related families comprising the tribe. These men claimed authority based on family connections and personal merit. Tribes tended to be made up of three-generation families employing a gendered division of labor. The Bedouin led a precarious existence, moving their flocks from one pasture to the next, often following set patterns of migration. Aside from maintaining their herds, these nomads traded animal products for goods from the settled areas. They also relied on plunder from raids on settlements, on passing caravans, and on one another.

Their nomadic existence, its hardships, and the beauty of the desert landscape are all celebrated in the poetry of pre-Islamic Arabia.

The Bedouin enjoyed a degree of personal freedom unknown in more agrarian and settled societies. They developed a code of ethics represented in the word *muru'a* (moo-ROO-ah), or "manly virtue." Far from being abrasive and rough, men proved *muru'a* through grace and restraint, loyalty to obligation and duty, a devotion to do what must be done, and respect for women. The tribe shared a corporate spirit, or *'asabiyya* (AHS-ahb-ee-yah), which reflected the shared interests and honor of the tribe.

Although Bedouin society was patriarchal (dominated by the senior males), women enjoyed a great degree of independence. They engaged in business and commerce and could sometimes wed men of their own choosing. As in all traditional agricultural societies, however, women were under the protection of men, and the honor of the tribe was vested in the sexual honor of the women. The relative freedom of the Bedouin sprang from the realities of life in the desert, as did their values and ethics. One rule of conduct was unqualified hospitality to strangers. A nomad never knew when the care of a stranger might be essential to provide the necessary water and shade to save his or her own life.

The Bedouin of the seventh century did not have a highly structured religious system. They apparently looked at life as a brief time during which to take full advantage of daily pleasure. Ideas of an afterlife were not well defined or described. The Bedouin were animists; they worshipped a large number of gods and spirits, many of whom they believed to inhabit trees, wells, and stones. Each tribe had its own gods, sometimes symbolized by sacred stones.

The Bedouin of the Arabian interior led a relatively primitive and isolated existence, but it was not in their herding camps that the message of Islam was first spoken. In the Arabian cities along the trade routes, the people came into contact with traders and travelers who brought a complex mix of artistic, religious, and philosophical influences. Among these were the monotheistic beliefs of Judaism and Christianity. Some parts of Arabia were greatly influenced by the neighboring and more highly sophisticated cultures of Byzantium, Sassanid Persia, and Ethiopia. It was out of this more urban and commercial context that the early Islamic state would emerge.

Early Mecca

On the western side of the Arabian peninsula along the Red Sea is a region known as the Hijaz, or "barrier."

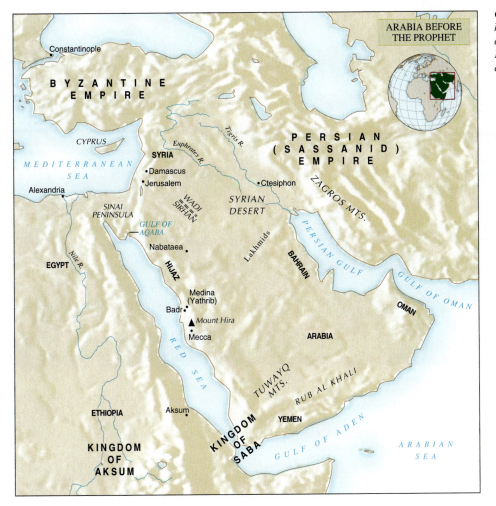

ARABIA BEFORE
THE PROPHET

The Hijaz extends along the western coastal plain from Yemen in the south to the Sinai peninsula in the north. One of the oases in the Hijaz is Mecca, set among barren hills 50 miles inland from the sea. This site had several advantages: Mecca possessed a well (the Zamzam) of great depth, and two ancient caravan routes met there. One route ran from Africa through the peninsula to Iran and central Asia, and another, a southeast-northwest route, brought the textiles and spices of India and Southeast Asia to the Mediterranean world.

A second significant advantage for Mecca was its importance as a religious sanctuary. An ancient temple, an almost square structure built of granite blocks, stood near the well of Mecca. Known as the *Ka'ba* ("cube"), this square temple contained the sacred Black Stone. According to tradition, the stone, probably a meteorite, was originally white but had become blackened by the sins of all those who touched it. Later Muslim historians would attribute the building of the Ka'ba to the prophet Abraham or even to Adam. The Ka'ba itself was draped with the pelts of sacrifi-

cial animals and supposedly held the images and shrines of 360 gods and goddesses. For centuries, the Ka'ba had been a holy place of annual pilgrimage for the Arab tribes and a focal point of Arab culture and ritual practice. As a pilgrimage site, it also brought prestige and wealth to the tribes who controlled the city of Mecca.

By the sixth century, Mecca was controlled by the Quraysh (KOO-raysh) tribe, whose rulers organized themselves into an aristocracy of merchants and wealthy businessmen. The Quraysh engaged in lucrative trade with Byzantium and Persia, as well as with the southern Arabian tribes and the kingdom of Aksum across the Red Sea in what is now Ethiopia. In addition, a number of annual merchant fairs, such as one usually held at nearby Ukaz, were taken over by the Quraysh to extend the economic influence of Mecca. The Quraysh were also concerned with protecting the religious shrine of the Ka'ba, in addition to ensuring that the annual pilgrimage of tribes to the holy place would continue as a source of revenue for the merchants of the city.

This nineteenth-century engraving depicts the city of Mecca with, at its center, the Ka'ba, a square building of stone draped with black cloth that became the focal point of Muslim worship. Each year Muslims make the pilgrimage to celebrate their unity and to worship at this most sacred shrine of Islam. The site itself and its buildings (as shown here) have been greatly expanded over the centuries since the Prophet Muhammad's time, and the number of pilgrims has dramatically increased.

MUHAMMAD, PROPHET OF ISLAM

- *What role did Muhammad play in the creation of Islam?*

Into this environment at Mecca was born a man who would revolutionize the religious, political, and social organization of his people. Muhammad (c. 570–632) came from a family belonging to the Quraysh. An orphan, he suffered the loss of both his parents and his grandfather, who cared for him after his parents' death. He was then raised by his uncle, Abu Talib, a prominent merchant of Mecca. His early years were spent helping his uncle in the caravan trade. Even as a young man, Muhammad came to be admired by his fellow Meccans as a sincere and honest person who earned the nickname al-Amin, "the trustworthy." When he was about 25 years old, he accepted employment from a wealthy widow, Khadija (cah-DEE-jah), whose caravans traded with Syria. He later married Khadija and began to take his place as a leading citizen of Mecca. Muhammad's marriage to Khadija was a long and happy one that produced two sons, who both died as infants, and two daughters. The younger, Fatima,

would play an important role in the future of the fledgling Islamic state.

Biographies of the Prophet, written after his death by his followers, describe him as a handsome, large man with broad shoulders and black, shining eyes, a man who was reserved and gentle but possessed of impressive energy. Tradition relates that Muhammad was an introspective man. Often he would escape from Meccan society, which he considered too materialistic and irreligious, and spend long hours alone in a cave on nearby Mount Hira. During these hours of meditation, Muhammad searched for answers to the metaphysical questions that many thoughtful people have pondered. Muhammad's meditations sometimes produced nearly total mental and physical exhaustion. During one such solitary meditation, Muhammad heard a call that was to alter history. This initial communication from heaven came in the form of a command:

> *Recite! In the name of your Lord, who created*
> *all things, who*
> *created man from a clot [of blood].*
> *Recite! And your Lord is Most Bounteous*
> *Who teaches by the Pen,*
> *Teaches man that which he would not have*
> *otherwise known. (Qur'an 96:1–5)*

The collected revelations given to Muhammad are known as the **Qur'an** (or Koran), an Arabic word meaning "recitation" or "reading." The revelations that continued to come over the next 20 years or so were sometimes terse and short, at other times elaborate and poetic. The early revelations did not immediately persuade Muhammad that he was a messenger of God. In fact, his first reactions were fear and self-doubt. Anxious about the source and nature of his revelations, he sought the comfort and advice of Khadija.

As the revelations continued, Muhammad was persuaded that he had been called to be a messenger of divine revelation. He began to think of himself and his mission as one similar to those of prophets and messengers who had preceded him in announcing the existence of the one God, *Allah*. Allah, *"the God,"* was the same God worshiped by the Christians and Jews, but Allah had now chosen Muhammad to be his last and greatest prophet to perfect the religion revealed earlier to Abraham, Moses, the Hebrew prophets, and Jesus. The religion Muhammad preached is called *Islam,* which means "submission" to the will of God. The followers of Islam are called *Muslims,* "those who submit" to God's law.

Muhammad's Message and Its Early Followers

At first Muhammad had little success in attracting followers in Mecca. The early message he brought to the Arabs was strong and direct: that Allah was the one God and majestic, all-powerful, and demanding of the faith of his followers. Furthermore, Allah decreed that his followers be compassionate, ethical, and just in all their dealings:

> *In the name of Allah, the most Beneficent, the*
> *   Most Merciful*
> *by the night as it enshrouds*
> *by the day as it illuminates*
> *by Him Who created the male and female*
> *indeed your affairs lead to various ends.*
> *For who gives [of himself] and acts righteously,*
> *   and conforms to goodness,*
> *We will give him ease.*

> *But as for him who is niggardly deeming*
> *   himself self-sufficient and rejects goodness,*
> *We will indeed ease his path to adversity.*
> *Nor shall his wealth save him as he perishes*
> *for Guidance is from Us*
> *and to Us belongs the Last and First.*
> *   (Qur'an 92:1–14)*

Muhammad was able to win the early support of some of his relatives and close friends. His first converts were his wife, his cousin Ali, and Abu Bakr, a leading merchant of the Quraysh tribe, who was highly respected for his integrity. Abu Bakr remained the constant companion of the Prophet during his persecution and exile and later succeeded him as the leader of Islam. But opposition to Muhammad's message was very strong, especially from Mecca's leading citizens. Many thought Muhammad was an ambitious poet attempting to pass on his own literary creations as the word of God. Others believed him to be possessed by demons. Muhammad challenged the status quo; his strong monotheism threatened the polytheistic beliefs of Mecca and the people who obtained their income from the pilgrims to the Ka'ba. Many of Muhammad's early converts were among the poorest of the city's residents, and Mecca's leading citizens feared the possibility of social revolution.

Since Muhammad was himself a member of the Quraysh tribe, its leaders first approached his uncle Abu Talib to persuade his nephew to stop preaching. Next they tried to bribe Muhammad with the promise of a lucrative appointment as an official. When he rejected such offers, actual persecution of Muhammad's converts began, and the Quraysh attempted a commercial and social boycott of the Prophet's family. During this time of trial, Abu Talib and Khadija both died, and Muhammad's faith and resolution were greatly tested. But inspired by the spirit and example of earlier prophets such as Abraham and Moses, who were also tested and persecuted, Muhammad persevered in his faith and continued his preaching.

The Hijra

To the north of Mecca is the city of Medina, which was then called Yathrib. The residents of Medina were somewhat familiar with monotheistic beliefs, in part because of the Jewish community in residence there. While visiting Mecca, some pilgrims from Medina judged Muhammad to be a powerful and influential mediator and invited him to come to Medina to settle differences among that city's tribal chiefs. As opposition to his message increased in Mecca, Muhammad sent some of his followers to take up residence in Medina in order to escape persecution. Finally, Muhammad and Abu Bakr fled Mecca when it became known that

---

Qur'an—Literally "recitation" or "reading" in Arabic; the Islamic holy book containing the word of God (Allah) as revealed to the Prophet Muhammad through the angel Gabriel. Written in Arabic and to be read only in this language by believers.

Allah—"The God" in Arabic; the Arabic word for the same God worshipped in Christianity and Judaism.

Islam—The religion founded by the Prophet Muhammad in the seventh century A.D., a monotheistic faith drawing on elements from Judaism, Christianity, and the indigenous beliefs of the Arabian peninsula; literally "submission" in Arabic, as in "submission" to God's will.

the Quraysh intended to kill the Prophet. They were followed, but escaped, the story goes, by hiding in a narrow cave whose entrance was quickly covered by a spider's web. The Quraysh pursuers saw the web and passed on, thinking that the cave had been abandoned for a long time.

The *Hijra* (or *Hegira*), Muhammad's "migration" from Mecca to Medina, took place in September in the year 622. The event was such a turning point in the history of Islam that 622 is counted as year 1 of the Islamic calendar, because it marked the beginning of the Islamic state. In Medina, the Prophet met with entirely different circumstances from those in his birthplace. Muhammad's leadership turned Medina (*Madinat al-Nabi*, "City of the Prophet") into the major center of power in the Arabian peninsula.

The Community at Medina

Muhammad was received in Medina as a leader and a spiritual visionary. There, he and his followers set about the establishment of the Muslim **umma** or community. This new community established relations with the Medinan tribes, including the Jewish and Christian residents. Those who did not choose to accept Muhammad's faith were allowed to continue their way of life, since Christians and Jews were thought to be "people of the Book" to whom God had made himself known through earlier prophets. Ultimately, however, the Prophet's new polity came into conflict with some of the Jewish tribes of Medina and the tribes were expelled. This conflict illustrates the tension between the expansionist political policies and generally tolerant religious policies of the new state.

Hijra—The departure of the Prophet Muhammad from Mecca for Medina in 622 A.D.; considered to be the formal starting point for Islam.

umma—The community or nation of believers in Islam.

The Early Islamic State

622   The Hijra, Muhammad's migration from Mecca to Medina, year 1 of the Islamic calendar

630   The Prophet returns and takes control of Mecca, Ka'ba consecrated to Allah

632   Death of the Prophet

632–661   Rule of the first four caliphs: Abu Bakr, Umar, Uthman, Ali

638   Muslim armies take Jerusalem

651   Defeat of the Sassanids in Persia

Muhammad and his followers became steadily more aggressive in their attempts to win converts to Islam. The word **jihad**, meaning "struggle," was applied to the early efforts of the *umma* to win converts and conquer territory. Military encounters with the opponents of Islam began in 624, with the battle of Badr. Muhammad defeated a stronger Quraysh troop from Mecca, and the victory reinforced the resolve of the new religion's followers. Succeeding battles established the Muslims as the dominant force in Arabia, and a truce with Mecca was arranged, under which the Muslims could visit the holy city.

Return to Mecca

In 630 Muhammad returned to take control of the city of Mecca and to cleanse the Ka'ba of idols. The temple itself, together with the Black Stone, was preserved as the supreme religious center of Islam and rededicated to the One God. It is to this shrine that all devout Muslims, if able, make pilgrimage during their lifetime. Muhammad urged unbelievers and his old enemies to accept Islam and become part of the *umma*. By 632 almost all of the Arabian peninsula had (at least nominally) accepted Islam, and Muhammad had even sent ambassadors to the neighboring Byzantine and Persian Empires to announce the new religion and encourage converts. Just as Christianity began as a religion of the Jews, Islam began as a religion of the Arabs. But, over time, like Christianity, and unlike Judaism, Islam became a universal religion with a missionary spirit.

The Death of Muhammad

Muhammad died on June 8, 632, in Medina. Muslims at first refused to accept his death but were reassured by Abu Bakr, who recited this verse from the Qur'an: "Muhammad is only a messenger: many are the messengers who have died before him; if he dies, or is slain, will you turn back on your heels?" (3:144).

Muhammad had no surviving son and had not designated a successor. On the day of his death, his close companions solved the question of leadership of the faithful by agreeing on the election of Abu Bakr, who became the first successor, or **caliph** (kal-IF). Abu Bakr could not really replace Muhammad, the last prophet. However, as caliph, he was regarded as the head of the Islamic *umma*; he combined the roles

jihad—Literally "struggle" in Arabic; an Islamic term with broad meaning, ranging from the internal struggle of an individual to overcome sin to the external struggle of the faithful to address a social challenge or to fight against enemies and unbelievers in what is essentially a holy war.

caliph—The religious and political leader of the Islamic nation; successor of Muhammad.

of religious leader and head of state. Abu Bakr and his three successors in the office, Umar, Uthman, and Ali, are often referred to as the *Rashidun* (RAHSH-ee-deun), the "Rightly Guided" caliphs.

The significance of Muhammad to the birth and growth of Islam is impossible to overestimate. The Prophet and his message inspired his followers to create and work for the betterment of a society united by the Islamic faith. Ideally, tribal loyalties were replaced by loyalty to the *umma* and faith in the One God, who chose to speak to his people in their own language through a messenger who was also one of their own.

Soon after Muhammad's death, his followers began to collect and codify his teachings and actions. The result of their efforts was the **hadith,** or reports of the sayings and activities of Muhammad. The hadith have

hadith—A collection of the sayings, deeds, and traditions of the Prophet Muhammad, compiled by the Prophet's followers after his death to further clarify Islamic values and ethics.

This miniature depicts one of the legends of the Prophet, the Miraj or Night Journey. Muhammad, mounted on a winged part-human, part-horse steed, is believed miraculously to have ascended to heaven from Jerusalem, there enjoying a vision of God, and returning in a single night.

become an important source of values and ethical paths of behavior for the Islamic world. The **sunna,** the custom or practice of the Prophet, is grounded in the hadith and serves as a pattern for a model way of life to be imitated by the faithful.

ISLAMIC FAITH AND LAW

■ *What is the relationship between the Qur'an and Islamic faith and law?*

Islam places great emphasis on the necessity of obedience to God's law in addition to faith. The Qur'an is the fundamental and ultimate source of knowledge about Allah. This holy book contains both the theology of Islam and the patterns of ethical and appropriate conduct to which a Muslim must subscribe. Included in the Qur'an are some basic concepts that the Islamic community holds in common as fundamental to the faith.

The Qur'an

Muslims believe that the Qur'an contains the actual word of God as it was revealed to Muhammad through divine inspiration. These revelations to the Prophet took place over a period of more than 20 years. Before Muhammad's death, many of these messages were written down. Muhammad himself began this work of preservation, and Abu Bakr, as caliph, continued the process by compiling revelations that up to that time had been memorized by the followers and passed on by word of mouth. A complete written text of the Qur'an was produced some years after Muhammad's death, with particular care taken to eliminate discrepancies and record only one standard version. This "authorized" edition was then transmitted to various parts of the new Islamic Empire and used to guide the faithful and assist in the conversion of unbelievers. The text of the Qur'an has existed virtually unchanged for nearly 14 centuries.

The Qur'an was intended to be recited aloud; anyone who has listened to the chanting of the Qur'an can testify to its beauty, melody, and power. Much of the power of the Qur'an comes from the experience of reciting, listening, and feeling the message. The Qur'an is never to be translated from the Arabic for the purpose of worship because it is believed that translation distorts the divine message. But over time, the Qur'an was indeed translated into many languages to facilitate

DOCUMENT

The Holy Qur'an

sunna—The custom or practice of the Prophet Muhammad, grounded in the hadith; intended to serve as a model by which Muslims should conduct their lives.

Document   The Qur'an

The Qur'an is one of the most significant of all religious works and one of the world's most beautiful works of literature. The following is a selection celebrating God's creation, from sura 23, titled "The Believers." It illustrates Islam's connection, through the prophets Moses and Jesus, to the sacred texts and beliefs of Judaism and Christianity. But it also points out the Islamic doctrine that God has no son. The Qur'an makes a point of rejecting the notions that God had either sons (e.g., Jesus) or daughters (goddesses in the Arabian pantheon). Note too, that the Qur'an urges men, as well as women, to "guard their modesty."

*In the name of Allah, the Beneficent, the Merciful.
Successful indeed are the believers
Who are humble in their prayers,
And who shun vain conversation,
And who are payers of the poor-due;
And who guard their modesty—
Save from their wives or the [slaves] that their
    right hands possess, for then they are not
    blameworthy,
But whoso craveth beyond that, such are
    transgressors—
And who are shepherds of their pledge and their
    covenant, and who pay heed to their prayers.
These are the heirs
Who will inherit Paradise. There they will abide.
Verily We created man from a product of wet
    earth;
Then placed him as a drop [of seed] in a safe
    lodging;
Then fashioned We the drop a clot, then fashioned
    We the clot a little lump, then fashioned We
    the little lump bones, then clothed the bones
    with flesh, and then produced it as another
    creation. So blessed be Allah, the Best of
    Creators!
Then lo! after that ye surely die.
Then lo! on the Day of Resurrection ye are raised
    [again].
And We have created above you seven paths, and
    We are never unmindful of creation.
And We send down from the sky water in
    measure, and We give it lodging in the earth,
    and lo! We are able to withdraw it.
Then We produce for you therewith gardens of
    date-palms and grapes, wherein is much fruit
    for you and whereof ye eat;
And a tree that springeth forth from Mount Sinai
    that groweth oil and relish for the eaters.
And lo! in the cattle there is verily a lesson for
    you. We give you to drink of that which is in
    their bellies, and many uses have ye in them,
    and of them do ye eat;
And on them and on the ship ye are carried.
Then We sent Moses and his brother Aaron with
    Our tokens and a clear warrant*

*Unto Pharaoh and his chiefs, but they scorned
    [them] and they were despotic folk.
And they said: Shall we put faith in two mortals
    like ourselves, and whose folk are servile unto
    us?
So they denied them, and became of those who
    were destroyed.
And We verily gave Moses the Scripture, that haply
    they might go aright.
And We made the son of Mary and his mother a
    portent, and We gave them refuge on a height,
    a place of flocks and water-springs.
O ye messengers! Eat of the good things, and do
    right. Lo! I am Aware of what ye do.
And lo! this your religion is one religion and I am
    your Lord, so keep your duty unto Me.
Say: In Whose hand is the dominion over all
    things and He protecteth, while against Him
    there is no protection, if ye have knowledge?
They will say: Unto Allah [all that belongeth]. Say:
    How then are ye bewitched?
Nay, but We have brought them the Truth, and lo!
    they are liars.
Allah hath not chosen any son, nor is there any
    God along with Him; else would each God
    have assuredly championed that which he
    created, and some of them would assuredly
    have overcome others. Glorified be Allah
    above all that they allege.
Knower of the invisible and the visible! and
    exalted be He over all that they ascribe as
    partners [unto Him]!*

Questions to Consider

1. What kind of God is suggested in these verses? Characterize him.
2. What clues do these verses give us about the society and environment of Arabia?
3. Compare this account of creation to other creation accounts you are aware of.

From Marmaduke William Pickthall, *The Meaning of the Glorious Koran: An Explanatory Translation* (London: Unwin Hyman/HarperCollins). Reprinted by permission.

scholarship and the spread of the Islamic message. As Islam spread, so too did the Arabic language. Arabic replaced many local languages as the language of administration, and gradually, some of the conquered territories adopted Arabic as the language of everyday use. The Qur'an remains the basic document for the study of Islamic theology, law, social institutions, and ethics. It forms the core of Muslim scholarship, from legal and linguistic inquiry to scientific and technical investigation.

IMAGE
The Holy
Qur'an

The Tenets of Islamic Faith

Monotheism is the central principle of Islam. Muslims believe in the unity or oneness of God; there is no other God but Allah, and this belief is proclaimed five times daily as the believers are called to prayer with these words:

> *God is most great. I testify that there is no God but Allah. I testify that Muhammad is the Messenger of Allah. Come to prayer, come to revelation, God is most great! There is no God but Allah.*

Allah is the one and only God, unchallenged by other false divinities and unlike all others in the strength of his creative power. All life—all creation—is the responsibility of Allah alone. His nature is described in many ways and through many metaphors:

> *Allah is the light of the heaven and the earth. . . . His light is as a niche wherein is a lamp. The lamp is in a glass. The glass is as it were a shining star. [The lamp is] kindled from a blessed tree, an olive neither of the East nor of the West, whose oil would almost glow forth [of itself] though no fire touched it. Light upon light, Allah guided unto His light whom He will. And Allah speaketh to mankind in allegories, for Allah is Knower of all things.*
>
> *[This lamp is found] in houses which Allah hath allowed to be exalted and that His name shall be remembered therein. Therein do offer praise to Him at noon and evening. (Qur'an 24:35–36)*

Islam also recognizes the significance and the contributions of prophets who preceded Muhammad. From the beginnings of human history, Allah has communicated with his people either by the way of these prophets or by written scriptures:

> *Lo! We inspire thee as We inspired Noah and the Prophets after him, as We inspired Abraham and Ishmael and Isaac and Jacob and the tribes, and Jesus and Job and Jonah and Aaron and Solomon and as We imparted unto David the Psalms. (Qur'an 4:164)*

Twenty-eight such prophets are mentioned in the Qur'an as the predecessors of Muhammad, who is believed to have been Allah's final messenger. Muham-

mad is given no divine status by Muslims; in fact, Muhammad took great care to see that he was not worshipped as a god. He told his followers, for example, that it was not appropriate for them to bow down before him.

The creation of the universe and of all living creatures within it is the work of Allah; harmony and balance in all of creation were ensured by God. In addition to humans and other creatures on the earth, angels exist to protect humans and to pray for forgiveness for the faithful. Satan, "the Whisperer," attempts to lead people astray, and mischievous spirits called *jinn* can create havoc for believers and unbelievers alike.

Men and women are given a special status in the pattern of the universe. They can choose to obey or to reject Allah's will and deny him. Allah's message includes the belief in a Day of Resurrection when people will be held responsible for their actions and rewarded or punished accordingly for eternity. The Qur'an graphically describes heaven and hell. Those who have submitted to Allah's law—the charitable, the humble, and the forgiving—and those who have preserved his faith shall dwell in the Garden of Paradise, resting in cool shade, eating delectable foods, attended by "fair ones with wide, lovely eyes like unto hidden pearls," and hearing no vain speech or recrimination but only "Peace! Peace!" This veritable oasis is far different from the agonies of the hell that awaits sinners, the covetous, and the erring. Cast into a pit with its "scorching wind and shadow of black smoke," they will drink boiling water and suffer forever.

The Five Pillars

Over time, the Muslim community developed doctrines, laws, and institutions (like schools and courts) to put into practice its evolving religious ideals. As in other religious traditions, the spread and institutionalization of Islam was a gradual and contested process. And, as in all societies, government and social practice did not always match the religious ideals expressed in the sacred texts. But certain practices became basic to the believers.

Islam is united in the observance of the **Five Pillars,** or five essential duties that all Muslims are required to perform to the best of their abilities. These obligations are accepted by Muslims everywhere and thus serve further to unite the Islamic world. The first obligation is a basic *profession of faith,* by which a

---

Five Pillars—The five essential duties of all Muslims: (1) a profession of faith *(shahada);* (2) prayer *(salat)* five times a day; (3) giving of alms *(zakat);* (4) fasting *(sawm)* during the holy month of Ramadan; and (5) making a pilgrimage *(hajj)* to Mecca at least once during one's lifetime if possible.

These illustrations from a sixteenth-century Persian manuscript depict scenes from the lives of the prophets: Jesus multiplying the loaves and fishes and the staff of Moses transformed into a dragon. Artistic representation of people, events, and landscapes varies considerably from place to place, culture to culture, and over time. Moses is depicted in Jewish, Christian, and Muslim texts, but the same story can be "told" artistically in very different ways.

believer becomes a Muslim. The simple proclamation (*shahada*) is repeated in daily prayers. Belief in the One God and imitation of the exemplary life led by his Prophet are combined in the profession of faith.

Prayer (*salat*) is said five times a day, when Muslims are summoned to worship by the *muezzin* (myeu-EZ-in), who calls them to prayer from atop the minaret of the mosque (*masjid,* meaning "place of prostration"). During prayer, Muslims face Mecca and in so doing give recognition to the birthplace of Islam and the unity of the Islamic community. Prayer can be said alone, at work, at home, or in the mosque.

A Muslim is required to give *alms (zakat)* to the poor, orphans, and widows and to assist the spread of Islam. The payment of alms is a social and religious obligation to provide for the welfare of the *umma.* Muslims are generally expected to contribute annually in alms a percentage (usually 2.5 percent) of their total wealth and assets.

Muslims are requested to *fast (sawm)* during the holy month of Ramadan, the ninth month of the Islamic lunar calendar. From sunrise to sunset, adult

Muslims in good health are to avoid food, drink, tobacco, and sexual activity. Finally, every Muslim able to do so is called to make a *pilgrimage (hajj)* to Mecca at least once in his or her lifetime, in the twelfth month of the Islamic year. The focus of the pilgrimage is the Ka'ba and a series of other sites commemorating events in the lives of the prophets Muhammad and Abraham. The *hajj* emphasizes the unity of the Islamic world community and the equality of all believers regardless of race or class.

Islamic Law

Islam is a way of life as well as a religion, and at its heart is the **Sharia,** the law provided by Allah as a guide for a proper life. The Sharia is based on the Qur'an and hadith; it gives the believers a perfect pattern of human conduct and regulates every aspect of

Sharia—Islamic law based on the word of God as manifested in the teachings of the Qu'ran and hadith.

a person's activities. God's decrees must be obeyed even if humans are incapable of understanding them, since the Sharia is greater than human reason. Those who study, interpret, and administer the Sharia are called *ulama*, "those who know." These men emerged, in the era after the Prophet's death, as religious scholars and leaders who administered the institutions of worship, education, and law. But there is no priesthood in Islam; all believers are equal members of the community.

Islamic law, then, permeates all aspects of human conduct and all levels of activity, from private and personal concerns to those involving the welfare of the whole state. The Sharia became the universal law of the Islamic lands. In practice, it worked in conjunction with the decrees of rulers and with customary laws that varied from region to region. Family law, set forth in the Qur'an, is based on earlier Arab tribal patterns. Islamic law emphasizes the patriarchal nature of the family and society. Marriage is expected of every Muslim man and woman unless physical infirmity or financial inability prevents it. Muslim men can marry non-Muslim women, preferably Christians or Jews, since they too are "people of the Book," but Muslim women are forbidden to marry non-Muslim men. This law reflects the notion, common in traditional societies, that the children "belong" to the father and his family. Thus, the children of a Muslim father and non-Muslim mother would be Muslims. The Qur'an had the effect of improving the status and opportunities of women, who could contract their own marriages, keep and maintain their own dowries, and manage and inherit property (unlike many Western Christian women at that time).

The Qur'an allows Muslim men to marry up to four wives, but only if each wife is treated with equal support and affection. Many modern-day Muslims interpret the Qur'an as encouraging monogamy. Polygamy, in any case, is not required; it is a practice that may have arisen to provide protection and security in early societies where women may have outnumbered men because of the toll of constant warfare.

Islamic law is considered to be God's law for all humankind, not only for the followers of Islam. Non-Muslim citizens of the Islamic state were called *dhimmis* (DHEE-mees); they received protection from the state and paid an extra head tax called the *jizya* (JIZ-yah). The Sharia courts were open to *dhimmis*,

Women associated with the Prophet are revered by the Muslim community. This manuscript image shows Fatima, Muhammad's daughter, along with Aisha and Umm Salama, two of his wives. Their fiery halos and veiled faces suggest their religious significance. Fatima is often held up as a model of Islamic womanhood and Aisha was a prominent political figure and transmitter of Islamic tradition (hadith).

who could also appeal to juridical authorities, such as rabbis or priests, within their own communities. Disputes between Muslims and *dhimmis* were handled in the Sharia court, but a dispute between Christians might be handled within the Christian community. Islamic law sometimes designated certain dress markers for *dhimmis* to set them apart. Bearing arms, engaging in ostentatious religious displays, and corrupting Muslims (by selling them wine, for example) were also prohibited. But repeated allusions to such violations in court records suggest that these laws often were not enforced.

Thus, in addition to its theology, Islam offers to its believers a system of government, a legal foundation, and a pattern of social organization. The Islamic *umma* was, and is, an excellent example of a theocratic state, one in which power ultimately resides in God, on whose behalf political, religious, and other forms of authority are exercised. Ideally, the role of the state is to serve as the guardian of religious law. Islamic monarchs ruled in the name of Allah and called on the Sharia law to legitimize their rule. Of course, as the Islamic state evolved, some rulers were more pious than others. Some came into conflict with the *ulama* over matters of law (as happened with brahmans and kings in India and priests and kings in Europe). But all Muslim kings, like all Christian kings in this era, claimed to be defenders of their faith.

THE EXPANSION OF COMMUNITY AND STATE

■ *What factors contributed to the rapid expansion of Islam?*

The Islamic state expanded very rapidly after the death of Muhammad through remarkable successes in the form of military conquest and conversion. Immediately after the Prophet's death in 632, Caliph Abu Bakr continued the effort to abolish polytheism among the Arab tribes and also to bring all of Arabia under the political control of Medina. The Muslim polity succeeded in strengthening its power throughout the Arabian peninsula and even began to launch some exploratory offensives north toward Syria.

Expansion Under the First Four Caliphs

Under the first four caliphs (632–661), the Islamic state rapidly expanded the territory under its control. The wars of expansion were aided by the devotion of the faithful to the concept of *jihad*, a term that is sometimes glossed as "holy war" and sometimes interpreted to mean simply "struggle." Muslims were obliged to extend the faith to unbelievers and to defend Islam from attack. *Jihad* was responsible in part for Islam's early conquests beyond the Arabian peninsula.

Arab Expansion and the Islamic World, 570–800 C.E.

But various factors account for the triumph of the early Muslim armies. A long series of wars waged between the Byzantine and Persian (Sassanid) Empires to the north left both sides exhausted and open to con-

EXPANSION OF ISLAM TO 750 C.E.
- Under Muhammad, 622–632
- Under the first four caliphs, 632–661
- Under the Umayyad caliphs, 661–750
- → Expansion routes

The Islamic conquests were rapid and far-reaching. By 750 Islamic monarchs controlled kingdoms stretching from central Asia to Spain.

quest. In addition, the inhabitants of Syria and Egypt, alienated by religious dissent and resenting the attempts of the Byzantine Empire to impose its brand of Christianity on the population, sought freedom from Byzantine rule. The Arabs' combined use of camels for long distance travel and swift horses for attacks was extremely effective. In 636 Arab armies conquered Syria and occupied the city of Damascus. Jerusalem was taken in 638. The Muslims then won Iraq from the Persians and in 651 defeated the last Sassanid ruler, thereby ending the 400-year-old Persian Empire. Most of Egypt had fallen with little resistance by 646, and raids had begun into the lands the Muslims called the Maghrib (MUG-reb) in North Africa west of Egypt and north of the Sahara. Within 30 years of Muhammad's death, Islam had become the dominant faith of a vast empire connecting western Asia with the Mediterranean and Africa. This area possessed a certain cultural unity under Islam, but it was politically divided.

The new Islamic territories were governed with remarkable efficiency and flexibility. The centralization of authority typical of effective military organization aided in the incorporation of new peoples. Unbelievers in the conquered territories became increasingly interested in the new religion and accepted Islam in great numbers. In addition to the power of the religious message of Islam, the imposition of a head tax on all non-Muslims and some restrictions on unbelievers' holding political office encouraged many to become converts. Accounts of the coercive imposition of Islam on conquered peoples are inexact: Jews and Christians outside Arabia generally enjoyed tolerance because they worshiped the same God as the Muslims, and many non-Muslims were active participants in the Islamic state and prospered financially and socially.

Islam was and remains one of the most effective religions in overcoming the potential barriers of race and nationality to conversion. In the early days of the spread of Islam, apart from a certain privileged position allowed Arabs and the Prophet's earliest supporters, distinctions were mostly those of economic and political rank. The new religion converted and included peoples of many ethnic origins and cultures. This egalitarian ideal of Islam undoubtedly aided its rapid and successful expansion.

Defining the Community

All Muslims shared belief in the unity of God and the practice of the Five Pillars. But Islamic civilization, like other traditions, was marked by debate and conflict over the interpretation of the law. As Islamic law was codified and as the Islamic state expanded, four main schools of legal interpretation emerged. Schol-

ars struggled with questions of faith and reason, just as their Christian and Buddhist counterparts did. Inspired in part by the spiritual thought and practices of India, Islam also developed a set of mystical traditions that challenged the orthodoxy of the *ulama*. Meanwhile, in the political realm, not long after the death of the Prophet, the new Islamic state underwent a crisis that split the community over the question of authority.

Islam's first three caliphs—Abu Bakr (632–634), Umar (634–644), and Uthman (644–656)—were chosen in consultation with the elders and leaders of the Islamic community, setting a pattern for selecting the caliph exclusively from the Quraysh tribe of Mecca. When Uthman was assassinated by a fellow Muslim, the ensuing struggle for power ultimately split the community into two major divisions, **Sunni** and **Shia** (or Shi'ites). The Shi'ites believed that only descendents of the Prophet could command authority in the Islamic state. Because Muhammad had no surviving sons, his bloodline passed through his grandsons, the sons of his daughter Fatima and her husband Ali, the fourth caliph. Thus for the Shi'ites, the first three caliphs before Ali had been usurpers. Ali and his descendents were the only legitimate heads of the community, *imams*, who were believed to have a special knowledge of the inner meaning of the Qur'an. The Sunnis, rather than insisting on a caliph who was a direct descendant of the Prophet, accepted the first three caliphs and upheld the principle that the caliph owed his position to the consent of the Islamic community. The Sunnis argued that they followed the *sunna* of the Prophet, the patterns of behavior modeled on Muhammad's life.

The Shi'ites did not refute the validity of the sunna, but they insisted on the Qur'an as the sole and unquestioned authority on the life and teachings of the Prophet. Though originally an Arab party, the Shia in time became a more widespread Islamic movement that stood in opposition to the ruling Umayyad dynasty. That the Shia remained, in general, a minority and opposition party in part explains the evolution of its doctrine of opposition to political authorities. Notwithstanding the several major Shi'ite dynasties in Islamic history, Sunni Muslims have remained numerically dominant. Some 85 percent of the modern world's Muslims are Sunnis,

Sunni—The largest division within Islam, comprising more than 85 percent of all Muslims; the form of Islam embraced by the Umayyad state, which accepts the legitimacy of the first three caliphs and holds that the caliph's authority stems from the consent of the Islamic community.

Shia—A division in Islam representing some 10 to 15 percent of all Muslims, principally in Iran, Iraq, and Lebanon; Shi'ites deny the legitimacy of the first three caliphs and hold that the true caliphs were descended from the Prophet Muhammad through Ali, his cousin and son-in-law.

The Early Islamic Dynasties

661	Umayyad dynasty established; Damascus becomes capital
680	Muhammad's grandson Husayn killed by Umayyads at Karbala in Iraq
711	Tariq ibn Ziyad invades Spain from North Africa
750	Abbasids defeat the Umayyads and establish a new dynasty
756	Umayyads set up a new dynasty in Spain; Córdoba later becomes capital
786–809	Reign of Abbasid caliph Harun al-Rashid
909–1171	Fatimid Shi'ite dynasty in North Africa, Egypt, and Syria
1055	Seljuk Turks gain control of Baghdad but leave Abbasid caliph in place
1095	First Crusade mobilized
1250	Mamluk kingdom established in Egypt, will endure until 1517
1258	Mongols conquer Baghdad and kill Abbasid caliph, ending Abbasid dynasty

although large Shi'ite communities exist, particularly in Iran, Iraq, and Lebanon.

Umayyad Rule

Ali and his followers were opposed first by Muslims under the leadership of Muhammad's widow and favorite wife, Aisha, daughter of Abu Bakr, and later by the forces of Muawiya (MOO-AH-wee-ah), the governor of Syria and a relative of the third caliph. The power struggle for leadership in the Muslim community thus erupted into civil war. In 661, after Ali was assassinated, Muawiya proclaimed himself caliph, made Damascus his capital, and founded the Umayyad (oo-MAI-yad) dynasty, which lasted until 750. In this manner the Umayyads made the caliphate in fact, although never in law, a hereditary office rather than one chosen by election.

The Umayyads expanded the borders of Islam, but not with the spectacular successes of the years immediately after Muhammad's death. The Umayyads held Cyprus, Rhodes, and several Aegean islands, which served as bases for naval attacks on the Byzantine Empire. The Byzantines successfully defended Constantinople against persistent Umayyad attacks, and the Islamic advance toward eastern Europe was checked for the first time. The Umayyads established garrisons in central Asia to further their conquests northward across the Oxus River and southwest into India. Westward across North Africa, Umayyad armies were eventually victorious. The Berbers, a nomadic tribal people inhabiting the Maghrib, initially resisted stubbornly but eventually converted to Islam. The Berbers then aided the Umayyad armies in expanding across the Strait of Gibraltar into the weak Visigoth kingdom in Spain. General Tariq ibn Ziyad (TAHR-ik ib-in zee-YAHD) led an army across the strait into Spain in 711 (according to legend, the name *Gibraltar* is derived from *Jabal Tariq,* or "Mountain of Tariq"). After the kingdom of the Visigoths swiftly crumbled, the Muslims were able to make conquests throughout the Iberian peninsula, which they called *al-Andalus.*

The Muslims in Spain seem never to have had serious intentions of expanding their territorial holdings across the Pyrenees into what is now France, but they did engage in seasonal raids to the north. One such raiding party was defeated by Charles Martel near Tours in 732 in a battle that Europeans portrayed later as a decisive blow to Muslim expansion in Europe. But the Byzantines indeed delivered such a blow: In 717 the Byzantine emperor Leo III won a major victory over the Muslims that halted the Umayyad advance into eastern Europe.

To the east, however, the Umayyads successfully extended their rule into central Asia; by the middle of the eighth century they could claim lands as far east as Turkestan and the Indus valley. To celebrate the enduring power of Islam in the 690s the Umayyads built the Dome of the Rock in Jerusalem on the site of the old Jewish Temple. This sacred shrine is built around an enormous rock where, according to tradition, God asked Abraham to sacrifice his son Isaac. A monumental building, it reflected the power of the dynasty and its god; its interior is decorated with Qur'anic inscriptions. The Dome of the Rock has endured to the present day and has become a major site of struggle between Muslim and Jewish claims to the city they both consider holy.

The mainstay of the Umayyad dynasty's power was the ruling class, composed of an Arab military aristocracy. The Arabs formed a privileged class greatly outnumbered by non-Arab converts to Islam. Many of these converted peoples had cultures much more highly developed than that of the Arabs, and the economic and cultural life of this Islamic empire came to be dominated by these non-Arab Muslims, called **mawali,** or

IMAGE

Arabs on Horseback

Document   The Early Islamic Conquests

Traditional Western historiography used the rhetorics of medieval Christian writers to portray the early Islamic conquests as sweeping and brutal. The following two excerpts from the Arabic chronicle of al-Tabari (839–923) suggest that wisdom, pragmatism, mercy, and intimidation all played a role in the early Islamic conquests. The Qur'an enjoined mercy as well as warfare, and Abu Bakr's rules of war suggest that the wise conqueror did not kill the citizens and livestock of the lands he wished to rule. In the first reading, the people who have "shaved the crown of their heads" may well be monks. But, earlier on, the passage admonishes the conquerors to leave those in hermitages alone—so the reference here is unclear. In the second passage, although the general initially calls upon God (customary in military and diplomatic messages of this era), he focuses on the power and violence of men. The Arab general Khalid ibn al-Walid's letters to the Persians offer mercy in exchange for submission, but they follow up that offer with a challenge. The *jizya* is the head tax that all non-Muslim citizens must pay to the Muslim state.

Abu Bakr (Muhammad's successor) on the Rules of War (632)

Oh People! I charge you with ten rules; learn them well!

Do not betray, or misappropriate any part of the booty; do not practice treachery or mutilation. Do not kill a young child, an old man, or a woman. Do not uproot or burn palms or cut down fruitful trees. Do not slaughter a sheep or a cow or a camel, except for food. You will meet people who have set themselves apart in hermitages; leave them to accomplish the purpose for which they have done this. You will come upon people who will bring you dishes with various kinds of food. If you partake of them, pronounce God's name over what you eat. You will meet people who have shaved the crown of their heads, leaving a band of hair around it. Strike them with the sword. Go, in God's name, and may God protect you from sword and pestilence.

Letters to the Persians (633)

In the name of God, the Merciful and the Compassionate.

From Khalid ibn al-Walid to the kings of Persia.

Praise be to God who has dissolved your order, frustrated your plans, and split your unanimity. Had he not done this to you, it would have been worse for you. Submit to our authority, and we shall leave you and your land and go by you against others. If not, you will be conquered against your will by men who love death as you love life.

In the name of God, the Merciful and the Compassionate.

From Khalid ibn al-Walid to the border chiefs of Persia.

Become Muslim and be saved. If not, accept protection from us and pay the jizya. If not, I shall come against you with men who love death as you love to drink wine.

Questions to Consider

1. Why would Abu Bakr urge his soldiers to exercise restraint and curb the destructive impulses of war?
2. Think about the idea of submission. Why does the general insist that his enemy submit and what do you think submission means for the conquered peoples?
3. What does Khalid ibn al-Walid mean when he says he shall attack "with men who love death as you love to drink wine"?

From *Islam: From the Prophet Muhammad to the Capture of Constantinople, Volume 1: Politics and War*, ed. Bernard Lewis. Translation copyright © 1974 by Bernard Lewis. Used by permission of Oxford University Press, Inc.

"affiliates." Because they were not Arab by birth, they were treated to a certain extent as citizens of inferior status. They were granted fewer privileges and received less from the spoils of war than did the Arabs. Resentment grew steadily among some of the non-Arab Muslims, who objected to their inferior status as a violation of the Islamic laws advocating equality. Eventually the resentment of the *mawali* and the opposition of the Shi'ites, who had been forced from power on the accession of Muawiya, helped bring about the downfall of the Umayyads.

---

mawali—Non-Arab Muslims; resentment against discrimination by Arab Muslims led them to oppose Umayyad rule.

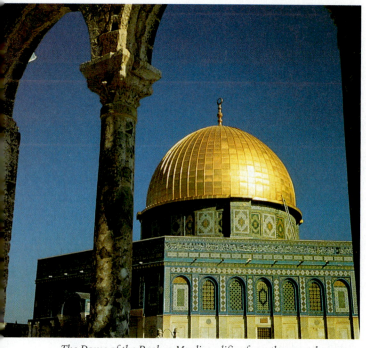

The Dome of the Rock, a Muslim edifice from the seventh century, is built above the Temple Mount in Jerusalem, the site of Solomon's Temple. According to tradition, the site is also the place where Muhammad ascended into heaven on his "Night Journey." Intricate mosaic decoration covers the outer walls of the building.

Support for Umayyad rule was never universal. Hostility to the Umayyads was inflamed in 680 when an Umayyad troop massacred Husayn, the second son of Ali, and his followers at Karbala in Iraq. The killing of the grandson of the Prophet was considered a horrible affront to the Islamic community. It helped spur resentment against the ruling dynasty and made it appear illegitimate. This event introduced the theme of martyrdom into Shi'ite tradition around which opposition party unity could be mobilized. To this day, a "passion play" commemorating Husayn's death is a dramatic and important element in Shi'ite ceremonial in many communities.

THE ABBASID ERA, ZENITH OF CLASSICAL ISLAMIC CIVILIZATION

■ *What roles did the cities of Baghdad, Cairo, and Córdoba play in classical Islamic civilization?*

A new dynasty, the Abbasid, was founded when a rebel army, with Shi'ite support, defeated the Umayyads. The first Abbasid caliph was Abu al-Abbas, a descendant of Muhammad's uncle, Abbas. His dynasty ruled most of the Muslim world from 750 to 1258 and built the city

of Baghdad in 762 as a symbol of its wealth, power, and legitimacy. The Abbasids owed their initial support and successes in part to the discontent of the non-Arab Muslims, many of whom had become prominent leaders in Islam's cities.

The fall of the Umayyad dynasty marked the end of Arab domination within Islam. The Arab "aristocracy" had led the forces of conquest during the great period of Islamic expansion, but over time, as new dynasties established themselves, the dominant status previously held only by Arab soldiers was shared with non-Arab administrators, merchants, and scholars.

Under the Abbasids, traditional Arab patterns of tribal organization and warfare gave way to patterns of military organization and governance based on the imperial traditions of the conquered lands. The new

This sixteenth-century Persian manuscript depicts the gendered division of space in a mosque scene. Women of various ages and their children are shown in an area separated from the main mosque area by a barrier. Cultural practice has varied from region to region, but today one will often see such a separation of females and younger children from the males in rituals of worship.

Abbasid polity fostered economic prosperity, the growth of town life, and the promotion of the merchant class.

The founding of the new capital at Baghdad shifted Islam's center of gravity to the province of Iraq, whose soil, watered by the Tigris and Euphrates Rivers, had nurtured the earliest civilizations. Here the Abbasid caliphs set themselves up as potentates in the traditional style of the ancient East (particularly Persia), so that they were surrounded by a lavish court that contrasted sharply with the simplicity of the lifestyle of the Prophet and the first caliphs. One historian described the amazement of the Byzantine envoys who, on entering the Abbasid court, found a magnificent tree of silver and gold, with singing birds, also of silver and gold, perched in its leaves. The Abbasid caliph forecast that Baghdad would become the "most flourishing city in the world"; indeed, it rivaled Constantinople for that honor, situated as it was on the trade routes linking East and West. Furthermore, Abbasid patronage of scholarship and the arts produced a rich and complex culture far surpassing that in western Europe at the time. In Baghdad they founded one of the great medieval libraries, the House of Wisdom.

The Abbasid dynasty marked the high point of classical Islamic power and civilization. The empire ruled by the Abbasid caliphs was greater in size than the Roman Empire at its height; it was the product of an expansion during which the Muslim state assimilated peoples, customs, cultures, learning, and inventions on an unprecedented scale. This Islamic empire, in fact, drew from the resources of the entire known world.

Abbasid power, however, did not go unchallenged, even in the Muslim world. While the Abbasids ruled in Baghdad, rival dynasties established their sovereignty in other areas that had been incorporated into the Islamic state during the early conquests. Members of the deposed Umayyad dynasty established a new dynasty in Muslim Spain in 756 and eventually set up a glorious court in Córdoba, famous for its scholarship and patronage of the arts. In Egypt the Fatimids established a Shi'ite ruling house and developed a formidable navy that dominated the eastern Mediterranean. To bolster their legitimacy, the Fatimids claimed descent from the Prophet's daughter, Fatima; hence, the name of the dynasty. They, too, founded a new and glorious capital at Cairo, where they established al-Azhar, the famous institution of Islamic learning that has attracted scholars from throughout the Muslim world since the tenth century. Thus, the eighth to the twelfth centuries were not only the period of the classical glory of the Islamic state but also an era during which rulers in three different Muslim capitals all claimed the title "caliph." This political division stood in contrast to the Islamic world's civilizational unity, which was based on the universal Sharia law and the spread of the Arabic language.

The Islamic world was embedded in a network of trading connections extending from the Atlantic to the Pacific.

Trade, Industry, and Agriculture

From the eighth century to the twelfth, the Muslim world enjoyed enormous prosperity. In close contact with three continents, merchants from the Islamic lands could move goods back and forth from China to western Europe and from Russia to central Africa. The absence of tariff barriers within the empire and the tolerance of the caliphs, who allowed non-Muslim merchants and craftsmen to reside in their territories and carry on commerce with their home countries, further facilitated trade. The presence of such important urban centers as Baghdad, Cairo, and Córdoba stimulated trade and industry throughout the Muslim world; the courts of the monarchs were great consumers of textiles, foodstuffs, arts, and crafts.

The cosmopolitan nature of Baghdad was evident in its bazaars, which contained goods from all over the known world. There were spices, minerals, and dyes from India; gems and fabrics from central Asia; honey, furs, and wax from Scandinavia and Russia; and ivory and gold from Africa. Muslim trade with Southeast Asia increased, and a large Muslim trading community established itself in the Chinese port of Guangzhou (GWANG-JOH; Canton). One bazaar in Baghdad specialized in goods from China, including silks, musk, and porcelain. In the slave markets Muslim traders bought and sold Scandinavians, Mongolians from central Asia, and Africans. Joint-stock companies flourished along with branch banking organizations, and checks (an Arabic word) drawn on one bank could be cashed with commercial agents throughout this vast network of traders. Muslim textile industries turned out excellent cottons (muslins) and silks. The steel of Damascus and Toledo, the leather of Córdoba, and the glass of Syria became internationally famous. Notable also was the art of papermaking, learned from the Chinese. Under the Abbasids, vast irrigation projects in Iraq increased cultivable land, which yielded large crops of fruits and grains. Wheat came from the Nile valley, cotton from North Africa, olives and wine from Spain, wool from eastern Asia Minor, and horses from Persia.

By the tenth century Islam was also making inroads into Africa south of the Nile and the Maghrib. Trade routes through the Sahara brought spices, leatherwork, and eventually slaves from the south to the northern coast, and, in return, caravans from the north brought luxury goods, salt, and the Islamic reli-

In the Muslim world, merchants transported goods by both land and sea. Camels carried merchants and goods on the overland routes, as shown in this manuscript illumination from the thirteenth century (above left). Sound vessels with space for both passengers and cargo, like the Indian ship depicted in this Iraqi manuscript from 1238 (above right), and reliable navigation techniques facilitated the sea trade.

gion to the early African kingdoms of Ghana and Mali. Commercial agents and missionaries carried Islam along the sea routes to central and southeastern African ports such as Mogadishu and Manda and to South and Southeast Asia.

Because the Islamic realms encompassed such a great expanse of territory, languages, and cultures, it is difficult to generalize about Islamic society. Most of the population of the Islamic world was illiterate and engaged in subsistence agriculture. In part because Muhammad was a merchant, trade was considered an honorable profession, and some merchants became quite wealthy. In general, however, the military and administrative classes possessed the greatest wealth and status. Religion, profession, gender, and class could be more important determinants of status than race (even though racism of different varieties was common here as it was in the rest of the world).

The Spectacular Reign of Harun al-Rashid

The rule of Harun al-Rashid (786–809), hero of the tales of *The Arabian Nights*, was the most spectacular of the Abbasid reigns. A contemporary of Charlemagne, who had revived the idea of a Roman Empire in the West (see Chapter 9), Harun was surely the more powerful of the two and the ruler of the more advanced culture. The two monarchs were on friendly terms, based on self-interest. Charlemagne wanted to exert pressure on the Byzantine emperor to recognize his new imperial title. Harun saw Charlemagne as an ally against the Umayyad rulers of Spain, who had broken away from Abbasid dominion. The two emperors exchanged embassies and presents. The Muslim sent the Christian rich fabrics, aromatics, and even an elephant named Abu-Lababah, meaning "the father of intelligence." Another gift, an intricate water clock from Baghdad, seems to have been regarded as miraculous in the West.

Relations between the Abbasid caliphate and the Byzantine Empire were never very cordial, and conflicts often broke out along the shifting borders that separated Christian and Muslim territories. Harun al-Rashid once responded to a communiqué from the Byzantine emperor with the following answer:

> In the name of God, the Merciful, the Compassionate. From Harun, Commander of the Faithful, to Nicepherus, the dog of the Greeks, I have read your letter, you son of a she-infidel, and you shall see the answer before you hear it.

This response was followed up with Abbasid raids on Byzantine possessions in Asia Minor.

In the days of Harun al-Rashid, Baghdad's wealth and splendor equaled that of Constantinople, and its chief glory was the royal palace. With its annexes for offi-cials, the harem, and eunuchs, the caliph's residence occupied one-third of the city of Baghdad. The caliph's audience chamber was the setting for an elaborate ceremonial, which mirrored that of the Byzantines and Persians. Such court ceremonial was designed to impress the Abbasid citizens with the justice, power, and magnificence of the caliph and to intimidate foreign envoys.

Challenges to Abbasid Authority

In the tenth century a movement of migration and conquest out of central Asia began that would have a dramatic impact on the political and cultural configuration of the central Islamic lands. By the early eleventh century, Turkish peoples had moved from central Asia into the Abbasid lands, where, over time, they converted to Islam. One group, the Seljuks, after annexing most of Persia, gained control of Baghdad in 1055 and subjugated Iraq. Subsequently, they conquered Syria and Palestine at the expense of the Fatimids and proceeded to take most of Asia Minor from the Byzantines. The Seljuks permitted the Abbasids to retain nominal authority, in part to secure political legitimacy for their reign, but they themselves ruled the state. By the time of the First Crusade in 1095, which was provoked in part by the Seljuk advances, the Abbasid dynasty had lost much of its power and status in the Islamic world.

Seljuk dominance of much of the old Abbasid Empire was later challenged by the arrival of Turco-Mongol invaders from the northeastern steppes of central Asia. Early in the thirteenth century Chinggis (Genghis) Khan succeeded in uniting the animistic, tribal horsemen of Mongolia and conquering much of China and Russia; he and his successors moved on to eastern and central Asia (see Chapter 10) and ultimately conquered Persia and Iraq. In 1258 a grandson of Chinggis Khan captured Baghdad and had the caliph executed. Unlike the Seljuks, the Mongols were contemptuous of the caliph and felt no need to preserve an Abbasid successor as a figurehead to secure their legitimacy. Not only did the Abbasid dynasty come to an end, but so did most of the vast irrigation system that had supported the land. The dynasty established there by the Mongols survived for almost a century, but the Mongol invaders were eventually acculturated and absorbed into the local population.

Egypt was "saved" from the Mongol advance by the Mamluks (1250–1517). The Fatimids had been replaced by one of their own commanders, Salah al-Din, who established a new dynasty, the Ayyubids (ay-YOO-bids), who reigned from 1169–1252. Famed in the West as Saladin, it was Salah al-Din who took Jerusalem from the crusaders. The Ayyubids were in turn overthrown by their own elite "slave" guard, called *mamluks*. *Mamluk* literally means "slave," but these men were not slaves in the sense of people of low status who did menial tasks. Taken as captives or purchased as young men in the slave market, they were trained in the military and political arts to serve their commanders. They were converted to Islam and hence could not be held as true slaves. Indeed, they often wielded great power and wealth. After overthrowing the Ayyubids and founding their own ruling group, they formed the elite military caste of Egypt. It was the Mamluks who stopped the Mongol advance in Syria and later ejected the last of the crusaders in 1291. They ruled in Egypt and Syria until 1517, claiming the title "Protector of the Holy Places" as a result of their governance of Mecca, Medina, and also Jerusalem, the three holy cities of Islam.

ISLAMIC CULTURE

■ *What were the achievements of Islamic culture in medicine, science, mathematics, literature, art, and architecture?*

The attainments of the Muslims in the intellectual and artistic fields can be attributed not only to the Arabs but also to the peoples who embraced Islam in Persia, Iraq, Turkey, Syria, Egypt, North Africa, and Spain. Muslim learning benefited both from Islam's ability to absorb other cultures and from the native talents of the Islamic peoples. Under Abbasid rule, a great synthesis of culture and scholarship emerged, strands of which were then transmitted by traveling scholars, traders, and missionaries throughout the known world from the Mediterranean to the Indian Ocean.

MAP

The Spread of Islam

The cosmopolitan spirit permeating the Abbasid dynasty supplied the tolerance necessary for a diversity of ideas, so that the science, philosophies, and literatures of ancient Greece and India alike received a cordial reception in Baghdad. Under Harun al-Rashid and his successors, the writings of Aristotle, Euclid, Ptolemy, Archimedes, Galen, and other great Greek philosophers and scientific writers were translated into Arabic. This knowledge, together with the teachings of the Qur'an, formed the basis of Muslim learning, which was in turn transmitted to scholars in Europe and Asia. In addition to being valuable transmitters of learning, Muslim scholars crafted a unique synthesis based on the genius of Arab civilization and on a continuing dialog among Muslim and non-Muslim thinkers and artists.

Advances in Medicine

The years between 900 and 1100 can be regarded as the golden age of Muslim learning. This period was particularly significant for its medical advances. Muslim students of medicine were by all measures far superior to their European contemporaries. Muslim cities had excellent pharmacies and hospitals, where physicians received instruction and training. Muslim scholars perfected surgical techniques, figured out the mode for the spread of the plague, and described the course of many diseases.

Perhaps the greatest Muslim physician was the Persian Abu Bakr Muhammad al-Razi (d. 925), better known in the West as Rhazes. Chief physician in Baghdad, he wrote more than 100 medical treatises, in which he summarized Greek medical knowledge and added his own clinical observations. His most famous work, *On Smallpox and Measles*, is the first clear description of the symptoms and treatment of these diseases.

The most influential Muslim medical treatise is the vast *Canon of Medicine*, in which the great scholar Ibn Sina, or Avicenna (d. 1037), systematically organized all Greek and Muslim medical learning. In the twelfth century, the *Canon* was translated into Latin. It was so much in demand in the West that it was issued 16 times in the last half of the fifteenth century and more than 20 times in the sixteenth, and it continued to be used until the modern era.

Progress in Other Sciences

Muslim physicists were also highly creative scientists. Al-Hasan ibn al-Haytham, or Alhazen (d. 1038), of Cairo, developed optics to a remarkable degree and challenged the theory of Ptolemy and Euclid that the eye sends visual rays to its object. The chief source of all medieval Western writers on optics, Alhazen was interested in optical reflections and illusions and examined the refraction of light rays through air and water.

Although astronomy continued to be strongly influenced by astrology, Muslim astronomers built observatories, recorded their observations over long periods, and achieved greater accuracy than the Greeks in measuring the length of the solar year and in calculating eclipses. Interest in alchemy—the attempt to change base metals into precious ones and to find the magic elixir for the preservation of human life—produced the first chemical laboratories and caused attention to be given to the value of experimentation. Muslim alchemists prepared many chemical substances (sulfuric acid, for example) and developed methods for evaporation, filtration, sublimation, crystallization, and distillation. The process of distillation, invented around 800, produced what was called *al-kuhl* ("the essence"), or alcohol, a new liquor that brought its inventors great honor in some circles.

In mathematics the Muslims were indebted to the Hindus as well as to the Greeks. From the Hindus

In an empire that straddled continents, where trade and administration made an accurate knowledge of lands imperative, the science of geography flourished. The Muslims added to the geographical knowledge of the Greeks, whose treatises they translated, by producing detailed descriptions of the climate, manners, and customs of many parts of the known world. Developments in mapping went hand in hand with the progress of Arab seafaring, which aimed at exploiting commercial possibilities along the seaborne routes of trade.

Islamic Literature and Scholarship

To Westerners, Islamic literature may seem somewhat alien. Early Western literary styles tried to emphasize restraint and simplicity, but Muslim writers have long enjoyed literature that makes use of elegant expression, subtle combinations of words, and fanciful and even extravagant imagery.

Westerners' knowledge of Islamic literature tends to be limited to *The Arabian Nights* and the poetry of Omar Khayyám. The former is a collection of often erotic tales told with a wealth of local color that sheds light on racial and gender relations and on practices of food, dress, and cleanliness. Although *The Arabian Nights* professedly covers different facets of life at the Abbasid capital, the story is in fact

DOCUMENT
The Rubáiyát of Omar Khayyám

Husayn ibn Ishaq's Book of the Ten Treatises on the Eye *shows the Islamic scientist's outstandingly accurate understanding of the anatomy of the eye. Written in the tenth century, the work was still standard in the thirteenth century, when the copy shown here was made.*

came arithmetic, algebra, the zero, and the nine signs known in the West as Arabic numerals. From the Greeks came the geometry of Euclid and the fundamentals of trigonometry, which Ptolemy had established. Two Muslim mathematicians made significant contributions: al-Khwarizmi (al-KWAHR-iz-mee; d. c. 844), whose *Arithmetic* introduced Arabic numerals and whose *Algebra* first employed that mathematical term, and Omar Khayyám (d. c. 1123), the mathematician, astronomer, and poet whose work in algebra went beyond quadratics to cubic equations. Other Islamic scholars developed plane and spherical trigonometry.

often based on life in medieval Cairo. It took the literary influences of India and Persia, combined them with conventions of Arabic literature, and passed them on to the West, where they can be seen in the works of Chaucer and Boccaccio. These tales present an interesting combination of the courtly and the vulgar. The fame of Omar Khayyám's *Rubáiyát* (reu-BAI-yaht) is due at least in part to the musical (though rather free) translation of Edward Fitzgerald. The following stanzas indicate the poem's beautiful imagery and gentle resignation:

*A Book of Verses underneath the Bough,
A Jug of Wine, a Loaf of Bread—and Thou*

An Islamic Map of the World

Which way is up? We tend to take the orientation of maps for granted, with north as up. For example, American world maps often depict the United States at the center and north at the top. But not all maps make those same assumptions. The world map of al-Idrisi, an Arab geographer, is a case in point. Al-Idrisi's map is oriented, as was common in Arab maps of his time, with south at the top. It is centered on the world of his own experience, the sacred city of Mecca in Arabia and the civilized realm of the Mediterranean. The map includes several distinctive features typical of this type of medieval map. The world is shown as an island encircled by a world sea. The extent of Africa is unknown; it is depicted as a giant mass occupying the upper half of the map. The Americas are not included at all.

Al-Idrisi was born in Morocco in 1100. Educated in Córdoba, he began his travels as a youth and ended up at the cosmopolitan court of King Roger of Sicily around 1138. There the king asked him to construct a world map complete with written commentary. In collaboration with other scholars, al-Idrisi crafted the map, which was engraved on silver, around the year 1154. Although the original is lost, there are various manuscript versions of al-Idrisi's world map, one of which is shown here. The Arab scholar's map was very influential and widely copied in Europe and Asia for centuries after his death in 1165. Al-Idrisi's map suggests one type of medieval worldview, and his life confirms the notion that cartographers were a valuable commodity in the Afro-Eurasian courts of the time. Rulers valued cartographers because they provided information that was practical and enlightening. They pieced together information about the world from classical sources, old maps, and the accounts of seamen, traders, and travelers. But, cartographers were also artists who made images of the ways in which peoples envisioned their own world and regions beyond their reach. Maps legitimized the power of rulers, cultures, kingdoms, and religions.

Turn the map upside down and see if you can identify the Mediterranean Sea, the Arabian Peninsula, and the Maghrib.

Questions to Consider

1. What does the world "look like" when *you* imagine it? Where and how did you learn your vision of the world?
2. The ways in which the world is represented change over time and place. Not all peoples depict land and sea in the same way. Try drawing a map of your childhood "world." What would it look like?
3. Are maps depictions of reality or do they suggest points of view?

Beside me singing in the Wilderness—
Oh, Wilderness were Paradise enow!—
Some for the Glories of This World; and some
Sigh for the Prophet's Paradise to come;
Ah, take the Cash, and let the Credit go,
Nor heed the rumble of a distant Drum! . . .
The Moving Finger writes; and, having writ,
Moves on: nor all your Piety nor Wit
Shall lure it back to cancel half a Line,
Nor all your Tears wash out a Word of it.
And that inverted Bowl they call the Sky,
Whereunder crawling coop'd we live and die,
Lift not your hands to It for help—for It
As impotently moves as you or I.[1]

DOCUMENT
A Mirror for Princes

The same rich imagery characterizes much Islamic prose, but *The Arabian Nights* and the *Rubáiyát* merely hint at the breadth and diversity of Islamic literature. As the first important prose work in Arab literature, the Qur'an set the stylistic pattern for all Arabic writers. With classical Arabic then "fixed" in the Qur'an, Muslim writers, spurred on by the generosity of the Islamic kings, produced a great corpus of literature. Arabic and then Persian were the languages of high culture. Poetry contests were a standard of the early Islamic courts, where the poets who contrived the most beautiful or wittiest verses received honors and rich rewards. Poetry was also used for satire. Poets used pointed verse to wound or defame their rivals, and kings used the talents of their poets to send insulting messages to their enemies. Muslim philosophy, essentially Greek in origin, was developed and modified by Islamic scholars. Like the medieval Christian philosophers, Muslim thinkers were largely concerned with reconciling the rationalism of Aristotle on the one hand and religious faith on the other. Some sought to harmonize Platonism, Aristotelianism, and Islam. The philosopher Ibn Sina (980–1037) sought to extract what was purely Aristotelian from later additions and to articulate the truths of Islam in terms of Aristotelian logic. His work had a profound effect on Islamic philosophy and was widely read in the West, where it was translated into Latin in the twelfth century.

Another great Islamic philosopher, Ibn Rushd, or Averroës (ah-VEHR-oh-eez; d. 1198), lived in Córdoba,

DOCUMENT
The Sea of Precious Virtues

where he was the caliph's personal doctor. He is famous for his marvelous commentaries on Aristotle. Ibn Rushd rejected the belief in the ultimate harmony between faith and reason along with all earlier attempts to reconcile Aristotle and Plato. He argued that parts of the Qur'an were to be taken metaphorically, not literally. But Ibn Rushd thought that most people were unable to understand either philosophy or the metaphorical meanings of the Qur'an. Those were questions for the philosophers.

In contrast, Moses Maimonides (mai-MON-e-deez), Ibn Rushd's contemporary who was also born in Muslim Spain, sought, in his still influential *Guide to the Perplexed,* to harmonize Judaism and Aristotelian philosophy. St. Thomas Aquinas, who in the next century undertook a similar project for Christianity, was influenced by these earlier attempts to reconcile faith and reason. Although Western historiography has focused on the clash of Muslim and Christian armies in Spain, it might be better to view that territory in particular as a place where Muslim, Christian, and Jewish thinkers and writers interacted and learned from each other through a series of ongoing debates.

Islamic historiography found its finest expression in the work of Ibn Khaldun of Tunis (d. 1406), who has been called the "father of sociology." Ibn Khaldun wrote a large general history dealing particularly with human social development, focusing on the interaction of society with the physical environment. He delineated guidelines for the writing of history and ridiculed earlier historical writing, saying it was often full of stupid or thoughtless errors. Ibn Khaldun defined history in this manner:

> *It should be known that history, in matter of fact, is information about human social organization, which itself is identical with world civilization. It deals with such conditions affecting the nature of civilization as, for instance, savagery and sociability, group feelings, and the different ways by which one group of human beings achieves superiority over another. It deals with royal authority and . . . with the different kinds of gainful occupations and ways of making a living, with the sciences and crafts that human beings pursue as part of their activities and efforts, and with all the other institutions that originate in civilization through its very nature.*[2]

Ibn Khaldun conceived of history as an evolutionary process, in which societies and institutions change continually. He traveled widely in the Islamic world, serving as a judge and scholar in the courts of the Mamluks and other rulers. When he beheld the city of Cairo, he described it as a pinnacle of Islamic civilization, full of shops, gardens, scholars, and institutions of higher learning.

The Sufis

As Islamic civilization produced traditions of scholarship and philosophy, it also produced a tradition of mysticism that came to be a significant factor in the spread of Islam throughout the world. The Arabic word *tasawwuf* (tah-SAHW-woof, "mysticism") is related to the word *suf,* for the coarse woolen clothes some of the early mystics wore. The early sufis were lone ascetics who practiced physical and spiritual dis-

Document — Ibn Sina's Path to Wisdom

The ways in which a person obtains an education vary considerably over time and from place to place. In the medieval Islamic world, it was customary for students to go from teacher to teacher or even from city to city seeking knowledge. Recitation and memorization were important elements of learning. Rather than working on a fixed "semester" system, a student often studied with a teacher until he mastered a particular text or body of knowledge (whether it took three months or three years). Only affluent students could afford their own books. As in many societies, formal education was reserved primarily for men; and, even among men, only an elite few were literate. Although some Muslim women became distinguished scholars and poets, girls generally received only a rudimentary education.

Ibn Sina, the famous Muslim philosopher who died in 1037, recorded the progress of his own education. His diligence, but not his pride, might in some ways serve as a model for modern students. As a young boy, Ibn Sina began his education in religion and the sciences. He remembers himself as a determined and independent student who had little patience with or respect for some of his teachers. By the time he was 16, his education was already far-reaching. Ibn Sina was raised in Bukhara, an important center of Islamic learning in Central Asia. There, he writes:

I was put under teachers of the Qur'an and of letters. By the time I was ten I had mastered the Qur'an and a great deal of literature, so that I was marvelled at for my aptitude. . . . My father sent me to a certain vegetable-seller who used the Indian arithmetic, so that I might learn it from him. Then, there came to Bukhara a man called Abu 'Abd Allah al-Natili who claimed to be a philosopher; my father invited him to stay in our house, hoping I would learn from him also. I had already occupied myself with Muslim jurisprudence, attending Isma'il the Ascetic; so I was an excellent enquirer, having become familiar with the methods of expostulation and the techniques of rebuttal according to the usages of the canon lawyers. . . . Whatever problem he [al-Natili] stated to me, I showed a better mental conception of it than he. So I continued until I had read all the straightforward parts of Logic with him; as for the subtler points, he had no acquaintance with them. From then onwards I took to reading texts by myself; I studied the commentaries, until I had completely mastered the science of Logic. Similarly with Euclid I read the first five or six figures with him, and thereafter undertook on my own account to solve the entire remainder of the book. . . . I now occupied myself with mastering the various texts and commentaries on natural science and metaphysics, until all the gates of knowledge were open to me. Next I desired to study medicine, and proceeded to read all the books that have been written on this subject. Medicine is not a difficult science, and naturally I excelled in it in a very short time, so that qualified physicians began to read medicine with me. I also undertook to treat the sick, and methods of treatment derived from practical experience revealed themselves to me such as baffle description. At the same time I continued between whiles to study and dispute on law, being now sixteen years of age.

Questions to Consider

1. Ibn Sina does not focus on the idea of learning as something that takes place in a specific building or one location. In what terms does he describe the learning process?

2. Think about writing an autobiography. When adults think back and describe their student days, is that history? What roles do memory and sense of identity play in the process?

From A. J. Arberry. *Aspects of Islamic Civilization* (Ann Arbor: University of Michigan Press, 1967), pp. 136–137.

cipline in order to transcend the material world and gain a special kind of closeness to Allah. Later, sufi orders were founded in which the devotees practiced rules of discipline, followed the path shown them by a spiritual master or *shaykh*, divorced themselves to some extent from the community, and developed rituals that ranged from the simple to the elaborate. There are many similarities between some of the sufi orders and the medieval monastic orders of Christian Europe. To be a sufi, however, one does not need to join a spiritual order; many sufis live and work in the community. What is essential to **Sufism** is the belief

Sufism—A broad term used to designate any of ascetic and mystic movements within Islam. Sufi movements have borrowed elements from Christian monasticism and Indian mysticism. The essential aim of Sufism is to achieve mystical communion with Allah.

in following a path of discipline that leads to mystical communion with Allah.

The early Muslim mystics expressed their desire for union with God in a language of love, longing, and ecstasy. This longing came to be embodied in the mystical poetry of sufis like that of the famous Jalal al-Din Rumi (1207–1273), who compared the sufi to a man "drunk with God." The *dhikr*, collective repetition of the name of God, sometimes accompanied by rhythmic movements and breathing, became part of sufi practice. It was a way of both glorifying God and transcending (like yoga) the distractions of the body and the world. In their quest for communion with God, the sufis also ran afoul of Islamic orthodoxy, because their beliefs and practices were sometimes considered extreme or blasphemous.

In the ninth century, sufis began systematically to write down the ways of the path. Communion with God meant the losing of self, however briefly. That losing or merging of self with God smacked of polytheism to many members of the *ulama*. Thus the sufis were accused of claiming to be divine and of believing they were above the law. In 922 al-Hallaj, a famous teacher and sufi in Baghdad, was executed for blasphemy after he claimed, "I am the Truth." Al-Hallaj had also alienated the authorities by claiming that the *hajj*, the pilgrimage to Mecca, was not necessary, because the sufi could pursue the pilgrimage to God from his own room. The pathos of the death of al-Hallaj is graphically described in the words of his servant, Ibrahim ibn Fatik, who wrote that al-Hallaj asked Allah to forgive those who were preparing to kill him:

> *Then he was silent. The Headsman stepped up and dealt him a smashing blow which broke his nose, and the blood ran onto his white robe. The mystic al-Shibli, who was in the crowd, cried aloud and rent his garment, and Abu Husayn al-Wasiti fell fainting, and so did other famous sufis who were there, so that a riot nearly broke out. Then the executioners did their work.*[3]

Al-Hallaj gave the sufi community in Baghdad a martyr. But in the end, the message of Sufism was too powerful and compelling for Islamic orthodoxy to ignore. Sufis were very effective in spreading the message of Islam beyond its Middle Eastern heartlands. In South and Southeast Asia, sufi asceticism and belief in mystical communion found resonances in the ascetic and mystical practices of those areas and aided the conversion of non-Muslims to Islam. By the end of the Abbasid era, Sufism had been brought into the mainstream of Islamic thought as a result of its widespread appeal and through the systematic efforts of scholars like al-Ghazali (1058–1111), who legitimized the sufi way as an acceptable path toward God. Sufism remains a powerful tool in the spread of Islam. In the United States today, Rumi's poetry remains popular, and American college students may get their first taste of Islam through the words of sufi masters.

Art and Architecture

Religious attitudes played an important part in shaping Islamic art. Because the Prophet warned against idols and their worship, there was a prohibition against pictorial representation of human and animal figures; that prohibition, however, was not always obeyed. The effect of this injunction was to encourage the development of stylized and geometrical designs. Islamic art, like other artistic traditions, borrowed extensively to forge a new and unique synthesis. Artists and craftspeople followed chiefly Byzantine and Persian models, but Central Asian, South Asian, and African motifs were also integrated into Islamic styles.

The ultimate stage of refinement of Moorish architecture, which combines Spanish and Islamic elements, is the Alhambra in Granada, the last Islamic stronghold in Spain during the Middle Ages. Slender, rhythmically spaced columns and arches covered with an intricate design of molded stucco frame the Court of the Lions, the most luxurious portion of the palace.

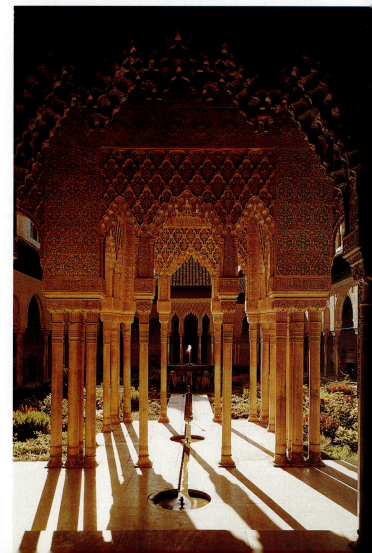

The Muslims excelled in the fields of architecture and the decorative arts. That Islamic architecture can boast of many large and imposing structures is not surprising; monumental building was a natural extension of the power and glory of the Islamic dynasts who wanted to celebrate their own power and glorify God. In time, original styles of building evolved; the great mosques embody such typical features as domes, arcades, and minarets, the slender towers from which the faithful are summoned to prayer. The horseshoe arch is another graceful and familiar feature of Muslim architecture.

On the walls and ceilings of their buildings, the Muslims gave full rein to their love of ornamentation and beauty of detail. The Spanish interpretation of the Islamic tradition is particularly delicate and elegant. A superb artistic example of the sophistication and wealth of the Muslim world is the Alhambra, built between 1248 and 1354 by Muslim kings in Granada, Spain. Some authorities consider it the apogee of Muslim architecture.

Restricted in their subject matter, Muslim craftspeople conceived beautiful patterns from flowers and geometrical figures. The Arabic script, one of the most graceful ever devised, was often used as a decorative motif. Muslim decorative skill also found expression in such fields as carpet and rug weaving, brass work, and the making of steel products inlaid with precious metals.

CONCLUSION

The great power of Islam's message enabled the fragmented Arab tribes to unify and expand across three continents in an astoundingly brief period. During the reigns of the first four caliphs and the century of dominance by the Umayyad dynasty, great gains were made in conquering new territories and peoples. But the Umayyad dynasty was based on a ruling hierarchy of Arabs, and the resentment of the non-Arab Islamic community helped establish the Abbasid dynasty in a new caliphate in Baghdad.

While traders, scholars, and sufis exported variants of the Islamic worldview, the Abbasid Empire provided the security, patronage, and institutional framework for a great cultural synthesis and an expanding network of international trade. As in all traditional empires of the time, agriculture provided the base for the economy of the Abbasid state, but its prosperity evolved from a combination of successful agriculture, trade, and industry.

The Islamic worldview both challenged and integrated the worldviews of the peoples it encountered in Asia, Africa, and Europe. Intellectual life was a product of that evolving synthesis. Muslim scholars participated in the rediscovery of classical (Greek) learning and the emergence of the Renaissance in Europe. They elaborated their cosmology in the course of a contentious but continuing dialog with the scholars, texts, and customs of other traditions.

Islam remains an extremely powerful force in the world. The Islamic community today is made up of leading industrialized societies as well as nations just emerging from colonialism. Present-day Muslims still derive great meaning from the teachings of Muhammad and the community he and his disciples constructed. They face the challenge of melding the world-view embedded in Islam's sacred text with the evolving conditions of the modern era, where the power of the ancient message still plays a dominant role.

Suggestions for Web Browsing

You can obtain more information about topics included in this chapter at the websites listed below. See also the companion website that accompanies this text, http://www.ablongman.com/brummett, which contains an online study guide and additional resources.

Internet Islamic History Sourcebook: Muhammad and Foundations—to 632 C.E.
http://www.fordham.edu/halsall/islam/islamsbook.html

Extensive online source for links about the early history of Islam, including a biography of Muhammad and the many aspects of Islam, including the role of women.

Islam and Islamic History in Arabia and the Middle East: The Message
http://www.islamic.org/Mosque/ihame/Sec1.htm

Islam and Islamic History in Arabia and the Middle East: The Golden Age.

http://www.islamic.org/Mosque/ihame/Sec7.htm

Extensive site details the origins of Islam and provides information and images about Muhammad, the Hijra, the Qur'an, Arabic writing, science and scholarship, Arabic literature, and Arabic numerals.

The Qur'an
http://islam.org/mosque/arabicscript/1/1.htm

The entire text of the Qur'an, with audio.

Islamic and Arabic Arts and Architecture
http://www.islamicart.com/

A rich and attractively designed general site, with information and images regarding architecture, calligraphy, and textiles. Includes a glossary of terms and names of important artists and architects. A subsite offers a portfolio of shrines and palaces including the Ka'ba, the Mosque of the Prophet Muhammad, the Dome of the Rock, and the Alhambra.

http://www.georgetown.edu/labyrinth

A wonderful site on medieval history which includes sections on texts and cartography.

Literature and Film

For literary sources suitable for class reading assignments and available in paperback, see the following: Robert L. Mack, ed., *Arabian Nights' Entertainments* (Oxford University Press, 1995), an annotated and historigraphically grounded edition of the Arabian Nights. Nizami, *The Story of Layla and Majnun*, trans. Rudolph Gelpke (Omega Publications, 1997), a twelfth-century classic Persian version of an Arabian folk epic of poetry, renunciation, and forbidden love. *The Legend of Seyavash* (Penguin, 1992)—one episode of the famous Persian Epic of Kings, penned in the eleventh century by Ferdowsi—is a wonderful study in notions of kingship, virtue, womanly wiles, and the mingling of Islam and animism. Usamah Ibn Munqidh, *An Arab-Syrian Gentleman and Warrior in the Period of the Crusades*, trans. P. K. Hitti (Princeton University Press, 1987), is an engaging memoir that reveals the mechanisms of cross-cultural exchange in twelfth-century Syria. Ruzbihan Baqli, *The Unveiling of Secrets: Diary of a Sufi Master*, trans. Carl Ernst (Parvardigar Press, 1997), records the personal reflections of a twelfth-century Persian Sufi. *The Adventures of Sayf Ben Dhi Yazan*, trans. Lena Jayyusi (Indiana University Press, 1999), is a folk romance composed during the medieval period of Mamluk rule in Egypt (magic, weddings, heroic feats, and day-to-day life). Ross E. Dunn, *The Adventures of Ibn Battuta: A Muslim Traveler of the 14th Century* (University of California, 1989), and Amin Maalouf, *Leo Africanus* (Dee, Ivan R., 1992), are also good student reading selections.

Films suitable for classroom presentation include *Mohammed, Messenger of God*, by Moustafa Akkad (Anchor Bay, 1976; also known as *The Message*), a popular commercial film, but one that has been acceptable in general to the Muslim community in the United States; and *Islam: Empire of Faith* (PBS, 2001), a historical assessment with commentary by various scholars of Islam.

Suggestions for Reading

Major scholarly surveys are Marshall Hodgson, *The Venture of Islam: Conscience and History of a World Civilization*, 3 vols. (University of Chicago Press, 1974), Ira Lapidus, *A History of Islamic Societies* (Cambridge University Press, 1988), and Albert Hourani, *A History of the Arab Peoples* (Warner, 1992). See also Philip K. Hitti, *The Arabs: A Short History* (Regnery, 1996), an excellent abridgment of a scholarly general history; and H. A. R. Gibb, *Mohammedanism: A Historical Survey*, 2nd ed. (Oxford University Press, 1969). See also the clear introduction to Islam by John L. Esposito, *Islam: The Straight Path*, 3rd ed. (Oxford University Press, 1998); Nehemia Levtzion and Randall Pouwels, eds., *The History of Islam in Africa* (Ohio University Press, 2000); J. Spencer Trimmingham, *The Sufi Orders in Islam* (Oxford, 1998); and Richard Fletcher, *Moorish Spain* (University of California Press, 1991).

W. Montgomery Watt, *Muhammad: Prophet and Statesman* (Oxford University Press, 1974), is a brief account of the Prophet's life and teachings. See also Karen Armstrong, *Muhammad: A Biography of the Prophet* (Harper Collins, 1992); Frederick Denny, *An Introduction to Islam*, 2nd ed. (Macmillan, 1996); and Martin Lings, *Muhammad: His Life Based on the Earliest Sources* (Inner Traditions International, 1983). For an interpretation and translation of the Qur'an, see Marmaduke William Pickthall, ed., *The Meaning of the Glorious Koran: An Explanatory Translation* (Unwin Hyman/HarperCollins). For primary source selections in translation, see James Kritzeck, ed., *Anthology of Islamic Literature* (Meridian, 1975). John Renard, *Islam and the Heroic Image* (University of South Carolina Press, 1994), is an excellent introduction to heroic Muslim personalities.

RELIGION AND GOVERNMENT

How do societies manage the relationship between their spiritual concerns and their temporal concerns?

Byzantine wall mosaic,
*Christ Pantocrator
Between Emperor
Constantine IX
Monamachus and
Empress Zoe.*

Throughout history, religion and government have served as foundational institutions in the world's many societies. These two institutions (often referrred to as "church" and "state" in the West) may seem to deal with different areas of human experience, but in reality the goals of both institutions are similar. Each in its own way seeks to maintain social order, foster a sense of community, and provide hope for a more satisfying future. Nevertheless, the relationship between these two institutions has varied significantly. Some societies fused religion and government into one entity. Other societies chose to maintain mutually cooperative relationships between the two institutions. Yet in further instances, societies consciously strove to separate one institution from the other.

The origins of religion are found in humanity's spiritual concerns while the origins of government stem from humanity's temporal (worldly) concerns. Humans' spiritual concerns essentially attempt to resolve the questions of how and why the universe came into being, what humans' proper role is in the world, and what the significance is of suffering and death. Temporal concerns, on the other hand, focus at their most basic level on how best to address humans' needs for food, water, and shelter. The answers to this question involve the specialization of tasks and social organization, which inevitably form the foundation of government.

The earliest humans made little if any distinction between their spiritual concerns (religion) and their temporal concerns (government). Our earliest ancestors believed that everything in the world around them and the heavens above, both animate and inanimate, possessed a spiritual essence. Because human beings were an integral part of this holistic universe, everything they did, particularly the activity of food gathering and production, was steeped in spiritual significance.

The earliest forms of separation between religion and government probably came about as human societies grew larger, more complex, and required greater specialization from their members. Because of the increasing interdependence of individuals that naturally results from specialization, some groups or individuals within a given society showed greater ability to address the community's spiritual concerns and became their society's priests. Similarly, others showed greater ability in addressing people's temporal concerns and became their society's chiefs. These two new social groups stood at the top of their societies' social hierarchies because of the vital significance of each of their responsibilities. While the two may have often competed with one another for power, they also tended to support each other's authority. We know of only a small number of early human societies in which primary spiritual and temporal roles were likely exercised by one individual.

Many of the world's earliest civilizations, however, eventually combined religious and political authority in the person of one ruler—a priest-king. In Egypt, a truly theocratic state evolved, in which the pharaoh was seen to be a living god who governed the state. In Mesopotamia, it is likely that initially the *patesi* was both a temporal ruler and a religious authority, administering the city-state as its patron god's representative on earth. Throughout most of the history of ancient Mesopotamia, rulers were held to be mortals governing on behalf of the gods.

In ancient China, the emperor, as head of the imperial government, used a religious concept to justify his rule. "The mandate of heaven" held that the emperor ruled with the blessing of heaven, and that if the emperor ruled wisely heaven would reward the nation; if, however, he ruled unwisely, heaven would be displeased and the mandate would pass to another. In Japan, ancient tradition held that the emperor was a divine being, descended from the great sun goddess Amaterasu, the supreme deity of the Shintō religion and queen of all the *kami*, the forces inherent in nature. As civilization emerged in South Asia, the forces of religion and government became permanently intertwined in the development of the caste system, which formally enshrined priests (Brahmans) and rulers (Kshatriyas) at the top of the Hindu socioreligious hierarchy. The earliest pre-Columbian civilizations in the Americas all appear to have combined religious and governmental authority in the person of priest-kings or emperors who functioned as temporal rulers and intermediaries to the gods.

The three monotheistic religions of Judaism, Christianity, and Islam have each had different relationships with government over the course of their histories. Judaism, in its formative stages, combined many religious responsibilities of the community with the political leadership. Moses served as both a temporal leader and a prophet with religious obligations to lead his people according to God's commands. The later kings of Israel and Judah constantly sought to influence the actions of priests and prophets, who, in turn, never hesitated to involve themselves in the politics of the monarchy.

The first Christians were much more focused on spiritual matters than on temporal matters, yet they were not blind to political authority. A strong advocacy of separation of religion and government may be found in Christ's own admonition to "Leave unto Caesar that which is Caesar's, and to God the things that are God's." As Christianity became established and institutionalized in Europe, both Roman emperors and the church realized the mutual benefit of cooperation. At times that cooperation could be more accurately called dependence, especially as strong emperors such as Constantine effectively unified religious and governmental authority, giving rise to caesaropapism—the domination of the church by the emperor. As Rome fell from influence and various European monarchies were established, the church, under the direction of its popes, exerted what political influence it could. Later, as Christian Europe moved through the Renaissance, Reformation, and Enlightenment, religious influence over government weakened, ultimately giving rise to the call for separation of church and state.

Islam, from its origins, sought to unify the two institutions of religion and government. Muhammad served as both political and religious leader of the community of believers. The Prophet's successors, the caliphs, shared the same responsibility: to govern in accordance with the word of Allah as written in the Qur'an.

Religion and government, of course, continue to stand at the foundation of the world's societies today, and the appropriateness of each institution's proper or improper influence over the other is still a matter of debate. In some Islamic countries, the institutions of religion and government still overlap. The political course of Iran is currently determined by its ayatollahs (religious leaders). In Afghanistan, the mullahs, authorities on the Qur'an and Sharia (Islamic law), have strong political influence through their status as tribal spokesmen. In India, while the constitution formally separates religion and government, Hindu nationalism remains a strong force in politics. In 1998, the Hindu nationalist Bharatiya Janata party won the national elections, giving rise to new fears that non-Hindu minorities would suffer under Hindu majority rule.

In western Europe and the United States, tension continues between the two institutions on a number of levels. The French government recently banned religious dress and ostentatious display of religious symbols from its schools in an attempt to assimilate the children of Muslim immigrants into French secular culture. In the United States, religion and government run up against each other over issues such as abortion, stem cell research, public prayer, and religious symbolism in public places.

The tension between the two institutions of government and religion has been present in human society throughout history. Today, the manner in which these two institutions interact can shape a society in profound ways. In general, the separation of religion and government is thought to be more conducive to the democratic principles of equality and pluralism because such a relationship prevents religious majorities from imposing their faith on others through the power of the state. On the other hand, the unification of religion and government may promote political stability and cohesion in societies where members of one religion make up the vast majority of the population. Every society in the modern world continues to grapple with the problems related to one institution's influence over the other, with the appropriate influence of government on religion and religion on government. It is most likely that the disagreement over the proper impact each institution should have on the other will be debated into the foreseeable future.

Questions

1. Why are religion and government such powerful social institutions?
2. Should religion have some influence over government and vice versa, or should the two institutions be separated from one another?
3. What has history taught us regarding the separation of religion and government?

African Beginnings

African Civilizations to 1500 C.E.

"Unless you know the road you've come down, you cannot know where you are going." This proverb from the Temne people of West Africa reflects the importance that Africans place on understanding the past. And, in Africa's case, there is an extraordinarily vibrant history to consider, stretching from the emergence of our human ancestors to the development of major kingdoms and empires to the creation of modern states. Africa's geography and environment presented formidable challenges to human development, but African peoples have displayed a remarkable genius for adaptation, innovation, and ingenuity and have developed a rich tapestry of cultures, societies, and civilizations. Although there are certain cultural traits that most Africans share, Africans have created a diverse variety of social and political systems, ranging from small-scale communities in which extended families and lineages met most of their needs to large states such as Nubia, Mali, and Great Zimbabwe, with hereditary rulers, elaborate bureaucracies, and extensive trading networks.

An enduring image of Africa is that it is a collection of unchanging societies that were isolated and unaware of developments in other parts of the world. This depiction is erroneous. Africans have shared ideas and innovations with each other and been receptive to technological advances and influences from outside the continent. The trans-Saharan trade linked West African Sudanic states to the Mediterranean and Middle East; Indian Ocean trade tied the East African coastal city-states and southern Africa kingdoms to Arabia, Persia, and Asia; and the Red Sea served as a bridge connecting Aksum and Ethiopia to the Mediterranean and the Indian Ocean.

3000

c. 3000 B.C.E. Beginning of Bantu migrations

1000

700–400 B.C.E. Ironworking introduced in Nok culture, Nigeria

1 C.E.

c. 100 C.E. Establishment of kingdom of Aksum

First century Camel introduced from Asia into trans-Saharan trade

300s Rise of kingdom of Ghana, West Africa

320–350 Reign of Ezana, king of Aksum

1000

1000–1500 Peak of Swahili civilization along East African coast

1076 Almoravid attack on Ghana

1100 Building of rock churches in Ethiopia

c. 1234–1260 Reign of Malinke ruler, Sundiata Keita, founder of Mali Empire

1270 Beginning of Solomonid dynasty, Ethiopia

1290–1450 Peak of kingdom of Zimbabwe

1300s Founding of kingdom of Kongo

1307–1337 Reign of Mansa Musa in Mali

1400–1600 Rise of Edo kingdom of Benin

1434–1468 Reign of Zar'a Ya'kob, emperor of Ethiopia

THE AFRICAN ENVIRONMENT

■ *How did African farmers adapt to different environmental zones?*

Many Americans have thought of the African continent as a place of two extremes: oceans of sand dunes in the north and, to the south, an immense "jungle" teeming with wild animals. In reality, more than half of the area south of the Sahara consists of grassy plains, known as **savanna,** whereas "jungle" or tropical rain forests make up only 7 percent of the continent's land surface.

The most habitable areas have traditionally been the savannas, as their grasslands and trees favor both human settlement and long-distance trade and agriculture. The northern savanna, a region sometimes called the Sahel or Sudan (not to be confused with the modern state by the same name), stretches across the continent just south of the Sahara. Other patches of savanna are interspersed among the mountains and lakes of East Africa and another belt of grassland that runs east and west across southern Africa, north and east of the Kalahari Desert.

Between the northern and southern savannas, in the region of the equator, is dense rain forest. Although the rain forest is lush, its soils are poor because torrential rains cause soil erosion and intense heat leaches the soil of nutrients and burns off humus or organic matter that are essential for soil fertility. The rain forests also harbor insects that carry deadly diseases. Mosquitoes transmit malaria and yellow fever, and the tsetse fly is a carrier of sleeping sickness to which both humans and animals such as horses and cattle are susceptible.

Whether they sustained a living through hunting, gathering, fishing, **pastoralism,** or farming, Africans had to contend with the continent's harsh and fragile environments. Thus, African cultivators accumulated sophisticated knowledge of what food crops to grow in particular areas and how to manage their environments and sustain a living from marginal or poor soils. Permanent cultivation was a luxury that few Africans farmers were able to practice. A more prevalent approach in sparsely populated areas was "slash and burn," or **shifting cultivation.** Farmers knew that they could stay on a piece of land for a few growing seasons before soils were exhausted. Thus, every growing season, they would clear land with iron hoes and machetes and fertilize it by burning natural vegetation such as brush and tree leaves for ash. Usually after two to three years, the land lost its fertility and a family had to move on and start the cycle in another area. Shifting agriculture was especially necessary in the rain forests, where, as noted, heavy rainfall and high temperatures produced poor soils.

Cultivators learned what crops were best suited for the soils and rainfall in certain climatic zones. In rain forest areas where vegetation was dense, they favored root crops such as yams and cassava, while in the grasslands of the savanna, they grew cereal crops such as sorghum and millet.

AFRICAN CULTURAL PATTERNS

■ *What is the connection between kinship relations and African political systems?*

Although African societies are remarkably diverse, they often share common values, belief systems, and aesthetic styles that are reflected in their family and kinship relations and political, economic, religious, and cultural institutions.

Africans place great importance on family and kinship ties. The primary unit of social organization is the extended family, which includes not only parents and children but also a network of wives and relatives—grandparents, aunts, uncles, and cousins. Relations within families are based on descent patterns. Most African societies are patrilineal, with descent traced through the father to his sons and daughters who belong to their father's kin group. When a woman marries, she becomes part of her husband's kin group and usually no longer shares in the economic resources of her father's group. About 15 percent of African societies are matrilineal, in which descent is passed through the mother's side of the family to a mother's brother. In matrilineal societies, when a man marries, he usually goes to live at his wife's family homestead and has to work for her family for a number of years. In these societies, women live with their own kin and have at least some independent access to economic resources such as land. Many of the matrilineal societies are found in forest areas with poor soils. Because farming required large numbers of laborers, an advantage of matrilineal relationships is that they can bring together a wide network of families from both the mother's and father's side who contribute laborers to agricultural production.

Historically, families also played an important role in decisions about marriages. Marriage was not solely a private issue between a bride and a groom but was a uniting of two larger groups, such as families or clans. Strict rules stipulated whether a person could marry outside a clan or lineage. Marriage was typi-

---

savanna—A flat grassland dotted with trees.

pastoralism—The raising of grazing animals such as sheep and cattle.

shifting cultivation—An agricultural system in which cultivators farm land for a few growing seasons; as the soil loses its fertility, they move to another area.

cally accompanied by an exchange of **bridewealth,** the husband's payment of money, goods, services, or cattle to his new wife's family. Bridewealth gave a husband certain domestic rights—to establish a homestead with his wife, to use his bride's labor in his household and fields, and to attach their offspring to his kinship group. Bridewealth also cemented a social relationship between a husband and his wife's family. If a wife could not bear children or deserted her husband, her parents had to return the bridewealth. This gave the wife's family a vested interest in preserving the marriage.

Another characteristic of both matrilineal and patrilineal African societies is that they accepted **polygyny,** a man's marrying more than one wife. Although a minority of men actually took a second wife, polygyny was seen as a necessity because of high infant mortality, the need for more manpower in farming, and the desire to express status and wealth.

The family household was the foundation for building larger identities and communities—one's *lineage* contained people who could trace their descent to a common ancestor, and one's *clan* contained many lineages or people who shared kinship. Within a society, lineages and clans could be used to mobilize people for self-defense and work parties, to allocate rights to land, to raise bridewealth, and to perform religious rituals. African societies also contained groups of people who were not bound by kinship and who created larger social identities. These were secret societies that often guarded medicines, performed ritual activities, and organized defense and were cohorts of people of roughly the same age who had gone through rites-of-passage ceremonies such as circumcision.

The lineage and clan also provided the basis for political units, ranging from the most basic to the largest kingdoms. Many African societies were formed without chiefs, rulers, or centralized political institutions and operated at the village level. These are known as "stateless" societies. Authority was usually vested in a group of elders or senior members of families and lineages who conferred to work out approaches to common concerns such as deciding when to plant and to harvest, whether to move or migrate, and how to resolve disputes within a community or handle conflicts with other communities. In these egalitarian societies, reaching a consensus was an essential part of the decision-making process.

Other African societies developed slowly into chiefdoms and kingdoms that incorporated larger populations, featured elaborate hierarchies and extensive bureaucracies, and engaged in long-distance trade with other states. Even though kingdoms could be made up of many lineages or clans, they were usually dominated by one. These kingdoms were governed by hereditary rulers who wielded religious as well as political power. However, their tendencies to abuse power were often held in check by councils and courts.

There were many ways in which women shared or influenced decision-making with men. On occasion women served as officials and advisers, religious leaders, and even soldiers, and some states had women rulers. The king's wife (the queen), his sisters, and the queen mother were often powers behind the throne. In the kingdom of Abomey in West Africa, each wife of a king represented one of the kingdom's lineages and advocated its interests to the king.

The queen mother could be the actual mother of a king, or she could be an in-law, an appointee, an influential person in a society, or the wife or sister of a former ruler. She was responsible not only for looking after the king's interests, but also for serving as a unifying presence. She mediated rivalries between court factions, maintained alliances, and represented groups who were excluded in succession disputes.

Work within communities was carried out by families and kinship groups. However, specific tasks were usually determined by sex and age. Women were primarily responsible for maintaining the homestead, cultivating the fields, preparing the food, and running local markets, while men took the lead in building houses, constructing paths and roads, clearing fields, raising livestock, hunting, and conducting long-distance trade. Work parties consisting of age-mates of one or both sexes could be mobilized for communal tasks such as harvesting and planting, clearing fields, weeding, threshing, and house building. Although men usually controlled technological advances such as ironworking and blacksmithing, there were exceptions to this practice. Among the Pare of eastern Africa, women were given the responsibility for gathering and smelting iron.

An important aspect of the African heritage was its value system, which shaped all aspects of life. Paramount were a profound awareness of human interdependence and an appreciation for communal harmony and unity within the family and the larger society. The African conception of land ownership, for instance, stressed that individuals had the right to cultivate untilled land but that they could not sell or rent the land to others or pass it on to their children. Land was held in trust by the larger community.

Religion permeated the everyday experiences of Africans and was an integral part of their social and political life. Specific religious beliefs and institutions varied from society to society, but several tenets were

---

bridewealth—A payment a groom and his family make to the bride's family to arrange for a marriage.

polygyny—A system of marriage that allows a man to have more than one wife.

shared. African societies were polytheistic. Most had a belief in a high god or creator who was usually remote and rarely concerned with the everyday affairs of humans. Therefore, Africans were more directly engaged with other divinities, such as nature and ancestral spirits that maintained an active interest in the affairs of the living and could intercede for humans with the high god. Political leaders were often imbued with ritual authority to approach the ancestors, who provided legitimacy to the moral order and reinforced political authority.

As individuals and as communities, Africans were concerned with identifying the causes of illness and disasters such as drought, crop failures, and plagues. One way of explaining misfortune was that the high god or the ancestors were unhappy with the actions of humans. Thus, people sought the goodwill of the ancestors with prayers and ritual offerings and sacrifices at shrines. Africans also attributed misfortune to witches, who wielded evil powers and inflicted suffering on people. Those afflicted by witchcraft appealed to specialists such as diviners to diagnose the sources of evil and provide remedies for them. Women enhanced their status and prestige by serving in religious rituals as priestesses, healers, rainmakers, diviners, and spirit mediums.

Some African religious systems were extremely complex, with elaborate priesthoods and cults. The Yoruba traditionally had four levels of spiritual beings. At the top was the supreme being, Oludumare, who was served by his subordinate gods on the second level. The secondary gods had their own priests, who presided over temples and shrines. Then came the ancestors, known as *Shango*. Finally, there were the nature spirits found in the earth, mountains, rivers, and trees.

Africans were traditionally skilled and sensitive artists, particularly in sculpture, which they used to record historical events. They carved expertly in wood, ivory, and soapstone. They also fashioned statues from baked clay and cast them in bronze. An innovative technique was the *cire perdue* (SIR purdee; "lost wax") technique, which involved making a cast of the object in wax, covering it with clay, and then melting the wax and replacing it with molten bronze. The famous bronze statuary of Benin, which drew on a long tradition of metalworking in the region of present-day Nigeria, has gained international recognition for its craftsmanship and beauty. Other specific artistic traditions, producing naturalism and symbolism in a rich tapestry of styles, flourished in many early African cultures.

Many African religious ceremonies featured masked male dancers. In this photo of the Dogon people of West Africa, the masked dancers performing at a funeral ceremony are driving the spirit of the dead person from its home. The dancers also act out the Dogon myth explaining how death entered the world through the disobedience of young men.

THE PEOPLING OF AFRICA

■ *How did the knowledge of pastoralism and agriculture spread throughout Africa?*

During the late Stone Age, human communities in Africa were small bands of foragers who based their existence on hunting wild animals and gathering wild plants. Their technology was relatively simple but effective. Small bands of hunters, armed with bows and arrows with stone barbs treated with poisons, tracked down and killed the small and large game that roamed the plains of Africa. While men conducted hunts, women were primarily responsible for gathering. With a tool kit of digging sticks, gourds, and carrying bags, they "collected a variety of wild fruits, nuts, and melons, and dug up edible roots and tubers from the ground."[1] For many foraging groups all over the world, hunting and gathering satisfied all their dietary requirements and remained a preferred way of life long after the invention of agriculture.

About 15,000 to 20,000 years ago foraging groups along the Nile River added more protein to their diets by fishing in rivers and lakes and gathering shellfish. From 10,000 B.C.E. to 6000 B.C.E., the northern half of Africa went through a wet phase known as the Aquatic Age. The region that is now the Sahara became a savanna of grassland and woodland, with an abundance of rivers and lakes. Lake Chad, for instance, formed part of a large inland sea. By fashioning bone harpoons and fishnets, people lived off the rich aquatic life. Around 3000 B.C.E. an extended dry phase set in and the vast barren area that we know now as the Sahara began to form.

Agriculture

The dry period largely cut off sub-Saharan Africa from developments in the Mediterranean, but it was also likely a major stimulus for the development of agriculture in West Africa as communities experimented with new crops to supplement their diets. They began growing barley, wheat, and flax with simple tools such as digging sticks and wooden hoes.

In the past it was widely assumed that sub-Saharan African communities acquired agriculture by diffusion from Nile civilizations, but more recent scientific investigations have shown that plant domestication began independently in four regions: the Ethiopian highlands, the central Sudan, the West African savanna, and the West African forests. In all cases African farmers adapted crops suited to particular environments that were tested over long periods of time. For instance, around 5000 B.C.E. in the dry West African savanna, farmers developed sorghum and pearl millet, both crops requiring short growing sea-

Before the Sahara became a desert, the region was home to pastoralists who herded cattle, sheep, and goats. On a plateau at Tassili n-Ajjer in the central Sahara, these pastoralists left an impressive array of wall paintings depicting their lifestyles and the wild animals that roamed the region. In this painting from the Tassili frescoes, women ride oxen as their community migrates to a new settlement.

sons and minimal rainfall. Around 3000 B.C.E. in the grasslands of the Ethiopian highlands, farmers began cultivating *teff* (a tiny grain), finger millet, *noog* (an oil plant), sesame, and mustard. In the forests they planted *ensete* (a source of starch that looks like a banana), coffee, and qat. People chewed coffee and qat leaves as a stimulant. Around 1000 B.C.E. wheat and barley were imported from across the Red Sea. In the central Sudan agricultural communities began producing sorghum, millet, rice, cowpeas, and groundnuts as far back as 4000 B.C.E. In the West African forests, oil palms, cowpeas, and root crops such as yams were produced.

Africans also began to use domesticated animals about the same time as they adopted agriculture. The

Early African Civilizations

10,000–6000 B.C.E.	Aquatic Age
c. 4000 B.C.E.	Domestication of food crops in central Sudan
c. 3100 B.C.E.	Beginning of unification of Upper and Lower Egypt
c. 3000 B.C.E.	Sahara region begins changing into desert
c. 730 B.C.E.	Kushite conquest of Egypt
c. 700 B.C.E.	Spread of knowledge of ironworking from Egypt to Kush

earliest evidence of livestock is found in the western Egyptian desert about 8000 B.C.E. Cattle, sheep, goats, and pigs were introduced from western Asia to Egypt and North Africa and then spread much later to western, eastern, and southern Africa.

Iron Technology

Another major breakthrough for sub-Saharan African cultures was the introduction of ironworking. Although bronze and copper toolmaking had developed in western Asia, the technology had not spread to sub-Saharan Africa. This was not the case with iron technology, which reached sub-Saharan Africa by two routes. It moved first from Assyria to Egypt around 700 B.C.E. and from Egypt to Nubia in the seventh century B.C.E. Ironworking then spread southward to the Lake Victoria area around 250 B.C.E. It also appeared in West Africa around 1000 B.C.E., apparently brought south across the Sahara by Berbers, in contact with Phoenician or Carthaginian traders.

The production of several pounds of iron requires ten to 15 trees to fuel smelters. Hence, two of the earliest centers of iron smelting were in forested areas at Meroe (MEHR-oh-wee), in the Nubian kingdom of Kush, and Nok, situated on the Jos plateau in central Nigeria. Located on the Nile River in a region rich in iron ore deposits, Meroe became well-known in the fourth century B.C.E. for iron smelting and making iron tools and weapons that were key to the kingdom's success. Huge iron slag heaps still exist around the ruins of Meroe.

Archaeologists have dated ironworking sites at Nok from 1000 to 500 B.C.E. Although some contend that ironworking was an independent invention at Nok, other ironworking sites of about the same time period

have recently been identified in Mauritania, southern Mali, and central Nigeria. Nevertheless, it is clear that Nok had one of the earliest ironworking sites. The Nok workers' preheating techniques and their ability to produce steel with a high carbon content were equal to those of Egypt and Rome. The Nok population included ironsmiths, craftspeople, and artists, who produced terra-cotta sculptures of remarkable realism that were strikingly similar to later art forms among the Yoruba kingdoms of Ife and Benin.

Iron production in most African societies usually took place in the dry months when rain and floods were not disruptive and agriculture was less intensive. Because their products were highly valued and could be exchanged for animals and food, ironworking specialists were persons of wealth and status who usually passed on their knowledge to close kin. Magical, ritual, and spiritual powers were often attributed to them. In some societies the ironworking craft assumed such ritualistic significance that the furnaces were hidden in secluded places.

Some scholars see the ironworking process as a metaphor that reinforced age and gender relationships. Ironworking was a preserve of the elders who

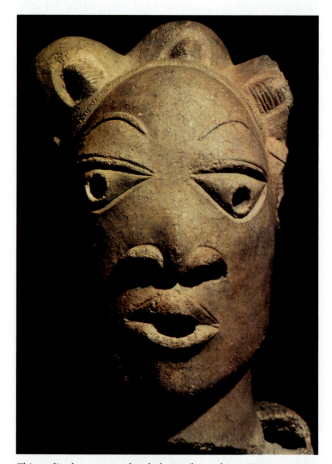

This stylized terra-cotta head, dating from about 500 B.C.E., is an outstanding example of a sculpture from the Nok culture of central Nigeria. The head, which has a human face, was probably used for religious purposes.

passed on their knowledge to young apprentices, while the smelting process was likened to a woman conceiving and giving birth. The Phoka, an ethnic group in Malawi, "described their smelting furnace as a fertile young woman while under construction, and as their 'wife' once smelting began."[2] To ensure success, male ironworkers had to observe strict abstinence while smelting, and menstruating and pregnant women were not allowed near the furnaces.

Ironworking allowed African societies to make the transition from stone to metal tools. Iron tools such as hoes, knives, sickles, spearheads, and axes made a significant difference in clearing forests and thick vegetation for agriculture, in hunting, and in waging war. When combined with the introduction of agriculture and pastoralism, the knowledge of ironworking contributed to population growth, craft specializations, trade between communities, and more complex political and economic systems. Ironworking was also a factor in the spread of Bantu groups to central, eastern, and southern Africa.

search of new areas to farm and fish. Another explanation is that the acquisition of ironworking gave Bantu groups access to iron tools that they could use in clearing the thicker vegetation of the forest regions. However, archaeological evidence now suggests that Bantu groups did not use iron tools until after their migrations began.

Using archaeological and linguistic data, historians have had some success in reconstructing the complex movements of Bantu groups. Around 3000 B.C.E., bands of Bantu began slowly moving out of their original homeland. These Bantu groups had common lifestyles—they lived in scattered homesteads and villages and farmed root crops, foraged for food, and fished. One stream of peoples moved south into the equatorial rain forests of west Central Africa and settled in present-day Angola and Namibia. Their agriculture relied heavily on root crops and palm trees. The other stream moved east through the Congo basin and eventually settled in the area east of Lake Victoria

Around 3000 B.C.E. groups of Bantu speakers began migrating from west Central Africa and establishing farming and pastoral communities in eastern, central, and southern Africa.

THE BANTU DISPERSION

■ *Why did Bantu-speaking groups migrate from their original home area?*

One of the striking features of many African societies from central to eastern to southern Africa is that their languages (called Niger-Congo) and cultures have many similarities. How these societies—known as **Bantu** ("people")—came to spread over this vast area is a question that has long vexed scholars.[3]

Authorities generally agree that the original homeland for Bantu speakers was an area in present-day Cameroon near the Nigerian border. They are still not sure, however, what prompted Bantu groups to start migrating from their homeland. One explanation relates to environmental changes—as the Sahara region dried up, small groups were forced to move southward in

AFRICAN CLIMATE ZONES AND BANTU MIGRATION ROUTES

→ East Bantu migrations
→ West Bantu migrations
☐ Desert
▨ Dry woodland & bushland
▨ Moist woodland
▨ Montane forest
▨ Macchia
▨ Lowland forest

0   500   1000
MILES

Bantu—A word meaning "people," it refers to a family of related languages spoken in central, eastern, and southern Africa.

in East Africa. There they came into contact with Cushitic-speaking peoples that had migrated from the Ethiopian highlands. The Bantu adopted their mixed farming practices—growing cereal crops such as millet and sorghum and herding cattle, sheep, and goats.

From that point, wherever Bantu groups migrated, they searched for areas that had enough summer rainfall to support cereal cultivation and their animal herds. As soils were not rich and could not support farmers for long periods, groups of people practiced shifting cultivation. The need to move on after two or three years in an area may explain why some Bantu groups, after spreading throughout East Africa, migrated southward, along tributaries of the Congo River, through the equatorial rain forest to present-day southern Congo and Zambia, where they settled in the savannas and woodland areas. Others migrated south, crossing the Zambezi and Limpopo Rivers by the fourth century of the Common Era.

As Bantu communities moved into eastern and southern Africa, they also acquired knowledge of ironworking and adopted new food crops such as the banana and the Asian yam, brought to Africa by sailors from Malaysia and Polynesia who settled on the island of Madagascar several thousand years ago. The banana had many attractive qualities. It could be grown more abundantly than root crops such as yams and without as much labor. Farmers did not have to clear out all the trees in an area for the banana to thrive. Moreover, bananas did not collect standing water and thus attracted fewer mosquitoes. In moist regions, it became a staple food and a source of mash for beer.

Throughout their migrations, Bantu societies came into contact with hunting and gathering groups. Although some scholars have portrayed the Bantu as a superior culture that overwhelmed hunting and gathering groups, recent scholarship has shown that the relationship was complex rather than one-sided. At the same time that Bantu were practicing agriculture and pastoralism, they relied on foraging for subsistence and turned to hunting and gathering bands for assistance and knowledge of local conditions. In addition, hunters and gatherers married into Bantu groups or attached themselves to Bantu groups for periods of time.

ETHIOPIA AND NORTHEASTERN AFRICA

■ *What role did the church play in strengthening the rule of Ethiopia's Solomonid dynasty?*

Situated along and inland from Africa's Red Sea coast, Ethiopia has been one of Africa's most enduring and richest civilizations. Indeed, the region between the Nile River and the Red Sea had been recognized as a major source of trade goods several thousand years before the kingdom of Ethiopia came into existence. To the Egyptians the area on the southern Red Sea coast was known as the Land of Punt, and from the Fifth Dynasty (c. 2494–2345 B.C.E.) on, Egypt's rulers regularly sent expeditions to trade for frankincense, myrrh, aromatic herbs, ebony, ivory, gold, and wild animals. The Egyptian queen Hatshepsut's funerary temple recorded a major expedition that she sent to Punt around 1470 B.C.E.

Around 800 B.C.E. traders from Saba', a kingdom on the southwestern Arabian peninsula, crossed the Red Sea, first founding trading settlements on the Eritrean coast and later a kingdom, Da'amat. The Sabaeans tapped into the ivory trade in the interior highlands, but because they were also proficient at farming in arid environments, they interacted well with farming communities of the coastal interior. The Sabaean language was similar to the Semitic languages spoken in the area, and a language called Ge'ez evolved that became the basis for oral and written communication of the elites.

By the start of the Common Era, a new state, Aksum, emerged to dominate the Red Sea trade. Taking advantage of its location between the Mediterranean and the Indian Ocean, Aksum developed extensive trading ties with Ptolemaic Egypt and the Roman Empire as well as with Asia as far east as Sri Lanka and India. In the fourth century Aksum captured elephants for Ptolemaic rulers to use in warfare against Babylon, which was

DOCUMENT·

Strabo on Africa

Aksum and Ethiopia

c. 800 B.C.E.	Sabaean traders establish trading settlements on the Eritrean coast
320–350 C.E.	Reign of Ezana, king of Aksum
c. 350	Aksum conquers Kush
700–800	Aksum's control of Red Sea trade ended by Persian and Muslim forces
c. 1185–1225	Reign of Lalibela, emperor of the Ethiopian Zagwe dynasty; beginning of construction of rock churches
c. 1314–1344	Reign of Amde-Siyon, emperor of Ethiopia
1434–1468	Reign of Zar'a Ya'kob, emperor of Ethiopia

brothers, Frumentius and Aedisius, have been credited with winning over Ezana to the Christian faith. Shipwrecked on the Red Sea coast, the brothers were brought to Aksum's royal court as slaves when Ezana was a child. Frumentius became an influential figure in the royal court, serving as main adviser to Ezana's mother, the queen regent. Following Ezana's conversion, Frumentius was chosen Aksum's first bishop, and Christianity was made the official state religion. Subsequently, the head of the Ethiopian church (*abuna*) was traditionally chosen by leaders of the Coptic Church in Egypt, even after Muslims gained control over Egypt.

Although Aksum's court language remained Greek, Ge'ez assumed a new prominence as the language of the Ethiopian church. The Old and New Testaments were translated into Ge'ez, which, much like Latin in the Catholic Church, became the primary language of literature and the liturgy. Several centuries after Ezana's conversion, a group of Syrian monks called the Nine Saints played a major role in spreading Christianity among rural people. The Nine Saints were known for their belief in the **Monophysite** doctrine, which held that Christ's human and divine qualities were inseparable.

The key to Aksum's continued prosperity was maintaining control over Red Sea trade. However, the Aksumites' influence in the Arabian peninsula ended in the late seventh century when a Persian expeditionary force ousted them. In 615 C.E. the Aksumite king El-Asham gave refuge to followers and family of the prophet Muhammad, who were being persecuted in Arabia. Although Muhammad directed Muslims to "leave the Abyssinians in peace,"[4] Islamic expansion late in the eighth century totally removed Aksum as a trading force in the Red Sea.

Despite Aksum's decline, some Ethiopian products such as perfume and coffee were still highly sought after. A highly prized musk was made from the glandular secretions of the civet cat. Coffee originated in Ethiopia. The coffee bean was initially chewed as a stimulant but then was made into a drink by brewing the coffee plant's leaves and berries in boiled water. Another quick-energy snack was a blend of ground coffee beans and animal fat. Finally, after someone came up with the idea of grinding roasted coffee beans, the drink rapidly spread to Arab cultures. Muslim monks drank coffee to stay awake during long periods of meditation and prayer, while coffee houses became popular gathering places throughout the Muslim world. *Qahwa* is the Arabic word from which the name *coffee* is derived.

Aksum's decline as a Red Sea power forced its rulers to migrate to the central highlands of the interior,

The kingdom of Kush was northeastern Africa's preeminent power until the rise of Aksum in the third and fourth centuries C.E.

importing elephants from India. The elephants were transported on specially constructed vessels.

Aksum also controlled trade with its interior, exporting slaves, gold, ivory and exotic items such as tortoise shells and rhinoceros horns in exchange for cloth, glassware and ceramic items, spices, vegetable oils, sugarcane, and wine. Aksum's capital, also called Aksum, was a major entrepot for the trade with the interior, while its bustling seaport, Adulis, prospered as the middleman for trade between the Mediterranean and the Indian Ocean. Monsoon winds dictated the rhythm of Indian Ocean trade. After July, when the summer monsoon winds were favorable, Adulis's traders set forth on their journeys. They returned in October when the prevailing winds reversed direction.

By the third and fourth centuries C.E., Aksum was at its zenith as a trading power, conquering its rival, Meroe, on the Nile, and replacing Rome as the dominant trading power on the Red Sea. Aksum minted its own bronze, silver, and gold coins with Greek inscriptions, something that only a handful of other states, such as Persia and Rome, were doing.

Aksum's best-known ruler was Ezana (320–350), who converted to Christianity toward the end of his reign, about the same time as the Roman emperor Constantine the Great. Some historians contend that Ezana conveniently converted to strengthen trading relations with the Greek-speaking world. Two Syrian

Monophysite—The doctrine that held that Christ has only one nature and that Christ's human and divine natures are inseparable.

where their rule continued to be plagued by conflict and warfare. There they mixed with a Cushitic-speaking people, the Agaw, who were assimilated into Aksum's political elite and also converted to Christianity. Some historians contend that the loss of commerce and revenues from the Red Sea trade led Aksum's rulers to develop a form of feudalism based on tribute from peasants that subsequent dynasties based their rule on.

The highland nobility formed the core of the Zagwe dynasty that took over in the mid-twelfth century. The Zagwes stressed their continuity with the Aksumite political order by claiming that they were descendants of Moses and encouraging the faithful to make pilgrimages to Jerusalem and Palestine. In this regard, the most enduring cultural expressions of the Zagwe dynasty were its churches, the most famous of which are the 11 awe-inspiring rock-hewn cathedrals of Roha, commissioned by the legendary Emperor Lalibela (law-lee-BAY-lah; c. 1185–1225). These impressive architectural feats, with ornate decorations and intricate workmanship, drew on Byzantine, Greek, and Roman motifs. The rock churches became the sites of pilgrimages by Christians cut off from Jerusalem by Muslim forces.

Lalibela's reign was the high point of Zagwe rule. Rivalries between feudal nobles and Muslim merchants and kingdoms were fierce, and Lalibela's successors were unable to maintain the kingdom. Yikunno-Amlak, a southern noble once imprisoned by the Zagwes, led the rebellion that overthrew them in 1270 and founded a new dynasty, the Solomonids. Like the Zagwes, the Solomonid emperors (each known as *negus*, or "king of kings") legitimized their rule by claiming a direct tie to the Aksumite past. In their royal chronicle, the *Kebre Negast* ("Glory of the Kings"), they gave an epic account of their dynasty's direct descent from the Old Testament's King Solomon. The tale related how Makeda, the queen of Sheba (Saba'), had visited Solomon to learn his techniques of rule. Instead, Solomon seduced Makeda, who bore him a son, Menelik. When Menelik later visited his father's court, he tricked Solomon and spirited the Ark of the Covenant out of Israel to Ethiopia—which church officials claim is in the Church of St. Mary of

Ethiopia's Emperor Lalibela oversaw the construction of 11 churches carved out of red volcanic rock at Roha. Shaped in the form of a Greek cross, the Church of St. George was an impressive architectural feat. Workers chipped away at the stone until they reached 40 feet down and then molded the church and hollowed out its interior.

Seyon (Zion). This story was interpreted as a sign of the covenant God was establishing with Ethiopia. Thus to the kings of the Solomonid dynasty, it was an article of faith that they were directly descended from Solomon.

To avoid the same fate as the Zagwes, the Solomonid rulers set strict rules to ensure orderly successions. To insulate royal princes from palace infighting and forming alliances with nobles in the countryside, the first Solomonid emperor crowned in 1285, Yikunno-Amlak, took the bold step of placing the princes in a remote retreat, Mount Geshen (the "mountain of the kings"). The princes lived a comfortable but monastic existence, totally isolated from the outside world. Many of them followed an ascetic life, absorbed in religious issues and gaining reputations as accomplished writers of Ge'ez poetry and composers of sacred music. When an emperor died without a designated heir, the princes provided a pool of candidates for the throne.

The first Solomonid rulers concentrated on consolidating their rule over the central highlands of Ethiopia and refrained from carrying out aggressive wars of expansion. These goals changed dramatically during the reign of Emperor Amde-Siyon ("Pillar of Zion"; c. 1314–1344), who conquered territories to the west and toward the coast and carried out aggressive campaigns against Muslim principalities to the south and east. Amde-Siyon's army had to be in a constant state of readiness because of his repeated campaigns. His soldiers were recruited from two elements: fiercely loyal regiments attached to the royal court and militias from Christian provinces that were called out for specific campaigns. The latter were based on ethnic identities and were commanded by local chiefs. Many women also followed armies, providing food for their husbands.

Amde-Siyon's campaigns against the Muslims were aimed not only at securing control over the lucrative trade in slaves and ivory but also at putting pressure on the Muslim rulers of Egypt to allow the Coptic church to send a new bishop to Ethiopia. Amde-Siyon was so successful in vanquishing his opponents that an Arab historian reported, "It is said that he has ninety-nine kings under him, and that he makes up the hundred."[5]

The Ethiopian emperor had to be constantly on guard against potential revolts against his authority by local hereditary rulers. Although he generally allowed local rulers to remain in place, he strategically placed his officials around the kingdom. Because all land within the kingdom belonged to the emperor, he maintained loyalty by granting **gults,** or fiefs, to nobles and to soldiers who distinguished themselves in his service, especially in newly conquered areas.

Gult-holders were bound to the emperor because he could revoke a *gult* at any time. Moreover, a *gult* owner did not own the land; he had to pay regular tribute to the emperor. In turn, the *gult* owner had the right during his lifetime to exact tribute and taxes in the form of grain, honey, cattle, and sheep from peasants who owned and worked the land. In Ethiopia tribute cattle were called "burning" because the cows were branded or "touched with fire" before they were handed over. Peasants were also expected to support any soldiers and clergy residing in their area. The major difference between the Ethiopian and European feudal systems was that the European nobility owned large estates and lived off the labor of tenants and serfs, while Ethiopian peasants kept their lands and gave up a portion of their production to the nobility.

Until Gondar was designated as the capital in the seventeenth century, Ethiopian emperors did not have a centralized bureaucracy or a fixed capital for more than a few decades at a time. Rather, they created a mobile court of family members, high officials, soldiers, priests, and retainers that moved regularly around the kingdom. This mobile court allowed the emperor to show off his power as well as encourage trade with outlying regions and to collect tribute from all his subjects. Mobile courts encamped in areas for up to four months, but they put such a strain on local resources that they were encouraged not to return for many years.

The Ethiopian monarchy assumed even greater power during the reign of Zar'a Ya'kob ("Seed of Jacob"; r. 1434–1468). Kings were usually crowned in the area where they found themselves when they took power. But Zar'a Ya'kob resurrected the tradition of kings' being crowned at the ancient capital of Aksum and stayed there an additional three years.

Within his immediate environs Zar'a Ya'kob ruled as an absolute monarch, surrounded by hundreds of courtiers and servants. To consolidate his rule, he dismissed provincial governors and replaced them with his own daughters and other female members of his family. When he held audiences at his court, he was positioned behind a curtain and communicated through a royal spokesman. When he traveled about his kingdom, his subjects had to avert their eyes on the penalty of death.

When Zar'a Ya'kob launched new campaigns of conquest to expand Ethiopia's boundaries, he was faced with the challenge of governing a diverse kingdom of many ethnic, linguistic, and religious backgrounds. He achieved his goal by exploiting the traditional feudal relationships his predecessors established with their nobles and also by reorganizing and aggressively promoting the Ethiopian church.

---

gult—The right to collect tribute granted to nobility and clergy by a king.

A characteristic art form of Ethiopia is wall murals. In this painting the bishop of Aksum confers a blessing on the emperor of Ethiopia at the Cathedral of St. Mary of Zion. When Zar'a Ya'kob became emperor in 1434, he chose to be crowned in Aksum because he wanted to link the monarchy with the historical prestige of that kingdom.

Under previous emperors, the state had perceived churches and monasteries as centers of Zagwe influence and struggled to win them over with gifts and land grants. Monks were especially difficult to influence because they led unpretentious lives and took their commitment to the poor seriously. Turning down a generous gift of gold and fine cloth from the Emperor Dawit, the abbot of the Dabra Halle Luya monastery in central Ethiopia provided an explanation for his decision: "We have no need for this. We have food which God ordered for us, the green of the earth and the roots of the trees. As for grain [it has] to be from the labour of our own hand." The emperor replied. "You say, 'We consume the fruit of our own labour,' but a church does not stand without land. Would it not be like a woman who has no husband?"[6] Dawit's persistence and more gifts eventually wore down the abbot's resistance.

Under Zar'a Ya'kob the Ethiopian church became a royal church, an extension of the crown that actively promoted its expansion throughout the kingdom. He granted the church extensive estates in newly conquered provinces. He appointed several bishops in these provinces. Clerics, who had previously led ascetic lives more concerned with their personal salvation, were now expected to play active roles in spreading the Christian faith. Monks recruited from monasteries were commissioned to establish churches and wage evangelical crusades to convert "pagans" and Muslims. At the same time, Zar'a Ya'kob declared war on traditional religious cults and imposed death sentences on those who practiced divination and sacrifices to gods.

The monarchy also sponsored monastic schools. The schools, mostly for boys, primarily accepted children from clerical families and the royal elite. Education typically consisted of reading and reciting religious tracts.

This was a period of the blossoming of the arts in which priests—and even Zar'a Ya'kob—played a leading role. They produced innumerable biblical translations, theological treatises, biographies of saints, historical chronicles, illuminated manuscripts, and mural paintings.

Although Zar'a Ya'kob's policies may have revived the church, they came at a cost. The church became intimately identified with imperial power and less able to develop deep roots among the common people.

Zar'a Ya'kob's reign was a high point in the Solomonid dynasty. His successors did not have the skills to hold the kingdom together, and Ethiopia went into a decline. Provincial officials and nobles seized on the weakness of the emperor to refrain from paying taxes and build up their own power. The Oromo, a pastoral people, began challenging Ethiopian control of the highland areas, and Muslims stopped sending tribute. Muslim states also grew restive. Under the military leadership of Ahmad al-Ghazi Ahmad Gran, the state of Adal launched a holy war against the Christian kingdom in 1527 that continued until 1543, when Ahmad was killed in battle.

EMPIRES OF THE WESTERN SUDAN

■ *How did trans-Saharan trade influence West African Sudanic states?*

Muslim writers called the savannas of West Africa *Bilad al-Sudan* ("Land of the Blacks"), and this region has been characterized by the long-standing trans-Saharan trade between the western savanna and the Mediterranean coast. Large camel caravans made regular trips across the dangerous desert carrying North African salt in exchange for West African gold. To the Berbers who organized these caravans,

African Empires in the Western Sudan

Document   **Emperor Zar'a Ya'kob's Coronation and His Concern for the Church**

Beginning with the Solomonid dynasty in the twelfth century, Ethiopian monarchs commissioned courts scribes to record their accomplishments in royal chronicles. Although the chronicles were produced to glorify and lionize the ruler, they do provide valuable insights into Ethiopian political and economic life. The following passages come from the chronicles of Zar'a Ya'kob, who centralized royal administration and reshaped the church as an institution of imperial rule. They describe his coronation at Aksum and his involvement in church affairs.

When our King Zar'a [Ya'kob] went into the district of Aksum to fulfill the law and to effect the coronation ceremony according to the rites followed by his ancestors, all the inhabitants, including the priests, came to meet him and welcomed him with great rejoicing; the chiefs and all the soldiers of Tigre were on horseback carrying shield and lance, and the women, in great numbers, gave themselves up, according to the ancient custom, to endless dancing. When he entered the gates of the town the King had on his right and left the governors of Tigre and Aksum who, according to custom, both waved olive branches. . . . After arriving within the walls of Aksum the King had gold brought to him which he scattered as far as the city gate on the carpets spread along his route. This amount of gold was more than a hundred ounces. . . .

On the twenty-first of the month of Ter [January 16] the day of the death of our Holy Virgin Mary, the coronation rite was carried out, the King being seated on a stone throne. This stone, together with its supports, is only used for the coronation. There is another stone on which the King is seated when he receives the blessing, and several others to the right and left on which are seated the twelve chief judges. There is also the throne of the metropolitan bishop.

While at Aksum the Emperor made a number of regulations for the church.

During his stay at Aksum our King regulated all the institutions of the church and ordered that prayers which had up to that time been neglected should be recited each day at canonical hours. For this purpose he convened a large number of monks and founded a convent, the headship of which he entrusted to an abbot with the title of Pontiff of Aksum, who received an extensive grant of land called Nader. The King accomplished this work through devotion to the Virgin Mary and to perpetuate his own memory and that of his children and his children's children. He summoned some catechists and presented to the church a great number of ornaments and a golden ewer, revived all the old traditions, spread joy in these places, and returned thence satisfied.

Zar'a Ya'kob also founded churches and regulated religious affairs in other provinces.

Arriving in the land of Tsahay in Amhara, he went up a high and beautiful mountain, the site of which he found pleasing; at the top of this mountain and facing east he found a wall which had been raised by his father, King Dawit, with the intention of erecting a shrine. His father, however, had not had the time to complete the work, in the same way that the ancient King David, who planned to build a temple to the Lord, could not accomplish his task which was completed by his son Solomon. Our king Zar'a Ya'kob fulfilled his father's intention by building a shrine to God on the west of the mountain. Everyone, rich and poor alike and even the chiefs, were ordered to carry the stones with the result that this edifice was speedily erected. They embellished this locality, which underwent a great transformation; two churches were built there, one called Makana Gol and the other Dabra Negwadgwad. The King attached to them a certain number of priests and canons to whom he gave grants of land. He also founded a convent and placed in it monks from Dabra Libanos, whom he endowed in a similar manner.

Questions to Consider

1. Why do you think Zar'a Ya'kob selected Aksum as the site for his coronation?
2. What do these passages tell us about the relations between the Ethiopian monarchy and the church?
3. What comparisons can be made between church-state relations in Ethiopia and in European kingdoms during the same time period?

From Richard K. Pankhurst, ed., *The Ethiopian Royal Chronicles* (Oxford: Oxford University Press, 1967), pp. 34–36.

West African Sudanic Kingdoms

c. 250 B.C.E.	Jenne-jeno on Niger River settled
c. 100–40 B.C.E.	Camel introduced to trans-Saharan trade
c. 900 C.E.	State of Kanem founded
1000–1200	Hausa city-states founded
1076	Almoravid attack on Ghana
c. 1200–1235	Reign of Sumaguru, Sosso king
1300–1400	Rise of kingdom of Oyo
1307–1337	Reign of Mansa Musa in Mali
1352	Visit of Berber geographer Ibn Battuta to Mali
1464–1492	Reign of Sunni Ali, Songhai emperor
1493–1528	Reign of Askia Muhammad, Songhai emperor
1591	Morocco invades Songhai

season and was much safer for trade than other settlements. Over time, Jenne-jeno became an interregional trade center for farmers, herders, and fishermen that long predated any involvement in the trans-Saharan trade. Jenne-jeno exported food via the Niger to points to the east.

Although the Sahara was not easy to traverse, it was not impenetrable. As early as 1000 B.C.E., Carthaginians, Romans, and perhaps Greeks began establishing several routes across the Sahara for their horse- and ox-drawn chariots. One route stretched from Libya and Tunisia through the Fezzan, while the other connected Morocco to Mauritania. Trade declined with the collapse of the Roman Empire in the fourth century C.E. but was revived several centuries later, first by the Byzantine Empire and then by Arabs.

The camel, introduced from the Middle East in the first century B.C.E., became the main conveyor of goods in the trans-Saharan trade. As pack animals, camels had several advantages over horses and oxen. Carrying loads of 250 to 300 pounds, camels could travel extended distances with little water. However, they were slow and inefficient. Averaging about 20 to 30 miles a day, they generally took over two months to cross the Sahara. Moreover, attendants had to load and unload their cargo once or twice each day, and much of the provisions were used to feed attendants. Whatever the camel's liabilities, its introduction boosted the vol-

the bend of the Niger River offered a secure watering and resting place. Here they found people who had conducted local trade for centuries before the caravans came, who knew the savanna well, and who could acquire gold from distant places. Their resulting control of the lucrative gold and salt trade brought great accumulations of wealth and was a key factor in the rise of major West African kingdoms.

Before the formation of these kingdoms, there was already a thriving interregional trade among the savanna communities. Archaeological evidence shows that in the ninth century B.C.E. some savanna communities began harnessing the floodwaters of the Niger River and started raising livestock and cultivating cereals. They formed settlements of 800 to 1000 people. The villages they lived in were unwalled and in open areas, an indication that relations between communities were mostly peaceful and cooperative. However, between 600 and 300 B.C.E., the pattern changed as villages erected walls and retreated to more remote and defensible sites—a sign that they were responding to external threats, possibly from nomadic Berbers who roamed the Sahara and occasionally raided savanna societies.

One of the earliest urban settlements, Jenne-jeno, was begun around 250 B.C.E. Situated on an inland delta of the Niger River, Jenne-jeno was ideally located because it was surrounded by water during the rainy

Introduced from the Middle East in the first century B.C.E., the camel was the main transporter of goods in the trans-Saharan trade between North Africa and the West African savanna.

Sudanic kingdoms such as Ghana, Mali, Songhai, and Kanem-Bornu owed their power and wealth to controlling the southern part of the trans-Saharan trade.

EMPIRES OF THE WESTERN SUDAN

- Ghana, 4th–11th centuries
- Mali, 13th–15th centuries
- Songhai, 15th–16th centuries
- Other major states

ume of trade. The camel remained an essential part of the trans-Saharan trade until the twentieth century, when it was replaced by the automobile.

Ghana

The earliest of the Sudanic kingdoms, first known as *Aoukar* or *Wagadu*, later took the name of its war chief, Ghana (not to be confused with the modern nation of the same name). It arose on the upper Niger during the fourth century C.E. as a loose federation of village-states, inhabited by Soninke farmers. This set a pattern for future kingdoms of the savanna as a lineage or a clan asserted its authority over other groups.

The introduction of ironworking allowed the Soninke farming communities to form larger political systems. In the face of drier conditions, they applied iron tools to improving agricultural production and devised iron swords and spears to conquer neighboring groups. They also used these weapons to fend off Saharan nomads who grazed their animals in the Sahel (the southern fringe of the Sahara) and occasionally raided Soninke communities.

By about 800 C.E. Ghana had established itself as a powerful kingdom able to exact tribute from vassal states in the region. Although agricultural production contributed to Ghana's wealth, it was the expanding trans-Saharan trade with Europe and the Mediterranean world that gave Ghana even more influence. From their strategic position on the upper Niger River, the Soninke were well positioned as intermediaries to barter the salt produced from the Taghaza salt mines in the Sahara, the gold coming from Bambuk, and kola nuts and slaves captured from areas south of the savanna.

Ghana's king controlled the supply of gold within his kingdom and claimed every gold nugget coming into the country, leaving ordinary citizens the right to buy and sell only gold dust. The king was reputed to own a gold nugget so large that he bragged he could tether his horse to it. In addition, taxes were levied on every load of goods entering and leaving the country.

Ghana's gold was actually mined in Bambuk, a region eight days' journey to the west of Ghana's capital, Kumbi-Saleh, from the beds of the Senegal and Faleme Rivers. Ghana's rulers did not have direct control over Bambuk, and the persons who worked the goldfields jealously guarded information about where and how they produced the gold. They devised a strategy for negotiating with Mande traders without actually coming into direct contact with them. Al Masudi, a noted Arab traveler, described this "silent trade" around 950:

> They have traced a boundary which no one who sets out to them ever crosses. When the merchants reach this boundary, they place their wares and cloth on the ground and then depart, and so the people of the Sudan come bearing gold which they leave beside the merchandise and then depart. The owners of the merchandise then return, and if they are satisfied with what they have found, they take it. If not, they go away again, and the people of the Sudan return and add to the price until the bargain is concluded.[7]

Outsiders who tried to interfere in gold production soon found that less gold was offered for trade.

Traders avidly sought salt from the trans-Saharan trade because it was a crucial element in diets and a preservative for foods and skins. It was also a scarce commodity in savanna communities. A certain amount of salt could be extracted from vegetable matter or from soil, but not enough to satisfy the requirements of these savanna communities. However, in the Sahara there were large salt deposits, the best known at Tag-haza, in the middle of the Sahara, about a three-week journey from both Mediterranean and Sudanese trading centers. Salt was quarried in huge 200-pound slabs, loaded on camels, and transported to trading centers like Timbuktu (tim-buk-TOO), where these slabs were distributed to other places.

Another item featured in the trade was kola nuts, which were primarily grown in the forest areas to the south of the savanna. Used to quench thirst, kola nuts were consumed mainly in the drier savanna. They did not become a major staple of the trans-Saharan exchange.

Slaves were the final component of the trans-Saharan trade. Although slavery was an established practice in some, though not all, sub-Saharan African societies, it took many shapes and forms. A common practice was that a family sent a family member—usually a child or a young adult—to serve in another household to pay off a debt or some other obligation (such as compensation for a crime) or to raise food in times of famine. In those cases, slaves were integrated into a master's family. Servile status could be of limited duration, and the slave would be sent back home as soon as the debt was repaid.

With centralized kingdoms such as Ghana and, later, Mali, slaves were bought and sold in trading transactions and were called on to perform a variety of roles—as servants, farm laborers, porters, traders, and soldiers. Most household slaves were women and children; slave women were often selected as marriage partners or concubines because a man did not have to pay bridewealth for them. Their children had all the rights of free persons.

Slave warriors had a privileged status; they could serve in high capacities as military officers, administrators, and diplomats in a king's court. Slave soldiers were the mainstays of armies and were used in raids to kidnap and capture more slaves. Most slaves were kidnapped or captured in raids on weaker communities by the stronger savanna states, especially in the forest region to the south. Muslim law enjoined Muslims from enslaving other Muslims, but this was not always observed when raiding parties were sent out.

Although savanna kingdoms created their own internal trade in slaves, the trans-Saharan slave trade was fueled primarily by demands from North African Mediterranean states. Slaves were typically taken in caravans, where they were exchanged for salt and horses. In Senegambia (si-neh-GAM-bee-ah) in the mid-fifteenth century, nine to 14 slaves could fetch one horse, while in Kanem-Bornu a horse would cost 15 to 20 slaves. In later centuries some slaves, especially those sold in Libya, were traded on to the eastern Mediterranean, the Italian peninsula, and other southern European areas. From the eighth century, when the trade was initiated, to the early twentieth century, an estimated 3.5 to 4 million slaves were taken across the Sahara.[8]

The 1200-mile journey across the desert was as perilous as the trans-Atlantic slave trade's infamous Middle Passage. Many slaves lost their lives to the harsh conditions. The majority of slaves were women who worked as domestic servants in royal households and courts or were designated as concubines. Male slaves were pressed into service in the salt mines and as caravan porters, agricultural labor, and soldiers. Because many slaves were freed or died of diseases and because so few children were born in captivity, there was a constant demand for more slaves to be sold on the market.

To reconstruct the histories of the Sudanic kingdoms, historians draw heavily on the accounts of Arab geographers, travelers, holy men, and scholars. One Arab chronicler, Al-Bakri, described Ghana at its peak in 1067. He claimed that the army was some 200,000 strong, with many contingents wearing chain mail. The king, who had not converted to Islam, was considered divine and able to intercede with the gods. He appointed all officials and served as supreme judge. His government was organized under ministers, with one responsible for his capital, Kumbi-Saleh. Princes of tributary states were held hostage at his court. When the king appeared in public, he was surrounded by highborn personal retainers holding gold swords, horses adorned with gold cloth blankets, and dogs wearing gold collars.

Ghana's capital, Kumbi-Saleh, was situated on the edge of a crop-growing area and had 15,000 to 20,000 residents. The capital was really two towns, 6 miles apart. One was a large Soninke village, where the king and his retinue lived. Close to the village was a sacred grove where traditional religious cults were practiced. The other town was occupied by Muslim merchants. The merchants' town had 12 mosques, two-story stone houses, public squares, and a market. Besides the traders, the town was also home to religious and legal scholars. Ghana's king relied on literate Muslims as treasurer, interpreters, and counselors. However influential the Muslims were, the king had to make sure that his own religious leaders were regularly consulted and that he participated in shrine and other religious activities. The first king to convert to Islam did not do so until after the Almoravid invasion in 1076.

Document

Ghana, as Described by Al-Bakri

Accounts by Muslim scholars and travelers are important sources for writing the history of West Africa's Sudanic kingdoms. A Muslim geographer and theologian who lived in Spain, Al-Bakri's account of the kingdom of Ghana appeared in his *Kitab al-maslik wa-'l-mamalik ("The Book of Routes and Realms")*, published in 1040 C.E. Al-Bakri relied extensively on people who traveled to the places he describes. The following passages describe contending religious factions at Ghana's royal capital, Kumbi-Saleh.

The city of Ghana consists of two towns situated on a plain. One of these towns, which is inhabited by Muslims, is large and possesses twelve mosques, in one of which they assemble for the Friday prayer. There are salaried imams and muezzins, as well as jurists and scholars. . . . Between these two towns there are continuous habitations. The houses of the inhabitants are of stone and acacia *(sunt)* wood. The king has a palace and a number of domed dwellings all surrounded with an enclosure like a city wall *(sur)*. In the king's town, and not far from his court of justice is a mosque where the Muslims who arrive at his court *(yafid 'alayh)* pray. Around the king's town are domed buildings and groves and thickets where the sorcerers of these people, men in charge of the religious cult, live. In them too are their idols and the tombs of their kings. These woods are guarded and none may enter them and know what is there. . . . The king's interpreters, the official in charge of his treasury and the majority of his ministers are Muslims. Among the people who follow the king's religion only he and his heir apparent (who is the son of his sister) may wear sewn clothes. All other people shave their beards, and women shave their heads. The king adorns himself like a woman [wearing necklaces' round his neck] and [bracelets] on his forearms, and he puts on a high cap *(tartur)* decorated with gold and wrapped in a turban of fine cotton. He sits in audience or to hear grievances against officials *(mazalim)* in a domed pavilion around which stand ten horses covered with gold-embroidered materials. Behind the king stand ten pages holding shields and swords decorated with gold, and on his right are the sons of the [vassal] kings of his country wearing splendid garments and their hair plaited with gold. The governor of the city sits on the ground before the king and around him are ministers seated likewise. . . . The audience is announced by the beating of a drum which they call *duba*, made from a long hollow log. When the people who profess the same religion as the king approach him they fall on their knees and sprinkle dust on their heads, for this is their way of greeting him. As for the Muslims, they greet him only by clapping their hands.

Their religion is paganism and the worship of idols *(dakakyr)*. When their king dies they construct over the place where his tomb will be an enormous dome of *saj* wood. Then they bring him on a bed covered with a few carpets and cushions and place him beside the dome. At his side they place his ornaments, his weapons, and the vessels from which he used to eat and drink, filled with various kinds of food and beverages. They place there too the men who used to serve his meals. They close the door of the dome and cover it with mats and furnishings. Then the people assemble, who heap earth upon it until it becomes like a big hillock and dig a ditch around it until the mound can be reached at only one place.

They make sacrifices to their dead and make offerings of intoxicating drinks.

Question to Consider

1. What insights does Al-Bakri provide into how Sudanic kings balanced their Islamic faith with traditional religious institutions?

From N. Levtzion and J. F. P. Hopkins, *Corpus of Early Arabic Sources for West African History* (Cambridge: Cambridge University Press, 1981), pp. 79–81.

The Almoravid invasion followed Ghana's conquest of Adoghast, a Sanhaja Berber trading center, when Sanhaja Berbers rallied around an Islamic revivalist movement called the Almoravid and attacked Ghana. Although it is still a subject of debate whether the Almoravid attack was a full-scale invasion or a series of raids, Ghana had to give up Adoghast and its dominance over trade. Ghana's dominance over the gold trade was further weakened when the Bure goldfield opened up on the Niger River.

Mali

In the early thirteenth century Ghana's rule was ended by an uprising led by Sumaguru (c. 1200–1235) of the Sosso, who were related to the Soninke. Oral traditions characterize Sumaguru as a tyrant who wielded magical powers over his people. Sumaguru was overthrown in 1235 by Sundiata (SOON-dee-AH-tah), a noted hunter and magician of the Malinke Keita clan, who forged an alliance of Malinke clans and chiefdoms for that purpose. Lengthy wars followed in which Sundiata's army defeated and killed Sumaguru and routed the Sosso. Sundiata's army then embarked on campaigns of conquest throughout the territory that had been Ghana.

Eventually, Sundiata's Malinke created a vast empire called Mali that stretched from the Atlantic south of the Senegal River to Gao on the middle Niger River. Mali gained control of the desert gold trade and the gold-producing regions of Wangara and Bambuk. When Europeans made gold a currency in 1252, West Africa became Europe's leading supplier of gold. Several tons of gold were produced annually. Two-thirds of it was exported, while the rest was kept for conspicuous display by Mali's ruling elites.

The kingdom of Mali was at the height of its power and prosperity during the reign of Sundiata's nephew, Mansa Musa (1307–1337). Musa was perhaps the most widely known sub-Saharan African ruler throughout western Asia and Europe. He was an accomplished soldier who consolidated his kingdom's control over a vast domain. Malian and Arab merchants carried on trade with the Mediterranean coast, particularly with Algeria, Tunisia, Egypt, and the Middle East.

Mansa Musa ruled over an efficiently organized state. On the north and northeast were loosely held tributary kingdoms of diverse populations, including some Berbers. To the south were more closely controlled tributary states under resident governors appointed by the king. Elsewhere, particularly in the cities such as Timbuktu, provincial administrators governed directly in the king's name and at his pleasure. Mali's central government included ministries for finance, justice, agriculture, and foreign relations. Agricultural settlements produced food for the court, the army, and the administration, and taxes and tribute were collected from subject communities.

A devout Muslim, Musa lavishly displayed his wealth and power on a pilgrimage he took to Mecca in 1324–1325. His retinue included thousands of porters and servants and a hundred camels bearing loads of gold. In Egypt he spent so lavishly and gave away so much gold that its value in that country plummeted and did not recover for a generation:

This man spread upon Cairo the flood of his generosity. . . . So much gold was current in Cairo that it ruined the value of money. Let me add that gold in Egypt had enjoyed a high rate of exchange up to the moment of their arrival. But from that day onward, its value dwindled. That is how it has been for twelve years from that time, because of the great amounts of gold they brought to Egypt and spent there.[9]

When he returned to his kingdom, Musa brought along an architect who designed mosques in Gao and Timbuktu as well as an audience chamber for Musa's palace. Musa sent students to study at Islamic schools in Morocco. They returned to found Qur'anic schools, the best known of which was at Timbuktu.

Mansa Musa's pilgrimage also caught the attention of Muslim scholars. Among them was the Moroccan geographer and traveler Ibn Battuta, who visited Mali in 1352 during the reign of Musa's brother, Mansa Sulayman (1336–1358). Battuta's account is one of the key sources for understanding the kingdom of Mali. He was favorably impressed by Mali's architecture, literature, and institutions of learning but was most laudatory about its law and justice, which guaranteed that no person "need fear brigands, thieves, or ravishers" anywhere in the vast domain. Battuta praised the king's devotion to Islam but was disappointed that so many subjects of Mali were not Muslims. He noted also that the unveiled women were attractive but lacking in humility. He was astounded that they might take lovers without arousing their husbands' jealousy and could discuss learned subjects with men.

As Mali's empire grew, Islam became an important unifying element among the political and commercial elite. Key agents for the spread of Islam were Mande traders known as Dyula (DJOO-lah), Jahanke, and Wangara, which created an extensive trading network that stretched from Senegambia on the Atlantic coast to the kingdom of Bornu to the east. Although they were largely responsible for the trade in such items as gold and kola nuts, they were Muslim teachers as well. Wherever they went, they became the lifeblood of small Muslim communities, establishing Qur'anic schools and arranging for the faithful to make pilgrimages to Mecca.

Since they operated in areas where most people were not Muslims, the Mande traders formulated religious precepts that allowed them to coexist with and accept the rule of non-Muslims. However, because there were concerns that the traders would not remain devout Muslims, they were encouraged to visit centers of Islamic learning periodically to deepen their faith.

One of the few regions where Muslims actively converted people in the countryside was in Senegambia. Despite the devoutness of kings such as

Mansa Musa and The Catalan Atlas of 1375

Mali's King Mansa Musa literally put himself on the map on his pilgrimage to Mecca in 1324–1325. During a lengthy stay in Cairo, he advertised his kingdom's wealth to the Mediterranean commercial world in a way that modern-day business people would appreciate. He spent extravagantly and gave away large quantities of gold. This reinforced Europe's awareness of Mali's special status—that it was a major source of gold at a time when Europe was exchanging silver for gold as its principal hard currency. Thus, when the Portuguese began exploring the African coast, one of their objectives was to establish direct contact with Mali's king.

Mansa Musa's actions left an indelible impression on outsiders' perceptions of his kingdom. Thus, it was not surprising that when Abraham Cresques, a cartographer from Majorca, was drawing the Catalan Atlas a half-century later, he made a point of highlighting Mansa Musa and his kingdom.

The Catalan Atlas was designed to promote trade between Europe and different parts of the world. For each of the atlas's 12 leaves, Cresques depended on information provided by travelers and traders, even if it was outdated. For instance, the map of Asia drew heavily from Marco Polo's travels a century earlier, while the map of West Africa relied on information passed on by Moroccan Jews who were familiar with trans-Saharan trade routes.

The map of West Africa contained several inscriptions. One was placed next to a Tuareg trader mounted on a camel. "All this region is occupied by people who veil their mouths; one only sees their eyes. They live in tents and have caravans of camels." Cresques clearly believed that Islam had a strong presence in the Sudan, as evidenced by the domes that identified Muslim centers such as Timbuktu and Gao. The map also gave an exaggerated importance to Mali's king, Mansa Musa, who is depicted holding a gold nugget in one hand and a scepter in the other as he awaits the arrival of a Muslim trader. The inscription beside him reads: "The Negro lord is called Musa Mali, lord of the Negroes of Guinea. So abundant is the gold which is found in his country that he is the richest and most noble king in all the land."

Questions to Consider

1. Why was King Mansa Musa of Mali so prominently featured in this map of the Catalan Atlas?

2. The maps in the Catalan Atlas were drawn before the European "Age of Discovery." What sources did the Catalan cartographers rely on for their knowledge of West Africa and other regions of the world?

Musa and the presence of Muslim traders in many areas, Islam was mainly a religion of court and commerce. Most people in the countryside remained faithful to their traditional religious beliefs. Muslim rulers who neglected their people's spiritual practices did so at the risk of provoking opposition. Hence, Islamic festivals were usually celebrated alongside traditional rites.

After Mansa Musa's death, his successors found the large empire increasingly difficult to govern. They were plagued by dynastic disputes, raids by desert nomads such as the Tuaregs and Sanhaja, and the restlessness of tributary states. One of the rebellious states was Songhai, centered around the bend of the Niger. Songhai had been in existence for many centuries before it was absorbed into the Malian Empire in the thirteenth century, and its principal city, Gao, was an entrepot for trade with the Maghrib and Egypt. Before the end of the fifteenth century, Songhai had won its independence, and, within another century, it had conquered Mali.

After Sunni Ali drowned in the Niger River, his son ruled for a few months before Askia Muhammad, who came from Sunni Ali's slave officer corps, deposed him and established his own dynasty. Askia Muhammad set about consolidating and reorganizing the whole empire. Although his armies seized control of the Taghaza saltworks in the Sahara, their attempts to expand control over the Hausa states to the east were not successful.

Reigning from his capital at Gao, Askia Muhammad created a centralized bureaucracy to manage finances, agriculture, and taxation, appointed administrators (usually relatives) to oversee newly created provinces, and built up a professional army featuring a cavalry of chain-mailed horsemen and an enlarged fleet of canoes, which constantly patrolled the Niger.

Unlike Sunni Ali, Askia Muhammad made peace with Muslim scholars and became their benefactor. He declared Islam the official religion. During his reign Timbuktu, Jenne-jeno, and Walata achieved recognition as centers of Islamic scholarship. Several hundred

Songhai

Songhai became the largest of the Sudanic empires, reaching its zenith during the reigns of Sunni Ali (1464–1492) and Askia Muhammad (1493–1528). Sunni Ali is remembered for his military exploits. His armies ventured out on constant campaigns of conquest, largely to the west along the Niger in what had been Mali's heartland, and captured the trading centers of Timbuktu, Walata, and Jenne-jeno.

Sunni Ali regularly feuded with Muslim scholars and clerics who accused him of not observing Muslim practices such as praying in public. They issued a condemnation of his behavior and ruled that because he was not a Muslim, he could not be recognized as a legitimate ruler. He tried to suppress his dissidents and expelled Muslim scholars from Timbuktu.

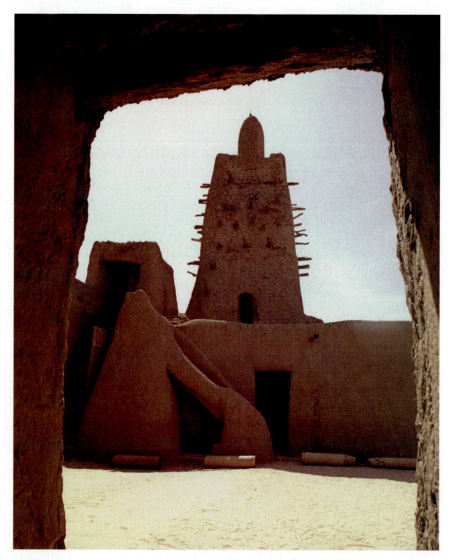

The Sankore mosque is the oldest surviving mosque in West Africa. Its pyramidlike minaret rises above the city of Timbuktu, the center of Islamic culture in the kingdom of Mali.

Muslim schools were established in Timbuktu, whose scholars developed extensive links and exchanges with scholars in the Middle East and North Africa. Its Sankore mosque became so renowned that a contemporary Arab traveler noted that more profits were being made from selling books and manuscripts there than from any other trade.

Like Mansa Musa, Askia Muhammad made a much publicized pilgrimage to Mecca. Traveling in 1497 with a large group of pilgrims, he brought thousands of gold pieces, which he freely distributed as alms to the poor and used to establish a hostel in Mecca for pilgrims from the western Sudan. Muhammad was not just expressing his faith; he was also drumming up trade with Songhai and shoring up his credentials with Muslims throughout his far-flung empire. On Muhammad's return home the Egyptian caliph recognized him as the **Caliph** of the lands of Takrur, an important distinction for any Muslim ruler.

Although a son deposed Askia Muhammad in 1528 and the kingdom was weakened by internal rivalries, Songhai remained a savanna power until 1591, when Morocco's King Ahmad al-Mansur launched an invasion of Songhai to prevent European rivals from gaining access to Sudanese gold. Taking offense at Songhai's refusal to pay a tax on salt from the Taghaza mines, al-Mansur sent a contingent of 4000 mercenaries to secure control over the Sudanic goldfields. Many died in the harsh march across the Sahara, but the survivors, armed with arquebuses (firearms mounted on a forked staff) and muskets, proved superior to the spears, swords, and bows and arrows of Songhai's soldiers. Although Morocco's impact was fleeting, Songhai was not able to recover, and the empire fragmented into many smaller kingdoms.

Kanem, Bornu, and the Hausa States

In the central Sudan, which stretches from the bend of the Niger to Lake Chad, a series of Muslim states emerged that took advantage of the fertile agricultural lands and their strategic location between the trans-Saharan trade routes to the north and the forest regions to the south. The kingdoms of Kanem and Bornu and the Hausa city-states became the most important dominant political actors.

Kanem, which lay to the northeast of Lake Chad, had been formed around 900 C.E. when groups of nomadic pastoralists unified and established the Saifawa dynasty. The ruling elite converted to Islam in the late eleventh century. As in other Sudanic states, Saifawa power and wealth were based on control of the Saharan trade. The main trade route cut through the central Sahara to the Fezzan and on to Tripoli and Egypt. Because Kanem was too far away from any sources of gold, its rulers exported ivory, ostrich feathers, and, especially, war captives from societies to the south. In return Kanem received horses that its rulers used to create a cavalry that fueled further raiding. Under Mai (king) Dunama Dibalemi (1210–1248), Kanem boasted a cavalry of 40,000 horsemen.

In the fourteenth century, one of Kanem's tributary states, Bornu, became a power in its own right, organizing its own trade and refusing to pay tribute to Kanem. During this period, Kanem's rulers were challenged by the Bulala, a non-Muslim clan, and by the deterioration of their pasturage. About 1400, the Saifawa dynasty came under attack from peoples living east of Lake Chad and moved to Bornu west of Lake Chad, where they gained access to new trading networks. At first they paid tribute to Bornu, but during the sixteenth century, Kanem's leaders gradually took over the Bornu state and began carrying out raids over an extensive area. Their rule was financed by tribute, taxes on peasants and customs levies on the trade in slaves, gold, salt and weapons between Bornu and Tripoli and Cairo.

Bornu's rulers maintained excellent relations with the Muslim world. In the early thirteenth century they established a **madrasa** in Cairo for their students studying at al-Azhar University. They developed a strong relationship with the Ottoman rulers of Tripoli and imported firearms and contracted Turkish mercenaries to train Bornu's army.

To the west of Kanem and Bornu, a group of Hausa city-states had been founded by nomadic cattle-keepers and farmers between 1000 and 1200. A common feature of Hausa villages was wooden stockades for protection. When villages grew into larger towns, they were enclosed by large walls.

Hausa city-states became important political and economic forces in the fifteenth century. All of the Hausa states were centralized, with a king and council making decisions. Islam was an important part of the trading and merchant class and the political elite.

Kano was one of the most powerful of the city-states. In the late fourteenth and fifteenth centuries, Kano's rulers made Muslim officials an integral part of their administration and invited scholars from Egypt, Tunis, and Morocco to establish centers of scholarship.

One way in which Kano's rulers thwarted lineages that were contesting for power was by appointing slaves to important state offices such as treasurer and as palace guards. They also relied on a cavalry with an officer corps to maintain their power and to raid for the slaves who labored on large royal farms. The cavalrymen wore iron helmets and coats of mail.

Caliph—The religious and political leader of the Islamic nation; successor of Muhammad.

madrasa—A theology school, usually for Sunni Muslims.

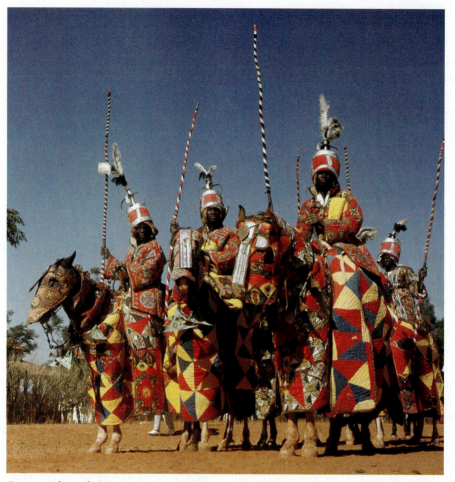

Ceremonial cavalry procession in contemporary northern Nigeria. Historically the military strength of kingdoms of the western Sudan was partly based on cavalry.

Kano produced and exported textiles, dyed cloth, and leatherwork through an extensive network in the trans-Saharan trade as well as with Yoruba and Akan states to the south.

Other significant Hausa city-states were Zazzau (ZA-zow), a supplier of slaves to Hausa states and to North Africa; Gobir, which traded with Songhai and Mali; and Katsina, an important terminus for the trans-Saharan trade. Katsina also successfully produced textiles from its cotton fields and leather goods from goat, sheep, and cattle hides. However prosperous they were, some of the Hausa states still had to pay tribute to Songhai to the west and Kanem and Bornu to the east. The Hausa states usually coexisted peacefully, although Kano and Katsina carried on a periodic war for almost a century.

A legendary Hausa ruler of the sixteenth century was Zazzau's Queen Amina. She led her armies on campaigns all the way to the banks of the Niger River and conquered Kano and Katsina. Under her rule, Zazzau controlled not only the intra-regional trade but also the region's trans-Saharan trade. Her reign is associated with the building of earthen walls around

Hausa cities. She is remembered in a popular song still sung in contemporary Nigeria: "Amina, daughter of Nikatau, a woman as capable as a man."[10]

WEST AFRICAN FOREST KINGDOMS

■ *How did trade in the forest kingdoms compare with those in the savannah region?*

Between the savanna grasslands and the Atlantic was forest land. Some of the forests were extensions of the savannas and were suitable for extensive human settlements; closer to the coast were rain forests that required considerable energy to clear for settlement and cultivation. The rain forests were also the home of the tsetse fly, the carrier of sleeping sickness, which limited the herding of highly susceptible livestock.

IMAGE

Yams as Sources of Traditional Power in West Africa

Most forest societies were built around villages and small chiefdoms sustained by agriculture and hunting. Root crops such as yams and, later, cassava were the main staples. Although they did not approach the same size as the savanna empires, some of these small chiefdoms merged and formed vibrant kingdoms.

In southwestern Nigeria, a Yoruba city-state, Ife, emerged around the eleventh century C.E. According to oral traditions, the Yoruba god of the sky, Olorun, had sent a founding ancestor, Oduduwa, to establish Ife. Anyone who subsequently made a claim to the kingship of Ife or other Yoruba states had to trace descent from Oduduwa.

To the southeast of Ife was the Edo kingdom of Benin, which rose to prominence in the fifteenth and sixteenth centuries. Benin's prosperity was based not only on commerce with the Hausa states, trading food, ivory, and kola nuts for copper and possibly salt, but also on the strength of its fishing communities on the Niger delta.

Benin was ruled by hereditary kings, known as *obas*. Advising the king was the *ozama*, a council composed of hereditary leaders who represented the main Edo lineages. They acted as a restraint on the *oba's* powers until a thirteenth-century *oba* named Ewedo undermined the *ozama's* powers by creating a court of men who were not members of the royal elite and who were given nonhereditary titles.

Benin remained a minor state until the rule of *Oba* Ewuare, who usurped the throne by killing his younger brother in 1440. He took over in a period of instability following the conquest of Benin by a neighboring state. Ewuare ensured that his line would succeed him by arranging that his heir be added to the *ozama* council.

Noted for his magical and healing powers, Ewuare was famous for rebuilding the capital, surrounded by a wall and featuring a broad avenue. He constructed an extensive royal palace that provided quarters for his family as well as for advisers, guilds of craftsmen, and servants. All of his freeborn subjects were expected to spend a period in the service of the palace. During Ewuare's three decades of rule, his armies expanded Benin's borders, conquering some 200 towns and extending Benin's influence far to the north and to coastal regions to the east and west. However, Ewuare did not tightly control his empire. Although he placed loyal officials in subject territories, he gave local rulers autonomy as long as they paid tribute on a regular basis. Ewuare's successors did not fare so well. The *ozama* chiefs asserted themselves and replaced, exiled, or killed a series of *obas*.

Other states developed along the forest fringe of the northern savanna. Most of them profited from the long-distance Saharan trade through the Hausa states to the north, exchanging slaves and forest products such as kola nuts for salt, leather goods, and glassware. In the Niger River region, the kingdom of Oyo emerged in the fourteenth century. The kings *(alafins)* of Oyo presided over a complex of palace councils, subkings, secret organizations, and lineage organizations at the village level. Although *alafins* claimed absolute power, they were held in check by a prime minister *(basorun)* and a council of ministers *(oyo mesi)*, composed of men from the seven wards of the city of Oyo. If an *alafin* abused his authority, the prime minister could rebuke him, "The Gods reject you, the people reject you, the earth rejects you." The *alafin* then had to commit suicide.[11] This happened rarely because an *alafin's* suicide meant that a member of the council also had to take his life. This system of checks and balances worked well until the seventeenth and eighteenth centuries.

The *alafins'* wealth was built on tolls collected from traders and their control of a slave labor force that they placed on royal farms. Oyo's rise as a regional power was due to its permanent officer corps and its cavalry, assembled with horses traded from the savanna. Because horses did not survive in the tsetse-infested forests, the cavalry was most effective in the open savannas to the southwest of Oyo.

All of these forest states are noted for their artistic achievements. Yoruba artisans created sculptures in bronze, copper, brass, and terra-cotta. Most of these artworks were used in religious contexts, as funereal pieces placed in tombs to honor ancestors and in temples. These objects showed continuity with the artistic styles of earlier civilizations such as the Nok culture of central Nigeria.

SWAHILI CITY-STATES IN EAST AFRICA

■ *Why were small city-states established on the East African coast rather than the large states in West Africa?*

For the past 2000 years the East African, or Swahili, coast has been part of a much wider maritime trading network that linked Africa with the Near East, India, and Asia. Indeed, one scholar argues that the Indian Ocean would be better named the Afrasian Sea.[12] However, unlike the trans-Saharan trade that opened up extensive trade throughout western Africa, trade along the East African coast, with some exceptions, did not have the same impact on the East African interior until the nineteenth century.

Trade Routes in Africa

The historical and cultural development of the East African coast was intimately linked to the creation of a coastal culture that dates from 100 B.C.E. to 300 C.E. with the establishment of Bantu-speaking communities along the coast north of the Tana River.

They took advantage of the fertile soils and forests along the coast to pasture their animals and to raise a great variety of food crops. They also found the creeks, rivers, lagoons, mangrove swamps, and seas ideal for fishing. Although Bantu farmers relied on subsistence agriculture and fishing, they began to expand their local and regional trading contacts and eventually linked up with merchants from the Arabian peninsula and the Persian Gulf.

Trade between the coastal Swahili city-states and Indian Ocean trading partners was regulated by monsoon winds that blow in a southwesterly direction between November and March and in a northeasterly direction between April and October.

The language that evolved on the coast and islands was Swahili, which was based on a Bantu language spoken on the Kenyan coast. Indeed, the word *Swahili* is taken from an Arabic word *sawahil*, meaning "coast." As the language evolved, it adopted Arabic loan words, especially after the seventeenth century.

The earliest known record of the East African trade is *The Periplus of the Erythrean Sea*, a navigational guide written by a Greek trader in Alexandria, Egypt, around the first century C.E. The *Periplus* chronicles shipping ports of the Red Sea and the Indian Ocean and identifies a string of market towns on the "Azanian" (East African) coast that actively participated in the Indian Ocean trade, especially with Arabia. The most important was a port named Rhapta. Market towns exported such goods as ivory, rhinoceros horn, copra, and tortoise shells in exchange for iron tools and weapons, cloth, glass, and grain.

The Indian Ocean trade continued between 300 and 1000, but it was given a great stimulus by the spread of Islam and the settling of Muslims from Arabia and the Persian Gulf along the East African coastline from the ninth century C.E. onward. This was about the same time as Islam reached western parts of North Africa, but the spread of Islam in eastern Africa was not associated with conquest. Muslims intermixed with African communities and helped expand trading links with the Arab world. An Arab traveler described this trade on a visit to the "land of Zanj" (the East African coast) in 916:

> The land of Zanj produces wild leopard skins. The people wear them as clothes, or export them to Muslim countries. They are the largest leopard skins and the most beautiful for making saddles. . . . They also export tortoise-shell for making combs, for which ivory is likewise used. . . . There are many wild elephants in this land but no tame ones. The Zanj do not use them for war or anything else, but only hunt and kill them for their ivory. It is from this country that come tusks weighing fifty pounds and more. They usually go to Oman, and from there are sent to China and India.[13]

Arab boats or dhows made the Indian Ocean trade possible. They had the ability to cross the Indian Ocean three times as fast as a camel could cross the Sahara, and, with a capacity of up to 200 tons, they could carry a thousand times as much. The dhows' lateen (triangular) sails made it possible for sailors to take advantage of seasonal monsoon winds in the Indian Ocean that blow in a southwesterly direction between November and March and northeasterly between April and October. As with the Red Sea trade, the monsoon winds governed the trading calendar. It took about a month for a dhow to make the 2000-mile journey from East Africa to the Persian Gulf, and the

The Arab dhow was the primary transporter of trade goods in the Indian Ocean. The dhow's lateen sails made it possible to navigate the monsoon winds that dictated the direction of trade at different times of the year.

traders had to carry out their business according to the favorable winds, or they could not transport their goods at all. Along the East African coast itself, however, it was possible to move between the islands at most times of the year. Because the coastal trade was conducted in shallower waters, traders built small dhows with capacities of about 50 tons. These dhows typically had no deck, one mast, and palm-leaf mats for sails.

Swahili civilization flourished between 1000 and 1500, when hundreds of city-states, many of them on offshore islands, sprang up along the 1800-mile stretch from Mogadishu to Sofala on the Mozambique coast. They began as fishing villages and gradually evolved into trading centers. Most were short-lived, but those that were situated at the mouth of a river or had deep harbors and were connected to established trade routes on the African mainland—such as Malindi, Pemba, Pate, Mombasa, Mafia, and Kilwa—became regional trade centers and thrived for centuries.

Kilwa peaked as a trading center between 1250 and 1330 C.E. Kilwa had the advantage of a good supply of fresh water and several natural harbors that could handle large ships. But it became the wealthiest of the city-states because of its near monopoly over gold exported

from the Zimbabwe interior. Kilwa's merchants claimed a sphere of influence over the East African coast from Kilwa southward to Sofala on the Mozambique coast, where they established an outpost to facilitate the gold trade with Africans from the interior.

The Swahili city-states were never part of an empire, nor were they dominated by any one of the city-states. Indeed, they usually competed fiercely with one another. The lack of high walls around the cities suggests that they were more concerned with protecting themselves from stray elephants than from rivals. At times, one city might exact tribute from its neighbors or a number of states might federate in time of war. Commercial competition made such cooperation difficult to maintain and curtailed political expansion on the African mainland, where kingdoms like Great Zimbabwe played one coastal city against another. Indian Ocean trade was largely free from major conflicts until the Portuguese arrived in the early sixteenth century.

Within the city-states, a Muslim commercial aristocracy exercised exclusive control over political institutions. Although they provided the capital, skills, and boats for their piece of the Indian Ocean trade, they always remained in the shadow of the Indian Ocean trading powers. The Swahili commercial elite was primarily descended from Arab and Indian settlers and indigenous Africans. A myth developed that that they were descendants of Shirazi Persians. Because the Persian Empire had once been an Indian Ocean trading power, Swahili elites probably manufactured a connection to the Persians who settled along the coast many centuries earlier. Many scholars question whether this claim has any validity.

As the Muslim Middle East became the commercial center of Eurasia, the maritime trade of the Swahili city-states figured significantly in the commercial networks of three continents. Gold, ivory, mangrove poles, amber, and slaves were the main exports. Other products commonly exported were hides and skins, cloth, rhinoceros horn, spices, and grain, in exchange for cloth, silk, beads, porcelain, gum, incense, spices (i.e., cinnamon, nutmeg, and cloves), glass, cloth, perfume, bronze, copper, and silver. Copper and silver coins were minted at Kilwa, Pate, and Mogadishu and used up and down the coast.

Kilwa, with its access to the Zimbabwean gold fields, became the major port for gold sent to Indian Ocean states and through Egypt to Europe. Gold was a mainstay of Swahili trade until gold and silver began to flow in the sixteenth century from Spanish possessions in the Americas. After that, Swahili traders turned more to exporting ivory. Iron ore, exported from Malindi and Mombasa, supplied the iron industries of India. Mangrove trees, typically found where rivers emptied into the Indian Ocean, were stripped of their branches and shipped to treeless areas throughout the southern Persian Gulf. Because mangrove poles are straight and sturdy, they made excellent materials for house construction. This trade remained healthy until the late twentieth century when oil revenues allowed Persian Gulf states to turn to steel for building materials. Slaves were shipped to the Arabian peninsula and Cambay, the capital of Gujarat, in India. There they served as domestic slaves or, as in southern Iraq, as laborers draining marshes. Their oppressive work conditions sparked off a revolt in 869 C.E. that lasted for nearly two decades. One consequence of the revolt was that few Persian Gulf households continued to rely on Africa as a source of slaves.

The Swahili coast attracted trading expeditions from as far away as China. In the early 1400s, a Chinese fleet under the command of Admiral Zheng He (JUHNG HUH) visited Swahili towns such as Malindi and Mogadishu, bearing porcelain, silks, lacquerware, and fine art objects and exchanging them for ivory, rhinoceros horns, incense, tortoise shell, rare woods, and exotic animals such as ostriches, zebras, and giraffes.

In the early 1400s, the Chinese commissioned seven expeditions to visit all the lands of the Indian Ocean to promote trade. A Chinese fleet under the command of Admiral Zheng He visited some of the Swahili towns and took back several envoys from Malindi who brought along a giraffe as a gift to the Chinese court in 1414. The presentation of this giraffe was memorialized in a tapestry.

Zheng He's ships also took back African envoys, who stayed at the Chinese court for several years.

The governments of the city-states were usually headed by monarchs or sultans, assisted by merchant councils and advised by holy men or royal relatives. Political leadership was equated with commercial success. The king of Pate, for instance, "owned much wealth, . . . acted as an entrepreneur in ship building, trading and even mining and relied for emergency on a private army as distinct from the regular troops which he also commanded. . . ."[14] Elite families maintained their privileged status by building political and commercial alliances through intermarriage and exchanging gifts.

Although the sultans were typical Muslim rulers in most respects, the common order of succession was according to matrilineal rules. When a sultan died at Kilwa, Pate, or any of numerous other cities, the throne passed to one of the head queen's brothers. Swahili civilization was an urban culture. Most towns had a central mosque, a Qur'anic school, a marketplace, a palace, and government buildings. Some towns, such as Kilwa, Mombasa and Lamu, were densely settled; in others, settlements were dispersed. The towns were the preserves of the commercial elite, who lived in houses made of wood with coral stone foundations until the mid-fifteenth century when they replaced wood with coral rag (broken coral stone) with lime mortar. Some of the homes were two or three stories high and reflected the wealth, status, and rank of their owners. A Portuguese account of the late fifteenth century described the layout of Kilwa, a prosperous city of 12,000 people: "The streets of the city are very narrow, as the houses are very high, of three and four stories, and one can run along the tops of them upon the terraces, as the houses are very close together. . . ."[15]

With the exception of the most loyal household slaves, the Swahili traders were the only ones who lived inside the walled cities. Most slaves slept outside the city in houses made of sun-dried mud and palm-matted roofs. They came into the city to work every day. Because the towns were not self-sufficient, the traders relied on the farmers and fishermen on the mainland for foodstuffs and meat.

Swahili masons and craftsmen were celebrated for building ornate stone and coral mosques and palaces, adorned with gold, ivory, and other wealth from nearly every major port in southern Asia. Perhaps because it borrowed architectural styles from the Middle East, Kilwa impressed the famous Muslim scholar-traveler Ibn Battuta in 1331 as the most beautiful and well-constructed city he had seen anywhere. Archaeological excavations have confirmed this evaluation, revealing the ruins of enormous palaces, great mansions, elaborate mosques, arched walkways, town squares, and public fountains. The Husuni Kubwa (hoo-SOO-nee KOO-bwah) palace and trade emporium at Kilwa, built on the edge of an ocean cliff, featured domed and vaulted roofs and contained over 100 rooms, with eight to ten apartments for visiting merchants as well as their goods, and an eight-sided bathing pool in one of its many courtyards.

Constructed in the thirteenth century by the Muslim sultans of Kilwa, the Great Mosque was built from coral blocks. In the mosque's center, its arches supported a domed ceiling.

KINGDOMS OF CENTRAL AND SOUTHERN AFRICA

■ *How were southern African kingdoms tied to the Indian Ocean economy?*

By the third century C.E. central and southern Africa had been settled by migrating groups of Bantu farmers who lived in scattered homesteads or small villages and subsisted on cereal crops and animal herds. Around 1000 C.E. some of these societies began to grow in size and complexity. States were formed with ruling elites that displayed their wealth through their cattle herds. They accumulated cattle through a variety of means—raids, tribute, death dues, court fines, and bridewealth exchanges for marriages. Cattle exchanges through marriages and loans gave ruling families the opportunity to establish broader social and political networks with other powerful families. Cattle herds also financed their participation in regional trading networks and links with the Indian Ocean economy.

A common feature of the ruling elites of these new states was that they built walls, dwellings, palaces, and religious centers made of stone. Throughout the region north and south of the Limpopo River archaeologists have identified more than several hundred political centers. An early state was Mapungubwe, situated south of the Limpopo River. Mapungubwe's rulers lived in stone residences on a hilltop, while commoners lived in their traditional settlements in the surrounding valley. An estimated 3000 to 5000 people lived at Mapungubwe's political center. The elites maintained their privileged status through their control over cattle herds; the trade in such metals as tin, copper, iron, and gold; and the hunting of elephants for ivory. Tin, copper, and iron were traded regionally, but ivory and gold were designated primarily for the expanding trade with the Indian Ocean coast. Mapungubwe peaked during the thirteenth century, but its main settlement had to be abandoned soon thereafter because farmers were not able to sustain production when a climatic change produced a colder, drier environment.

Mapungubwe's successor was Great Zimbabwe ("houses of stone"), centered on a well-watered plateau north of the Limpopo. Its grandeur as a state is symbolized by its imposing granite structures, left after its rulers were forced to move northward to the Zambezi. Extending over 60 acres and supporting about 18,000 residents, the complex at Great Zimbabwe contained many structures built over several centuries. At its center was a large complex of stoneworks where the political and religious elite lived. The most impressive structure was the Great Enclosure, which likely served as the royal family's main residence. Over 800 feet in circumference, the Great Enclosure was built without mortar and featured massive freestanding walls 12 feet thick and 20 feet high. Undoubtedly, Great Zimbabwe's rulers intended their monumental architecture to enhance their power and prestige among their subjects.

Zimbabwe's king presided over an elaborate court and administration. His key advisers included the queen mother and a ritual sister, a half-sister who was appointed when a king was installed. She had to give her consent to decisions made by the royal coun-

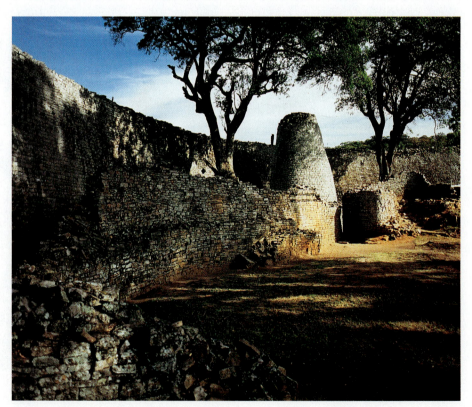

The Great Enclosure was Great Zimbabwe's most impressive structure and likely served as the royal family's main residence. Over 800 feet in circumference, the Great Enclosure was built without mortar and featured massive, freestanding granite walls 12 feet thick and 20 feet high.

cil before they could be enacted, she kept the ritual medicines that protected the well-being of the king, and she had considerable input into the choice of a new king.

Zimbabwe's rulers combined political and sacred power. Great Zimbabwe contained a rainmaking shrine, where its rulers prayed for abundant rainfall. On a nearby hillside was a temple where they prayed and offered sacrifices to the high god Mwari and the ancestors to ensure the fertility of the land and the prosperity of the people.

Great Zimbabwe's political elite based their power on their vast cattle herds as well as the control of regional trade, particularly copper and gold. The principal sources of gold were located on the plateau west of Great Zimbabwe. Women and children were responsible for mining most gold, which they did during the dry season, when they could take time off from their farming responsibilities. They sank narrow shafts as deep as 100 feet, brought the ore to the surface, crushed it, and sifted out the gold in nearby streams. Although some of the gold was fashioned into ornamental bangles and jewelry for Zimbabwe's rulers, most of the gold was transported as a fine powder for the external trade with the coastal Swahili cities, especially Kilwa, whose prosperity depended on its ties to Zimbabwe. One historian has estimated that 7 to 10 million ounces of gold were exported from this region from the late tenth to the nineteenth centuries. Besides gold, ivory and animal skins were traded for glass beads, Indian cloth, ceramic vessels from Persia, and blue-and-white porcelain from China.

Great Zimbabwe's zenith was between 1290 and 1450. A common explanation for its sudden collapse is environmental degradation. The land no longer supported large numbers of people living in a concentrated area; trees, chopped down for firewood, had become scarce; and many wild animals had been hunted down. However, part of this interpretation is not supported by data showing that rainfall actually increased around that time. A more likely explanation for the kingdom's decline is the rise to prominence of two of its former tributary states: Torwa to the northwest and Mutapa to the north.

Oral tradition relates that Mutapa's founder was Nyatsimbe Mutota, whom Great Zimbabwe's rulers had sent north to search for an alternative source of salt. He founded the Mutapa kingdom in the well-watered Mazoe Valley south of the Zambezi River. By 1500 Mutapa's ruler, the *mwene mutapa* ("conqueror"), and his army held sway over a vast part of the upper Zimbabwe Plateau. The *mwene mutapa* did not adopt the stone building traditions of Great Zimbabwe. Instead, he lived in a palace complex within a wooden palisade. With his family, military, bureaucracy, and representatives of tributary chiefdoms, he ruled over a federation of tributary states through governors that he appointed. They paid tribute in the form of agricultural produce, iron, cattle, and especially gold, which was still the mainstay of the trade with the East African coast.

Another notable kingdom in west Central Africa was Kongo, located in a fertile agricultural area near the Atlantic coast at the mouth of the Congo River. It was formed in the fourteenth century when a petty prince named Wene led a migration, married into the local ruling family, and began developing a loose federation of states. Wene took the title of *Manikongo* ("lord of Kongo"). However, as kings of Kongo centered their political rule at their capital, Mbanza Kongo, they developed a centralized state. By the time the Portuguese arrived in the late fifteenth century, Kongo had already developed a sophisticated political system. The king, who had a professional army resident at his capital, appointed officials, usually close relatives, as his provincial administrators. The Kongo kingdom also controlled interregional trade, exchanging its cloth, woven from fibers of the raffia palm, for salt and seashells from neighboring societies.

IMAGE

Loango, the Capital of the Congo (Kongo)

CONCLUSION

By 1500 C.E. Africans had successfully adapted to the opportunities and constraints of Africa's challenging environments by creating a diverse range of communities and states. Critical turning points in the histories of African cultures occurred with the introduction of agriculture, herding, and ironworking. These developments spurred population growth, migrations, craft specialization, trade between communities, and more complex political and economic systems. Most Africans in 1500 still lived in scattered homesteads and small communities and earned their livelihoods from farming, herding, and hunting. However, because of trading relations with one another and with other continents, Africans began to establish kingdoms and empires in all parts of the continent and in a variety of environments. Like other early world civilizations, Egypt and Nubia evolved in the Nile River valley, but Aksum and Ethiopia emerged on a mountain plateau; Ghana, Mali, Songhay, and Great Zimbabwe in savannas; Oyo and Benin in rainforests; and the Swahili city-states on the Indian Ocean.

While Africans created their own distinct cultures and traditions, states in the West African Sudan, northeastern Africa, and the East African coast carried on vigorous commercial, technological, and intellectual exchanges with the cultures of the Indian Ocean, the Mediterranean, the Near East, and Asia, largely by tapping Muslim trading networks. The kingdom of Aksum became a major Red Sea power, serving as a bridge between the Mediterranean and the Indian Ocean. The Swahili city-states on the East African coast and the states of the Zimbabwe Plateau carried on extensive relations with Indian Ocean trading networks. West African savanna kingdoms created the most extensive trading network through their position overseeing trade between North Africa, the savanna, and forest regions to the south. However, within these long-distance trading networks, African states were primarily producers of raw materials.

Although most Africans remained faithful to their traditional religious beliefs and practices, many converted to Christianity and Islam in specific areas. Egypt became an early center of Christianity, while Ethiopia's rulers firmly established Christianity as their kingdom's state religion. Islam became the dominant religion of North Africa, while some rulers and traders in the West African savanna, northeastern Africa, and along the Swahili coast adopted Islam. However, until the eighteenth century, Islam remained primarily a religion of court and commerce in sub-Saharan Africa. It won few followers in small-scale societies that did not have ruling elites. This pattern is similar to other places such as Indonesia where Muslim traders established themselves but did not initially win many converts.

Suggestions for Web Browsing

You can obtain more information about topics included in this chapter at the websites listed below. See also the companion website that accompanies this text, **http://www.ablongman.com/brummett,** which contains an online study guide and additional resources.

Internet African History Sourcebook
http://www.fordham.edu/halsall/africa/africasbook.html

Extensive online source for links about the history of ancient Africa, including the kingdoms of Ghana, Mali, and Songhai.

Art of Benin
http://www.si.edu/ofg/Units/sorsnmafa.htm

Site of the Smithsonian Institution's National Museum of African Art displays art objects from the kingdom of Benin before Western dominance.

Great Zimbabwe
http://www.mc.maricopa.edu/~reffland/anthropology/anthro2003/legacy/africa/zimbabwe/

A 23-slide series, with commentary, that will take you through the ruins of Great Zimbabwe in southern Africa.

The Story of Africa
http://www.bbc.co.uk/worldservice/africa/features/storyofafrica/index.shtml

The radio service of the BBC presents a history of Africa from the origins of humankind to modern nation-states.

African Voices
http://www.mnh.si.edu/africanvoices/

The African Voices exhibit at the Smithsonian Institution's Museum of Natural History features discussions of history, culture and politics.

Literature and Films

The Sundiata epic of the Malian Empire is recorded in D. T. Niane, *Sundiata: An Epic of Old Mali* (Longman, 1995). For Ethiopian royal literature, see G. W. B. Huntingford, ed., *Royal Chronicles of Abyssinia: The Glorious Victories of Ama Seyon King of Ethiopia* (Clarendon Press, 1965).

Caravans of Gold (Home Vision, 1984) treats the gold trade between the Sudanic kingdoms of West Africa and the Muslim and European worlds. It is one film in an eight-part series, *Africa: The Story of a Continent,* presented by Basil Davidson, a British writer on African issues. *Lost Cities of the South* (PBS, 1999) presents a discussion of African civilizations of southern Africa, such as Mapungubwe and Great Zimbabwe. It is part of a six-part series, *Wonders of the African World,* narrated by Harvard professor Henry Louis Gates, Jr.

Suggestions for Reading

The best detailed coverage of African history can be found in two multivolume series, each containing chapters by leading scholars: *The Cambridge History of Africa,* 8 Vols. (Cambridge University Press, 1982–1984) and *The UNESCO General History of Africa.* Among other general surveys of African history are Robert July, *A History of the African People,* 4th ed. (Waveland Press, 1992); Erik Gilbert and Jonathan Reynolds, *Africa in World History from Prehistory to the Present* (Pearson Education, 2004); and Christopher Ehret, *The Civilizations of Africa: A History to 1800* (University Press of Virginia, 2002).

The best general reference work on early African history is Joseph Vogel, ed., *Encyclopedia of Precolonial Africa: Archaeology, History, Languages, Cultures, and Environments* (AltaMira Press, 1997). Another general work that examines Africa's history with a disciplinary focus is James Newman, *The Peopling of Africa: A Geographic Interpretation* (Yale University Press, 1995). A general synthesis on women in African history is Iris Berger and E. Frances White, *Women in Sub-Saharan Africa: Restoring Women to History* (Indiana University Press, 1995).

On Ethiopia, see Richard K. Pankhurst, *The Ethiopians* (Blackwell, 1998).

General works on West Africa include J. F. Ajayi and Michael Crowder, eds., *History of West Africa,* 3rd ed., Vol. 1 (Longman, 1985). A comprehensive study on Islam in Africa is Randall Pouwels and Nehemia Levtzion, eds., *The History of Islam in Africa* (Ohio University Press, 2000).

The East African coast and Swahili city-states are well covered in John Middleton, *The World of the Swahili: An African Mercantile Civilization* (Yale University Press, 1992).

The best general study on early central and southern African history is David Birmingham, ed., *History of Central Africa to 1870* (Cambridge University Press, 1981). The kingdom of Great Zimbabwe is extensively treated in Joseph Vogel, *Great Zimbabwe: The Iron Age in South Central Africa* (Garland, 1994). A detailed study of central and eastern African states is David Schoenbrun, *A Green Place, a Good Place: Agrarian Change, Gender, and Social Identity in the Great Lakes Region to the 15th Century* (Heinemann, 1998).

The European Middle Ages, 476–1348 C.E.

The absence of the political unity and military security once provided by the Roman Empire became an obvious fact of life in almost all of western Europe in the fourth and fifth centuries. As the unity and security of the old Roman order collapsed and Germanic chieftains claimed lands and asserted what authority they could, very slowly the civilization of Rome evolved into a culture that was a unique blending of Roman and Germanic institutions. Out of this blending of cultures emerged a distinct pattern of life in western Europe.

One of the institutions that survived the collapse of Roman order was the Christian Church, which, by the beginning of the sixth century, was still in the process of unification under the direction of the bishop of Rome, the Pope. The church increased its efficiency through the centralization of its administration, and unified its efforts to convert all of Europe and eliminate rival religions. Christian efforts to preserve knowledge and learning centered on saving art and literature of the past that was supportive exclusively of the Christian faith; for the most part the art and literature of the non-Christian past was destroyed, suppressed, or ignored—much of the intellectual heritage of the ancient world was lost forever.

The first significant state to emerge out of the fragmentation of old Roman order was that established by the Germanic tribe of the Franks, who gave northern Europe an interim of stability and progress. Military and political security was improved, and Roman Christianity was extended among the barbarian tribes of the north.

But the accomplishments of the Franks were not to be permanent. Their empire did not endure, partly because it lacked the solid economic foundation that had supported the Romans, and because of new and violent invasions. Viking, Magyar, and Muslim incursions had to be addressed through local resistance, since no effective response existed on a national or international level.

Out of the disintegration of the Frankish empire evolved an alternative political order sometimes described as feudalism. Based on formally stated agreements between individuals, this method of government was designed to provide social stability and military security in Europe. And the manorial system, the economic foundation of medieval life, provided stability to the rural economy of Europe. Both institutions attempted to insure security by resisting change and fostering self-sufficiency.

Gradually, the political and military goals of the feudal nobility became aggressive and expansionist. Monarchs once again attempted to increase their authority over the feudal nobility. The growth of trade and commerce slowly provided an economic alternative to the manorial system, and the society of the West changed in the process. In addition, the church increased its power as a political and economic force in European society, in addition to its religious leadership. The church's sponsorship of the Crusading movement of the later Middle Ages was indicative of that power and influence.

The culture of the Later European Middle Ages emerged as greatly distinct from that of the period before 500. The collective and conservative society of the earlier period gave way to a culture becoming more familiar with religious challenge, economic growth, and political centralization. The cultural conservatism and conformity that typified the earlier patterns of medieval life gave way to a society that had to adjust to a more rapid rate of change and challenge in virtually all facets of life. The roots of modern European society are easily found in the civilization of the Late Middle Ages.

THE CHURCH IN THE EARLY MIDDLE AGES

■ *What role did the Church play in stabilizing western European society after the fall of the Roman Empire?*

As Europe formed a unique culture out of the remnants of Roman influence and the injection of Germanic peoples and their traditions, the church played a formative role in shaping this new social fabric. In the Early Middle Ages (500–1000), the administration of the church was centralized through the efforts of the popes and the ever more efficient bureaucracy at Rome. Missionary activity spread Christianity to the borders of the continent and provided a unified cultural and religious foundation for early European society. And, in large part, the church, its missionaries, and its copyists in monasteries should be credited with keeping at least some of the intellectual heritage of the ancient world alive in an age when learning, other than that which supported Christian belief, was considered useless and unnecessary.

The Early Medieval Papacy, 500–1000

Chapter 5 examined the growing authority of the bishops of Rome, the popes, over the Christian Church in western Europe. Not only were the bishops of Rome able to establish control over the church's hierarchy and supervise the spiritual concerns of the believers; often the early popes were looked to for political leadership and guidance in troubled times. During the pontificate of Gregory I, the Great (590–604), the papacy aggressively began to assert its political as well as its spiritual authority. After his election as pope, Gregory assumed the task of protecting Rome and its surrounding territory from the threat of invasion from the Germanic tribe of the Lombards. After successfully negotiating a peace treaty with this tribe, Gregory became the first pope to conduct himself as actual ruler of a part of what later became the Papal States.

Gregory also laid the foundation for the papal machinery of church government. He took the first step in asserting papal control of the church outside Italy by sending a mission of Benedictine monks to convert the non-Christian Anglo-Saxons. The pattern of church government that Gregory established in England—bishops supervised by archbishops, who reported to the pope—became standard.

The task of establishing papal control of the church and extending the pope's **temporal** authority was continued by Gregory's successors. In the eighth century English missionaries transferred to Germany and France the pattern of papal government they had known in England; the Donation of Pepin, a sizable grant of territory in Italy given to the pope by the Merovingian (meh-roh-VIN-gee-ahn) king (see p. 261), greatly increased the pope's temporal power by creating the Papal States.

Missionary Activities of the Church

The early Middle Ages were years of widespread and intense missionary activity. By spreading Christianity,

---

temporal—Having to do with time, or the present life and this world. Worldly or transitory concerns.

The bejeweled front cover of the Lindau Gospels, a work dating from the third quarter of the ninth century, is an example of Carolingian art. The Celtic-Germanic metalwork tradition has been adapted to the religious art produced during the era of Charlemagne. The main clusters of semi-precious stones adorning the gold cover have been raised so that light can penetrate beneath them to make them glow.

missionaries contributed to the confluence of Germanic and Roman cultures. Monasteries, many of which were established in remote territories far from urban centers, served not only as missionary outposts, but also as refuges for those seeking a life of contemplation and prayer, as centers of learning for scholars, and even as progressive farming centers. The dedication and enthusiasm with which many of these monks approached their faith often extended beyond the monastic walls, and resulted ultimately in the virtual elimination of paganism in Europe.

One of the most successful of early Christian missionaries was Ulfilas (OOL-fi-lahs) (c. 311–383), who spent 40 years with the Visigoths and translated most of the Bible into Gothic. Ulfilas and many other early missionaries were followers of Arius, and the heresy of Arianism (see p. 154) was adopted by all the Germanic tribes in the empire, with the exception of the Franks and the Anglo-Saxons.

Missionary activities in Ireland resulted in the founding of numerous monasteries on that island, many of them in remote and isolated locations. In the late sixth and seventh centuries, many of these Irish monks, moved by a passionate devotion to Christianity and dedicated to the elimination of heresy, traveled to Scotland, northern England, the kingdom of the Franks, and even Italy as missionaries to renew the

faith and erase the effects of worldly corruption. Irish monks also eagerly pursued scholarship and the preservation of early Christian literary works, and their monasteries became storehouses for priceless manuscripts and exquisite copies of original works.

Early in the seventh century, the papacy, along with the monasteries, took a more aggressive part in directing Christian missionary efforts. Under the direction of the pope, Roman Catholicism was established throughout England, and the Irish church acknowledged the primacy of Rome.

The English church, in turn, played an important role in the expansion of Roman Catholic Christianity on the European mainland. Boniface, the greatest English missionary in the eighth century, spent 35 years among the Germanic tribes and established several important monasteries and bishoprics before he turned to the task of reforming the church in France. There, he revitalized the monasteries, organized a system of local **parishes** to bring Christianity to the countryside, and probably was instrumental in forming the alliance between the papacy and the Carolingian dynasty of kings of the Franks. Roman Catholic missionaries were also sent to work among the Scandinavian peoples and the Slavs.

The Preservation of Knowledge

One of the great contributions of the monasteries was the preservation of the learning of the early church, and some of the literature of the Greek and Roman world that early Christian leaders found compatible with the Christian faith. After the fall of Rome, learning did not entirely die out in western Europe; the knowledge of the classical world was preserved through the efforts of a small number of concerned intellectuals who recognized its lasting value. Seeing that the ability to read Greek was quickly disappearing, the sixth-century Roman scholar Boethius (boh-EE-thee-uhs) (c. 480–525) determined to preserve Greek learning by

---

parish—A local church, with its own priest, and the people under the religious care of that priest.

translating all of Plato and Aristotle into Latin. But only Aristotle's treatises on logic were translated, and these works remained the sole writings of that philosopher available in Europe until the twelfth century. Unjustly accused of treachery by the emperor, Boethius was thrown into prison, where he wrote *The Consolation of Philosophy* while awaiting execution, which eventually became a medieval textbook on philosophy.

Cassiodorus (cah-si-oh-DOH-ruhs; c. 490–c. 585), a contemporary of Boethius, devoted most of his life to the collection and preservation of classical knowledge. By encouraging the monks to copy valuable manuscripts, he was instrumental in making the monasteries centers of learning. Following his example, many monasteries established *scriptoria*, departments concerned exclusively with copying manuscripts.

During the early Middle Ages, most education took place in the monasteries. In the late sixth and seventh centuries, when political stability was not yet reestablished throughout much of the European continent, Irish monasteries provided a safe haven for learning. There, men studied Greek and Latin, copied and preserved manuscripts, and, in illuminating them, produced masterpieces of art. The *Book of Kells* is a surviving example of their skill. In the early Middle Ages, women were provided no opportunities for such pursuits; the Church limited access to reading and writing to men involved in clerical and business occupations.

DOCUMENT

Rule of St. Benedict

Visigothic belt buckle, circa 525–560. This elaborately crafted buckle is inlaid with finely polished red garnets and was probably worn by a prominent Spanish Visigothic woman. Most Visigothic belt buckles are of the same shape, but the patterns of decoration vary greatly, perhaps to signify the family or clan of the owner.

THE MEROVINGIANS AND CAROLINGIANS

■ *How successful were the Merovingian and Carolingian monarchs in preserving Roman institutions and culture?*

In the blending of Roman and Germanic customs and institutions, the Franks played a particularly significant role. Not only was the kingdom of the Franks the most enduring of the early Germanic states, but it became, with the active support of the church, the first European kingdom that attempted to take the place of the Roman Empire in the West.

The Kingdom of the Franks Under Clovis

Before the Germanic invasions of the fourth century, the Franks lived close to the North Sea; late in the fourth century they began to migrate south and west into Roman Gaul. By 481 they occupied the northern part of Gaul as far south as the old Roman city of Paris, and in that same year, Clovis I of the Merovingian dynasty became ruler of one of the small Frankish kingdoms. By the time of his death in 511, Clovis had united the Franks into a single kingdom that stretched south to the Pyrenees.

Clovis was an intelligent manipulator of alliances and a shrewd diplomat who also used religion for political gain. He was converted to Christianity—perhaps through the influence of his Christian wife—and was baptized together with his whole army. He thus became the only Orthodox Christian ruler in the West, since the other Germanic tribes were either still pagan or followers of Arian Christianity (the heresy that maintained that Jesus was not equal to the Father and thereby not completely divine). This conversion of the Franks to Roman Christianity ultimately led to a close alliance of the Franks and the papacy.

Decline of the Merovingians—Rise of the Carolingians

Clovis's sons and grandsons extended Frankish control south to the Mediterranean and east into Germany. But after Clovis's death, the Merovingian dynasty began to decay. The Germanic tradition of treating the kingdom as personal property and dividing it among all the king's sons resulted in constant and bitter civil wars. But most importantly, the Merovingian kings proved themselves incompetent and ineffectual. Soon the Frankish state broke up into three separate kingdoms; in each, power was

The Merovingians and the Carolingians

481–511	Clovis unites Franks; beginning of Merovingian dynasty
714–741	Charles Martel mayor of the palace
732	Charles defeats Muslims at Tours
741–768	Pepin the Short mayor of the palace
751	Pepin crowned king of the Franks; beginning of Carolingian dynasty
768–814	Reign of Charlemagne
800	Charlemagne crowned emperor by the pope; beginning of Carolingian Empire
814–840	Reign of Louis the Pious
843	Treaty of Verdun divides Carolingian Empire

concentrated in the hands of the chief official of the royal household—the mayor of the palace, a powerful noble who hoped to keep the king weak and ineffectual. The Merovingian rulers became puppets—"do-nothing kings."

By the middle of the seventh century, the Frankish state had lost most of the essential characteristics of Roman civilization. The Roman system of administration and taxation had collapsed. The dukes and counts who represented the Merovinginan king received no salary and usually acted on their own initiative in commanding the fighting men and presiding over the courts in their districts. International commerce had ceased except for a small-scale trade in luxury items carried on by adventurous Greek, Syrian, and Jewish traders. The old Roman cities served mainly as centers housing the local bishops and their staffs. The virtual absence of a middle class meant that society was composed of the nobility, a union through intermarriage of aristocratic Gallo-Roman and German families who owned and exercised authority over vast estates, and, at the other end of the social scale, the peasants *(coloni)* who worked the land and were considered bound to that estate. These peasants included large numbers of formerly free German farmers. Only about 10 percent of the peasant population of Gaul maintained their status as free individuals.

Coinciding with the Merovingian decay, new waves of invaders threatened every region of Europe. A great movement of Slavic peoples from the area that is now Russia had begun around 500 C.E. From this region the Slavs pushed west, inhabiting the areas left by the Germanic tribes when they advanced into the Roman Empire. By 650 the western Slavs had reached the Elbe River, which they crossed to raid German territory. Another danger threatened western Europe from the south: in the late seventh century the Muslim Moors prepared to invade Spain from North Africa.

The kingdom of the Franks gained strength when Charles Martel became mayor of the palace (or the king's court) in 714. His military skill earned him the surname Martel, "The Hammer." Charles was responsible for introducing a major innovation in European warfare. To counteract the effectiveness of the quick-striking Muslim cavalry, Charles recruited a force of professional mounted soldiers. He rewarded his soldiers with land to enable each of them to support a family, equipment, and war horses. With such a force, Charles Martel won an important victory over the Muslim cavalry at Tours in 732.

Charles's son, Pepin the Short (741–768), legalized the power already being exercised by the mayors of the palace by requesting and receiving from the pope a decision that whoever exercised the actual power in the kingdom should be the legal ruler. In 751 Pepin was elected king by the Franks; the last Merovingian was sent off to a **monastery,** and the Carolingian dynasty came to power. In 754 the pope reaffirmed the election of Pepin by personally anointing him as king of the Franks.

Behind the pope's action was his need for a powerful protector against the Lombards, who had conquered the **Exarchate** of Ravenna (the center of Byzantine government in Italy) and were demanding tribute from the pope. Following Pepin's coronation, the pope secured his promise of armed intervention in Italy and his pledge to give the Exarchate to the papacy, once it was conquered. In 756 a Frankish army forced the Lombard king to withdraw, and Pepin gave Ravenna to the pope. The so-called Donation of Pepin made the pope a temporal ruler over the Papal States, a strip of territory that extended diagonally across northern Italy.

The alliance between the Franks and the papacy affected the course of politics and religion for centuries. It furthered the separation of the Roman from the Greek Christian Church by giving the papacy a dependable Western ally in place of the Byzantines, previously its only protector against the Lombards.

---

monastery—A house or residence of a community of religious men (monks), who live in seclusion from the world and maintain a self-sufficient communal lifestyle.

Exarchate—In the Byzantine empire, the office and/or the area ruled by an official named an exarch—a bishop ranking below the patriarch of the Eastern Orthodox Christian church.

Charlemagne and His Achievements

Under Pepin's son Charlemagne (CHAHR-leh-mayn), or Charles the Great, the Frankish state and the Carolingian dynasty reached the height of its power. Although he was certainly a successful warrior-king, leading his armies on yearly campaigns, Charlemagne, who ruled from 768 to 814, also tried to provide an effective administration for his kingdom. In addition, he had great appreciation for learning; his efforts at furthering the arts produced the revival in learning and letters known as the Carolingian Renaissance.

Charlemagne sought to extend his kingdom southward against the Muslims in Spain. He crossed the Pyrenees and eventually drove the Muslims back to the Ebro River, establishing a frontier area known as the Spanish March, centered near Barcelona. French immigrants moved into the area, later called Catalonia, giving it a character culturally distinct from the rest of Spain.

Charlemagne conquered the Bavarians and the Saxons, the last of the independent Germanic tribes, on his eastern frontier. Even farther to the east, the empire's frontier was continually threatened by the Slavs and the Avars (AY-vahrs), Asiatic nomads related to the Huns. In six campaigns, Charlemagne nearly eliminated the Avars and then set up his own military province in the Danube valley to guard against any future advances by eastern nomads. Called the East March, this territory later became Austria. Like his father Pepin, Charlemagne was deeply involved in Italian politics. The Lombards resented the attempts of the papacy to expand civil control in northern Italy. At the request of the pope, Charlemagne attacked the Lombards in 774, defeated them, and named himself their king.

One of the most important events in Charlemagne's reign took place on Christmas Day, 800. In the previous year the Roman nobility had removed the pope from office, charging him with corruption. But Charlemagne came to Rome and restored the pope to his position. At the Christmas service, Charlemagne knelt before the altar and the pope placed a crown on his head while the congregation shouted: "To Charles Augustus crowned of God, great and pacific Emperor of the Romans, long life and victory!"

This ceremony demonstrated that the memory of the Roman Empire still survived as a meaningful tradition in Europe and that there was a strong desire to reestablish political unity. In fact, Charlemagne had named his capital at Aix-la-Chapelle (AX-lah-shah-PEL), "New Rome," or Aachen (AH-ken), and considered taking the title of emperor in an attempt to revive the idea of the Roman Empire in the West.

The Carolingian Empire

The extent of Charlemagne's empire was impressive. His territories included all of the western area of the old Roman Empire except north Africa, Britain, southern Italy, and the majority of Spain. Seven defensive provinces, or *marches*, protected the empire against hostile neighbors.

The Carolingian territories were divided into some 300 administrative divisions, each under a count *(graf)* or, in the marches along the border, a margrave *(markgraf)*. In addition, there were local military officials, the dukes. In an effort to supervise the activities of local officials, Charlemagne issued an ordinance creating the *missi dominici,* the king's envoys. Pairs of these itinerant officials, usually a bishop and a lay noble, traveled throughout the realm to check on the local administration. So that the *missi* were immune to bribes, they were chosen from men of high rank, were frequently transferred from one region to another, and no two of them were teamed for more than one year.

This gold bust of Charlemagne was made in the fourteenth century and is housed now in the treasury of the Palace Chapel of Charlemagne in Aachen, Germany. The reliquary bust contains parts of the emperor's skull.

Charlemagne's Legacy

Charlemagne is considered one of the most significant figures of early European history. He created a state in which law and order were again enforced

Document   Charlemagne: A Firsthand Look

Einhard, born in the kingdom of the Franks in circa 770 C.E., was the emperor Charlemagne's secretary and biographer. The following is an excerpt from Einhard's *Life of Charlemagne*, which he completed some years after the emperor's death. Einhard's biography of the emperor is considered one of the finest works of biography produced in the early Middle Ages. It was modeled after Roman biographies of the later emperors, and intended to give its readers an intimate glimpse of Charlemagne's character, as well as to convince them of the emperor's wisdom and majesty. The following except deals mainly with the emperor's physical appearance and private pleasures:

Charles was large and strong, and of lofty stature, though not disproportionately tall (his height is well known to have been seven times the length of his foot); the upper part of his head was round, his eyes very large and animated, nose a little long, hair fair, and face laughing and merry. Thus his appearance was always stately and dignified, whether he was standing or sitting; although his neck was thick and somewhat short, and his belly rather prominent; but the symmetry of the rest of his body concealed these defects. His gait was firm, his whole carriage manly, and his voice clear, but not so strong as his size led one to expect. His health was excellent, except during the four years preceding his death, when he was subject to frequent fevers; at the last he even limped a little with one foot. Even in those years he consulted rather his own inclinations than the advice of physicians, who were almost hateful to him, because they wanted him to give up roasts, to which he was accustomed, and to eat boiled meat instead. In accordance with the national custom, he took frequent exercise on horseback and in the chase, accomplishments in which scarcely any people in the world can equal the Franks. He enjoyed the exhalations from natural warm springs, and often practiced swimming, in which he was such an adept that none could surpass him; and hence it was that he built his palace at Aix-la-Chapelle, and lived there constantly during his latter years until his death. He used not only to invite his sons to his bath, but his nobles and friends, and now and then a troop of his retinue or bodyguard, so that a hundred or more persons sometimes bathed with him.... Charles was temperate in eating, and particularly so in drinking, for he abominated drunkenness in anybody, much more in himself and those of his household; but he could not easily abstain from food, and often complained that fasts injured his health. He very rarely gave entertainment, only on great feastdays, and then to large numbers of people. His meals ordinarily consisted of four courses, not counting the roast, which his huntsmen used to bring in on the spit; he was more fond of this than of any other dish. While at table, he listened to reading or music....

Charles had the gift of ready and fluent speech, and could express whatever he had to say with the utmost clearness. He was not satisfied with command of his native language merely, but gave attention to the study of foreign ones, and in particular was such a master of Latin that he could speak it as well as his native tongue; but he could understand Greek better than he could speak it. He was so eloquent, indeed, that he might have passed for a teacher of eloquence. He most zealously cultivated the liberal arts, held those who taught them in great esteem, and conferred great honors upon them. He took lessons in grammar of the deacon Peter of Pisa, at that time an aged man. Another deacon, Albin of Britain, surnamed Alcuin, a man of Saxon extraction, who was the greatest scholar of the day, was his teacher in other branches of learning. The King spent much time and labor with him studying rhetoric, dialectics, and especially astronomy; he learned to reckon, and used to investigate the motions of the heavenly bodies most curiously, with an intelligent scrutiny. He also tried to write, and used to keep tablets and blanks in bed under his pillow, that at leisure hours he might accustom his hand to form the letters; however, as he did not begin his efforts in due season, but late in life, they met with ill success.

Questions to Consider

1. What do you suppose is Einhard's real purpose in writing this biography? Do you think it is an impartial account?

2. What could such a biography be used for, especially since it appeared after Charlemagne's death?

3. Do you think there are some exaggerations contained in this except? If so, what might they be, and why do you think they were included?

From Samuel Epes Turner, trans., *Life of Charlemagne by Einhard* (Ann Arbor: University of Michigan Press, 1960), pp. 50–57.

after three centuries of disintegration. His patronage of learning began a cultural revival that later generations would build on, producing a European civilization distinct from the Byzantine to the east and the Muslim to the south.

Charlemagne's empire was not long-lived, however, for its territories were too vast and its nobility too divisive to be held together after the dominating personality of its creator was gone. Charlemagne had no standing army; his foot soldiers were essentially the old Germanic war band summoned to fight by its war leader. The king did not have a bureaucratic administrative machine comparable to that of Roman times. The Frankish economy was agricultural and localized, and there was no system of taxation adequate to maintain an effective and permanent administration. Under Charlemagne's weak successors, the empire collapsed in the confusion of civil wars and devastating new invasions. Progress toward a centralized and effective monarchy in Europe ended with Charlemagne's death.

When he died in 814, Charlemagne was succeeded by his only surviving son, Louis the Pious, a well-meaning but ineffective ruler. Louis, in accordance with Frankish custom, divided the kingdom among his three sons, and bitter rivalry and warfare broke out among the brothers even before Louis died in 840.

In 843 the three brothers met at Verdun, where they agreed to split the Carolingian lands among themselves. Charles the Bald obtained the western part of the empire, and Louis the German the eastern; Lothair, the oldest brother, retained the title of emperor and obtained an elongated middle kingdom, which stretched 1000 miles from the North Sea to central Italy.

The Treaty of Verdun contributed to the shaping of political problems that continued into the twentieth century. Lothair's middle kingdom soon collapsed into three major parts: Lorraine in the north, Burgundy, and Italy in the south. Lorraine included Latin and German cultures, and, although it was divided in 870 between Charles and Louis, the area was disputed for centuries. Lorraine became one of the most frequent battlegrounds of Europe.

Europe Under Attack

During the ninth and tenth centuries, coinciding with the collapse of the Carolingian Empire, western Europe came under attack by Scandinavians from the

Charlemagne was able to rule the largest empire in the West since the collapse of Rome. Although today the emperor is probably remembered most for his administrative and cultural contributions, he conducted campaigns to enlarge his empire during nearly all of his reign.

north and Muslims from the south, while the Magyars, a new band of Asiatic nomads, conducted destructive raids on central Europe and northern Italy. Christian Europe was hard pressed to repel these warlike newcomers who were more threatening to life and property than the Germanic invaders of the fifth century.

From bases in North Africa, Muslim adventurers, in full command of the sea, raided the coasts of Italy and France. In 827 they began the conquest of Byzantine Sicily and southern Italy. From forts erected in southern France they penetrated far inland to attack merchant caravans even in the Alpine passes. What

New invasions in the ninth and tenth centuries threatened the stability of western Europe in much the same way the Germanic invasions had challenged the Roman Empire. Muslim, Viking, and Magyar attacks posed serious threats to Christian European political stability.

trade still existed between Byzantium and western Europe, except for that undertaken by Venice and several other Italian towns, was now almost totally cut off, and the Mediterranean Sea came under almost complete Muslim control.

The most widespread and destructive raids, however, came from Scandinavia. Swedes, Danes, and Norwegians—collectively referred to as Vikings—began to move south. Overpopulation and a surplus of young men are possible reasons for this expansion, but some scholars suggest that these raiders were defeated war bands expelled from their homeland by the emergence of strong royal power. The Vikings had developed seaworthy ships capable of carrying 100 men, powered by long oars or by sail when the wind was favorable. Viking sailors had also developed expert sailing techniques; without benefit of the compass, they were able to navigate by the stars at night and the sun by day.

The range of Viking expansion reached as far as North America to the west, the Caspian Sea to the east, and the Mediterranean to the south. Between 800 and 850, Ireland was raided repeatedly. Many monasteries, the centers of the flourishing Irish Celtic culture, were destroyed. The Icelandic Norsemen ventured on to Greenland and, later, to North America. Other raiders traveled the rivers of Russia as merchants and soldiers of fortune and founded the nucleus of a Russian state. Danes raided Britain and the shores of Germany, France, and Spain. By 840 they had occupied most of Britain north of the Thames. They devastated northwest France, destroying dozens of abbeys and towns. Unable to fend off the Viking attacks, the weak Carolingian king accepted the local Norse chieftain as duke of a Viking state, later called Normandy. Like Viking settlers elsewhere, these Northmen, or Normans, became Christian converts and eventually played an important role in shaping the future of medieval Europe.

FEUDALISM AND MANORIALISM

■ *What influences did feudalism and manorialism have in shaping European society during the Middle Ages and beyond?*

Europe's response to the invasions of the ninth and tenth centuries was not uniform. By 900 the Viking occupation of England had initiated a strong national reaction, which soon led to the creation of a united British kingdom. Germany in 919 repelled the Magyar threat through the efforts of a new and able line of kings who went on to become powerful European

monarchs. But Viking attacks on France accelerated a political fragmentation. Since the monarchy could not hold together its vast territory, small independent landowners surrendered both their lands and their personal freedoms to the many counts, dukes, and other local lords in return for protection and security. The decline of trade further strengthened the position of the landed nobility, whose large estates, or manors, sought to become economically self-sufficient. In addition, the nobility became increasingly dependent on military service provided by a professional force of heavily armed mounted knights, many of whom lived in the houses of their noble retainers in return for their military service.

In most parts of western Europe, where an effective centralized government was entirely absent, personal safety and security became the primary concerns of most individuals. Many historians have used the term *feudalism* to apply to the individual and unique political and social patterns resulting from political decentralization and the resulting attempts to ensure personal security.

Feudalism can be described as a system of rights and duties in which political power was exercised locally by private individuals rather than through the bureaucracy of a centralized state. In general, western European feudalism involved three basic elements: (1) a personal element, called *lordship* or *vassalage*, by which one nobleman, the *vassal*, became the follower of a stronger nobleman, the *lord;* (2) a property element, called the **fief** or *benefice* (usually land), which the vassal received from his lord to enable him to fulfill the obligations of being a vassal; and (3) a governmental element, the private exercise of governmental functions over vassals and fiefs.

Feudal Society

In theory, feudalism was a vast hierarchy. At the top stood the king; all the land in his kingdom in theory belonged to him. He kept large areas for his personal use (royal or crown lands) and, in return for the military service of a specified number of mounted knights, invested the highest nobles—such as dukes and counts (in Britain, earls)—with the remainder. Those nobles, in turn, in order to obtain the services of the required number of mounted warriors owed to the king, parceled out large portions of their fiefs to lesser nobles. This process, called *subinfeudation,* was continued in theory until the lowest in the scale of vassals

---

fief—A grant made to a vassal by a feudal lord in exchange for services. The grant usually consisted of land and the labor of the peasants who were bound to that estate. The income the land provided supported the vassal. Dignities, offices, and money rents were also given in fief.

was reached—the single knight whose fief was just sufficient to support one mounted warrior.

By maintaining the king at the head of this theoretical feudal hierarchy, the justification for monarchy was preserved, even though some feudal kings were little more than figureheads who were less powerful than their own vassals.

Relation of Lord and Vassal: The Contract

Personal bonds between lord and vassal were sometimes formally recognized. In the ceremony known as **homage,** the vassal knelt before his lord, or **suzerain,** and promised to be his "man." In the *oath of fealty* that followed, the vassal swore on the Bible or some other sacred object that he would remain true to his lord. Next, in the ritual of *investiture,* a lance, a glove, or even a clump of dirt was handed to the vassal to signify his jurisdiction over the fief. As his part of the contract, the lord was usually obliged to give his vassal protection and justice. In return, the vassal's primary duty was military service. But in addition, the vassal could be obliged to assist the lord in rendering justice in the lord's court. At certain times, as when the lord was captured and needed to be ransomed, the lord also had the right to demand special money payments, called *aids.*

The lord also had certain rights, called feudal *incidents,* regarding the administration of the fief. These included *wardship*—the right to administer the fief during the minority of a vassal's heir—and forfeiture of the fief if a vassal failed to honor his feudal obligations.

Feudal Warfare

The final authority in the early Middle Ages was force, and the general atmosphere of the era was one of potential violence. Aggressive vassals frequently made war upon their lords. But warfare was also considered the normal occupation of the nobility, for success offered glory and rich rewards. If successful, warfare might increase a noble's territory; and, if they produced nothing else, wars and raids kept nobles active. To die in battle was an appropriate end for a warrior, much preferred to death in restful circumstances.

Medieval society essentially consisted of three classes: nobles, peasants, and the clergy. Each of these groups had its tasks to perform. The nobles were primarily fighters, belonging to an honored level of society distinct from peasant workers—freemen or serfs. In an age of violence, society obviously accorded prominence to the man with the sword rather than to one with a hoe. The church drew on both the noble and peasant classes for the clergy. Although most higher churchmen were sons of nobles and held land as vassals under the feudal system, the clergy formed a class that was considered separate from the nobility and the peasantry.

The Church and Feudalism

A natural development linked to the decentralization of political power in the early Middle Ages was the involvement of the church in feudalism. The unsettled conditions caused by the Viking and Magyar invasions forced church officials to enter into close relations with the only power able to offer them protection—the feudal nobles in France and Germany. Bishops and abbots often became vassals, receiving fiefs for which they were obligated to provide the usual feudal services. The papacy was also affected; during much of the tenth and early eleventh centuries, the papacy became a political prize sought by Roman nobles.

In spite of its inevitable involvement in politics, the church also sought to influence for the better the behavior of the feudal warrior nobility. In addition to attempting to add Christian virtues to the code of knightly conduct (chivalry), the church sought to impose limitations on feudal warfare. In the eleventh century bishops urged the knights to observe the "Peace of God" and the "Truce of God." The Peace of God banned from the sacraments all those who pillaged sacred places or harmed noncombatants. The Truce of God established "closed seasons" on fighting: from sunset on Wednesday to sunrise on Monday and certain longer periods, such as Lent. These attempts to impose peace, however, were generally unsuccessful.

Chivalry

One of the most interesting legacies of the Middle Ages is its concept of chivalry, a code of conduct that was to govern the behavior of all knights. Early chivalric conduct, emerging during the eleventh century, stressed the warrior virtues that were essential in medieval society: prowess in combat, courage, and loyalty to one's lord and fellow warriors. By the twelfth and thirteenth centuries, many of the rigorous aspects of earlier feudal life had given way to a more peaceful and relaxed lifestyle made possible in a more settled and secure Europe. In a sense, when feudal knights began to occupy themselves with chivalric deeds and

---

homage—A pledge by a vassal to be the lord's "man" (*homo* in Latin means "man"), vowing loyalty and service to his superior. Homage created an unconditional bond between a vassal and his lord.

suzerain—A ruler, or even a state, that exercises political control over a dependent individual or state; a feudal overlord.

gentlemanly pursuits of court life, feudalism itself became a dying institution.

At the height of its development, chivalry was a combination of three elements: warfare, religion, and reverence toward women. It required the knight to fight faithfully for his lord, champion the church, aid the humble, and honor women. Unfortunately, practice often differed from theory. The average knight was more superstitious than religious, and he continued to fight, plunder, and abuse women, especially those of the lower class.

From boyhood, men of the nobility underwent a rigid training for knighthood. At the age of seven, a boy was usually sent to the household of a relative, a friend, or the father's lord. There he became a page, learning the rudiments of manners, hawking, and hunting and undergoing training in the fundamentals of religion. At about 15 or 16, he became a squire and prepared himself seriously for the art of war. He learned to ride a war house with dexterity and to handle a sword, shield, and lance correctly. The squire also waited on his lord and lady at the table and learned music, poetry, and games.

If not already knighted on the battlefield for valor, the squire was usually considered eligible for knighthood at the age of 21. By the twelfth century, the church claimed a role in the ceremony, investing it with impressive symbolism. The future knight took a bath to symbolize purity and washed his weapons before the altar in an all-night vigil, confessing his sins and making a resolution to be a worthy knight. During the solemn Mass that followed, his sword was blessed on the altar by a priest. The climax of the ceremony came when the candidate, kneeling before his lord, received a light blow on the neck or shoulder (the *accolade*). The ceremony was designed to impress upon the knight that he must be virtuous and valiant, loyal to his overlord and his God.

The Lives of the Nobles

Life for the nobles centered around the castle. The earliest of these structures, mere wooden blockhouses, were built in the ninth century. Not until the twelfth and thirteenth centuries were massive castles constructed entirely of stone.

The donjon, or central tower, was the focal point of the castle; it was surrounded by an open space that contained storerooms, workshops, and a chapel. The outside walls of the castle were surrounded by turrets from which arrows, boiling oil, and various missiles might be showered upon attackers. Beyond the wall was the moat, a steep-sided ditch filled with water to deter the enemy. The only entrance to the castle lay across the drawbridge. The portcullis, a heavy iron grating that could be lowered rapidly to protect the gate, was a further barrier against intrusion.

Bodiam Castle, England

Life in the castle was anything but comfortable or ideal. The lord at first dwelt in the donjon, but by the thirteenth century, most had built more spacious quarters. Because the castle was designed for defense, it possessed no large windows, and the rooms were dark and gloomy. The stone walls were bare except for occasional tapestries hung to cut down on drafts and dampness, and a huge fireplace provided the only warmth.

The average noble derived his pleasures primarily from outdoor sports, among which warfare might be included. In peacetime the joust and tournament substituted for actual battle. The joust was a conflict between two armed knights, each equipped with a blunted lance with which one attempted to unseat the other. The tournament was a general melee in which groups of knights attacked each other. Often fierce fighting ensued, with frequent casualties.

The nobles were fond of hunting, and the constant demand for fresh meat afforded a legitimate excuse for galloping over the countryside. Most hunting was done in the nearby forests, but at times an unlucky peasant's crops might be ruined during hunts.

A similar outdoor pastime, which lords, ladies, and even high church dignitaries delighted in, was falconry: hunting with predatory birds. The hawks were reared with great care, and large groups of lords and ladies spent many afternoons eagerly wagering with one another as to whose falcon would bring down the first victim. Nobles often attended Mass with hooded falcons on their wrists.

Indoor amusements included the universally popular diversions of backgammon, dice, and chess. Nights were sometimes enlivened by the entertainment of jesters. At other times, a wandering minstrel entertained his noble hosts in exchange for a bed and a place at the table.

Noble women generally shared the lifestyles of their husbands. Even the nobility had to make the most of life in a crude and often brutal age devoid of many refinements. Like her husband, a medieval woman was expected to devote herself to days of hard work with little time for leisure. Many a noble woman was charged with the administration of the manor and the regulation of its peasants while the lord was otherwise occupied. She may also have presided over the court of the lord's vassals on occasion and generally been charged with the control of the finances for the manor.

The Early Medieval Economy: Manorialism

The economy of the early Middle Ages reflected the localism and self-sufficiency that resulted from the

The manor, the self-contained economic unit of early medieval life, operated on a system of reciprocal rights and obligations based on custom. In return for protection, strips of arable land, and the right to use the nonarable common land, the peasant paid dues and worked on the lord's demesne. Under the three-field system, one-third of the land lay fallow so that intensive cultivation did not exhaust the soil.

lack of an effective central government in Europe. The economic and social system based on the manors, the estates held by the nobles, was referred to as *manorialism.*

The manor usually varied in size from one locality to another; a small one might contain only about a dozen households. Since the allotment of land to each family averaged about 30 acres, the smallest manors probably had about 350 acres of land suitable for farming, not counting meadows, woods, wasteland, and the lord's **demesne**—the land reserved for the lord's use alone. A large manor might contain 50 families in a total area of 5000 acres.

The center of the manor was the village, in which the thatched cottages of the peasants were grouped together along one street. Around each cottage was a space large enough for a vegetable patch, chicken yard, haystack, and stable. An important feature of the landscape was the village church, together with the priest's house and the burial ground. The lord's dwelling might be a fortified house or a more modest dwelling.

Distribution of the Land

Every manor contained arable and nonarable land. Part of the arable land was reserved for the lord and was cultivated for him by his serfs; the remainder was held by the villagers. The nonarable land, consisting of meadow, wood, and wasteland, was used in common by the villagers and the lord.

---

desmesne—Part of the land that is owned by the lord. The demesne is the land upon which the lord built his manor house.

From one-sixth to one-third of the arable land was given over to the lord's demesne. The arable land not held in demesne was allotted among the villagers under the open-field system, in which the fields were subdivided into strips. The strips, each containing about an acre, were separated by narrow paths of uncultivated land. The serf's holding was not all in one plot, for all soil throughout the manor was not equally fertile, and an attempt was made to give each of the villagers land of the same quality. Each tenant was really a shareholder in the village community, not only in the open fields but also in the meadow, pasture, wood, and wastelands.

Wooded land was valuable as an area to graze pigs, the most common animal on the manor. Tenants could also gather dead wood in the forest, but cutting down green wood was prohibited unless authorized by the lord.

Medieval Farming Methods

It is difficult to generalize about agricultural methods, because differences in locality, fertility of soil, crop production, and other factors resulted in a variety of farming approaches. Farming as practiced in northwestern Europe was characterized by some common factors. The implements the peasants used were extremely crude; the plow was a cumbersome instrument with heavy wheels, often requiring as many as eight oxen to pull it. (By the twelfth century the use of plow horses had become common.) Other tools included crude harrows, sickles, beetles for breaking up clods, and flails for threshing.

Inadequate methods of farming soon exhausted the soil. The average yield per acre was only 6 to 8 bushels of wheat, one-fourth the modern yield. In classical times farmers had learned that soil planted continually with one crop rapidly deteriorated. As a counteraction, they employed a two-field system: half of the arable land was planted while the other half lay fallow to recover its fertility. Medieval farmers learned that wheat or rye could be planted in the autumn as well as in the spring. As a result, by the ninth century, they were dividing the land into three fields, with one planted in the fall, another in the spring, and the third left lying fallow. This system not only kept more land in production but also required less plowing in any given year.

Both peasant men and women usually had to endure backbreaking labor. While the men usually attended to the daily manual labor of farming, peasant women cooked, cleaned, made clothing, maintained the animals, milked cows, made butter and cheese, brewed ale and beer, and nurtured the gardens. Women assisted the men during planting and

Both peasant men and women toiled in the fields. Here women reap with sickles, while behind them a man binds the sheaves.

harvesting seasons and with any seasonal or special projects endorsed by the lord. The sexes were treated fairly equally on the lower social levels in the Middle Ages—there was not much difference in the demanding lifestyle all had to endure.

Administration of the Manor

Although the lord might live on one of his manors, each manor was usually administered by such officials as the steward, the bailiff, and the reeve. The steward was the general overseer who supervised the business of all his lord's manors and presided over the manorial court. It was the bailiff's duty to supervise the cultivation of the lord's demesne; collect rents, dues, and fines; and inspect the work done by the free peasants (freemen) and the nonfree peasants (serfs). The reeve was the "foreman" of the villagers, chosen by them and representing their interests.

Freemen often lived on the manor, although they constituted only a small portion of its population. Freemen were not subject to the same demands as the serfs. The freeman did not have to work in the lord's fields himself but could send substitutes. Serfs, however, were bound to the manor and could not leave without the lord's consent. Serfdom was a hereditary status; the children of serfs were attached to the soil, just as their parents were.

The lord of the manor was bound by custom to respect certain rights of his serfs. As long as they paid their dues and services, serfs could not be evicted from their hereditary holdings. Although a serf could not appear in court against his lord or a freeman, he could appeal to the manor court against any of his fellows. To the serfs, the manor was the center of their very existence, but to the lord the manor was essentially a source of income and subsistence.

Life of the Peasants

On the manors of the Middle Ages, the margin between starvation and survival was narrow, and the life of the peasant was not easy. Famines were frequent; warfare was a constant threat; and grasshoppers, locusts, caterpillars, and rats repeatedly destroyed the crops. Men, women, and children alike had to toil long hours in the fields.

Home life offered few comforts. The typical peasant dwelling was a cottage with mud walls, clay floor, and thatched roof. The fire burned on a flat hearthstone in the middle of the floor; unless the peasant was rich enough to afford a chimney, the smoke escaped through a hole in the roof. The window openings had no glass and were stuffed with straw in the winter. Furnishings were meager, usually consisting of a table, a kneading trough for dough, a cupboard, and a bed, often either a heap of straw or a box filled with straw, which served the entire family. Pigs and chickens wandered about the cottage continually; the stable was often under the same roof, next to the family quarters.

The peasants, despite their hard, monotonous life, enjoyed a few pleasures. Wrestling was popular, as were cockfighting, a crude type of football, and fighting with quarterstaves, during which contestants stood an excellent chance of getting their heads bashed in. Dancing, singing, and drinking were popular pastimes, especially on the numerous holy days and festivals promoted by the church.

THE REVIVAL OF TRADE AND TOWNS

■ *How did the revival of trade and towns impact the feudal and manorial systems?*

Even though manorialism attempted to secure economic self-sufficiency, an increase in trade and commercial activity in Europe was obvious after the tenth century. The opening of the Mediterranean to European trade was instrumental in increasing trade and commerce. In the eleventh century Normans and Italians broke the Muslim hold on commerce in the eastern Mediterranean, and the First Crusade (see p. 275) revived trade with the Near East. Early in the fourteenth century an all-sea route connected the Mediterranean with northern Europe via the Strait of Gibraltar. The old overland route from northern Italy through the Alpine passes to central Europe was also reopened.

Along the main European trade routes, lords set up fairs, where merchants and goods from Italy and northern Europe met. During the twelfth and thirteenth centuries the fairs of Champagne in France functioned as the major clearinghouse for this international trade.

Factors in the Revival of Towns

The resurgence of trade in Europe was a prime cause of the revival of towns; the towns arose because of trade, but they also stimulated trade by providing greater markets and by producing goods for the merchants to sell. Rivers were important in the development of medieval towns; they were natural highways on which articles of commerce could be easily transported.

Another factor contributing to the rise of towns was population growth. In Britain, for example, the population more than tripled between 1066 and 1350. The reasons for this rapid increase in population are varied. The ending of bloody foreign invasions and, in

some areas, the stabilization of feudal society were contributing factors. More significant was an increase in food production brought about by the cultivation of wastelands, clearing of forests, and draining of marshes. Medieval towns were not large by modern standards. Before 1200 a European town of 20,000 was considered very large, in contrast to such cities as Baghdad, Cairo, and Constantinople—all of which were well over 50,000 in population.

Merchant and Craft Guilds

In each town the merchants and artisans organized themselves into **guilds**. There were two kinds of guilds: merchant and craft. The merchant guild, whose members were the more prosperous and influential of the town's commercial leaders, existed to ensure a monopoly of trade for its members within a given locality. All foreign merchants were supervised closely and made to pay tolls. Disputes among merchants were settled at the guild court according to its

guilds—An organization of people who practice a similar occupation and come together to protect their own professional standards and social interests.

A guild master judges the work of two craftsmen, a mason and a carpenter.

own legal code. The guilds also tried to ensure that the customers were not cheated: they checked weights and measures and insisted on a standard quality for goods. To allow only a legitimate profit, the guild fixed a "just price," which was fair to both producer and customer.

With the increase of commerce in the towns, artisans and craftspeople in each of the medieval trades—weaving, cobbling, tanning, and so on—began to organize as early as the eleventh century. The result was the craft guild, which differed from the merchant guild in that membership was limited to artisans in one particular craft.

The craft guild also differed from the merchant guild in its recognition of three distinct classes of workers: apprentices, journeymen, and master craftsmen. The apprentice was a youth who lived at the master's house and was taught the trade thoroughly. Although the apprentice received no wages, all his physical needs were supplied. Apprenticeship commonly lasted seven years. When the apprentice's schooling was finished, the youth became a journeyman. He was then eligible to receive wages and to be hired by a master. About age 23, the journeyman sought admission into the guild as a master. To be accepted he had to prove his ability. Some crafts demanded the production of a "master piece," for example, a pair of shoes that the master shoemakers would find acceptable in every way.

Very few women, usually widows of guild members, were allowed admittance into a craft guild. In Paris in 1300, for instance, there were approximately 200 craft guilds, with nearly 80 including members of both sexes. There were, however, about a dozen guilds restricted to female trades, such as the making of garments, silk, and lace.

In spite of restrictions placed on women's full participation in the guild structure, women played a vital role in the functioning of every craft guild. The home remained the center of production in every medieval town, and the wife and daughters of the master craftsman assisted him in every facet of his profession. Not only did they oversee domestic household duties, they also were relied upon to assist in the production of whatever goods the guildsman produced. They would work with the apprentices and the journeymen; if girls were placed as apprentices, they were usually supervised directly by the wife of the guildsman. The wife of the master craftsman was essential to the operation of business; in most cases, she sold merchandise, kept the financial records, and fed and paid the employees. Because of their experience and skills, such women often took over the shop after their husband's death.

The guild's functions stretched beyond business and politics into charitable and social activities. A guild member who fell into poverty received aid from the guild. The guild also provided financial assistance for the burial expense of its members and looked after their dependents. Members attended social meetings in the guildhall and periodically held processions in honor of their patron saints.

The guilds played an important role in local government. Both artisans and merchants were subject to the feudal lord or bishop in whose domain the city stood. Gradually, the citizens of the towns came to resent their overlord's collecting tolls and dues as though they were serfs. The townspeople demanded the privileges of governing themselves—of making their own laws, administering their own justice, levying their own taxes, and issuing their own coinage. The overlord resisted these demands for self-government, but the towns were able to win their independence in various ways.

THE CHURCH IN THE HIGH MIDDLE AGES: 1000–1348

■ *How did the church and its leaders hold such power and influence over European society?*

During the High Middle Ages the church became more extensively involved in the structure of society and, of necessity, more concerned with temporal affairs. Always a spiritual force in Europe, the church grew in political and economic importance through the assertive and able leadership of the papacy and the bureaucracy that served the popes in Rome. By the middle of the fourteenth century, the church had emerged as a dominant political as well as spiritual force in European life.

Monastic Reform

A religious revival, often called the "medieval reformation," began in the tenth century and grew to exercise strong influence in the twelfth and thirteenth centuries. The first manifestation of the revival was the reformed Benedictine order of monks at Cluny (KLOO-nee), in present-day France, founded in 910. The ultimate goal of these Cluniac reformers was to free the church from secular control and subject it to papal authority.

CASE STUDY

Monks and Warriors

The most aggressive advocate of church reform in the High Middle Ages was Pope Gregory VII (1073–1085), who claimed unprecedented power for the papacy. In 1075 Gregory VII formally prohibited lay investiture (bestowal of the symbols of the churchman's office by a secular official such as a king) and threatened to excommunicate (expel from the Roman Catholic Church) any layman who performed it. The climax to the struggle occurred in Gregory's clash with the German emperor Henry IV (see p. 282).

Late in the eleventh century a second wave of monastic reform produced several new orders of monks, among which were the Cistercians. The Cistercian movement received its greatest inspiration from the efforts of St. Bernard of Clairvaux (klahr-VOH; 1091–1153). This order's abbeys were intentionally located in solitary places, and their strict discipline emphasized fasts and vigils, manual labor, and a vegetarian diet. Their churches contained neither stained glass nor statues, and Bernard denounced the beautification of churches in general as unnecessary distraction from spiritual dedication.

The Papacy's Zenith: Innocent III

Under Innocent III (1198–1216) a new type of administrator-pope emerged, and papal power reached an unprecedented height. Unlike Gregory VII and other earlier reform popes, who were monks, Innocent and other great popes of the late twelfth and thirteenth centuries were lawyers trained in the newly revived and enlarged church, or canon, law.

The unity and power of the church rested not only on a systematized, uniform religious creed but also on the most highly organized and efficient administrative system in western Europe. The church was far ahead of secular states in developing a system of courts and a body of law. Canon law was based on the Scriptures, the writings of the church fathers, and the decrees of church councils and popes. But the papacy's chief weapons to support its authority were spiritual penalties. The most powerful of these was excommunication. A person who

was excommunicated was deprived of the sacraments of the church and in effect condemned to hell should a person die while excommunicated.

Interdict was also a powerful instrument of punishment and control. While excommunication was directed against individuals, interdiction suspended all public worship and withheld most sacraments in the realm of a disobedient subject. Pope Innocent III successfully applied or threatened the interdict 85 times against disobedient kings and princes.

Heresy

Heresy, the belief in doctrines officially condemned by the church, once again became a great concern in the High Middle Ages. Numerous spiritual ideas found new audiences particularly in the newly revived towns, where changing social and spiritual needs went largely ignored by churchmen more traditional in outlook.

For ten years Innocent III tried to combat the growth and popularity of new heretical groups. Unsuccessful, he instigated a crusade against the prosperous and cultured French region of Toulouse, where

Giotto, Pope Innocent III (1198–1216) Approves the Franciscan Rule. *In this predella (part of a series of paintings on the base of an altar) by the Florentine painter Giotto (1266–1337), Innocent III, accompanied by high-ranking churchmen, is shown approving the Franciscan order of monks by giving the approving document to St. Francis (center) and his humble followers. Legend says that the pope had a dream in which he was instructed by God to give approval to the Franciscans.*

the heretics were attacked in 1208 with the approval of the pope. Soon, the original religious motive was lost in a selfish rush to seize the wealth of the accused.

In 1233 a special papal court, the Inquisition, was established to cope with the rising tide of heresy and to bring about religious conformity. Those accused were tried in secret without the aid of legal counsel. Those who confessed and renounced heresy were "reconciled" with the church on performance of penance. Those who did not voluntarily confess could be tortured. If torture failed, the prisoners could be declared heretics and turned over to the secular authorities, usually to be burned at the stake.

Franciscans and Dominicans

As a more positive response to the spread of heresy and the conditions that caused it, Innocent III approved the founding of the Franciscan and Dominican orders of *friars* ("brothers"). Instead of living in remote monasteries, the friars of these orders moved among the people—especially in the quickly growing towns—ministering to their needs, preaching the Gospel, and teaching in the schools.

The Franciscans were founded by St. Francis of Assisi (c. 1182–1226), who rejected riches and emphasized a spiritual message of poverty and Christian simplicity. Love of one's fellow human beings and all God's creatures, even "brother worm," was basic in the Rule of St. Francis.

The second order of friars was founded by St. Dominic (1170–1221), a well-educated Spaniard who had fought the heretics in southern France. There, he decided that to combat the strength and zeal of its opponents, the church should have champions who could preach the Gospel with the dedication of the apostles. The friar-preachers of Dominic's order dedicated themselves to preaching as a means of maintaining the doctrines of the church and of converting heretics.

The enthusiasm and sincerity of the friars in their early years made a profound impact on an age that had grown increasingly critical of the worldliness of the church. But after they took charge of the Inquisition, became professors in the universities, and served in the papal bureaucracy in a variety of capacities, the original simplicity of the spiritual message became lost. Yet their message and zeal had done much to provide the church with moral and intellectual leadership at a time when such leadership was badly needed.

Education and the Origins of Universities

Before the twelfth century, almost all education was under the control and direction of the church. When schools run by monasteries began limiting their admissions to men preparing for church careers, students interested in educations for careers outside the church began to pressure for admittance to schools administered by cathedrals. Although the cathedral schools were still run by churchmen and taught a curriculum centered on religion, these schools steadily expanded their subject offerings to attract students who were pursuing secular careers. Cathedral schools were also more accepting of the new knowledge made available to western Europe by Byzantine and Moslem scholars. Translations of classical works of philosophy (most importantly the works of Aristotle on logic), medicine, and Roman law, accompanied by analyses and commentaries by Islamic scholars, were reintroduced to western Europe. Much of this revived interest can be attributed to an increasing interest in Islamic culture, brought about partially through contacts established during the crusades, and through the revival of international trade. The result was an intellectual revival that invigorated the interest of scholars and students in the cathedral schools.

The development of professional studies in law, medicine, and theology led to the development of universities, which soon eclipsed or expanded the cathedral schools as centers of learning. The word *university* meant a group of persons pursuing a common purpose—a guild of learners, both teachers and students, similar to a craft guild with their masters and apprentices. In the thirteenth century universities had no campuses and little or no money, and the masters taught in rented rooms or religious buildings. If the university was dissatisfied with its treatment by townspeople or the administration, it could move elsewhere. The earliest universities—at Bologna, Paris, and Oxford—were not officially founded, but in time popes or kings granted them and other universities charters of self-government.

Scholasticism

Most medieval scholars did not think of truth as something to be discovered by themselves: They saw it as already existing in the authoritative Christian and a select few non-Christian texts of antiquity. By employing reason (through the use of logic or **dialectic**), scholars of the twelfth and thirteenth centuries attempted to understand and express truth through this process of explanation. Since this task was carried out almost exclusively in the schools, these scholars are known as Scholastics, and the intellectual method they designed is called *Scholasticism*.

Scholasticism reached its highest development in the works of Thomas Aquinas (ah-KWAI-nahs;

---

dialectic—Logical discussion or logical argumentation.

c. 1225–1274). In his *Summa Theologica* ("summation of theology") this brilliant Dominican philosopher and theologian attempted to reconcile the works of Aristotle with church **dogma**—in other words, the truths obvious through natural reason with the truths held through faith. There can be no real contradiction between the two, he argued, since all truth comes ultimately from God. In case of an unresolved contradiction, however, faith won out because of the possibility of human error in reasoning.

Women and Learning

In the early Middle Ages, and especially after the eighth century, the convents of Europe served as centers of learned activity for a very select group of aristocratic and middle-class women who pursued an intellectual life as well as one devoted to faith. But outside the convents, a life devoted to scholarship was almost impossible for a medieval woman; the church taught that a woman should be either a housewife or a virgin in service to her God. Rarely was it possible for a woman to write, compose, or create works of scholarship or literature in such a society.

But intellectual achievement by some exceptional medieval women was possible. One such remarkable example was Hildegard of Bingen (1098–1179), the leader of a community of Benedictine nuns in Germany. Hildegard wrote a mystical work describing her visions, which she began to receive at the age of 42. She was also a skilled composer and the author of a morality play and several scientific works, which cataloged nearly 500 plants, animals, and stones, assessing their medicinal values.

THE CRUSADES

■ *What was the influence of the Crusades on European and world history?*

DOCUMENT

An Arab-Syrian Discusses the Franks

The Crusades, a series of campaigns that began toward the end of the eleventh century, were a remarkable expression of European self-confidence and expansion in the High Middle Ages. The church was instrumental in beginning these efforts to recapture the Holy Land from Muslim control. But by the conclusion of the crusading era, the church, and the papacy in particular, had suffered a serious loss of prestige, largely because of its actions related to the crusading movement.

dogma—A set of beliefs that are accepted as true by a church. A doctrine put forward with authority. From a Greek word meaning "to seem (good)."

For hundreds of years peaceful pilgrims had been traveling from Europe to worship at the sites held to be significant to events described in the New Testament. But during the eleventh century, Christian pilgrims to the Holy Land became especially concerned when the Seljuk Turks, recent and fervent converts to Islam, took over Jerusalem from the more lenient Abbasid Muslims.

In 1095 Pope Urban II proclaimed the First Crusade to establish Christian control of the Holy Land. Preaching at the Council of Clermont in that year, he called on Christians to take up the cross and strive for a cause that promised not merely spiritual rewards but material gain as well. Following Urban's appeal, there was a spontaneous outpouring of religious enthusiasm. The word *crusade* itself is derived from "taking the cross," after the example of Christ.

The Crusading Expeditions

From the end of the eleventh through the thirteenth century, seven major crusades, as well as numerous small expeditions, warred against the Muslims, whom the crusaders called *Saracens*. The First Crusade, composed of feudal nobles from France, parts of Germany, and Norman Italy, marched overland through eastern Europe to Constantinople. Expecting the help of skilled European mercenaries against the Seljuk Turks, the Byzantine emperor Alexius Comnenus was shocked when confronted by a disorderly mob of crusaders and quickly ushered them out of Constantinople to fight the Turks. This First Crusade was the most successful of the seven; with not more than 5000 knights and infantry, it overcame the resistance of the Turks, who were at the time no longer united. It captured Jerusalem and a narrow strip of land stretching from there to Antioch, which became known as the Latin Kingdom of Jerusalem, and over which crusaders and Islamic armies continued to battle until the region was finally retaken by the Muslims in 1291.

IMAGE

Crusaders Besieging a Medieval Castle

The fall of Jerusalem to the Muslims, reinvigorated under the leadership of Salah-al-Din (SAH-lah-ahl-DEEN) or Saladin, the sultan of Egypt and Syria, inspired the Third Crusade in 1189. Its leaders were three of the most famous medieval kings—Frederick Barbarossa of Germany, Richard the Lion-Hearted of England, and Philip Augustus of France. Frederick drowned in Asia Minor, and, after many quarrels with Richard, Philip returned home. Saladin and Richard remained to fight but finally agreed to a three-year truce and free access to Jerusalem for Christian pilgrims.

The Fourth Crusade (1202–1204) was a disaster from both a religious and economic perspective. No kings answered the call of Pope Innocent III for the crusade, and the knights who did participate were unable to pay the Venetians

MAP

The Crusades

the agreed-on transport charges. The Venetians persuaded the crusaders to pay off their debts by capturing the Christian town of Zara on the Adriatic coast, which had long proved a successful rival to Venetian trading interests. Then, in order to eliminate Byzantine commercial competition, the Venetians pressured the crusaders to attack Constantinople itself. After conquering and sacking the great city, the crusaders set up the Latin Empire of Constantinople and forgot about their intentions of recovering the Holy Land.

The thirteenth century produced other crusading failures. The boys and girls participating in the Children's Crusade of 1212 fully expected the waters of the Mediterranean to part and make a path from southern France to the Holy Land, which they would take without fighting; instead, thousands of them were sold into slavery by the merchants of Marseilles. The Seventh Crusade was the last major attempt to regain Jerusalem; the crusading movement ended in 1291 when Acre, the last stronghold of the Christians in the Holy Land, fell to the Muslims.

The Crusader States

Four crusader states, with the kingdom of Jerusalem dominant, were established along the eastern Mediterranean coast as a result of the crusading movement. By the time Jerusalem fell to Saladin in 1187, however, only isolated pockets of Christians remained, surrounded by Muslims. The crusader states were able to cling to survival only through frequent delivery of supplies and manpower from Europe.

The crusader states were defended primarily by three semimonastic military orders: the Templars, or Knights of the Temple, so called because their first headquarters was on the site of the old Temple of Jerusalem; the Hospitalers, or Knights of St. John of Jerusalem, who were founded originally to care for the sick and wounded; and the Teutonic Knights, exclusively a German order. Combining monasticism and militarism, these orders served to protect all pilgrims and to wage perpetual war against the Muslims.

From the eleventh to the thirteenth century, seven major crusades were launched from western Europe for the purpose of taking possession of the Holy Land—portions of the eastern Mediterranean significant to Christians because of their association with the life of Jesus. Although the Crusades eventually failed to annex large amounts of territory for western states, they brought about a broadening perspective and appreciation for Byzantine and Muslim culture on the part of many western Europeans.

Muslim and Christian: Two Contemporary Perspectives

This first selection describes the bloody fall of Jerusalem to the Christians during the First Crusade in 1099, as witnessed by the author, a Frankish knight. He writes with the certainty of religious justification for his cause, and cultural superiority to the Muslim enemy.

In comparison to the Frankish evaluations of their Islamic rivals, the second account, from the Muslim perspective, appears in the writings of a Muslim physician who encountered the crusaders and obviously found their culture not as impressive as his own.

During this siege, we suffered so badly from thirst that we sewed up the skins of oxen and buffaloes, and we used to carry water in them for the distance of nearly six miles. We drank the water from these vessels, although it stank, and what with foul water and barley bread we suffered great distress and affliction every day, for the Saracens used to lie in wait for our men by every spring and pool, where they killed them and cut them to pieces; moreover they used to carry off the beasts into their caves and secret places in the rocks.

At last, when the pagans were defeated, our men took many prisoners, both men and women, in the Temple. They killed whom they chose, and whom they chose they saved alive. After this our men rushed round the whole city, seizing the gold and silver, horses and mules, and houses full of all sorts of goods, and they all came rejoicing and weeping from excess of gladness to worship at the Sepulchre of our Savior Jesus, and there they fulfilled their vows to him. Next morning they went cautiously up on to the Temple roof and attacked the Saracens, both men and women, cutting off their heads with drawn swords. No-one has ever seen or heard of such a slaughter of pagans, for they were burned on pyres like pyramids, and no-one save God alone knows how many there were.

From Rosalind Hill, ed., *Gesta Francorum* (London: Nelson, 1962). Reprinted by permission of Oxford University Press, Oxford.

Glory be to Allah, the creator and author of all things! Anyone who is acquainted with what concerns the Franks can only glorify and sanctify Allah the All-Powerful; for he has seen in them animals who are superior in courage and in zeal for fighting but in nothing else, just as beasts are superior in strength and aggressiveness.

I will report some Frankish characteristics and my . . . surprise as to their intelligence. . . .

Among the curiosities of medicine among the Franks, I will tell how the governor of Al-Mounaitira wrote to my uncle to ask him to send him a doctor who would look after some urgent cases. My uncle chose a Christian doctor named Thabit (?). . . . Thabit replied: "They brought before me a knight with an abscess which had formed in his leg and a woman who was wasting away with a consumptive fever. I applied a little plaster to the knight; his abscess opened and took a turn for the better; the woman I forbade certain food and improved her condition." It was at this point that a Frankish doctor came up and said: "This man is incapable of curing them." Then, turning to the knight, he asked, "Which do you prefer, to live with one leg or die with two?" "I would rather live with one leg," the knight answered. "Bring a stalwart knight," said the Frankish doctor, "and a sharp hatchet." Knight and hatchet soon appeared. I was present at the scene. The doctor stretched the patientís leg on a block of wood and then said to the knight, "Strike off his leg with the hatchet; take it off at one blow." Under my eyes the knight aimed a violent blow at it without cutting through the leg. He aimed another blow at the unfortunate man, as a result of which his marrow came from his leg and the knight died instantly. As for the woman, the doctor examined her and said, "She is a woman in whose head there is a devil who has taken possession of her. Shave off her hair!" His prescription was carried out, and like her fellows, she began once again to eat garlic and mustard. Her consumption became worse. The doctor then said, "It is because the devil has entered her head." Taking a razor, the doctor cut open her head in the shape of a cross and scraped away the skin in the centre so deeply that her very bones were showing. He then rubbed the head with salt. In her turn, the woman died instantly. After having asked them whether my services were still required and obtained an answer in the negative, I came back, having learnt to know what I had formerly been ignorant of about their medicine.

—*Usamah Ibn-Munqidh*

From G. R. Potter, trans., *The Autobiography of Ousama (1095–1188)* (London: George Routledge and Sons, 1929), pp. 172–175, 181–182, in Perry M. Rogers, *Aspects of Western Civilization*, Vol. I, 4th ed. (Prentice Hall, 2000), pp. 311–312.

Questions to Consider

1. What seem to be the most significant obstacles to cultural understanding and tolerance in these two accounts of contact between Christian and Muslim cultures?

2. How might we, as modern analysts of this medieval clash of cultures, misinterpret the sentiments expressed in these two documents? What insights might be gained from a comparison of these two viewpoints?

Significance of the Crusades

Even though the Crusades failed to achieve their permanent objective, they were much more than mere military adventures. Much of the crusading fervor spilled over into the Christian attacks against the Muslims in Spain and the Slavs in eastern Europe. The Crusades crucially weakened the Byzantine Empire and accelerated its fall. Although the early Crusades strengthened the moral leadership of the papacy in Europe, the misadventures of the later Crusades, together with the church's preaching of Crusades against Christian heretics and political opponents, weakened both the crusading ideal and respect for the papacy.

But contact with the East through the crusading movement widened the scope of many Europeans, ended their isolation, and exposed them to a civilization with much within it to be admired. The Crusades did influence the reopening of the eastern Mediterranean to Western commerce, a factor that in itself had an effect on the revival of cities and the emergence of a money economy in the West.

THE DEVELOPMENT OF EUROPEAN STATES: 1000–1348

■ *How successful were European monarchs in establishing authority over their territories?*

The first three centuries of the Later Middle Ages in Europe are often described as the High Middle Ages, since many experts see in this period the full development of the earlier culture of post-Roman Europe. In this era, European monarchies struggled to emerge from the decentralized feudal organization of an earlier time. The church rose to great heights of power and authority. The revival of trade and the rebirth of towns altered the economy of Europe and offered an alternative to manorialism. And this period gave birth to developments in art, architecture, and literature that stand as some of the most significant achievements in European civilization.

The High Middle Ages witnessed the efforts of kings to assert themselves once again as forceful rulers of their lands. As we have seen, feudalism was a system founded on the decentralization of authority; the king was often no more than a figurehead in the feudal order. Now, the monarchs of most European states gradually increased their powers at the expense of their feudal nobility. Through such efforts, several of which took centuries to bear results, national monarchies began to take form on the European continent.

The Capetians and the Beginnings of France

In France, by the beginning of the tenth century, more than 30 great feudal princes were vassals of the king, but they gave him little or no support. When the last Carolingian monarch died in 987, the nobles elected one of their number, Hugh Capet (kah-PAY), count of Paris, as successor. The territory that Hugh Capet (987–996) actually controlled was a small feudal county, the Île-de-France (EEL-duh-FRAHNS), extending from Paris to Orléans. These royal lands were surrounded by many large duchies and counties, such as Flanders, Normandy, Anjou, and Champagne, which were fiercely independent.

The major accomplishment of the first four Capetian (kah-PEE-shi-ahn) kings was their success at keeping the French crown within their own family and at slowly expanding their influence, largely through marriage alliances and the efficiency of the royal courts. With the support of the church, the Capetians cleverly arranged for the election and coronation of their heirs. For 300 years the House of Capet never lacked a male heir.

Philip II Augustus

The first great expansion of the royal domain was the work of Philip II Augustus (1180–1223). Philip's great ambition was to seize from the English kings the vast territory they held in France. Philip took Normandy, Maine, Anjou, and Touraine from the English, and by doing so, he tripled the size of the monarchy's land holdings.

After the brief reign of Philip II's son Louis VIII, France came under the rule of Louis IX (1226–1270), better known as St. Louis. Louis's ideal was to rule justly, and in so doing, he became one of the most beloved kings of France. The king believed himself responsible only to God, who had put him on the throne to lead his people out of a life of sin. Just, sympathetic, and peace-loving, Louis IX convinced his subjects that the monarchy was the most important agency for ensuring their happiness and well-being.

Nation-Building in France

987–996	Reign of Hugh Capet
1108–1137	Reign of Louis VI
1180–1223	Reign of Philip II Augustus
1226–1270	Reign of Louis IX
1285–1314	Reign of Philip IV, the Fair

Height of Capetian Rule Under Philip IV

The reign of Philip IV, known as Philip the Fair (1285–1314), culminated three centuries of Capetian rule. The opposite of his saintly grandfather, Philip was a man of violence and cunning, tireless in his effort to make the monarchy supreme in France. Aware that anti-Semitism was growing in Europe in the wake of the Crusades, he expelled the Jews from France and confiscated their possessions.

DOCUMENT
Summa de legibus

Philip's need for money also brought him into conflict with the last great medieval pope. Boniface VIII refused to allow Philip to tax the French clergy and made sweeping claims to supremacy over secular powers. But Philip IV would not tolerate papal interference, and the result was the humiliation of Boniface (see Chapter 14), a blow from which the influence of the medieval papacy never recovered. In domestic affairs, the real importance of Philip's reign lay in the king's ability to increase the power and improve the organization of the royal government. Philip's astute civil servants, recruited mainly from the middle class, sought to make the power of the monarch absolute.

Philip enlarged his feudal council to include representatives of the third "estate" or class, the townspeople. This Estates-General of nobles, clergy, and burghers was used to obtain popular support for Philip's policies, including the announcement of new taxes. Philip did not ask the Estates-General's consent for his tax measures; thus, this body did not acquire a role in decisions affecting taxation. By the middle of the fourteenth century, France was well organized, unified in support of a strong monarch, and ready to assert itself as a power on the continent.

England to 1348

Most of England in 1000 was ruled by an Anglo-Saxon monarchy threatened by conquest from the Danish king Canute (ka-NOOT). In 1016 Canute conquered the island and ruled it until his death in 1035, when England returned to an Anglo-Saxon monarchy that was challenged both by the Danes and by William, the duke of Normandy, who claimed the throne on a questionable hereditary right.

William and his army of 5000 men crossed the English Channel to enforce his claim to the throne. In 1066 the duke's mounted knights defeated the English infantry at Hastings, and William became king of England (1066–1087), where he began to introduce the Norman, feudal style of administration. The new king retained some land as his royal domain and granted the remainder as fiefs to royal vassals called *tenants-in-chief*. In return for their fiefs, the tenants-in-chief provided William with a number of knights to serve in his royal army. From all the landholders in England, regardless of whether they were his immediate vassals, William exacted an oath that they would "be faithful to him against all

The Bayeux tapestry, a woolen embroidery on linen, dates from the eleventh century. Over 230 feet long, it depicts the events in the Norman conquest of England in 1066, accompanied by a commentary in Latin and surrounded by a decorative border portraying scenes from fables and everyday life.

other men." Both tenants-in-chief and lesser vassals owed their first allegiance to William.

Henry II

William was succeeded by a number of average or ineffectual rulers, but the monarchy was strengthened by Henry II (1154–1189), the founder of the Plantagenet (plahn-TAH-jehn-et), or Angevin, dynasty. As a result of his inheritance (Normandy and Anjou) and his marriage to Eleanor of Aquitaine (AH-kwi-tayn), the richest heiress in France, Henry's possessions extended from Scotland to the Pyrenees. Henry's great military skill and restless energy were important assets to his reign. He quickly began rebuilding the power of the monarchy in England.

Henry's chief contribution to the development of the English monarchy was to increase the jurisdiction of the royal courts at the expense of the feudal courts. Henry's courts also used the jury system to settle private lawsuits; circuit judges handed down quick decisions based on evidence sworn to by a jury of men selected because they were acquainted with the facts of the case. His judicial reforms stimulated the growth of the common law, one of the most important factors

Henry II's claims to lands in France threatened to absorb the kingdom of France. Note the sizable territory claimed by the English king through his marriage to Eleanor of Aquitaine, once wife of the French king. Though it took hundreds of years, the French eventually gained control of all of the French territories claimed by England.

in unifying the English people; the decisions of the royal justices became the basis for future decisions made in the king's courts and became the law common to all English people.

Thomas à Becket

Although Henry strengthened the royal courts, he was not as successful in regulating the church courts. When he appointed his trusted friend Thomas à Becket archbishop of Canterbury, the king assumed that Becket could easily be persuaded to cooperate, but the new archbishop proved stubbornly independent in upholding the authority of the church courts over the king's. After a number of disagreements in which Becket defended the independence of the English church from royal authority, Henry was reputed to have remarked that he would be relieved if someone would rid England of the troublesome Becket. Responding to this angry remark, four knights went to Canterbury and murdered Becket before the high altar of the cathedral. Popular outrage over this murder destroyed Henry's chances of reducing the power of the church courts.

The Successors of Henry II

Henry's many accomplishments were marred by the mistakes of his successors. Richard the Lion-Hearted (1189–1199) spent only five months of his ten-year reign in Britain, which he regarded as a source of money for his overseas adventures. Richard's successor, his brother John (1199–1216), was an inept and cruel ruler whose unscrupulousness cost him the support of his barons, at the time he needed them most, in his struggles with the two ablest men of the age, Philip II of France and Pope Innocent III. As feudal overlord of John's possessions in France, Philip declared John an unfaithful vassal and his claims to lands in France unwarranted. He also became involved in a struggle with Innocent III that ended in John's complete surrender.

In the meantime, the king alienated the British barons, who rebelled and in 1215 forced him to agree to the Magna Carta, a document that bound the king to observe all feudal rights and privileges. Although in later centuries people looked back on the Magna Carta as one of the most important documents in the history of political freedom, to the English nobility of John's time, the Magna Carta did not appear to break any new constitutional ground. It was essentially a feudal agreement between the barons and the king, the aristocracy and the monarchy. However, two great principles were contained in the charter: The law is above the king, and the king can be compelled by force to obey the law of the land.

A detail of the Carrow Psalter depicts the murder of Thomas à Becket by the knights of Henry II in Canterbury Cathedral. One knight has broken his sword over the archbishop's head.

The Origins of Parliament

The French-speaking Normans commonly used the word *parlement* (from *parler,* "to speak") for the great council. Anglicized as *parliament,* the term was used interchangeably with *great council* and *Curia Regis.*

Nation-Building in England	
871–899	Reign of Alfred the Great of Wessex
1016–1035	Reign of Canute
1066	Battle of Hastings
1066–1087	Reign of William the Conqueror
1154–1189	Henry II begins Plantagenet dynasty
1189–1199	Reign of Richard I, the Lion-Hearted
1199–1216	Reign of John I
1215	Magna Carta
1272–1307	Reign of Edward I

Modern historians, however, generally apply the term to the great council only after 1265, when its membership was radically enlarged. Parliament first became truly influential during the reign of Edward I (1272–1307), one of England's most outstanding monarchs. Beginning with the so-called Model Parliament of 1295, Edward followed the pattern of summoning representatives of shires and towns to meetings of the great council. In calling parliaments, Edward had no intention of making any concession to popular government; rather, he hoped to build popular consensus to support his own policies.

Early in the fourteenth century the representatives of the knights and the townsmen, called the Commons, adopted the practice of meeting separately from the lords. This resulted in the division of Parliament into what came to be called the House of Commons and the House of Lords. Parliament, particularly the Commons, soon discovered its power as a major source of revenue for the king. It gradually became the custom for Parliament to exercise this power by withholding its financial grants until the king had redressed grievances, made known by petitions. Parliament also presented petitions to the king with the request that they be recognized as statutes (laws drawn up by the king and his council and confirmed in Parliament). Gradually, Parliament assumed the right to initiate legislation through petition.

Edward I was the first English king with the goal of being master of the whole island of Great Britain—Wales, Scotland, and England. In 1284, after a five-year struggle, English law and administration were imposed on Wales, and numerous attempts were made to conquer the Scots, who continued to offer Edward serious resistance up to the time of his death. By the time of Edward's death in 1307, England was efficiently organized under a strong monarchy and ready to assert itself in the quest for power on the continent.

Spain to 1348

Unification in Spain took a different course from that in either France or England. Customary rivalry between the Christian feudal nobles and royal authority was complicated by another element: religious fervor. Unification of Christian Spain was not thought possible without the expulsion of the Muslims, with their non-Christian religion and culture.

During the long struggle to drive the Muslims from Spain, patriotism blended with fierce religious devotion. This movement became known as the *Reconquista* (ree-kon-KEE-stah)—the reconquest of Spain from Muslim control. As early as the ninth century, northern Spain became committed to a religious effort to drive all Muslims out of territory Christian Spaniards considered theirs. In the early thirteenth century they captured first Cordova and Seville. The conquest of Seville effectively doubled the territory of the Spanish kingdom. From the end of the thirteenth century, when the Reconquista slowed, until the latter part of the fifteenth century, Muslim political control was confined to Granada. Until the fifteenth century, the Christian victors usually allowed their new Muslim subjects to practice their own religion and traditions. Muslim traders and artisans were protected because of their economic value, and Muslim culture—art in particular—influenced Christian designs and preferences.

Disunity in Germany and Italy

When the last Carolingian ruler of the kingdom of the East Franks died in 911, the great German dukes elected the weakest of their number to hold the title of king. But an exceptionally strong ruler inherited the throne in 936—Otto the Great (936–973), duke of Saxony and

Ivory plaque of Christ and the Emperor Otto I (962–968). This ivory carving shows Christ on a throne and in the process of blessing a model of a church presented to him by the German emperor Otto I (left) and a number of saints (right), including St. Peter, who holds his symbolic keys to the kingdom of heaven. The artist was probably influenced by both Carolingian and Byzantine artistic traditions.

founder of the Saxon dynasty of kings. Otto attempted to control the great dukes by appointing his own relatives and favorites as their rulers. Through alliance with the church, he constructed a stronger German monarchy. Otto himself appointed German bishops and abbots, a practice known as lay investiture; since their offices were not hereditary, he expected that their first obedience was to the king.

Otto the Great wanted to establish a German empire, modeled after Roman and Carolingian examples. The conquest and incorporation of the Italian peninsula into that empire were Otto's primary objectives. He proclaimed himself king of Italy, and in 962 he was crowned emperor by the pope. His empire later became known as the Holy Roman Empire.

The Saxon rulers were the most powerful in Europe. They had permanently halted Magyar advances and, by utilizing the German church as an ally, reduced feudal fragmentation in their homeland. They also fostered economic progress. German eastward expansion had begun, and the Alpine passes had been freed from Muslim control and made safe for Italian merchants.

The Salian Emperors

The Saxon kings were succeeded by the Salian dynasty (1024–1125), whose members also tried to establish a centralized monarchy. Under the emperor Henry IV (1056–1106) the monarchy reached the height of its power, but it also experienced a major reverse. The revival of a powerful papacy led to a bitter conflict with Henry, centering on the king's right to appoint church officials who were also his most loyal supporters (lay investiture). This disagreement between state and church culminated in Henry's begging the pope's forgiveness at Canossa in 1077. This conflict, the Investiture Controversy, resulted in the loss of the monarchy's major sources of strength: the loyalty of the German church, now transferred to the papacy; and the support of the great nobles, now openly rebellious and insistent on their "inborn rights."

The second emperor of the new Hohenstaufen (HOH-hen-stahw-fen) dynasty, Frederick I Barbarossa ("Redbeard"), who ruled from 1152 to 1190, also sought to force the great nobles to acknowledge his overlordship. To maintain his hold over Germany, Frederick needed the resources of Italy. But encouraged by the papacy, the cities of northern Italy had joined together in the Lombard League to resist him. Frederick spent about 25 years fighting intermittently in Italy, but the final result was failure: opposition from the popes and the Lombard League was too strong. Frederick did, however, succeed in marrying his son to the heiress of the throne of the kingdom of Naples and Sicily.

The Holy Roman Empire

962	Otto the Great crowned emperor by the pope
1056–1106	Reign of Henry IV
1152–1190	Frederick I Barbarossa begins Hohenstaufen dynasty
1212–1250	Reign of Frederick II

Barbarossa's grandson, Frederick II (1212–1250), was a remarkable individual. Orphaned at an early age, Frederick was brought up as the ward of Innocent III, the most powerful medieval pope. With the pope's support, Frederick was elected emperor in 1215, one year before Innocent's death. Frederick sacrificed Germany in his efforts to unite Italy under his rule. He transferred crown lands and royal rights to the German princes in order to win their support for his Italian wars. Born in Sicily, he remained devoted to the southern part of his empire. He shaped his kingdom there into a vibrant state. Administered by paid officials who were trained at the University of Naples, which he founded for that purpose, his kingdom was the most centralized and efficiently administered in Europe.

After Frederick's death in 1250, the Holy Roman Empire never again achieved the brilliance it had once enjoyed. Later emperors usually did not try to interfere in Italian affairs, and they ceased going to Rome to receive the imperial crown from the pope. In German affairs the emperors no longer even attempted to assert their authority over the increasingly powerful nobles. By the middle of the fourteenth century Germany was hopelessly divided into more than two hundred political units, each striving for separation from the control of the other.

In 962, Otto the Great was crowned as Holy Roman Emperor by the pope. The dreams of recreating a Christian empire to rival the achievements of ancient Rome were never to be realized. Resistance from powerful German nobles and forceful opposition from the northern Italian communes continually frustrated the ambitions of Otto and his successors, so that the Holy Roman Empire was never able to achieve political centralization.

CONCLUSION

This chapter discusses almost one thousand years of European history: from the collapse of Roman political and economic organization, the migrations of new peoples into the old empire, and the growth in influence of a new religion and culture, to the emergence of strong European states under the leadership of ambitious monarchs. Most of the centuries that we call the European Middle Ages were times typified by conservatism and preservation. Political and economic disunity gave rise to institutions that sought to provide protection and security to all segments of society. That quest for security and stability was also evident in early European Christianity, which rejected the cultural heritage of the ancient world in return for a uniform orthodoxy of belief which sought to provide stability in troubled times. But by the eleventh century European self-imposed isolation and the quest for changelessness was challenged on several fronts. Monarchs disrupted the feudal order by setting in motion the drive toward creation of the modern nation-state. The growth of towns and revival of trade brought about new economic and social priorities. The church, once the partner of the state and the unchallenged authority in matters of spirituality and culture, came under increasing examination and challenge. The unique circumstances brought about in Europe by the collapse of Rome, the rise of Christianity, and the Germanic migrations had produced a society unlike any other in world history—one that would emerge by the fourteenth century as vibrant, creative, aggressive, and about to take a more active part in events on a world stage.

Suggestions for Web Browsing

You can obtain more information about topics included in this chapter at the websites listed below. See also the companion website that accompanies this text, http://www.ablongman.com/brummett, which contains an online study guide and additional resources.

Medieval Studies
http://labyrinth.georgetown.edu/

The Labyrinth project at Georgetown University offers numerous links categorized by national cultures and by artistic genre.

Women in the Middle Ages
http://info-center.ccit.arizona.edu/~ws/ws200/fall97/grp7/grp7.htm

An excellent site for examining the many activities and responsibilities of medieval women, from peasants to nobility.

Internet Medieval Sourcebook
http://www.fordham.edu/halsall/sbook.html

Extremely helpful site containing original course materials from medieval authors and secondary sources dealing with a large variety of medieval subjects.

Middle Ages
http://www.learner.org/exhibits/middleages/

This site, under the direction of the Annenberg/CBS Project, features information and exhibits illustrating what daily life was really like during the Middle Ages.

Medieval Women
http://labyrinth.georgetown.edu/display.cfm?Action=View&Category=Women

Site details the individual lives and works of medieval women, including Hildegard of Bingen; women rulers and creators; and the impact of the Crusades on women, in addition to numerous general resources.

Women Writers of the Middle Ages
http://lib.rochester.edu/camelot/womenbib.htm

Site offers bibliographies of primary and secondary sources by and about medieval women writers.

World of the Vikings
http://www.worldofthevikings.com/

This well-indexed site provides links to almost everything there is to know about these medieval seafarers—their everyday life, their travels, their influence.

Literature and Film

An excellent new edition of the Beowulf epic is Seamus Heaney, ed., *Beowulf: A New Verse Translation* (W. W. Norton, 2001). Outstanding video presentations on the Middle Ages are *Charlemagne* (2000; 5 tapes, Acorn Media); *Landmarks of Western Art: The Medieval World*, Vol. I (Kultur Video, 1999); *The Vikings* (Nova, 2000); *Just the Facts—The Middle Ages* (Goldhil Home Media, 2001); *Music of the Middle Ages* (Timeless Multimedia, 1994); *Sienna: Chronicle of a Medieval Commune* (Home Vision Entertainment, 2000); *Living in the Past: Life in Medieval Times* (Kultur Video, 2000); and *Medieval Warfare* (2000; 3 tapes, Kultur Video). An award-winning feature film set in France during this period is *The Return of Martin Guerre* (Nelson Entertainment, 1982).

Suggestions for Reading

Three excellent surveys of the early Middle Ages are Robert Bartlett, *The Making of Europe: Conquest, Colonization, and Cultural Change, 950–1350* (Princeton University Press, 1993); Rosamond McKitterick, ed., *The Early Middle Ages: Europe 400–1000* (Oxford University Press, 2001); and Richard W. Southern, *The Making of the Middle Ages* (Yale University Press, 1992). For economic and social history, see Werner Roesener, *Peasants in the Middle Ages* (Polity Press, 1996) and Frances Gies and Joseph Gies, *Women in the Middle Ages* (Perennial, 1991), *Life in a Medieval Village* (HarperPerennial, 1991), and *Marriage and Family in the Middle Ages* (HarperPerennial, 1989). For the history of the church, see Peter Brown et al., *The Rise of Western Christendom*, 2nd ed. (Blackwell, 2003), and Jaroslav Pelikan, *The Growth of Medieval Theology*, Vol. 3: The Christian Tradition (University of Chicago Press, 1978), and Michael Haren,

Medieval Thought (Dublin University Press, 1992). On the Crusades, see Jonathan Riley-Smith, ed., *The Oxford History of the Crusades* (Oxford University Press, 1997), and Malcolm Billings, *The Cross and the Crescent* (Sterling, 1987). John Burrow, *The Ages of Man: A Study in Medieval Writing and Thought* (Oxford University Press, 1989) is an outstanding review of medieval literature.

Culture, Power, and Trade in the Era of Asian Hegemony, 220–1350

Asia served as an incubator and transmitter of cultures and religions with global reach from 220 to 1350. As empires consolidated and expanded their boundaries, trade and commerce accompanied cultural diffusion. Human cultures had long migrated globally, but during this long millennium, the pace of international contacts accelerated. Religions, philosophies, and arts deepened their roots in areas that had spawned them, and at the same time, new ideas spread throughout the region.

The first half millennium was, in some ways, Asia's Buddhist Age. In South Asia, Hinduism, and in East Asia, Daoism and Confucianism as well as indigenous religions continued to play important roles. But a Buddhist traveler from East Asia would find co-religionists in lands with remarkably distinct cultures. Buddhism was spread by both missionary activity and commercial activity along the Silk Roads. The second half of the millennium was likewise influenced by a global religion—Islam. South and Southeast Asian rulers either adopted Islam or resisted it, and power and trade networks were influenced by Islamic missionary and commercial activities. China and Northeast Asia felt the impact of nomadic cultures throughout the millennium, and in the twelfth and thirteenth centuries much of East and Central Asia was integrated into a trade and power network controlled by originally nomadic Mongols. Disease—bubonic plague—took advantage of these networks to spread the hand of death throughout Eurasia in the mid-fourteenth century, and ironically, fatally weakened the Mongols, whose dominance in China created fourteenth-century globalism. While Asian power and culture were in many ways hegemonic until that time and Asia would continue to grow and dominate world trade until the eighteenth century, the door was open to the rise of new sites of power, particularly in Europe, during the next few hundred years.

Each Asian civilization produced significant contributions to the world's common culture. India made remarkable advances in mathematics, medicine, chemistry, textile production, and literature, and Buddhism continued its dramatic spread to East and Southeast Asia. China excelled in political organization, scholarship, and the arts, and at the same time produced such revolutionary technical inventions as printing, gunpowder, and the mariner's compass. Maritime trade flourished as Arab, Jewish, and Indian traders crisscrossed the Indian Ocean to the west of the subcontinent, while Indian and Southeast Asian traders plied the waters to the east as far as China and Japan.

Growth in the old Asian centers led naturally toward outward cultural diffusion and a varied exchange of goods, philosophies, literatures, and fashions with bordering civilizations. In Southeast Asia these arose from increasing contacts with India and China through trade, missionary efforts, colonizing, and conquest. First Korea, and then Japan, imported cultural bases from China. Similarly, nomads of Central Asia—Turks, Uighurs (WEE-ghers), Mongols, and numerous other steppe peoples—engaged in a vigorous exchange with China and India (often assimilating the cultural patterns of those civilizations) as merchants, subjects, or conquerors. The conquest of China by the Mongols during the thirteenth and fourteenth centuries facilitated the passing of those influences to the peoples of the Middle East and Europe. Nor was the diffusion of cultural influences and material culture a one-way process. The great cultural centers of Persia, India, and China adapted dress styles, military tactics, literature, and the hardy Mongol horse from the Central Asians.

INDIA IN THE CLASSICAL AND MEDIEVAL ERAS

■ *What factors contributed to a diversity of religions and cultures in classical and medieval India?*

The Classical Age

The political fragmentation of India during the 500 years from 184 B.C.E. to 320 C.E. permitted the spread of new Indian religions and the introduction of ideas and technologies from east and west of India. But it was not until the reunification of India's north under the Guptas that the classical age of Hindu culture emerged. India's cultural renaissance took root in the Gupta dynasty (320–500) and attempted to recapture the territorial and cultural grandeur of the Mauryas (MOW-ree-yahs). Its monarchs gained control over northern India while fostering traditional religions, Sanskrit literature, and indigenous art. Hindu and Buddhist culture also spread widely throughout Southeast Asia in this period.

The Gupta state began its rise in 320 with the accession to power of Chandra Gupta I (not related to his earlier Mauryan namesake). His son Samudra Gupta (r. 335–375) and grandson Chandra Gupta II (r. 375–415) were successful conquerors, extending the boundaries of an original petty state in Maghada (mah-GAH-dah) until it included most of northern India, from the Himalayas to the Narmada River and east to west from sea to sea. Within this domain the Gupta monarchs developed a political structure along ancient Mauryan lines, with provincial governors, district officials, state-controlled industries, and an imperial secret service. This centralized system, however, was effective only on royal lands, which were much less extensive than in Mauryan times. With a smaller bureaucracy, the Gupta rulers depended on local authorities and communal institutions. Peasants were obligated to pay as taxes to the state one-fourth of their harvest, one-fiftieth of their cattle and gold, one-sixth of their wealth in meat, fruit, honey and trees, and a day of labor per month for road repair or irrigation maintenance. Despite such high taxes, Indian farmers appeared in reports by foreign visitors to successfully produce an abundance of food. Artisans were organized in guilds which negotiated relationships with state and religious institutions. Military forces were raised by feudal levy.

Gupta India	
320	Accession of Chandra Gupta I
c. 335–375	Reign of Samudra Gupta
c. 376–414	Reign of Chandra Gupta II
515	Huna (Huns) seize northwest India; Gupta Empire collapses

Marriage alliances aided the Guptas' rise to power. Chandra Gupta I married a princess from the powerful Licchavi (leek-CHAH-vee) clan; his coins show the king and his queen, Kumaradevi (koo-MAH-rah-DEH-vee), on one side and a lion with his queen's clan name on the other. Chandra Gupta II gave his daughter, Prabhavati (prah-bah-VAH-tee) Gupta, in marriage to Rudrasena II (roo-DRAH-seh-nah), king of the powerful Vakataka dynasty in central India. Rudrasena died after a short reign, and his wife then took control of his kingdom for about 20 years as regent for her minor sons. The two kingdoms maintained close ties even after her death.

Peace and stable government under the later Guptas increased agricultural productivity and foreign trade. Commerce with Rome brought a great influx of gold and silver as well as Arabian horses into the Gupta Empire in exchange for Indian textiles, jewels, spices, perfumes, and wood. In fact, Rome's net deficit in gold exports led to the weakening of its economy. Indian traders were also active in Southeast Asia, particularly in Burma, Vietnam, and Cambodia, where they brought not only new products but also Buddhist culture. India's resulting prosperity was reflected in great public and religious buildings and in the luxuries of the elite, particularly at the Gupta court.

Although the Gupta rulers generally favored Hinduism, they practiced religious pluralism, patronizing and building temples for Hindus, Buddhists, and Jains. The Brahmans provided the Guptas with religious legitimacy, and the Guptas rewarded them with significant grants of land. Hinduism dominated the subcontinent. The Hindu revival of this period brought a great upsurge of devotion to Vishnu, Shiva, and Durga. This religious fervor was reflected in a series of religious books, the *Puranas,* which emphasized the compassion of the personal gods. The *Puranas* are a collection of myths, philosophical dialogues, ritual prescriptions, and dynastic genealogies gathered in the third and fourth centuries. The tales of the gods were popular. Among their legends, for example, is a recounting of the deeds of the goddess Durga and her fight against the buffalo demon. By promoting the devotional Hinduism reflected in these tales, the Gupta monarchs gained great favor among all classes of their subjects.

The *Bhagavad-Gita* (BAH-gah-vahd-GHEE-tah; *Song of the Blessed One*), written during this time, assured Hindus that salvation was possible, regardless of one's station in life. **Bhakti** (BAHK-tee; "devotion") was introduced as a path to salvation. Revealing himself as the Divine Savior Vishnu, the *Gita*'s protagonist Krishna explained: "Those who revere me with devotion (bhakti), they are in me and I too am in them. . . . Even those who may be of base origin, women, men of the artisan caste, and serfs, too."[1] Though inequality remained embedded in the status system that differentiated one's religious duties by caste, Hindu salvation was, in the *Bhagavad-Gita,* made accessible to all.

Much of our knowledge of Gupta society comes from the journal of a Chinese Buddhist monk, Faxian (fah-SHEN), who traveled in India for 14 years at the opening of the fifth century. Despite the Guptas' preference for Hinduism, thousands of Buddhist monks and nuns practiced their religion. Buddhist stupas (funerary mounds) dotted the landscape. In the fourth century, only Sri Lanka was more Buddhist than India. Buddhism was an important bridge linking China and India and stimulating commerce in both East and Southeast Asia.

Faxian was primarily interested in Buddhism in India, but he also commented on social customs. He reported the people to be happy, relatively free of government oppression, and inclined toward courtesy and charity. He mentions the caste system and its associations with purity and impurity, including "untouchability," the social isolation of a lowest class that is doomed to menial labor. Of course, travelers' accounts never tell the entire story and must be read with some caution. Each traveler sees bits and pieces of the society he or she is visiting and looks at the society in ways that may be very different from those of other travelers of different

The Guptas extended their rule over northern and central India but never managed to control the southern peninsula.

bhakti—Hindu devotion.

Document   Faxian: A Chinese Buddhist Monk in Gupta India

Faxian is an important source on India around 400 C.E. A Buddhist monk, he left China as a pilgrim to India in search of spiritual knowledge and Buddhist texts; he was away from home for 14 years. Faxian reached northern India on foot, via the grueling route over the mountains from China. When he returned home, he translated various Indian works and wrote the account of his travels. Faxian's story and long arduous journey illustrate both the effects of the spread of Buddhism and the draw that the Indian heartland had on Buddhists abroad. Here he describes Pataliputra (modern Patna), where Ashoka once reigned. The festival illustrates the amalgamation of Buddhist and Hindu ritual and suggests the joyous nature of some popular urban religious celebrations. Faxian's account of hospitals gives us some insight into the quality of medical care available free to the poor.

By the side of the tower of King Ashoka is built a monastery belonging to the Great Vehicle [Mahayana Buddhism], very imposing and elegant. There is also a temple belonging to the Little Vehicle [Theravada Buddhism]. Together they contain about 600 or 700 priests; their behavior is decorous and orderly. . . . Of all the kingdoms in Mid-India, the towns of this country are especially large. The people are rich and prosperous; they practice virtue and justice. Every year on the eighth day of the second month, there is a procession of images. On this occasion, they construct a four-wheeled cart, and erect upon it a tower of five stages, composed of bamboos lashed together, the whole being supported by a center post resembling a large spear with three points, in height twenty-two feet or more. So it looks like a pagoda. They then cover it with fine white linen, which they afterward paint with gaudy colors. Having made figures of the *devas* [gods], and decorated them with gold, silver, and glass, they place them under canopies of embroidered silk. Then at the four corners [of the vehicle] they construct niches in which they place figures of Buddha in a sitting posture, with a Bodhisattva [a Buddha in the making] standing in attendance. There are perhaps twenty cars thus prepared and differently decorated. During the day of the procession both priests and laymen assemble in great numbers. There are games and music, whilst they offer flowers and incense.... Then all night long they burn lamps, indulge in games and music, and make religious offerings. Such is the custom of all those who assemble on this occasion from the different countries round about. The nobles and householders of this country have founded hospitals within the city, to which the poor of all countries, the destitute, cripples, and the diseased may repair. They receive every kind of requisite help gratuitously. Physicians inspect their diseases, and according to their cases order them food and drink, medicine or decoctions, everything in fact that may contribute to their ease. When cured they depart at their convenience.

Questions to Consider

1. What does this story suggest about the institutionalization of Buddhism and its integration into city life in India?

2. Why might the people in Patna place figures of the Hindu gods and of the Buddha on the same float or cart used in a festival procession?

From Samuel Beal, ed., *Buddhist Records of the Western World*, translated from the Chinese of Hiuen Tsiang (629) (Delhi: Oriental Books, 1969), pp. lvi–lvii.

---

class, gender, upbringing, or motive for travel. Nonetheless, travelers like Faxian, who wrote down their observations in some detail, often provide us with the clearest glimpse we can obtain of past societies.

Gupta Art and Literature

Indian art of the Gupta period depicts a golden age of classical brilliance, combining stability and serenity with an exuberant love of life. The Gupta artistic spirit is well expressed in the 28 monasteries and temples at Ajanta, hewn out of a solid rock cliff and portraying in their wall frescoes not only the life of Buddha but also life in general: lovers embracing, beds of colorful flowers, musicians, and dancers. These sculptures reveal the beauty of the human form and provide us with a sense of Indian culture beyond that found in theological texts. The various incarnations of Vishnu and the deeds of the goddess Durga were also common subjects of Gupta sculpture. Hundreds of workers and artisans were employed in this work of building and

IMAGE

Classical
Indian
Sculpture

The Gupta era is justly renowned for its sculpture. This fifth-century terra-cotta piece shows the young Lord Krishna fighting the horse demon. According to Hindu religious tradition, Krishna, even as a baby, was formidably powerful; he battled a whole assortment of demons before reaching adolescence.

decorating temples that might, as Faxian points out, house hundreds of monks.

The Gupta era was also a golden age for literature, written in Sanskrit, the ancient language of the Brahmans. Authors supported by royal patronage poured forth a wealth of sacred, philosophical, and dramatic works in prose and poetry, including fables, fairy tales, and adventure stories featuring a wide range of characters—thieves, courtesans, hypocritical monks, and strange beasts. The *Panchatantra* is a manual of political wisdom employing animal tales to advise the king on proper rule.

The most renowned literary figure of the Gupta era was India's greatest poet and dramatist, Kalidasa, who wrote at the court of Chandra Gupta II. His best-known work in the West is *Shakuntala*, a great drama of lovers separated by adversity for many years and then by chance reunited. This universal theme of separated lovers is found in the epic stories

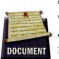

DOCUMENT

Tales of Ten Princes

of many Eurasian peoples in this era—the Arabian story of *Layla and Majnun*, for example.

Gupta Scholarship and Science

The Gupta era brought a great stimulus to learning. Brahman traditions were revitalized, and Buddhist centers, which had spread after the Mauryan period, were given new support. The foremost Indian university, founded in the fifth century, was the Buddhist university at Nalanda in northeastern India. Accomplishments in science were no less remarkable than those in art, literature, scholarship, and philosophy. The university had a diverse population, with students from China and Southeast Asia also attending classes. The most famous Gupta scientist was the astronomer-mathematician Aryabhatta (AH-ree-ah-BAHT-tah), who lived in the fifth century. He elaborated (in verse) on quadratic equations, solstices, and equinoxes, along with the spherical shape of the earth and its rotation. Other Hindu mathematicians of this period popularized the use of a special sign for zero, passing it on later to the Arabs. Mathematical achievements were matched by those in medicine. Hindu physicians sterilized wounds, prepared for surgery by fumigation, performed cesarean operations, set bones, and were skilled in plastic surgery. They used drugs then unknown in the West, such as chaulmoogra oil for leprosy, a treatment still used during the first half of the twentieth century. With these accomplishments in pure science came many effective practical applications by Gupta craftsmen, who made soap, cement, superior dyes, and the finest tempered steel in the world.

India is famous for its rock carved temples. Kings or affluent families often financed such temples (both Hindu and Buddhist) with spectacular carvings as acts of devotion. This is the Kailasanatha Temple at Ellora, dedicated to the Hindu god Shiva and dating to approximately 765 C.E.

New Political and Religious Orders

Gupta hegemony began to collapse in the second half of the fifth century with attempted invasions by the Huna (called Xiongnu (SHONG-noo) in China and Huns in Europe) from the north. Although the Guptas held out for several decades, they ruled only in parts of northern India after 497. In 515 the Huna—who had already menaced the Roman Empire and successfully invaded Persia—seized first northwestern India and then the Ganges plain. Huna rule did not endure, but it led to several smaller kingdoms breaking free of the Gupta and prompted the migration of more Central Asian tribesmen into India. This resulted in a period in which India was generally divided into regional kingdoms rather than more expansive empires like that of the Guptas. The Central Asian tribesmen also intermarried with local populations to produce a class of fighting aristocrats known as *Rajputs* (RAHJ-poots). These fierce warriors carved out kingdoms among the Hindu states of northern India. Extensive intermarriage was common in frontier areas, blurring the boundaries between ethnolinguistic groups and even creating new identities.

In the seventh century the unity of northern India was revived for a short while by Harsha (r. 606–647), a strong leader. In 6 years he reconquered much of what had been the Gupta Empire, restoring order and partially reviving learning. However, Harsha failed in his bid to conquer the Deccan, and no ruler would do so until 1206. A tolerant leader, he was a strong supporter of Buddhism; during his reign Hinduism also grew in popularity. Harsha's support for Buddhism made possible several successful visits by Chinese ambassadors. In 643 the large delegation sent by the Tang court was received by Harsha who held a Buddhist ceremony in their honor. This diplomatic mission visited Buddhist sites and brought along an artisan to copy Buddhist architecture and sculpture. In addition to making spiritual overtures, the Chinese mission had a key commercial success—acquiring sugar-making technology from the South Asians.

When Harsha died in 647, regional kingdoms again prevailed. The period of the regional kingdoms was not a sterile one. In this era the great Hindu philosopher Shankara (c. 788–820) brilliantly argued a mystical philosophy based on the *Upanishads;* literature, especially in Tamil in the south, flourished; and Brahmans and

Buddhist monks continued to carry their religious and cultural ideas to Southeast Asia and China. Their crucial role in the "Indianization" of Southeast Asia is reflected in the great temples there. It is also reflected in Chinese sources that note 162 visits of Buddhist monks from the fifth to the eighth centuries.[2]

The Chola kingdom on India's southeastern coast played a significant role in the commercial and cultural exchange with Southeast Asia as well. The Chola had long lived in the Tamil south but were apparently a tributary lineage to the more powerful Pallavar dynasty. They began to challenge the Pallavars in the late ninth century and emerged as a ruling force in their own right within a century. Chola rulers in the eleventh century exchanged embassies with China, Sumatra, Malaya, and Cambodia; Chola fleets took Sri Lanka (Ceylon) and challenged the power of the Southeast Asian kingdom of Srivijaya (SHREE-vee-JAH-yah). When a Chola king conquered Bengal, he ordered the defeated princes to carry the holy water of the Ganges River to his new capital to celebrate his victory. Through this ceremony, he not only forced his enemies to perform a ritual act of submission but enhanced his legitimacy in Hindu terms by linking his own lands to those watered by the sacred Ganges.

Muslims in India

The prophet Muhammad founded an Arab Muslim state in Arabia in the seventh century (see Chapter 7); soon the Arab conquerors had defeated the Sassanids in Persia, and Muslim armies arrived at the boundaries of the Indian subcontinent. In 712 an Arab force seized Sind, a coastal outpost in northwestern India. During the next 300 years, Arabic-speaking Muslims established trading posts throughout the Indian Ocean region. Although the existence of the Muslim kingdom at Sind did not serve as a springboard for Arab Muslim penetration of India, Muslim traders did facilitate the integration of India into an Islamic world system. This system was a trading network that did not require participants to be Muslim but did take advantage of Muslim political expansion. The significant expansion of Muslim political control in India 300 years later, beginning in 997, had Turkish, Persian, and Afghan rather than Arabian roots.

Armies of Central Asian and Turkish slaves, originally purchased to support Muslim rulers at Baghdad, began to form independent kingdoms in Afghanistan and Persia. One of them, a kingdom ruled by Mahmud of Ghazni (MAH-mood, GAHZ-nee), launched a series of campaigns into northwestern India. He gained a reputation as a destroyer for his 17 campaigns over the course of 25 years that devastated northern India. One notable episode during these campaigns was Mahmud's destruction of Shiva's large temple complex

DOCUMENT

Al-Biruni on India's Hindus

in Gujarat and the slaughter of its defenders who, according to legend, numbered 50,000 men. These campaigns of pillage rather than conquest made Mahmud a name that to the present day evokes powerful emotions among Hindus.

Mahmud is also known for the famous scholars at his court, among them Firdawsi (feer-DOW-see; 940–1020), who wrote the great epic Persian poem the *Shahnamah* (SHAH-NAH-mah), and al-Biruni (b. 973), author of a major history of India. Al-Biruni wrote that it was the caste system that prevented Muslims and Hindus from ever reaching any understanding because the Muslims considered "all men as equal, except in piety."[3] Of course, al-Biruni was minimizing the hierarchies that existed in Muslim society. But the caste system did indeed serve as a significant barrier between Hindus and Muslims (although, over time, Hindus and Muslims intermarried and some Muslim groups adapted castelike social divisions).

Firdawsi's career is an illustration of the vagaries of life at court. He spent many years writing the 60,000 verses of the *Shahnamah* but was then disappointed when the king did not reward him properly. So he penned a savage satire of Mahmud and fled to his home region of Khurasan in Persia. Legend has it that Mahmud later realized the value of Firdawsi's work and sent a large reward after him, but by the time it arrived, the poet was already dead.

The date 1206 stands out as the next significant marker of Muslim conquest in India. In the same year that the Mongol Chinggis (Genghis) Khan mobilized his campaigns of conquest and expansion in Central Asia, the general Qutb ud-Din Aibak (KOOT-buh ood-DIN ai-BAHK) seized power as sultan at Delhi. Qutb ud-Din had been a commander in the army of the Afghan ruler Muhammad of Ghur, who seized Delhi in 1193 from the Rajputs, Hindus who mounted a staunch defense in the northwest. Qutb ud-Din founded a new dynasty in 1206 that lasted for 320 years. He was followed on the throne by his son-in-law, Iltutmish (il-TOOT-mish; r. 1211–1236), and by the latter's daughter, Raziyya (ra-ZEE-yah; r. 1236–1240). According to the Muslim chronicler Minhaju-s Siraj, Sultana Raziyya was "wise, just and generous. . . . She was endowed with all the qualities befitting a king, but she was not born of the right sex, so in the estimation of men all these virtues were worthless."[4] Raziyya's father Iltutmish had himself been formally consecrated in 1229 as sultan of Delhi by a representative of the Abbasid sultan in Baghdad. Even though the Abbasid sultan wielded little power at this time, he was still a source of Islamic legitimacy for South Asian Muslim rulers. Less than 30 years later, the Abbasid caliphate would fall prey to the Mongol descendants of Chinggis Khan.

At the peak of its power in the thirteenth century, the Delhi Sultanate held not only the north but also part of the Deccan Plateau in the south. When Sultan

Muslim rulers established a sultanate in northern India, and Delhi flourished as its imperial capital.

DOCUMENT

The Ideal Muslim King

Ala ud-Din (r. 1296–1316) invaded the Deccan, he called himself the "Second Alexander," a title that was emblazoned on his coins. The Delhi Sultanate also managed to ward off the Mongol invaders who seized the Punjab (poon-JAHB), thus avoiding the fate of Persia and Iraq. Delhi, under the sultanate, emerged as a great imperial capital. The Delhi sultans were patrons of the arts, builders of splendid monuments, and proponents of philosophy. The Tughluks (TOOG-looks), a Muslim dynasty who ruled Delhi for most of the fourteenth century, held an uneasy rule over the majority Hindu populace as well as over rival Muslim rulers. Ibn Battuta (IH-buhn bah-TOO-tah), the famed Muslim world traveler from north Africa, served the Tughluk court as its chief judge, observing it closely and leaving a detailed historical record. By the

DOCUMENT

A World Traveler in India

middle of the fourteenth century, the Tughluks had lost control of the south (upon the rise of the Hindu Vijayangar (vee-JAH-yahn-gahr) Empire in 1336) and the northeast (Sufi Muslim leaders there declared their independence of Delhi in 1338). Although experiencing brief periods of revival, the regime continued to decline internally before it was terminally fragmented by the brutal destruction of Delhi at the hands of the Turco-Mongol Timur (Tamerlane) in 1398. Timur's army wrought such destruction in Delhi that in his autobiography he denied

responsibility and blamed the slaughter on his soldiers. Numerous rulers, espousing a variety of religious faiths, emerged throughout India as Delhi declined, until a century later, when Timur's great-grandson Babur would return to establish the Mughal dynasty.

Pre-Mughal Muslim rule in India brought some cultural integration as local lords and warriors were incorporated into the new Muslim court. Some Hindus found emotional appeal in the Muslim faith, which had no caste system, or sought to lighten their taxes and qualify for public service by converting to Islam. Others

DOCUMENT

Indian Poetry

formed new religious groups synthesizing aspects of Hinduism and Islam—for example, **Sikhism.** Another typical example of cultural integration was the spread of Urdu, a spoken Indian language incorporating Persian, Arabic, and Turkish words. The Sikh religion and the Urdu language illustrate how difficult it is to maintain strict boundaries (whether ethnic, linguistic, or spiritual) between peoples who regularly interact with each other, especially in frontier areas.

Cultural synthesis, however, could not eliminate Hindu-Muslim contention over polytheism, religious images, and closed castes. Many aristocratic Hindu leaders continued to resist Islam. The Muslim centuries should not be seen as a takeover of Indian society and culture by foreigners. Scholars today stress that though the rulers were Islamic, their governments ruled in ways similar to non-Islamic Indian rulers. Religion and caste remained significant barriers to assimilation, and mass conversions did not occur. The Delhi Sultanate remained a Muslim military-administrative class that ruled over a predominantly Hindu population. The impact on Buddhism was, however, far greater. The university at Nalanda and other major Buddhist centers were destroyed in 1202, driving thousands of monks and scholars to Nepal and Tibet. Buddhism was, then, effectively erased from India.

MAP

The Delhi Sultanate and Mughal India

CHINA: CULTURAL AND POLITICAL EMPIRES

■ *How did cross-cultural interaction with indigenous culture and ideology define China as a nation?*

The fall of the Han in 220 was followed by three and a half centuries of political disunity. Unity was regained under the Sui dynasty (589–618), consolidated under the Tang (618–907), maintained precariously under the Song (960–1279), and reasserted

---

Sikhism—Indian religion blending elements of Hinduism and Islam.

under the Yuan (1279–1368). Despite periods of internal disruption, this political system, recreated from Han precedents, survived repeated invasions and civil wars. For the 90-year Yuan dynasty, China was ruled by Central Asian invaders, the Mongols, but despite foreign control at the top, Chinese culture survived and reclaimed the emperorship in 1368. Throughout the millennium, stability resulted from a common written language, a strong family structure, an enduring Confucian tradition, an elite of scholar bureaucrats who shared power while contending for dominance, and the strength of China's economy and material culture. In the first half millennium, including the centuries of political disunity, China was part of the expanding Buddhist world. In the second half, the efforts of China's Confucian scholars promoted a flowering of Chinese culture during the expansionist Tang period, when China was the largest state in the world; during the ensuing economic prosperity of the Song; and in the Yuan period, in which China's economy dominated Eurasian trade.

Period of Division

No single dynasty was able to unite North and South China and establish a long-lasting dynasty from the fall of the Han to the rise of the Sui more than 360 years later. Yet this was a vibrant age of artistic creation, intellectual growth, and profound religious development. The divisions between north and south created dynamic differences in the two regions over time, and the reuniting of the two in the late sixth century led to a fertile synthesis of ideas and practices. Following the fall of the Han Empire various nomadic peoples, mainly Xiongnu and Yuezhi (yoo-EH-juh; "Turks"), interacted with Chinese in the border areas. At the same time, Chinese claimants to power—the ideal of a unified country persisted throughout the age of division—struggled with other Chinese as well as with sinified non-Chinese for dominance. (*Sinification* or *sinicization* meant adopting varying degrees of Chinese civilization, culture, governance, philosophy, and economic organization.) During the third century, three kingdoms vied for supremacy, and one, Jin, seemed to be on the verge of reuniting China in 280. Soon, however, succession disputes pitted Jin factions, joined by Chinese and non-Chinese allies, against one another. Unity was not to be at that time.

Xiongnu and other northern people had been invited inside the Han dynasty's borders in the second century as a way of gaining their support and decreasing the possibility of barbarian conquest. Many were used as soldiers by Chinese generals. By 304, some Xiongnu, sensing an opportunity during the fratricidal wars of the Jin, rose up, declared themselves the new kings of Han, and sacked Luoyang and Chang'an.

For the next century (304–439), China was involved in constant warfare during the period known as the Sixteen Kingdoms. Many aristocrats fled southward, populating the south and bringing Chinese culture with them. This was a demographically significant move, extending the reach of Chinese civilization and developing the south's fertile agricultural economy. When, centuries later, the Grand Canal was built, food could be transported from this "rice basket" to the north, where China's defensive armies had long been dependent on either growing their own food or striking bargains with their barbarian neighbors.

In the North, a clan originally from Manchuria but sinified by the fifth century established the Northern Wei dynasty (439–534). Like other successful outsiders, the Northern Wei had adopted Chinese methods, creating an effective administration by blending their indigenous ways with Chinese ways. Throughout history, China was challenged by the question of maintaining Chinese culture and institutions—especially rule by scholars according to Confucian principles—while learning from the outsider (or barbarians, as they were ungenerously called) to create a hybrid culture, economy, and military. The question of how to maximize borrowing without compromising Chinese culture was most evident in times of strong central government. But religious, cultural, and economic blending occurred at all times. The Northern Wei instituted an **equal-field system** of land tenure that resembled the ancient "well-field" system to overcome the rise of powerful land owners whose control of land and serfs cut the tax roles. They also adopted Chinese language and dress. Their capital at Luoyang was a grand Chinese city, with palaces, 500,000 inhabitants, and 1000 Buddhist temples.

While the Northern Wei controlled the North, other rulers controlled the South. Northern aristocratic families contributed to state building through their interest in Confucianism, while leading southern families were more focused on religion and the arts. Southerners seemed somewhat effete to northerners, but when the two regions reunited in 589, the blend of both styles led to a stronger and more cultured civilization. Each region was differently influenced by foreign cultures as well, stimulating intellectual inquiry and encouraging trade.

The hallmark of the period of political disunity was its cultural growth. At the beginning of the period, the incessant military struggles led many intellectuals to abandon public service. Why bother being a serious Confucian scholar in such times, many concluded, giving themselves up to hedonism and artistic performance, often simultaneously expressing itself in

---

equal-field system—Division of land to peasants, who tilled it, rather than to wealthy landholders; adopted in China, spread to Korea and Japan.

Huge Buddhist rock carvings (these are around 50 feet tall) were commissioned by the Northern Wei at the end of the fifth century. These large figures are part of a collection of thousands of carvings at Yungang in North China. They may have been inspired by earlier Buddhist carvings, recently destroyed by the Taliban in Afghanistan.

poetry or unconventional behavior. The Seven Sages of the Bamboo Grove were the most famous of many talented poets and although one was executed for scandalous behavior, they continue to be celebrated to this day.

Buddhism and Daoism emerged as more spiritual alternatives to Confucian government service. While Daoism had indigenous roots, Buddhism came to China as part of a great expansion of a universal religion. From its origins in India, Buddhism traveled along trade routes to China, bringing international (Greek, Afghan, and Indian) arts and ideas. Missionaries aided the transmission of Buddhism as did Chinese travelers like Faxian.

Buddhism provided comfort in times of crisis. Its promise of salvation (to all, including common people), special appeal to the supposed natural compassion of women and men, offer of monastic security to men in troubled times, and long incubation within Chinese culture all ensured its popularity. China's dominant form of Buddhism, Mahayana, focused on **bodhisattvas** (BOH-dee-SAHT-vahs), individuals who had achieved salvation but chose to postpone their release from the cycle of birth and rebirth in order to save others. Bodhisattvas were technically sexless beings (though identified in popular forms of religion as female) and transcended class and culture as well as gender. The notion of salvation through faith was developed in the **Pure Land** sect of Buddhism in the fourth century; this made Buddhism increasingly appealing to those not able to enter

monastic life. Developments in the Tang dynasty would broaden Buddhism's appeal further.

Daoism was encouraged to enhance its dogma and organization by the rise of Buddhism. Like Buddhists, Daoists formed monastic communities and wrote scriptures, although many of these scriptures were kept hidden from non-Daoists, unlike the widely circulated Buddhist texts. Daoists were particularly important in the study of alchemy as a route to immortality; alchemy, in turn, led to scientific discoveries. Although challenged by native Daoism, scorned by some Confucian intellectuals, and periodically persecuted by rulers jealous of its strength, Buddhism ultimately won adherents throughout China. The monarchs of the North patronized Buddhism by building splendid temples and generously endowing monasteries. From the fourth to the ninth centuries, Buddhism interacted with Chinese religious and philosophical traditions to create a complex new synthesis of ideas and art.

The Sui dynasty (589–618), descended from the Northern Wei, presented themselves as Chinese defenders of Buddhism. Emperor Wendi (r. 581–604), the first Sui ruler, and his son Yangdi (r. 604–618) established an imperial military force and a land-based militia, centralized the administration, and revived the civil service system. Between 605 and 609, Yangdi built a great waterway, the Grand Canal, to link the rice-growing Yangzi basin with northern China; this helped to overcome regional differences. This canal eventually stretched 1200 miles and permitted some later governments to locate their seats of power in the less productive but strategically important North. Building this canal, in addition to a massive conscription of soldiers (over one million) to fight in Korea, took huge amounts of labor. Disgust with this exploitation led to numerous rebellions, and in 618 Yangdi's cousin overthrew the Sui. The new Tang dynasty, like the Sui, was a hybrid of North and South, Chinese and foreign.

---

bodhisattvas—In Mahayana Buddhism, an enlightened being who chooses to postpone salvation to aid others in reaching enlightenment.

Pure Land—A place for those saved by faith in the Amida Buddha.

Political Developments Under the Early Tang Dynasty, 618–756

During the first half of the Tang period, China attained a new pinnacle of glory. The first three emperors, Gaozu (GOW-dzuh; r. 618–626), Taizong (TAI-dzong; r. 626–649), and Gaozong (GOW-dzong; r. 650–683), subjugated Turkish Central Asia and conquered Annam (northern Vietnam). Tang cultural influence extended north to Manchuria, east to Korea and Japan, and south to parts of Southeast Asia. It controlled Central Asia all the way to Afghanistan during the seventh century and maintained extensive trade routes. Along with territorial expansion came a deepening of state power.

The legal code of 653 combined northern and southern legal traditions, and the reemphasized **examination system** recruited officials from all regions and, in theory, all classes. This system was based on Confucian texts that were, in principle, accessible to all men (women were not allowed to take the examinations), but in reality were more likely studied in families financially able to educate their sons. This bought the elite's loyalty and focused the ideology of those who wished to be rulers, who were selected by their answers on exams based on the Confucian classics, on a unified body of scholarship. Thus, although the expansion of the empire depended on the promotion of *wu* (military), its maintenance was even more dependent on its promotion of *wen* (civil arts). Though strong supporters of Buddhism, early Tang rulers elevated the principles of Confucianism to rule the state and to define its Chinese nature.

The era of growth and grandeur was marked by the extraordinary reign of the able Empress Wu (r. 690–705), a concubine of the second and third emperors, who controlled the government for 20 years after the latter's death, eliminating her political opponents and firmly establishing the Tang dynasty. She greatly weakened the old aristocracy by favoring Buddhism and strengthening the examination system for recruiting civil servants. Moreover, she decisively defeated the Koreans, making Korea a loyal vassal state. As a woman and a widow, she was considered a usurper and was later criticized by Chinese historians and politicians who emphasized her vices, particularly her many favorites and lovers. She was overthrown in 705. Her grandson, Emperor Xuanzong (SHWAHN-dzong; r. 712–756), was also known for his long reign filled with cultural growth.

Tang rulers perfected a highly centralized government, using a complex bureaucracy organized in specialized councils, boards, and ministries, all directly responsible to the emperor. Local government functioned under 15 provincial governors, aided by subordinates down to the district level. Military commanders supervised tribute collections in semiautonomous conquered territories. Officeholders throughout the empire were, by the eighth century, usually degreeholders from government schools and universities who had qualified by passing the regularly scheduled examinations. These scholar-bureaucrats were steeped in Confucian conservatism but were more efficient than the remaining minority of aristocratic hereditary officials. The Tang retained the nationalized land register under the equal-field system, designed to check the growth of large estates, guarantee land to peasants, and relate their land tenure to both their taxes and their militia service. Until well into the eighth century, when abuses began to appear, the system worked to merge the interests of state and people.

Tang Economic and Social Changes

The early Tang economy was extremely prosperous, supported by thriving cities and the always busy trade routes through Central Asia, along the southeastern coast, and up and down the Grand Canal. Economic productivity, both agricultural and industrial, rose steadily during the early Tang period. The introduction of tea and wet rice from Annam turned the Yangzi area into a vast irrigated food bank and the economic base for Tang power. Tea became a staple throughout China during the Tang. More food and rising population brought increasing manufactures. Population growth was most impressive in the south, where it increased form one-quarter of the realm's population in the early seventh century to half by 742. Chinese techniques in the newly discovered craft of papermaking, along with iron casting, porcelain production, and silk processing, improved tremendously and spread west to the Middle East.

Foreign trade and influence increased significantly under the Tang emperors in a development that would continue through the Song era (960–1279). Chinese control in Central Asia facilitated trade along the old overland silk route; but as porcelain became the most profitable export and could not be easily transported by caravan, it swelled the volume of sea trade through Southeast Asia. Most of this trade left from southern ports, particularly from Guangzhou (gwahng-JOH; Canton), where more than 100,000 non-Chinese Indians, Persians, Arabs, and Malays handled the goods. Foreign merchants were equally visible at Chang'an, the Tang capital and eastern terminus of the silk route. Chang'an, a planned city of 30 square miles, not counting the imperial palace, was the largest planned city in the world, and the most populous. The imperial palace at the north of the city was flanked on either side by a market. The "West Market" dealt in foreign goods, food, and wine and exhibited foreign entertainers and magi-

---

examination system—The selection of scholar-officials through examination in Confucian texts.

cians; the "East Market" was for domestic items. The city was vibrant, but it was also controlled, for Chang'an was planned on a grid, and every resident lived in a rectangular ward, surrounded by walls. The gate to the ward was locked at night.

Although largely state-controlled and aristocratic, Tang society was particularly responsive to new foreign stimuli, which it swiftly absorbed. A strongly pervasive Buddhism, a rising population, and steady urbanization fostered this cross-cultural exchange. Many city populations exceeded 100,000, and four cities had more than a million people. Their cosmopolitan residents enjoyed products from foreign lands, including luxury goods, musical instruments, and textiles. The foreign practice of sitting on chairs replaced sitting on floor mats. Hairstyles and games were adopted from abroad. Foreign religions, including Islam, Nestorian Christianity, Judaism, Zoroastrianism, and Manichaeism (MAN-ih-KEE-ism), were practiced freely by the thousands of international residents in Chang'an and Luoyang, though few Chinese converted to these religions as they had earlier to Buddhism. Merchants clearly benefited, but despite their wealth, they were still considered socially inferior. They often used their wealth to educate their sons for the civil service examination, thus promoting a rising class of scholar-bureaucrats. The latter, as they acquired land, gained status and power at the expense of the old aristocratic families. Conditions among artisans and the expanding mass of peasants improved somewhat, but life for them remained hard and precarious.

By the eighth century, Tang legal codes had imposed severe punishments for wifely disobedience or infidelity to husbands. New laws also limited women's rights to divorce, inheritance of property, and remarriage as widows. Women were, however, still active in the arts and literature. Although some wielded influence and power at royal courts, many were confined to harems. This subordinate position was partly balanced by the continued high status and authority of older women within families.

Class and education played an important role in women's status. Women poets were sought after by men of distinction, and one father of a poet, himself a writer of note, was promoted to a prestigious government position on the strength of his daughter's writing. Empress Wu wrote powerful poetry, some of it recalling her mother, some longing for her late husband, some expressing political ideas. Other women wrote of love and longing, military events, affairs at court, and a wide variety of topics. Not all Tang women poets were genteel. In a poem entitled "Getting It Off My Chest," Xu Yueying (SHOO yoo-eh-YING), a late Tang poet wrote: "I've broken the rules—obedience to father, husband, son. That's why I cry so much. This body? What way, what use to stick to what proper people do?"[5]

Fashions in female beauty change from place to place and over time. Figurines like this one of a mounted woman, possibly playing polo, show that physical activity and a plump physique were esteemed. This style also influenced standards of beauty in Korea and Japan at that time.

Tang Religion and Culture

Buddhism and Daoism blossomed alongside Confucian scholarship and government service. Poets, artists, architects, and painters were all inspired by religious as well as secular themes. Buddhism was particularly dynamic in the early Tang dynasty. Buddhist monasteries and temples educated children in their schools, rural temples gave lodging to travelers, and monasteries ran large-scale farms. Buddhist themes permeated folk tales. Most important, faith-based Buddhist sects, especially Pure Land, spread throughout China, offering peasants a route to salvation. Pure Land Buddhism was a vastly different form of devotion from the earlier sects that required years of good living and often many rebirths on earth before attaining salvation. **Chan** (Zen in Japanese) Buddhism developed in the Tang as well. Chan appealed more to the elite and focused on sudden enlightenment rather than scripture.

Chan—A form of Buddhism that seeks sudden enlightenment through techniques and rituals intended to quiet the mind. Known as Zen in Japan.

A fresh flowering of literature occurred during the early Tang period. It followed naturally from a dynamic society, but it was also furthered by the development of papermaking and the invention, in about 600, of block printing, which soon spread to Korea and Japan. Movable type, which would later revolutionize Europe, was little used in China during this period because it was less efficient in printing Chinese characters. Printing helped meet a growing demand for the religious and educational materials generated by Buddhism and the examination system.

Tang scholarship is best remembered for historical writing. Chinese of this period firmly believed that lessons from the past could be guides for the future. As an early Tang emperor noted, "By using a mirror of brass, you may . . . adjust your cap; by using antiquity as a mirror you may . . . foresee the rise and fall of empires."[6] In addition to universal works, the period produced many studies of particular subjects. History itself came under investigation, as illustrated by *The Understanding of History*, a work that stressed the need for analysis and evaluation in the narration of events. Writers produced works of all types, but poetry was the accepted medium, composed and repeated by emperors, scholars, singing courtesans, and common people in the marketplaces. Tang poetry was marked by ironic humor, deep sensitivity to human feeling, concern for social justice, and a near-worshipful love of nature. Two of the most famous among some 3000 recognized poets of the era were Li Bo (701–763; also known as Li Bai) and Du Fu (712–770). The former was an admitted lover of pleasure, especially of wine. A famous story about him is that during a drinking party on a lake, he leaned over the side of the boat in order to scoop out the moon and drowned. But he also had his philosophical side as seen in the following poem inspired by Daoism:

DOCUMENT
Poems by Li Bai (also known as Li Bo) and Du Fu

> *Zhuangzi in a dream*
> *became a butterfly,*
> *And the butterfly became*
> *Zhuangzi at waking.*
> *Which was the real, the*
> *butterfly or the man?*[7]

Du Fu, one of the great landscape poets, also wrote of suffering, especially suffering brought about by rebellions toward the end of his life.

> *The war-chariots rattle,*
> *The war-horses whinny.*
> *Each man of you has a bow and quiver at his*
> *   belt. . . .*
> *At the border where the blood of men spills like*
> *   the sea—*

> *And still the heart of Emperor Wu is beating for*
> *   war. . . .*
> *In thousands of villages, nothing grows but*
> *   weeds,*
> *And though strong women have bent to the*
> *   ploughing,*
> *East and west the furrows are all broken down*
> *   . . .*

> *It is very much better to have a daughter*
> *Who can marry and live in the house of a*
> *   neighbor,*
> *While under the sod we bury our boys. . . .*[8]

The Tang literary revival was paralleled by movements in painting and sculpture. The plastic arts, dealing with both religious and secular subjects, became a major medium for the first time in China. Small tomb statues depicted both Chinese and foreign life with realism, verve, and diversity. These figures—warriors, servants, and traders—were buried with the dead and believed to serve them in the afterlife. Religious statuary, even in Buddhist shrines, showed strong humanistic emphases, often juxtaposed with the naive sublimity of Buddhas carved in the Gandaran (Greek Hellenistic) style of northwestern India. Similar themes were developed in Tang painting, but the traditional preoccupation with nature prevailed in both the northern and southern landscape schools. The most famous Tang painter was Wu Daozi (WOO DOW-zuh), whose landscapes and religious scenes were produced at the court of the emperor Xuanzong in the early eighth century.

Tang Decline and the Transition to Premodern China

The cultural flowering of Xuanzong's reign was matched, in its early years, by vigorous and effective leadership. He fixed problems in the tax system, curbed the power of imperial relatives, and strengthened defenses against the Turks, Uighurs, and Tibetans. His method of strengthening border defenses by giving authority to commanders of military provinces backfired, however. One of these commanders, a protégé of the emperor's favorite concubine, Yang Guifei (YAHNG gwei-FAY), was doted on by the emperor to please his concubine. The commander, An Lushan, built up an army of 160,000 troops along the border, but then turned and marched on Chang'an and Luoyang in 755.

The aged emperor Xuanzong, while fleeing for his life from the capital, was forced by his troops to approve the execution of Yang Guifei, who was seen as having dominated him and his court. According to legend, he died of sorrow less than a month later. Yang

Bo Juyi (772–846): "The Song of Everlasting Sorrow"

This poem by one of the late Tang dynasty's most respected poets recounts the love of Emperor Xuanzong and his beloved concubine, Yang Guifei, who was blamed by her contemporaries for the An Lushan Rebellion. Bo Juyi's poem was esteemed not only in China but also in Japan. Lady Murasaki cited it repeatedly in *The Tale of Genji*.

China's Emperor, craving beauty that might shake
    an empire,
Was on the throne for many years, searching,
    never finding,
Till a little child of the Yang clan, hardly even
    grown,
Bred in an inner chamber, with no one knowing
    her,
But with graces granted by heaven and not to be
    concealed,
At last one day was chosen for the imperial
    household.
If she but turned her head and smiled, there were
    cast a hundred spells,
And the powder and paint of the Six Palaces faded
    into nothing.
. . . There were other ladies in his court, three
    thousand of rare beauty,
But his favours to three thousand were
    concentered in one body.
. . . Her sisters and her brothers all were given
    titles;
And, because she so illumined and glorified her
    clan,
She brought to every father, every mother through
    the empire,
Happiness when a girl was born rather than a
    boy.
. . . The Emperor's eyes could never gaze on her
    enough—
Till war-drums, booming from Yuyang, shocked
    the whole earth
And broke the tunes of The Rainbow Skirt and the
    Feathered Coat.
The Forbidden City, the nine-tiered palace, loomed
    in the dust
From thousands of horses and chariots headed
    southwest.
The imperial flag opened the way, now moving
    and now pausing—
But thirty miles from the capital, beyond the
    western gate,
The men of the army stopped, not one of them
    would stir
Till under their horses' hoofs they might trample
    those moth-eyebrows.
Flowery hairpins fell to the ground, no one picked
    them up,
And a green and white jade hair-tassel and a
    yellow gold hair-bird.

The Emperor could not save her, he could only
    cover his face.
And later when he turned to look, the place of
    blood and tears
Was hidden in a yellow dust blown by a cold
    wind.
. . . And people were so moved by the Emperor's
    constant brooding
That they besought the Daoist priest to see if he
    could find her.
. . . He searched the Green Void, below, the Yellow
    Spring;
But he failed, in either place, to find the one he
    looked for.
And then he heard accounts of an enchanted isle
    at sea,
. . . And the lady, at news of an envoy from the
    Emperor of China,
Was startled out of dreams in her nine-flowered
    canopy.
. . . She took out, with emotion, the pledges he
    had given
And, through his envoy, sent him back a shell box
    and gold hairpin,
But kept one branch of the hairpin and one side of
    the box,
Breaking the gold of the hairpin, breaking the shell
    of the box;
Our souls belong together," she said, "like this gold
    and this shell—
Somewhere, sometime, on earth or in heaven, we
    shall surely meet."
. . . Earth endures, heaven endures; some time
    both shall end,
While this unending sorrow goes on and on for
    ever.

Questions to Consider

1. Why did the Emperor's soldiers execute Yang Guifei, and why was the Emperor unable to protect her?

2. What does this poem suggest about the role of women in the Emperor's court in the Tang?

3. Why was this poem loved not only in China but also throughout East Asia?

Excerpted from Bo Juyi (Po Chi-yi), "A Song of Unending Sorrow," in Cyril Birch, ed., *Anthology of Chinese Literature: From Early Times to the Fourteenth Century* (New York: Grove Press, 1965), pp. 266–269.

Guifei became a model of female perfidy, fueling misogynistic notions of women's control over men.

It took 8 years to put down An Lushan's rebellion, but the ensuing disruption was so extensive that the late Tang emperors never recovered their former power. In several key areas, military governors acted as independent rulers, paying no taxes to Chang'an. In the rest of China, the equal-field system was replaced with twice yearly taxation on the value of the land. This **two tax system** persisted for the next 700 years in China. Regions were allowed to fill their tax responsibilities as they wished with little government supervision. In addition, the government instituted salt, wine, and tea monopolies to raise revenues. Government receipts to merchants came to be used as a kind of currency, becoming the antecedent for paper money that was developed during the Song dynasty. Though private trade was stimulated by the government's declining economic role, government revenues declined, and taxes on peasants were raised. Falling revenues brought deterioration of the state education establishment and a corresponding drop in administrative efficiency. The government further alienated some groups by seizing Buddhist property and persecuting

---

two tax system—Twice yearly tax payment based on value of land rather than on output as under the earlier equal field system.

all "foreign" religions. Buddhism was suppressed in 841. Tens of thousands of monasteries and temples were destroyed and 250,000 monks and nuns were returned to lay life. Except for the popular sects of Pure Land and Chan, most other sects of Buddhism soon declined.

In response to the threat posed by autonomous regional commanders, the court created armies led by eunuchs, originally personal servants to the emperor or to his women's quarters. In time, these eunuchs gained their own power, manipulating and even murdering emperors and scholar-officials. Bandits and other gangs ravaged the country after 860. Chang'an was captured in 881, and the brutal warlord who took the city killed all the foreign residents. Chang'an would never again be capital of China. In 907, the pretense of Tang rule was ended.

Political Developments During the Song Era, 960–1279

For a half-century after the fall of the Tang dynasty, China experienced political division, at times approaching anarchy. During this period of five dynasties in the north and ten kingdoms in the south, attacks by "barbarian" raiders alternated with internal con-

China expanded to the south, west, and north during the Tang dynasty. Northern Vietnam (Annam) and Turkish Central Asia came under Chinese control.

flicts among contending warlords. One military leader in the north—who reigned as Song Taizu (r. 960–76)—was finally able to unify all of China, founding the Song dynasty in 960. Taizu and his successors were never able to regain all the territories, however. Militarily powerful non-Chinese states bordered the Song, and the new rulers had to devise ways to keep them in check. Several were hybrid states, using Chinese methods of governance to rule over populations that included many Chinese immigrants. The Song responded by building a large military—their army had 1.25 million men by 1040—and producing large quantities of armaments. Military technology advanced as well; after using gunpowder to launch grenades, the Song invented the cannon. At the same time, scholar-officials were used to strengthen the centralizing power of the state. While this did help consolidate Song authority, in time excessive bureaucratization crept in, and rules and regulations began to impede creative governing.

Another consequence of the Song's strong focus on rule by scholar-officials was the rise of factionalism. As the state experienced mounting budgetary deficits and confronted peasant unrest, the emperor Shenzong (SHEN-dzhong; r. 1067–1085) called on an eminent statesman, Wang Anshi (WAHNG ahn-SHUH), to resolve these difficulties. Wang sponsored a thoroughgoing—and therefore threatening—reform program that granted interest-bearing agricultural loans to peasants, fixed commodity prices, provided unemployment benefits, established old-age pensions, converted labor service to monetary taxes, mobilized local militias, increased the number of schools, and reformed the examination system by stressing practical rather than literary knowledge. Although these measures brought some improvements, they evoked fanatical opposition from scholars, bureaucrats, and moneylenders. The internal debate resembled that of more than 1000 years earlier (the Salt and Iron Debates of the Han dynasty) over the propriety of the government's involvement in the economy. In the next generation most of Wang Anshi's reforms were rescinded.

Song ministers faced continuous threats along their northern and western frontiers. To placate their neighbors, the Liao (around Beijing) and the Xia (in the northwest), the Song paid them annual tribute payments in silk and silver. These payments indicated Song subordination or at least a desire for peace. In 1115, the Jurchen, a nomadic people from Manchuria, challenged the Liao. Believing the Jurchen would be good allies against their old rivals in Liao, the Song made a pact with them to divide Liao. Soon the alliance broke apart, and the Jurchen took the Song capital at Kaifeng (kai-FUHNG) in 1126. Ruling northern China, the Jurchen became increasingly sinified,

ruling according to Chinese ways and intermarrying with Chinese. The Song court fled in panic to Nanjing and later set up a new capital at Hangzhou (hahng-JOH), thus bringing to an end the Song effort to govern a realm united from north to south. The period from 960 to 1127 is often called the Northern Song, and that from 1127 to 1279 the Southern Song.

After a decade of indecisive war, a treaty in 1142 stipulated that the Song had to pay tribute of silk and silver to the Jurchen whose new dynasty was called Jin (1115–1234). It also prescribed that the Jin monarch be addressed as "lord" and the Song emperor as "servant" in all official communications. The subordination of the Song was thus formalized in language and in tribute payments.

Despite these disasters, the Song rulers enjoyed somewhat better economic conditions. The country experienced unprecedented economic and cultural advances, particularly after its territory was reduced to only southern China, and it turned increasingly toward using the many canals and streams throughout the South to move products. In addition, trade with the Jin state continued as before. One and a half centuries later, a new band of Central Asian nomads, the Mongols, conquered the Jin and went on to take

Tang, Song, and Yuan China

618–907	Tang dynasty
c. 690–705	Reign of Empress Wu
701–763	Poet Li Bo
712–756	Cultural flowering under Emperor Xuanzong
712–770	Poet Du Fu
755–763	An Lushan Rebellion
960–1279	Song dynasty
1005, 1042	Song sign treaties of subordination with Liao and Xia
1019–1086	Sima Guang, historian
1067–1085	Emperor Shenzong and Wang Anshi Reforms
1126–1134	Jin dynasty established in north
1162–1227	Chinggis becomes Mongol Khan (Supreme King)
1260–1294	Khubilai becomes Khan
1279–1368	Yuan dynasty

all of the Southern Song. From 1279 to 1368, China was ruled by Mongols who established a dynasty they called Yuan.

Song Economic and Social Conditions

Economic growth was rapid. Agricultural growth sustained a population that doubled between 750 and 1100. Farmers used their surpluses to buy charcoal, tea, and wine. Many raised and sold silk, sugar, vegetables, cotton, fruit, and wood products. The government maintained some monopolies, taxed trade moderately, built great water-control projects, and aided intensive agriculture, but otherwise loosened control over individual enterprise. Rice production doubled within a century after 1050, and industry grew rapidly, pouring out, for home and foreign markets, fine silk, lacquer wares, porcelain, and paper for writing, books, money and wrapping gifts. Heavy industry, especially iron, grew rapidly, and was used for tools, suspension bridges, and nails for construction. Song economic advances were furthered by such technical innovations as water clocks, explosives for mining, hydraulic machinery, paddleboats, seagoing junks, the stern post rudder, and the mariner's compass. These commercial developments were paralleled by the development of an oceangoing navy. The resulting commercial expansion prompted banks to depend on paper currency and specialized commercial instruments. Trade with the outside world, formerly dominated by Indians and Southeast Asians, was taken over by the Chinese, who established trading colonies throughout East Asia.

The Song economic revolution exerted tremendous foreign influence abroad. Paper money, dating from the eleventh century in the south, was soon copied in the Liao state and issued by the Jin government in 1153; its use then spread steadily in all directions. Other Song economic innovations appeared quickly in coastal areas from Japan and Korea to the East Indies, where Chinese merchants were immigrant culture carriers. Song technology also spread to India, the Middle East, and even Europe. From China, Europe acquired metal horseshoes, the padded horse collar, and the wheelbarrow. Chinese mapping skills, along with the compass and the stern post ship rudder, helped prepare the way for Europe's age of expansion. Later, gunpowder and movable type, both pioneered in Song China, arrived in Europe via Asian intermediaries.

Profound and rapid change brought many tensions to Song society. Some arose from urban expansion in a population that swelled from 60 to 115 million, a growth rate of more than twice the world average. A rise in population unaccompanied by a rise in the number of officials meant that passing the exams to enter officialdom became increasingly, and frustratingly, difficult. On the other hand, life was dynamic and cosmopolitan. Cities offered residents and travelers alike access to international culture, restaurants, plays, artwork, and civic organizations. Rural life was far less exciting, but farmers could go to regularly scheduled rural markets and read printed books published on a variety of topics, including agriculture, rituals, and childbirth. The spread of books and literacy created a national culture that transcended the localism of most rural societies. Unlike Europe, cities were not islands of merchant liberation in a rural sea of aristocratic domination; rather, scholar-officials ruled everywhere. Merchants did not have power, although they could take the exams to enter the scholarly class.

Women's lives were varied though lacking in power. While lively physical activity had been encouraged in the Tang—as evidenced in art work showing women playing vigorous sports like polo—a more demure and modest demeanor was expected of women in the Song. To be sure, the extant records of the Song show women who ran inns, delivered babies as midwives, worked as entertainers, sold their sewing and weaving, wrote poetry, and served as shamans (religious mediums). As wives and mothers, women had a voice in childrearing and spouse selection for their children, despite Confucian ideas that called for women to take a back seat to men in the family. Court records in inheritance cases indicate that judges made sure that daughters received money for dowries by which they could make more successful marriages. The availability of a great number of printed materials opened doors to literature for women of educated families.

At the same time, however, the resurgence of Confucian thinking reinforced a view that demure and even physically weak women were attractive. Women were told to be modest, which limited their public role, and footbinding carried this injunction to an extreme. Begun by dancers in the tenth century, the tight binding of a little girl's feet till they were broken, bent, and ideally just three inches long came to be a symbol both of beauty and of a girl's modesty and refinement. Bound feet attracted better marriage prospects but did little to expand girls' horizons. Though it began in the Song, footbinding was still uncommon at that time and was never mentioned by the Song's greatest woman poet, Li Qingzhao (LEE ching-JOW; 1094–1152). Female infanticide, restriction on remarriage of widows, and harsh legal penalties, including death, for violating the accepted code of prescribed wifely conduct were also Song social phenomena. Women were told to put their families first, but so, too, were men. All family members were under the rule of the patriarchal (male) family head, but women were additionally burdened by their subordinate position in society as a whole.

Song Philosophy, Literature, and Art

The rapidly changing Song society was reflected in its philosophy, literature, and art. Poets wrote of people's inner lives, joys, and misfortunes. Song aesthetic expression encouraged versatility; as during the later European Renaissance, the universal man, public servant, scholar, poet, or painter was the ideal. Song's most famous woman poet, Li Qingzhao, whose work was enthusiastically promoted by her scholar husband, wrote personalized verse describing the early years of her marriage in which she and her husband engaged in lively intellectual discussions. Su Shi (1037–1101) was a northern Song poet who excelled in painting and calligraphy as well as writing. Writing his poems on his paintings, he combined the three arts of the Confucian gentleman-scholar in a single work. In another genre, Sima Guang (SUH-muh GWAHNG; 1019–1086) was an outstanding Confucian historian. Known for his bitter attacks on his contemporary Wang Anshi, he also was an astute observer of the past, looking to it for moral guidance, and a critic of those who misread historical sources. Artists depicted the beauty of nature in

This Song landscape painting, Snow Mountain and Forest, *was painted by the artist Fan Kuan.*

widely varied styles, all involving great attention to detail. Landscapes embraced all of nature in a single work, removing humans from the central position they had had in earlier works. Darker tones and sharper lines replaced the decorative lightness of Tang works. The greatest Song landscape painter was Fan Kuan (FAHN KWAHN; active 990–1020).

Buddhism lost its appeal to Song's rulers as it was associated with their Liao, Xia, and Jin rivals, all of whom were ardent Buddhists. Confucianism, as a result, had a revival. The brothers Cheng Hao (1032–1085) and Cheng Yi (1033–1108) developed metaphysical approaches to Confucianism. They asserted that *li* (principle or pattern) was inherent in all things. *Qi* (CHEE; material force or energy) gives substance to things for which *li* is the blueprint. Mencius's contention that humans are fundamentally good (see Chapter 2) was always hard to explain in light of people's bad behavior. The Song **"Neo-Confucians"** could now claim that humankind's blueprint *(li)* was good but *qi* was sometimes impure and in need of cleaning. The Cheng brothers' most important follower was Zhu Xi (JOO SHEE; 1130–1200). His White Deer Grotto Academy was one of many that trained students in new approaches to Confucianism. He differed from the Chengs by ascribing greater importance to *li* over *qi* and by positing the existence of a Supreme Ultimate to which all *li* was connected. Zhu Xi contended that self-cultivation required the extension of knowledge, best achieved by the "investigation of things." In time, Neo-Confucianism was identified with Zhu Xi's philosophy, though it had many varieties and proponents.

The Song renaissance in scholarship was accompanied by significant advances in the experimental and applied sciences. Chinese doctors introduced inoculation against smallpox, and their education and hospital facilities surpassed anything in the West. In addition, there were notable achievements in astronomy, chemistry, zoology, botany, cartography, and algebra.

The Yuan Dynasty (1279–1368)

The Mongol conquest of the Song followed three-quarters of a century of Mongol growth and expansion in Central and Western Asia. The Mongol Khubilai's (1215–1294) takeover of the southern Song in 1279 furthered China's position as the center of Eurasia. Thus, although the Mongol era was a short dynasty despised by many Chinese and having a relatively minor impact on Chinese culture, it played a very significant role in world history. More than during the

Neo-Confucianism—Metaphysical form of Confucianism developed by the Cheng brothers and Zhu Xi; later became the dominant form of Confucianism throughout East Asia.

Song dynasty, with its lively international trade, and the early Ming, with its unprecedented maritime explorations, during the Yuan the five main areas of Eurasia—China, Southeast Asia, South Asia, Central Asia, and Europe—were part of a single world trading system. Europe was able to acquire Asian goods at low cost during this period; thus, when the Ming drove the Mongols out of China in 1368 and the Turks came to dominate western Asian trade routes, Europeans were inspired to seek maritime access to Asia. This, in turn, led to Europe's encounter with the Americas. Therefore, the brief Mongol period has an importance that belies both its brevity and its very limited demographic extent (the total Mongol population of about 1.5 million ruled over 100 times as many non-Mongols). Some background on earlier Central Asian tribes is helpful to understand the rise of the Mongols.

An earlier precedent for invasions out of Central Asia came from the Turkic peoples, who had figured in Eurasian history for a thousand years before the emergence of the Mongols. Between the sixth and eighth centuries, Turkic and Chinese regimes competed for control of the steppes. With Chinese support, the first Turkish Empire emerged in 552 and extended its dominion over much of Central Asia before it was conquered by the early Tang emperors. (An Lushan was of Turkish background.) During and after their imperial expansion, the Turks absorbed and transmitted much of the culture from their more advanced neighbors. Trade, religion, and warfare facilitated the process. Eastern Turks borrowed early from China, adopting

Buddhism and converting their western kinsmen in far distant Ferghana. After the eighth century, when the Abbasid caliphate brought Islam to the steppes, Turkic invaders launched conquests in the Middle East and India. Through the fifteenth century, there were waves of migration and conquest out of Central Asia and into the settled territories of Eurasia. Such incursions usually brought short-term disaster to occupied regions, but effected a great synthesis of peoples and cultures and ultimately led to the establishment of Turkic regimes from India to the Middle East.

For more than five centuries before the Mongol conquests, this process had been growing in intensity. Westward and to the north of the Chinese frontiers, a series of large states, partially settled but still containing nomadic or seminomadic populations, rose and fell. Among them were the Uighur Empire of the ninth century and the Tangut state. Both of these regimes prospered by providing goods, protection, and transport for the overland trade with China, which continued to grow. For many peoples of Central Asia—Turks, Uighurs, Tanguts, Tibetans, Mongols, and a host of others—trade, especially the silk trade, was one of many stimuli that turned their attention toward the outside world in the thirteenth century.

Debate continues over what sparked Mongol expansion: climatic changes that ruined Mongol pasture lands, military capability, or the inspiration of an ambitious warlord. The Mongols, horse- and sheep-raising nomads and formidable mounted warriors, began conquering cities and trade routes in the early

Two views of Mongols as seen by their contemporaries. Left is a Persian miniature showing Mongols preparing food at their tents. Right is a Chinese painting of a mounted Mongol archer. Tents and horses were critical elements of Mongol life and status. The Mongol khans gave tents and horses as gifts to honor their subordinates and Central Asian horses were in great demand in China and Japan. In Central Asian culture a warrior was, by definition, a horseman.

thirteenth century on the way to establishing an empire that controlled most of Eurasia a century later. Beginning with Temujin, known in the West as Chinggis (1162–1227), who was selected Great Khan (Supreme King) in 1206, they claimed that they were destined by "heaven" to subdue all peoples. Chinggis was likely motivated to begin his quest for power to avenge his father's death. The Mongols were remarkably successful in launching large-scale military operations throughout Eurasia. They seized Persia, toppled the Islamic Abbasid caliphate in Baghdad, established their rule in Russia, and sacked Delhi, though they made no further inroads into India before moving on to China. From North China, they invaded Korea (1231 and 1258) and attempted unsuccessfully to invade Japan (1274 and 1281) and Java (1281 and 1292).

The Mongols have often been represented as destroyers par excellence, sacking cities, disrupting trade, and building towers of the heads of their conquered foes. The Mongols often used terror to control conquered peoples, particularly during the early conquests. Mongol commanders regularly imposed mass murder, torture, and resettlement on resisting populations. One million residents of the Chinese city of Chengdu (chuhng-DOO) were slaughtered in 1236 although that city had already been taken with little fighting. But Mongol presence also facilitated trade and diplomatic activity by providing security and postal service on Eurasian trade routes.

The Mongols Before the Conquest of the Song

Prior to their expansion in the early thirteenth century, Mongols had ranged widely in Central Asia, pitching their black felt tents, pasturing their animals, and fighting the elements much like other peoples who had raided and traded with settled Eurasian populations since the fourth century B.C.E. Mongol chiefs contended to be the "first among equals," decisions were made by councils of warriors, and women enjoyed a high degree of respect and influence. Polygamy was practiced among the warriors, but not all marriages were polygamous, and marital fidelity was enforced equally for men and women. Wives sometimes rode and fought beside their husbands; in a harsh environment where raiding and warfare were common, women as well as men had sometimes to defend the hearth and livestock.

At the opening of the thirteenth century, the Mongols began their campaign of conquests and empire building. Within less than a century, they had subdued most populations from the Pacific to the Caspian Sea,

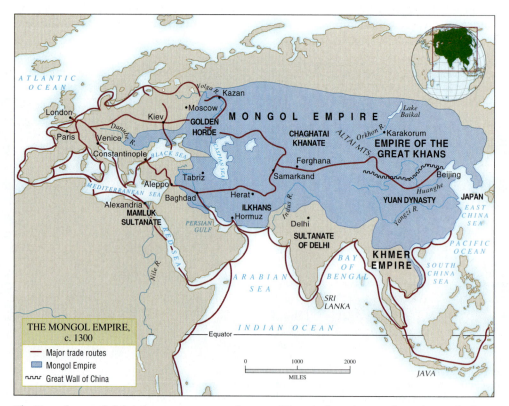

The Mongols extended their hegemony over a major part of Eurasia from the Danube to the Pacific from the mid-thirteenth to the mid-fourteenth centuries.

terrorized the rest, and gained luxuries beyond their imaginings. Trade and travel across Eurasia were facilitated. In most cases, however, they left a light cultural footprint. While the population of China did, indeed, decline from 120 million in 1207 to 60 million in 1290 (after the Mongol conquest), the cultural effects were less drastic. Chinese religion, painting, poetry, and social structure were not touched by the Mongols. Tolerance for foreign religions was promoted, but few Chinese changed their religious beliefs because of the presence of new sects.

During the first stage of their empire building, to 1241, the Mongols concentrated on the Central Asian steppe and its less developed border areas. Chinggis subordinated the Uighurs and Tanguts, seized Turkestan and Afghanistan, and invaded Persia. After his death in 1227, the campaigns halted and the Mongol forces reassembled in Mongolia to elect Chinggis's designated successor, his son Ögödei (EU-guh-dai; 1229–1241). Ögödei was granted Mongolia, from which he took the Jin Empire in northern China in 1234.

Between 1251 and 1259, during the reign of Ögödei's son, Möngke (MUHNG-kuh), Mongol armies conquered eastern Tibet (1252) and Korea (1259) while Möngke's brother, Hülegü (hoo-LEH-goo), toppled the Abbasid caliphate, absorbing every subsidiary state in Persia, Palestine, and Syria. Hülegü's campaign reflected the cosmopolitan nature of the Mongol army, with its Chinese catapult operators, and its court, with its Chinese physicians. The Mongols integrated the commanders, bureaucrats, artisans, and professionals of the conquered peoples into their armies and courts, thereby enhancing their ability to conquer and govern through borrowing the best practices of the conquered people.

Khubilai Khan (r. 1260–1294) emerged as dominant following a struggle from power among Mongol kings in 1260. After 1264 the empire broke up into four parts with only nominal central administration: Mongolia and China under Khubilai; and three other khanates in western Turkestan, Russia, and Persia and Iraq.

Mongol rulers of the mid-thirteenth century were forced to learn quickly how to organize and operate the largest imperial state that had ever existed. Although the ultimate base of authority in the sprawling Mongol territories was military power whose nucleus was a cavalry force of potentially 130,000 Mongols, civil administration and taxation were necessary. They developed a complex courier system linking the empire and created a written form of their language by using the script of the conquered Uighur people to transmit messages and records. The nomadic methods of the steppes were obviously no longer effective and had to be integrated with those of more experienced conquered bureaucrats.

Khubilai Khan hunting with his wife or a consort in a scroll painted in the late thirteenth century. Mongol women and men were expected to be vigorous and talented equestrians.

Before the conquest of the Song dynasty, Möngke revised the law code of Chinggis Khan to accommodate native cultural differences and meet practical needs. He minted coins, issued paper currency, collected taxes in money, and perfected a census system as a basis for taxes and military service. To support military operations, his state industries mined ores and produced arms. Other measures regularized trade tolls, improved roads, and provided for the safety of travelers, especially merchants. These reforms encouraged support from subject peoples, many of whom were now employed in the khan's service. Other areas were under lighter Mongol control. In these, local rulers proclaimed their submission publicly, left hostages with the khans, paid annual tribute, and provided troops for military campaigns. Such tributary rulers who served the khans loyally were guaranteed political security, honored publicly, and rewarded with lavish gifts (e.g., horses, daggers, furs, or silk garments).

China Under the Yuan Dynasty

Khubilai, who reigned as Great Khan from 1260 to 1294, turned his sights to the conquest of the Southern Song. After moving his capital to Beijing in 1264, he adopted a Chinese name for his dynasty in 1271. Like other Central Asian rulers who sought power in the east, Khubilai relied heavily on the advice of his Chinese and non-Chinese sinified advisors. One Song general offered advice on the construction of boats capable of navigating the many rivers and canals of South China. Khubilai, who had relied on cavalry and massive armies for his earlier conquests, thus became the first Central Asian conqueror of South China. Making use of a multiethnic force of Jurchen, Mongols, Persians, Uighurs, Koreans, and Chinese, Khubilai's forces laid siege to the Song. When the Yuan conquered all of China in 1279, Khubilai had gained the richest empire on earth. But even as he gained the wealth of China, the Mongol Empire had already ceased to be a unified Asian empire. Each of the four major khanates had developed its own state, and these were often at odds with one another. Though it is inaccurate to consider the Mongol realm a single political entity, the Mongol bonds of the khanates facilitated trade across the numerous Central Asian routes. Moreover, Turks and other West-Central Asians who had tried to take advantage of the commercial caravans themselves were suppressed during this period, making transport cheaper and easier.

Life under the Mongols was hard for most Chinese. While the Mongols did not prevent Chinese cultural expression, they did treat ethnic Chinese as distinctly inferior. A hierarchy dominated by foreigners was established: Mongols at the top, other peoples of Central Asia on the next rung, northern Chinese in lower positions, and southern Chinese almost completely excluded from office or public life. Taxation of Chinese was high. Many southern Chinese were subjected to serfdom or slavery. Though Khubilai retained the traditional ministries and local governmental structure, he staffed them with those in higher hierarchical positions. Generally, Mongol law prevailed, but the conquerors were often influenced by Chinese legal precedents, as in the acceptance of brutal punishments for loose or unfaithful women. Most religions were tolerated unless they violated Mongol laws.

According to Marco Polo, a Venetian traveler who arrived at Khubilai's court around 1275 and served the Khan for 17 years, the ethnic Chinese deeply resented unequal treatment. On the other hand, Polo also noted that the state insured against famine, kept order, and provided care for the sick, the aged, and the orphaned. To the awed Venetian, the Yuan state appeared fabulously wealthy, as indicated by the khan's 12,000 personal retainers, bedecked in silks, furs, fine leathers, and sparkling jewels.[9] Polo's fabulous story, dictated to a fellow prisoner of war in Genoa, reported the wondrous world of Cathay (China)—its canals, granaries, social services, technology, and such customs (strange to much of Europe) as regular bathing. Polo's account, like many travelogues of the period, is an interesting mix

DOCUMENT

Marco Polo on Chinese Society

of fact and fantasy based on impressionistic observations and probably prompted by the desire to entertain as well as inform a specific audience. Polo was not the only observer of China, but his work at the court gave him an unusual vantage point.

The Yuan court's social practices, in addition to the discriminatory ethnic hierarchy, included the requirement that individuals register by occupation in order to pay labor services. In the realm of culture, the Yuan borrowed some Chinese traditions. At first, Daoism and Confucianism were subordinated to Buddhism, but both were revived during Khubilai's reign. The examination system was sporadically revived after 1315 but was weighted in favor of Mongols, so ethnic Chinese grew disillusioned. Chinese drama remained popular, influenced somewhat by the dance of Central Asia. Interest in drama encouraged the development of classical Chinese opera, a combination of singing, dancing, and acting, which reached maturity in the Yuan period. Some of the most influential Chinese painters were also producing at this time, and the novel emerged as a reflection of Chinese concerns. An example is *Romance of the Three Kingdoms*, a long and rambling tale set in late Han times but written in the fourteenth century.

During the Yuan dynasty, hosts of missionaries, traders, and adventurers continued to journey to and from Asia, Africa, and Europe. These travelers describe the opulence of China and the Mongol court. Even before the Polos, Christian missionaries had proceeded eastward, encouraged by hopes of converting the Mongols and, more important, gaining allies against the Muslims. John of Plano Carpini (PLAH-noh car-PEE-nee), dispatched by Pope Innocent IV, visited the Great Khan in 1246 but failed to convert the ruler or enlist him as a papal vassal. In fact, the khan sent him home with a letter demanding that Europe's monarchs submit to him and that the pope attend the khan's court to pay homage. Later, a Flemish Franciscan, William of Rubruck, visited Möngke's court in 1254 and 1255 and met with similar results; but another Franciscan, John of Monte Corvino, attracted thousands of converts to Christianity between his arrival in Beijing in 1289 and his death in 1322. Meanwhile, Mongol religious toleration had drawn Christians into Central Asia and Buddhists into the Middle East.

In addition to the missionaries, swarms of other people visited China and Mongolia. One was Guillaume Boucier, a Parisian architect, who trekked to Karakorum, where he constructed a palace fountain capable of dispensing four different alcoholic beverages. Other adventurers, equally distinct, moved continuously on the travel routes. Between 1325 and 1354, Ibn Battuta, the famous Muslim globetrotter from Morocco, visited Constantinople, every Middle Eastern Islamic state, India, Sri Lanka, Indonesia, and China. In Hangzhou he encountered a man from

Gog and Magog in the Ebstorf Mappamundi

Maps depict more than geographical observations; they tell us the beliefs and imaginings of the people who produce them and reflect the point of view of the mapmaker. Historically, when people lacked a clear picture of far-off lands, they employed fantastic stories to describe what lay beyond their own known world. Like myths and folktales, maps from different eras illustrate some of the ways that societies have imagined apparently "strange" or "foreign" lands. We have seen that there was considerable commercial and intellectual exchange among Europe, India, China, and Central Asia in the years 220–1350 C.E. Nonetheless, the "Orient" remained a mysterious place in the imagination of many Westerners, a sometimes frightening place inhabited by strange creatures.

The thirteenth-century Ebstorf Mappamundi (map of the world), discovered in a Benedictine monastery in Germany, presents a geographical vision that combines Christian historiography, geographical observation, biblical mythology, the legends of Alexander the Great, and ancient tales of beastlike races inhabiting the "ends of the earth." It incorporates the idea of Gog and Magog, the homelands of apocalyptic destroyers, drawn from the New Testament (Revelation 20:7–8), into the description of the territory of northeastern Asia, the Mongol territory to the north of the Caucasus Mountains. On medieval Christian maps

Gog and Magog were equated with barbarian races, with the Ten Lost Tribes of Israel, and with the armies of the Anti-Christ. According to legend, these ferocious peoples had been trapped by Alexander the Great, who built a great wall to contain them; they would break out at the end of time and overwhelm civilized societies. On the Ebsdorf map the people of Gog and Magog are tribes of savages who are shown eating human body parts and drinking blood. They are walled off in the far northeast of the world. Their identification with the Tartars suggests the fear of Turco-Mongol invaders that pervaded the mapmaker's society in the thirteenth century. Given the striking success of the Mongols' conquests in this era, it is no wonder that they came to be associated with Gog and Magog. Gog and Magog also appear on the twelfth-century Islamic world map of al-Idrīsī (see Chapter 7).

Questions to Consider

1. Why might medieval Europeans have imagined that a "hero" like Alexander the Great put a wall around such fearsome peoples?

2. Do you think the mapmakers took the idea of Gog and Magog literally? Why or why not?

3. What other examples do you know reflecting ideas about frightful peoples that live in far-off lands or about terrible events occurring at the "end of time?"

Morocco whom he had met before in Delhi. Some travelers went the opposite way. Rabban Sauma, a monk from Central Asia, traveled to Paris; and a Chinese Christian monk from Beijing, while in Europe as an envoy from the Persian khan to the pope, had audiences with the English and French kings.

Eurasian traders—Persians, Arabs, Greeks, and western Europeans—were numerous and worldly wise travelers. They were enticed by Mongol policies that lowered tolls in the commercial cities and provided special protection for merchants' goods. Land trade between Europe and China, particularly in silk and spices, increased rapidly in the fourteenth century. The main western terminals were Nizhni Novgorod, east of Moscow, where the China caravans made contact with merchants of the Hanseatic League, a coalition of German merchant companies; Tabriz, in northeastern Persia, which served as the eastern terminal for Constantinople; and the Syrian coastal cities, where the caravans met Mediterranean ships, mostly from Venice.

Expanding land trade along the old silk route did not diminish the growing volume of sea commerce. Indeed, the Mongol devastation of Middle Eastern cities provided a quick stimulus, particularly to the spice trade, which was partly redirected through the Red Sea and Egypt to Europe. Within a few decades, however, the Mamluk monopoly in Egypt drove prices up sharply, and the European demand for cheaper spices helped revive overland trade. By now, however, the southern sea route was thriving for other reasons. The Mongol conquest of China had immediately opened opportunities to Japanese and Malayan sea merchants, causing a modest commercial revolution. Later, after the government in China stabilized and became involved in the exchange, the volume of ocean trade between northeastern Asia and the Middle East surpassed that of Song times.

Although their conquests were accompanied by horrifying slaughter and wrought considerable havoc, Mongol control also spread knowledge of explosives, printing, medicine, shipbuilding, and navigation from China to the West. In the Middle East they furthered art, architecture, and historical writing. To China they brought Persian astronomy and ceramics, in addition to sorghum, a new food from India.

In the end, the Yuan dynasty was short-lived. Khubilai was its last effective leader. A powerful chancellor attempted to build a new canal to transport southern grain after the Yellow River burst its dikes in the 1340s, but his conscription of 150,000 laborers strained China's resources. In response, a messianic religion, the **White Lotus Society,** claimed numerous adherents anxious for Maitreya, the messiah Buddha, to bring about an end to suffering and injustice. Devastating epidemics hit cities already weakened by Mongol subjection; in 1232, Kaifeng lost one million

people to the plague in three months. By mid-century, plague ravaged China and spread via the trade routes to the rest of Eurasia. A great rebellion, beginning in southern China and led by Zhu Yuanzhang (JOO yoo-ahn-JAHNG; 1328–1398)—known to history as Taizu, the first emperor of the Ming dynasty—ultimately ended the weakened Yuan. After the Chinese reconquered most of Mongolia and Manchuria, many northern Mongols reverted to nomadism. Others, on the western steppes, were absorbed into Turkic states.

KOREA: FROM THREE KINGDOMS TO ONE

■ *How did Buddhism and Confucianism contribute to Korean culture and politics?*

In the third century C.E. the land inhabited by modern Koreans was divided in three kingdoms—one in the north and two in the south. Despite the common stereotype of Korea as an isolated "hermit kingdom," these three kingdoms were very much part of East Asian international culture. They adopted religion, arts, philosophy, and means of governance from China, transmitted culture and material goods to Japan, and fought battles against and in alliance with Chinese and Japanese rulers at various times. The fate of Koreans was closely integrated with the rise and fall of empires on the continent. By the fourteenth century, domestic and international influences led to the merger of the Korean kingdoms into one kingdom.

Southeast Asia, Japan, and Korea

According to legend, Ko Chosŏn (KOH CHO-son), the earliest kingdom of Korea, was established in the third millennium B.C.E., but bronze age remnants date it from about 1500 B.C.E. Archaeological remains show that Koreans grew millet, soybeans, red beans, and rice; used ploughs and knives; developed metallurgy; and had an animistic form of religion in which all natural objects had spirits. Labor became specialized into peasant and artisan categories. In 109 B.C.E., this productive territory attracted the attention of the Han dynasty in China. Emperor Wudi conquered Ko Chosŏn and established four Chinese provincial commanderies in the north, permitting the introduction of Chinese culture. The decline of the Han allowed the newly arising Korean states to push the Chinese out and compete for dominance.

Koguryŏ (KOH-goo-ree-oh) was founded in 37 B.C.E. and by the first century C.E. had adopted a Chi-

---

White Lotus Society—Messianic religion that blended Manichaeism, Maitreya Buddhism, Daoism, and Confucianism. Appealed to people in times of crisis.

Korea

57 B.C.E.	Silla established
37 B.C.E.	Koguryŏ established
200s C.E.	Paekche established
383	Buddhism adopted in Korea
668	Silla defeats Paekche and Koguryŏ, unites Korea
936–1392	Koryŏ dynasty
1238	Mongol Invasion

nese style of kingship. Free peasants, living in villages under headmen, formed the bulk of society. Legal codes punished murder, theft, and bodily injury as well as female (though not male) adultery and jealousy—underscoring the importance of life and property in addition to the centrality of the polygamous, patriarchal family. The rise of the southern state of Paekche (PAIK-cheh) in the third century led Koguryŏ to strengthen its institutions: Koguryŏ's King Sosurim (r. 371–384) adopted Buddhism, set up a National Confucian Academy, and developed an administrative law code, all of which made Koguryŏ a centralized aristocratic state. In 433 Paekche formed an alliance with Silla (SHIL-lah; founded 57 B.C.E.), the other southern state. Koguryŏ fought against its Korean neighbors, sometimes in alliance with Chinese or Japanese forces. Koguryŏ was a powerful kingdom, later launching attacks on the Sui in China. (Its victories against the Sui army are part of the Korean annals of resistance.)

All three kingdoms were culturally Buddhist; Paekche adopted Buddhism in 384 and Silla in 528. Their poetry and arts followed Buddhist themes. Because most buildings were made of wood, none remain, but paintings and sculpture from this period, many with religious themes, are plentiful. A major **pagoda** (the East Asian form of the stupa) was built in Silla in 645, and lasted till it was destroyed by the Mongols in the thirteenth century.

Silla began to assert its power in the fifth century. Silla had an aristocratic society in which officials' positions were determined by "bone-rank" (that is, one's bloodline or status). Officials met in the Council of Nobles, and young men were placed in the Flower of Youth Corps, a powerful military organiza-

tion. Silla allied with the Tang to defeat Koguryŏ and Paekche in the 660s, but, worried about Tang expansionism, Silla decided to push the Tang out of the Korean peninsula in 676. Lively trade between Silla and the Tang ensued, taking the place of conquest. Koreans were drawn into the international system promoted by the Tang; a Silla general in service to the Tang conquered Tashkent and Silla monks traveled to India. The eighth century, in which Pure Land Buddhism and Zen were introduced to Korea and the agricultural output was plentiful and varied, was the high point of Silla rule. By the ninth and tenth centuries, powerful landowners emerged, breaking apart the equal-field system applied in Silla.

In 936, one of many rebels succeeded in unifying the peninsula under a new dynasty he called the Koryŏ (KOH-ree-oh). This leader, King Taejo, and his immediate successors emancipated slaves (while retaining some forms of labor taxes), instituted an examination system (though preserving some aristocratic privilege), collected all arms held by private individuals, built a major university, supported Buddhism, and attempted to model the kingdom on Song Confucianism. Throughout its early years, Koryŏ faced threats from the Liao. The Jurchen's defeat of Liao and then of the northern Song left Koryŏ temporarily at peace with its neighbors. Domestically, however, the civilian leadership of Koryŏ was removed by a bloody coup by military officials in 1170, and peasant uprisings

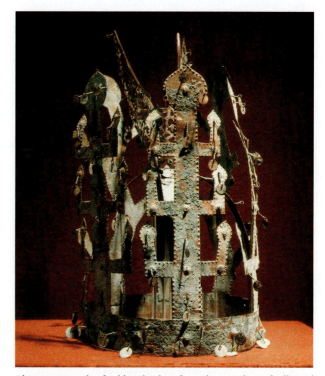

This crown made of gold and jade is from the Kingdom of Silla and was made in the fifth or sixth century. Its opulence is a symbol for the national unification of Korea under a monarch.

---

pagoda—A Buddhist reliquary/monument, the East Asian equivalent of the Indian stupa.

around the same time weakened, but did not destroy, the state.

The Mongols invaded the weakened Koryŏ state in 1238. In the 1270s and 1280s, Koryŏ joined the Mongols in two unsuccessful invasions of Japan. Destructive Mongol rule led to uprisings throughout Korea in the 1340s, and soon King Kongmin (r. 1351–1374) restored Koryŏ rule. But he was doomed to failure. His bold initiatives at land reform were resisted by officials, tensions between Buddhists and Neo-Confucians of the Zhu Xi school erupted, and Japanese pirates plagued coastal trade. When he was assassinated in 1374, uprisings broke out all over Korea. The newly risen Ming dynasty in China took advantage of Koryŏ's instability, and was poised to invade in 1392. The Koryŏ general facing the Ming saw the writing on the wall, negotiated a treaty that made Korea a Ming tributary state, and marched back to the court to take over as the founder of the Yi or Chosŏn dynasty (1392–1910).

Even in times of trouble, however, Korean culture blossomed. When the great royal library was burnt in 1126, a new collection of Buddhist works was commissioned. Movable type to print this great collection was cast and used three centuries before Gutenberg first used movable type in Europe. Buddhist works of literature, painting, and sculpture as well as a beautiful stone pagoda were also produced during the Mongol era.

of aristocratic society that developed in the classical age that followed the tomb period. How did Japan develop before the tomb period?

Classical Asian culture—religions, philosophies, arts, and means of governance developed on the continent—flowed into Japan first from Korea and later from China. During the Ice Age, land bridges had connected Japan with the continent. Tools dating from 30,000 B.C.E. and pottery dating from 10,000 B.C.E. (the world's oldest examples of pottery) have been found by archaeologists. Whether these were developed in Japan itself or transmitted from elsewhere is uncertain. An increasingly sophisticated Neolithic culture, called Jōmon (JOH-mon) by scholars, developed distinctive pottery and, between 5000 and 3500 B.C.E., the ancient Japanese language. But it was around 300 B.C.E. that a large migration of Koreans to Japan's westernmost large island, Kyūshū, brought about a revolution in agricultural technology (paddy-field rice) as well as bronze and iron technology. By the time the Chinese observers commented on life in Japan in the late third century, the civilization that blended the new continental ideas with indigenous culture had been established for over 600 years. The period from about 300 B.C.E. to 300 C.E. is called the Yayoi (yah-YOI) period for the district in Tokyo in which the period's pottery was first unearthed.

THE EMERGENCE OF JAPAN IN EAST ASIA

■ *Did Japan's distance from the continent allow it to retain more of its indigenous culture than the other countries of Asia in the classical and medieval eras?*

Separated from the Asian mainland by more than 100 miles of open sea since the end of the last Ice Age (around 12,000 B.C.E.), Japan was something of a curiosity to Chinese observers in the late third century C.E. These Chinese chroniclers found the Japanese law-abiding, adept at farming, fond of alcohol, expert at weaving and fishing, interested in divination, and perhaps most surprising, governed by both male and female shamanistic rulers. They described one of these rulers, Queen Himiko (also known as Pimiko), as a powerful priestess/monarch who, after her death, was interred in a remarkably large funeral mound. These tombs, some of which were twice the volume of the Great Pyramid in Egypt, tell historians that Japan was likely a hierarchical society able to mobilize labor during the tomb period, c. 300–645 C.E. The existence of religious leadership, especially female religious leadership, helps to explain the type

Clay figures like this happy dancing peasant couple were placed in the huge tombs built for Japanese uji *leaders in the third, fourth, and fifth centuries.*

The following era, the tomb period, gave birth to what might be called Japan's first organized governments, ruled by those whose remains are in the great tombs. At first, the extent of a leader's control was likely no more than a clan located in one village, but in time, successful leaders brought more and more villages under their control until they had something like a province. Political authority was intimately connected to religious authority. The original clans, called *uji*, were led by a head priest or priestess believed to be descended from the clan's own deity or *kami*. In ancient Japanese religion—later called **Shintō** ("Way of the Gods") when the introduction of Buddhism made it obvious that Japan's intrinsic belief system deserved a religious name—*kami* were believed to be everywhere in nature. The world of the living was seen as connected to the world of the gods, and governance was a part of religious ritual. Thus, women were not barred from what we would consider administrative leadership, and the Chinese observers found that fact sufficiently interesting to comment on it.

The *uji* in the Yamato region, near the area in which the cities of Nara and Kyoto were later built, possessed the most fertile agricultural land in ancient Japan. It is small wonder that the Yamato leaders, able to build on their productive wealth to support military strength, emerged as the most powerful *uji* by the fifth century. The Japanese language did not yet have its own written form, so historians rely on Chinese observers' reports from the fifth century, rich archaeological remains in tombs, and Japanese histories (*Kojiki*—Records of Ancient Matters—and *Nihongi*—Records of Japan), written in the early eighth century and based on orally transmitted tales, for evidence about people's lives at that time. Tomb artifacts throughout the period included jewels, mirrors, and, most interestingly, clay statues of human figures like warriors, musicians, courtiers, and dancing peasants, all showing expressions of joy, as well as of horses, boats and model houses. From the fifth century on, these tombs increasingly held military objects brought in by a new wave of people from the Korean peninsula. Outside the tombs, archaeological remains of peasant villages suggest farmers lived in pit dwellings.

The power of the Yamato *uji* vis-à-vis the other *uji* throughout Japan was bolstered by its alliance with Paekche. Korean artisans and scribes brought a wealth of Korean and Chinese culture with them to Japan, strengthening the prestige, authority, and administrative competence of the Yamato state. Imported weapons allowed the Yamato warriors to hold sway over their neighbors. As in Korea, Chinese characters were used to transcribe Japanese. Confucian scholarship was introduced around 513, and Buddhism made

Shintō—Indigenous Japanese religion focused on innumerable gods in nature; animistic belief system tied to government in antiquity.

Japan	
c. 300 B.C.E.–300 C.E.	Yayoi period
late 200s	Queen Himiko of Yamato
c. 300	Yamato clan dominates central Japan
c. 538	Buddhism introduced to Japan
645	Taika Reform
710–784	Nara period
760s	Compilation of *Man'yōshū*
794–1181	Heian period
c. 800	Introduction of Tendai and Shingon Buddhism
995–1027	Regency of Fujiwara Michinaga
c. 1000	Lady Murasaki, *The Tale of Genji*
1185–1333	Kamakura Shogunate
1274, 1281	Mongol Invasions

a grand entrance, possibly in 538, when the king of Paekche sent Yamato a statue of the Buddha and copies of Buddhist scriptures. Though the ties with Paekche soon ended, the coming of continental culture in general and Buddhism in particular set in motion a cultural and intellectual revolution in Japan. After Silla's unification of the Korean peninsula in the 670s, the Yamato leaders turned to the Tang dynasty for cultural models, diplomatic ties, and trade. At the same time, the Japanese retained significant indigenous customs. These included marriage practices that emphasized the central role of the bride and her family, practices that would later play an important political role. They also included the old religions of Japan. The Yamato family, while welcoming Buddhism following a sixth-century struggle between Shintō ritualists and proponents of Buddhism that was won by the latter, nevertheless retained the worship of the Shintō gods. At some earlier time, as the Yamato were rising to power, a myth of Japan's creation that blended several *uji*'s founding myths and placed the Yamato's ancestral deity Amaterasu **(AH-mah-teh-RAH-soo)**, the sun goddess, at the top of the hierarchy, developed. The Yamato would use this to legitimize their political dominance for many centuries to come.

The victorious proponents of Buddhism, the Soga family, greatly influenced the Yamato family. During his aunt's reign as the Yamato ruler, Prince Shōtoku (SHOH-toh-koo), head of the Soga, apparently undertook so many reforms that Japan was forever changed. He is credited with scholarly commentary (in flawless Chinese) on Buddhist scriptures; with building many temples, including, in 607, Hōryūji (hoh-ree-OO-jee), which contains the world's oldest extant wooden buildings; with opening diplomatic relations with the Sui and later Tang; with adopting the Chinese calendar; with reorganizing the Yamato governing structure on the model of the Confucian state to make it the central monarchy of Japan; and with writing, in 604, the "Seventeen-Article Constitution." These accomplishments were detailed in one of the eighth-century histories of Japan and undoubtedly exaggerated the Prince's personal contributions, but most of them did take place either during his service as regent to the throne or in the decades after his death. Shōtoku's death in 622 led to a struggle for power, ending with the victory of one courtly faction led by the head of the Nakatomi family (renamed Fujiwara in 645). The Yamato family retained the throne, as they do to this day, but the Fujiwara family replaced the Soga as their main advisors. In 645, the Fujiwara carried out the Taika (Great change) Reforms, which centralized economic control under the equal-field system imported from China and Korea. Two rulers, Emperor Temmu (r. 672–686) and Empress Jito (r. 686–697), implemented additional changes; they and their successors were simultaneously continental-style rulers empowered by the prestige of Confucian authority and Shintō rulers legitimized by descent from Amaterasu.

Government in the Classical Era— Nara and Heian

An important step toward Chinese-style centralization was the building of a permanent capital. In 710, the Yamato, by then considered the imperial family, built the city of Nara on the model of Chang'an. Although today's Nara is located in a different site, the eighth-century capital's grid of streets and ancient Buddhist temples are still evident in the Japanese countryside. The rise of powerful Buddhist monasteries and temples may have challenged the power of the court sufficiently to force it to abandon Nara in 784 and build a new capital, Heian (now called Kyoto), in 794. Like Nara, Heian was originally laid out on a grid pattern preserved in modern Kyoto's downtown boulevards and streets. Historians designate the years 710–784 as the Nara Period and 794–1181 (or 1185) as the Heian Period.

To make the capital the sole seat of power, the court enticed all *uji* leaders, who might be potential rivals for power, to live there by granting them titles of nobility and making the court too glamorous to avoid. Many of these *uji* families' provincial lands were con-

A fine example of architecture during the mid-Heian period in Japan is Phoenix Hall, near the modern city of Kyoto. Used by Fujiwara Michinaga as a villa, it later became a temple honoring Amida.

fiscated and redistributed under the equal-field system in the seventh and eighth centuries, but the *uji* were allowed to retain some lands, as were religious institutions and individual farmers who opened new fields to cultivation. Such private estates, unlike the lands farmed by average peasants, were exempt from taxation by the court. Though these estates, called **shōen,** were but a small percentage of Japan's cultivated fields in the eighth century, during the next several centuries peasants wishing to escape taxation commended their lands to private estate owners. This led to the gradual reduction in taxable lands, as farmers paid rents to large owners rather than the often higher taxes to the court. The replacement of tax revenues by rents did not at first appear problematic, however. The great families not only lived at or near the court but also, as we shall see, were often tied by blood to the imperial family. By the eleventh century, however, the gradual erosion of the tax base undermined the central authority of the court. In addition, the absence of a government-run military—a conscript army was one of the Chinese institutions not implemented by the Japanese court because Japan appeared not to face external enemies as did the Chinese—induced estate owners to hire guards to protect their provincial economic interests. These guards eventually became the samurai or warrior class. When they served as guards, they presented no threat to the throne, but when they banded together, as they did in the tenth century and then, most disastrously for the court, in 1181, they could become an alternate political authority to the throne.

Even during the height of the throne's power, its authority was dependent on a balance with one great family, the northern branch of the Fujiwara family. The Fujiwara had earned a special role as advisors at the time of the Taika Reform, but they preserved their dominant position through Japan's traditional marriage practices. Japanese couples married extremely young by today's standards—often as young as 12 or 13. Though girls of the elite spent most of their time indoors and spoke with men not of their immediate families from behind a screen to maintain their propriety, they were very well educated and could communicate easily by letters. Literature describes the lives of women and girls at the court as much more open, and these courtly women communicated more freely with men and with one another. In either case, women and girls played an important role in selection of their sexual and marital partners.

CASE STUDY

Women in the Imperial Courts of China and Japan

A young man interested in a woman at court might find few barriers to a liaison with her. If the young woman lived at home with her parents, courtship was a bit more complicated. The suitor would call on a potential lover by slipping, under cover of night, through the windows of her room, taking care not to wake her parents. She would speak to him, exchanging poetry and observing his character and attractiveness, from behind her screen. If his clothes, language, scholarly ability, scent, musical talent, and sensitive heart were sufficiently appealing, it was proper for her to invite him behind her screen. If not, she sent him packing, and her propriety was not compromised. If he spent the night, he would have to sneak out at the first rays of morning light. Repeated visits would trigger the parents' investigation of the young man and his career prospects, and if they approved, they would indicate the couple's marriage by leaving ritual food and drink outside their daughter's bedroom door. Thereafter, the young man could come and go during the day, as he was now part of the family as the daughter's husband. The young man would be known as the husband of his bride's house, her parents would make sure he was beautifully outfitted to present himself well at court, and in some cases, once the bride was mature enough to run her own household, the parents and other children might move to another house and leave the teenage bride in charge of her own home. Most likely, she would already have one or two children, raised in their early years by their maternal grandparents, as women usually had their first child in their teens. Grandparents thus had a particularly strong bond with their grandchildren. Property was inherited by daughters, children were their mothers' and maternal grandparents' responsibility, and respectable men and women—though not *married* women—could have more than one sexual partner. Once married, a woman should be unavailable to other men, but serial monogamy was practiced.

Fujiwara influence over the throne depended on marriage customs and family relations. When an 8-year-old boy ascended the throne as emperor in 858, his maternal grandfather, a Fujiwara who was already Grand Minister to the court, assumed even greater control as regent for his grandson. This pattern of Fujiwara patriarchs' control of child emperors, and even some adult emperors who were their grandsons or other relatives, continued for the next 200 years. The pinnacle of Fujiwara dominance was in the early eleventh century. Fujiwara Michinaga (MEE-chee-NAH-gah), who held dominion over the court from 995 to 1027, was the brother of two empresses and the father of four, the uncle of two emperors, the grandfather of two more, and the great-grandfather of another. Some non-Fujiwara protested, but until an emperor whose mother had not been a Fujiwara ascended the throne in the late eleventh century, the Fujiwara controlled the throne. Through this control, the Fujiwara were able to have the tax-free ownership status of their shōen estates confirmed, as only an official could grant that status. For the next century, retired emperors took the place of the Fujiwara as

---

shōen—A tax-free estate in Heian Japan.

regents for their youthful sons whom they placed on the throne. In the late twelfth century, disputes over succession to the throne led to the development of factions at court, and with each faction backed by a powerful samurai family, civil war raged throughout the country from 1181 to 1186. When it was over, the imperial institution survived, but it no longer had the authority to rule Japan. That power fell to the victorious samurai leader, Minamoto Yoritomo (MEE-nah-MOH-toh YOH-ree-TOH-moh; 1147–1199), his wife, Hōjō Masako (HOH-joh MAH-sah-ko; 1157–1225), and her family, who exercised their power from the medieval town of Kamakura in eastern Japan.

Classical Arts and Literature

Japanese emperors sent numerous embassies to the Tang court and brought back a continuing stream of up-to-date culture and material goods. New developments in Chinese poetry were reflected in Japanese verse; new schools of Buddhism influenced Japanese religion; and plump Tang beauties set the standard for female pulchritude at the Japanese court. Yet Japan preserved many of its own practices, including an emphasis on aristocracy, a rejection of eunuchs at court, and unique marriage customs. In 839, as the Tang dynasty was clearly declining, the court ceased to send embassies to China.

Courtly society from the Nara through the Heian periods was extraordinarily refined. The record left from those centuries includes great volumes of poetry, diaries, the world's first novel—the massive *Tale of Genji* by Lady Murasaki—as well as paintings, sculpture, temples, monasteries, and other buildings. Art works from distant lands in Eurasia, brought to Japan by travelers to China, show Japan's integration with the international culture of the Buddhist Age in the Nara and early Heian eras. And music preserved in Japan's court until the present day is the only extant record of Tang musical styles borrowed in the classical era. Impressive though this body of culture is, it was the creation of just a tiny group of people; aristocrats were no more than one tenth of one percent of the population, with urban residents influenced by those aristocrats perhaps an additional several percent.

Unlike aristocrats, farmers were not literate. Tax rates appear high, as evidenced by peasants' attempts to escape the tax roles. Pestilence devastated farmers and city-folk alike. Men, women, and children worked hard. Despite these difficulties, folk tales and written stories abound with examples of farm women's high status relative to their husbands. Women likely selected their own spouses, and many made important economic contributions to their households. Wives' infidelity was treated as a joke rather than as a capital crime in folk tales.

The poetry of the literate elite reflected the importance of sentiment. The *Man'yōshū* (mahn-YOH-shoo; *The Collection of Ten Thousand Leaves*), compiled in the 760s, contains over 4000 poems, many of which date to the fifth century, composed by emperors, empresses, courtesans, frontier guards, and commoners. These brief and direct compositions covered such themes as parting of lovers, loyalty to one's lord, love of nature, grief over the death of a child, and the Buddhist theme of the fleeting nature of human life, give us a rich sense of early Japanese society and culture. Two *Man'yōshū* poems, the first a love poem by a woman, the second a poem of grief for his wife by a man, give a sense of this collection:[10]

Court ladies and their maids in The Tale of Genji. *Heian court women were ideally plump, had hair longer than their bodies, and wore many layers of robes. The* Genji *scrolls integrated text and images.*

Oh, how steadily I love you—
You who awe me
Like the thunderous waves
That lash the seacoast of Ise!

> Lady Kasa

In our chamber, where our two pillows lie,
Where we two used to sleep together,
Days I spend alone, broken-hearted:
Nights I pass, sighing till dawn.

> Kakinomoto Hitomaro

The imperial treasury at Nara, built in the eighth century, contains works of art by both Japanese and continental artists, indicating Japan's increasing international contacts in the Nara period. This small silver jar depicts a hunting scene that includes a deer, still one of the symbols of Nara.

Because the Japanese language did not have a written form, it was represented with Chinese characters. Aristocratic men and some women were able to read and write in Chinese and thus sought to use characters to record Japanese. The two languages are not related linguistically, so the characters were used in several different ways. One was to represent meaning—the Chinese character for "tree," for example, would be applied to the Japanese word for "tree." The other was to represent sounds without any consideration for the meaning of the character. This led to a virtually indecipherable script, so *kana*, a syllabic script, was devised in the early ninth century. Soon poetry, diaries, essays, and novels were written in this script. Aristocratic authors, especially but not exclusively women, produced an outpouring of creative works. Women's dominance in the literary arts at that time was due, in part, to the fact that men spent a lot of their time writing government documents in Chinese. But the fact that creativity, including calligraphic, artistic, and sensory abilities, was not gendered at that time, as well as the leisure time their aristocratic privilege gave them, may have had more to do with offering women opportunities to produce fine works.

The most important work of the Heian period—and some might say of the entire body of Japanese literary arts—was *The Tale of Genji*, written over the course of perhaps two decades by Lady Murasaki, who

DOCUMENT

Excerpt from Lady Murasaki Shikibu's Diary

was sometimes praised, sometimes ridiculed for her exceptional knowledge of both Japanese and Chinese scholarship.[11] *The Tale of Genji* describes the life, loves, escapades, and sorrows of the sensitive and talented Prince Genji, a paragon of male virtue; his son Kaoru; Genji's steadfast male friends; and his beloved wife Murasaki. The novel is an intriguing look into courtly life around the year 1000. An excellent parallel to *Genji* is *The Pillow Book* by Sei Shōnagon (SAY SHOH-nah-gon), a contemporary and professional rival of Lady Murasaki at another empress's court. *The Pillow Book* contains often racy, amusing and satirical essays that give good insight into the life of the court.

From the sixth century through the first half of the Heian period, religious themes predominated in the arts. Statues and paintings of various manifestations of the Buddha, indicating changes in artistic style and notions of physical beauty over the centuries, were common. But decorated items for aristocratic pleasure, such as musical instruments, boxes, and tables are also among the treasury of early Japanese art. By the tenth century, paintings of highly secular themes emerged. Fans with themes from literature were made and used by court ladies, and the *Genji* scrolls of the eleventh century were a multimedia production interspersing gorgeous paintings with Murasaki's text. Comic scrolls appeared by the late Heian period. The architecture of the court and of private mansions was elegant, with raised floors of polished wood, sliding screen doors, wooden buildings connected to one another by covered corridors, windows with hinged shutters (through which suitors could climb), all surrounded by carefully landscaped gardens with streams and ponds.

Japanese Buddhism in the Classical and Early Medieval Eras

Mahayana Buddhism reached entered Japan in the sixth century and was well established among the aristocracy by the eighth. To further the secular reach of the Nara state, the court established branch temples throughout the country, staffed by monks trained in the capital. Most commoners, especially those in the countryside, continued to carry out Shintō rituals. Except for the struggles in the sixth century, there was little conflict between Buddhism and either indigenous Shintō and the imported philosophy of Confucianism as there had been in China, and Buddhism was eventually

Document   Sei Shōnagon: *The Pillow Book*

Sei Shōnagon was a contemporary and literary rival of Lady Murasaki. The two served different empresses of the reigning emperor; Sei Shōnagon's court was considered more fashionable and Lady Murasaki's more erudite. Sei Shōnagon was a witty and talented writer. In her diary, Murasaki describes Sei Shōnagon as "a very proud person. She values herself highly and scatters her Chinese writings all about. . . . How can such a vain and reckless person end her days happily!"[11] Below is an excerpt from Sei Shōnagon's *Pillow Book* in which she describes distressing things.

One has been expecting someone, and rather late at night there is a stealthy tapping at the door. One sends a maid to see who it is, and lies waiting, with some flutter of the breast. But the name one hears when she returns is that of someone completely different, who does not concern one at all. Of all depressing experiences, this is by far the worst.

It is very tiresome when a lover who is leaving at dawn says that he must look for a fan or a pocket-book that he left somewhere about the room last night. . . . Instead of experiencing the feelings of regret proper to such an occasion, one merely feels irritated at his clumsiness. . . . It is important that a lover should know how to make his departure. To begin with, he ought not to be too ready to get up, but should require a little coaxing. . . . He should not pull on his trousers the moment he is up, but should first of all come close to one's ear and in a whisper finish off whatever was left half-said in the course of the night. . . . If he springs to his feet with a jerk and at once begins fussing around, one begins to hate him.

I like to think of a bachelor . . . returning at dawn from some amorous excursion. . . . As soon as he is home . . . he begins to write his next-morning letter. . . . When he has washed and got into his court cloak . . . he takes the sixth chapter of the Lotus Sutra and reads it silently. Precisely at the most solemn moment of his reading, the messenger returns. . . . With an amusing if blasphemous rapidity the lover transfers his attention from the book he is reading to the business of framing an answer.

Questions to Consider

1. How important was romantic love to Heian aristocrats?
2. The ideal bachelor Sei Shōnagon describes reads Buddhist scriptures before heading off to work at the court. What other tasks take priority over his religious practice?
3. Did women have a choice in the selection of their suitors?

From "The Pillow Book of Sei Shōnagon," in Donald Keene, *Anthology of Japanese Literature* (New York: Grove Press, 1955), pp. 137–139.

---

indigenized as the dominant religion of Japan following new theological directions in the Heian period.

Two new sects of Buddhism were brought to Japan by student monks who had journeyed to China in 804. Tendai, introduced by Saichō in 805, and Shingon, brought back by Kūkai in 806, both made it possible to develop mass participation in Buddhist worship. Tendai doctrine stated that those who led a life of purity and contemplation could realize enlightenment and their "Buddha nature." Saichō established an important monastery at Mt. Hiei (HEE-ay), which several centuries later became a source of trouble for the court as it supported not only devotion and learning but also a large army of warrior-monks who demanded land rights and privileges. Shingon was an esoteric faith, with secret and seemingly magical rites. It was extremely popular in the Heian period, as it encouraged art, medicinal use of herbs, incantations, and pageantry. It also appealed to Shintō adherents, as its

IMAGE
Buddhist Monks

central deity was Dainichi (DAI-nee-chee), the "Great Sun" Buddha, who was identified with the Sun Goddess in the popular mind.

In the mid-tenth century, itinerant monks spread a simplified version of the Tendai doctrine of enlightenment, stating that salvation was possible only for those who called on the name of Amida, the Buddha of the Pure Land. But it was not until the end of the Heian period, with its natural disasters, earthquakes, fires, and fearsome warfare that a proponent of Pure Land Buddhism succeeded in establishing a new type of Buddhism. The monk Hōnen (1133–1212) preached that faith in Amida alone, without relying on good works, was the only route to salvation. He endured persecution for his propagation of Pure Land ideas. His follower Shinran (1173–1262) took these ideas even further. He said that perfect faith was shown by uttering the name of Amida just once, and that an evil man of perfect faith was able to enter the Pure Land. Shinran broke with Buddhist tradition—eating meat,

The pagodas of Yakushi-ji at Nara. Built in the eighth century, Yakushi-ji is one of Japan's earliest wooden temple compounds. Buddhist temples of that era challenged the secular power of the government, so the emperor's court moved to Heian in 794.

marrying a nun, and advocating the equality of all occupations if performed with a pure heart. His True Pure Land sect eventually became the largest in Japan. The other important faith sect was Nichiren (NEE-chee-ren) Buddhism, founded by the monk Nichiren (1222–1282), who stated that one should place faith in the Lotus Sutra, a key Buddhist scripture, rather than Amida. Known for his Japanese nationalism, he predicted the Mongol invasions. By the twelfth century, Buddhism had spread to all classes of society.

Two major **Zen** sects were also brought back to Japan by Japanese student monks. Eisai (1141–1215) introduced the Rinzai sect and Dōgen (1200–1253) the Sōtō sect. Rinzai stressed complicated riddles to achieve enlightenment, while Sōtō emphasized long hours of meditation. Both methods were increasingly popular with samurai who were attracted to the sudden enlightenment they promised.

Early Medieval Government and Culture

Minamoto Yoritomo's victory over the other major warrior band, the Taira, in 1185 ushered in the era of warrior dominance. He never claimed the throne, as victorious generals elsewhere in Asia had, but rather had the emperor confer on him a new position, *shōgun* (great general), a title which would remain in use for most of the next 700 years. The shōgun theoretically served at the pleasure of the emperor, but (until 1868) when emperors attempted to assert their rights, the struggle was always won by the shōgun, who, of course, claimed to be serving the emperor. (An

attempted imperial uprising in 1221 was suppressed.) The shōgun set up his seat of power in Kamakura, away from the capital, and the era of Kamakura dominance is called the Kamakura Period (1185–1333).

Minamoto Yoritomo's legitimacy as a ruler was based on his own institutions in addition to his symbolic subordination to the emperor. First, he made use of the loyalty of his samurai. Like feudal lords in Europe, he used a bond of loyalty to motivate his samurai warriors, whom he called "honorable house men" or vassals. These vassals were appointed constables of provinces, with the duty to raise up armies if necessary, and stewards or overseers on the shōen estates owned by the rich old Heian families. To show his authority over the estates, he allowed the stewards to collect a small amount of revenue—so small that owners did not bother to contest it as they had contested the imperial court's ability to collect taxes on private lands. By paying the small fees, however, owners acknowledged the legitimacy of Kamakura's right to collect it. During the next century, the stewards would use these locally collected resources to establish their own landed power base in the countryside, and they would eventually turn on their supposed overlords in Kamakura. Second, Minamoto Yoritomo and his successors made use of much of the provincial governing structure of the old imperial system for most of the next century. The vassal samurai were too few in number to rule on their own, so the previous system was retained in many places. Third, Minamoto established three new offices: the samurai board, which controlled the vassals; the judicial board, which settled suits over land holdings as well as criminal issues; and the administrative board, to carry out his policies. The judicial board was particularly important in gaining the support of the people, as it was known for its impartiality in settling disputes. The administrative board was headed by his Hōjō in-laws, and was used by them to increase their power after Yoritomo's death in 1199. Indeed, power passed into Hōjō hands, where it remained until the Kamakura shogunate (government by shōgun) was overthrown.

Zen—The Japanese form of Chan Buddhism. Popular with the samurai.

By the end of the thirteenth century, samurai ties to Kamakura had become attenuated. Allegiance to the dominant Hōjō was not as certain as allegiance to the Minamoto had been earlier. Far from Kamakura, samurai stewards out in the provinces developed local ties, both political and economic. When the Mongols attacked in 1274 and again in 1281, the samurai, especially those of the western island of Kyūshū, where the attack came, fought bravely, but none was rewarded, because there were no spoils of war to divide. The invasion in 1274 threw 30,000 attackers against Japan; the second invasion was mounted by 140,000. Commoners built a sea wall whose remnants are still visible today to keep the Mongols out; it helped the Japanese warriors hold the Mongols out until typhoon winds, called *kamikaze* (divine winds), blew many of the Mongol vessels out to sea, forcing them to withdraw. Japan was saved, but the invasions had some very significant outcomes. Disgruntled warriors who had fought, commoners whose labor had built the fortifications, and religious people who claimed their prayers brought about the divine winds eventually moved against Kamakura when succession disputes at court gave them an excuse to join one side or the other in the 1330s. Also, the practice of daughter inheritance and multiple inheritance gave way to unigeniture or inheritance by one son in order to keep samurai lands intact to support a mounted warrior now deemed necessary for national defense. Single inheritance weakened family ties, as younger sons sought new patrons to protect them. This strengthened the lord-vassal bond at the heart of feudalism, which became increasingly important in the next three centuries.

Kamakura was home to numerous beautiful temples, built in harmony with the verdant hills, a new style of construction. A huge outdoor Great Buddha statue that still attracts thousands of tourists every day was cast in the early Kamakura period. But much of Japan's culture in this era emanated from Heian (now increasingly called Kyoto). The court commissioned great collections of poetry as they had in earlier centuries, and court ladies wrote, for an aristocratic readership, tales of great emotional depth. Periodic markets began to bring rural people into a larger national culture, but the arts were still fairly elite. This would change in the next century, as a national culture, enhanced by new infusions of Asian styles, entered Japan.

CONCLUSION

During the centuries following the collapse of the Mauryan dynasty in India (184 B.C.E.) and, much later, the Han dynasty in China (220 C.E.), significant cultural revivals occurred in Asia. First India and then China experienced golden ages when political unity was restored and social systems were revitalized. In India, the Gupta era encouraged the development of Hindu thought, along with notable advances in painting, architecture, literature, drama, medicine, and the physical sciences. At the same time, India continued to be part of an emerging international Buddhist culture, helping to link it to other Buddhist countries along the East-West trade routes. Later, international Islam tied rising Indian dynasties, some of them Islamic, to other centers of power and trade. China experimented with blending "barbarian" and indigenous means of government in the millennium from the fall of the Han to the fall of the Mongols. Cosmopolitan blending of culture made China the East Asian center of both cultural consumption and production. Scholarship and art blossomed even in the period of disunity and flourished in the lively international Tang dynasty and the technologically sophisticated early modern Song dynasty. Korea and Japan, while retaining much of their own culture, adopted a number of aspects of Chinese governance, art, philosophy, religion, and means of communication. Rivalries at times impeded trade, but diffusion of material and other forms of culture made Eurasia a single system, often dominated by its eastern side, during much of the millennium. Over the centuries, cultural diffusion gained increasing momentum throughout Eurasia. Goods and cultural patterns spread through migrations, invasions, missionary activities, and trade to China, India, Southeast Asia, Japan, Korea, the Asian steppes, and Europe.

Suggestions for Web Browsing

You can obtain more information about topics included in this chapter at the websites listed below. See also the companion website that accompanies this text, **http://www.ablongman.com/ brummett,** which contains an online study guide and additional resources.

Ancient and Medieval India
http://www.fordham.edu/halsall/india/indiasbook.html
> *Extensive collection of materials on ancient and medieval India; most entries include subsites with text and images.*

Gupta Period
http://www.wsu.edu:8080/~dee/ANCINDIA/GUPTA.HTM
> *Indian history in the Gupta era.*

Medieval India
http://www.goindiago.com/history/medieval.htm
> *Site discussing the history, sites and monuments, and classical texts of medieval India, 600 B.C.E.–1526 C.E.*

Chinese Empire
http://www.wsu.edu/~dee/CHEMPIRE/CHEMPIRE.HTM
> *Chinese history from 256 B.C.E. to 1300 C.E., with details about philosophy and culture.*

The Heian Era
http://www.wsu.edu:8080/~dee/ANCJAPAN/HEIAN.HTM
> *This site gives a valuable context to the Heian era.*

Ancient Japan

http://www.wsu.edu:8080/~dee/ANCJAPAN/ANCJAPAN.HTM

Website on ancient Japan includes political, religious, and cultural history, details about women and women's communities, and a portfolio of art from the era.

Samurai Archives

http://www.samurai-archives.com/

Extensive collection of information about individuals and events in the samurai millennium.

Empires Beyond the Great Wall: The Heritage of Chinggis Khan

http://web.archive.org/web/20000815214514/http://vvv.com/khan/

A rich site (now archived) offering a biography of Chinggis Khan and information about the history and culture of the Mongol Empire.

Literature and Film

The following works give the flavor of this long millennium in India: *The Panchatantra,* trans. Arthur W. Ryder (University of Chicago, 1967); Prince Ilangô Adigal, *Shilappadikaram (The Ankle Bracelet),* trans. Alain Daniélou (New Directions, 1965); Somadeva, *Tales from the Kathāsaritsāgara,* trans. Arshia Sattar (Penguin, 1994); Cornelia Dimmitt, ed., *Classical Hindu Mythology: A Reader in Sanskrit Puranas,* trans. J. A. Van Buitenen (Temple University, 1994).

For a fictional treatment about Empress Wu that offers a picture of Tang court opulence and intrigue see Evelyn McCune, *Empress* (Fawcett Columbine, 1994). For Japan, Lady Murasaki's *Tale of Genji* is available in several excellent translations. The newest is by Royall Tyler (Penguin Publishers, 2002). A 1991 animated film (subtitled) is a good introduction to the first third of the book.

Suggestions for Reading

Informative surveys of India's medieval history include Hermann A. Kulke, *A History of India,* 3rd ed. (Routledge, 1998); and Tej Ram Sharma, *The Political History of the Imperial Guptas* (Concept, 1989). On the Delhi Sultanate, see Peter Jackson, *The Delhi Sultanate: A Political and Military History* (Cambridge University Press, 2003). On women, see Tracy Pintchman, *The Rise of the Goddess in the Hindu Tradition* (State University of New York Press, 1994); and Leslie Orr, *Donors, Devotees, and Daughters of God: Temple Women in Medieval Tamilnadu* (Oxford University Press, 2000).

Two of many fine general histories of China in the post-Han, Tang, Song, and Yuan periods are Patricia Buckley Ebrey, *Cambridge Illustrated History of China* (Cambridge University Press, 1996); and Charles O. Hucker, *China's Imperial Past* (Stanford University Press, 1975). A comprehensive work on Chinese painting is *Three Thousand Years of Chinese Painting,* eds. Richard M. Barnhart, Nie Chongzheng, Lang Shaojun, James Cahill, and Wu Hung (Yale University Press, 1998). Dorothy Ko, Jahyun Kim Haboush, and Joan R. Piggott's *Women and Confucian Cultures in Premodern China, Korea, and Japan* (University of California Press, 2003) is an excellent overview of the role of women in each of the three countries. For a classic though still excellent introduction to the Song, see Jacques Gernet, *Daily Life in China on the Eve of the Mongol Invasion, 1250–76* (Stanford University Press, 1962). Valerie Hansen, *The Open Empire: A History of China to 1600* (W. W. Norton, 2000) explicates Tang and Song foreign relations and the domestic repercussions of economic expansion. On women and family relationships see Patricia Buckley Ebrey, *The Inner Quarters: Marriage and the Lives of Chinese Women in the Sung Period* (University of California Press, 1993). Katherine Bernhardt's *Women and Property in China, 960–1949* (Stanford University Press, 1999) gives us a legal history of family law in Song China with its social repercussions. On the Yuan dynasty see Elizabeth Endicott West, *Mongolian Rule in China* (Harvard University Press, 1989).

An excellent study of networks of trade and communication in the Mongol era is Janet Abu-Lughod, *Before European Hegemony: The World System, A.D. 1250–1350* (Oxford University Press, 1989). A recent work that treats Asia as an interacting unit is Warren I. Cohen, *East Asia at the Center: Four Thousand Years of Engagement with the World* (Columbia University Press, 2000).

A solid survey of Korean history is Carter J. Eckert, et al., *Korea Old and New: A History* (Harvard University Press, 1990). Surveys of Japanese history in the classical and medieval eras include *The Cambridge History of Japan: Ancient Japan,* eds. Delmer M. Brown, John Whitney Hall, Marius B. Jansen, Madoka Kanai, and Denis Twitchett (Cambridge University Press, 1993); John W. Hall, *Government and Local Power in Japan, 500–1700* (University of Michigan Press, 1999); and Wayne Farris, *Heavenly Warriors: The Evolution of Japan's Military, 500–1300* (Harvard University Press, 1996). Karen Brazell's translation of *The Confessions of Lady Nijo* (Stanford University Press, 1976) offers a fascinating account by an itinerant woman, once a court lady, now a nun, in the early thirteenth century, and is a wonderful addition to the larger body of work on women writers in the Heian period.

CHAPTER 11

The Americas to 1492

Early civilizations in the Americas followed a social sequence similar to that found in Africa and Eurasia. As agriculture became more diversified, food supplies increased and some cultures became more and more able to support cities, highly skilled crafts, expanding commerce, complex social structures, and the emergence of powerful states. The most noteworthy were the civilizations of the Mayas in Yucatán and Guatemala, the Aztecs in central Mexico, and the Incas in Peru. The Mayas are particularly recognized for their mathematics, solar calendar, and writing system—70 percent of which has only recently been deciphered. The Aztecs and Incas conquered large populations and governed extensive states. Each civilization produced distinctive customs, values, art, and religion, many of which have become part of the Latin American heritage. Spanish adventurers who invaded these civilizations were shocked by the religious sacrifices of human beings but astonished by the wealth, grandeur, technical efficiency, urban populations, and institutional complexity they saw in Central America and Peru. For example, Tenochtitlán (te-nohch-teet-LAHN), the Aztec capital with its 150,000 inhabitants, was larger and probably better administered than any European city of its time.

To the north of Mesoamerica, hundreds of Amerindian tribes developed diverse social patterns, languages, and economic pursuits as they adapted to the differing environments they faced. Around 4000 B.C.E. Amerindians in the southwestern part of present-day Florida founded villages along the coast in which they enjoyed a rich diet of fish, shellfish, grains, and berries and lived in accord with a sophisticated religious system that included the burial of the dead in funeral mounds. Recent archaeological finds indicate that still earlier in the present-day state of Washington, Amerindians founded villages with their own unique cultures and economic activities. The Amerindians to the north never attained the centralized power or wealth of the Mayas, Aztecs, and Incas. However, they left behind a variety of archaeological sites that attest to their sophistication and creativity.

40,000

c. 40,000–10,000 B.C.E. Movement back and forth across the Bering Strait land bridge

10,000

10,000 B.C.E. Nomadic migrations from Asia reach tip of South America

c. 5000 B.C.E. Development of maize agriculture

2000

c. 2000 B.C.E. Divergence of Inuits and Aleuts

c. 1200 B.C.E.–150 C.E. Formative period of Mesoamerica culture (Olmec)

c. 800 B.C.E.–600 C.E. Adena and Hopewell cultures

1 C.E.

c. 150–900 Classical period in Mesoamerica culture (Maya)

c. 300 Beginning of Anasazi culture

500

c. 500–600 Beginning of Mississippian culture

c. 900–1500 Postclassical period of Mesoamerican culture (Toltec, Aztec)

1000

c. 1100–1500 Development of Inca empire

c. 1300 Height of Cahokia culture

1500

c. 1500s Inca Empire in South America reaches maturity

ORIGINS OF AMERICANS AND THEIR CULTURES

■ *Does the development of Amerindian cultures support or negate the theory of parallel development?*

Many of the American cultures can be traced back to nomadic migrations from Asia to Alaska, across the Bering Strait land bridge. During the Pleistocene epoch, coinciding with the last great ice age, humans established themselves in Siberia where they built underground shelters and hunted large mammals such as mammoths. The most recent ice advance, beginning some 65,000 years ago, locked up immense amounts of global water and lowered sea levels, creating a land bridge that enabled Paleolithic people to follow the animals they hunted into North America. Later, as increasing global temperatures melted the ice and raised water levels, the bridge slowly disappeared around 10,000 years ago, after an estimated 30,000 years of sporadic human migrations. Recent discoveries indicate that there also may have been other routes of entry into the Americas, including those by sea from Iceland and Greenland and across the Pacific into Chile and Peru.

Archaeological work throughout the twentieth century continually pushed back the estimates of the time of the first permanent residents. Artifacts known as Clovis spear points, the oldest of which are about 11,200 years old, were found from Mexico to Nova Scotia. Continued discoveries across North America revised the estimates of when human beings settled in the Americas to around 20,000 years ago. Some archaeologists think humans could have lived in North America even earlier. However, the most widely accepted estimates of the first human settlement in the Americas are 14,000 years ago, with humans reaching southern Chile by circa 12,500 years ago. Recent discoveries in Peru indicate that the first city in the Americas was that at Caral, founded around 2600 B.C.E. Archaeologists believe that the pyramids built there were constructed a century before the Great Pyramid at Giza in Egypt.

Over this protracted period the Amerindians split into eight major ethnolinguistic groups and hundreds of subgroups and adapted to numerous physical environments. New research has shown the Americas to be far more densely populated in the fifteenth century than the European invaders believed—perhaps by as many as 75 million people before the massive population decline caused by climatic changes and foreign diseases such as small pox in the fifteenth and sixteenth centuries.

The development of agriculture in the Mexican highlands, along the Peruvian coastal plain, and in what is now the southwestern United States caused major changes in indigenous American culture after 7000 B.C.E. This development occurred considerably later than in the Near East, and the plants that the Amerindians domesticated were different from those in other parts of the world. They also domesticated animals such as alpacas and llamas in the Andes—there were no cattle, sheep, or horses until the Europeans arrived in 1492. The major agricultural contribution came with the cultivation of maize (corn), shortly before 5000 B.C.E., in the Tehuacán (ti-wah-CAN) valley of Mexico. From this center, maize culture spread widely. After 1000 B.C.E. it became the staple food for hundreds of societies, from the Mississippi River valley to the Argentine pampas. The Aztec Confederacy and Inca Empire, which so awed the Spanish *conquistadores* after 1500, were dependent on the raising of maize.

Beyond these mature civilizations, cultural levels varied widely among the Amerindians by the end of the fifteenth century. Some powerful cultures, like that of the Mound Builders of the Mississippi valley, borrowed heavily from Mexico. Cahokia, a major capital and trade center near contemporary St. Louis, Missouri, housed approximately 25,000 people during the thirteenth century. Other sophisticated cultures north of the Rio Grande ranged from the Pueblo of the southwest to the large Iroquois Confederacy of the eastern woodlands. In South America, complex cultures lived along the north coast and near the mouth of the Amazon. Other societies developed on Caribbean islands, in the South American pampas, and in Chile. Other Amerindians—probably a majority of them—were still hunters and gatherers. These included the Eskimo peoples of Alaska and the Inuit peoples of Arctic Canada; jungle groups such as the Jivaro (he-VAR-oh) of the upper Amazon; and the peoples of Tierra del Fuego, at the southern tip of South America.

Despite differing timeframes, Amerindian cultures differed little from cultures in Africa and Eurasia in their progression from Paleolithic hunting and food gathering to Mesolithic semifixed communities to Neolithic food production and settled communal life and then to urban centers and the emergence of political states. They also displayed common traits with other civilizations in their theocratic systems, sun cults, and human sacrifices. Like the African cultures, they were in transition from matriarchal to patriarchal institutions, although further along in the process. Finally, a common belief in monarchy among Aztecs and Incas was also typical of many other peoples in the ancient river civilizations of Eurasia.

EMERGING CIVILIZATIONS IN MESOAMERICA

▪ *What geographical and climatic factors permitted the rise of Mesoamerican civilization?*

Central and South American Civilizations

A variety of related cultures flourished in **Mesoamerica,** a zone ranging from roughly 100 miles north of Mexico City to Costa Rica. The region varies greatly in landforms, climate, and vegetation. Two mountain ranges run through northern Mexico to join a central highland block in the region of the Valley of Mexico. The Pacific coastal region is relatively narrow while that on the Atlantic side is wide. The north and west have dry lands with sparse vegetation; the south and east are marked by tropical rain forests and savannas.

Despite these physical differences, the early cultures were unified by their economic interdependence, because no one region was self-sufficient. They shared a complex calendar, hieroglyphic writing, bark paper, deerskin books, team games played with balls of solid rubber, chocolate bean money, widespread upper-class polygamy, large markets, and common legends. A popular one featured a god-man symbolized by a feathered serpent. We may conveniently divide Mesoamerican history into three main periods: formative (to 150 C.E.), classical (150–900), and postclassical (900–1492).

The Formative Period

For a millennium after 1500 B.C.E., villages in the regions of Mexico and Central America grew steadily to become cities. Scattered throughout this region at the beginning of this period were some 350,000 people, living in relatively sparsely populated ceremonial trading centers and villages. Labor and stone for the massive construction projects, jade for carving, luxury goods, raw materials for the crafts, and food were brought to the centers often from distant places—without the use of horses, mules, or oxen. These goods were probably not the spoils of conquest; Olmec society left little evidence of war or violence, although some security would have been present to protect trading missions.

In these settlements artisans worked at pottery making, weaving, feather design, and masonry. Merchants ranked second only to the priesthood in social status, as they conducted trade among the temple cities. As population increased and society became

Mesoamerica—A cultural zone in Central America ranging from roughly 100 miles north of Mexico City to Costa Rica.

Mesoamerican and South American Civilizations	
2500s B.C.E.–400s C.E.	Olmec
300s–900s C.E.	Mayas
900s–1200s C.E.	Toltecs
1100s–1500s C.E.	Incas
1300s–1500s C.E.	Aztecs

more complex, priests came to dominate governments. They governed by enjoying respect and exploiting fear rather than relying on force. The general theocratic orientation is reflected most clearly in the great temple mounds; in the huge stone conical pyramid at La Venta, rising some 100 feet; and in the characteristic carved statuary that represented the dominance of the Olmec cults.

In time the common culture, known as the Olmec, centered in five geographical areas. One was in the Oaxaca (wah-HAHK-ah) region of western Mexico; another was in the inland Valley of Mexico; a third straddled the present Mexican-Guatemalan border; and a fourth (the later Mayan) arose in the southern highlands and lowlands of Yucatán, Honduras, and Guatemala. The fifth, and at the time most significant, area spread over some 125 miles of the eastern Mexican coast and its hinterlands, near present-day Veracruz.

Archaeological research in Olmec sites reveals exceptional wealth, technical efficiency, and artistic sensitivity. In many Olmec sites, the oldest at San Lorenzo, there were great stone buildings and pyramids dating from 1200 B.C.E. The culture is perhaps best known for its colossal heads and its fine jade carving, featuring jaguars. This cultural maturity was not matched by military advancements: San Lorenzo was destroyed by invaders about 900 B.C.E.; another ceremonial center at La Venta, in Tabasco, assumed leadership until it, too, fell, six centuries later.

Olmec influence permeated most of present-day Mexico and Central America. A few independent Olmec centers may have been established farther to the north, but it was probably more common for a number of Olmec priests and traders to live among native populations, conducting religious rites and arranging for the transport of goods to the homeland. Such enclaves were typical of regions as distant as the Pacific coast of Central America. In other places, such as the Oaxaca valley to the west, the southwestern

Ranging from the lowland and jungles of Central America to the arctic cold of the Andes, the civilizations of Central and South America exhibited a rich and sophisticated diversity.

Mexican highlands, or the southern Mayan regions, Olmec influence was more indirect, possibly resulting from trade or Olmec marriage into local elites. By such varied means, Olmec foundations were laid for the religion, art, architecture, and characteristic ball games—and possibly for the calendars, mathematics, and writing systems—of later civilizations, including the Mayan and the Aztec.

The Classical Period

After the fall of La Venta, Olmec prestige waned, but by the second century C.E., cultural developments progressed to a point known as the classical period, which

would last until the tenth century. This was a golden age when, across the region, written communication, complex time reckoning, a pantheon of gods, interregional trade, and a 40-fold population increase over the Olmec period occurred. Hundreds of communities raised great buildings, decorated them with beautiful frescoes, produced pottery, figurines, and sculptures in large quantities. Although classical Mayan culture of the Yucatán lowlands is perhaps best known, Teotihuacán (te-oh-tee-wah-KAHN*)*, in the northeastern valley, also generated an impressive culture.

At its peak about 500 C.E., Teotihuacán was the sixth largest city in the world, with a population of 125,000 to 200,000. Three and a half miles long and nearly two miles wide, it was laid out in a grid of sorts

The colossal Pyramid of the Sun rose above the metropolis of Teotihuacán. Measuring 650 feet at its base and 213 feet high, the structure is more than four times larger than the Great Pyramid of Khufu (Cheops) in Egypt.

and paved with a plaster floor on which clusters of imposing edifices were erected. This ceremonial center is dominated by the temple-pyramids dedicated to the moon and the sun. The first pyramid was cut off at the top to provide for a temple with a broad step ascending from a wide rectangular court. Running south is a long ceremonial axis, and adjacent to it the Pyramid of the Sun. Also truncated, it measures 650 feet at the base and rises in four terraces to 213 feet above the valley floor. The interior contains more than a million cubic yards of sun-dried bricks, and the exterior was once faced entirely with stone. As with other pyramids throughout Mesoamerica, these structures, with their ceremonial staircases, led to temples at the summit where rites and sacrifices were offered to the gods.

Teotihuacán was noted for its specialized craftspeople who came from all over Mexico and occupied designated quarters of the city. Its streets were studded with bustling markets, where all types of goods were available from foreign as well as local sources. This wealth permitted a governing elite of priests, civil officials, military leaders, and merchants to enjoy great luxury. Teotihuacán exerted a powerful influence over other states, including some among the lowland Mayas, because of its cultural reputation, social connections, and commercial advantages. When necessary, it used its formidable military power to enforce trade and tribute agreements. Above all, Teotihuacán marks the high point of priestly power over the rest of society. Thereafter, especially with the Toltecs, the cultures came to be far more military in character.

Another impressive classical center in Mexico was located at Monte Alban in the Oaxaca valley. In 200 B.C.E. it already had a population of 15,000, and its fortifications dominated the valley. In Teotihuacán's era, this concentration of temples, pyramids, and shrines was a theocratic state, still drawing tribute from adjacent hill settlements and a valley population of over 75,000 people. Although developed on a smaller scale than Teotihuacán, Monte Alban produced a similar pattern of foreign trade, class distinctions, elaborate religious architecture, artistic creativity, writing, and time reckoning. It derived most of its art styles from Teotihuacán and some from the Mayas but synthesized both in its own traditions. Politically, it remained independent through the classical era, although its elite sought the luxury goods and favor of Teotihuacán.

CLASSICAL MAYAN CIVILIZATION

■ *What were the economic, political, cultural, and religious characteristics of Mayan civilization?*

While Teotihuacán and Monte Alban flourished, Mayan peoples farther south in Yucatán and Guatemala brought artistic and intellectual activity to new heights in more than 100 Mayan centers, each boasting temples, palaces, observatories, and ball courts. Although it borrowed from Teotihuacán before the latter's decay in the eighth century C.E., Mayan civilization subsequently cast a brilliant light over the whole of Mexico and Central America.

IMAGE

A Mayan Town

The earliest Mayas are thought to have migrated from the northwest coast of California to the Guatemalan highlands during the third millennium B.C.E. From that homeland, Yucatec- and Cholian-speaking peoples settled the northern and central lowlands, respectively, between 1500 B.C.E. and 100 C.E. Mayan villages developed steadily, many becoming ceremonial centers by the start of the Common Era. In the highlands, Kaminaljuyu (kah-MEEN-ah-leu-yeu) had by then developed architecture and primitive writing under the influence of Oaxaca and Teotihuacán. But in the early classical period, before 550 C.E., Tikal, in the central lowlands, assumed Mayan leadership as it traded with Teotihuacán and allied itself with Kaminaljuyu. The fall of Teotihuacán brought temporary confusion, soon followed by the glorious renaissance of the late classical era at Tikal, Palenque, Yaxchilán (yahks-chee-LAHN), Uxmal, and other Mayan centers.

A number of distinguished scholars such as Linda Schele and David Friedel, Jeremy Sobloff, and Michael D. Coe have given us a detailed view of the Mayas. Their communities had productive economies based not only on agriculture but also on handicrafts and long-distance trade. In often barren soil, except in some parts of the highlands, Mayan farmers used intensive agriculture, clearing, irrigating, and terracing to raise squash, chili peppers, and many other crops, including maize—which supplied 80 percent of their food. Mayan metalwork, cotton cloth, and chipped stone implements were traded widely, carried in large dugout canoes along the rivers and the Atlantic coast. Exchange was facilitated by the use of common goods as media of exchange, including cocoa beans, polished beads, salt, and lengths of cotton cloth.

Mayan society in this period was a rich mixture of old and new. An ancient kinship system prevailed among all classes, with lands assigned and controlled by the clans. Matriarchal values persisted, as indicated by some queens who retained power and influence. Women were generally respected, held some legal rights, and did some of the most important work, such as weaving. The shift toward patriarchy, however, was definite and unmistakable, as was seen in priorities accorded men in most social situations, such as being served first by women at meals. A more fundamental change involved the rise of social classes. Hereditary male nobles and priests were in most positions of authority and power, but craftspeople and merchants enjoyed privileges and status. Slaves, captured in military campaigns or kidnapped, did most of the hard work, particularly in the continuous heavy construction of ceremonial buildings. They were also subject to being used in religious sacrifice, although this was far less common than among the later Aztecs.

A hereditary priest-king, usually considered to be a descendant of a god, governed each Mayan center. He was assisted by a council of priests and nobles. His government levied taxes, supervised local government in outlying villages, and administered justice. It also was responsible for conducting foreign relations and making war. The Mayas were not very successful in large-scale military operations because their armies were drawn mainly from the nobility and were therefore limited in size. Nevertheless, armed with their obsidian-bladed weapons, they were equal to their neighbors in making war. Indeed, as time passed and

cities vied for supremacy, wars became increasingly common. In the process, some centers remained independent, but most joined loosely organized leagues, based on common religious traditions, dynastic marriages, or diplomatic alignments.

Religion permeated all phases of Mayan life. Like the later Aztecs, the Mayas saw life as a burden and time as its measure, and they deified many natural phenomena, particularly the planets and stars, as powers to be appeased by human pain and suffering. Public bloodletting was part of normal ritualistic worship. Human sacrifice, usually accomplished by decapitation, was common, and wars to obtain prisoners for sacrifice were sometimes waged. The dominance of religion over everyday life is further illustrated by the general interpretation of law as religious principle and taxation as religious offerings. Economic value derived as much from the religious sanctity of a thing as from its material utility or scarcity. Moreover, education was aimed primarily at training priests; reading and writing were considered necessary religious skills, and mathematics and astronomy were valued mainly because they were required in scheduling ceremonies honoring the gods.

The two most significant achievements of the Mayas were their calendar and their writing system. Neither of these was original, but both were more efficient than those of earlier peoples. The Mayan astronomers, using only naked-eye observation, surpassed their European contemporaries. Their constant scanning of the heavens allowed them to perfect a solar calendar with 18 months of 20 days each and a five-day period for religious festivals. Using an ingenious cyclical system of notation known as the "long count," they dated events of the distant past for accurate record keeping and the scheduling of astronomical observations. Their notational mathematics, based on 20 rather than 10 as in the decimal system, employed combinations of dots and bars in vertical sequences, to indicate numbers above 20. For nonnumerical records, they combined **pictographs** and **glyphs,** which have recently been deciphered sufficiently to reveal specific historic events and their human dimensions.

These remarkable accomplishments in mathematics, astronomy, and writing were more than matched by the magnificent Mayan art and architecture. The plaza of each Mayan community was marked by at least one pyramid, topped by a temple. The one at Tikal towered to 229 feet, 16 feet higher than the Pyramid of the Sun at Teotihuacán. With their terraced sides and horizontal lines, Mayan pyramids showed a skilled sense of proportion. The highly stylized sculpture dec-

DOCUMENT

Anonymous: Victory over the Underworld

---

pictographs—Picture symbols.

glyphs—Symbolic characters in writing.

The Mesoamerican societies were at the same time sophisticated, complex, and powerful—and bloody in their human sacrifices to the gods. This seated figure, surrounded by winged messengers, seems to be looking off in the distance to anticipate what the divine powers might next demand from him.

orating their terraces is regarded by some authorities as the world's finest, even though the Mayan sculptors accomplished their intricate carving with only stone tools—there were no bronze or iron implements in the Americas at that time. The Mayas also developed mural painting to a high level of expression. Even their crafts, such as weaving, ceramics, and jewelry making, reveal a great aesthetic sense, subtlety of design, and manipulative skill.

THE POSTCLASSICAL ERA

▪ *Which civilizations rose to prominence after the end of the classical era of Mesoamerican civilization?*

The region's classical artistic development ended during the eighth and ninth centuries. The causes, not yet fully uncovered, have been generally attributed to factors ranging from overpopulation and internal struggles to soil exhaustion and Chichimec invasions from the north. Amid the accompanying upheavals, urban populations dwindled, and most of Teotihuacán's residents scattered in all directions, even into the Mayan lands. But there was no complete collapse; trade continued on a large scale, and the expanded use of writing indicated more social complexity and interstate competition, which contributed to intensified politi-

cal conflict. Consequently, the age produced a new cultural mode, with heavier emphases on militarism, war, and gods thirsting for human blood. Among many smaller but thriving city-states, in addition to the dying Teotihuacán, were the Mayan polities of Tikal, Chichén Itzá (cheech-EN eet-SAH), and Mayapán. Farther north, the Oaxacan centers were still flourishing after the tenth century, as were Atzcapotzalco (ahts-kah-poh-TSAL-koh), Xochicalco (hoh-chee-KAL-koh), and Cholula, with its colossal pyramid.

The Toltecs

Most prominent of all these centers was Tollan, the Toltec capital. Toltec history is unclear before 980, when Topiltzin (to-PIL-tzin), a legendary king, founded the city and created a new power located in the central Valley of Mexico. His subjects were a mixture of Chichimecs and former urbanites of the area, who may have served for a while as peacekeepers in the north. Over the next two centuries, the city became a great urban complex of 120,000 people, a hub of trade, and the center of an evolving Toltec confederacy that assumed the leading role formerly played by Teotihuacán. Meanwhile, Tollan's future was shaped by a struggle for power between Topiltzin and his enemies. The king had early adopted the Teotihuacán god **Quetzalcoatl** (kets-al-koh-AHT-el), who opposed human sacrifice; but followers of the traditional Toltec war god, **Tezcatlipoca** (tez-kat-le-POH-ka), ultimately rebelled and forced Topiltzin into exile. The victorious war cult took over, steadily expanding its hegemony, by conquest and trade, into an empire stretching from the Gulf of Mexico to the Pacific, including some Mayan cities of the south.

The tumultuous political conditions of the early postclassical period finally brought disaster to the Toltecs. Failing crops and internal dissension caused great outward migrations from Tollan and abandonment of the capital at the end of the twelfth century. Shortly after, the city was burned by Chichimecs. For two centuries thereafter, the area was a land of warring states and constantly forming and dissolving federations. Some cultural continuity, however, was maintained by peoples in the Oaxaca valley, notably the Zapotecs, whose culture was as old as the Olmec. Although they struggled constantly with neighboring peoples for supremacy and survival, the Zapotecs maintained towns, temples, ball courts, and art that helped preserve Mesoamerican traditions for later times.

Quetzalcoatl—The Toltec god of the civilization, goodness, and light; literally "plumed serpent."

Tezcatlipoca—The god of the night sky and sorcery; literally "smoking mirror"; initially Toltec in origin but also adopted by subsequent peoples, including the Aztecs.

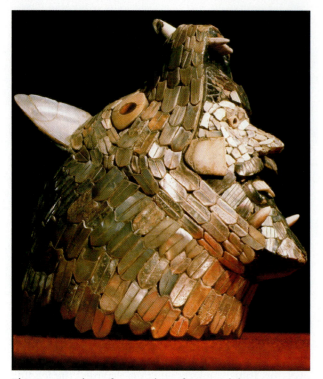

This Aztec mask is a figure within a figure, and the person wearing the mask would hope to project animal strength and unearthly terror.

Toltec militarism spread from central to southern Mexico. It left the less developed Mayan highlands relatively undisturbed but brought decline and reorientation to the old lowland centers, such as Tikal. Severe droughts also drove migrants into northern Yucatán, where a developing cistern technology provided more water. At Chichén Itzá in the tenth century, a cosmopolitan Mexican-Mayan military elite established their dominance and maintained a trading network, by land and sea, throughout the southern region. From the early thirteenth into the fifteenth century, Mayapán was a fortified center, defended by mercenaries and maintaining leverage over subkingdoms by holding hostages from dependent royal families. Trade continued to grow, along with population, among the postclassical Mayas; but art, cultural pursuits, and even architecture deteriorated. The Spaniards were later to describe the Mayan people as fiercely independent, bloodthirsty, and, like the Aztecs, inclined to sacrifice war captives' hearts on their gods' altars.

The Aztecs

Arising in the confusion of the late postclassical era, the Aztec Confederacy came to conquer and dominate central Mexico from coast to coast in less than two centuries. The Aztecs, like the Toltecs before them, retained many of their old traditions while freely bor-

rowing from the culture, religion, and technology of their neighbors and victims. The most significant example of this borrowing was their hydraulic agriculture. It was the major factor by which they increased population in the central Mexico to more than a million people living in some 50 city-states.

The Aztecs' story really begins with the founding of the capital at Tenochtitlán; their earlier history is quite obscure. They evidently migrated from the north into central Mexico some time before 1200. For a while they were dominated by other peoples, including the Toltecs. About 1325 they settled on an island in Lake Texcoco (the site of present-day Mexico City), later connecting their new town to the mainland by causeways. In its later days Tenochtitlán was an architectural wonder. The Aztecs built a dam to control the lake level, completed a freshwater aqueduct, and created floating artificial islands where irrigated fields supplied food for the capital. Within the imperial metropolis, beautiful avenues, canals, temples, and monuments symbolized increasing Aztec power, particularly after the early fifteenth century.

IMAGE
Aztec Warriors

The Aztecs completed the formation of their confederacy at the same time. During the early decades at Tenochtitlán, the Aztecs had fought as tributaries of Atzcapotzalco, the dominant city-state in the valley. In 1370 they accepted a king of assumed Toltec lineage. For decades they won victories and prospered in concert with their overlords, but in 1427 they rebelled, forming a "triple alliance" with nearby Texcoco and Tlacopán, which defeated Atzcapotzalco and became the major power in the region. For the Aztecs, these events brought great change. Internally, they shifted power from the old clan leaders to a rising military aristocracy. Externally, they started a series of conquests and trading agreements. A new imperial order developed, shared at first by the other two allies but increasingly dominated by Tenochitlán, whose ruler imposed his will as head of the army, leader of the state, and chief priest. The reigns of the Aztec kings Itzcoatl (1427–1440) and his nephew Montezuma I (1440–1468), ushered in this new era of rising centralism, efficiency, and expansion. It was still in progress under the ninth monarch, Montezuma II (1502–1520), at the time of the Spanish invasion.

DOCUMENT
Xicohtencatl, the Elder: "I Say This"

As the empire expanded, so did the state-controlled economy. Its base was agricultural land, particularly floating plots installed on the lake after the 1430s. Most were built by the government. Some were allotted to the *calpulli* (clans)—made up of the remnants of diverse ethnic groups that came together on the island of Tenochtitlán—for distribution to families. Others were developed as estates for the monarch

---

calpulli—Aztec social units based on family clans.

and the nobility; the latter were worked by tenants under government supervision. Rising agricultural production supported not only the engineering, dredging, stonework, and carpentry required for heavy construction but also artisans turning out weapons, cloth, ceramics, feather work, jewelry, and hundreds of other goods. Porters from distant places backpacked over mountains to the markets of the valley. A later Spanish observer reported that the great market at Tlatelolco (tlah-tel-LOHL-koh), serving Tenochtitlán, attracted 25,000 people daily.

DOCUMENT

"Song of Tlaltecatzin"

Conquest and the increasing wealth that accompanied it modified the ancient social structure. The old *calpulli* developed into city wards, identified largely by occupational specialties. By 1500 most *calpulli* families were headed by men. Women could inherit property and divorce their husbands but were confined mostly to household tasks, except for midwives, healers, and prostitutes. Kinship still promoted social cohesion, but class status provided major incentives. The appointed nobility *(pipiltin)*, along with the priests, held both power and social status, but they were burdened with heavy responsibilities. Moreover, they held appointed rather than hereditary posts, although they could inherit property. Commoners could be made nobles by performing superior service, particularly in war. Craftspeople and merchants paid taxes but were exempt from military service; some long-distance merchants *(pochteca)* served the government as diplomats or spies in foreign states. Peasants worked their plots and served in the army; nonmembers of *calpulli* were tenants. Their lot was hardly better than that of the numerous slaves, except for the latter's potential role as ceremonial sacrifice victims.

Official documents of the period and other written accounts focus mainly on Mesoamerican social and political elites and conditions in the imperial capitals. However, recent archaeological studies throw fresh light on the lives of the Aztec common people and conditions in the provinces. Surveys of settlement patterns show that Aztec society experienced one of the most significant population explosions of premodern times. In the Valley of Mexico, the heartland of the Aztec Empire, population increased from 175,000 in the early Aztec period (1150–1350) to almost one million in the late period (1350–1519). This pattern of growth was duplicated elsewhere in the empire. To cope with this population explosion, the environment was altered: Farmers built dams and canals to irrigate cropland, constructed terraced stone walls on hillsides to form new fields, and drained swamps outside Tenochtitlán to create **chinampas** or

floating gardens. With these changes emerged new villages and towns.

Excavations of rural sites near modern Cuernavaca (kwehr-nah-VAH-kah) disclose that provincial society was much more complex than previously thought. Commoners created a thriving marketing system whereby craft goods produced in their homes were exchanged for a variety of foreign goods. Houses at these sites were small, built of adobe brick walls supported on stone foundations. These houses were furnished with mats and baskets and had a shrine with two or three figurines and an incense burner on one of the walls. In this region the household production of cotton textiles was the major craft. All Aztec women spun and wove cloth, which provided garments, constituted the most common item of tribute demanded by the state, and served as currency in the marketplaces for obtaining other goods and services. In addition to textiles, some residents made paper out of the bark of the wild fig tree, used to produce books of pictographs and to burn in ritual offerings. According to written sources, Aztec commoners were subject to the nobles, who possessed most of the land and monopolized power in the polity. But new archaeological excavations show that the commoners were relatively prosperous people whose market system operated largely beyond state control.

The Aztec polity included subordinated allies and 38 provinces. The latter were taxed directly; most of the former paid tribute in some form; and all were denied free foreign relations. This polyglot empire was headed by a member of the royal family proclaimed to be the incarnation of the sun-god. His household was more lavish than many in Europe and swarmed with servants. A head wife supervised the concubines and scheduled their assignments, but Aztec queens rarely engaged in court intrigues or offered advice to the emperor, for he usually ruled without concern for other opinions. He was assisted in his official duties by a chief minister and subordinate bureaucracies for war, religion, justice, treasury, storehouses, and personnel. The capital and each province were administered directly by governors, most of whom were descended from former kings. They collected taxes, held court, arranged religious ceremonies, regulated economic affairs, and directed police activities. In addition, urban guilds, villages, and tribes had their own local officials. Vassal states were governed under their own laws but observed by resident Aztec emissaries. This whole system was defended by a large military organization, comprising allied forces, local militias, and an imperial guard of elite troops.

Aztec religion developed from the worship of animistic spirits, symbolizing natural forces seeking balance while in constant conflict. A pessimistic obsession with human futility also dominated the Aztec world-

---

Chinampas—The floating gardens the Aztecs of Tenochtitlán built and tended on Lake Texcoco.

view, perpetuating the common belief that the gods required human blood to sustain life. Thus, as they assembled their empire, the Aztecs came to envision their sun deity, **Huitzilopochtli** (wheet-tsee-loh-POHCHT-lee), as a bloodthirsty war god with an appetite for warriors captured in battle. In every city, the Aztecs built pyramids, topped by their two temples to the sun deity and Tlatelolco, god of rain. Here they honored Huitzilopochtli in great public ceremonies such as one in 1487 when bloodstained priests at the high altars tore out the living hearts of thousands of victims and held them up, quivering, to the sun. The need for sacrificial victims forced continuing conquests and later weakened the state as it faced the Spanish threat.

DOCUMENT
Admonishing Those Who Seek No Honor in War

Comparing the Aztecs and Mayas with the Romans and Greeks can be an interesting theoretical exercise. The Aztec calendar, mathematics, and writing were derived mainly from Mayan sources, somewhat the way that Roman philosophy and science were based on Greek models. Although Aztec culture spawned skilled sculptors, painters, and craftspeople who produced in great numbers, they lacked the imagination of the Mayas, whom they indirectly copied, just as Roman artists largely imitated their Greek predecessors. Similarly, both Roman and Aztec cultures were characterized by respect for discipline, practicality, directness, and force. Each was highly skilled in engineering, as attested, for example, by their aqueducts and other feats for furnishing copious amounts of water to their respective capitals. They also shared a militaristic ethos and powerful standing armies.

The Inca

The great Inca Empire in the Andean highlands of South America reached its height in the early 1500s.

MAP
Inca Expansion

It extended 3500 miles between Ecuador and Chile, including almost impassable mountain ranges that separate the upper Amazon forests from the Pacific. The empire contained at least ten million people in 200 ethnolinguistic groups. It was six times the size of Texas. The capital, Cuzco, which had an estimated 200,000 inhabitants, was governed in a more centralized way than any city in Europe at the time. The Incas produced fine art and architecture and were superb engineers, but their major achievement was imperial organization. In this respect they compared favorably with the Romans and the Chinese.

A long tradition of scholarship, exemplified by researchers such as Ian Cameron, Richard W. Keating,

and J. Alden Mason, gives us a detailed idea of Inca society. Although it rose very rapidly just before the Spanish conquest, Inca civilization evolved from ancient cultural foundations. Ceremonial and commercial centers had existed on the Peruvian plateau well before the Common Era. About 600 C.E. cities began rising in the highlands of the interior. During the next two centuries, tributary kingdoms drew together formerly isolated ceremonial centers of the Peruvian highlands. Some of the resulting states exercised control over the plain, along with territories in what are now Bolivia and Chile. Two kingdoms had capitals at Huari (WHA-ree) and Tiahuanaco (tee-ah-wah-NAH-koh) in south central Peru. When these states collapsed in the tenth century, they were succeeded by independent agrarian villages, which were nearly consumed by continuous warfare. A completely different situation developed along the northern coast, where the kingdom of Chimu developed a civilization, marked by extensive irrigation, rising population, centralized government, public works, high craft production, widespread trade, and an expanding tributary domain. This polity was conquered and its culture absorbed by the Incas in 1476.

The Incas created their empire while waging ruthless struggles in the highlands. According to their own legends, these "children of the sun" settled the valley of Cuzco, in the heartland of the Andes, about 1200 C.E., having migrated from the south, possibly from the region of Tiahuanaco. During the next hundred years they were a simple peasant people, organized by kinship in clans *(ayllu)*, living in villages, fulfilling mutual labor obligations, and worshipping their local demigods *(chuacas)*. To strengthen their unity and better protect themselves in constant wars for survival, they formed a monarchy, developed their military, and began taking over territory near Cuzco. In this competition they were only moderately successful during the reigns of the first seven kings, to the early fifteenth century.

Like the Aztec state at almost the same time, the Inca polity began a climactic period of rapid development with a memorable series of rulers. Viracocha (veh-rah-CO-cha) (d. 1438), the eighth emperor, turned his ragtag army into a formidable fighting machine, conquered adjoining territories, and instituted a divine monarchy, with his lineage accepted as descendants of the sun-god. His son, Pachacuti (pahch-ah-KEU-tee) (1438–1471), was a reformer, religious leader, and builder who stands among the most powerful people ever to rule in the New World, and received the admiration of the Spanish occupiers. He began arduous campaigns to the north and south, notably against Chimu. Topa Yupanqui (yeu-PAHN-kee) (1471–1493), Pachacuti's son and successor who commanded the Inca armies after 1463, completed the

---

Huitzilopochtli—The patron deity of the Aztecs, god of the sun and of war.

Document   Father Bernabé Cobo, "Pachacuti, the Greatest Inca"

Bernabé Cobo (1582–1657) spent 61 of his 75 years in the Americas, from his first arrival in the Antilles to his death in Lima. During that time the Jesuit priest combined his duties with his qualities as a scientist and observer to write at great length about the flora and fauna of Latin and southern America. He entered into close relations with the Indians, as he spread the faith, and came to have a deep understanding of respect for them.

This selection is from Chapter 12 of his *History of the Inca Empire*. Cobo relied on Indian legends and contemporary Indian testimony, as well as earlier Spanish writings as he dealt with the civilization his countrymen had attacked. Far from viewing the Incans as barbaric and "uncivilized" as later, nineteenth-century missionaries would do, Cobo showed the capacity to understand and even admire them.

Viracocha Inca left four sons by his principal wife; they were called Pachacuti Inca Yupanqui, Inca Roca, Tupa Yupanqui, and Capac Yupanqui. The first one succeeded him in the kingdom, and concerning the rest, although they were lords and grandees, nothing is said. Pachacuti married a lady named Mama Anahuarque, native to the town of Choco, near Cuzco, and he founded a family that they call Iñaca Panaca. This king was the most valiant and warlike, wise and statesmanlike of all the Incas, because he organized the republic with the harmony, laws, and statutes that it maintained from that time until the arrival of the Spaniards. He injected order and reason into everything; eliminated and added rites and ceremonies; made the religious cult more extensive; established the sacrifices and the solemnity with which the gods were to be venerated, enlarged and embellished the temples with magnificent structures, income, and a great number of priests and ministers; reformed the calendar; divided the year into twelve months, giving each one its name; and designated the solemn fiestas and sacrifices to be held each month. He composed many elegant prayers with which the gods were to be invoked, and he ordered that these prayers be recited at the same time that the sacrifices were offered. He was no less careful and diligent in matters pertaining to the temporal welfare of the republic; he gave his vassals a method of working the fields and taking advantage of the lands that were so rough and uneven as to be useless and unfruitful; he ordered that rough hillsides be terraced and that ditches be made from the rivers to irrigate them. In short, nothing was overlooked by him in which he did not impose all good order and harmony; for this reason he was given the name of Pachacuti, which means "change of time or of the world"; this is because as a result of his excellent government things improved to such an extent that times seemed to have changed and the world seemed to have turned around; thus, his memory was very celebrated among the Indians, and he was given more honor in their songs and poems than any of the other kings that either preceded him or came after him.

After having shown himself to be so devoted to the sun and having taken the care just mentioned that all worship him in the same way that his ancestors had done, one day Pachacuti began to wonder how it was possible that a thing could be God if it was so subject to movement as the Sun, that it never stops or rests for a moment since it turns around the world every day; and he inferred from this meditation that the Sun must not be more than a messenger sent by the Creator to visit the universe; besides, if he were God, it would not be possible for a few clouds to get in front of him and obscure his splendor and rays so that he could not shine; and if he were the universal Creator and lord of all things, sometimes he would rest and from his place of rest he would illuminate all the world and command whatever he wished; and thus, there had to be another more powerful lord who ruled and governed the Sun; and no doubt this was Pachayachachic. He communicated this thought to the members of his council, and in agreement with them, he decided that Pachayachachic was to be preferred to the Sun, and within the city of Cuzco, he built the Creator his own temple which he called Quishuarcancha, and in it he put the image of the Creator of the world, Viracocha Pachayachachic.

Questions to Consider

1. What was there in Pachacuti's quest to understand the universe that would appeal to Bernabé Cobo?

2. Discuss Pachacuti's accomplishments as enumerated by Cobo. Do you think that the Spaniard's admiration came because the Incan chief possessed "European" qualities, or because he chose local solutions to local problems?

3. Would you like to be a citizen in a state led by Pachacuti? Why? Why not?

From *History of the Inca Empire*, trans. and ed. Roland Hamilton from the holograph manuscript in the *Biblioteca Capitular y Colombina de Sevilla*, © 1979. Reprinted by permission of the University of Texas Press.

Machu Picchu, a natural fortress on a narrow ridge between two mountains, was built by the Incas probably after 1440. When the last Inca ruler died, the fortress was abandoned and lost until its rediscovery in 1911.

annexation of Chimu and extended the empire south into central Chile. The next emperor, Huayna Capac (WHAY-nah KAH-pahk) (1493–1527), completed the subjugation of Ecuador, put down rebellions, and attempted to impose order, although the empire was seething with internal discontent when the Spaniards arrived in 1532.

Despite internal problems, intensified by the steep slopes and harsh weather of the Andes, the Incas demonstrated rare technical skills in fashioning their civilization in difficult and often dangerous circumstances. They were master engineers, carrying water long distances by canals and aqueducts, using techniques borrowed from the Chimu Empire, building cities high in the Andes, and constructing networks of roads along the coast and through the mountains, along with suspension bridges and interconnecting valley roadways. All were designed to knit together a vast region that in the Inca Empire covered some 380,000 square miles.

Archaeologists have long known that the Incas gained a knowledge of canals and irrigation systems from the Chimu: Recent excavation have revealed new evidence about their sophisticated use of that technology. Canals are difficult to construct: If the slope is too narrow, the canal silts up; if it is too steep, its sides erode. Inca engineers devised different canal shapes to control the water's speed and prevent its velocity from ruining the canal. One "intervalley" canal carried water to a city from 60 miles away; it was only one of many networks, involving thousands of feeder canals, that stretched for hundreds of miles. These hydraulic

techniques have been described as deserving to stand with Egypt's pyramids and China's Great Wall as among the world's greatest engineering feats. With irrigation canals constructed far removed from the water's source, the Incas farmed 40 percent more land than is achieved today. But if skills fail, land can quickly return to desert conditions. We have yet to learn what caused the destruction or abandonment of these canal systems—was it human or environmental forces, or both?

Hydraulic feats were matched by sophisticated organizational skills. To link the empire together, Inca leaders established a communication service, using state-built roads, runner-messengers, rest houses, and smoke signals. Governing by means of a divide-and-rule technique, they appealed wherever possible to traditional prejudices among conquered peoples, perpetuating feuds, courting native leaders, settling colonies of subjects among their enemies, and generally provoking disunity among potentially rebellious areas. They also relied on a common official language and the cult of divine monarchy to unify their own people, particularly the elite. Every part of their system was fitted together in a highly disciplined and integrated whole. Before the Incas, few other states had succeeded so effectively in regimenting millions of people over such great distances and against such formidable obstacles.

Like all civilized peoples, the Incas faced the problem of population expansion and a limited food supply. They solved it well enough to support large military, bureaucratic, and priestly establishments by developing what economists call a *command economy*. They used no money, no credit, and very little trade beyond local barter. The state planned all economic operations and kept all accounts. Government assigned to families the land to be worked; local family heads, under government supervision, directed workers who produced the crops and saw that harvests were brought to state warehouses. Labor taxes provided work done on public projects, the nobles' estates, and royal lands. A similar approach was used in manufacturing, with craftspeople producing in local guilds, noble households, and palace workshops. From its storehouses, the government distributed goods to individuals, to the military, and to government projects. In the process, it built roads, operated hospitals, and maintained schools. All property, even the nobles' land, was state-owned and assigned, except for distinctly personal possessions, including some luxury goods owned by the privileged classes.

This state-controlled economy functioned by way of a precisely defined class structure, built on the lingering kinship tradition. Commoners were kept loyal and disciplined by identifying the state with their ancient *ayllus*. Inca nobles maintained respect because they were all related directly or indirectly to the royal lineage and therefore shared the divine mandate to rule. They held the highest positions in government, the army, and the priesthood. A notch lower were lesser aristocrats and nobles among conquered peoples, who held local offices, up to subgovernors in the provinces. The two upper classes made up a privileged elite. Trained in special schools, they were rewarded with luxuries in food, dress, and housing. They were also exempted from taxes and cruel punishments. At the third level were common workers. They were generally confined to their villages; their work was prescribed; their dress and food were restricted; and government checked even the cleanliness of their houses. Commoners were thus little better off than the lowest class of slaves, who were often taken as prisoners of war and assigned to serve the upper classes.

The shift from kinship toward class division was accompanied by a decline of matriarchal values. Upper-class women shared some social status with their husbands, and all women could inherit property when they were widowed; but they were generally subordinated and exploited. Indeed, a fifteenth-century royal decree prohibited women from testifying in court because they were by nature "deceitful, mendacious, and fainthearted."[1] Female commoners worked in the fields, while women of all classes were expected to keep house, mind the children, and serve the needs of men. Many were concubines or surplus wives, the number depending on the husbands' wealth and status. The most beautiful and intelligent young girls were drafted as "chosen women." Some would become "virgins of the sun," serving as nuns and weavers in the temple workshops; others would become concubines of the emperor or nobles; a few would be sacrificed. All were honored as servants of the state.

All authority in the Inca state originated with the hereditary divine emperor, who exercised the power of life and death over all his subjects. He was usually aloof, even with his own immediate family, although he might, if he chose, delegate authority to the queen (his full sister after 1438) or take advice from his mother. With its thousands of servants and concubines, his court was a magnificent display of wealth and power. It was also the locus of a central government that included agencies for rituals (religion), war, treasury, accounts, and public works. The chief ministers were advisers to the Imperial Council, consisting of the emperor and four viceroys, who governed the four provinces. Each province, about the size of New York State, was divided into approximately 40 districts, under subgovernors and their assistants. Authority in the districts was further subdivided, ultimately into units of ten families. Officials at each level reported regularly to superiors and were subject to

frequent inspections. This system regulated every aspect of life, including labor, justice, marriage, and even morals.

The power of the ruler depended largely on an excellent military system, which featured compulsory service. Instructors in the villages trained peasant boys for the army; the most promising were marked for advancement when they were called to active service in their twenties. They served for two years before retiring to the labor reserve and militia. The army was organized in units of 10, 50, 100, 1000, and 10,000, under officers who held complete authority over subordinates. A combat force of 200,000, with support units, was always under arms. It was supplied from military storehouses throughout the country and garrisoned in mighty stone fortresses, each with independent water sources. Troops from these centers ruthlessly suppressed any resistance to the regime.

A second base for Inca authority was religion. As the empire grew, its priests appropriated the gods of conquered peoples and included them in a vast pantheon, headed by the Inca sun-god. For example, the virgins of the sun, with their ceremonies and temples, evolved from an earlier moon goddess cult among **matrilineal** societies. War victims would on occasion be sacrificed to the sun, as would some children of "chosen women." In later times the servants of an emperor, as well as his favorite concubines, were sent with him, at his death, to serve him in the hereafter. To emphasize the emperors' divinity and symbolize the state's continuity, dead emperors were mummified, seated on thrones in their sacred palaces, and attended by living servants, wives, and priests. On public occasions these figures were paraded before the people, who bowed before them in reverence. Such ceremonies were conducted by a clerical establishment of 4000 priests in the capital and many scores of thousands more throughout the country.

CASE STUDY
Death in War and Childbirth in the Americas

There was a remarkable exception to this religious mind-set in the person of the emperor Pachacuti. A highly successful military leader who largely laid the empire's foundation by consolidating the area around Cuzco and annexing the rich Titicaca basin, this multitalented innovator established **Quechua** (KECH-wah) as the administrative language, reformed the calendar, introduced methods of terracing the hillsides and extending irrigation, and created an efficient public service. Although regarded as a direct descendant of the sun-god, Pachacuti asked himself how the sun could be the supreme deity since it never rested but

---

matrilineal—Tracing hereditary descent through the mother, not the father.

Quechua—A language of the Central Andes, spoken by the Incas and today the most widely spoken indigenous tongue of the Americas.

revolved endlessly around the earth. He concluded that the sun was itself a messenger sent by a more powerful being who from his place of rest could illuminate and command the world. This must be the universal Creator, Viracocha ("Lord"), who governed the sun and had brought into being all other deities. And in his honor the emperor constructed a temple in Cuzco. But, as in the case of Akhenaton, his conceptual forerunner in Egypt, Pachacuti's nascent monotheism did not prevail; later rulers continued to sacrifice victims to the sun-god—though not to the extent practiced by the Aztecs.

Order and security were dominant values in Inca cultural expression, and neither aesthetic concerns nor philosophical speculation received much attention. As we have seen, religious innovation was given short shrift, and any theorizing was subordinated to the practicalities of a state cult and the morality of power—treason and cowardice were considered the worst sins. The Incas had no written records and seem to have lacked even the pictographs of Mesoamerica. Instead they relied on oral traditions, supplemented by mnemonic devices such as the system of knotted strings called *quipus* (KE-peuz). These oral traditions were dealt a lethal blow by the Spanish conquest.

The Inca lunar calendar was inaccurate and provided no starting point for the identification of historical events. Although the Incas were excellent craftspeople, capable of producing fine pottery and metalwork in copper and gold, their most striking technical and cultural accomplishments were in engineering and massive architecture. Without using mortar, they fitted immense slabs of stone into temple and fortress walls. This efficiency is still exhibited in existing roads, bridges, terraced fields, and stone fortresses, such as Machu Picchu.

THE AMERINDIANS OF NORTH AMERICA

■ *Why was there no unification of the North American Amerindians, such as there was in Mesoamerica?*

In the past century Hollywood and the popular media reinforced the fallacy that all Native Americans in North America constituted a single culture with a common lifestyle. The mounted, war-bonneted warrior of the plains has too often been considered the archetype of the "Red Man," presented in the "Wild West Shows" of the last century. Some Plains Indians were indeed fine mounted warriors, but they were only a fraction of the complex family of North American Indians.

European settlers found the Native Americans more diverse in their languages and appearances than the Europeans themselves. Two hundred distinct North American languages have been classified. Amerindian societies presented a wide spectrum of variation: from small bands of hunter-gatherers and farmers to well-organized states. A similar diversity was found in their arts and crafts; various regions excelled in basketry, weaving, sculpture, totem-carving, and boat making.

There is a serious debate among scholars as to the number of Native Americans at the time of the European invasions. Estimates range from as low as 2 million to as many as 18 million people in the area north of Mexico—most estimates fall between these extremes. In any case, much of North America was well populated at the end of the fifteenth century. Amerindians north of the Rio Grande did not produce the massive technological and governmental achievements found in Mesoamerica and South America. As with Paleolithic and Neolithic societies in Asia, Africa, and Europe before the Common Era, their populations were smaller, and consequently, they did not create large cities, with their complex division of labor and urban way of life. More often, they typically survived by hunting and fishing until knowledge of food raising spread north from Mesoamerica.

For North American Indians before 1492, agriculture where it could be practiced had the same effect as elsewhere in the world. A more dependable food supply made possible stable settlements in which men cleared the fields and women tended the crops. Marked population growth, with accompanying large village or town centers, and political and military power occurred in the Rio Grande, Ohio, Mississippi, and St.

---

quipus—A mnemonic system based on knotted strings used by the Inca to keep records and send messages.

North American Civilizations

c. 3000–2500 B.C.E.	Watson Brake settlements
c. 800 B.C.E.–600 C.E.	Adena and Hopewell cultures
c. 900–1300	Cahokia flourishes
c. 300 B.C.E.–1350 C.E.	Mogollon culture
c. 1100	Establishment of Navajo culture
c. 1300	Arrival of Mandans in Great Plains

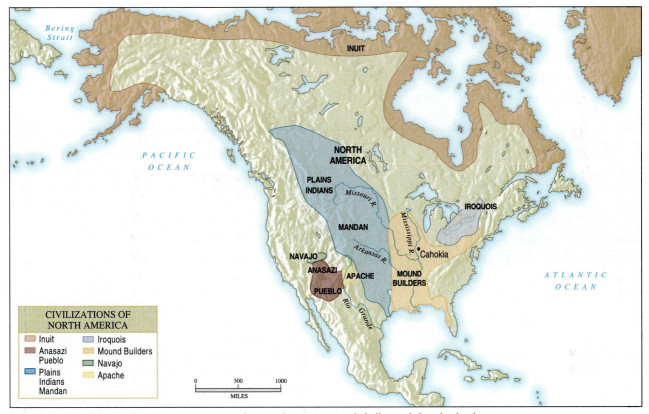

In the vastness of the North American continent, the varied environmental challenges led to the development of hundreds of different Indian tribes—more than 250 alone in the present-day state of California.

Lawrence valleys. In these places, overpopulation exhausted the soil and occasionally created environmental problems that led to the decline of the urban centers. Climate changes and European-borne pandemics in the fifteenth and sixteenth centuries devastated the Native American population, both those settled in the cities and the nomadic peoples.

The Iroquois of the Northeast Woodlands

Europeans arriving in what is now upper New York State found various groups speaking dialects of a common Iroquoian language. They had created a distinctive culture by 1000 C.E. and subsequently formed the League of the Five Nations. They used the metaphor of the longhouse, their traditional communal dwelling, to describe their political alliance: the Mohawk along the Hudson were the "keepers of the eastern door," adjoined in sequence by the Oneida, Onondaga, and Cayuga, with the Seneca, "keepers of the western door." When the Tuscarora joined in the early eighteenth century, the confederacy became known as the Six Nations. The Iroquois eventually extended their control from the Great Lakes toward the Atlantic by subjugating the nomadic, food-gathering Algonquin people.

The Iroquois had the advantage of being agriculturists with permanent villages. Some of these had several hundred residents and extensive fields where maize, beans, squash, and tobacco were grown. Fish traps were built across streams, and smokehouses preserved joints of game. Related families lived in the longhouses, long rectangular buildings protected by high wooden palisades. Women played a notable part: They owned the homes and gardens, and, since descent was matrilineal, chose the leaders. If the men chosen did not give good leadership, they could be replaced.

The Adena and Hopewell of the Ohio Valley

In the area of present-day Kentucky and Ohio, important Amerindian settlements took root between 800 B.C.E. and 600 C.E. Known generally as the Adena and Hopewell cultures, these Amerindians developed complex societies from the Missouri River to the Appalachians and from the Great Lakes to the Gulf of Mexico. Their settlements were based on the work of Indian women who, over two to three millennia,

The Great Serpent Mound in Ohio is a rich repository of the North American Indian life centered in the Adena culture. Active between 500 B.C.E. and 100 C.E. the Indians of the Adena culture had a well-developed village life and traded with other peoples from Canada to the Gulf of Mexico.

mastered the cultivation of seed plants such as sunflowers and squash and maize that arrived in the area in the fourth century B.C.E. As in Mesoamerica and South America, by 1000, maize cultivation sustained the peoples of the Ohio and Mississippi valley regions. Archaeologists think that the Hopewell and Adena cultures survived on a diet of fish, game, nuts, and other plant life.

The Adena and Hopewell cultures developed differing ways to construct their homes: the Adena chose to live in circular houses made out of poles and covered with mats and thatched roofs, while the Hopewell built round or oval houses with more protective roofs made of skins, bark from trees, and a combination of thatch and clay. They had a sophisticated view of the afterlife, as can be seen in the effort they took to bury their dead. The Native Americans near Watson Brake in northeast Louisiana (3000–2500 B.C.E.) and the peoples of the Adena culture at the beginning of the Common Era built thousands of earthen mounds for their dead. The Adena interred their deceased in vast cone-shaped mounds of earth, sometimes 500 feet around. Sometimes the dead were cremated, and the ashes were placed in the mounds along with all sorts of relics such as carved stone tablets, pipes smoked during religious ceremonies, and jewelry. The Hopewell did the same on an even larger scale for the more distinguished members of their families. Archaeologists have found evidence in these mounds of stone and clay items from both coasts, imported copper from the Great Lakes, and flaked stone items from the Tennessee valley.

Along with the impressive burial mounds, archaeologists have found indications of other projects indicating the combined efforts of hundreds of people in addition to a substantial investment of wealth. At Newark, Ohio, for example, the ceremonial site covers 4 square miles. Such enterprises indicate a long period of relative peace, generations remaining in the same place, and a substantial level of wealth. Archaeologists have also found indications of contacts with tribes across North America. Whether through trading or tribute, the Ohio valley societies had access to metals and goods found only in the Rocky Mountain area and shells from the Gulf coast. They had mastered the manufacture of tools, pottery, and copper jewelry.

The Mississippian Culture

At the end of the sixth century C.E. another major Amerindian culture made its appearance in the area just east of present-day St. Louis. Archaeologists are still investigating the origins and extent of this culture from the various burial sites, the most important of which is that at Cahokia, Illinois. Unlike the Adena and Hopewell cultures, the Mississippian culture lived in houses made out of thin pieces of wood (laths) covered with clay—so-called wattle-and-daub houses. These took various shapes in the large villages of the area. So influential was this culture that it came to dominate most of the region west of the Mississippi to the Plains, as can been seen in the Spiro Mounds in eastern Oklahoma.

The Mississippian peoples benefited from mastering the raising of maize, beans, and squash, and they tied their religion to the planting and harvesting cycles. Their burial mounds took the form of flat-topped pyramids, arranged around a central square. In the most developed regions, fortresslike palisades surrounded the site. The Cahokia complex was constructed over a period of nearly three centuries (c. 900–c. 1150). The centerpiece of the Cahokia site is a pyramid with a base of more than 18 acres, reaching a height of almost 100 feet. This is only one of more than 80 such mounds to be found at Cahokia, a city more than 6 miles long. There was no set burial practice for the Mississippian culture—remains have also been found in cemeteries, in urns, and under the floors of houses.

After the twelfth century the peoples in the Mississippian culture passed a highly complex religion along from generation to generation—an indication of their stability, continuity, and sophistication. The extent of their wealth enabled them to construct temples filled with ceremonial objects such as large stone scepters and copper plates. Their religion used symbols such as the cross, the sun, arrows surrounded by

An artist's creation of what Cahokia might have been like at its height.

semicircles, a sunburst, and—most intriguing—an outstretched hand with an eye in the palm. The art that derived from the religion featured portrayals of gods based on animals, rattlesnakes with feathers and wings, and people portrayed as birds. Vessels found at the sites indicate the presence of human sacrifice: jars with human faces painted on them and portrayals of the heads of sacrificed victims. These are indications that not only adults but also infants were given up to the higher deity the Mississippi culture believed controlled their lives.

Excavations of the Cahokia mounds give evidence of an hierarchical society that maintained order and productivity through brutality. Even though it was far distant from the Aztec and Incan Empires, there were several similarities between the political and religious systems and social repression of Cahokia and the systems in Mesoamerica and South America. For a while at the beginning of the thirteenth century, Cahokia was probably the largest city in North America, with a population larger than that of medieval London. At the end of the fourteenth century Cahokia began to decline. Archaeologists point to climate change, soil exhaustion, and the unification of those peoples Cahokia had repressed as an effective enemy force as likely causes for the end of Cahokia as a major power.

The Mogollon, the Hohokam, the Anasazi, and the Fremont Culture

The southwestern Amerindian cultures lived in the most environmentally challenging part of the continental United States, the dry and rocky regions of present-day Utah, Arizona, New Mexico, and Colorado. In response to their surroundings, they produced the most advanced levels of technology and agriculture around 300 B.C.E. The Mogollon, Hohokam, and Anasazi grew maize, beans, and squash, each group evolving its own techniques. The homes of each group were built out of adobe brick or other techniques of masonry, sometimes on extremely challenging sites.

Each group also produced pottery that could rank in beauty with any in the world.

The Mogollon culture of southwestern New Mexico lasted almost 1600 years, from around 300 B.C.E. to 1350 C.E. Its people built their homes low to the ground along the tops of ridges. Villages were built around large underground buildings used for religious ceremonies and as pit houses until the eleventh century; thereafter, they built these structures at ground level. Because of the constant threat of drought, they developed a diversified economy based on hunting, gathering, and farming. Relatively isolated, they saw little need to change over the centuries.

The Hohokam culture grew along the valleys of the Salt and Gila Rivers. Its architecture was similar to that of the early Mogollon, although the Hohokam built not just ceremonial structures but also their homes inside underground pits. Perhaps learning from the Mesoamerican cultures, the Hohokam constructed an impressive network of canals, some more than 30 miles long, 6 to 10 feet deep, and 15 to 30 feet wide. The extent of these canals proves the existence not only of wealth but also of substantial social organization. The Hohokam also borrowed their religion, their burial practices, and even some of their games from the Mesoamericans.

Deriving from these two cultures was the Anasazi, which appeared around 300 C.E. Of the three cultures, the Anasazi had the most sophisticated and most impressive architecture and the largest area of influence—from the Idaho-Utah border to the Gulf of California. Early on, they built their homes in the shape of beehive-shaped domes made out of logs held together by a mudlike mortar. They grew maize and made pottery, like the Mississippian culture, and stored both in warehouse-like structures. Around 700 C.E. they took their economic development one step further by beginning the manufacture of cotton cloth. Their technological genius is apparent from their use of two forms of irrigation: runoff by building dikes and terracing hills and subsoil by constructing sand dunes at the base of hills to hold the runoff of the

The Cliff Palace of the Anasazi, Mesa Verde National Park, Colorado, is among the important Anasazi ruins to be found in the southwestern United States.

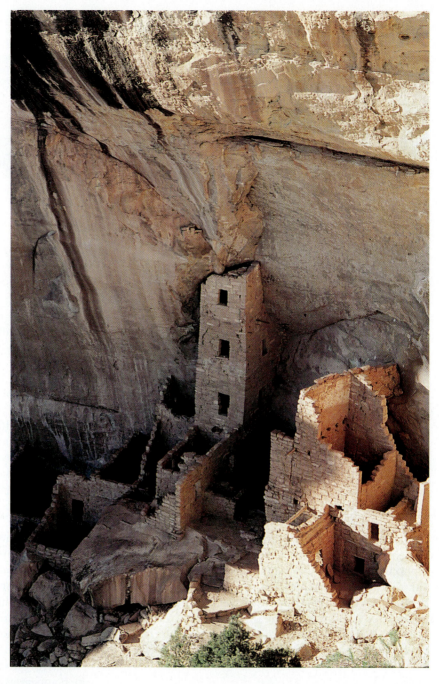

sometimes torrential rains. Their lives revolved around their religion, with ceremonies to placate the gods to hold off storms and to ensure fertility.

The Anasazi are best known today for their architectural accomplishments. Around the eleventh century they began to construct cities, with houses built in the shapes of squares and semicircles. They used all of the available materials to build these settlements; with wood, mud, and stone, they erected cliff dwellings and the equivalent of terraced apartment houses. One such structure, with some 500 living units, was the largest residential building in the North America until the completion of an apartment house in New York in 1882. At their height, these master architects constructed around a dozen towns and nearly 200 villages. The disappearance of the Anasazi around 1300 remains a mystery. It is believed that a combination of a long drought, internecine conflicts, and the arrivals of the Navajo and the Apache led to their demise.

To the north of the Anasazi there were a number of different societies spread across the Colorado Plateau and into Idaho. They were a diverse group: Some depended on farming while others were hunters and they spoke different languages. Anthropologists have labeled this group the Fremont culture. They shared traits with the Navajo in that they raised corn, used the same kinds of tools, and lived in pit houses. The culture flourished between the sixth and the fourteenth centuries. Recently one of the best-preserved settlements of the Fremont culture was revealed to have been found near Horse Canyon, Utah in the Range Creek site.

The Navajo, the Apache, and the Mandan

Three other Amerindian civilizations established their presence before the arrival of Europeans. The Navajo, the largest Native American group in the United States, came down from the north to the Southwest sometime in the eleventh century. There they borrowed extensively from the indigenous cultures.

A century or so later, the Apache, who speak a language close to that of the Navajo, arrived in the southwest and by the end of the 1500s lived in parts of the present states of Arizona, Colorado, and New Mexico. They, too, were heavily influenced by the cultures present there.

Finally, the Mandan, who based their economy on fur trading and hunting, came to the vast valley of the Missouri River from east of the Mississippi in the late 1300s. There had been Amerindians in this region since 12,000–8,000 B.C.E. who hunted on foot on the Great Plains for mammoths, mastodons, and bison using spears tipped with Clovis points. Archaeological sites in Canada indicate that Indians hunted and slaughtered buffalo for more than 7000 years. By 1000 C.E. the use of bows and arrows was common throughout the plains. When the Mandan moved west, they became yet another in a long series of Amerindians who harvested the animal wealth of the mid-continent.

The Far North: Inuit and Aleut

The appearance of the Inuit, also known as the Eskimos, is shrouded in controversy. Some observers assert that they descended from ancient seagoing peoples; others believe that they developed their culture in Alaska after the last ice age. They speak much the same language as the Aleut, whose origins are similarly unclear. It is accepted that the two groups split apart more than 4000 years ago and that they are tied more closely to Asians than the Amerindians are.

The Aleut stayed largely in the area that is now known as the Alaskan peninsula, the Aleutian Islands, and the far eastern portion of Russia. The Inuit spread along the area south of the Arctic Circle from the Bering Strait across the top of Canada to Greenland. Both peoples lived by hunting and fishing. The Aleut hunted sea lions, otters, and seals from kayaks—small boats made of a wood frame over which skins were stretched. The Inuit showed more flexibility, hunting both sea and land animals, fishing in fresh and salt water. Their diet was based primarily on the caribou, musk-ox, walruses, and whales. They used the kayak too, but supplemented it with canoes and dogsleds.

The Navajos constructed houses called hogans *to shelter themselves from the often harsh climate of the high desert in the American Southwest.*

Their greatest accomplishment in seafaring, whaling vessels was the umiak, a larger boat with a wood frame covered with caribou hide, in which several people could row.

By about 100 C.E. the Inuit had established large villages; one of the biggest, with around 400 homes, was near present-day Nome, Alaska. To counter the arctic cold, they dug as much as 20 inches into the permafrost to erect their homes, which they then covered with poles and sod. In settlements such as that near present-day Nome, archaeologists have found large structures for the performance of religious rites, led by shamans who claimed to be able to heal diseases and wounds.

CONCLUSION

Before the European invasions and colonization, the Americas produced a rich variety of highly sophisticated and complex civilizations in response to the varied environmental challenges and opportunities of the Western Hemisphere. Some of these groups made the transition from food hunting to food raising, and some did not.

In Central and South America advanced agriculture supplied the foundation to support growing populations. This in turn led to the establishment of villages, and then cities, and, finally, far-flung states. More food and more wealth made possible leisure and priestly classes who had the time and resources to consolidate their power through control of religion as well as producing an advanced art, architecture, and discoveries in mathematics and astronomy.

In North America, environmental conditions were harsher and did not permit a similar accumulation of wealth as in Central and South America. Some Indian tribes remained hunter-gatherers. Others established settled villages and complex civilizations, but without the power and sophistication of the peoples to the south.

Tragically, a combination of climate changes, pandemics—both indigenous and foreign—and European invasions diminished the population by an estimated 80 percent by 1650. Those who survived were subjugated or later forced from their lands. Although they fought bravely against overwhelming odds, the Amerindians would have to struggle to maintain their identities in the centuries to come.

Suggestions for Web Browsing

You can obtain more information about topics included in this chapter at the websites listed below. See also the companion website that accompanies this text, **http://www.ablongman.com/ brummett,** which contains an online study guide and additional resources.

Mesoweb, including Illustrated Encyclopedia of Mesoamerica
http://www.mesoweb.com/

Mesoweb is devoted to ancient Mesoamerica and its cultures: the Olmec, Mayas, Aztecs, Toltecs, Mixtecs, Zapotecs, and others.

University of Pennsylvania Museum of Archaeology and Art: Mesoamerica
http://www.museum.upenn.edu/new/exhibits/galleries/mesoameric aframedoc1.html

A history of Mesoamerican culture as reflected by the many artifacts in the university's museum.

National Museum of the American Indian
http://www.nmai.si.edu/

Website of the Smithsonian Institution's National Museum of the American Indian offers a look at one of the finest and most complete collections of items from the indigenous peoples of the Western Hemisphere.

Arctic Studies Center
http://www.mnh.si.edu/arctic/

Smithsonian Institution site dedicated to the study of Arctic peoples, culture, and environments includes numerous images, as well as audio and video segments of dance and discussion.

Literature and Film

For a sensitive and moving portrayal of the Indian life before Columbus in North America see Ruth B. Hill's *Hanta Yo: An American Saga* (Doubleday, 1979). Kathleen King's *Cricket Sings: A Novel of Pre-Columbian Cahokia* (Ohio University Press, 1983) gives an imaginative presentation of life in that Mississippian metropolis. An amusing concoction is A. Tanner Smith's *Anasazi and the Viking* (Sunstock, 1992), a not-totally-inconceivable meeting of Europeans and Amerindians. Insights into the Iroquois world can be gained from Joseph Bruchac, *The Boy Who Lived with the Bears and Other Iroquois Stories* (HarperCollins, 1995). A penetrating novel first published in 1826 has been recently translated by Guillermo I. Castillo-Feliis Félix Varela, *Xicoténcatl: An anonymous historical novel about the events leading up to the conquest of the Aztec Empire* (University of Texas, 1999). Another viewpoint on the Spanish conquest from the viewpoint of Atahualpa is given in Suzanne Alles Blom, *Inca, the Scarlet Fringe* (Forge, 2000). David Drew provides a window into the rich Mayan culture in his *The Lost Chronicles of the Maya Kings* (University of California, 1999).

PBS offers presentations on the Incas and the Mayas in their *Odyssey* series. See also the PBS series: *Seeking the First Americans, Surviving Columbus, Myths and Moundbuilders,* and the *Chaco Legacy*.

Suggestions for Reading

For a useful summary of the theories of migration into the Americas, see Sasha Nemecek, "Who were the First Americans," in *Scientific American,* September 2000, pp. 80–87. A sound, in-depth introduction to indigenous cultures in the New World is Alvin M. Josephy, ed., *America in 1492* (Knopf, 1992). See also Robert Wauchope's *Indian Background of Latin American History* (Knopf, 1970).

Among the most informative works on pre-Columbian Mesoamerica are Ross Hassig, *War and Society in Ancient Mesoamerica* (University of California Press, 1992); Richard A. Dieh and Janet C. Berlo, eds., *Mesoamerica After the Decline of Teotihuacán* (Dumbarton Oaks, 1989); and Robert R. Miller, *Mexico: A History* (University of Oklahoma Press, 1989). Special insights into the Mayan experience are provided in Jeremy A. Sobloff, *A New Archeology and the Ancient Maya* (Scientific American Library, 1990). A recent study of the darker side of Aztec society is David L. Carrasco and Micah Kleist, eds., *City of Sacrifice: The Aztec Empire and the Role of Violence in Civilization* (Beacon, 1998). Michael A. Malpass presents *Daily Life in the Inca Empire* (Greenwood Press, 1996).

E. James Dixon's *Bones, Boats, and Bison* (University of New Mexico Press, 1999) guides the reader through complex archaeological questions surround the question of the first colonization in western North America. Colin G. Galloway's documentary survey of American Indian History, *First Peoples* (Bedford/St. Martin's, 1999), is the best introduction to the general discussion of Native Americans in North America.

Credits

Chapter 1

2 University of Pennsylvania Museum (neg #30-12-702); **3** John Reader/Science Photo Library/Photo Researchers, Inc.; **4** John Reader/Science Photo Library/Photo Researchers, Inc.; **6** Drawing of Paleolithic tools; **7** Des & Jen Bartlett/Bruce Coleman; **8** James Mellaart; **11** Erich Lessing/Art Resource, NY; **16** Courtesy, The Oriental Institute of the University of Chicago. Photo by Victor J. Boswell, Jr. (sm8601); **18** Kurt Scholz/Egyptian National Museum, Cairo/SuperStock; **20** ©The Trustees of the British Museum (EA 921); **21** ©The Trustees of the British Museum; **23** ©The Trustees of the British Museum; **24** ©Sandro Vannini/CORBIS; **26** The Metropolitan Museum of Art, Gift of Norbert Schimmel Trust, 1989. (1989.281.10) Photograph ©1992 The Metropolitan Museum of Art; **32** ©The Trustees of The British Museum

Chapter 2

38 Gansu Provincial Museum,Wang Lu/China Stock; **41** The Avery Brundage Collection, B60P377 ©Asian Art Museum of San Francisco, Chong-Moon Lee Center For Asian Art and Culture. Used by permission.; **43** Imagine China; **44** Musée Cernuschi, Musées des Arts de l'Asie de la Ville de Paris; **48** ©Bettmann/CORBIS; **53** Don Hamilton Photo & Film; **55** Werner Forman/Art Resource, NY; **58** Christie's Images; **58** Robert Harding Picture Library Ltd.

Chapter 3

65 Jean-Louis Nou/akg – images; **67** MacQuitty International Collection, London; **68** Jean-Louis Nou/akg – images; **68** National Museum of India, New Delhi/Bridgeman Art Library; **76** Jean-Louis Nou/akg – images; **82** Burstein Collection/CORBIS; **84** British Library/The Art Archive; **85** Ministero per I Beni e le Attivitá Culturali Soprintendenza Archeologica; **86** Jean-Louis Nou /akg – images; **90** ©Adam Woolfitt/CORBIS; **91** "Vessel in the Form of an Ax," 2nd cent. B.C. to 5th cent. A.D. The Metropolitan Museum of Art, Purchase, George McFad-den Gift and Edith Perry Chapman Fund, 1993. (1993.525) Photograph by Bruce White. ©1993 The Metropolitan Museum of Art

Global Issue Essay

94 ©Reuters/CORBIS

Chapter 4

97 Scala/Art Resource, NY; **99** Michael Holford Photographs; **100** Nimatallah/Art Resource, NY; **101** Scala/Art Resource, NY; **105** Réunion des Musées Nationaux/Art Resource, NY; **113** Courtesy, The Manchester Museum, The University of Manchester (Fx 568); **118** akg – images; **119** ©Charles O'Rear/CORBIS; **121** "Dionysos, Ariadne & Pan." Hellenic Ministry of Culture/Archaeological Receipts Fund/TAP Service; **126** Erich Lessing /Art Resource, NY; **127** ©Araldo de Luca/Corbis

Chapter 5

130 Vanni/Art Resource, NY; **133** Scala/Art Resource, NY; **136** Scala/Art Resource, NY; **143** Archivo Fotografico Musei Capitolini/INDEX, Firenze; **146** Werner Forman Archive/Art Resource, NY; **148** The Art Archive/Museo della Civilta Romana Rome/Dagli Orti; **149** Scala/Art Resource, NY; **149** The J. Paul Getty Museum, Villa Collection, Malibu, California. ©J. Paul Getty Museum; **150** Scala/Art Resource, NY; **151** Israel Museum, Jerusalem, Israel/Ancient Art and Architecture Collection Ltd/Bridgeman Art Library; **156** ©Araldo de Luca/Corbis;**159** Scala/Art Resource, NY

Chapter 6

164 ©Diego Lezama Orezzoli/CORBIS; **167** Duane Preble; **171** ©Christel Gerstenberg/CORBIS; **171** Woodfin Camp & Associates; **172** Ronald Sheridan/Art Resource, NY; **174** akg – images; **176** The Granger Collection, New York; **179** Scala/Art

Resource, NY; **183** Bibliothèque Nationale, Paris, France/Bridgeman Art Library; **187** Roger-Violett/Getty Images; **190** ©The State Russian Museum/CORBIS

Chapter 7

194 Bibliotek Nationale/akg – images; **198** By permission of the British Library; **201** "The Night Journey of Muhammad on His Steed, Buraq," 1514. Leaf from the "Bustan" (underline) of Sa'di, copied by calligrapher Sultan-Muhammad Nur. The Metropolitan Museum of Art, Purchase, Louis V. Bell Fund and Astor Foundation Gift, 1974. (1974.294.2) Photograph by Schecter Lee. Photograph ©1986, The Metropolitan Museum of Art; **204** Qisas al-Anibiya, folio 152v, illustration: "Jesus Performs Miracle of Loaves." (Spencer Persian MS 46) Spencer Collection, The New York Public Library, Astor, Lenox and Tilden Foundations; **204** Qisas al-Anibiya, "Moses Turns Staff into a Dragon." Spencer Persian Manuscript, 46, folio 82. Courtesy, the Spencer Collection, The New York Public Library, Astor, Lenox and Tilden Foundations; **205** Reproduced by kind permission of the Trustees of the Chester Beatty Library, Dublin; **210** The Imagebank Films/Getty Images; **210** The Bodleian Library, University of Oxford (MS Ouseley Add 24 folio 55v); **212** Bibliothèque Nationale de France (Ms. Ar. 5847 fol. 138v.); **212** akg – images; **215** The Art Archive/Egyptian Museum Cairo/Dagli Orti; **216** The Bodleian Library, University of Oxford (MS Pococke 375 folio 3v-4r); **219** ©SuperStock, Inc.

Global Issue Essay

223 ©Gianni Dagli Orti/CORBIS

Chapter 8

224 bpk, Berlin/Art Resource, NY; **228** Sarha Errington/Hutchinson Library of Holland Park, Ltd.; **229** Erich Lessing/Art Resource, NY; **230** Werner Forman/Art Resource, NY; **234** Georger Gerster/Photo Researchers, Inc.; **236** Marc & Evelyn Bernheim/Woodfin Camp & Associates; **238** Bibliothèque Nationale de France, Paris; **241** Bibliothèque Nationale de France, Paris; **243** Bibliothèque Nationale de France, Paris; **244** ©Ferdinando Scianna/Magnum Photos, Inc.; **246** ©Paul Almasy/CORBIS; **249** akg – images; **250** National Palace Museum, Taipei, Taiwan, Republic of China; **251** Marc & Evelyn Bernheim/Woodfin Camp & Associates; **252** Robert Aberman/Art Resource, NY

Chapter 9

256 ©Archivo Iconografico, S.A./CORBIS; **259** The Pierpont Morgan Library/Art Resource, NY; **259** Belt Buckle, Visigothic (Spain), Migration Period, c. 525–560. Bronze with garnets, mother-of-pearl, green glass, traces of gilding, gold foil, W 6.7 x LL 13.3 cm. ©The Cleveland Museum of Art, 2004. Purchase from the J.H. Wade Fund, 2001.119; **262** Foto Marburg /Art Resource, NY; **270** ©Archivo Iconografico, S.A./CORBIS; **271** "Des Proprietez des Choses," 1482. British Library, London, UK/ Bridgeman Art Library; **273** St. Francis Receives Approval of his 'Regula Prima' from Pope Innocent III (1160–1216) in 1210, 1297–1299 (fresco), Giotto di Bondone (c.1266–1337)/San Francesco, Upper Church, Assisi, Italy, Giraudon/Bridgeman Art Library; **279** Giraudon/Art Resource, NY; **281** Carrow Psalter detail: "The Martyrdom of Thomas a Becket," English, 1250. MS W. 34 f. 15v. The Walters Art Museum, Baltimore; **282** The Metropolitan Museum of Art, Gift of George Blumenthal, 1941. (41.100.157) Photograph ©1986 The Metropolitan Museum of Art

Chapter 10

286 Werner Forman/Art Resource, NY; **291** "Krishna Battling the Horse Demon, Keshi," 5th cent. The Metropolitan Museum of Art, Purchase, Florence and Herbert Irving Gift, 1991. (1991.300) Photograph by Bruce White. Photograph ©1994 The Metropolitan Museum of Art; **292** Ric Ergenbright Photography; **296** ©Wolfgang Kaehler/CORBIS; **298** Anonymous, Chinese, Equestrienne, Tang dynasty (618–907 CE), 2nd quarter of 8th century, Earthenware with traces of polychromy, 56.2 x 48.2 cm. Mr. and Mrs. Potter Palmer Collection, 1970.1073 Photography ©The Art Institute of Chicago; **304** Fan Kuan, "Snow Mountain and Forest." ChinaStock (WL-16); **305** Bibliothèque Nationale de France, Paris; **305** Victoria & Albert Museum, London/Art Resource, NY; **307** The National Palace Museum, Taipei, Taiwan, Republic of China (detail); **309** Special Collections, New York Public Library, Astor, Lenox and Tilden Foundations; **311** Art Resource, NY; **312** TNM Image Archives Source:http:// TnmArchives.jp/; **314** Kyoto News Service; **316** Tokugawa Reimeikai Foundation, Tokyo, Japan/

Bridgeman Art Library; **317** ©Sakamoto Photo Research Library/CORBIS; **319** ©Royalty-Free/CORBIS

Chapter 11

322 ©Werner Forman/CORBIS; **327** Bruce Coleman; **329** Justin Kerr; **330** Museo Nacional de Antropologia, Mexico City/Werner Forman/Art Resource, NY; **334** Ewing Krainin; **338** Mark C. Burnett, Ohio Historical Society, Columbus/Photo Researchers, Inc.; **339** Cahokia Mounds State Historic Site; **340** International Color Stock, Ltd./eStock Photo; **341** ©L. Clarke/CORBIS

Global Issue Essay

344 ©Asian Art & Archaeology, Inc./CORBIS

Notes

Chapter 1

1. Harold C. Conklin, *The Relation of Hanunóo Culture to the Plant World*, doctoral dissertation, Yale University, 1954 (microfilm), p. 9. See also Claude Levi-Strauss, *The Savage Mind* (Chicago: University of Chicago Press, 1970), Chapter 1, "The Science of the Concrete."
2. Rob Stein, *Archaeology: Astronomical Structures in Ancient Egypt* (Washington, D.C.: Washington Post Company, 1998).
3. *The Code of Hammurabi*, Reverse Side, xxiv: 43–48, as quoted in Jean Bottero, *Mesopotamia: Writing, Reasoning, and the Gods* (Chicago: University of Chicago Press, 1992).
4. *The Code of Hammurabi*, Reverse Side, xxiv: 43–48.
5. From the *Epic of Gilgamesh*, trans. E. A. Speiser, in *Ancient Near Eastern Texts Relating to the Old Testament*, 2nd ed., ed. James B. Pritchard. Copyright © 1950, 1955, 1969, renewed 1978 by Princeton University Press. Reprinted by permission of Princeton University Press.
6. From the *Epic of Gilgamesh*, in Pritchard.
7. From Miriam Lichtheim, *Ancient Egyptian Literature: A Book of Readings, Three Volumes*, Vol. 2. Copyright © 1973–1980 Regents of the University of California. Reprinted by permission of the University of California Press.
8. John A. Wilson, *The Burden of Egypt* (Chicago: University of Chicago Press, 1951), p. 117.
9. Lichtheim, *Ancient Egyptian Literature*, Vol. 2, pp. 96, 98.
10. John Foster, *Love Songs of the New Kingdom* (New York: Charles Scribner's Sons, 1974), p. 72.
11. Amy Dockser Marcus, *The View from Nebo* (Little, Brown, and Company: 2000), pp. 22–28.
12. I. Finkelstein and Neil A. Silberman, *The Bible Unearthed* (New York: The Free Press, 2002), pp. 123–145 passim.

Chapter 2

1. From *The Book of Songs*, quoted in Patricia Buckley Ebrey, *The Cambridge Illustrated History of China* (Cambridge: Cambridge University Press, 1996), p. 34.
2. Michael Loewe, *The Pride That Was China* (New York: St. Martin's Press, 1990), p. 99.
3. Loewe, p. 99.
4. Loewe, p. 99.
5. Mencius, VA:5, in W. Theodore de Bary et al., trans., *Sources of Chinese Tradition* (New York: Columbia University Press, 1960), p. 96.
6. From the *Laozi*, quoted in Ebrey, p. 48.
7. Arthur Waldron, *The Great Wall of China: From History to Myth* (Cambridge: Cambridge University Press, 1990).
8. Loewe, p. 106.
9. W. Theodore de Bary, *East Asian Civilizations: A Dialogue in Five Stages* (Cambridge, Mass.: Harvard University Press, 1988), p. 19.
10. R. G. Collingwood, *The Idea of History* (New York: Galaxy Books, 1956), p. 22.
11. Kwang-Chih Chang, *The Archaeology of Ancient China*, 4th ed. (New Haven, Conn.: Yale University Press, 1987), p. 5.
12. Christopher Cullen, *Astronomy and Mathematics in Ancient China: The Zhou bi su an jing* (Cambridge: Cambridge University Press, 1996).
13. Nancy Lee Swann, *Pan Chao: Foremost Woman Scholar of China* (Ann Arbor, Mich.: University of Michigan, 2001).
14. See Loewe, ch. 18.

Chapter 3

1. Kautilya, *The Kautiliyan Arthasastra*, Part II, 2nd ed., trans. R. P. Kangle (Bombay: University of Bombay, 1972), pp. 327, 339–341.
2. Kautilya, pp. 327, 339–341.
3. Quoted in Vincent Smith, *The Oxford History of India* (Oxford: Oxford University Press, 1958), p. 131.
4. Quoted in Charles Drekmeier, *Kingship and Community in Early India* (Stanford, Calif.: Stanford University Press, 1962), p. 175.
5. From *The Interior Landscape: Love Poems from a Classical Tamil Anthology*, trans. A. K. Ramanujan (Bloomington: Indiana University Press, 1975), p. 54.
6. *The Bhagavad-Gita*, trans. Barbara Stoler Miller (New York: Bantam, 1986), pp. 46–47.
7. *The Ramayana of Valmiki*, Vol. 1, trans. Robert P. Goldman (Princeton, N.J.: Princeton University Press, 1984), p. 121.

Global Issues: Migration

1. B. Weiss, "The Decline of Late Bronze Age Civilizations as a Possible Response to Climatic Change," *Climatic Change*, Vol. 4 (1982), pp. 172–198.

Chapter 6

1. Procopius of Caesarea, *History of the Wars*, Vol. 1, 24:36–38, trans. S. R. Rosenbaum, in Charles Diehl, *Theodora: Empress of Byzantium* (New York: Ungar, 1972), pp. 87–88.
2. Geoffrey de Villehardouin, "The Conquest of Constantinople," in M. R. B. Shaw, *Chronicles of the Crusades* (Baltimore: Penguin, 1963), pp. 79, 92.
3. *The Russian Primary Chronicle*, trans. Samuel H. Cross and O. P. Sherbowitz-Wetzor (Cambridge: Mediaeval Academy of America, 1953), pp. 110–118.

Chapter 7

1. *Rubáiyát of Omar Khayyám*, trans. Edward Fitzgerald, stanzas 12, 13, 71, and 72.
2. Ibn Khaldun, *The Muqaddimah: An Introduction to History*, Vol.1, trans. Franz Rosenthal (London: Routledge & Kegan Paul, 1958), p. 71.
3. John Williams, ed., *Islam* (New York: Braziller, 1962), p. 142.

Chapter 8

1. Kevin Shillington, *History of Africa* (New York: St. Martin's Press, 1989), p. 10.
2. Terry Childs and David Killick, "Indigenous African Metallurgy: Nature and Culture," *Annual Review of Anthropology* (1993), pp. 326–327.
3. The latest synthesis of research on Bantu migrations is Jan Vansina, "A Slow Revolution: Farming in Subequatorial Africa," *Azania* 29–30 (1994–1995), pp. 15–26.
4. Richard Pankhurst, *The Ethiopians: A History* (Oxford: Blackwells, 1998), p. 40.
5. Al Omari, quoted in Tadesse Tamrat, "The Horn of Africa: The Solomonids in Ethiopia and the States of the Horn of Africa," in D. T. Niane, ed., *UNESCO General History of Africa: Africa from the Twelfth to the Sixteenth Century* (Berkeley: University of California Press, 1984), p. 435.
6. Donald Crummey, *Land and Society in the Christian Kingdom of Ethiopia from the Thirteenth to the Twentieth Century* (Oxford: James Currey, 2000), p. 29.
7. Joseph Vogel, *Encyclopedia of Precolonial Africa: Archaeology, History, Languages, Cultures, and Environment* (Walnut Creek, Calif.: AltaMira Press, 1997), p. 490.
8. Ralph Austen, "Slave Trade: Trans-Saharan Trade," in Seymour Drescher and Stanley Engerman, eds., *A Historical Guide to World Slavery* (Oxford: Oxford University Press, 1998), p. 368.
9. Al Omari, quoted in Vogel, *Encyclopedia of Precolonial Africa*, p. 492.
10. Barbara Callaway, *Muslim Hausa Women in Nigeria: Tradition and Change* (Syracuse University Press, 1989), p. 9.
11. Adu Boahen, *Topics in West African History* (Longman, 1966), p. 9.
12. Michael Pearson, *Port Cities and Intruders: The Swahili Coast, India, and Portugal in the Early Modern Era* (Johns Hopkins University Press, 1998), pp. 36–37. Pearson defines the Afrasian Sea as extending from Sofala in Mozambique to the southern tip of India.
13. Al Masudi, quoted in G. S. P. Freeman-Grenville, *The East African Coast* (Oxford: Oxford University Press, 1962), pp. 15–17.
14. A. H. J. Prins, *The Swahili-Speaking Peoples of Zanzibar and the East African Coast* (International African Institute, 1961), p. 93, quoted in Chapurukha Kusimba, *The Rise and Fall of Swahili States* (AltaMira Press, 1999), pp. 134–5.
13. Eric Gilbert and Jonathan Reynolds, *Africa in World History from Prehistory to the Present* (Upper Saddle River, N.J.: Pearson, 2004), p. 113.

Chapter 10

1. Stanley Wolpert, *A New History of India*, 7th ed. (New York: Oxford University Press, 2004), p. 79.
2. Hermann Kulke and Dietmar Rothermund, *History of India*, 3rd ed. (London: Routledge, 1998), p. 147.
3. *Alberuni's India*, trans. Edward Sachau (New York: Norton, 1971), p. 100.
4. Minhaju-s Siraj, quoted in John Keay, *India: A History* (New York: Grove Press, 2000), p. 245.
5. Excerpt from poem by Xu Yeueying, in Kan-I Sun Chang and Haun Saussy, eds., *Women Writers of Traditional China* (Stanford, Calif.: Stanford University Press, 1999), p. 78.
6. Quoted in H. H. Gowen and H. W. Hall, *An Outline History of China* (New York: Appleton, 1926), p. 117.
7. *The Works of Li Po*, trans. Shigeyoshi Obata (New York: Dutton, 1950), no. 71.

8. Du Fu, "A Song of War Chariots," in Cyril Birch, ed., *Anthology of Chinese Literature* (New York: Grove Press, 1965), pp. 240–241.

9. Marco Polo, *The Travels of Marco Polo* (New York: Grosset & Dunlap, 1931), pp. 30, 133–149.

10. Donald Keene, ed., *Anthology of Japanese Literature: From the Earliest Era to the Mid-Nineteenth Century* (New York: Grove Press, 1955), pp. 39–41.

11. Murasaki Shikibu, "The Diary of Murasaki Shikibu," in Donald Keene, ed., *Anthology of Japanese Literature* (New York: Grove Press, 1960), p. 152.

Chapter 11

1. Quoted by Clements Markham, in Edward Hyams and George Ordish, *The Last of the Incas* (New York: Simon & Schuster, 1963), p. 88.

Global Issues: Location and Identity

1. Emanuel Bowen, *Complete Atlas of the Known World* (London, 1752), cited in Martin W. Lewis and Kären Wigen, *The Myth of Continents: A Critique of Metageography* (Berkeley: University of California Press, 1997), p. 29.

2. Just as the European-initiated paradigm of East and West influenced people outside of Europe in the past century, China's view of itself as the "Middle Kingdom" has influenced non-Chinese views of the rest of Asia. On maps of Asia, Japan sometimes gets chopped off, and in teaching about East Asia, Korea and Vietnam have only recently joined China and Japan as deserving of treatment.

3. Cited by Lewis and Wigen, p. 69.

4. Robert B. Marks, *The Origins of the Modern World: A Global and Ecological Narrative* (Lanham, Md.: Rowman and Littlefield, 2002), pp. 52–53.

5. Lewis and Wigen, p. 23.

6. An early critic of the arbitrary binary divide between East and West is Edward W. Said, *Orientalism* (New York: Pantheon, 1978).

7. Karl Wittfogel, *Oriental Despotism: A Comparative Study of Total Power* (New Haven, Conn.: Yale University Press, 1957). Because Asian agriculture—uniquely—required irrigation, Wittfogel alleged, autocratic government came into being there. The argument may be logical, but the ecological premise is wrong.

Index

Note: Page numbers followed by letters *i* and *m* indicate illustrations and maps, respectively. Boldface page numbers indicate key terms.

Contemporary
Political Map
of the World